MW01233336

Project Management Professional (PMP)® Training: Aligned with PMBOK® Guide Fifth Edition

A Guide to the Project Management Body of Knowledge (PMBOK® Guide) – Fifth Edition, Project Management Institute (PMI)®, Project Management Professional (PMP)®, and Certified Associate in Project Management (CAPM)® are registered trademarks of Project Management Institute, Inc. - Version 2.1 Published September 30, 2014

Project Management Professional (PMP)® Training: Aligned with PMBOK® Guide Fifth Edition

Part Number: 095001
Course Edition: 2.1

Acknowledgements

PROJECT TEAM

Author	Media Designer	Content Editor	Technical Reviewers
Kelly L Popen Cathleen M. Frank, PMP	Alex Tong	Michelle Farney	Jean McKay, PMP Trina Jones, PMP

Notices

and Canada, 1-585-350-7000 in all other countries. Logical Operations' World Wide Web site is located at **www.logicaloperations.com.**

Project Management Professional (PMP)® Training: Aligned with PMBOK® Guide Fifth Edition

A Guide to the Project Management Body of Knowledge (PMBOK® Guide) – Fifth Edition, Project Management Institute (PMI)®, Project Management Professional (PMP)®, and Certified Associate in Project Management (CAPM)® are registered trademarks of Project Management Institute, Inc. - Version 2.1 Published September 30, 2014

A Guide to the Project Management Body of Knowledge (PMBOK® Guide) – Fifth Edition, Project Management Institute (PMI)®, Project Management Professional (PMP)®, and Certified Associate in Project Management (CAPM)® are registered trademarks of Project Management Institute, Inc. - Version 2.1 Published September 30, 2014

A Guide to the Project Management Body of Knowledge (PMBOK® Guide) – Fifth Edition, Project Management Institute (PMI)®, Project Management Professional (PMP)®, and Certified Associate in Project Management (CAPM)® are registered trademarks of Project Management Institute, Inc. - Version 2.1 Published September 30, 2014

A Guide to the Project Management Body of Knowledge (PMBOK® Guide) – Fifth Edition, Project Management Institute (PMI)®, Project Management Professional (PMP)®, and Certified Associate in Project Management (CAPM)® are registered trademarks of Project Management Institute, Inc. - Version 2.1 Published September 30, 2014

About This Course

If you are taking this course, you probably have some professional exposure to the duties of a project manager, or you may be considering embarking on a career in professional project management. Your ability as a project manager to demonstrate best practices in project management—both on the job and through professional certification—is becoming the standard to compete in today's fast-paced and highly technical workplace. In this course, you will apply the generally recognized practices of project management acknowledged by the Project Management Institute (PMI)® to successfully manage projects.

Project managers who have proven skills and experience can find exciting, high-visibility opportunities in a wide range of fields. This course is specifically designed to provide you with the proven, practical body of project management knowledge and skills that you need to demonstrate project management mastery on the job. Additionally, this course can be a significant part of your preparation for the Project Management Professional (PMP)® Certification Exam. The skills and knowledge you gain in this course will help you avoid making costly mistakes and increase your competitive edge in the project management profession.

Course Description

Target Student

This course is designed for individuals who have on-the-job project management experience (whether or not project manager is their formal job role), who are not certified project management professionals, and who might or might not have received formal project management training. The course is appropriate for these persons if they wish to develop professionally, increase their project management skills, apply a formalized and standards-based approach to project management, and seek career advancement by moving into a formal project manager job role, as well as to apply for Project Management Institute, Inc. (PMI) Project Management Professional (PMP) certification.

Course Prerequisites

Familiarity with project management concepts and some working experience with project management are required. Experience with a specific project management software tool is not required. Basic computing skills and some experience using Microsoft Office is desirable but not required.

Course Objectives

Upon successful completion of this course, students will be able to apply the generally recognized practices of project management acknowledged by the Project Management Institute (PMI) to successfully manage projects.

You will:

- Get started with project management fundamentals.
- Identify organizational influences and project life cycle.
- Work with project management processes.
- Initiate a project.
- Plan a project.
- Plan for project time management.
- Plan project budget, quality, and communications.
- Plan for risk, procurements, and stakeholder management.
- Execute a project.
- Manage project work, scope, schedules, and cost.
- Control a project.
- Close a project.

The LogicalCHOICE Home Screen

The LogicalCHOICE Home screen is your entry point to the LogicalCHOICE learning experience, of which this course manual is only one part. Visit the LogicalCHOICE Course screen both during and after class to make use of the world of support and instructional resources that make up the LogicalCHOICE experience.

Log-on and access information for your LogicalCHOICE environment will be provided with your class experience. On the LogicalCHOICE Home screen, you can access the LogicalCHOICE Course screens for your specific courses.

Each LogicalCHOICE Course screen will give you access to the following resources:

- eBook: an interactive electronic version of the printed book for your course.
- LearnTOs: brief animated components that enhance and extend the classroom learning experience.

Depending on the nature of your course and the choices of your learning provider, the LogicalCHOICE Course screen may also include access to elements such as:

- The interactive eBook.
- Social media resources that enable you to collaborate with others in the learning community using professional communications sites such as LinkedIn or microblogging tools such as Twitter.
- Checklists with useful post-class reference information.
- Any course files you will download.
- The course assessment.
- Notices from the LogicalCHOICE administrator.
- Virtual labs, for remote access to the technical environment for your course.
- Your personal whiteboard for sketches and notes.
- Newsletters and other communications from your learning provider.
- Mentoring services.
- A link to the website of your training provider.
- The LogicalCHOICE store.

Visit your LogicalCHOICE Home screen often to connect, communicate, and extend your learning experience!

How to Use This Book

As You Learn

This book is divided into lessons and topics, covering a subject or a set of related subjects. In most cases, lessons are arranged in order of increasing proficiency.

A Guide to the Project Management Body of Knowledge (PMBOK® Guide) – Fifth Edition, Project Management Institute (PMI)®, Project Management Professional (PMP)®, and Certified Associate in Project Management (CAPM)® are registered trademarks of Project Management Institute, Inc. - Version 2.1 Published September 30, 2014

The results-oriented topics include relevant and supporting information you need to master the content. Each topic has various types of activities designed to enable you to practice the guidelines and procedures as well as to solidify your understanding of the informational material presented in the course. Procedures and guidelines are presented in a concise fashion along with activities and discussions. Information is provided for reference and reflection in such a way as to facilitate understanding and practice.

Data files for various activities as well as other supporting files for the course are available by download from the LogicalCHOICE Course screen. In addition to sample data for the course exercises, the course files may contain media components to enhance your learning and additional reference materials for use both during and after the course.

At the back of the book, you will find a glossary of the definitions of the terms and concepts used throughout the course. You will also find an index to assist in locating information within the instructional components of the book.

As You Review

Any method of instruction is only as effective as the time and effort you, the student, are willing to invest in it. In addition, some of the information that you learn in class may not be important to you immediately, but it may become important later. For this reason, we encourage you to spend some time reviewing the content of the course after your time in the classroom.

As a Reference

The organization and layout of this book make it an easy-to-use resource for future reference. Taking advantage of the glossary, index, and table of contents, you can use this book as a first source of definitions, background information, and summaries.

Course Icons

Watch throughout the material for these visual cues:

Icon	Description
	A **Note** provides additional information, guidance, or hints about a topic or task.
	A **Caution** helps make you aware of places where you need to be particularly careful with your actions, settings, or decisions so that you can be sure to get the desired results of an activity or task.
	LearnTO notes show you where an associated LearnTO is particularly relevant to the content. Access LearnTOs from your LogicalCHOICE Course screen.
	Checklists provide job aids you can use after class as a reference to performing skills back on the job. Access checklists from your LogicalCHOICE Course screen.
	Social notes remind you to check your LogicalCHOICE Course screen for opportunities to interact with the LogicalCHOICE community using social media.
	Notes Pages are intentionally left blank for you to write on.

A Guide to the Project Management Body of Knowledge (PMBOK® Guide) – Fifth Edition, Project Management Institute (PMI)®, Project Management Professional (PMP)®, and Certified Associate in Project Management (CAPM)® are registered trademarks of Project Management Institute, Inc. - Version 2.1 Published September 30, 2014

| About This Course |

1 | Getting Started with Project Management

Lesson Time: 1 hour

Lesson Objectives

In this lesson, you will:

- Get started with project management fundamentals.
- Examine the relationship between project management and the business.

Lesson Introduction

Welcome to *Project Management Professional (PMP)® Training: Aligned with PMBOK® Guide Fifth Edition* In this first lesson, we will take you through some foundational concepts and information that will set the stage for the remaining lessons presented in this course. Understanding how the PMI *PMBOK® Guide* processes provide a framework in which project management can be applied is key in not only managing successful projects, but can assist you in preparing for the Project Management Profession (PMP)® or the Certified Associate in Project Management (CAPM)® certification exams.

In this lesson, you will identify the components of project management and how they relate to other disciplines within an organization. You will also explore the relationship project management has to business and how it can be applied to align with business objectives.

TOPIC A

Components of Project Management

As you may already know, project management is made up of many different areas of focus and components. Through experience and application of project management fundamentals, you will understand how PMI's project management framework can be a powerful tool within an organization. In this first topic, we will take a look at the basic concepts of project management and how PMI influences how project management processes and tasks are followed by project managers.

What Is a Project?

A *project* is a temporary effort to create a unique product, service, or result. It has a defined beginning and end. The end is reached when the objectives of the project have been achieved or when the project is terminated. Projects can vary by size, number of team members, outcomes, duration, and stakeholders. The outcome or number of outcomes of a project may be tangible or intangible.

A Guide to the Project Management Body of Knowledge (PMBOK® Guide) – Fifth Edition, Project Management Institute, Inc., 2013, p. 3

Project Outcomes

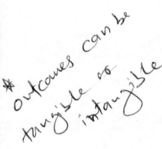

 # outcomes can be tangible or intangible

As stated in the *PMBOK® Guide,* a project can create:

- A product that can be either a component of another item, an enhancement of an item, or an end item in itself.
- A service or a capability to perform a service (for example, a business function that supports production or distribution).
- An improvement in the existing product or service lines (for example, a Six Sigma project undertaken to reduce defects).
- A result, such as an outcome or document (for example, a research project that develops knowledge that can be used to determine whether a trend exists or a new process will benefit society).

A Guide to the Project Management Body of Knowledge (PMBOK® Guide) – Fifth Edition, Project Management Institute, Inc., 2013, p. 3

Project Examples

There are many different types of projects that can be implemented by using PMI processes:

- Developing a new product, service, or result.
- Effecting a change in the structure, processes, staffing, or style of an organization.
- A home improvement project.
- Developing or acquiring a new or modified information system (hardware or software).
- Conducting a research effort whose outcome will be aptly recorded.
- Implementing, improving, or enhancing existing business processes and procedures.
- Planning a wedding.

A Guide to the Project Management Body of Knowledge (PMBOK® Guide) – Fifth Edition, Project Management Institute, Inc., 2013, p. 4

Subprojects

Subprojects are smaller components that relate directly to a larger project. In many cases, subprojects will be created to manage a third-party contract or service that can be tracked separately from the main project.

A Guide to the Project Management Body of Knowledge (PMBOK® Guide) – Fifth Edition, Project
Management Institute, Inc., 2013, p. 564

Project Management

Project management is the "application of knowledge, skills, tools, and techniques to plan activities to
meet the project requirements," according to the *PMBOK® Guide.* Properly managing projects
involves a number of tasks, with the most important being communication. Tasks include proper
planning, scheduling, identifying project requirements; applying quality, scope, time, and cost
requirements; and effectively managing all the project stakeholders. *A Guide to the Project Management
Body of Knowledge (PMBOK® Guide) - Fifth Edition,* on which this course is based, provides guidelines
for managing individual projects and defines project-management–related concepts. It also describes
the project management life cycle and its related processes as well as the project life cycle.

Project management is an iterative, cyclical process that involves back-and-forth progression
through many of the processes and phases. For the purposes of this course, we will take a linear
approach through the processes presented in the PMI framework.

A Guide to the Project Management Body of Knowledge (PMBOK® Guide) – Fifth Edition, Project
Management Institute, Inc., 2013, pg. 5-6

Portfolios, Programs, and Projects

The relationship among portfolios, programs, and projects is such that a portfolio is a collection of
projects, programs, sub-portfolios, and operations managed as a group to achieve strategic business
results. Programs are grouped in a portfolio and are made up of subprograms, projects, or other
work that supports that portfolio. Individual projects that are either within or outside of a program
are still considered part of a portfolio. All items in a portfolio are linked to the organization's
strategic plan.

A Guide to the Project Management Body of Knowledge (PMBOK® Guide) – Fifth Edition, Project
Management Institute, Inc., 2013, p. 4

A Guide to the Project Management Body of Knowledge (PMBOK® Guide) – Fifth Edition, Project Management Institute (PMI)®, Project Management Professional
(PMP)®, and Certified Associate in Project Management (CAPM)® are registered trademarks of Project Management Institute, Inc. - Version 2.1 Published September 30, 2014

Lesson 1: Getting Started with Project Management | *Topic A*

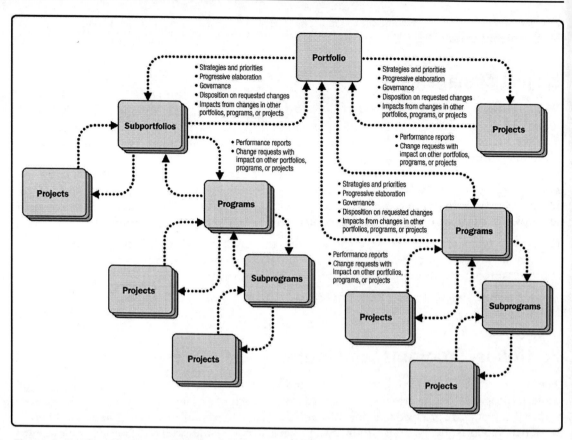

Figure 1-1: The relationship between portfolios, programs, and projects.

A Guide to the Project Management Body of Knowledge (PMBOK® Guide) – Fifth Edition, Project Management Institute, Inc., 2013, p. 5

Projects and Strategic Planning

Projects are a way of achieving objectives within an organization's strategic plan. Projects are typically authorized as a result of one or more of the following strategic considerations:

- Market demand
- Strategic opportunity/business need
- Social need
- Environmental consideration
- Customer request
- Technological advance
- Legal requirement

A Guide to the Project Management Body of Knowledge (PMBOK® Guide) – Fifth Edition, Project Management Institute, Inc., 2013, p. 10

Organizational Project Management

Portfolio, program, and project management are part of and support *organizational project management (OPM)*. OPM is a strategy execution framework that relies on project, program, and portfolio management and organizational practices to deliver a robust organizational strategy that will ultimately produce better organization-wide performance and results. This strategy gives an organization a more sustainable, competitive advantage in a predictable and consistent manner.

A Guide to the Project Management Body of Knowledge (PMBOK® Guide) – Fifth Edition, Project Management Institute, Inc., 2013, p. 7

Organizational Project Management			
	Projects	**Programs**	**Portfolios**
Scope	Projects have defined objectives. Scope is progressively elaborated throughout the project life cycle.	Programs have a larger scope and provide more significant benefits.	Portfolios have an organizational scope that changes with the strategic objectives of the organization.
Change	Project managers expect change and implement processes to keep change managed and controlled.	Program managers expect change from both inside and outside the program and are prepared to manage it.	Portfolio managers continuously monitor changes in the broader internal and external environment.
Planning	Project managers progressively elaborate high-level information into detailed plans throughout the project life cycle.	Program managers develop the overall program plan and create high-level plans to guide detailed planning at the component level.	Portfolio managers create and maintain necessary processes and communication relative to the aggregate portfolio.
Management	Project managers manage the project team to meet the project objectives.	Program managers manage the program staff and the project managers; they provide vision and overall leadership.	Portfolio managers may manage or coordinate portfolio management staff, or program and project staff that may have reporting responsibilities into the aggregate portfolio.
Success	Success is measured by product and project quality, timeliness, budget compliance, and degree of customer satisfaction.	Success is measured by the degree to which the program satisfies the needs and benefits for which it was undertaken.	Success is measured in terms of the aggregate investment performance and benefit realization of the portfolio.
Monitoring	Project managers monitor and control the work of producing the products, services, or results that the project was undertaken to produce.	Program managers monitor the progress of program components to ensure the overall goals, schedules, budget, and benefits of the program will be met.	Portfolio managers monitor strategic changes and aggregate resource allocation, performance results, and risk of the portfolio.

Figure 1–2: Organizational project management comparison.

A Guide to the Project Management Body of Knowledge (PMBOK® Guide) – Fifth Edition, Project Management Institute, Inc., 2013, p. 8

Portfolio Management

A *portfolio* is a collection of projects, programs, sub-portfolios, and operations managed as a group to achieve organizational strategic results. *Portfolio management* is the centralized management of one or more portfolios to achieve strategic objectives.

A Guide to the Project Management Body of Knowledge (PMBOK® Guide) – Fifth Edition, Project Management Institute (PMI)®, Project Management Professional (PMP)®, and Certified Associate in Project Management (CAPM)® are registered trademarks of Project Management Institute, Inc. - Version 2.1 Published September 30, 2014

Lesson 1: Getting Started with Project Management | Topic A

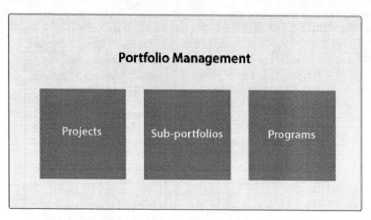

Figure 1-3: Portfolio management.

Portfolio management selects the right programs or projects, prioritizes the work, and provides resources. Program management solidifies its programs and projects and controls interdependencies, whereas project management develops and implements plans to achieve a specific scope that is driven by the objectives of the program or portfolio.

A Guide to the Project Management Body of Knowledge (PMBOK® Guide) – Fifth Edition, Project Management Institute, Inc., 2013, p. 9

Program Management

A *program* is defined as a group of related projects, subprograms, and program activities managed in a coordinated way to achieve benefits not available from managing them individually. A project may or may not be part of a program, but a program will always have projects.

A Guide to the Project Management Body of Knowledge (PMBOK® Guide) – Fifth Edition, Project Management Institute, Inc., 2013, p. 9

PMO

As stated in the *PMBOK® Guide,* a *project management office (PMO)* is a management structure that standardizes the project-related governance processes and facilitates the sharing of resources, methodologies, tools, and techniques. PMOs are more common in larger organizations because of the amount of projects that can be in process all at the same time. A PMO can offer assistance and guidance for all projects in progress. PMI does not provide official guidelines or standards for a PMO, so large organizations must use PMI principles and best practices to implement their PMO. There are several types of PMO structures, each varying in the degree of control and influence they have on projects within the organization:

- *Supportive PMOs* provide a consultative role to projects by supplying templates, best practices, training access to information, and lessons learned from other projects.
- *Controlling PMOs* provide support and require compliance through various means. Compliance may involve adopting project management frameworks or methodologies; using specific templates, forms, and tools; or conforming to governance.
- *Directive PMOs* take control of the projects by directly managing the projects.

A Guide to the Project Management Body of Knowledge (PMBOK® Guide) – Fifth Edition, Project Management Institute, Inc., 2013, pg. 10-11

Role of the Project Manager

The *project manager* is the individual assigned by an organization to lead the team that is responsible for carrying out and achieving the project objectives. A project manager could report to a functional manager, or a program or portfolio manager who is responsible for the alignment of a number of related projects.

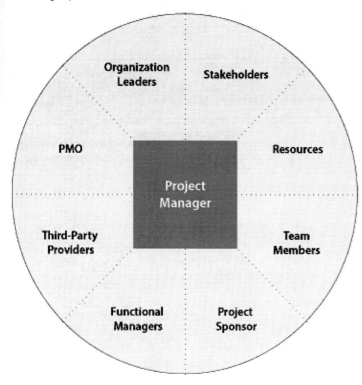

Figure 1-4: Role of a project manager.

A Guide to the Project Management Body of Knowledge (PMBOK® Guide) – Fifth Edition, Project Management Institute, Inc., 2013, p. 16

Responsibilities of the Project Manager

Project managers are responsible for satisfying the task, team, and individual needs for a project. The project manager is the link between what the business must have and the project team that will produce deliverables to meet the project objectives. There are many competencies that enable a project manager to effectively manage projects:

- Knowledge—refers to what the project manager knows about project management.
- Performance—refers to what the project manager is able to do or accomplish while applying his or her project management knowledge.
- Personal—refers to how the project manager behaves when performing the project activity. Personal effectiveness encompasses attitude, core personality characteristics, and leadership, which provides that ability to guide the project team while achieving project objectives and balancing the project constraints.

 Note: To further explore dealing with project team issues, you can access the LearnTO **Handle Pushback** presentation from the **LearnTO** tile on the LogicalCHOICE Course screen.

A Guide to the Project Management Body of Knowledge (PMBOK® Guide) – Fifth Edition, Project Management Institute, Inc., 2013, pg. 16-17

Interpersonal Skills of a Project Manager

Interpersonal skills are unique abilities that an individual has to conduct themselves in a professional manner when interacting with others. Because project managers accomplish work through the

A Guide to the Project Management Body of Knowledge (PMBOK® Guide) – Fifth Edition, Project Management Institute (PMI)®, Project Management Professional (PMP)®, and Certified Associate in Project Management (CAPM)® are registered trademarks of Project Management Institute, Inc. - Version 2.1 Published September 30, 2014

Lesson 1: Getting Started with Project Management | Topic A

project team and other stakeholders, they must have the skills needed to enable a good working environment. This requires a balance of ethical, interpersonal, and conceptual skills that help you analyze situations and interact appropriately. Because project managers work with and communicate with a number of different people throughout the life cycle of a project, using interpersonal skills is very important.

 Note: To explore how to say "no" comfortably, you can access the LearnTO **Say No Comfortably** presentation from the **LearnTO** tile on the LogicalCHOICE Course screen.

Interpersonal Skill	Description
Leadership	The ability to step up and guide others to help you achieve results. Leadership abilities are gained through experience, building relationships, and taking on initiatives.
Team building	Building a strong team can be challenging, but through continuous support and working collaboratively you can enable a team to work together to solve problems, diffuse interpersonal issues, share information, and tackle project objectives as a unified force. The team mentality is extremely effective and can be a powerful tool in achieving project objectives.
Motivation	Motivation skills are key in any management role. Motivation is what keeps people involved and wanting to complete excellent work on time. Every team member will be driven by different factors such as job satisfaction, achievement and recognition in the workplace, the room to grow, and finally, financial compensation. Understanding how these factors can play into a team member's motivation will help you provide the support they need while completing project work.
Communication	Communication can arguably be the most important skill needed to effectively manage projects. Information regarding project work and team members must be shared and dispersed among the team and can get tainted if the project manager is not addressing it properly. Good communication skills will help project managers resolve conflicts, make decisions, and support solutions.
Influencing	The ability to influence people can be a powerful tool when managing a team. Influencing can result in positive outcomes when resolving an issue because you can state a good case and explain why an idea, decision, or problem should be handled a certain way without resistance from other individuals.
Decision making	Decision making can be a very important skill to use when working with others to come up with a result. In the business work, decisions are usually produced by a group of individuals. Demonstrating that you have the ability to make decisions will show that you can be a strong advocate in any decision-making process, meeting, or group. Decision making can be broken up into a series of phases, including: • Defining the problem • Generating potential solutions • Planning for solution actions • Putting ideas into action • Planning for solution evaluations • Evaluating the outcomes and processes

Interpersonal Skill	Description
Political and cultural awareness	Understanding and being aware of the cultural and political views and beliefs of not only the organization you are working within, but the individuals on your project team will help you develop better communication skills and trust.
Negotiation	Negotiation is an approach used by more than one individual to come to an agreement or resolution. Being able to successfully negotiate will have a huge impact on how you resolve issues and conflicts that arise during the course of a project.
Trust building	Trust is at the foundation for many interpersonal relationships. As a project manager, you must build trusting relationships between the individuals you will be working with on a project. Trust building can be accomplished through a variety of ways, including good communication, following up on expectations, and proving that you can follow through.
Conflict management	Conflict management involves intervening before a negative result of a conflict can occur. Successfully managing conflicts throughout a project's life cycle can be challenging. As a project manager, you will be the point person for any conflict that arises. You will determine how it will be handled. The goal is to try to increase any positive outcomes of a conflict so it can be viewed as a learning experience.
Coaching	Coaching is the act of giving guidance and direction to another person so that he or she can make better decisions in the future. As the manager of a project, you will need to coach team members to get them to perform to the desired level.

A Guide to the Project Management Body of Knowledge (PMBOK® Guide) – Fifth Edition, Project Management Institute, Inc., 2013, pg. 17-18, 513-519

The *PMBOK® Guide*

A Guide to the Project Management Body of Knowledge (PMBOK® Guide) - Fifth Edition provides guidelines for managing individual projects and defines project management concepts. It describes the project management life cycle and its processes, and the project life cycle. It is a globally recognized standard that describes the established norms, methods, processes, and practices that provide a base of best practices for the project management profession. The acceptance of project management as a profession indicates that the application of knowledge, processes, skills, tools, and techniques can have a significant impact on project success. It provides and promotes a common methodology and vocabulary for project management processes.

The *PMBOK® Guide* contains the standard for managing most projects most of the time across many types of industries. It contains project management processes that are used to manage a project toward a more successful outcome. The standard is unique to the project management field and has interrelationships to other project management disciplines, such as program and portfolio management.

There are two Project Management Institute (PMI)® project management certifications available:

- *Certified Associate in Project Management (CAPM)* is a valuable entry-level certification for project practitioners with little or no project experience that demonstrates your understanding of the fundamental knowledge, terminology, and processes of effective project management. This can be achieved by having the required project management experience, passing an exam, and then maintained by re-testing every five years.

A Guide to the Project Management Body of Knowledge (PMBOK® Guide) – Fifth Edition, Project Management Institute (PMI)®, Project Management Professional (PMP)®, and Certified Associate in Project Management (CAPM)® are registered trademarks of Project Management Institute, Inc. - Version 2.1 Published September 30, 2014

Lesson 1: Getting Started with Project Management | Topic A

- *Project Management Professional (PMP)* is the most important industry-recognized certification for project managers. Globally recognized and demanded, the PMP® demonstrates that you have the experience, education, and competency to lead and direct projects. This can be achieved by having the required project management experience, passing an exam, and then maintained by obtaining *Professional Development Units (PDUs)*. This is similar to the Certified Public Accountant (CPA) exam and professional development requirements.

 Note: To further explore PMI's PDU requirements, you can access the LearnTO **Earn PDUs** presentation from the **LearnTO** tile on the LogicalCHOICE Course screen.

A Guide to the Project Management Body of Knowledge (PMBOK® Guide) – Fifth Edition, Project Management Institute, Inc., 2013, pg. 1-2, 18

Ethics and Professional Conduct

The PMI *Code of Ethics and Professional Conduct* describes the ethical and professional behavior expectations of any individual working as a project management professional. There are many values that PMI expects a project manager to have while interacting with anyone related to a project, including being respectful, being fair, and being honest.

A Guide to the Project Management Body of Knowledge (PMBOK® Guide) – Fifth Edition, Project Management Institute, Inc., 2013, p. 1

A Guide to the Project Management Body of Knowledge (PMBOK® Guide) – Fifth Edition, Project Management Institute (PMI)®, Project Management Professional (PMP)®, and Certified Associate in Project Management (CAPM)® are registered trademarks of Project Management Institute, Inc. - Version 2.1 Published September 30, 2014

Lesson 1: Getting Started with Project Management | Topic A

ACTIVITY 1-1
Discussing Components of Project Management

Scenario
In this activity, you will identify and explore the project management field.

---

1. What projects have you worked on and what was your role in those projects? Were you ever a project manager of a project?

2. What interpersonal skills do you think are most important for a project manager to use within a project team?

3. A large organization's PMO provides templates and other tools for the project managers to use on various projects. They also provide support to the project management team and require compliance with PMI methodologies from each project manager with respect to the project work. What type of PMO is used by this organization?

4. Navigate to PMI's web page at **http://www.pmi.org/About-Us/Ethics/Code-of-Ethics.aspx** and review the Code of Ethics and Professional Conduct document.

A Guide to the Project Management Body of Knowledge (PMBOK® Guide) – Fifth Edition, Project Management Institute (PMI)®, Project Management Professional (PMP)®, and Certified Associate in Project Management (CAPM)® are registered trademarks of Project Management Institute, Inc. - Version 2.1 Published September 30, 2014

Lesson 1: Getting Started with Project Management | Topic A

TOPIC B

Project Management and the Business

Now that you have a better understanding of project management fundamentals and what the role of the project manager is, you can take a closer look at how project management can be implemented within the context of a business or organization. There are projects being conducted in a variety of different industries, organizations, and businesses, and understanding how the management aspect of a project can relate to the business as a whole is very important to its success. In this next topic, you will examine the relationship between project management and the business.

Business Value

Business value is a concept that is unique to each organization. It is defined as the entire value of a business, the total sum of all tangible and intangible elements. The value may be created and grow through consistent and effective management of all ongoing operations throughout the business. Through the effective use of portfolio, program, and project management, organizations will possess the ability to employ reliable, established processes to meet strategic objectives and obtain greater business value from their project investments. As a project manager, your role is to manage projects within this business framework and ensure that each project is on track with what the business is trying to accomplish.

A Guide to the Project Management Body of Knowledge (PMBOK® Guide) – Fifth Edition, Project Management Institute, Inc., 2013, pg. 15-16

Business Value Development

Successful business value realization begins with comprehensive strategic planning and management by company leaders. Through proper portfolio management, projects can be aligned directly to the organizational strategy so that the organization has an overall view of how project investments support the organizational plan for growth and development. Next, program management provides the ability to align multiple projects for optimized or integrated costs, scheduling, effort, and benefits. And finally, project management applies knowledge, processes, skills, tools, and techniques that enhance the likelihood of success over a wide range of projects that deliver products, services, or results.

A Guide to the Project Management Body of Knowledge (PMBOK® Guide) – Fifth Edition, Project Management Institute, Inc., 2013, p. 16

Operations Management

Operations management is a business function that is responsible for overseeing, directing, and controlling business operations. Operations support the day-to-day business to achieve the strategic and tactical goals of the business. Operations areas or departments can include manufacturing, accounting, payroll, human resources, sales, marketing, quality assurance, and more. Projects can help achieve the organizational goals when they are aligned with the organization's business strategy and result in a beneficial outcome or result to the related operational area.

A Guide to the Project Management Body of Knowledge (PMBOK® Guide) – Fifth Edition, Project Management Institute, Inc., 2013, p. 13

Operations and Project Management

Changes to business operations may be driven by a project, especially if the changes are a result of a new product or service delivery. Projects can intersect with ongoing operations at points in the product life cycle, such as:

- At each close-out phase
- When developing new product, upgrading a product, or expanding outputs
- While improving operations of the product development process
- The end of the product life cycle

Deliverables and knowledge are transferred between project managers and operations for implementation of the delivered work at each point. Operations management is concerned with the ongoing production of goods or services, and the transfer of inputs to outputs. The needs of stakeholders who perform and conduct business operations must be considered in projects that will affect their operations. These stakeholders' needs should be identified and tracked, and their influence addressed as part of the risk management plan.

A Guide to the Project Management Body of Knowledge (PMBOK® Guide) – Fifth Edition, Project Management Institute, Inc., 2013, pg. 12-13

Organizational Strategy and Governance

Organizations use governance guidelines to establish strategic direction and performance parameters. The strategic direction provides the purpose, expectations, goals, and actions to guide business pursuits and is aligned with business objectives. Project management activities should be, and must stay, aligned with business direction to increase project success.

Organizational strategy should provide guidance and direction to the project management function. If the goals of a project are in conflict with an established organizational strategy, it is incumbent upon the project manager to document and identify such conflicts as early as possible in the project.

Projects and programs are initiated to achieve strategic business outcomes, for which many organizations adopt formal organizational governance processes and procedures. Organizational governance criteria, such as HIPPA in the health care field, can impose restrictions and constraints on projects. It is important for the project manager to be knowledgeable about the corporate or organizational governance policies and procedures pertaining to the subject matter of the product or service being delivered by the project. For example, if the organization has adopted sustainability practices for new construction, the project manager must be aware of these sustainability requirements.

A Guide to the Project Management Body of Knowledge (PMBOK® Guide) – Fifth Edition, Project Management Institute, Inc., 2013, pg. 14-15

PBOs

Project-based organizations (PBOs) refer to various organizational forms that create temporary systems for carrying out their work. In this project-focused environment, work success is measured by the final result, not position or politics. A PBO can refer to either an entire firm or it can be nested within subsidiaries or divisions of larger corporations.

A Guide to the Project Management Body of Knowledge (PMBOK® Guide) – Fifth Edition, Project Management Institute, Inc., 2013, p. 14

A Guide to the Project Management Body of Knowledge (PMBOK® Guide) – Fifth Edition, Project Management Institute (PMI)®, Project Management Professional (PMP)®, and Certified Associate in Project Management (CAPM)® are registered trademarks of Project Management Institute, Inc. - Version 2.1 Published September 30, 2014

Lesson 1: Getting Started with Project Management | Topic B

ACTIVITY 1-2
Discussing the Relationship Between Projects and the Business

Scenario
In this activity, you will examine the relationship between project management and business.

1. What are operational areas?

2. Describe how a past project supported or changed your organization's operational area.

3. Describe how a past project contributed to the business and why.

A Guide to the Project Management Body of Knowledge (PMBOK® Guide) – Fifth Edition, Project Management Institute (PMI)®, Project Management Professional (PMP)®, and Certified Associate in Project Management (CAPM)® are registered trademarks of Project Management Institute, Inc. - Version 2.1 Published September 30, 2014

Summary

In this lesson, you identified what project management is and how your role as the project manager can be influenced by an organization's portfolios, programs, and projects. With a good foundation set in this first lesson, you have a better understanding of how project management can be used at a high level within an organization and the impact a project can have on an organization's business strategy.

What is the relationship among portfolio management, program management, project management, and organizational project management?

What is the role of the project manager?

Note: Check your LogicalCHOICE Course screen for opportunities to interact with your classmates, peers, and the larger LogicalCHOICE online community about the topics covered in this course or other topics you are interested in. From the Course screen you can also access available resources for a more continuous learning experience.

A Guide to the Project Management Body of Knowledge (PMBOK® Guide) – Fifth Edition, Project Management Institute (PMI)®, Project Management Professional (PMP)®, and Certified Associate in Project Management (CAPM)® are registered trademarks of Project Management Institute, Inc. - Version 2.1 Published September 30, 2014

2 Project Management and the Organization

Lesson Time: 3 hours

Lesson Objectives

In this lesson, you will:

- Identify and analyze organizational influences and how they affect the project.

- Identify how project stakeholders and governance can influence a project.

- Identify a project team.

- Identify the phases of the project life cycle and determine how a project evolves through each phase.

Lesson Introduction

In the previous lesson, you set the foundation for building the framework of project management. With the basic concepts presented in that lesson, you can now focus on how an organization's culture, business frameworks, processes, procedures, and business requirements can influence how projects are conducted and managed. You will also examine how an organization can directly affect a project's life cycle. In this lesson, you will explore how projects are managed within an organization.

A Guide to the Project Management Body of Knowledge (PMBOK® Guide) – Fifth Edition, Project Management Institute (PMI)®, Project Management Professional (PMP)®, and Certified Associate in Project Management (CAPM)® are registered trademarks of Project Management Institute, Inc. - Version 2.1 Published September 30, 2014

TOPIC A

Identify Organizational Influences

Projects and project management take place in an environment that is broader than that of the project itself, and an organization's culture, style, and structure influence how projects are performed. Understanding this broader context helps ensure that work is carried out in alignment with the organization's goals and managed in accordance with the organization's established practices. In this topic, you will analyze how organizational influences affect the methods used for staffing, managing, and executing the project.

Organizational Cultures and Styles

Organizations are groups of people or departments that are in place to accomplish a purpose, such as providing health care to patients. Every organization develops a unique culture and style that represents its cultural norm and affects how projects are performed. For example, flex hours versus an 8 to 5 work day can directly affect how a project manager schedules resources and how the team interacts. Culture is shaped by people's common experiences, such as:

- Shared visions, missions, values, beliefs, and expectations
- Regulations, policies, methods, and procedures
- Motivation and reward systems
- Risk tolerance
- View of leadership, hierarchy, and authority relationships
- Code of conduct, work ethic, and work hours
- Operating environments

A project manager should understand that cultures have a strong influence on a project's ability to meet its objectives. He or she also needs to know which individuals in the organization are the decision makers or influencers and work with them to increase the probability of project success.

A Guide to the Project Management Body of Knowledge (PMBOK® Guide) – Fifth Edition, Project Management Institute, Inc., 2013, pg. 20-21

Organizational Communications

Communication is a vital aspect of project management. Project management success depends on an effective communication style. Project managers need to communicate with all relevant stakeholders in all locations to facilitate decision making. Communication can be formal or informal and verbal or written. Formal communication can include reports, letters, presentations, contracts, and web conferencing. Informal communication can include e-mail, texting, instant messaging, social media, and video.

A Guide to the Project Management Body of Knowledge (PMBOK® Guide) – Fifth Edition, Project Management Institute, Inc., 2013, p. 21

Organizational Structures

An *organizational structure* dictates how the various groups and individuals within the organization interrelate. The organizational structure also affects how the project team is structured. The structure of an organization is an enterprise environmental factor, which affects the availability of resources and influences how projects are performed. These structures range from functional to projectized, with a variety of matrix structures in between. The structural model used by an organization will have a huge impact on how project managers interact with team members and stakeholders. In many cases, a project manager will interact with various levels in an organization, such as middle management, operations, strategic functions, and senior management. Several factors play into the interaction level of a project manager. Organizations will typically be configured in one of three main structural implementations: functional, matrix, or projectized.

A Guide to the Project Management Body of Knowledge (PMBOK® Guide) – Fifth Edition, Project Management Institute, Inc., 2013, p. 21

The Functional Organizational Structure

A classic *functional organization* is a hierarchy with each employee reporting into a specific supervisor or manager. The project team members in this structure complete project work along with their normal functional work. Employees are typically grouped by specialty or function, such as engineering, production, and sales. The main goal of using this structure is to share experience and knowledge within the functional group. Employees can grow and learn from one another because they are grouped by function. However, as a project manager this can be challenging because you will be working with a number of different functional managers and could have difficulty with resource availability, scheduling, and so on.

A Guide to the Project Management Body of Knowledge (PMBOK® Guide) – Fifth Edition, Project Management Institute, Inc., 2013, pg. 22-23

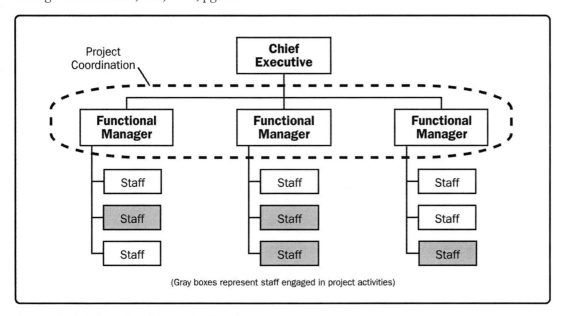

Figure 2-1: A functional organizational structure.

A Guide to the Project Management Body of Knowledge (PMBOK® Guide) – Fifth Edition, Project Management Institute, Inc., 2013, p. 22

The Projectized Organizational Structure

A *projectized organizational structure* is set up with the project management function overseeing and managing the resources and project work directly on a project-by-project basis. This structure is commonly used when most of the organization's resources are involved with project work and teams are primarily working virtually. This structure gives project managers a great deal of independence and authority over resources, budget, scheduling, and project work.

A Guide to the Project Management Body of Knowledge (PMBOK® Guide) – Fifth Edition, Project Management Institute (PMI)®, Project Management Professional (PMP)®, and Certified Associate in Project Management (CAPM)® are registered trademarks of Project Management Institute, Inc. - Version 2.1 Published September 30, 2014

Lesson 2: Project Management and the Organization | *Topic A*

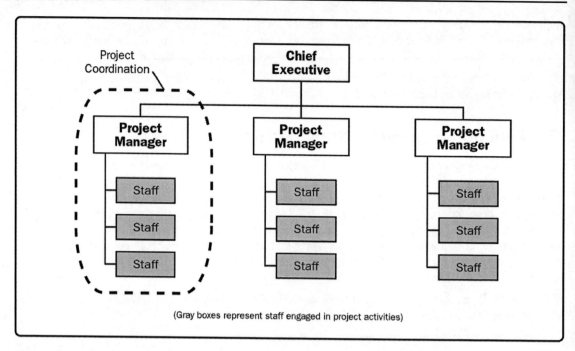

Figure 2-2: A projectized organization.

A Guide to the Project Management Body of Knowledge (PMBOK® Guide) – Fifth Edition, Project Management Institute, Inc., 2013, p. 25

Matrix Organizational Structures

The matrix organizational structure is a blend of both functional and projectized structures and can utilize characteristics from a variety of other structures. Depending on the level of power and influence between the project manager and the functional managers, the matrix categories can range from weak to strong. There are three basic types of matrix structures that you may come across in an organization.

Matrix Type	Description
Weak	A weak matrix organization is similar to a functional organization and the project manager is a coordinator (who has some authority and ability to make decisions) or an expediter (who has little decision-making authority). In this structure, the project manager does not have much control over the resources on a project and has to work within the functional departments and with a number of different managers and supervisors.

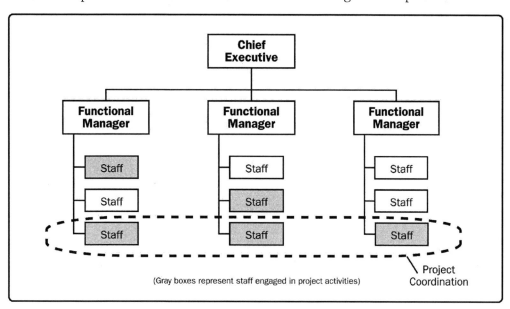

A Guide to the Project Management Body of Knowledge (PMBOK® Guide) – Fifth Edition, Project Management Institute, Inc., 2013, p. 23

Balanced	A balanced matrix organization has a project manager who does not have full authority over the project team members. The project manager shares authority over project team members with departmental functional managers.

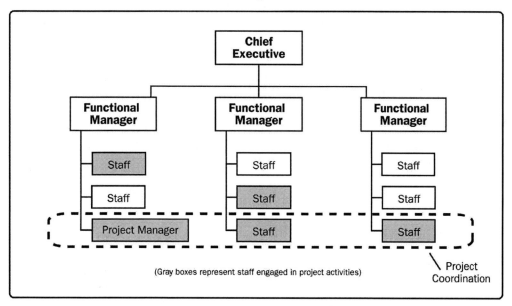

A Guide to the Project Management Body of Knowledge (PMBOK® Guide) – Fifth Edition, Project Management Institute, Inc., 2013, p. 24

A Guide to the Project Management Body of Knowledge (PMBOK® Guide) – Fifth Edition, Project Management Institute (PMI)®, Project Management Professional (PMP)®, and Certified Associate in Project Management (CAPM)® are registered trademarks of Project Management Institute, Inc. - Version 2.1 Published September 30, 2014

Lesson 2: Project Management and the Organization | Topic A

Matrix Type	Description
Strong	A strong matrix organization is similar to the projectized organization and has full-time project managers who have authority over the team members.

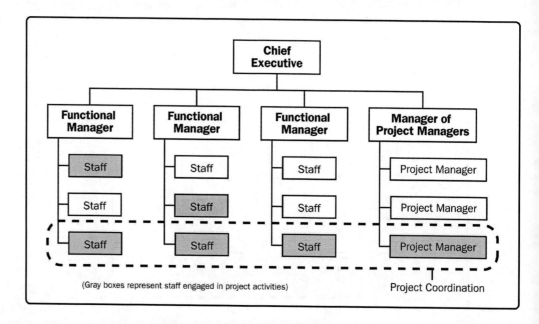

A Guide to the Project Management Body of Knowledge (PMBOK® Guide) – Fifth Edition, Project Management Institute, Inc., 2013, p. 24

A Guide to the Project Management Body of Knowledge (PMBOK® Guide) – Fifth Edition, Project Management Institute, Inc., 2013, pg. 22-26

The Composite Organizational Structure

The composite organizational structure is a combination of any structure. It can be composed of a matrix, a functional, or a projectized structure, or a combination of all three. This model is used most when special projects are identified that are critical to the organization as a whole. Therefore, the team members can come from any number of departments and levels within the structure. The team may develop its own set of operating procedures and operate outside the standard formalized reporting structure during the project. You may come across a composite structure when a project demands that the team work outside the normal operating procedures during the life of the project.

A Guide to the Project Management Body of Knowledge (PMBOK® Guide) – Fifth Edition, Project Management Institute, Inc., 2013, pg. 25-26

A Guide to the Project Management Body of Knowledge (PMBOK® Guide) – Fifth Edition, Project Management Institute (PMI)®, Project Management Professional (PMP)®, and Certified Associate in Project Management (CAPM)® are registered trademarks of Project Management Institute, Inc. - Version 2.1 Published September 30, 2014

Lesson 2: Project Management and the Organization | *Topic A*

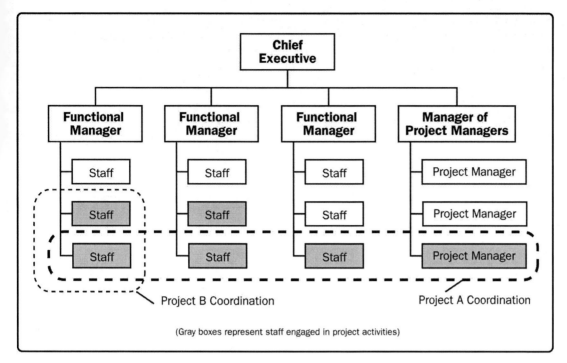

Figure 2–3: A composite organizational structure.

A Guide to the Project Management Body of Knowledge (PMBOK® Guide) – Fifth Edition, Project Management Institute, Inc., 2013, p. 26

Organizational Process Assets

Organizational process assets are the assets and resources that are specific to an organization, and that the organization will use throughout the life of the project. Assets can be broken into two types: processes and procedures, and corporate knowledge base. Process assets can include the lessons an organization has learned from previous projects and activities, and general historical information preserved by the organization. Assets can be resources plans, processes, policies, procedures, and knowledge bases specific to and used by the performing organization.

A Guide to the Project Management Body of Knowledge (PMBOK® Guide) – Fifth Edition, Project Management Institute, Inc., 2013, p. 27

Organizational Processes and Procedures

The organization's processes and procedures for conducting project work are intended to facilitate the project process.

Process Phase	Includes
Initiating and Planning	• Guidelines and criteria for aligning an organization's standard processes and procedures to meet the needs of each project initiated. • Specific organizational standards. This can include any number of policies and procedures that will need to be referenced for a specific project. For example, if you are working within the health care field, you may need to refer to and adhere to the HIPPA standards when planning your project. • Organizations may develop and manage a set of standard templates that you will be required to use throughout the initiating and planning phases of a project.

Process Phase	Includes
Executing, Monitoring, and Controlling	• Change control processes and procedures • Financial controls procedures • Procurement procedures • Issue and defect management procedures • Organizational communications requirements • Procedures for prioritizing, approving, and issuing work authorizations • Risk control procedures • Standardized guidelines, work instructions, proposal evaluation criteria, and performance measurement criteria
Closing	Organizations may provide specific closing procedures or requirements that must be completed for a project to be officially closed. This can include anything from documenting the lessons learned during the project to conducting a post-project audit or evaluation to verify that what the project intended was carried out successfully.

A Guide to the Project Management Body of Knowledge (PMBOK® Guide) – Fifth Edition, Project Management Institute, Inc., 2013, pg. 27-28

Corporate Knowledge Base

The corporate knowledge base is a repository for storing and retrieving useful information. There is a wide variety of information that can be available:

• Configuration management knowledge bases that can include baselines of performing organizational standards, policies, procedures, and documents.
• Financial databases that include historic financial information.
• Government and industry standards, such as regulations, codes of conduct, and quality standards.
• Project files, such as scope, cost, schedule, and quality baselines.
• Infrastructure documentation and reference materials, such as network diagrams and hardware and software inventory information.
• Personnel administration information, such as staffing and retention guidelines.
• Human resources documentation and standards.
• Marketplace or industry conditions.
• Company work authorization systems.

A Guide to the Project Management Body of Knowledge (PMBOK® Guide) – Fifth Edition, Project Management Institute, Inc., 2013, p. 28

Enterprise Environmental Factors

Enterprise environmental factors refer to internal or external conditions, not under the control of the project, that influence, constrain, or direct the project. These factors can either support or limit the project management options, act as inputs for planning processes, and have a negative or positive influence on a project outcome. In some cases, they may even be considered overhead to the project. Examples of enterprise environmental factors may include:

• Organizational culture, structure, and governance
• Geographic distribution of facilities and resources
• Government or industry standards
• IT infrastructure

- Existing human resources
- Personnel administration
- Company work authorization systems
- Marketplace conditions
- Stakeholder risk tolerances
- Political climate and situations
- Organization's established communications channels
- Commercial databases
- Project Management Information Systems   ← PMIS
- Languages, time zones, and other countries' holiday schedules

A Guide to the Project Management Body of Knowledge (PMBOK® Guide) – Fifth Edition, Project Management Institute, Inc., 2013, p. 29

A Guide to the Project Management Body of Knowledge (PMBOK® Guide) – Fifth Edition, Project Management Institute (PMI)®, Project Management Professional (PMP)®, and Certified Associate in Project Management (CAPM)® are registered trademarks of Project Management Institute, Inc. - Version 2.1 Published September 30, 2014

Lesson 2: Project Management and the Organization | *Topic A*

ACTIVITY 2-1
Discussing Organizational Influences on Projects

Scenario

In this activity, you will discuss the various organizational influences that affect project management.

1. Describe the organizational culture, style, communication, and structure of one of your projects.

2. If you were the project manager of the project described in the previous question, how would you work with those organizational cultures and styles? Describe the organizational process assets you have used on past projects.

3. Describe any enterprise environmental factors that you have experience with or factors that you can see coming across in the future as a project manager.

A Guide to the Project Management Body of Knowledge (PMBOK® Guide) – Fifth Edition, Project Management Institute (PMI)®, Project Management Professional (PMP)®, and Certified Associate in Project Management (CAPM)® are registered trademarks of Project Management Institute, Inc. - Version 2.1 Published September 30, 2014

Lesson 2: Project Management and the Organization | Topic A

TOPIC B

Project Stakeholders and Governance

In the previous topic, the focus was on the organizational aspects that can influence a project. Now we will build on that by identifying how the project stakeholders can influence a project. You will explore the way governance can affect how a project is conducted and managed. It is important to understand the different influences on a project in order to properly manage and monitor the project as a whole.

Project Stakeholders

A *project stakeholder* is an individual, group, or organization that has a business interest in the outcome of a project. Stakeholders may or may not be actively involved in project work and could affect or be affected by a decision, activity, or outcome of a project. Stakeholders take on a variety of roles and responsibilities on a project, and can include members of the project team, customers, end users, and many other individuals and groups of people. Managing stakeholders' influence and engagement throughout the project will have a large impact on the outcomes and success of a project.

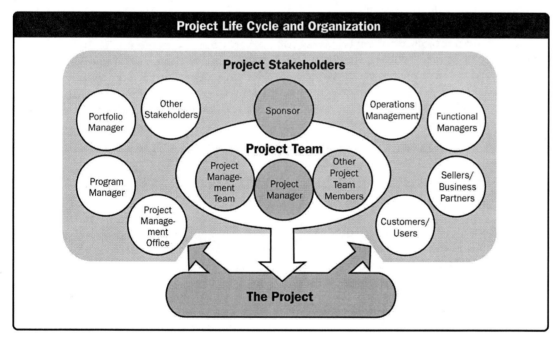

Figure 2–4: Stakeholders and the project.

A Guide to the Project Management Body of Knowledge (PMBOK® Guide) – Fifth Edition, Project Management Institute, Inc., 2013, p. 31

Stakeholders may have competing interests, needs, priorities, and opinions. They may have conflicting visions for the project's outcomes, so managing them carefully is an important part of the project manager's role. Project managers must identify the internal and external stakeholders of a project as early as possible, learn what their needs are, and secure their participation in defining the project's parameters and success criteria. Although it may be difficult to negotiate a consensus early in the project, it is far less painful and costly than getting to the end of the project only to learn that someone's needs were not met or were misunderstood.

A Guide to the Project Management Body of Knowledge (PMBOK® Guide) – Fifth Edition, Project Management Institute, Inc., 2013, pg. 30-33

Project Stakeholder Types

Project stakeholders can include:

- Sponsors, who may be individuals or groups, that provide the financial assistance, resources, and support for the project.
- Customers and users who will approve the project's deliverables.
- Sellers who will provide components or services to the project under a contract.
- Business partners who will have a special business relationship and role with the project, such as performing installation, training, or support.
- Organizational groups that are internal stakeholders affected by the activities of the project team, such as legal, finance, operations, sales, and customer service.
- Functional managers who manage organizational departments such as human resources, finance, procurement, or accounting and who need to support the project activities.
- Other stakeholders that contribute to or have an interest in the deliverables, such as government regulators, consultants, financial institutions, and more.

A Guide to the Project Management Body of Knowledge (PMBOK® Guide) – Fifth Edition, Project Management Institute, Inc., 2013, pg. 32-33

Positive and Negative Stakeholders

Positive stakeholders usually benefit from the successful outcome of a project, whereas negative stakeholders will view the successful outcome of the project as harmful in some way. Good examples of positive stakeholders are business leaders from a community who benefit from an industrial expansion project because it involves economic growth for the community. Negative stakeholders in this scenario could be environmental groups who are concerned about the environment and consider the project as harmful to the environment. Furthermore, positive stakeholders can go to the extent of getting the needed permits to proceed with the project because they are more interested in the project's success. The negative stakeholders can block the progress of the project by demanding more environmental reviews.

A Guide to the Project Management Body of Knowledge (PMBOK® Guide) – Fifth Edition, Project Management Institute, Inc., 2013, pg. 31-32

Project Governance

Project governance is a comprehensive methodology that provides oversight on the project life cycle for the organization and ensures its success. It provides the structure, processes, decision-making models, and tools for the project manager and team to manage the project. It provides critical support to the project and is a method of controlling the project and increasing the success of the project by defining, documenting, and communicating effective, reliable, and repeatable project practices for the project to use. In large organizations that utilize a Project Management Office (PMO), governance is generally managed and controlled by the PMO.

A Guide to the Project Management Body of Knowledge (PMBOK® Guide) – Fifth Edition, Project Management Institute, Inc., 2013, pg. 34-35

The Project Governance Framework

As stated in the *PMBOK® Guide,* a project governance framework can include:

- Project success and deliverable acceptance criteria
- Process to identify, escalate, and resolve issues
- Relationship between project team, organizational groups, and external stakeholders
- Project organization chart with project roles
- Communication processes and procedures
- Processes for project decision-making
- Guidelines for aligning project governance and organizational strategy

- Project life cycle approach
- Process for stage gate or phase reviews
- Process for review and approval of changes above the project manager's authority
- Process to align internal stakeholders with project process requirements

A Guide to the Project Management Body of Knowledge (PMBOK® Guide) – Fifth Edition, Project Management Institute, Inc., 2013, p. 34

Project Success

Because projects are temporary endeavors, the success of the projects should be measured in terms of completing the project within the constraints of scope, time, cost, quality, resources, customer satisfaction, and risk as approved between the project managers and the customer, whether the customer is an external, paying client or people and departments internal to the organization that are considered internal customers. Internal customers can include senior management.

A test period can be part of the total project time before handing it over to the permanent operations to ensure a smooth and successful transition.

A Guide to the Project Management Body of Knowledge (PMBOK® Guide) – Fifth Edition, Project Management Institute, Inc., 2013, p. 35

A Guide to the Project Management Body of Knowledge (PMBOK® Guide) – Fifth Edition, Project Management Institute (PMI)®, Project Management Professional (PMP)®, and Certified Associate in Project Management (CAPM)® are registered trademarks of Project Management Institute, Inc. - Version 2.1 Published September 30, 2014

ACTIVITY 2-2
Discussing Project Stakeholders Roles

Scenario

In this activity, you will discuss the different roles project stakeholders can have on a project.

---

1. From your experience, give some examples of project stakeholders and what value they added to a project.

2. What types of experiences have you had with project stakeholders? Were there any negative or positive impacts on the project?

3. What responsibilities apply to project sponsors?
   - ☑ Signs and publishes the project charter
   - ○ Keeps the sponsor and the stakeholders informed
   - ○ Provides input to define needs for the project output
   - ○ Supervises and coordinates the management of all projects in an organization

4. What responsibilities apply to a PMO?
   - ○ Signs and publishes the project charter
   - ○ Keeps the sponsor and the stakeholders informed
   - ○ Provides input to define needs for the project output
   - ☑ Supervises and coordinates the management of all projects in an organization

A Guide to the Project Management Body of Knowledge (PMBOK® Guide) – Fifth Edition, Project Management Institute (PMI)®, Project Management Professional (PMP)®, and Certified Associate in Project Management (CAPM)® are registered trademarks of Project Management Institute, Inc. - Version 2.1 Published September 30, 2014

Lesson 2: Project Management and the Organization | Topic B

TOPIC C

The Project Team

The project team can arguably be the most important aspect of a successful project. In the last few topics, you have discovered how outside influences are important and must be recognized throughout the project's duration, but more importantly, you must understand the dynamic of the project team and how the team can affect the successes and failures of a project. In this topic, you will identify a project team.

Project Teams

A project team is made up of a project manager and other people who have the skills necessary to perform the project work. The roles of the people on the project team can include:

- Project management staff that performs activities such as budgeting, scheduling, reporting and control, risk management, and project communications. This role may be supported by a PMO.
- Project staff that perform the work to create the project deliverables.
- Supporting experts who perform work to develop the project management plan. These roles can include legal, logistics, engineering, testing, and so on.
- User or customer representatives who will provide requirements and accept the project deliverables.
- Sellers that are external companies that have a contract to provide a product or service needed by the project.
- Business partners that are external companies that provide specialized support through a partnership.
- Business partner members that support the business partnership.

A Guide to the Project Management Body of Knowledge (PMBOK® Guide) – Fifth Edition, Project Management Institute, Inc., 2013, pg. 35-36

Project Team Composition

Project team composition can vary based on organizational culture, location, and scope. Composition refers to the flavor of the team and how the team members are brought together or combined on the team. For example, they can be a dedicated team in which most of the project team members are assigned to work on the project full-time, or they can be part-time team members who work on a project in addition to their regular work. Often, organizations have a mix of these two formats. The project team generally is comprised of the project manager, project management team, and other individual team members. The individual team members perform project work and might not be involved in the management side of the project. The project team contains people from different groups who possess knowledge on specific subjects or have unique skill sets to carry out project work.

A Guide to the Project Management Body of Knowledge (PMBOK® Guide) – Fifth Edition, Project Management Institute, Inc., 2013, pg. 37-38

ACTIVITY 2-3
Discussing Project Teams

Scenario
In this activity, you will discuss the dynamics of a project team.

1. What types of project teams have you worked with?

2. What were some of the pros and cons of that team's composition?

A Guide to the Project Management Body of Knowledge (PMBOK® Guide) – Fifth Edition, Project Management Institute (PMI)®, Project Management Professional (PMP)®, and Certified Associate in Project Management (CAPM)® are registered trademarks of Project Management Institute, Inc. - Version 2.1 Published September 30, 2014

TOPIC D

The Project Life Cycle

In the previous topics, you discovered how the organization affects project management and how individuals such as project stakeholders and the project team play a large role in the success of a project. But what about the project itself? The project is constantly evolving and changing as people, work, and other external influences are involved from initiation to close-out. In this topic, you will identify the phases of the project life cycle and determine how a project evolves through each phase and ultimately comes to a close.

The Project Life Cycle

Projects are typically broken down into manageable, sequential phases of work activities. These project phases, taken together, are referred to as the *project life cycle*. Each project phase has a time frame and a predetermined outcome, such as specific deliverables, a milestone, or intermediate results. A project life cycle may have four or five phases, which can vary because the life cycle is unique and customized to meet the needs of specific projects or the organization as a whole.

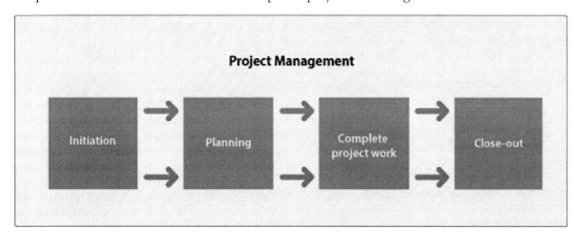

Figure 2-5: The project life cycle.

The project life cycle is marked by the beginning and end of the project. At the start-up, the project's general scope and timing are determined. In the next phase, detailed planning occurs followed by another phase of actual project work activities and the monitoring of those activities. In the final phase, project-closing activities occur. A project life cycle can be predictive, in which the deliverables are defined at the initiation of the project and changes are tightly managed, or adaptive, where the scope and deliverables are developed during multiple iterations.

A Guide to the Project Management Body of Knowledge (PMBOK® Guide) – Fifth Edition, Project Management Institute, Inc., 2013, p. 38

General Characteristics of the Project Life Cycle

Though projects differ in nature, size, and complexity, they display certain common characteristics. At the beginning of the project, the cost and staffing levels are quite low. They reach the peak once the work is carried out and drop rapidly upon project completion. The influences, uncertainties, and risks involved with stakeholders are high at the project start and diminish over the life of the project.

 Note: It is important to note that the project life cycle, as discussed here, refers to the cycle of work being performed as part of the project, and not to the phases of project management.

A generic life cycle for a project includes:

- Starting or initiating the project
- Organizing, planning, and preparing
- Carrying out or performing the project work and monitoring the project work
- Closing the project out

For most projects, cost and staffing levels are low to start, increase as the project work is being done and then decrease when the project closes.

A Guide to the Project Management Body of Knowledge (PMBOK® Guide) – Fifth Edition, Project Management Institute, Inc., 2013, pg. 38-40

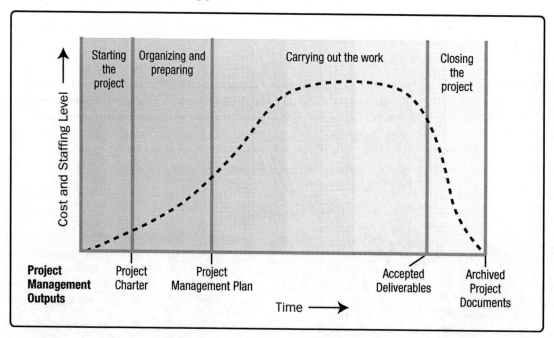

Figure 2-6: Cost and staffing levels.

A Guide to the Project Management Body of Knowledge (PMBOK® Guide) – Fifth Edition, Project Management Institute, Inc., 2013, p. 39

Project Risk and Costs

At the start of a project, risk and uncertainty are at a high level and decrease gradually throughout the project life cycle. The ability to influence the project and its objectives are high at the beginning of the project and decrease over time. That means that the costs of changes to the project start low and significantly increase over time.

A Guide to the Project Management Body of Knowledge (PMBOK® Guide) – Fifth Edition, Project Management Institute, Inc., 2013, pg. 40-41

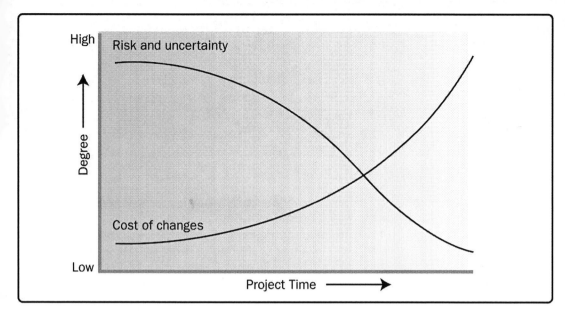

Figure 2-7: Project risks and costs comparison.

A Guide to the Project Management Body of Knowledge (PMBOK® Guide) – Fifth Edition, Project Management Institute, Inc., 2013, p. 40

Applying Governance within the Project Life Cycle

At the beginning of each phase, it is a good practice to verify and validate the former assumptions made to the project, analyze risks, and explain in detail the processes required to achieve a phase's deliverables. After the key deliverables of a particular phase are produced, a review at the end of the phase is necessary to ensure completeness and acceptance. Even though this method signifies the start of the subsequent phase, a phase can be closed or the project terminated when huge risks are involved for the project or when the objectives are no longer required.

A Guide to the Project Management Body of Knowledge (PMBOK® Guide) – Fifth Edition, Project Management Institute, Inc., 2013, pg. 34-35

Project Phases

A project can be divided into phases that represent activities that produce one of more deliverables. *Project phases* are usually performed sequentially, but can overlap. The output of one phase is often a hand-off, or input, to the next phase. Phases facilitate management, planning, and control as the work is represented in smaller, more focused segments. Some organizations have standard phases across all projects.

A Guide to the Project Management Body of Knowledge (PMBOK® Guide) – Fifth Edition, Project Management Institute, Inc., 2013, pg. 41-42

Phase-to-Phase Relationships

Projects that have multiple phases will generally follow a sequential process that ensures greater control over the project and aids in achieving the desired product, service, or result. Sometimes multi-phased projects will have more than one phase-to-phase relationship occurring during the life cycle of a project. In such cases, factors such as the level of control, effectiveness, and the degree of uncertainty decide the relationship that can be applied between phases. Based on these factors, both types of relationships can be applied between different phases of a project.

- *Sequential relationships* contain consecutive phases that start only when the previous phase is complete. This relationship reduces the level of uncertainty, which may eliminate the option for shortening a project's schedule.
- *Overlapping relationships* contain phases that start prior to the previous phase ending. This relationship increases the level of risk and may cause rework if something from the previous phase directly affects the next phase.

A Guide to the Project Management Body of Knowledge (PMBOK® Guide) – Fifth Edition, Project Management Institute, Inc., 2013, pg. 42-44

Progressive Elaboration

Progressive elaboration, also commonly referred to as *rolling wave planning,* is a method used to arrange project life cycle phases in a specific way to allow for progressive elaboration, in which successive layers of detail are added to the plans as the project progresses. Usually, the sequence of the phases defined by most project life cycles involves some type of handoff or deliverable. Most often, deliverables from one phase are approved before work begins on the next phase. For example, design specifications are approved and handed off before the design phase begins. However, a subsequent phase may begin before approval is gained on the deliverables of a previous phase if the risks are considered acceptable. It helps the project management team plan work to a greater level of detail as the project progresses.

A Guide to the Project Management Body of Knowledge (PMBOK® Guide) – Fifth Edition, Project Management Institute, Inc., 2013, p. 152

Predictive Life Cycles

Predictive life cycles determine project scope, time, and cost as early in the project as possible. This is a preferred cycle to use when project outcomes are well understood and known, such as enhancements to an established product. Predictive cycles are very formal and enable the project team to stay focused on each phase of the project before having to move forward into the next phase.

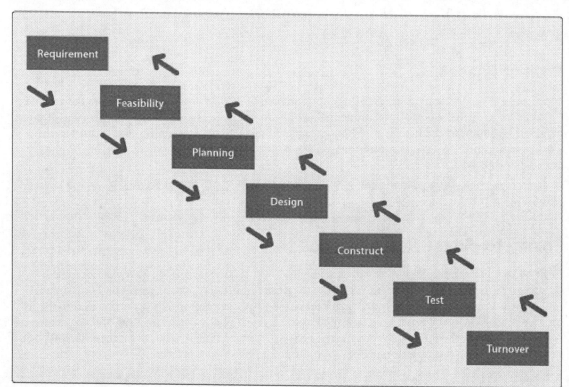

Figure 2–8: A predictive life cycle.

A Guide to the Project Management Body of Knowledge (PMBOK® Guide) – Fifth Edition, Project Management Institute, Inc., 2013, pg. 44-45

Iterative and Incremental Life Cycles

Iterative and *incremental* life cycles include project phases that are intentionally placed and repeated as the team's understanding of the deliverables is developed and understood. In most cases, the team will work with a high level vision, because the deliverables will be defined up front and developed with more detail and characteristics as the project moves through each phase. This cycle can be helpful in environments that are uncertain and undefined. For example, when developing a brand new product, the high level vision for the product exists, but all the details, such as limitations, size, and functions, will be discovered and identified as each phase is completed. This life cycle is also beneficial when managing a changing objective and scope or when partial delivery of the objectives provides value.

This cycle is like an extension or corollary of the overlapping relationship, but in this case the same phase repeats itself multiple times—once in every iteration.

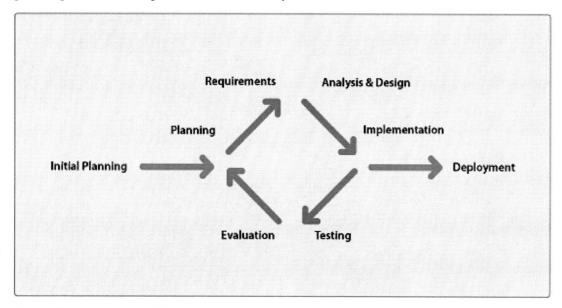

Figure 2-9: An iterative life cycle.

A Guide to the Project Management Body of Knowledge (PMBOK® Guide) – Fifth Edition, Project Management Institute, Inc., 2013, p. 45

Adaptive Life Cycle

Adaptive life cycles, also referred to as change-driven or agile methods, work well in environments with high levels of change and ongoing stakeholder involvement in a project. This is similar to iterative and incremental life cycles, but at a much more rapid pace. It is used in a highly flexible, interactive, adaptive organization where project outcomes are realized while the project work is being completed, and not at the beginning of the project. This method is used when dealing with a rapidly changing environment, scope and requirements are difficult to define in advance, and small incremental deliverables have value to stakeholders.

A Guide to the Project Management Body of Knowledge (PMBOK® Guide) – Fifth Edition, Project Management Institute (PMI)®, Project Management Professional (PMP)®, and Certified Associate in Project Management (CAPM)® are registered trademarks of Project Management Institute, Inc. - Version 2.1 Published September 30, 2014

Lesson 2: Project Management and the Organization | Topic D

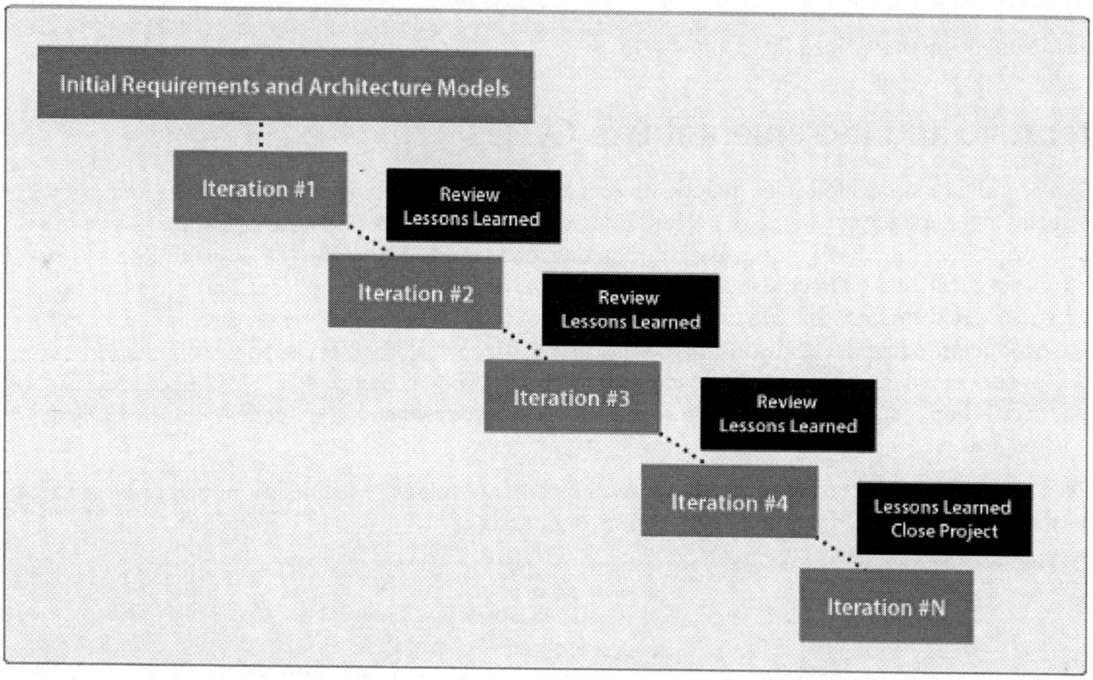

Figure 2-10: An adaptive life cycle.

A Guide to the Project Management Body of Knowledge (PMBOK® Guide) – Fifth Edition, Project Management Institute, Inc., 2013, p. 46

Agile Project Management

Agile project management refers to taking an iterative approach to managing a project throughout its life cycle. It allows the project manager to continually re-evaluate progress, development, and priorities and make adjustments as needed. It is a fluid, quick-paced, dynamic process that emphasizes face-to-face communication.

A Guide to the Project Management Body of Knowledge (PMBOK® Guide) – Fifth Edition, Project Management Institute, Inc., 2013, pg. 1, 114

A Guide to the Project Management Body of Knowledge (PMBOK® Guide) – Fifth Edition, Project Management Institute (PMI)®, Project Management Professional (PMP)®, and Certified Associate in Project Management (CAPM)® are registered trademarks of Project Management Institute, Inc. - Version 2.1 Published September 30, 2014

Lesson 2: Project Management and the Organization | Topic D

ACTIVITY 2-4
Examining Project Life Cycles

Scenario

In this activity, you will examine the different project life cycles.

1. What project life cycles, if any, do you have experience with? What life cycles do you think are used most often?

2. Which project life cycle type is best suited for a fast-paced project that is always changing?
   - ○ Predictive
   - ○ Iterative
   - ◉ Adaptive

3. Which life cycle type is best suited for a project that does not have well-defined deliverables?
   - ○ Predictive
   - ◉ Iterative
   - ○ Adaptive

4. Which life cycle type is best suited for a project that has a detailed and complete plan?
   - ◉ Predictive
   - ○ Iterative
   - ○ Adaptive

Summary

In this lesson, you discovered how project management fits into an organization's environment and structure. Understanding how organizations and enterprises are structured and what the environmental factors can be is one of the most important aspects of conducting a successful project within that organization. You were also exposed to the project life cycle at a high level and have a better idea of the general flow through the phases and how it can differ depending on the project's requirements and outcomes.

Why is it important for a project to conform to an organization's culture?

When thinking about your next project, why is it important to consider the project management concepts presented in this lesson?

Note: Check your LogicalCHOICE Course screen for opportunities to interact with your classmates, peers, and the larger LogicalCHOICE online community about the topics covered in this course or other topics you are interested in. From the Course screen you can also access available resources for a more continuous learning experience.

A Guide to the Project Management Body of Knowledge (PMBOK® Guide) – Fifth Edition, Project Management Institute (PMI)®, Project Management Professional (PMP)®, and Certified Associate in Project Management (CAPM)® are registered trademarks of Project Management Institute, Inc. - Version 2.1 Published September 30, 2014

Lesson 2: Project Management and the Organization |

3 | Working with Project Management Processes

Lesson Time: 1 hour, 30 minutes

Lesson Objectives

In this lesson, you will:

- Identify project management process groups and knowledge areas.

- Identify project information.

Lesson Introduction

In the previous lesson, you were introduced briefly to the project life cycle and how the project phases are conducted in a variety of ways depending on the specific needs of the project. In this next lesson, we will dive in a little further and start looking at the PMI project management processes in detail and examining how they apply to a project. This lesson will give you a good foundation for the remaining lessons in this course.

In this lesson you, will identify the five main PMI project management process groups and describe the purpose for each process group.

A Guide to the Project Management Body of Knowledge (PMBOK® Guide) – Fifth Edition, Project Management Institute (PMI)®, Project Management Professional (PMP)®, and Certified Associate in Project Management (CAPM)® are registered trademarks of Project Management Institute, Inc. - Version 2.1 Published September 30, 2014

TOPIC A

Project Management Processes and Knowledge Areas

Now you are ready to take a close look at what project management processes and knowledge areas are and how they can help you conduct, manage, and complete successful projects as a project manager. In this topic, you will identify the five project management process groups required for any project. You will examine the dependencies each group has on the others and how often the groups are iterated during the project life cycle.

Project Management Processes

A *process* is a set of interrelated actions and activities performed to create a specific product, service, or result. *Project management processes* are all the activities that underlie the effective practice of project management; they include all the phases of initiating, planning, executing, monitoring and controlling, and closing a project. Project management processes may produce project deliverables, such as schedules and performance reports, or product deliverables, such as software interface specifications or a building's foundation.

The *PMBOK® Guide* describes the project management processes in terms of the integration between the processes, their interactions, and the purposes they serve. There are five categories of project management process groups.

A Guide to the Project Management Body of Knowledge (PMBOK® Guide) – Fifth Edition, Project Management Institute, Inc., 2013, pg. 47-50

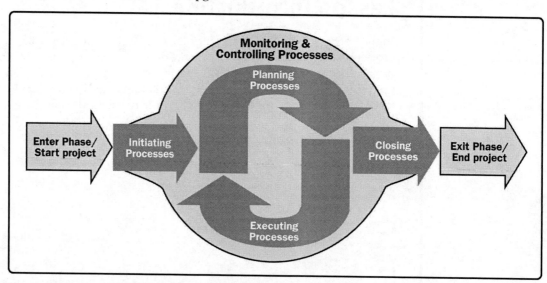

Figure 3-1: The project management processes.

A Guide to the Project Management Body of Knowledge (PMBOK® Guide) – Fifth Edition, Project Management Institute, Inc., 2013, p. 50

Tailoring the Project Management Processes

Project management processes are recognized within the profession as good practice; applying them appropriately improves the chances of success on nearly any project. Not every process takes place in every project, so determining which processes are appropriate for a given project is referred to as *tailoring*. The project manager and the project team are responsible for tailoring the applicable

A Guide to the Project Management Body of Knowledge (PMBOK® Guide) – Fifth Edition, Project Management Institute (PMI)®, Project Management Professional (PMP)®, and Certified Associate in Project Management (CAPM)® are registered trademarks of Project Management Institute, Inc. - Version 2.1 Published September 30, 2014

Lesson 3: Working with Project Management Processes | Topic A

processes to meet the needs of a specific project or phase. It is important to note that the project management process groups do not change; rather, the processes that make up each of those groups are what can be tailored to an individual project or project phase. For a project to be successful, the project team should:

- Select the appropriate processes necessary to meet the project objectives.
- Use a defined approach that can be tailored to meet requirements.

A Guide to the Project Management Body of Knowledge (PMBOK® Guide) – Fifth Edition, Project Management Institute, Inc., 2013, pg. 47-48

Project Process Categories

There are two categories of project processes that are performed by the project team. The *PMBOK® Guide* describes only the project management processes, not the product development processes, such as engineering or construction. The project management processes generate an effective flow of work throughout the project's life cycle. These processes have tools and techniques that use the skills and capabilities described in the knowledge areas.

A Guide to the Project Management Body of Knowledge (PMBOK® Guide) – Fifth Edition, Project Management Institute, Inc., 2013, pg. 48-49

Inputs, Tools and Techniques, and Outputs

Project management processes are implemented through *inputs, tools and techniques*, and *outputs*. Inputs are the information and data that project managers draw on, create, or gather to guide their work for a specific process to achieve project goals. Inputs can be new information or information that has been derived during the course of the project. Tools and techniques are the methods, templates, or approaches that project managers employ within a particular process, using a combination of inputs, to achieve stated goals. Outputs are the end results and deliverables achieved during project management processes and can become inputs into subsequent processes. Organizational process assets and enterprise environmental factors should be considered for every process in the project management processes life cycle.

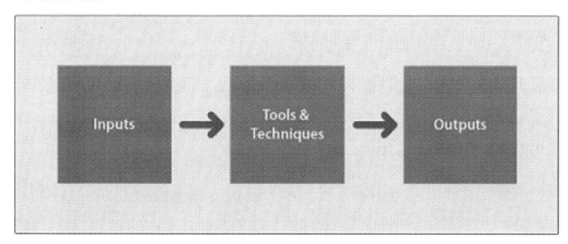

Figure 3–2: Inputs, tools, and techniques.

A Guide to the Project Management Body of Knowledge (PMBOK® Guide) – Fifth Edition, Project Management Institute, Inc., 2013, pg. 289-291, 296-297

Common Project Management Process Interactions

The project management processes are individual processes with well-defined interfaces, but in reality, they overlap and interface throughout the life of a project. There are no hard lines between each of the phases; outputs become inputs to the next phase. Feedback loops are built in, especially

A Guide to the Project Management Body of Knowledge (PMBOK® Guide) – Fifth Edition, Project Management Institute (PMI)®, Project Management Professional (PMP)®, and Certified Associate in Project Management (CAPM)® are registered trademarks of Project Management Institute, Inc. - Version 2.1 Published September 30, 2014

Lesson 3: Working with Project Management Processes | *Topic A*

between the planning, executing, and monitoring and controlling process groups. Although project management is an iterative, cyclical process in real life, continually re-entering a process, it is necessarily presented in a linear manner throughout this course.

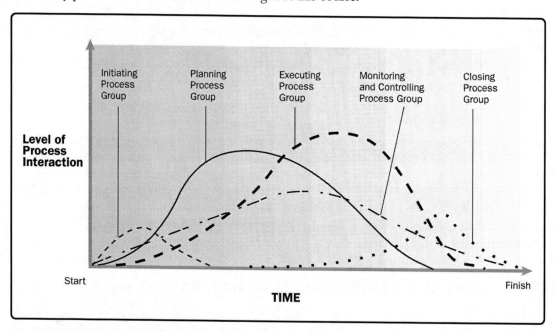

Figure 3–3: Project management process group interactions.

A Guide to the Project Management Body of Knowledge (PMBOK® Guide) – Fifth Edition, Project Management Institute, Inc., 2013, p. 51

The process groups are not phases and would usually be repeated for each subproject or phase. Typically, once a project is initiated, you move into the planning processes where you develop a project management plan. From there, you start executing the plan and controlling and monitoring work results in the executing and monitoring and controlling processes. The work results your team generates may indicate a need for modifications to the project schedule, budget, or scope statement, which requires more planning. The loop continues between planning, executing, and monitoring and controlling until the project's objectives are completely and satisfactorily met. Then, you move into the closing process group.

A Guide to the Project Management Body of Knowledge (PMBOK® Guide) – Fifth Edition, Project Management Institute, Inc., 2013, pg. 50-51

Initiating Process Group

The *Initiating Process Group* contains processes performed to define a new project or a new phase of an existing project by obtaining authorization to start the project or phase. The initial scope of the new project or phase is defined and financial resources are committed. Internal and external stakeholders are identified and the project manager is selected. This information is captured in the project charter and the stakeholder register. When the project charter is approved, the project becomes officially authorized. This is where we determine the scope of a project at a high level in a project charter document and obtain authorization to start the project.

A Guide to the Project Management Body of Knowledge (PMBOK® Guide) – Fifth Edition, Project Management Institute, Inc., 2013, pg. 54-55

Planning Process Group

The *Planning Process Group* contains processes performed to establish the total scope of the project, define and refine the objectives, and develop a course of action to obtain the project objectives.

The project management plan and the project documents that support the project are developed. As more project information is understood or changes are uncovered, additional planning may be required. The outputs from these processes will support all aspects of the scope, time, cost, quality, communications, human resources, risks, procurements, and stakeholder engagement for the project. This is where you create the roadmap or planning document of how you are going to do your project.

A Guide to the Project Management Body of Knowledge (PMBOK® Guide) – Fifth Edition, Project Management Institute, Inc., 2013, pg. 55-56

Executing Process Group

The *Executing Process Group* contains processes performed to complete the work defined in the project management plan to satisfy the project objectives. This involves coordinating people and resources, managing stakeholder expectations, and integrating and performing the activities of the project based on the project management plan. During the project execution, results may require planning updates and re-baselining, including changes to activity durations, resource productivity and availability, and unanticipated risks. This new information will generate change requests that initiate changes to the project management plan or other project documents. This is where we do the project work, such as the engineering for a new product.

A Guide to the Project Management Body of Knowledge (PMBOK® Guide) – Fifth Edition, Project Management Institute, Inc., 2013, p. 56

Monitoring and Controlling Process Group

The *Monitoring and Controlling Process Group* contains processes required to track, review, and orchestrate the progress and performance of the project, identify areas in which changes to the plan are needed, and initiate those changes. Project performance is measured and analyzed at regular intervals. This is the process used to keep a close eye on the pulse or health of the project, manage changes, and update project documents.

As stated in the *PMBOK® Guide,* this process group also involves:

- Controlling changes and recommending corrective or preventive action in anticipation of possible problems.
- Monitoring the ongoing project activities against the project management plan and the project performance measurement baseline.
- Influencing the factors that could circumvent integrated change control or configuration management, so only approved changes are implemented.

A Guide to the Project Management Body of Knowledge (PMBOK® Guide) – Fifth Edition, Project Management Institute, Inc., 2013, p. 57

Closing Process Group

The *Closing Process Group* contains processes performed to finalize all activities across all project management process groups to formally complete the project, phase, or contractual obligations. This process confirms that all the defined process group processes are complete so that the project or phase can be closed. This is when all project work is complete and resources are released.

A Guide to the Project Management Body of Knowledge (PMBOK® Guide) – Fifth Edition, Project Management Institute, Inc., 2013, pg. 57-58

Knowledge Areas

There are 10 areas identified as project management *knowledge areas* that are each defined by knowledge requirements. There are also 47 project management processes identified in the

A Guide to the Project Management Body of Knowledge (PMBOK® Guide) – Fifth Edition, Project Management Institute (PMI)®, Project Management Professional (PMP)®, and Certified Associate in Project Management (CAPM)® are registered trademarks of Project Management Institute, Inc. - Version 2.1 Published September 30, 2014

Lesson 3: Working with Project Management Processes | *Topic A*

PMBOK® *Guide* that are grouped into the 10 separate knowledge areas. These represent a complete set of concepts, terms, and activities for project management.

A Guide to the Project Management Body of Knowledge (PMBOK® Guide) – Fifth Edition, Project Management Institute, Inc., 2013, p. 60

(handwritten note, left margin:)
I – I
S – Saw
T – Two
C – Crows
Q – Quitly
H – Having
C – Coffee and
R – Reading
P – Poetic
S – Stories

Knowledge Areas	Initiating Process Group	Planning Process Group	Executing Process Group	Monitoring and Controlling Process Group	Closing Process Group
4. Project Integration Management	4.1 Develop Project Charter	4.2 Develop Project Management Plan	4.3 Direct and Manage Project Work	4.4 Monitor and Control Project Work 4.5 Perform Integrated Change Control	4.6 Close Project or Phase
5. Project Scope Management		5.1 Plan Scope Management 5.2 Collect Requirements 5.3 Define Scope 5.4 Create WBS		5.5 Validate Scope 5.6 Control Scope	
6. Project Time Management		6.1 Plan Schedule Management 6.2 Define Activities 6.3 Sequence Activites 6.4 Estimate Activity Resources 6.5 Estimate Activity Durations 6.6 Develop Schedule		6.7 Control Schedule	
7. Project Cost Management		7.1 Plan Cost Management 7.2 Estimate Cost 7.3 Determine Budget		7.4 Control Costs	
8. Project Quality Management		8.1 Plan Quality Management	8.2 Perform Quality Assurance	8.3 Control Quality	
9. Project Human Resource Management		9.1 Plan Human Resource Management	9.2 Acquire Project Team 9.3 Develop Project Team 9.4 Manage Project Team		
10. Project Communication Management		10.1 Plan Communications Management	10.2 Manage Communications	10.3 Control Communications	
11. Project Risk Management		11.1 Plan Risk Management 11.2 Identify Risks 11.3 Perform Qualitative Risk Analysis 11.4 Perform Quantitative Risk Analysis 11.5 Plan Risk Responses		11.6 Control Risks	
12. Project Procurement Management		12.1 Plan Procurement Management	12.2 Conduct Procurements	12.3 Control Procurements	12.4 Close Procurements
13. Project Stakeholder Management	13.1 Identify Stakeholders	13.2 Plan Stakeholder Management	13.3 Manage Stakeholder Engagement	13.4 Control Stakeholder Engagement	

Figure 3-4: Overview of the knowledge areas with associated processes.

A Guide to the Project Management Body of Knowledge (PMBOK® Guide) – Fifth Edition, Project Management Institute, Inc., 2013, p. 61

The 10 Knowledge Areas

Knowledge Area	Description
Project integration management	*Project integration management* includes the activities and processes needed to identify, define, combine, unify, and coordinate all of the various processes and project management activities in the Project Management Process Groups.
	A Guide to the Project Management Body of Knowledge (PMBOK® Guide) – Fifth Edition, Project Management Institute, Inc., 2013, pg. 63-104
Project scope management	*Project scope management* is the process of identifying project work and making sure that project work stays within the identified boundaries of a project. Project managers will ensure that all project work is directly aligned with the determined scope. The scope of a project can change, and will require changes to many of a project's processes, but with a good management plan in place, the scope can be updated and managed successfully. For example, the scope of a housing project includes a single family home on the lot at 122 East Main Street, not the other properties on the same street.
	A Guide to the Project Management Body of Knowledge (PMBOK® Guide) – Fifth Edition, Project Management Institute, Inc., 2013, pg. 105-140
Project time management	*Project time management* includes the processes to manage the time to complete a project. The plan for executing the project's activities is represented in a schedule model, which also contains the data (activity dependencies and durations) and calculations that produce that schedule. The baselined project schedule model is used in the control schedule process to manage the completion of the project work on time.
	Many organizations use project scheduling applications, such as Microsoft Project, Oracle® Primavera, and CA Clarity™, to plan and manage the project's schedule. It contains the schedule presentation, data and calculations for the schedule, and the schedule baseline for the project.
	A Guide to the Project Management Body of Knowledge (PMBOK® Guide) – Fifth Edition, Project Management Institute, Inc., 2013, pg. 141-192
Project cost management	The processes that make up *project cost management* include the processes required to plan, estimate, budget, finance, fund, manage, and control the project costs. These processes help ensure that the project can be completed within the approved project budget. Project scope definition, what the project includes or does not include, is critical so that the cost of the project resources (labor, materials, etc.) can be estimated accurately at the beginning of the project.
	A Guide to the Project Management Body of Knowledge (PMBOK® Guide) – Fifth Edition, Project Management Institute, Inc., 2013, pg. 193-226

Knowledge Area	Description
Project quality management	*Project quality management* includes processes that enable a project to meet expectations on the quality of its project work and deliverables. The quality standards that need to be met must be managed throughout the life of the project. Quality policies and procedures that will be used on the project need to be planned at the beginning of the project and managed and controlled throughout the project by using the organization's quality management system. Continuous process improvement activities also need to be considered for the benefit of the project, and the organization and its other and future projects. *A Guide to the Project Management Body of Knowledge (PMBOK® Guide) – Fifth Edition,* Project Management Institute, Inc., 2013, pg. 227-254
Project human resource management	*Project human resource management* contains the processes to organize, manage, and lead the people on the project team. These people have skills and may be assigned to the project part or full time at different times in the project life cycle. They have specific assigned roles and responsibilities on the project. *A Guide to the Project Management Body of Knowledge (PMBOK® Guide) – Fifth Edition,* Project Management Institute, Inc., 2013, pg. 255-285
Project communications management	*Project communications management* includes processes that enable project managers to effectively and efficiently manage the communications of a project. Project managers spend a great deal of their time communicating with the project team members and the project stakeholders. These communications can be internal (project team) and external (customers), formal (letters and reports) or informal (emails and phone calls), vertical and horizontal within the organization, official or unofficial, and written or verbal. *A Guide to the Project Management Body of Knowledge (PMBOK® Guide) – Fifth Edition,* Project Management Institute, Inc., 2013, pg. 287-308
Project risk management	*Project risk management* includes conducting risk management planning, identification, analysis, and response planning, and controlling risk on a project. A risk is an uncertain event that may occur during the project. For example, we want to increase the likelihood and impact of positive events or opportunities and decrease the likelihood and impact of negative events or threats. A risk could impact any aspect of the project. Known risks are those that have been identified and analyzed so that they can have a planned risk response. These can be managed proactively and have a contingency reserve to pay for the risk if it occurs. Unknown risks cannot be managed proactively and have a management reserve. Risk management must be addressed proactively and consistently throughout the project to reduce the potential for unmanaged threats to negatively impact the project. *A Guide to the Project Management Body of Knowledge (PMBOK® Guide) – Fifth Edition,* Project Management Institute, Inc., 2013, pg. 255-285

A Guide to the Project Management Body of Knowledge (PMBOK® Guide) – Fifth Edition, Project Management Institute (PMI)®, Project Management Professional (PMP)®, and Certified Associate in Project Management (CAPM)® are registered trademarks of Project Management Institute, Inc. - Version 2.1 Published September 30, 2014

Lesson 3: Working with Project Management Processes | Topic A

Knowledge Area	Description
Project procurement management	*Project procurement management* is the process used to properly manage the purchase or acquisition of the products, services, or results needed to perform project work external to the project team.
	A Guide to the Project Management Body of Knowledge (PMBOK® Guide) – Fifth Edition, Project Management Institute, Inc., 2013, pg. 255-285
Project stakeholder management	*Project stakeholder management* area includes processes to ensure that the project stakeholders are engaged, involved, and communicated with throughout the processes.
	A Guide to the Project Management Body of Knowledge (PMBOK® Guide) – Fifth Edition, Project Management Institute, Inc., 2013, pg. 391-415

* Total 47 processes

A Guide to the Project Management Body of Knowledge (PMBOK® Guide) – Fifth Edition, Project Management Institute (PMI)®, Project Management Professional (PMP)®, and Certified Associate in Project Management (CAPM)® are registered trademarks of Project Management Institute, Inc. - Version 2.1 Published September 30, 2014

Lesson 3: Working with Project Management Processes | Topic A

ACTIVITY 3-1
Identifying Project Management Process Groups

Scenario

In this activity, you will identify project management process groups.

1. Which process is performed to finalize all project work?
   - ○ Initiating
   - ○ Planning
   - ○ Executing
   - ○ Monitoring and Controlling
   - ○ Closing

2. Which project management process group will you apply to regularly measure progress and identify variances from the project management plan?
   - ○ Initiating
   - ○ Planning
   - ○ Executing
   - ○ Monitoring and Controlling
   - ○ Closing

3. Which process is performed to define a new project and get authorization to start the project?
   - ○ Initiating
   - ○ Planning
   - ○ Executing
   - ○ Monitoring and Controlling
   - ○ Closing

4. What process is performed to actually do the project work to meet the project objectives?
   - ○ Initiating
   - ○ Planning
   - ○ Executing
   - ○ Monitoring and Controlling
   - ○ Closing

5. Which project management process will you apply to refine program objectives and the courses of action the project team will take to meet program objectives?
   - ○ Initiating
   - ○ Planning
   - ○ Executing
   - ○ Monitoring and Controlling
   - ○ Closing

6. What process is performed to track the progress of the project and manage changes to the project?
   - ○ Initiating
   - ○ Planning
   - ○ Executing
   - ⊙ Monitoring and Controlling
   - ○ Closing

7. What process is performed to determine the scope of the project and the activities to achieve the project objectives?
   - ⊗ Initiating
   - ⊙ Planning
   - ○ Executing
   - ○ Monitoring and Controlling
   - ○ Closing

8. As a project manager, why is it important to use the five process groups for your project?

_____

A Guide to the Project Management Body of Knowledge (PMBOK® Guide) – Fifth Edition, Project Management Institute (PMI)®, Project Management Professional (PMP)®, and Certified Associate in Project Management (CAPM)® are registered trademarks of Project Management Institute, Inc. - Version 2.1 Published September 30, 2014

Lesson 3: Working with Project Management Processes | *Topic A*

TOPIC B

Identify Project Information

In the previous topic, you identified the five process groups and what activities are conducted in each process. You also identified the 10 different knowledge areas included in the *PMBOK® Guide*. These process groups and knowledge areas have many different processes associated with them, and each process generates project data. It is important to understand the different types of project information created and how to handle them all along the way. In this topic, we will take a close look at the types of information that projects can generate.

Project Information

Projects generate a significant amount of data and information to guide the project's path to completion. *Project information* is the raw data that is collected and gathered at each stage of a project. This data is then turned into information on which decisions can be made and is ultimately reported to stakeholders. As the project manager, it is your responsibility to manage how project information is managed, used, and reported throughout the project life cycle.

For example, project information is used to determine if the quality standards set for the project are being met. If a project has spent $50,000 at this point in time, that is work performance data. If the project should have spent $45,000, the variance of $5,000 is work performance information. This is included in the project status report as a work performance report.

A Guide to the Project Management Body of Knowledge (PMBOK® Guide) – Fifth Edition, Project Management Institute, Inc., 2013, pg. 58-59

Types of Project Information

As stated in the *PMBOK® Guide,* there are three types of project data.

Project Data	Description	Examples
Work performance data	The raw observations and measurements identified during activities performed to carry out the project work.	Reported percent of work physically complete, quality and technical performance measures, start and finish dates of schedule activities, number of change requests, number of defects, actual costs, actual durations, and more.
Work performance information	Performance information that is collected from various controlling processes, analyzed in context, and integrated based on relationships across areas.	Status of deliverables, implementation status for change required, and forecasted estimates to complete.
Work performance reports	The physical electronic representation of work performance information compiled in project documents, intended to generate decisions or raise issues, actions, or awareness.	Status reports, memos, justifications, information notes, electronic dashboards, recommendations, and updates.

A Guide to the Project Management Body of Knowledge (PMBOK® Guide) – Fifth Edition, Project Management Institute, Inc., 2013, p. 59

A Guide to the Project Management Body of Knowledge (PMBOK® Guide) – Fifth Edition, Project Management Institute (PMI)®, Project Management Professional (PMP)®, and Certified Associate in Project Management (CAPM)® are registered trademarks of Project Management Institute, Inc. - Version 2.1 Published September 30, 2014

Lesson 3: Working with Project Management Processes | Topic B

ACTIVITY 3-2
Identifying Project Data

Scenario

In this activity, you will identify the different project data you will come across when managing projects.

1. Which type of project information is a physical representation of electronic work performance information compiled in project documents, intended to generate decisions or raise issues, actions, or awareness?

   ○ Work performance data

   ○ Work performance information

   ⊘ Work performance reports

2. Which type of project information is composed of raw observations and measurements identified during activities performed to carry out the project work?

   ⊘ Work performance data

   ○ Work performance information

   ○ Work performance reports

3. Which type of project information consists of performance data collected from various controlling processes, analyzed in context, and integrated based on relationships across areas?

   ○ Work performance data

   ⊘ Work performance information

   ○ Work performance reports

A Guide to the Project Management Body of Knowledge (PMBOK® Guide) – Fifth Edition, Project Management Institute (PMI)®, Project Management Professional (PMP)®, and Certified Associate in Project Management (CAPM)® are registered trademarks of Project Management Institute, Inc. - Version 2.1 Published September 30, 2014

Lesson 3: Working with Project Management Processes | Topic B

Summary

In this lesson, you explored all the different process groups and knowledge areas. With a strong foundation for the PMI process and how each phase relates to the other, you are ready to tackle the next lessons and work your way through each process in detail.

What is project management and what do you think is the value of using the project management processes?

What is your experience with gathering project work performance data and using the derived work performance information to make decisions during a project?

 Note: Check your LogicalCHOICE Course screen for opportunities to interact with your classmates, peers, and the larger LogicalCHOICE online community about the topics covered in this course or other topics you are interested in. From the Course screen you can also access available resources for a more continuous learning experience.

A Guide to the Project Management Body of Knowledge (PMBOK® Guide) – Fifth Edition, Project Management Institute (PMI)®, Project Management Professional (PMP)®, and Certified Associate in Project Management (CAPM)® are registered trademarks of Project Management Institute, Inc. - Version 2.1 Published September 30, 2014

Lesson 3: Working with Project Management Processes |

4 | Initiating a Project

Lesson Time: 1 hour, 30 minutes

Lesson Objectives

In this lesson, you will:

- Develop a project charter.
- Identify project stakeholders.

Lesson Introduction

With project management fundamentals out of the way, you are ready to initiate a project. The processes within this group are performed to define a new project or a new phase of an existing project by obtaining authorization to start the project or phase. Every project will need some sort of authorization or go ahead from the proper individuals. Without this, a project can be delayed or can be interrupted until authorization is given. By following the processes within the Initiating a Project process group, you will ensure that the proper steps are taken to initiate a project.

In this lesson, you will use the Initiating a Project processes to gather and identify the project components you need to get a project started.

The following diagram highlights the next process group and knowledge areas covered in this lesson.

Project Management Process Groups					
Knowledge Areas	Initiating Process Group	Planning Process Group	Executing Process Group	Monitoring and Controlling Process Group	Closing Process Group
4. Project Integration Management	4.1 Develop Project Charter	4.2 Develop Project Management Plan	4.3 Direct and Manage Project Work	4.4 Monitor and Control Project Work 4.5 Perform Integrated Change Control	4.6 Close Project or Phase
5. Project Scope Management		5.1 Plan Scope Management 5.2 Collect Requirements 5.3 Define Scope 5.4 Create WBS		5.5 Validate Scope 5.6 Control Scope	
6. Project Time Management		6.1 Plan Schedule Management 6.2 Define Activities 6.3 Sequence Activites 6.4 Estimate Activity Resources 6.5 Estimate Activity Durations 6.6 Develop Schedule		6.7 Control Schedule	
7. Project Cost Management		7.1 Plan Cost Management 7.2 Estimate Cost 7.3 Determine Budget		7.4 Control Costs	
8. Project Quality Management		8.1 Plan Quality Management	8.2 Perform Quality Assurance	8.3 Control Quality	
9. Project Human Resource Management		9.1 Plan Human Resource Management	9.2 Acquire Project Team 9.3 Develop Project Team 9.4 Manage Project Team		
10. Project Communication Management		10.1 Plan Communications Management	10.2 Manage Communications	10.3 Control Communications	
11. Project Risk Management		11.1 Plan Risk Management 11.2 Identify Risks 11.3 Perform Qualitative Risk Analysis 11.4 Perform Quantitative Risk Analysis 11.5 Plan Risk Responses		11.6 Control Risks	
12. Project Procurement Management		12.1 Plan Procurement Management	12.2 Conduct Procurements	12.3 Control Procurements	12.4 Close Procurements
13. Project Stakeholder Management	13.1 Identify Stakeholders	13.2 Plan Stakeholder Management	13.3 Manage Stakeholder Engagement	13.4 Control Stakeholder Engagement	

A Guide to the Project Management Body of Knowledge (PMBOK® Guide) – Fifth Edition, Project Management Institute (PMI)®, Project Management Professional (PMP)®, and Certified Associate in Project Management (CAPM)® are registered trademarks of Project Management Institute, Inc. - Version 2.1 Published September 30, 2014

TOPIC A

Develop a Project Charter

Documenting and developing a project charter is an important first step in initiating your project. Before you can apply organizational resources such as people or money to project activities, you need formal authorization to do so.

A Guide to the Project Management Body of Knowledge (PMBOK® Guide) – Fifth Edition, Project Management Institute, Inc., 2013, pg. 66-67

The following data flow diagram illustrates how the Develop a Project Charter process relates to the other project management processes.

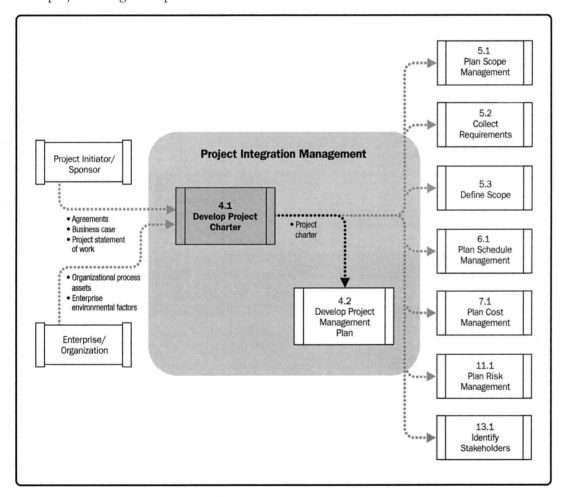

Figure 4-1: The Develop a Project Charter data flow diagram.

A Guide to the Project Management Body of Knowledge (PMBOK® Guide) – Fifth Edition, Project Management Institute, Inc., 2013, p. 67

What Is a Project Charter?

A *project charter* is a document developed by the project manager and approved by a project sponsor to formally authorize the existence of a project and authorizes the project manager to apply organizational resources, such as people and dollars, to project activities. The project initiator or sponsor is a person who provides resources and support for the project and is accountable for

A Guide to the Project Management Body of Knowledge (PMBOK® Guide) – Fifth Edition, Project Management Institute (PMI)®, Project Management Professional
(PMP)®, and Certified Associate in Project Management (CAPM)® are registered trademarks of Project Management Institute, Inc. - Version 2.1 Published September 30, 2014

Lesson 4: Initiating a Project | *Topic A*

enabling the success of the project. An effective project charter conveys why the project is being initiated, what the outcomes of the project will be, ensures that you have support for the project, and gives you the authority to apply resources to project activities.

Project Charter Template

A. General Project Information

Project Title:	
Brief Project Description:	
Sponsor:	
Date:	*Version:*

B. Project Objective:
Explain the measurable objectives and success criteria of the project.

C. Assumptions
List and describe the high level requirements and known assumptions and constraints.

D. Project Scope
Describe the scope of the project. The project scope establishes the boundaries of the project.

E. Project Milestones
List the major milestones and deliverables of the project.

Milestones	Deliverables	Date

Figure 4–2: A sample project charter.

As stated in the *PMBOK® Guide,* a project charter should include:

- Project purpose
- Measurable objectives and success criteria
- High-level requirements
- Assumptions and constraints
- High-level description and boundaries
- High-level risks
- Summary milestone schedule
- Summary budget
- Initial stakeholder list
- Project approval requirements
- Assigned project manager and authority levels
- Name and authority of sponsor

A Guide to the Project Management Body of Knowledge (PMBOK® Guide) – Fifth Edition, Project Management Institute, Inc., 2013, pg. 71-72

The Develop a Project Charter Process

Developing a project charter is the major output of Initiation. The purpose of developing a project charter is to formally launch and authorize a new project or new phase of an existing project. To be successful, a project must link to the ongoing work of the organization and it must align its goals and capabilities with relevant business requirements of that organization. The project charter may be developed by an initiator or sponsor, or it may be delegated to the project manager. Either way, the project manager should be involved in the development process.

A Guide to the Project Management Body of Knowledge (PMBOK® Guide) – Fifth Edition, Project Management Institute, Inc., 2013, pg. 66-67

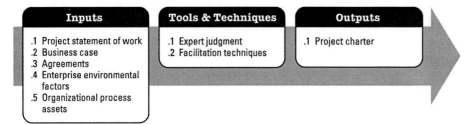

Figure 4-3: The Develop a Project Charter process.

A Guide to the Project Management Body of Knowledge (PMBOK® Guide) – Fifth Edition, Project Management Institute, Inc., 2013, p. 66

Develop a Project Charter Inputs

Various components provide input to the Develop Project Charter process.

Input	Description (as stated in the PMBOK® Guide)
Project statement of work (SOW)	A SOW is a narrative description of products, services, or results to be delivered by the project.
Business case	A business case is a documented economic feasibility study used to establish validity of the benefits of a selected component lacking suffixation definition and that is used as a basis for the authorization of further project management activities.
Agreements	Agreements are any document or communication that defines the initial intentions of a project. This can take the form of a contract, memorandum of understanding (MOU), letters of agreement, verbal agreements, email, and so on.
Enterprise environmental factors	Enterprise environmental factors are conditions, not under the immediate control of the team, that influence, constrain, or direct the project, program, or portfolio.
Organizational process assets	Organizational process assets are plans, processes, policies, procedures, and knowledge bases that are specific to and used by the performing organization.

A Guide to the Project Management Body of Knowledge (PMBOK® Guide) – Fifth Edition, Project Management Institute, Inc., 2013, pg. 68-70

Project SOW

A *SOW* is a document describing products, services, or results that will be delivered by the project. This document is based on business needs, product, or service requirements for a particular project.

Project SOWs can be initiated internally or externally. For internal projects, the project sponsor generally provides the SOW, and for external projects, generally the customer will provide the SOW as part of a bid document or a contract.

Statement of Work

Project Name	
Date Submitted	
Prepared By	

1. Business Need and Benefits

1.1 Business Need

1.2 Benefits to be achieved

1.3 Scope of Project

1.4 Summary of Work to be delivered

2. Strategic Business Information for the Organization

2.1 Vision

2.2 Goals

2.3 Objectives

2.4 High Level Mission Statement

3. High Level Schedule with Major Deliverable Milestones

Date	Milestone

Figure 4–4: A SOW.

The SOW generally includes:

- The business need for a project based on market demand, new technology, legal requirements, government regulations, or an environmental need.
- The scope of the product that documents the attributes of the project, services or results that the project will deliver.
- Strategic plan information that documents the organization's strategic vision, goals, and objectives and high-level mission statement.

A Guide to the Project Management Body of Knowledge (PMBOK® Guide) – Fifth Edition, Project Management Institute, Inc., 2013, p. 68

Business Case

Business case captures the reasoning for initiating a project or task from a financial perspective. It documents the investment needed to make the project successful and determines whether or not the deliverables from the project are worth the investment to the overall business.

It conveys the business need and the cost-benefit analysis information to determine what the boundaries are for a project. The business need is usually generated by a result of market demand, an organizational need, a customer request, a technological advance, a legal requirement, ecological impacts, and/or social needs. Once the need has been identified and the business case information developed, then risk should be identified and documented. For example, the business case for a new

A Guide to the Project Management Body of Knowledge (PMBOK® Guide) – Fifth Edition, Project Management Institute (PMI)®, Project Management Professional (PMP)®, and Certified Associate in Project Management (CAPM)® are registered trademarks of Project Management Institute, Inc. - Version 2.1 Published September 30, 2014

Lesson 4: Initiating a Project | Topic A

product would show that an investment of $500,000 in the development of the new product would result in potential profits of $1,000,000+ if the estimated demand of 10,000 units of the product are sold.

A Guide to the Project Management Body of Knowledge (PMBOK® Guide) – Fifth Edition, Project Management Institute, Inc., 2013, p. 69

Business Case Components

A number of components need to be included in a business case.

Component	Description
Business need	Substantiates the business reason for conducting the project.
Project contribution	Determines the project's contribution toward the organization's objectives.
Stakeholders	Lists the project stakeholders, along with their expectations and contributions toward the project.
Constraints	Compiles the limitations of the project.
Strategic risks	Lists the risks that the project may face and the possible risk management measures.
Benefits evaluation	Analyzes and outlines the key benefits to be obtained.
Project roles	Defines roles and responsibilities of the project and may note specific team member. (This is the pre-assigned team member.)
Benefits realization plan	Documents the benefits project outcomes can have on the business as a whole.
Contingency plan	Outlines the alternate solutions for unplanned events.

A Guide to the Project Management Body of Knowledge (PMBOK® Guide) – Fifth Edition, Project Management Institute, Inc., 2013, p. 69

Agreements

Agreements are used to document the intent of a project. Examples include contracts, MOUs, service level agreements (SLAs), letters of agreement, letters of intent, verbal agreements, email, or other written agreements. When a project is initiated with external customers or parties, then a formal contract agreement is needed so both parties are on the same page about project information.

A Guide to the Project Management Body of Knowledge (PMBOK® Guide) – Fifth Edition, Project Management Institute (PMI)®, Project Management Professional (PMP)®, and Certified Associate in Project Management (CAPM)® are registered trademarks of Project Management Institute, Inc. - Version 2.1 Published September 30, 2014

Lesson 4: Initiating a Project | Topic A

Sample Service Level Agreement

Service Scope and Description Statement

The agreement covers the provision and support of a Service, which provides end user computer support. The DESKTOP COMPUTING SERVICE consists of the hardware, software, and supporting infrastructure for user personal computers running the Windows operating system.

Service Availability

Desktop Service is required along with Network/Intranet for access to other services. Required availability for these services is 99.5 percent uptime, not counting planned maintenance times.
The 99.5 percent availability metric will be measured by a rolling 6-month period.

Reliability

The service is guaranteed not to break more than three times per year. A break is defined as the loss of access to a vital business function.

Service Performance

Designed for high performance, the desktop should not keep the user waiting for response to an input for more than two minutes out of any five-minute window. Any failures must be reported to the Service Desk for incident resolution.

Change Management Procedures

Any proposed changes by the Customer must be submitted through the Service Desk for review. A notice of acceptance/denial and reason for such must be within five business days of the next CAB meeting for Normal changes, or three days for Standard changes. Emergency changes will be dealt with immediately by the Service Desk Manager.

Service Reviews

Reviews of the service will be conducted by Service Level Management in conjunction with the Customer at least annually, as well as after a major outage or change.

Figure 4–5: A sample agreement.

A Guide to the Project Management Body of Knowledge (PMBOK® Guide) – Fifth Edition, Project Management Institute, Inc., 2013, p. 70

Enterprise Environmental Factors

Enterprise environmental factors that should be considered when developing the project charter can include governmental and industry standards, organizational structure and culture, and market conditions. For example, having to adhere to OSHA regulations can be an example of an environmental factor.

A Guide to the Project Management Body of Knowledge (PMBOK® Guide) – Fifth Edition, Project Management Institute, Inc., 2013, p. 70

Organizational Process Assets

Organizational process assets that should be considered for the development of the project charter could include:

- Organizational standard processes, policies, and process definitions
- Project charter templates
- Historical information and lessons learned from previous projects.

A Guide to the Project Management Body of Knowledge (PMBOK® Guide) – Fifth Edition, Project Management Institute (PMI)®, Project Management Professional (PMP)®, and Certified Associate in Project Management (CAPM)® are registered trademarks of Project Management Institute, Inc. - Version 2.1 Published September 30, 2014

Lesson 4: Initiating a Project | Topic A

A Guide to the Project Management Body of Knowledge (PMBOK® Guide) – Fifth Edition, Project Management Institute, Inc., 2013, p. 70

Project Charter Tools and Techniques

There are two tools and techniques used in the Develop Project Charter process.

Tools & Techniques	Description (as stated in the PMBOK® Guide)
Expert judgment	Expert judgment is based upon expertise in an application area, knowledge area, discipline, industry, and so on, as appropriate for the activity being performed. Such expertise may be provided by any group or person with specialized education, knowledge, skill, experience, or training.
Facilitation techniques	Facilitation techniques are various techniques to assist in the progress of the project.

A Guide to the Project Management Body of Knowledge (PMBOK® Guide) – Fifth Edition, Project Management Institute, Inc., 2013, p. 71

Expert Judgment

Expert judgment is used to evaluate the inputs used to document the project charter. Expert judgment can be given by any group or individual that has specific knowledge about the objectives of the project. Examples can include people from other areas of the organization, consultants, stakeholders, professional and technical associations (such as the Project Management Institute, PMI), industry groups, subject matter experts (SMEs), and the project management office (PMO).

It's important to understand that expert judgment is not only used for determining what should be included in the project charter, but also that it will be used throughout the project's life cycle in a number of project management processes.

A Guide to the Project Management Body of Knowledge (PMBOK® Guide) – Fifth Edition, Project Management Institute, Inc., 2013, p. 71

Facilitation Techniques

Facilitation techniques such as brainstorming, conflict resolution, problem solving, and meeting management are techniques that can be used by facilitators to help teams complete project activities.

A Guide to the Project Management Body of Knowledge (PMBOK® Guide) – Fifth Edition, Project Management Institute, Inc., 2013, p. 71

Project Charter Outputs

There is one output from the Develop a Project Charter process.

Output	Description
The project charter	As stated in the *PMBOK® Guide,* a project charter is a document issued by the project initiator or sponsor that formally authorizes the existence of a project and provides the project manager with the authority to apply organizational resources to project activities.

A Guide to the Project Management Body of Knowledge (PMBOK® Guide) – Fifth Edition, Project Management Institute, Inc., 2013, pg. 71-72

A Guide to the Project Management Body of Knowledge (PMBOK® Guide) – Fifth Edition, Project Management Institute (PMI)®, Project Management Professional (PMP)®, and Certified Associate in Project Management (CAPM)® are registered trademarks of Project Management Institute, Inc. - Version 2.1 Published September 30, 2014

Lesson 4: Initiating a Project | Topic A

Guidelines to Develop a Project Charter

An effective project charter clearly communicates the project's value to the organization and formally authorizes the project.

To create an effective project charter, use these guidelines:

- Use a corporate template, if your organization has one.
- Include the project and authority identification information:
    - Title of the project and date of authorization
    - Name and contact information of the project manager
    - Name, title, and contact information for the initiating authority, usually the customer or sponsor
- Include a clear, concise, description of the business need, opportunity, or threat that the project is intended to address:
    - The circumstances that generated the need for the project
    - The market demand for the product or service
- Any legal requirements associated with the project.
- Include summary descriptions of the product or service of the project:
    - What is the required outcome of the project?
    - What are the critical characteristics of the product or service?
- Include a description of the project's relationship to the business need it is intended to address:
    - Why is it important to do the project now?
    - How will the project address the business need, opportunity, or threat for which it is intended?
- Consider any known constraints and/or assumptions:
    - Are there any known time, cost, scope, quality, or resource issues or factors that will limit the way you and your project team can approach the project?
    - Are there any factors or issues that you and your project team will presume to be true, real, or certain in order to begin planning your project?
- Ensure the person with the required knowledge and authority signs the project charter.
- Distribute the signed project charter to the appropriate project stakeholders:
    - Project team members
    - Customer, and if relevant, sellers (vendors)
    - Relevant functional managers
    - Finance and/or accounting departments

A Guide to the Project Management Body of Knowledge (PMBOK® Guide) – Fifth Edition, Project Management Institute, Inc., 2013, pg. 66-72

A Guide to the Project Management Body of Knowledge (PMBOK® Guide) – Fifth Edition, Project Management Institute (PMI)®, Project Management Professional (PMP)®, and Certified Associate in Project Management (CAPM)® are registered trademarks of Project Management Institute, Inc. - Version 2.1 Published September 30, 2014

Lesson 4: Initiating a Project | Topic A

ACTIVITY 4-1
Creating a Project Charter

Data Files

C:\095001Data\Initiating a Project\Project Charter.doc

Scenario

You are a Project Manager for Building with Heart. Building with Heart is a not-for-profit organization that builds homes for low-income families in Greene City. The home build program's purpose is to build a two- or three-bedroom home for each qualifying family. These homes have a mortgage with a reasonable interest rate, and because many materials and labor are donated, the mortgage is much less than if everything had to be purchased outright. The mortgage for each home is $75,000 with 3 percent interest over 30 years. This program has been successfully completing homes on time, within budget, and passing Certificate of Occupancy inspections on the first pass 100 percent of the time.

Building with Heart is getting ready to build a new home for the Smith family. The family has qualified for the home build program and is the next family on the home list. You have been assigned to manage this project. Each new build project is named by the address and the next available lot is located at 122 East Main Street in Greene City. Each new build completes one single-family home.

The winter weather in Greene City can be very cold, snowy, and windy, and this must be taken into account for the scheduling of the home builds. Each house takes about six months to complete if the weather cooperates.

---

1. On your computer, open Windows Explorer, browse to the **C:\095001Data\Initiating a Project** folder, and open the **Project Charter.doc**.

2. Using the information provided in the scenario, complete each section of the project charter for the Building with Heart project.

3. Save the file as *My Project Charter.doc* and close the file.

A Guide to the Project Management Body of Knowledge (PMBOK® Guide) – Fifth Edition, Project Management Institute (PMI)®, Project Management Professional (PMP)®, and Certified Associate in Project Management (CAPM)® are registered trademarks of Project Management Institute, Inc. - Version 2.1 Published September 30, 2014

Lesson 4: Initiating a Project | Topic A

TOPIC B

Identify Project Stakeholders

To get a project started, you must understand who the stakeholders are so that you have the proper guidance and direction as to what the project will accomplish. Stakeholder identification is another important step in initiating your project. Stakeholders are the people who have a "stake" in the success of the project or are impacted by the deliverables that the project produces. In this topic, you will explore the Identify Stakeholder process and how it can be used as a tool to identify and acquire stakeholders.

A Guide to the Project Management Body of Knowledge (PMBOK® Guide) – Fifth Edition, Project Management Institute, Inc., 2013, pg. 393-394

The following data flow diagram illustrates how the Identify Stakeholders process relates to the other project management processes.

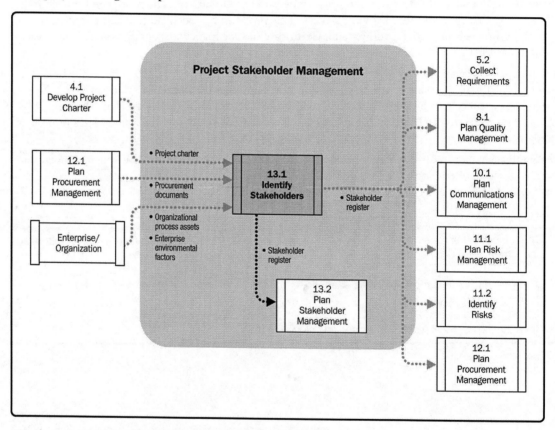

Figure 4-6: The Identify Stakeholders data flow diagram.

A Guide to the Project Management Body of Knowledge (PMBOK® Guide) – Fifth Edition, Project Management Institute, Inc., 2013, p. 393

Who Is a Stakeholder?

Stakeholders are people who may affect or be affected by the objectives of a project. Stakeholders can be of varying levels of project involvement and can have partial oversight of a project. Examples include customers, suppliers, end users of a product, the general public, sponsors, or the recipients of the project's deliverables. Stakeholders are those who may affect or be affected by a decision, activity, deliverable, or outcome of a project.

A Guide to the Project Management Body of Knowledge (PMBOK® Guide) – Fifth Edition, Project Management Institute (PMI)®, Project Management Professional (PMP)®, and Certified Associate in Project Management (CAPM)® are registered trademarks of Project Management Institute, Inc. - Version 2.1 Published September 30, 2014

It is important to understand that project stakeholders are always emerging throughout a project's life cycle. As new requirements are added, as project constraints change, new stakeholders will emerge and it is your job to make sure that they are identified as early as possible.

A Guide to the Project Management Body of Knowledge (PMBOK® Guide) – Fifth Edition, Project Management Institute, Inc., 2013, pg. 393-394

The Identify Stakeholders Process

Stakeholders should be identified early in the project so that their needs and expectations can be met. They are also the people best able to help the project succeed, as they have a specific interest in the project objectives and its success. It is important to understand and document the stakeholders' interest in and influence on the project.

A Guide to the Project Management Body of Knowledge (PMBOK® Guide) – Fifth Edition, Project Management Institute, Inc., 2013, pg. 393-394

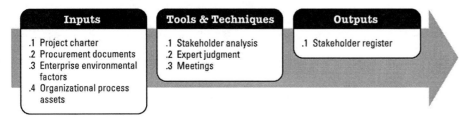

Figure 4-7: The identify stakeholders process.

A Guide to the Project Management Body of Knowledge (PMBOK® Guide) – Fifth Edition, Project Management Institute, Inc., 2013, p. 393

Identify Stakeholders Inputs

Various components provide input to the Identify Stakeholders process.

Input	Description
Project charter	Provides information about the internal and external people interested in the project, such as project sponsor, customers, team members, and other people and organizations affected by the project.
Procurement documents	As stated in the *PMBOK® Guide,* procurement documents are the documents utilized in bid and proposal activities, which include the buyer's Invitation for Bid, Invitation for Negotiations, Request for Information, Request for Quotation, Request for Proposal, and seller's responses.
Enterprise environmental factors	As stated in the *PMBOK® Guide,* enterprise environmental factors that influence identifying stakeholders can include: organizational culture and structure; governmental or industry standards; global, regional, or local trends; and practices or habits.
Organizational process assets	As stated in the *PMBOK® Guide,* organizational process assets that can influence identifying stakeholders can include: stakeholder register templates, lessons learned from previous projects, and stakeholder registers from previous projects.

A Guide to the Project Management Body of Knowledge (PMBOK® Guide) – Fifth Edition, Project Management Institute, Inc., 2013, pg. 394-395

Procurement Documents

Procurement is the acquisition of goods and services from an external organization, vendor, or supplier to enable the deliverables of the project. If a project has procurement activities, which is the need for external goods and/or services, and is based on an established contract, the people in that contract are also project stakeholders. Any suppliers that support or participate in the project should also be identified as stakeholders.

Sample Procurement of Goods Document

PART 1 – BIDDING PROCEDURES

Section I.   Instructions to Bidders (ITB) - This Section provides information to help Bidders prepare their bids.

PART 2 – SUPPLY REQUIREMENTS

Section VI.   Schedule of Requirements - This Section includes the List of Goods and Related Services, the Delivery and Completion Schedules, the Technical Specifications and the Drawings that describe the Goods and Related Services to be procured.

PART 3 – CONTRACT

Section VII.   General Conditions of Contract (GCC) - This Section includes the general clauses to be applied in all contracts. The text of the clauses in this Section shall not be modified.

Section VIII.   Special Conditions of Contract (SCC) - This Section includes clauses specific to each contract that modify or supplement Section VII, General Conditions of Contract.

Section IX: Contract Forms

This Section includes the form for the Agreement, which, once completed, incorporates corrections or modifications to the accepted bid that are permitted under the Instructions to Bidders, the General Conditions of Contract, and the Special Conditions of Contract.

The forms for Performance Security and Advance Payment Security, when required, shall only be completed by the successful Bidder after contract award.

Figure 4-8: A procurement document.

A Guide to the Project Management Body of Knowledge (PMBOK® Guide) – Fifth Edition, Project Management Institute, Inc., 2013, p. 394

Identify Stakeholders Tools and Techniques

There are three tools and techniques used in the Identify Stakeholders process.

Tools & Techniques	Description
Stakeholder analysis	As stated in the *PMBOK® Guide,* stakeholder analysis is a technique of systematically gathering and analyzing quantitative and qualitative information to determine whose interests should be taken into account throughout the project.
Expert judgment	Expert judgment used to help identify stakeholders could be obtained from senior management, identified key stakeholders, project managers, SMEs, industry groups, consultants, and professional and technical associations.
Meetings	As stated in the *PMBOK® Guide,* a meeting is a gathering of people for a business purpose.

A Guide to the Project Management Body of Knowledge (PMBOK® Guide) – Fifth Edition, Project Management Institute (PMI)®, Project Management Professional (PMP)®, and Certified Associate in Project Management (CAPM)® are registered trademarks of Project Management Institute, Inc. - Version 2.1 Published September 30, 2014

Lesson 4: Initiating a Project | Topic B

A Guide to the Project Management Body of Knowledge (PMBOK® Guide) – Fifth Edition, Project
Management Institute, Inc., 2013, pg. 395-398

Stakeholder Analysis

Stakeholder analysis is a process of gathering and analyzing data about people whose interests should
be considered and taken into account during the life cycle of the project. These are the people who
are interested in the project, have business expectations from the project, and can also influence the
progress of the project. Stakeholder analysis documents can contain sensitive information regarding
stakeholder rankings, opinions, and other factors, so they should be managed appropriately.

The power/interest grid is a classification method used to document stakeholder analysis results.

A Guide to the Project Management Body of Knowledge (PMBOK® Guide) – Fifth Edition, Project
Management Institute, Inc., 2013, pg. 395-397

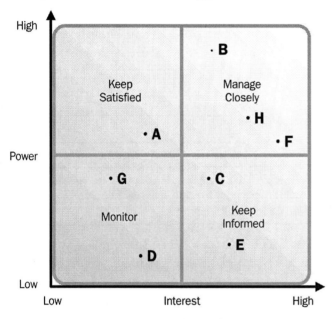

Figure 4-9: Power/interest stakeholder grid.

A Guide to the Project Management Body of Knowledge (PMBOK® Guide) – Fifth Edition, Project
Management Institute, Inc., 2013, p. 397

Steps to Perform Stakeholder Analysis

There are some general steps used when performing stakeholder analysis:

- Identify all potential project stakeholders. Anyone in a decision-making or management role who
  is affected by the project outcome (sponsor, project manager, and primary customer) is a key
  stakeholder.
- Analyze the support each stakeholder may provide and its impact on the project.
- Determine how key stakeholders might react or respond in various situations.
- Use known classification models to properly document stakeholder analysis data:
  - Power/interest grid: a classification model that groups stakeholders on the basis of their
    levels of authority and interest in the project.
  - Power/influence grid: a classification model that groups stakeholders on the basis of their
    levels of authority and involvement in the project.
  - Influence/impact grid: a classification model that groups stakeholders on the basis of their
    involvement in and impact on the project.

A Guide to the Project Management Body of Knowledge (PMBOK® Guide) – Fifth Edition, Project Management Institute (PMI)®, Project Management Professional
(PMP)®, and Certified Associate in Project Management (CAPM)® are registered trademarks of Project Management Institute, Inc. - Version 2.1 Published September 30, 2014

Lesson 4: Initiating a Project | *Topic B*

- Salience model: a classification model that groups stakeholders on the basis of their level of authority, their immediate needs, and how appropriate their involvement is in terms of the project.

A Guide to the Project Management Body of Knowledge (PMBOK® Guide) – Fifth Edition, Project Management Institute, Inc., 2013, p. 396

Meetings

Meetings should be held with targeted experts and the project team to define the required engagement levels of stakeholders. Stakeholder roles, knowledge of, and interests in the project should be reviewed during the meetings. This information can be used to prepare the stakeholder management plan. For example, this would be a meeting with a broad cross section of knowledgeable people that can participate in further identification of needed stakeholders for a project. Meeting discussion notes and results should also be handled with care due to the sensitivity of the information gathered during the meetings.

A Guide to the Project Management Body of Knowledge (PMBOK® Guide) – Fifth Edition, Project Management Institute, Inc., 2013, p. 398

Identify Stakeholders Outputs

There is one output from the Identify Stakeholders process.

Output	Description
Stakeholder register	As stated in the *PMBOK® Guide,* a stakeholder register is a project document that includes the identification, assessment, and classification of project stakeholders.

A Guide to the Project Management Body of Knowledge (PMBOK® Guide) – Fifth Edition, Project Management Institute, Inc., 2013, p. 398

Stakeholder Register

Stakeholder involvement and management is often documented in a *stakeholder register.* The stakeholder register contains specific information such as name, contact information, location, job role or position, and project involvement. Some registers might also include additional stakeholder information such as potential influence over the project or a specific phase of the project, and their classification based on stakeholder analysis completed during the identification process.

STAKEHOLDER REGISTER

Name	Organizational Position	Location	Role in Project	Contact Information	Major Requirements	Expectations	Influence	Areas of Interest	Internal/ External	Supporter?
Jane Smith	CEO, Building with Heart	Green City	Sponsor	585-555-1234	Budget, Schedule, Quality	Community involvement	Major	Community	Internal	Yes
Bob Matthews	Mayor, Green City	Green City	Mayor	585-555-9118	Neighborhood development	Growth	Major	Development	External	Yes
Smith Family	Homeowners	Green City	Homeowners	585-555-8372	New house	Engage family and friends	Major	House	Internal	Yes
Bill Lewis	Electrician	Green City	Electrician	585-555-1847	Electrical work	Pass inspection	Minor	Electrical system	External	Yes
You!	Project Manager	Green City	Project Manager	585-555-7248	Scope, schedule, cost, quality	Project goes as planned	Major	All	Internal	Yes

Figure 4–10: A stakeholder register.

A Guide to the Project Management Body of Knowledge (PMBOK® Guide) – Fifth Edition, Project Management Institute, Inc., 2013, p. 398

Guidelines to Identify Stakeholders

To identify the stakeholder for a project:

- Review the project charter for the scope, boundaries, deliverables, and outcomes to get a sense of who may be affected.
- Set up a meeting and use the stakeholder analysis techniques to determine who has an interest in the project.
- Identify the stakeholder and the support they might provide.
- Use a classification model to organize your stakeholders.
- Develop a stakeholder register to record all pertinent information for each stakeholder.

A Guide to the Project Management Body of Knowledge (PMBOK® Guide) – Fifth Edition, Project Management Institute, Inc., 2013, pg. 393-398

A Guide to the Project Management Body of Knowledge (PMBOK® Guide) – Fifth Edition, Project Management Institute (PMI)®, Project Management Professional (PMP)®, and Certified Associate in Project Management (CAPM)® are registered trademarks of Project Management Institute, Inc. - Version 2.1 Published September 30, 2014

Lesson 4: Initiating a Project | Topic B

ACTIVITY 4-2
Creating a Stakeholder Register

Data Files

C:\095001Data\Initiating a Project\Stakeholder Register.doc

Scenario

There are many people involved in the new 122 East Main build. The mayor, local government, an inspector, a master carpenter, a plumber, an electrician, a landscaper, a project manager, family and friends, volunteers, and so on. The CEO, Jane Dorand, reviews and approves each new build project. You need to create a stakeholder register based on the information you have gathered to this point.

1. On your computer, open Windows Explorer, browse to the **C:\095001Data\Initiating a Project** folder, and open the **Stakeholder Register.doc**.

2. Using the information provided in the scenario, complete the stakeholder register for the 122 East Main Building with Heart project.

3. Save the file as *My Stakeholder Register.doc* and close the file.

Summary

In this lesson, you examined the Develop a Project Charter process and the Identify Stakeholders process, which are both part of the Initiating Process Group. You identified the inputs, tools and techniques, and the outputs of both processes to ultimately develop a project charter document and a stakeholder register. You also were introduced to two of the Project Integration Management Knowledge Areas and how developing a project charter is the first step in initiating a project. You also learned about the Project Stakeholder Management Knowledge Area and how to identify project stakeholders.

What are some benefits of having a project charter?

Why do you think it's important to identify and document the project stakeholders?

Note: Check your LogicalCHOICE Course screen for opportunities to interact with your classmates, peers, and the larger LogicalCHOICE online community about the topics covered in this course or other topics you are interested in. From the Course screen you can also access available resources for a more continuous learning experience.

A Guide to the Project Management Body of Knowledge (PMBOK® Guide) – Fifth Edition, Project Management Institute (PMI)®, Project Management Professional (PMP)®, and Certified Associate in Project Management (CAPM)® are registered trademarks of Project Management Institute, Inc. - Version 2.1 Published September 30, 2014

Lesson 4: Initiating a Project |

5 | Planning a Project

Lesson Time: 2 hours, 30 minutes

Lesson Objectives

In this lesson, you will:

- Develop a project management plan.

- Plan scope management.

- Collect project requirements.

- Define project scope.

- Create a WBS.

Lesson Introduction

Now that you have been through the process of creating a project charter and identifying the stakeholders, you are ready to start the planning phase of project development.

This next lesson will take you through the different processes used to properly plan the management of the project as a whole, the scope, and how to create a work breakdown structure to meet the needs of the project. These processes can be used in many ways to plan specific parts of the overall project once the project authorization has been obtained.

The following diagram highlights the next process group and knowledge areas covered in this lesson.

Knowledge Areas	Project Management Process Groups				
	Initating Process Group	Planning Process Group	Executing Process Group	Monitoring and Controlling Process Group	Closing Process Group
4. Project Integration Management	4.1 Develop Project Charter	4.2 Develop Project Management Plan	4.3 Direct and Manage Project Work	4.4 Monitor and Control Project Work 4.5 Perform Integrated Change Control	4.6 Close Project or Phase
5. Project Scope Management		5.1 Plan Scope Management 5.2 Collect Requirements 5.3 Define Scope 5.4 Create WBS		5.5 Validate Scope 5.6 Control Scope	
6. Project Time Management		6.1 Plan Schedule Management 6.2 Define Activities 6.3 Sequence Activites 6.4 Estimate Activity Resources 6.5 Estimate Activity Durations 6.6 Develop Schedule		6.7 Control Schedule	
7. Project Cost Management		7.1 Plan Cost Management 7.2 Estimate Cost 7.3 Determine Budget		7.4 Control Costs	
8. Project Quality Management		8.1 Plan Quality Management	8.2 Perform Quality Assurance	8.3 Control Quality	
9. Project Human Resource Management		9.1 Plan Human Resource Management	9.2 Acquire Project Team 9.3 Develop Project Team 9.4 Manage Project Team		
10. Project Communication Management		10.1 Plan Communications Management	10.2 Manage Communications	10.3 Control Communications	
11. Project Risk Management		11.1 Plan Risk Management 11.2 Identify Risks 11.3 Perform Qualitative Risk Analysis 11.4 Perform Quantitative Risk Analysis 11.5 Plan Risk Responses		11.6 Control Risks	
12. Project Procurement Management		12.1 Plan Procurement Management	12.2 Conduct Procurements	12.3 Control Procurements	12.4 Close Procurements
13. Project Stakeholder Management	13.1 Identify Stakeholders	13.2 Plan Stakeholder Management	13.3 Manage Stakeholder Engagement	13.4 Control Stakeholder Engagement	

TOPIC A

Develop a Project Management Plan

Documenting a detailed project management plan is essential to the success of your project. It will be referred to and updated throughout the project's life cycle.

In this topic, you will identify the processes used to create a project management plan and how the inputs, tools and techniques, and the output are utilized to create the desired outcome that meets a project's needs. With a good project management plan, you will be able to react quickly and seamlessly to any issues, changes, or modifications needed during the course of your project.

A Guide to the Project Management Body of Knowledge (PMBOK® Guide) – Fifth Edition, Project Management Institute, Inc., 2013, pg. 72-74

The following data flow diagram illustrates how the Develop a Project Management Plan process relates to the other project management processes.

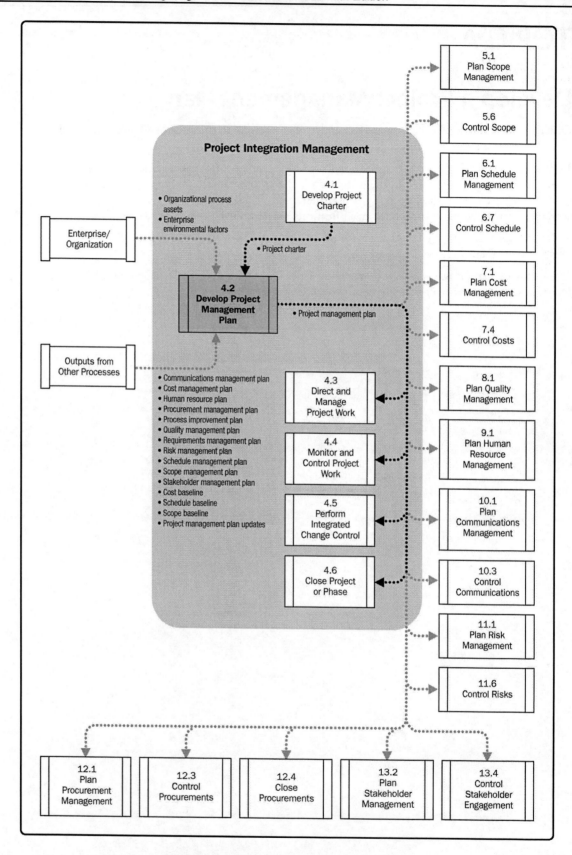

Figure 5-1: The Develop a Project Management Plan data flow diagram.

A Guide to the Project Management Body of Knowledge (PMBOK® Guide) – Fifth Edition, Project Management Institute, Inc., 2013, p. 73

What Is a Project Management Plan?

A *project management plan* is one or more documents that define how the project is executed, monitored, controlled, and closed. There is generally not one single plan but many plans that make up the project management plan. The contents and plans themselves will vary with every project and will be unique to a specific project's needs. A project's plan is always changing and is updated, altered, and tweaked as project demands change. Changes to the project management plan are controlled and managed through the integrated change control process.

A Guide to the Project Management Body of Knowledge (PMBOK® Guide) – Fifth Edition, Project Management Institute, Inc., 2013, p. 74

Program Management Plans

Projects that are contained within a program will most likely have to follow a single program management plan. If a program management plan exists for a project, then any changes made to a project management plan will need to conform with what is stated in the program management plan.

A Guide to the Project Management Body of Knowledge (PMBOK® Guide) – Fifth Edition, Project Management Institute, Inc., 2013, pg. 7-9

Project Management Plan Components

Collectively, the following plans make up the Project Management plan.

Component	Description
Baselines	Baseline management is a key component of the project management plan. Most plans will include a description of how the integrity of the project baselines will be maintained. There are a few common baselines used when developing a project management plan: • Scope baseline • Schedule baseline • Cost baseline
Subsidiary plans	There are a number of subsidiary plans that will be integrated in the overall project management plan. Any of the following plans may be used: • Scope management plan • Requirements management plan • Schedule management plan • Cost management plan • Quality management plan • Process improvement plan • Human resource management plan • Communication management plan • Risk management plan • Procurement management plan • Stakeholder management plan
Life cycle	The plan may include a specific life cycle selected for the project and processes that will be applied to each phase of the project.

A Guide to the Project Management Body of Knowledge (PMBOK® Guide) – Fifth Edition, Project Management Institute (PMI)®, Project Management Professional (PMP)®, and Certified Associate in Project Management (CAPM)® are registered trademarks of Project Management Institute, Inc. - Version 2.1 Published September 30, 2014

Lesson 5: Planning a Project | Topic A

Component	Description
Project processes	Project processes selected for a specific process will be stated within the plan. These descriptions can include: • Project management processes selected by the project management team • Level of implementation for each selected process • Descriptions of the tools and techniques to be used for accomplishing those processes • Description of how the selected processes will be used to manage the specific project, including dependencies and interactions among those processes and the essential inputs and outputs.
Work explanation	An explanation of how project work will be executed to meet the project's objectives.
Change management plan	A change management plan may be included to provide procedures on how to control change requests, which may include configuration management.

A Guide to the Project Management Body of Knowledge (PMBOK® Guide) – Fifth Edition, Project Management Institute, Inc., 2013, pg. 76-77

The Develop a Project Management Plan Process

The *Develop a Project Management Plan process* is the first process within the Planning Process Group. The purpose of developing a project management plan is to define, prepare, and coordinate all subsidiary plans and integrate them into a comprehensive project management plan.

A Guide to the Project Management Body of Knowledge (PMBOK® Guide) – Fifth Edition, Project Management Institute, Inc., 2013, pg. 72-74

The following diagram shows how this process relates to other connected processes.

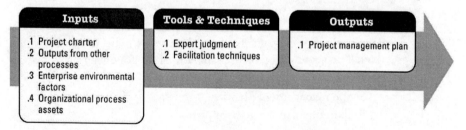

Figure 5–2: The Develop a Project Management Plan data flow diagram.

A Guide to the Project Management Body of Knowledge (PMBOK® Guide) – Fifth Edition, Project Management Institute, Inc., 2013, p. 72

Develop a Project Management Plan Inputs

There are a number of components that provide input into the Develop a Project Management Plan process.

Input	Description
The project charter	Used to determine what the high level project objectives are.

Input	Description
Outputs from other processes	As stated in the *PMBOK® Guide,* these are outputs from other processes.
Enterprise environmental factors	Enterprise environmental factors that affect the project management plan include: • Governmental or industry standards • Project Management Information Systems • Organizational structure, culture, management practices, and sustainability • Infrastructure • Personnel administration
Organizational process assets	Organizational process assets that can influence this process include standardized guidelines, work instructions, proposal evaluation criteria, performance measurement criteria, project management plan templates, change control procedures, project files from previous projects, historical information, configuration management, and other knowledge bases.

A Guide to the Project Management Body of Knowledge (PMBOK® Guide) – Fifth Edition, Project Management Institute, Inc., 2013, pg. 74-75

Outputs from Other Processes

Any outputs from the processes within the Planning Process Group can be inputs to this process. For example, any subsidiary plans or baselines that affect the overall project management plan will be used in developing the project management plan. Any updates or changes made to any of these other documents can alternately affect the project management plan and adjustments will need to be made. Changes to these documents may necessitate updates to the project management plan.

A Guide to the Project Management Body of Knowledge (PMBOK® Guide) – Fifth Edition, Project Management Institute, Inc., 2013, p. 74

Develop a Project Management Plan Tools and Techniques

There are two useful techniques used when you are developing a project management plan for your project.

Tools & Techniques	Description
Expert judgment	Expert judgment is used to adjust the process to meet the specific needs of a project. You will use this technique to: • Customize the process to meet specific project needs. • Develop technical and management details that will be used within the project management plan. • Determine the resources and skills needed for project work. • Define the level of configuration management needed to apply to a project. • Identify the project documents that will be subject to a formal change control process. • Prioritize the work on the project to ensure resources are allocated to the appropriate work at the appropriate time.

A Guide to the Project Management Body of Knowledge (PMBOK® Guide) – Fifth Edition, Project Management Institute (PMI)®, Project Management Professional (PMP)®, and Certified Associate in Project Management (CAPM)® are registered trademarks of Project Management Institute, Inc. - Version 2.1 Published September 30, 2014

Lesson 5: Planning a Project | Topic A

Tools & Techniques	Description
Facilitation techniques	Used to resolve issues, brainstorm ideas, enable problem solving, and manage conflicts that may arise over the course of a project. Facilitation techniques can be used by any project team member to assist other team members.

A Guide to the Project Management Body of Knowledge (PMBOK® Guide) – Fifth Edition, Project Management Institute, Inc., 2013, p. 76

Develop a Project Management Plan Output

There is one output from the Develop Project Management Plan process.

Output	Description
Project management plan	As stated in the *PMBOK® Guide,* this is the formal document that describes how the project will be executed, monitored, and controlled.

A Guide to the Project Management Body of Knowledge (PMBOK® Guide) – Fifth Edition, Project Management Institute, Inc., 2013, pg. 76-77

Guidelines to Develop a Project Management Plan

Guidelines to develop a project management plan are as follows:

* Review the project charter for the high level boundaries of the project.
* Review outputs from other processes such as baselines and subsidiary plans that are outputs of other planning processes.
* Review enterprise environmental factors including governmental or industry standards, Project Management Information Systems, organizational structure, culture, management practices, and sustainability, infrastructure and personnel administration, as applicable to your project.
* Review organizational process assets including standardized guidelines, work instructions, proposal evaluation criteria, performance measurement criteria, project management plan templates, change control procedures, project files from previous projects, historical information and configuration management knowledge base, as applicable to your project.
* Use tools and techniques such as expert judgment to tailor the process to meet the project needs, develop technical and management details, determine resources and skill levels needed to perform project work, define the level of configuration management to use on the project, and prioritize the work on the project to ensure resources are allocated to the appropriate work at the appropriate time, as applicable to your project.
* Use facilitation techniques such as brainstorming, conflict resolution, problem solving, and meeting management, which are examples of key techniques used by facilitators to help teams and individuals accomplish project activities and develop the project management plan.
* Document the project management plan.

A Guide to the Project Management Body of Knowledge (PMBOK® Guide) – Fifth Edition, Project Management Institute, Inc., 2013, pg. 72-78

TOPIC B

Plan Scope Management

With your project management plan and stakeholder management plan developed, you can move to the next logical process and plan how the project's scope will be managed from start to close-out. It is important to identify what the scope of a project is so that you can make sure the project is on the right course through every stage. In this topic, you will identify how project scope will be handled throughout the life cycle of a project.

A Guide to the Project Management Body of Knowledge (PMBOK® Guide) – Fifth Edition, Project Management Institute, Inc., 2013, pg. 107-108

The following diagram displays how the Plan Scope Management process is applied within the Project Scope Management knowledge area.

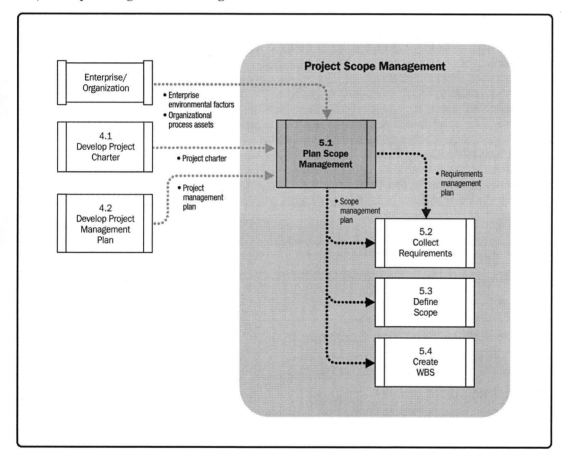

Figure 5–3: The Plan Scope Management data flow diagram.

A Guide to the Project Management Body of Knowledge (PMBOK® Guide) – Fifth Edition, Project Management Institute, Inc., 2013, p. 107

What Is a Scope Management Plan?

A *scope management plan* is a document that determines how project scope is to be managed throughout a project. This plan is a component of the project management plan or program management plan that describes how the project scope will be identified, explained, monitored, and controlled throughout a project's life cycle. As a project manager, you will reference the project charter and any subsidiary plans of the project management plan when developing the scope management plan. Another factor you must consider during the development is whether or not any environmental factors are pertinent to the project.

SCOPE MANAGEMENT APPROACH

It is important that the approach to managing the projects' scope be clearly defined and documented in detail. This section provides a summary of the Scope Management Plan in which it addresses the following:

- Who has authority and responsibility for scope management
- How the scope is defined (i.e. Scope Statement, WBS, WBS Dictionary, Statement of Work, etc.)
- How the scope is measured and verified (i.e. Quality Checklists, Scope Baseline, Work Performance Measurements, etc.)
- The scope change process (who initiates, who authorizes, etc.)
- Who is responsible for accepting the final project deliverable and approves acceptance of project scope

For this project, scope management will be the sole responsibility of the Project Manager. The scope for this project is defined by the Scope Statement, Work Breakdown Structure (WBS) and WBS Dictionary. The Project Manager, Sponsor and Stakeholders will establish and approve documentation for measuring project scope which includes deliverable quality checklists and work performance measurements. Proposed scope changes may be initiated by the Project Manager, Stakeholders or any member of the project team. All change requests will be submitted to the Project Manager who will then evaluate the requested scope change. Upon acceptance of the scope change request the Project Manager will submit the scope change request to the Change Control Board and Project Sponsor for acceptance. Upon approval of scope changes by the Change Control Board and Project Sponsor the Project Manager will update all project documents and communicate the scope change to all stakeholders. Based on feedback and input from the Project Manager and Stakeholders, the Project Sponsor is responsible for the acceptance of the final project deliverables and project scope.

Figure 5-4: An example of a scope management plan.

A Guide to the Project Management Body of Knowledge (PMBOK® Guide) – Fifth Edition, Project Management Institute, Inc., 2013, pg. 108-109

The Scope Management Plan Components

There can be a number of components included within a scope management plan. The components are determined by the specifics of the project and can vary on a project-by-project basis. Components of a scope management plan include:

- A process for preparing a detail project scope statement.
- A documented process to use when creating the Work Breakdown Structure (WBS).
- A process for establishing how the WBS will be approved and maintained throughout the project life cycle.
- A process to formalize the distribution of deliverables once a project is completed.
- A process to manage any changes requested to the overall project scope.

 Note: Please note that WBS will be covered in more detail later in this lesson.

A Guide to the Project Management Body of Knowledge (PMBOK® Guide) – Fifth Edition, Project Management Institute, Inc., 2013, p. 110

Scope Creep

The goal of a good scope management plan is to prevent the project work from exceeding the identified work targets. This is referred to as *scope creep*. Scope creep is the tendency of project work to exceed the expected limits stated in the project charter.

A Guide to the Project Management Body of Knowledge (PMBOK® Guide) – Fifth Edition, Project Management Institute, Inc., 2013, p. 137

The Requirements Management Plan

The *requirements management plan* is a component of the project management plan that describes how all project requirements will be determined, documented, updated, and managed.

A Guide to the Project Management Body of Knowledge (PMBOK® Guide) – Fifth Edition, Project Management Institute, Inc., 2013, p. 110

Components of a Project Requirements Plan

Components of the requirements management plan require project managers to choose the most effective relationships to aid the success of the project and document this approach in the plan. These components include:

- How requirements activities will be planned, tracked, and reported
- Configuration management activities such as how version control of project documents and changes to the product will be initiated; how impacts will be analyzed; how they will be traced, tracked, and reported; and what authorization level is required to approve these changes
- Requirements prioritization process, which defines how project requirements will be analyzed and prioritized
- Product metrics that will be used and the rationale for using them
- Traceability structure stating which requirement attributes will be captured on the traceability matrix, the forward and backward chain of traceability, and the categorization of requirements

A Guide to the Project Management Body of Knowledge (PMBOK® Guide) – Fifth Edition, Project Management Institute, Inc., 2013, p. 110

The Plan Scope Management Process

The *Plan Scope Management process* utilizes inputs from other project documents and processes, tools and techniques to generate the desired outputs, which include the scope management plan and the requirements management plan. These are all included in the following illustration.

A Guide to the Project Management Body of Knowledge (PMBOK® Guide) – Fifth Edition, Project Management Institute, Inc., 2013, pg. 107-108

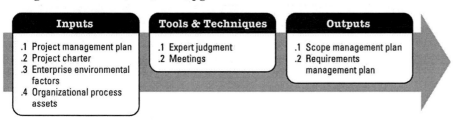

Figure 5-5: The Plan Scope Management process.

A Guide to the Project Management Body of Knowledge (PMBOK® Guide) – Fifth Edition, Project Management Institute, Inc., 2013, p. 107

Plan Scope Management Inputs

There are a number of various components that provide input to the Plan Scope Management process.

Input	Description
Project management plan	In this process, any subsidiary plans of the project management plan that have been approved will be referred to and used to create the scope management plan. Any information that was included in the project management plan will be used when determining how to manage the scope of a project. As the project management plan is the first plan created for the project, as other plans are developed, their impacts will be added to the project management plan. (This is known as iterative planning.)
Project charter	The project charter provides the context and the direction of the project. Therefore, the charter should be used when determining how to manage scope. The charter will include the high-level descriptions and what the end product of a project will be. With this information, you can determine what the scope is and what will need to be included in the management plan.
Enterprise environmental factors	Any enterprise environmental factors that can influence the scope of a project should be included in the plan. This may include: • An organization's culture • The infrastructure of an organization • Personnel administration • Marketplace conditions
Organizational process assets	Organizational process assets that can influence the development of a scope management plan include any policies and procedures that an organization might need to adhere to, or any historical information or lessons learned from previous projects.

A Guide to the Project Management Body of Knowledge (PMBOK® Guide) – Fifth Edition, Project Management Institute, Inc., 2013, pg. 108-109

Plan Scope Management Tools and Techniques

Tools and techniques are used to help develop the scope management plan.

Tools & Techniques	Description
Expert judgment	In this process, you can use external experts that specialize in scope management. These individuals can be consulted when you are ready to put the plan together.
Meetings	Meetings are held during this process with any team member who will be involved with the creation of the scope management plan.

A Guide to the Project Management Body of Knowledge (PMBOK® Guide) – Fifth Edition, Project Management Institute, Inc., 2013, p. 109

Plan Scope Management Outputs

There are two outputs from the Plan Scope Management process.

Output	Description (as stated in the PMBOK® Guide)
The scope management plan	A component of the project management plan that describes how the scope will be defined, developed, monitored, controlled, and verified.
The requirements management plan	A component of the project or program management plan that describes how requirements will be analyzed, documented, and managed.

A Guide to the Project Management Body of Knowledge (PMBOK® Guide) – Fifth Edition, Project Management Institute, Inc., 2013, pg. 109-110

Guidelines to Develop a Scope Management Plan

Guidelines to develop a scope management plan are as follows:

- Review the project management plan and subsidiary plans to create the scope management plan and influence the approach taken for planning scope and managing project scope.
- Review the enterprise environmental factors such as the organization's culture, infrastructure, personnel administration, and marketplace conditions.
- Review the organizational process assets such as policies and procedures, historical information, and lessons learned knowledge base.
- Use tools and techniques such as expert judgment, which provides expertise from any group or person with specialized education, knowledge, skills, experience, or training in developing scope management plans.
- Hold meetings to develop the scope management plan and include anyone with responsibility for any of the scope management processes.
- Document the scope management plan and the requirements management plan.

A Guide to the Project Management Body of Knowledge (PMBOK® Guide) – Fifth Edition, Project Management Institute, Inc., 2013, pg. 107-110

ACTIVITY 5-1
Researching Scope Management Plans

Scenario

Before you start developing the scope management plan for the 122 East Main project, you need to get an idea of what potential templates there are and which ones might suit the needs of the project. In this activity, you will research scope management plans.

1. Review scope management templates available on the Internet.
   a) From the desktop, launch Internet Explorer.
   b) In the search engine text box, enter *Scope Management Plan Template* Review the results of the search.
   c) In the address bar, enter *projectmanagementdocs.com*
   d) Select the **Project Planning** tab and scroll down to the **Scope Management Plan**.

2. Why is it important to properly manage the scope of your project?

3. Which of the following is not a component of the scope management plan?
   - ○ A scope statement
   - ○ The project management plan
   - ○ A process to manage changes
   - ○ A process to create the WBS

4. True or False? Scope creep includes new requirements that must be added to the project immediately.
   - ☐ True
   - ☐ False

A Guide to the Project Management Body of Knowledge (PMBOK® Guide) – Fifth Edition, Project Management Institute (PMI)®, Project Management Professional (PMP)®, and Certified Associate in Project Management (CAPM)® are registered trademarks of Project Management Institute, Inc. - Version 2.1 Published September 30, 2014

Lesson 5: Planning a Project | Topic B

TOPIC C

Collect Project Requirements

Now that you have familiarized yourself with the requirements management plan, you can start the process of collecting and gathering all the requirements that are needed for your project. In essence, you will be assembling a project "wish list" that includes all potential requirements that are collected from the project's sponsor and stakeholders. It is important to assemble all the requirements so that you can properly analyze each one, prioritize them, and then ultimately use them to define the scope for a project.

A Guide to the Project Management Body of Knowledge (PMBOK® Guide) – Fifth Edition, Project Management Institute, Inc., 2013, pg. 110-112

The diagram displays how the Collect Requirements process relates to the other knowledge areas.

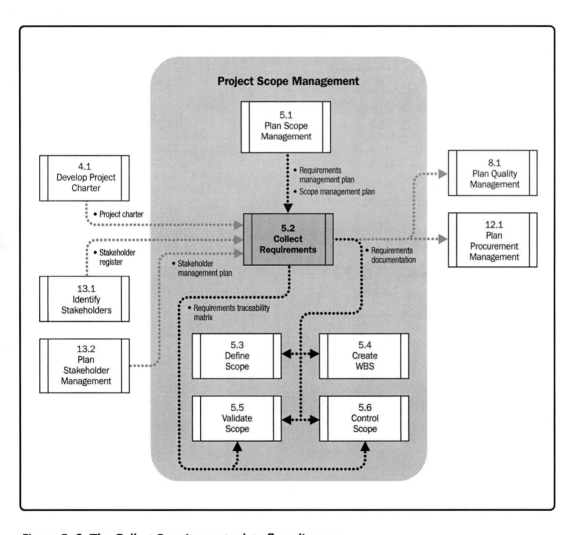

Figure 5-6: The Collect Requirements data flow diagram.

A Guide to the Project Management Body of Knowledge (PMBOK® Guide) – Fifth Edition, Project Management Institute, Inc., 2013, p. 111

Project Requirements

Project requirements are the conditions or capabilities that must be accomplished by the project outcomes. Requirements are the determined and documented needs and expected project outcomes and expectations of the project customer, sponsor, and stakeholders. Some high-level requirements may already be documented and in the project charter, but as the project manager you must verify that all requirements are determined and documented during this process. Requirements create the foundation for building the WBS, and are verified regularly during the project execution process.

A Guide to the Project Management Body of Knowledge (PMBOK® Guide) – Fifth Edition, Project Management Institute, Inc., 2013, pg. 112, 118

Requirements Documentation

Requirements documentation is an output in the collect requirements process. The documentation is composed of all the individual requirements needed in order for a project to meet the business and/or stakeholder needs for a project. The composition of the documents will vary depending on the specific needs of a project, so the range can be from very detailed and categorized, to a simple list of high-level requirements. Requirements documentation can include any or all of the following components:

- Business requirements:
    - Business and project objectives for traceability
    - Business rules for the performing organization
    - Guiding principles of the organization
- Stakeholder requirements:
    - Impacts to other organizational areas
    - Impacts to other entities inside or outside the performing organization
    - Stakeholder communications and reporting requirements
- Solution requirements:
    - Functional and nonfunctional requirements
    - Technical and standard compliance requirements
    - Support and training requirements
    - Quality requirements
    - Reporting requirements
- Project requirements:
    - Levels of service, performance, safety, compliance, and so on.
    - Acceptance criteria
- Transition requirements
- Requirements assumptions, dependencies, and constraints

A Guide to the Project Management Body of Knowledge (PMBOK® Guide) – Fifth Edition, Project Management Institute, Inc., 2013, p. 112

Requirements Classification

When analyzing and evaluating each project requirement gathered, you will most likely use a classification to help prioritization later in the process. There are a number of common classifications used when organizing and dividing requirements.

Classification	Description
Business	A business requirement is a high-level need of an organization.
Stakeholder	A need that comes directly from a project stakeholder.

A Guide to the Project Management Body of Knowledge (PMBOK® Guide) – Fifth Edition, Project Management Institute (PMI)®, Project Management Professional (PMP)®, and Certified Associate in Project Management (CAPM)® are registered trademarks of Project Management Institute, Inc. - Version 2.1 Published September 30, 2014

Lesson 5: Planning a Project | Topic C

Classification	Description
Solution	Solution requirements are any feature, function, product, service, or result of a project. These requirements are split into two types: • Functional, which are results of a specific product • Nonfunctional, which are any conditions that must be present for the outcome to be successful
Transition	Transition requirements are classified when requirements are temporary in order to enable project work to get done.
Project	Project needs are the high-level requirements that the overall project must meet. These can be actions, processes, or any other condition of the project.
Quality	Quality requirements are described as any condition that the outcomes of a project are validated against.

A Guide to the Project Management Body of Knowledge (PMBOK® Guide) – Fifth Edition, Project Management Institute, Inc., 2013, p. 112

Requirements Traceability Matrix

The *requirements traceability matrix* is a grid representation of project requirements that were determined and mapped directly to the outcomes of a project. The purpose of this matrix is to justify each requirement determined and to link it directly to the business and project objectives. This matrix can be used to track the progress of requirements throughout the project life cycle and to verify that the requirements have been met once the project closes out. It can also be very helpful to manage a project's scope and any proposed changes to the scope.

 Note: There are tools available to project managers to enable proper requirements tracking such as DOORS® (Dynamic Object-Oriented Requirements System).

There are a number of tracing requirements used when creating the traceability matrix:
- Business needs, opportunities, goals, and objectives
- Project objectives
- Project scope/WBS deliverables
- Product design
- Product development
- Test strategy and test scenarios
- High-level requirements to more detailed requirements
- Work package mapping
- Stakeholder reference, so you can track each individual requirement to a stakeholder

A Guide to the Project Management Body of Knowledge (PMBOK® Guide) – Fifth Edition, Project Management Institute, Inc., 2013, pg. 118-119

The following example shows how a matrix can be used to track requirements.

A Guide to the Project Management Body of Knowledge (PMBOK® Guide) – Fifth Edition, Project Management Institute (PMI)®, Project Management Professional (PMP)®, and Certified Associate in Project Management (CAPM)® are registered trademarks of Project Management Institute, Inc. - Version 2.1 Published September 30, 2014

Lesson 5: Planning a Project | Topic C

Requirements Traceability Matrix

Project Name:		
Cost Center:		
Project Description:		

ID	Associate ID	Requirements Description	Business Needs, Opportunities, Goals, Objectives	Project Objectives	WBS Deliverables	Product Design	Product Development	Test Cases
001	1.0							
	1.1							
	1.2							
	1.2.1							
002	2.0							
	2.1							
	2.1.1							
003	3.0							
	3.1							
	3.2							
004	4.0							
005	5.0							

Figure 5-7: An example of a requirements traceability matrix.

A Guide to the Project Management Body of Knowledge (PMBOK® Guide) – Fifth Edition, Project Management Institute, Inc., 2013, p. 119

The Collect Requirements Process

The *Collect Requirements process* is used to gather, analyze, document, and manage all the needs of a project. The requirements are assembled directly from the project stakeholders and the outcomes for a project. Using this process, you can actively engage with stakeholders to determine the project's needs, which will directly result in the specific requirements. This stage in the process is important to the success of a project. Without the proper requirements established at the planning phases of the project, all processes that rely on proper requirements collection will not be accurate.

A Guide to the Project Management Body of Knowledge (PMBOK® Guide) – Fifth Edition, Project Management Institute, Inc., 2013, pg. 110-111

The following diagram displays the Collect Requirements process.

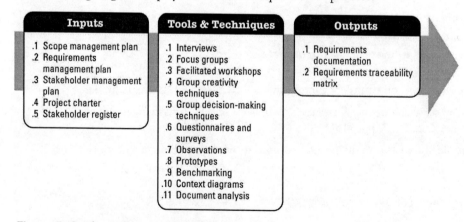

Figure 5-8: The Collect Requirements process.

A Guide to the Project Management Body of Knowledge (PMBOK® Guide) – Fifth Edition, Project Management Institute, Inc., 2013, pg. 111

A Guide to the Project Management Body of Knowledge (PMBOK® Guide) – Fifth Edition, Project Management Institute (PMI)®, Project Management Professional (PMP)®, and Certified Associate in Project Management (CAPM)® are registered trademarks of Project Management Institute, Inc. - Version 2.1 Published September 30, 2014

Lesson 5: Planning a Project | Topic C

Collect Requirements Inputs

Various components provide input to the Collect Requirements process.

Input	Description
Scope management plan	In this process, the scope management plan will be referenced to help the project team determine what type of requirements are needed for a project.
Requirements management plan	The requirements management plan is used to determine what the specific processes are to collect and document stakeholder needs for a project.
Stakeholder management plan	In this process, the stakeholder management plan is used to give the project manager and team members communication guidelines when working with the stakeholders of a project. The plan will also state how stakeholder involvement is managed during this process.
Project charter	The project charter provides direction during this process when determining the requirements needed for the project outcomes. The high-level project outcomes will act as a guide when determining the requirements.
Stakeholder register	The stakeholder register can be used as reference when you need to know what stakeholder can provide you with the right level of requirements information.

A Guide to the Project Management Body of Knowledge (PMBOK® Guide) – Fifth Edition, Project Management Institute, Inc., 2013, p. 113

Collect Requirements Tools and Techniques

There are numerous tools and techniques used in the Collect Requirements process.

Tools & Techniques	Description (as stated in the PMBOK® Guide)
Interviews	A formal or informal approach to elicit information from stakeholders by talking to them directly.
Focus groups	An elicitation technique that brings together pre-qualified stakeholders and subject matter experts to learn about their expectations and attitudes about a proposed product, service, or result.
Facilitated workshops	An elicitation technique using focused sessions that bring key cross-functional stakeholders together to define product requirements.
Group creativity techniques	Techniques that are used to generate ideas within a group of stakeholders.
Group decision-making techniques	Techniques to assess multiple alternatives that will be used to generate, classify, and prioritize product requirements.
Questionnaires and surveys	Written sets of questions designed to quickly accumulate information from a large number of respondents.
Observations	A technique that provides a direct way of viewing individuals in their environment performing their jobs or tasks and carrying out processes.

Tools & Techniques	Description (as stated in the PMBOK® Guide)
Prototypes	A method of obtaining early feedback on requirements by providing a working model of the expected product before actually building it.
Benchmarking	Benchmarking is the comparison of actual or planned practices, such as processes and operations, to those of comparable organizations to identify best practices, generate ideas for improvement, and provide a basis for measuring performance.
Context diagrams	A visual depiction of the product scope showing a business system (process, equipment, computer system, etc.) and how people and other systems (actors) interact with it.
Document analysis	An elicitation technique that analyzes existing documentation and identifies information relevant to the requirements.

A Guide to the Project Management Body of Knowledge (PMBOK® Guide) – Fifth Edition, Project Management Institute, Inc., 2013, pg. 114-117

Interviews

An *interview* is a formal or informal meeting or discussion that can be used to gather and document needed information from stakeholders by talking with them directly and asking targeted questions to generate discussion. Through discussion, you can record any pertinent information you need for your project requirements. With this information, you can further identify and define specific project outcome features and functions. For example, an interview might be helpful when you need to get specific feedback from an end user of a product or service to find out what is useful and what is not.

A Guide to the Project Management Body of Knowledge (PMBOK® Guide) – Fifth Edition, Project Management Institute, Inc., 2013, p. 114

Focus Groups

Focus groups are small events or discussions that are designed to be less structured and more for information-sharing sessions within a small group of people. Project managers will use focus groups to bring together both SMEs and stakeholders to gain further information and clarification on specific project requirements. These events are typically conducted by a trained moderator who will propose pre-selected questions and keep the discussions on track with the selected theme. For example, a focus group might be used to gather customer feedback for a product that is scheduled to be updated.

A Guide to the Project Management Body of Knowledge (PMBOK® Guide) – Fifth Edition, Project Management Institute, Inc., 2013, p. 114

Facilitated Workshops

Facilitated workshops are organized working sessions held by project managers to determine what a project's requirements are and to get all stakeholders together to agree on the project's outcomes. There are different types of workshops used depending on the industry you are working in:

- Joint application design/development (JAD) workshops include both SMEs and the development team together to discuss and improve on the software development process.
- Quality function deployment (QFD) workshops are commonly used in the manufacturing field to determine new product development requirements.
- Voice of the customer (VOC) sessions are used to gain customer feedback about a product or service that can then be used to determine new project requirements. User stories are a result of

A Guide to the Project Management Body of Knowledge (PMBOK® Guide) – Fifth Edition, Project Management Institute (PMI)®, Project Management Professional (PMP)®, and Certified Associate in Project Management (CAPM)® are registered trademarks of Project Management Institute, Inc. - Version 2.1 Published September 30, 2014

Lesson 5: Planning a Project | Topic C

a VOC workshop and can be used later on to validate a stakeholder's goal and motivation for a requirement.

A Guide to the Project Management Body of Knowledge (PMBOK® Guide) – Fifth Edition, Project Management Institute, Inc., 2013, p. 114

Group Creativity Techniques

Group creativity techniques can be used to help guide a group in determining project requirements. There are a number of techniques used based on the needs of the project manager and the participants.

Technique	Description
Brainstorm ideas	This technique allows participants to share any and all ideas that come to mind about a specific subject.
Use nominal voting	This technique is often used with brainstorming to further narrow ideas and thoughts. Participants can place a vote on what idea they feel is best. The information can then be used by project managers to rate ideas for requirement options.
Use idea/mind mapping	A technique that uses the results of a brainstorming session to construct a map of all legitimate ideas and how they might help to generate a project's requirements.
Use an affinity diagram	An affinity diagram allows you to group and organize ideas that relate to each other or are alike. The diagram allows you to then conduct further analysis.
Conduct multi-criteria decision analysis	This technique uses a decision matrix to reach decisions. It can be used to analyze ideas to ultimately evaluate and rank group ideas.

A Guide to the Project Management Body of Knowledge (PMBOK® Guide) – Fifth Edition, Project Management Institute, Inc., 2013, p. 115

Group Decision-Making Techniques

Group decision-making is a method used by a group to come to a decision. This technique is an assessment process that can have multiple alternatives and can lead to many outcomes. There are a number of methods used within the group decision-making technique to reach a group decision.

Method	Outcome
Unanimity	Using this method, everyone in the group agrees on the course of action to take. A useful technique to facilitate a unanimous outcome is called the Delphi method. When you use this method, a group of experts is brought in to answer specific questions and give their feedback on the results of each group gathering. Only the facilitator of the events can see the results.
Majority	The majority method can be used when you need to attain the majority of the group's decision or ideas. This is a good method to use with very large unevenly numbered groups.
Plurality	This method can be utilized when the largest group within a group agrees on a decision. This method is useful when the number of options is more than two.

A Guide to the Project Management Body of Knowledge (PMBOK® Guide) – Fifth Edition, Project Management Institute (PMI)®, Project Management Professional (PMP)®, and Certified Associate in Project Management (CAPM)® are registered trademarks of Project Management Institute, Inc. - Version 2.1 Published September 30, 2014

Lesson 5: Planning a Project | Topic C

Method	Outcome
Dictatorship	A dictatorship is used when someone in the group can override a group's decision. In most cases, this person will consider the larger group's ideas and decisions, and will then make their decision based on the best decision.

A Guide to the Project Management Body of Knowledge (PMBOK® Guide) – Fifth Edition, Project Management Institute, Inc., 2013, pg. 115-116

Questionnaires and Surveys

Questionnaires and surveys are used to get feedback and ideas quickly from a large group of people. They typically use sets of questions that target a specific area or subject. This technique is useful when the group is varied and located in multiple locations. The results of the questionnaires and surveys can be sent out and returned quickly and the results can be analyzed in a timely manner. In most cases, the results will be used to conduct a statistical analysis and used by decision makers to prioritize, categorize, and determine requirements. For example, you might survey users of a banking application to see how they are using the system.

A Guide to the Project Management Body of Knowledge (PMBOK® Guide) – Fifth Edition, Project Management Institute, Inc., 2013, p. 116

Observations

Observations, also referred to as *job shadowing*, is a technique used in order to gain knowledge of a specific job role, task, or function in order to understand and determine project requirements. This technique allows decision makers to directly observe a job when a job or task is complex and detailed and cannot be described easily. For example, for a product assembly improvement project, project team members might observe the actual assembling of the product in a manufacturing plant to better understand a process and determine what requirements are for the project.

A Guide to the Project Management Body of Knowledge (PMBOK® Guide) – Fifth Edition, Project Management Institute, Inc., 2013, p. 116

Prototypes

Prototyping is a method used to create and distribute a mocked-up model of a potential project outcome. The prototype can be used for evaluation and experimentation by project stakeholders and other team members. The results of the evaluation can then be analyzed and assembled into a prioritized list of redesign ideas for the prototype, or a detailed list of project requirements. This process can be cyclical with many prototype revisions until the project requirements are determined.

A Guide to the Project Management Body of Knowledge (PMBOK® Guide) – Fifth Edition, Project Management Institute, Inc., 2013, p. 116

Storyboarding

Storyboarding is a prototyping method that can use visuals or images to illustrate a process or represent a project outcome. Storyboards are useful to illustrate how a product, service, or application will function or operate when it is complete. For example, in software development, a storyboard might be used to show how a customer service application will function from a user's perspective by showing the results of each option available within the application.

A Guide to the Project Management Body of Knowledge (PMBOK® Guide) – Fifth Edition, Project Management Institute, Inc., 2013, p. 116

Benchmarking

Benchmarking is a method used to evaluate processes or practices against another organization's standard. This technique can be helpful in determining a project's requirements by comparing current requirements against a proven or best practice standard within the same professional field or product area. A benchmark can be used to measure performance and to generate ideas for project requirements.

A Guide to the Project Management Body of Knowledge (PMBOK® Guide) – Fifth Edition, Project Management Institute, Inc., 2013, p. 116

Context Diagrams

A *context diagram* is a visual representation of a product's scope. The diagram includes the business process, equipment, or computer system and what roles interact with those systems. The diagrams depict specific business and actor inputs to the business system, as well as the business and actor outputs of the system.

A Guide to the Project Management Body of Knowledge (PMBOK® Guide) – Fifth Edition, Project Management Institute, Inc., 2013, p. 117

Document Analysis

Document analysis is a technique used to gain project requirements from current documentation evaluation. This method can be used to derive new project requirements from existing documentation such as business plans, service agreements, marketing materials, current process diagrams, application software documentation, and more.

A Guide to the Project Management Body of Knowledge (PMBOK® Guide) – Fifth Edition, Project Management Institute, Inc., 2013, p. 117

Collect Requirements Outputs

There are two outputs from the Collect Requirements process.

Output	Description (as stated in the PMBOK® Guide
Requirements documentation	A description of how individual requirements meet the business need for the project.
Requirements traceability matrix	A grid that links product requirements from their origin to the deliverables that satisfy them.

A Guide to the Project Management Body of Knowledge (PMBOK® Guide) – Fifth Edition, Project Management Institute, Inc., 2013, pg. 117-119

Guidelines to Collect Project Requirements

Guidelines to collecting requirements are as follows:

- Review the scope management plan for clarity as to how project teams will determine which type of requirements need to be collected for the project.
- Review the requirements management plan for the processes that will be used throughout the collect requirements process to define and document the stakeholder needs.
- Review the stakeholder management plan to understand stakeholder communication requirements and the level of stakeholder engagement in order to assess and adapt to the level of stakeholder participation in requirements activities.

- Review the project charter for the high-level description of the product, service, or result so that detailed requirements can be developed.
- Review the stakeholder register to identify stakeholders who can provide information on the requirements.
- Use tools and techniques such as interviews, focus groups, facilitated workshops, group creativity techniques, group decision-making techniques, questionnaires and surveys, observations, prototypes, benchmarking, context diagrams, and document analysis to collect requirements for the project.
- Document the requirements and the requirements traceability matrix.

A Guide to the Project Management Body of Knowledge (PMBOK® Guide) – Fifth Edition, Project Management Institute, Inc., 2013, pg. 110-119

A Guide to the Project Management Body of Knowledge (PMBOK® Guide) – Fifth Edition, Project Management Institute (PMI)®, Project Management Professional (PMP)®, and Certified Associate in Project Management (CAPM)® are registered trademarks of Project Management Institute, Inc. - Version 2.1 Published September 30, 2014

Lesson 5: Planning a Project | Topic C

ACTIVITY 5-2
Collecting Project Requirements

Data Files

C:\095001Data\Planning a Project\Requirements Document.doc

C:\095001Data\Planning a Project\Requirements Traceability Matrix.xls

Scenario

At this point in the process, you are ready to start documenting your project requirements for the 122 East Main project. The stakeholders have provided some of the specifications for the new build. They determined that build must be completed within six months and must pass all required home inspections for Greene City. They have also determined that the total cost of the build should not exceed $75,000. They provided a list of specifications for the 122 East Main house:

- 1,400 square feet
- Full basement
- Two-car garage
- Flower boxes on each front-facing window
- Three bedrooms
- 1.5 baths
- Kitchen
- Family room
- Porch
- Landscaped yard

1. Complete the requirements document for the 122 East Main project by using the specification provided.
   a) Launch Windows Explorer and navigate to **C:\095001Data\Planning a Project\Requirements Document.doc**
   b) Complete the document with the information collected from the project stakeholders.
   c) Save the document as *My Requirements Document.doc*

2. Complete the traceability matrix.
   a) Launch **Windows Explorer** and navigate to **C:\095001Data\Planning a Project\Requirements Traceability Matrix.xls**
   b) Fill in the template with the information collected from the project stakeholders.
   c) Save the document as *My Requirements Traceability Matrix.xls*

3. Compare your completed document and Excel file with the files located at **C:\095001Data\Planning a Project\Solution\Requirements Document Solution.doc** and **Requirements Traceability Matrix Solution.xls.** Once you are done with your comparison, close all the files.

A Guide to the Project Management Body of Knowledge (PMBOK® Guide) – Fifth Edition, Project Management Institute (PMI)®, Project Management Professional (PMP)®, and Certified Associate in Project Management (CAPM)® are registered trademarks of Project Management Institute, Inc. - Version 2.1 Published September 30, 2014

Lesson 5: Planning a Project | Topic C

TOPIC D

Define Project Scope

Now that you have a better handle on what the project requirements are, you can take that "wish list" you gathered from the stakeholders and project sponsors and narrow it down to the actual requirements that will be included in the scope of the project. As a project manager, you will facilitate this process in order to determine the project's scope. This is an important step in planning project work and determining what tasks will be needed for a project. In this topic, you will define project scope.

A Guide to the Project Management Body of Knowledge (PMBOK® Guide) – Fifth Edition, Project Management Institute, Inc., 2013, pg. 120-121

The diagram displays how the Define Scope process relates to the other knowledge areas.

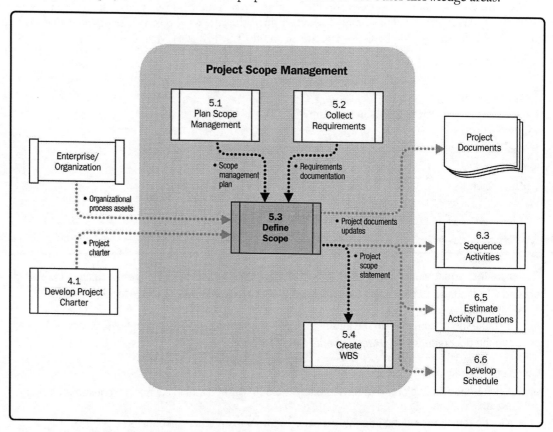

Figure 5–9: The Define Scope data flow diagram.

A Guide to the Project Management Body of Knowledge (PMBOK® Guide) – Fifth Edition, Project Management Institute, Inc., 2013, p. 120

Project Scope

Project scope is made up of the approved requirements that will get implemented through the project work, but not exceeded by the project work. The scope of a project gives the project manager a structure to work within when determining a project's work. The scope is what the actual project is and what the result should be.

A Guide to the Project Management Body of Knowledge (PMBOK® Guide) – Fifth Edition, Project Management Institute, Inc., 2013, p. 121

The Project Scope Statement

The *project scope statement* is a description that includes what the project scope is, quality requirements, project deliverables, constraints, and assumptions of the project work. The scope statement can be referred to by stakeholders and other project members when scope development needs to be verified against the scope baseline, updated, or changed during the course of a project.

A project scope statement will be different for every project, but as stated in the *PMBOK® Guide,* it may include any or all of the following components:

- Project scope description—progressively elaborates the characteristics of the product, service, or result described in the project charter and requirements documentation.
- Acceptance criteria—a set of conditions that is required to be met before deliverables are accepted.
- Deliverable - any unique and verifiable product, result, or capability to perform a service that is required to be produced to complete a process, phase, or project. This also includes ancillary results, such as project management reports and documentation.
- Project exclusion—generally identifies what is excluded from the project. Explicitly stating what is out of scope for the project helps to manage stakeholders' expectations.
- Constraints—limiting factors that affect the execution of a project or process.
- Assumptions—factors in the planning process that are considered to be true, real, or certain, without proof or demonstration. Also describes the potential impact of those factors if they prove to be false.

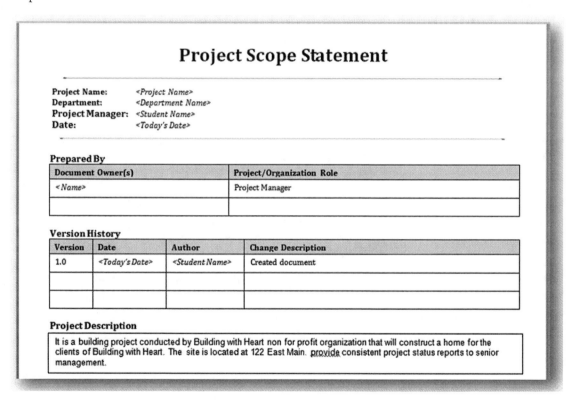

Figure 5–10: Project scope statement components.

A Guide to the Project Management Body of Knowledge (PMBOK® Guide) – Fifth Edition, Project Management Institute, Inc., 2013, pg. 123-124

Project Scope Statement vs. Project Charter

The project charter and project scope statement are similar, but contain different levels of detail. The project charter includes more high-level project objectives and goals, whereas the project scope statement is a detailed listing that focuses on the actual outcomes of the project. You can see the differences illustrated by the following diagram.

A Guide to the Project Management Body of Knowledge (PMBOK® Guide) – Fifth Edition, Project Management Institute, Inc., 2013, p. 124

The Define Scope Process

The *define scope process* is used to evaluate all the requirements collected during the Collect Requirements process and to determine what requirements will be included within the project scope and which ones will not. The project's scope encompasses all the project requirements, services, and results of the proposed project.

A Guide to the Project Management Body of Knowledge (PMBOK® Guide) – Fifth Edition, Project Management Institute, Inc., 2013, pg. 120-121

Figure 5-11: The Define Scope process.

A Guide to the Project Management Body of Knowledge (PMBOK® Guide) – Fifth Edition, Project Management Institute, Inc., 2013, p. 120

Define Scope Inputs

There are a number of components that provide input to the Define Scope process.

Input	Description
Scope management plan	In this process, the scope management plan establishes the activities for developing, monitoring, and controlling the project scope.
Project charter	In this process, the project charter provides high-level project description, product characteristics, and project approval requirements.
Requirements documentation	In this process, the requirements documentation will be used to select the requirements that will be included in the project.
Organizational process assets	In this process, the organizational process assets that can influence how scope is defined include: policies, procedures, templates for a project scope statement, project files from previous projects, and lessons learned from previous phases or projects.

A Guide to the Project Management Body of Knowledge (PMBOK® Guide) – Fifth Edition, Project Management Institute, Inc., 2013, pg. 121-122

Define Scope Tools and Techniques

There are four tools and techniques used in the Define Scope process.

Tools & Techniques	Description
Expert judgment	In this process, expert judgment is often used to analyze the information needed to develop the project scope statement. Such judgment and expertise can be applied to any technical detail.
Product analysis	For projects that have a product as a deliverable, product analysis is a tool that generally means asking questions about a product and forming answers to describe the use, characteristics, and other relevant aspects of what is going to be manufactured.
Alternatives generation	A technique used to develop as many potential options as possible to identify different approaches to execute and perform the work of the project.
Facilitated workshops	In this process, participation of key players in facilitated workshops can help to reach a cross-functional and common understanding of the project objectives and its limits.

A Guide to the Project Management Body of Knowledge (PMBOK® Guide) – Fifth Edition, Project Management Institute, Inc., 2013, pg. 122-123

Product Analysis

Product analysis is a different way to look at a project. This method is typically used for projects that have a product as a deliverable. Depending on the specific product, a number of analysis methods can be used such as product breakdown, systems analysis, requirements analysis, systems engineering, value engineering, and value analysis. For example, if your product was a camera, you would analyze all components of that product such as lens, battery, camera body, and user interface to help generate requirements.

A Guide to the Project Management Body of Knowledge (PMBOK® Guide) – Fifth Edition, Project Management Institute, Inc., 2013, p. 122

Alternatives Generation

Alternatives generation is a method used to draw out potential options to complete project work. There are a few common methods used to generate alternatives.

Method	Description
Lateral thinking	A creative approach to problem solving in which the team attempts to think about a problem in new ways and generate a fresh solution.
Brainstorming	A general creativity technique for generating possible alternatives. Brainstorming methods can be structured or unstructured in approach. The goal is to generate as many ideas as possible from as many team members as possible. *A Guide to the Project Management Body of Knowledge (PMBOK® Guide) – Fifth Edition,* Project Management Institute, Inc., 2013, p. 324
Delphi technique	A group technique that extracts and summarizes anonymous expert group input to choose among various alternatives. Often used to arrive at an estimate or forecast. *A Guide to the Project Management Body of Knowledge (PMBOK® Guide) – Fifth Edition,* Project Management Institute, Inc., 2013, p. 324

A Guide to the Project Management Body of Knowledge (PMBOK® Guide) – Fifth Edition, Project Management Institute (PMI)®, Project Management Professional (PMP)®, and Certified Associate in Project Management (CAPM)® are registered trademarks of Project Management Institute, Inc. - Version 2.1 Published September 30, 2014

Lesson 5: Planning a Project | Topic D

A Guide to the Project Management Body of Knowledge (PMBOK® Guide) – Fifth Edition, Project Management Institute, Inc., 2013, p. 123

Define Scope Outputs

There are two outputs from the Define Scope process.

Output	Description
Project scope statement	The description of the project scope, detailed deliverables, assumptions, and constraints.
Project documents updates	Updates as a result of this process could affect any project documents established to this point in the process, such as stakeholder register, requirements documentation, and requirements traceability matrix.

A Guide to the Project Management Body of Knowledge (PMBOK® Guide) – Fifth Edition, Project Management Institute, Inc., 2013, pg. 123-124

Guidelines to Develop a Project Scope Statement

Guidelines to defining scope are as follows:

- Review the scope management plan for the activities for developing, monitoring, and controlling the project scope.
- Review the project charter for the high-level project description, product characteristic, and project approval requirements.
- Review the requirements documentation to select the requirements that will be included in the project.
- Review the organizational process assets such as policies, procedures, template for a project scope statement, project files from previous projects, and lessons learned from previous phases or projects.
- Use tools and techniques such as expert judgment, product analysis, alternatives generation, and facilitated workshops to define the project scope.
- Document the project scope statement and update any project documents, as needed.

A Guide to the Project Management Body of Knowledge (PMBOK® Guide) – Fifth Edition, Project Management Institute, Inc., 2013, pg. 120-125

Lesson 5: Planning a Project | Topic D

ACTIVITY 5-3
Creating a Project Scope Statement

Data Files

C:\095001Data\Planning a Project\Scope Statement.doc

Scenario

Using the requirements that were documented in the previous activity, you can take a look at the project scope. Using the requirements document, create a scope statement for the 122 East Main project to verify that you are on track with the scope determined in the project charter.

---

1. Which documents can you use as a basis for your scope statement?

2. Develop the scope statement for the project.
   a) Launch Windows Explorer and navigate to **C:\095001Data\Planning a Project\Scope Statement.doc.**
   b) Fill in the template with the information collected from the project requirements.
   c) Save the file as *My Scope Statement.doc*

3. Compare your completed document with the **C:\095001Data\Planning a Project\Solution\Scope Statement Solution.doc.** Once you are done with your comparison, close all files.

A Guide to the Project Management Body of Knowledge (PMBOK® Guide) – Fifth Edition, Project Management Institute (PMI)®, Project Management Professional (PMP)®, and Certified Associate in Project Management (CAPM)® are registered trademarks of Project Management Institute, Inc. - Version 2.1 Published September 30, 2014

Lesson 5: Planning a Project | Topic D

TOPIC E

Create a WBS

Now that you have collected project requirements and determined the scope for the project, you are ready to determine what your actual project work will be and how it will be tracked during the course of the project. The work breakdown structure provides an organized vision of the work that needs to be done in order to achieve the project deliverables. In this topic, you will create a work breakdown structure (WBS) for your project.

A Guide to the Project Management Body of Knowledge (PMBOK® Guide) – Fifth Edition, Project Management Institute, Inc., 2013, pg. 125-126

The diagram displays how the Create WBS process relates to the other knowledge areas.

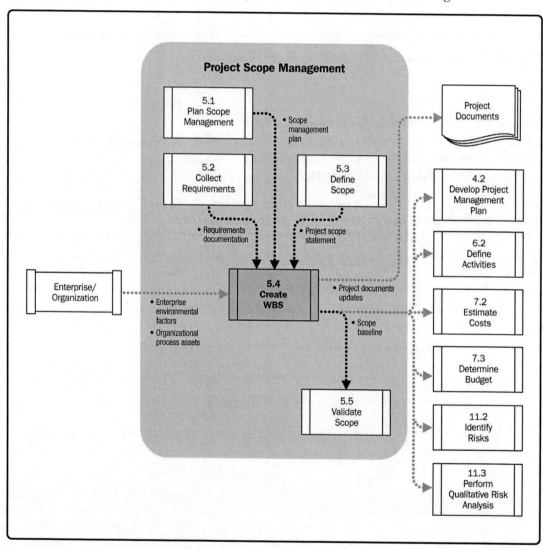

Figure 5-12: The Create WBS data flow diagram.

A Guide to the Project Management Body of Knowledge (PMBOK® Guide) – Fifth Edition, Project Management Institute, Inc., 2013, p. 126

What Is a WBS?

The *WBS* is a logical grouping of project deliverables arranged in a hierarchical structure. A WBS defines the total scope of work required to complete the project. The individual components are at the lowest level of the hierarchy and are referred to as work packages. Each level of the WBS breaks down the work into more and more layers until the work package is at a level that can be assigned, estimated for cost and duration, and tracked individually.

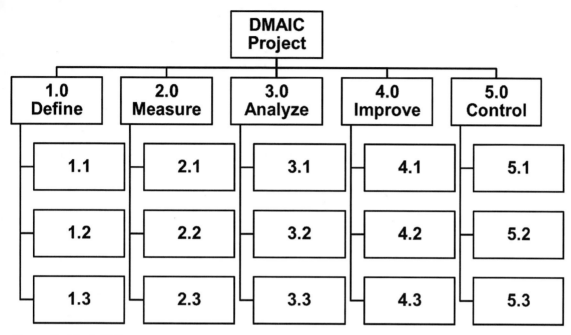

Figure 5–13: A WBS.

 Note: Large projects will sometimes have more than one WBS to represent different phases of the project or level of detail.

The WBS organizes and defines the total scope of the project, and represents the work specified in the current approved project scope statement. The planned work is contained within the lowest level of WBS components, which are called *work packages*. A work package is a small set of "to-do items" or work that needs to be done, resulting in a small deliverable that must exist to support the satisfaction of a requirement. An important distinction to be made here is that the "work" referred to in a WBS is actually the products or deliverables that are a result of an individual work package, not necessarily the work itself. The goal is to eventually roll up each work package into the level above within the WBS hierarchy to gain the overall time and budget requirements.

A Guide to the Project Management Body of Knowledge (PMBOK® Guide) – Fifth Edition, Project Management Institute, Inc., 2013, pg. 125-126

Control Accounts

Control accounts are points within the WBS that are tracked by finance to verify that costs are within budget. These accounts associated with different work packages within the WBS that can be tracked and verified against the earned value of a project to check performance. Work packages will be assigned to a control account and the work will be managed within that account throughout the project. Control accounts may contain more than one work package, but each work package should be assigned to only one control account.

A Guide to the Project Management Body of Knowledge (PMBOK® Guide) – Fifth Edition, Project Management Institute, Inc., 2013, p. 132

Planning Packages

A *planning package* is a placeholder for work that is yet to be determined by a requirement. It is placed within the control account but does not have specific activities applied. The planning package work can be anything that must be designated within the control account, but does not have a cost or a budget applied yet.

A Guide to the Project Management Body of Knowledge (PMBOK® Guide) – Fifth Edition, Project Management Institute, Inc., 2013, p. 132

Code of Accounts

A *code of accounts* is any system for numbering the elements in a WBS. A code of accounts system allows project managers to more easily track individual WBS components by using a *unique identification code*, which is especially helpful in the areas of performance, reporting, and cost.

For example, a school district requires its schools to comply with a uniform code of accounts so that it can easily record, track, and document specific types of revenues and expenditures in every school. The code of accounts could be shown as Function/Category/Program. If functions include administrative salaries (30), teacher salaries (31), and consultants' fees (32); categories include para-professional expenditures (100) and professional expenditures (101); programs include regular instructional (411), special education (417), and languages (419), then the fee paid to a consultant leading a teacher training workshop in special education services would be coded 32/101/417.

A Guide to the Project Management Body of Knowledge (PMBOK® Guide) – Fifth Edition, Project Management Institute, Inc., 2013, p. 132

WBS Dictionary

The *WBS dictionary* is a document that retains all WBS component information such as deliverables, activities, code assignments, and scheduling information. The document can be used as a reference when assigning and researching individual WBS component information.

A Guide to the Project Management Body of Knowledge (PMBOK® Guide) – Fifth Edition, Project Management Institute, Inc., 2013, p. 132

The Create WBS Process

The Create WBS process involves analyzing the project's scope and determining what the project deliverables are and what project work needs to be done to achieve the outcome. The process itself is executed by dividing up the project work into smaller chunks, which is known as decomposition, and then organizing them into a logical format that can be referenced, updated, and changed during the course of a project. The WBS provides a structured and organized vision of the work to be done to achieve the outcome.

A Guide to the Project Management Body of Knowledge (PMBOK® Guide) – Fifth Edition, Project Management Institute, Inc., 2013, pg. 125-126

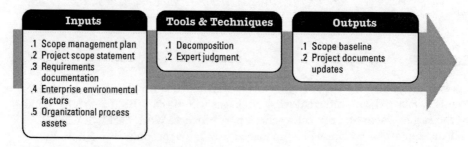

Figure 5-14: The Create WBS process.

A Guide to the Project Management Body of Knowledge (PMBOK® Guide) – Fifth Edition, Project Management Institute, Inc., 2013, p. 125

Create WBS Inputs

Various components provide input to the Create WBS process.

Input	Description (from PMBOK® Guide)
Management plan	In this process, the scope management plan specifies how to create the WBS from the detailed project scope statement and how the WBS will be maintained and approved.
Project scope statement	In this process, the project scope statement describes the requirements that are necessary to be satisfied and those that are excluded. It lists and describes the specific internal or external restrictions or limitations that may affect the execution of the project.
Requirements documentation	In this process, the detailed requirements documentation is essential for understanding what requirements were requested and what requirements were added to the project scope to be produced as the result of the project and also what needs to be done to deliver the project and its final products.
Enterprise environmental factors	In this process, the enterprise environmental factors that influence this process include industry-specific WBS standards (such as ISO) that are relevant to the nature of the project and that may serve as external reference sources for creating the WBS.
Organizational process assets	In this process, the organizational process assets that can influence how scope is defined include: policies, procedures, possible templates for the WBS, project files from previous projects, and lessons learned from previous projects.

A Guide to the Project Management Body of Knowledge (PMBOK® Guide) – Fifth Edition, Project Management Institute, Inc., 2013, p. 127

Create WBS Tools and Techniques

There are two tools and techniques used in the Create WBS process.

Tools & Techniques	Description (as stated in the PMBOK® Guide)
Decomposition	A technique used for dividing and subdividing the project scope and project deliverables into small, more manageable parts.
Expert judgment	In this process, expert judgment is often used to analyze the information needed to decompose the project requirements down into smaller component parts in order to create an effective WBS.

A Guide to the Project Management Body of Knowledge (PMBOK® Guide) – Fifth Edition, Project Management Institute, Inc., 2013, p. 128

Decomposition

Decomposition is the breaking down of project scope and requirements into smaller more manageable chunks. The work package is the smallest chunk from the WBS, which includes the to-do activities, so you can apply duration and estimated cost. The level of decomposition is based on specific project needs and to what level of granularity you need to manage the project effectively. There are a number of steps involved in the process of decomposition:

- Identify the deliverables and the work tasks necessary to accomplish the deliverable.
- Structure and organize the WBS.
- Decompose high-level WBS scope components into low-level components,
- Develop and assign a unique identification code to each component.
- Review the decomposition of work packages and verify that they align with the project requirements.

A Guide to the Project Management Body of Knowledge (PMBOK® Guide) – Fifth Edition, Project Management Institute, Inc., 2013, pg. 128-131

The following diagram illustrates how a WBS can be decomposed to the work package level.

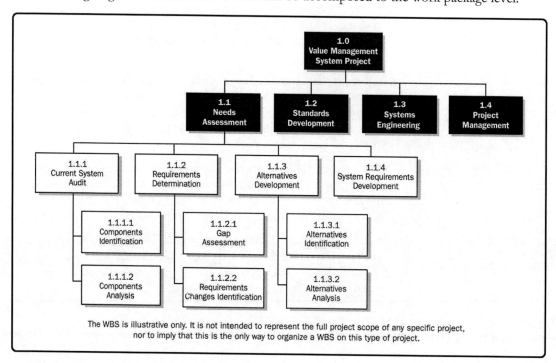

Figure 5–15: A sample decomposed WBS.

A Guide to the Project Management Body of Knowledge (PMBOK® Guide) – Fifth Edition, Project Management Institute, Inc., 2013, p. 129

Create WBS Outputs

There are two outputs from the Create WBS process.

Output	Description (as stated in the PMBOK® Guide)
Scope baseline	The approved version of a scope statement, WBS, and its associated WBS dictionaries, that can be changed only through formal change control procedures and is used as a basis for comparison.
Project documents updates	In this process, project documents that are updated could include requirements documentation to include approved changes.

A Guide to the Project Management Body of Knowledge (PMBOK® Guide) – Fifth Edition, Project Management Institute, Inc., 2013, pg. 131-132

Scope Baseline

The *scope baseline* is composed of the approved versions of the scope statement, the WBS, and the associated WBS dictionaries. With these approved versions, the scope baseline for a specific project can be incorporated into the project management plan. This is the baseline that you are monitoring and measuring against throughout the project. If the data collected does not align with the scope baseline, then action may need to be taken depending on the variance. A scope baseline may include any of the following components:

- The project scope statement
- The WBS
- The WBS dictionary
- Code account identification
- Description of work
- Assumptions and constraints
- Responsible organization
- Schedule milestones
- Associated schedule activities
- Resources required to complete the work
- Cost estimations
- Quality requirements
- Acceptance criteria
- Technical references
- Agreement information

A Guide to the Project Management Body of Knowledge (PMBOK® Guide) – Fifth Edition, Project Management Institute, Inc., 2013, p. 131

Guidelines to Create a WBS

Guidelines to creating a WBS are as follows:

- Review the scope management plan that specifies how to create the WBS from the detailed project scope statement and how the WBS will be maintained and approved.
- Review the project scope statement for a description of the requirement that needs to be satisfied and the requirements that have been excluded and a list and description of the specific internal or external restrictions or limitations that may affect the execution of the project.
- Review the requirements documentation to understand what needs to be produced as the result of the project and what needs to be done to deliver the project and its final products.
- Review the enterprise environmental factors such as industry specific WBS standards (such as ISO) that are relevant to the nature of the project and that may serve as external reference sources for creating the WBS.
- Review organizational process assets such as policies, procedures, template for the WBS, project files from previous projects, and lessons learned from previous projects.
- Use tools and techniques, such as decomposition, to divide and subdivide the project scope into small, more manageable parts.
- Use expert judgment to analyze the information needed to decompose the project requirements down into smaller component parts in order to create an effective WBS.
- Document the scope baseline and update any project documents, as needed.

A Guide to the Project Management Body of Knowledge (PMBOK® Guide) – Fifth Edition, Project Management Institute, Inc., 2013, pg. 125-132

ACTIVITY 5–4
Creating a WBS

Scenario

The next step in managing the 122 East Main project is to develop a WBS for the project. You have been given the high-level features of the project, and need to break down the lower-level detailed components.

1. When creating the WBS for the 122 East Main project, what types of reference materials and other inputs could you use?

2. Using the provided WBS, complete the components for each work package.

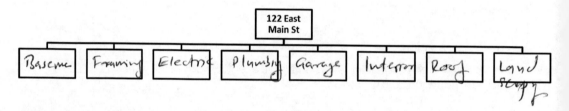

3. As the project manager, you are asked to decompose the WBS deliverables. Which activity will you perform during decomposition?

   ○ Assign unique ID numbers to each requirement.

   ☑ Break the requirements down into smaller components.

   ○ Arrange the requirement into categories, based on risk.

   ○ Organize the requirements based on which project team is responsible for their completion.

4. Close all open files.

A Guide to the Project Management Body of Knowledge (PMBOK® Guide) – Fifth Edition, Project Management Institute (PMI)®, Project Management Professional (PMP)®, and Certified Associate in Project Management (CAPM)® are registered trademarks of Project Management Institute, Inc. - Version 2.1 Published September 30, 2014

Lesson 5: Planning a Project | Topic E

Summary

In this lesson, you developed project, stakeholder, and scope management plans. This also involved collecting requirements, defining scope, and creating a work breakdown structure (WBS). With these plans established, you will have a better idea of what is needed to continue to the next phase of the overall project management process.

Why do you think developing project and scope management plans is important?

Why do you think it's important to collect requirements, define scope, and create a work breakdown structure?

Note: Check your LogicalCHOICE Course screen for opportunities to interact with your classmates, peers, and the larger LogicalCHOICE online community about the topics covered in this course or other topics you are interested in. From the Course screen you can also access available resources for a more continuous learning experience.

A Guide to the Project Management Body of Knowledge (PMBOK® Guide) – Fifth Edition, Project Management Institute (PMI)®, Project Management Professional (PMP)®, and Certified Associate in Project Management (CAPM)® are registered trademarks of Project Management Institute, Inc. - Version 2.1 Published September 30, 2014

Lesson 5: Planning a Project |

6 | Planning for Project Time Management

Lesson Time: 3 hours

Lesson Objectives

In this lesson, you will:

- Plan schedule management.

- Define project activities.

- Sequence project activities.

- Estimate activity resources.

- Estimate activity durations.

- Develop a project schedule.

Lesson Introduction

Now that you have initiated the planning phase of your project, you are ready to take a closer look at how the project time will be planned and managed throughout the project's life cycle. Planning for time management will give you a good foundation to determine who will be available as potential resources for the project. If you do not know what activities are needed and when they need to be completed then you cannot acquire the proper resources.

The following diagram highlights the next process group and knowledge areas covered in this lesson.

	Project Management Process Groups				
Knowledge Areas	**Initiating Process Group**	**Planning Process Group**	**Executing Process Group**	**Monitoring and Controlling Process Group**	**Closing Process Group**
4. Project Integration Management	4.1 Develop Project Charter	4.2 Develop Project Management Plan	4.3 Direct and Manage Project Work	4.4 Monitor and Control Project Work 4.5 Perform Integrated Change Control	4.6 Close Project or Phase
5. Project Scope Management		5.1 Plan Scope Management 5.2 Collect Requirements 5.3 Define Scope 5.4 Create WBS		5.5 Validate Scope 5.6 Control Scope	
6. Project Time Management		6.1 Plan Schedule Management 6.2 Define Activities 6.3 Sequence Activities 6.4 Estimate Activity Resources 6.5 Estimate Activity Durations 6.6 Develop Schedule		6.7 Control Schedule	
7. Project Cost Management		7.1 Plan Cost Management 7.2 Estimate Cost 7.3 Determine Budget		7.4 Control Costs	
8. Project Quality Management		8.1 Plan Quality Management	8.2 Perform Quality Assurance	8.3 Control Quality	
9. Project Human Resource Management		9.1 Plan Human Resource Management	9.2 Acquire Project Team 9.3 Develop Project Team 9.4 Manage Project Team		
10. Project Communication Management		10.1 Plan Communications Management	10.2 Manage Communications	10.3 Control Communications	
11. Project Risk Management		11.1 Plan Risk Management 11.2 Identify Risks 11.3 Perform Qualitative Risk Analysis 11.4 Perform Quantitative Risk Analysis 11.5 Plan Risk Responses		11.6 Control Risks	
12. Project Procurement Management		12.1 Plan Procurement Management	12.2 Conduct Procurements	12.3 Control Procurements	12.4 Close Procurements
13. Project Stakeholder Management	13.1 Identify Stakeholders	13.2 Plan Stakeholder Management	13.3 Manage Stakeholder Engagement	13.4 Control Stakeholder Engagement	

A Guide to the Project Management Body of Knowledge (PMBOK® Guide) – Fifth Edition, Project Management Institute (PMI)®, Project Management Professional (PMP)®, and Certified Associate in Project Management (CAPM)® are registered trademarks of Project Management Institute, Inc. - Version 2.1 Published September 30, 2014

TOPIC A

Plan Schedule Management

In the previous lesson, you initiated the planning phase of a project. You have now identified the project requirements and the project scope, and created the WBS for a project. With your WBS created, you can focus on how the actual management of the project time will be handled. In this topic, you will examine the planning tasks to create and manage the project's schedule.

A Guide to the Project Management Body of Knowledge (PMBOK® Guide) – Fifth Edition, Project Management Institute, Inc., 2013, pg. 145-146

The following data flow diagram illustrates how the Plan Schedule Management process relates to the other knowledge areas within the Planning Process Group.

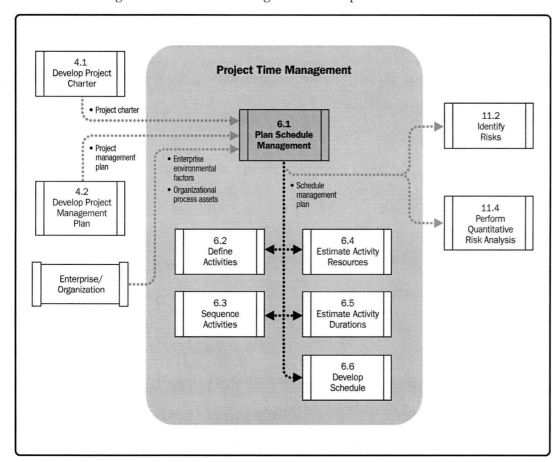

Figure 6–1: Plan Schedule Management data flow diagram.

A Guide to the Project Management Body of Knowledge (PMBOK® Guide) – Fifth Edition, Project Management Institute, Inc., 2013, p. 145

What Is a Schedule Management Plan?

A *schedule management plan* is a subsidiary plan of the project management plan. It identifies a scheduling method and scheduling tool that will be used for a project. It also determines the format of the schedule and establishes criteria for developing and controlling the project schedule. The following diagram shows how this process relates to other connected processes.

A Guide to the Project Management Body of Knowledge (PMBOK® Guide) – Fifth Edition, Project Management Institute, Inc., 2013, pg. 146, 148

Schedule Management Plan Components

The schedule management plan can document the following decisions for the project.

Component	Description
Project schedule model	The project schedule model is the methodology and tool that will be used to develop the project schedule. Maintenance of the project schedule describes how to update the status and record the progress of the project during the project execution.
Accuracy	Level of accuracy is the acceptable range used to determine realistic activity duration estimates, and may include an amount for risk contingency.
Units	Units of measure are defined for each resource, such as staff hours, days, weeks, etc.
Organizational procedures links	The WBS is used as the framework for the schedule management plan so that there is consistency with the estimates and resulting schedules.
Control thresholds	Control thresholds are the defined variance thresholds for monitoring schedule performance before action is taken. Expressed as percentage deviations from the baseline plan, for example, 10 percent behind schedule or 15 percent ahead of schedule.
Rules	This includes the rules of performance measurement, for example, Earned Value Management (EVM) rules: • Rules for establishing percent complete • Control accounts where progress and schedule will be measured • Earned value measurement techniques • Schedule performance measurements, such as schedule variance (SV) and schedule performance index (SPI)
Reporting	Reporting formats defines frequency and formats for schedule-related reports.
Process descriptions	Process descriptions describe how the schedule management processes are documented.

A Guide to the Project Management Body of Knowledge (PMBOK® Guide) – Fifth Edition, Project Management Institute, Inc., 2013, pg. 148-149

The Plan Schedule Management Process

The *Plan Schedule Management process* documents the policies, procedures, and documentation for planning, developing, managing, executing, and controlling the project schedule. It determines how the project schedule and any schedule contingencies will be managed throughout the project life cycle.

A Guide to the Project Management Body of Knowledge (PMBOK® Guide) – Fifth Edition, Project Management Institute, Inc., 2013, pg. 145-146

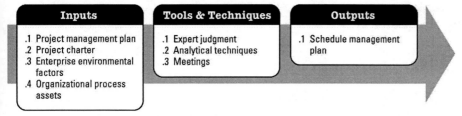

Figure 6-2: The Plan Schedule Management process.

A Guide to the Project Management Body of Knowledge (PMBOK® Guide) – Fifth Edition, Project Management Institute, Inc., 2013, p. 145

Plan Schedule Management Inputs

Various components provide input to the Plan Schedule Management process.

Input	Description
Project management plan	Provides information used to develop the schedule, such as the scope baseline and other scheduling-related information, such as risk decisions.
Project charter	Provides a summary, high-level milestone schedule for the project. It also states who may approve the project schedule.
Enterprise environmental factors	Enterprise environmental factors that can influence this process include organizational culture and structure, resource availability and skills, use of project management software, published commercial information, and organizational work authorization systems.
Organizational process assets	Organizational process assets that can influence this process include monitoring and reporting tools; historical information; schedule control tools; existing schedule control-related policies, procedures, and guidelines; templates; project closure guidelines; change control procedures; and risk control procedures.

A Guide to the Project Management Body of Knowledge (PMBOK® Guide) – Fifth Edition, Project Management Institute, Inc., 2013, pg. 146-147

Plan Schedule Management Tools and Techniques

There are three tools and techniques used in the Plan Schedule Management process.

Tools & Techniques	Description
Expert judgment	Expert judgment and historical information can give the project team advice on schedule development and management from previous similar projects.
Analytical techniques	The plan contains decisions to use fast tracking or crashing to shorten the duration of the project schedule. Other technique choices include rolling wave planning, leads and lags, alternatives analysis and methods for reviewing schedule performance. These choices can affect project risk.
Meetings	Meetings are held to develop the schedule management plan.

A Guide to the Project Management Body of Knowledge (PMBOK® Guide) – Fifth Edition, Project Management Institute, Inc., 2013, pg. 147-148

Plan Schedule Management Outputs

There is one output from the Plan Schedule Management process.

Output	Description
Schedule management plan	As stated in the *PMBOK® Guide,* the schedule management plan is a component of the project management plan that establishes the criteria and the activities for developing, monitoring, and controlling the schedule.

A Guide to the Project Management Body of Knowledge (PMBOK® Guide) – Fifth Edition, Project Management Institute, Inc., 2013, pg. 148-149

Guidelines to Develop a Schedule Management Plan

Guidelines to developing a schedule management plan are as follows:

- Review the project management plan for information to develop the schedule such as the scope baseline, and other scheduling-related information, such as risk decisions.
- Review the project charter for a summary, high-level milestone schedule for the project and who will approve the project schedule.
- Review the enterprise environmental factors such as organizational culture and structure, resource availability and skills, use of project management software, published commercial information, and organizational work authorization systems.
- Review the organizational process assets such as monitoring and reporting tools; historical information; schedule control tools; existing schedule control-related policies, procedures, and guidelines; templates; project closure guidelines; change control procedures; and risk control procedures.
- Use tools and techniques such as expert judgment and historical information to give the project team advice on schedule development and management from previous similar projects.
- Use meetings to develop the schedule management plan.
- Document the schedule management plan for the project.

A Guide to the Project Management Body of Knowledge (PMBOK® Guide) – Fifth Edition, Project Management Institute, Inc., 2013, pg. 145-149

ACTIVITY 6-1
Researching Schedule Management Plans

Data Files

C:\095001Data\Planning for Project Time Management\Schedule Management Plan.doc

Scenario

Before you start developing the schedule management plan for the 122 East Main project, you should always review the management plans used by previous projects. In this activity, you will review a management plan used for past Building with Heart projects.

1. On your computer, open Windows Explorer, browse to the **C:\095001Data\Planning for Project Time Management** folder, and open the **Schedule Management Plan.doc**.

2. Review the sample plan and determine how it may be used for current and future projects.

3. Why is managing the project schedule important?

4. Which of the following is not a component of the schedule management plan?
   - ○ Rules for establishing percent complete
   - ○ Schedule performance measurements
   - ○ Control thresholds
   - ✓ Cost estimates for each work package

5. Close all open files.

TOPIC B

Define Project Activities

Now that you have a plan to manage the schedule, you can start looking at the activities you need to produce the project outcomes. It is important to identify and define the specific project activities that need to be done on the project to meet the project requirements and objectives. This process includes all the steps to properly define the activities so that you don't miss an important outcome.

A Guide to the Project Management Body of Knowledge (PMBOK® Guide) – Fifth Edition, Project Management Institute, Inc., 2013, pg. 149-150

The following data flow diagram illustrates how the Define Activities process relates to the other project management processes.

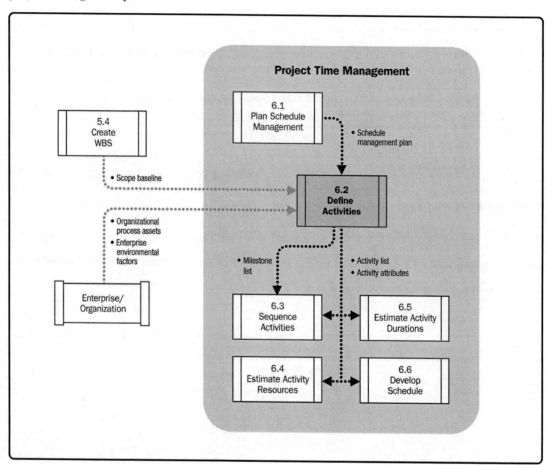

Figure 6-3: The Define Activities data flow diagram.

A Guide to the Project Management Body of Knowledge (PMBOK® Guide) – Fifth Edition, Project Management Institute, Inc., 2013, p. 150

Project Activities

An *activity* is an element of project work that requires action to produce a deliverable. Activities lay the foundation for estimating, scheduling, executing, monitoring, and controlling the project work. The characteristics of an activity are:

- It has an expected duration.

- It consumes budget and/or human resources.
- It is named in verb-noun format.

Examples include revising a user manual, making a sales presentation, and reserving a conference room. Each of these items requires action to produce a deliverable. Each has an expected duration and will consume budget and human resources. Finally, they are all named in verb-noun format.

Activities can be broken down into smaller components. For example, the activity "reserve conference room," could be broken down into multiple units, such as:

- Determine budget
- Determine size requirement
- Determine date needed
- Identify possible room alternatives
- Select room
- Call to reserve room
- File confirmation when received

A Guide to the Project Management Body of Knowledge (PMBOK® Guide) – Fifth Edition, Project Management Institute, Inc., 2013, p. 153

Activity vs. Task

Although the words "activity" and "task" may be interchangeable in common usage and in many organizations, they are not considered synonyms in the *PMBOK® Guide.* One of your goals as a professional project manager seeking certification should be to align your language with the language used in the *PMBOK® Guide* whenever possible. Use the word "activity" to refer to the components of work performed during the course of a project. Use the word "task" sparingly, typically only in reference to brands of project-management software or in relation to other work that you need to do.

A Guide to the Project Management Body of Knowledge (PMBOK® Guide) – Fifth Edition, Project Management Institute, Inc., 2013, p. 526

The Define Activities Process

The *define activities process* determines the activities that need to take place to deliver the project objectives and outputs that need to be defined and documented. The WBS that was defined in the Create WBS process provides the deliverables at the work package level. These work packages need to be broken down into lower-level activities that allow these activities to be estimated for how long they will take, scheduled, executed, monitored and controlled.

A Guide to the Project Management Body of Knowledge (PMBOK® Guide) – Fifth Edition, Project Management Institute, Inc., 2013, pg. 149-150

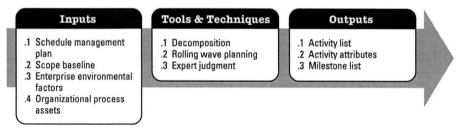

Figure 6–4: The Define Activities process.

A Guide to the Project Management Body of Knowledge (PMBOK® Guide) – Fifth Edition, Project Management Institute, Inc., 2013, p. 149

Define Activities Inputs

Various components provide input to the Define Activities process.

Input	Description
Schedule management plan	Provides level of detail needed to manage the project work.
Scope baseline	Provides the WBS, deliverables, assumptions, and constraints.
Enterprise environmental factors	Enterprise environmental factors include organizational culture and structure, published commercial information, and project management information systems.
Organizational process assets	Organizational process assets include lessons learned, standardized processes, templates and organizational policies, procedures, and guidelines for scheduling.

A Guide to the Project Management Body of Knowledge (PMBOK® Guide) – Fifth Edition, Project Management Institute, Inc., 2013, pg. 150-151

Define Activities Tools and Techniques

There are numerous tools and techniques used in the Define Activities process.

Tools & Techniques	Description
Decomposition	This technique involves dividing the scope and deliverables down to an actionable or activity level.
Rolling wave planning	*Rolling wave planning* is an iterative planning technique in which near-term work is defined at a detailed level and future work is left at a higher level, until it becomes the near term work. It is a form of progressive elaboration of developing the work packages into activities as more is known about those work packages.
Expert judgment	Experience with documenting detailed scope statements, WBS, and scheduling can help with defining activities at the appropriate level.

Progressive elaboration ← [handwritten annotation]

A Guide to the Project Management Body of Knowledge (PMBOK® Guide) – Fifth Edition, Project Management Institute, Inc., 2013, pg. 151-152

Define Activities Outputs

There are three outputs from the Define Activities process.

Output	Description
Activity list	An *activity list* includes all the activities for the project. Each activity should have an identifier, a title, and a scope-of-work description of what needs to be done to complete that activity. This list is used to build the project schedule.

Output	Description
Activity attributes	*Activity attributes* describe each activity on the activity list. Attributes can include duration of the activity, resource to do that activity, cost for the activity, components of the activity, an identifier, WBS ID, successor activities, logical relationships to other activities, leads and lags, and any imposed dates, constraints or assumptions about that activity. More detailed attributes include level of effort (LOE), discrete effort, and apportioned effort for the activity.
Milestone list	The *milestone list* contains the significant points or events in a project. The duration of milestones is zero because they represent a specific point in time.

A Guide to the Project Management Body of Knowledge (PMBOK® Guide) – Fifth Edition, Project Management Institute, Inc., 2013, pg. 152-153

Guidelines to Define Activities

To define activities for a project:

- Review the schedule management plan for information on the level of detail needed to manage the project work.
- Review the scope baseline for the WBS, deliverables, assumptions and constraints.
- Review the enterprise environmental factors such as organizational culture and structure, published commercial information, and project management information systems.
- Review the organizational process assets such as lessons learned, standardized processes, templates and organizational policies, and procedures and guidelines for scheduling.
- Analyze and decompose each work package of the WBS into activities that will be required to produce the deliverable:
  - Conduct brainstorming sessions with the project team to ensure that no required activities are overlooked.
  - Consult the scope statement to ensure that activities will enable you to meet the project objectives.
- Consult subject matter experts about unfamiliar material.
- Evaluate all constraints and assumptions for their possible impact on activity definition.
- Once you have decomposed each work package into activities, evaluate your activity list:
  - Ensure that the descriptions accurately reflect the actions to be performed.
  - Verify that the activity descriptions are as specific as possible. For example, if the desired outcome is a revised user manual, describe the activity as "revise user manual," rather than "produce new user manual."
  - Confirm that the activities listed for each work package are necessary and sufficient for satisfactory completion of the deliverable.
  - Verify that the list is organized as an extension of the WBS.

A Guide to the Project Management Body of Knowledge (PMBOK® Guide) – Fifth Edition, Project Management Institute, Inc., 2013, pg. 149-153

ACTIVITY 6-2
Creating an Activity List and a Milestone List

Data Files

C:\095001Data\Planning for Project Time Management\Activity List.doc

C:\095001Data\Planning for Project Time Management\Milestone List.doc

Scenario

There are a number of activities that must be completed for the 122 East Main project. You must define the activities for the build, and record them in an activity list, and determine the milestones for the project activities. In this activity, you will create an activity list for the framing work package and a milestone list for all the major milestones for the build project.

---

1. The first step in creating an activity list is to gather your resource materials. Which items will be helpful in creating your list?
   - ☑ The WBS
   - ☐ Cost-benefit analysis
   - ☑ The scope statement
   - ☑ Activity lists from similar projects

2. Brainstorm the possible activities for the framing work package.

3. Navigate to and open C:\095001Data\Planning for Project Time Management\Activity List.doc

4. Enter the activities with descriptions in the activity list template.

5. Add a unique identifier and code for each activity in the list.

6. Add any predecessor and successor activities for each entry and then the logical relationships.

7. If there are any activities where a lead or lag might apply, add them to the activity list.

8. Save the file as *My Activity List.doc* and close it.

9. Navigate to and open the C:\095001Data\Planning for Project Time Management\Milestone List.doc

10. Brainstorm the high-level milestones for the entire build project.

11. Enter each milestone and record if it is mandatory or optional for the project.

12. Save the file as *My Milestone List.doc* and close it.

A Guide to the Project Management Body of Knowledge (PMBOK® Guide) – Fifth Edition, Project Management Institute (PMI)®, Project Management Professional (PMP)®, and Certified Associate in Project Management (CAPM)® are registered trademarks of Project Management Institute, Inc. - Version 2.1 Published September 30, 2014

TOPIC C

Sequence Project Activities

After we define the specific project activities that need to be done on the project to meet the project deliverables and objectives, we next need to sequence these activities in a logical way so that the execution of the project is as efficient and cost effective as possible.

A Guide to the Project Management Body of Knowledge (PMBOK® Guide) – Fifth Edition, Project Management Institute, Inc., 2013, pg. 153-154

The following data flow diagram illustrates how the Sequence Activities process relates to the other project management processes.

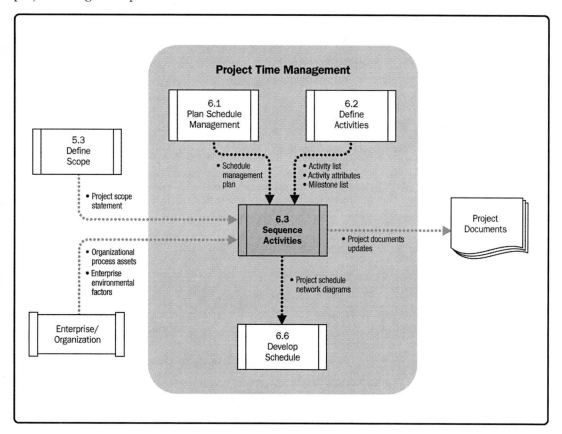

Figure 6–5: Sequence Activities management data flow diagram.

A Guide to the Project Management Body of Knowledge (PMBOK® Guide) – Fifth Edition, Project Management Institute, Inc., 2013, p. 154

The Sequence Activities Process

The *Sequence Activities process* looks at each activity on the activity list and determines the relationship between the activities. A logical sequence of activities is determined so that the project can be worked with the greatest efficiency, given any project constraints. As activities are sequenced, each relationship should have at least one predecessor and one successor. This information is used to build the project schedule.

A Guide to the Project Management Body of Knowledge (PMBOK® Guide) – Fifth Edition, Project Management Institute, Inc., 2013, pg. 153-154

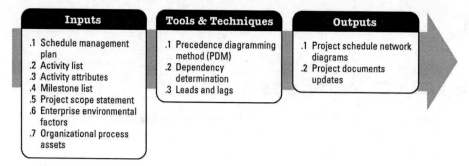

Figure 6–6: The Sequence Activities process.

A Guide to the Project Management Body of Knowledge (PMBOK® Guide) – Fifth Edition, Project Management Institute, Inc., 2013, p. 153

Project Schedule Network Diagrams

Project schedule network diagrams are graphical representations of the sequence of project activities and the dependencies among them. Project schedule network diagrams read from left to right and are typically accompanied by summary information. The diagram can either include the entire project or just specific parts of the project. Parts of a schedule network diagram may be referred to as a subnetwork or a fragmented network.

A Guide to the Project Management Body of Knowledge (PMBOK® Guide) – Fifth Edition, Project Management Institute, Inc., 2013, pg. 159-160

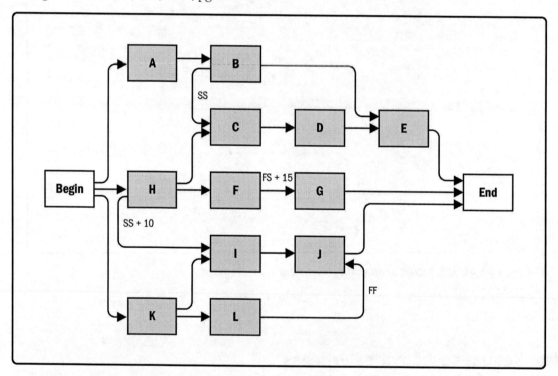

Figure 6–7: A sample project schedule network diagram.

A Guide to the Project Management Body of Knowledge (PMBOK® Guide) – Fifth Edition, Project Management Institute, Inc., 2013, p. 160

Sequencing Activities Inputs

Various components provide input to the Sequence Activities process.

A Guide to the Project Management Body of Knowledge (PMBOK® Guide) – Fifth Edition, Project Management Institute (PMI)®, Project Management Professional (PMP)®, and Certified Associate in Project Management (CAPM)® are registered trademarks of Project Management Institute, Inc. - Version 2.1 Published September 30, 2014

Lesson 6: Planning for Project Time Management | Topic C

Input	Description
Schedule management plan	Provides the scheduling method and tool, and guides how activities may be sequenced.
Activity list	Provides all project schedule activities.
Activity attributes	Provides attributes for each activity, including predecessor or successor relationships.
Milestone list	Provides the dates for specific schedule milestone events.
Project scope statement	Provides scope description, deliverables, constraints, and assumptions that may affect activity sequencing.
Enterprise environmental factors	Enterprise environmental factors include government or industry standards, Project Management Information System, scheduling tool, and work authorization systems.
Organizational process assets	Organizational process assets include activity planning policies, procedures, guidelines, and templates.

A Guide to the Project Management Body of Knowledge (PMBOK® Guide) – Fifth Edition, Project Management Institute, Inc., 2013, pg. 154-156

Sequencing Activities Tools and Techniques

There are three tools and techniques used in the Sequence Activities process.

Tools & Techniques	Description (as stated in the PMBOK® Guide)
Precedence Diagramming Method (PDM)	The precedence diagramming method is a technique used for constructing a schedule model in which activities are represented by nodes and are graphically linked by one or more logical relationship to show the sequence in which the activities are to be performed.
Dependency determination	Dependency determination is a technique used to identify the type of dependency that is used to create the logical relationships between predecessor and successor activities.
Leads and lags	Leads are the amount of time whereby a successor activity can be advanced with respect to a predecessor activity. A lag is the amount of time whereby a successor activity is required to be delayed with respect to a predecessor activity.

A Guide to the Project Management Body of Knowledge (PMBOK® Guide) – Fifth Edition, Project Management Institute, Inc., 2013, pg. 156-157

PDM

The *Precedence Diagramming Method (PDM)* is used to sequence activities to create a schedule model, which is the first pass at creating a schedule and may be adjusted until it fits the project as best as possible, for the project. Activities are represented as nodes and are graphically linked by their relationships. *Activity-on-node (AON)* is used by most project management software tools (for example, Microsoft Project).

A Guide to the Project Management Body of Knowledge (PMBOK® Guide) – Fifth Edition, Project Management Institute, Inc., 2013, pg. 156-157

A Guide to the Project Management Body of Knowledge (PMBOK® Guide) – Fifth Edition, Project Management Institute (PMI)®, Project Management Professional (PMP)®, and Certified Associate in Project Management (CAPM)® are registered trademarks of Project Management Institute, Inc. - Version 2.1 Published September 30, 2014

Lesson 6: Planning for Project Time Management | Topic C

Precedence Relationships

A *precedence relationship* is the logical relationship between two activities that describes the sequence in which the activities should be carried out. Each activity has two open points: Start and Finish points. Precedence relationship considers appropriate logic while connecting these points. Precedence indicates which of two activities should come first (the predecessor activity) and which should come later (the successor activity). Precedence relationships are always assigned to activities based on the dependencies of each activity. A finish-to-start relationship is an example of the precedence relationship: Drywall installation must finish before painting can begin.

A Guide to the Project Management Body of Knowledge (PMBOK® Guide) – Fifth Edition, Project Management Institute, Inc., 2013, pg. 156-157

Types of Precedence Relationships

There are four precedence relationship types. Predecessor activities come before a dependent activity and successor activities come after another activity.

- *Finish-to-start (FS)* is the relationship between two activities in which the successor activity cannot start until the predecessor activity has finished. For example, the foundation for the house must be finished (Activity A) before the framing can start (Activity B). The total time for these two activities is the sum of A + B.
- *Finish-to-finish (FF)* is the relationship between two activities in which the successor activity cannot finish until the predecessor activity has finished. For example, construction must be finished (Activity A) before the building inspection can be finished (Activity B). The total time to complete both activities is the sum of A + B, minus any overlap.
- *Start-to-start (SS)* is the relationship between two activities in which the successor activity cannot start until the predecessor activity has started. For example, the building design must start (Activity A) before the electrical layout design can start (Activity B). As with the FF example, the total time for activities A and B will vary, depending on when Activity B starts. But in SS, there is a longer window of time during which Activity B can begin.
- *Start-to-finish (SF)* is the relationship between two activities in which the successor activity cannot finish until the predecessor has started. For example, ticket sales (Activity B) don't end until the concert (Activity A) starts. The total time for two activities in an SF relationship is either A or B, whichever is longer.

A Guide to the Project Management Body of Knowledge (PMBOK® Guide) – Fifth Edition, Project Management Institute, Inc., 2013, pg. 156-157

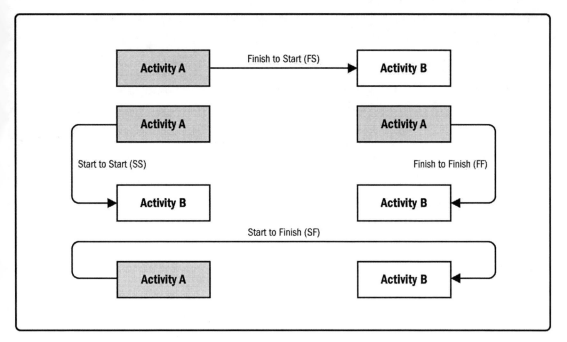

Figure 6–8: PDM relationship types.

A Guide to the Project Management Body of Knowledge (PMBOK® Guide) – Fifth Edition, Project Management Institute, Inc., 2013, p. 157

Summary Activities

A *summary activity* is a group of related activities that, for reporting purposes, is shown as a single aggregate activity in a bar chart or graph. It may also be called a "hammock activity." Some summary activities have their own internal sequence of activities, but others include separate activities. A summary normally spans several activities and encompasses fixed resources or costs associated with one type of activity.

A Guide to the Project Management Body of Knowledge (PMBOK® Guide) – Fifth Edition, Project Management Institute, Inc., 2013, p. 564

Conditional Diagramming Methods
Activity sequences that must be revisited or repeated are called loops, whereas activities that will be implemented only under specific conditions are called conditional branches. A conditional diagramming method is any network diagramming method that allows for non-sequential activities such as loops or conditional branches. Typically, activities in these types of diagrams are represented by rectangles, decision points are represented by diamonds, and directional flow is indicated by arrows. Conditional diagramming methods will vary based on which method is used. The most common conditional diagramming methods are the Graphical Evaluation Review Technique (GERT) and system dynamic models.

Dependency Determination

An *activity dependency* is a logical relationship that exists between two project activities. The relationship indicates whether the start of an activity is contingent upon an event or input from outside the activity. Activity dependencies shape the sequence among project activities. For example, an architect has designed a residence and has a vision for the room layouts. However, he will not be able to assess the functionality of the design until the builders have framed in the structure with walls, windows, and a roof. Once the structure is in place, he will be able to reassess the plans to determine if modifications are necessary.

A Guide to the Project Management Body of Knowledge (PMBOK® Guide) – Fifth Edition, Project Management Institute, Inc., 2013, p. 157

Types of Activity Dependencies

Activity dependencies can be categorized as either mandatory or discretionary, and they can be either internal or external. Activity dependencies categories include:

- *Mandatory dependencies* are legally or contractually required, or are due to the nature of the work. They are referred to as hard logic or hard dependencies, where there is no way around this sequence. For example, the sidewalk form must be built before the concrete can be poured.
- *Discretionary dependencies* are a desired sequence of activities that make sense for the project. They are also called soft logic. They are not necessary and can be modified as the project progresses and a better sequence is found or the schedule needs to be condensed.
- *External dependencies* are relationships between project activities and non-project activities and can be out of the project's control. For example, the delivery of a part needed to build a prototype.
- *Internal dependencies* are dependencies between project activities and are usually under the project's control. For example, the software testing is dependent on the software being written on a software development team.

A Guide to the Project Management Body of Knowledge (PMBOK® Guide) – Fifth Edition, Project Management Institute, Inc., 2013, pg. 157-158

Leads and Lags

A *lead* is the amount of time whereby a successor activity can be advanced with respect to predecessor activity. For example, if the activity **Landscape Parking Lot** can start two weeks before the predecessor activity **Complete Punch List** is finished, you would subtract two weeks of lead time from their finish-to-start dependency.

A *lag* is the amount of time whereby a successor activity will be delayed with respect to a predecessor activity. For example, if there must be a 15-day delay between the start of the **Write Draft** activity and the start of the **Edit Draft Activity** successor task, you would add 15 days of lag time to their start-to-start dependency.

A Guide to the Project Management Body of Knowledge (PMBOK® Guide) – Fifth Edition, Project Management Institute, Inc., 2013, pg. 158-159

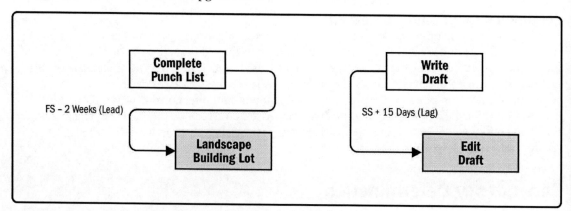

Figure 6-9: Examples of lead and lag.

A Guide to the Project Management Body of Knowledge (PMBOK® Guide) – Fifth Edition, Project Management Institute, Inc., 2013, p. 159

Lag and Lead Opportunities

There are many opportunities for lags to occur. For example, a permit application is going to take six weeks to procure. The activity that follows the submission of the permit application is going to be delayed by six weeks due to an external dependency of the application processing time.

A lead can occur when a programmer for a website decides to start programming the home page four days before the interface design is approved. Starting the programming may shorten the overall project schedule by four days. However, if the design is not approved, there may be significant rework for the programmer, resulting in the loss of some or all of the four day gain. This should be considered a risk.

A Guide to the Project Management Body of Knowledge (PMBOK® Guide) – Fifth Edition, Project Management Institute, Inc., 2013, p. 159

Sequencing Activities Outputs

There are two outputs from the Sequence Activities process.

Output	Description
Project schedule network diagrams	As stated in the *PMBOK® Guide,* project schedule network diagrams are graphical representations of the logical relationships among the project schedule activities.
Project documents updates	Project documents that could be updated include activity lists, activity attributes, milestone list, and risk register.

A Guide to the Project Management Body of Knowledge (PMBOK® Guide) – Fifth Edition, Project Management Institute, Inc., 2013, pg. 159-160

Guidelines to Sequence Project Activities

To sequence project activities effectively:

- Review the schedule management plan for information on the scheduling method and tool, and information on how activities may be sequenced.
- Determine the dependencies among project activities by using your activity list and product descriptions.
- Identify predecessor and successor activities by reviewing the activity attributes for each activity, including predecessor or successor relationships.
- Review the milestone list for the dates for specific schedule milestone events.
- Review the project scope statement for the scope description, deliverables, constraints, and assumptions that may affect activity sequencing.
- Review the enterprise environmental factors such as government or industry standards, Project Management Information System, scheduling tool, and work authorization systems.
- Review the organizational process assets such as activity planning policies, procedures, guidelines, and templates.
- Use tools and techniques such as precedence diagramming method (PDM), dependency determination, and leads and lags to develop the project schedule network diagram.
- Document the project schedule network diagram and update any project documents as needed.

A Guide to the Project Management Body of Knowledge (PMBOK® Guide) – Fifth Edition, Project Management Institute, Inc., 2013, pg. 153-160

A Guide to the Project Management Body of Knowledge (PMBOK® Guide) – Fifth Edition, Project Management Institute (PMI)®, Project Management Professional (PMP)®, and Certified Associate in Project Management (CAPM)® are registered trademarks of Project Management Institute, Inc. - Version 2.1 Published September 30, 2014

Lesson 6: Planning for Project Time Management | *Topic C*

ACTIVITY 6-3
Sequencing Activities

Data Files

C:\\095001\Planning for Project Time Management\My Activity List.doc

Before You Begin

Open your **My Activity List.doc** file.

Scenario

With the project activities identified for the framing work package, you must sequence those activities so that the work gets done in the most efficient order. You may need to add lag or lead time as appropriate. Tasks to be sequenced include:

- Install doors
- Install windows
- Frame exterior walls
- Install plywood flooring
- Frame interior walls
- Frame roof
- Frame garage
- Install drywall
- Install trim

---

1. During a recent meeting with your project team, a decision was made to add five days between the installing plywood flooring and frame interior walls activities due to other projects that some members of the team have already committed to. Will this be a lag or lead relationship that you should account for? Please explain.

2. Referring to the My Activity List document, draw your network diagram for the framing work package. Make sure that all the required activities are included in your network diagram. Make sure your diagram shows the sequence constraints from left to right. Check to make sure the activities that are connected by arrows correctly indicate their precedence relationship. Inside each node, include the activity codes and lag or lead time needed.

3. Close all open files.

A Guide to the Project Management Body of Knowledge (PMBOK® Guide) – Fifth Edition, Project Management Institute (PMI)®, Project Management Professional (PMP)®, and Certified Associate in Project Management (CAPM)® are registered trademarks of Project Management Institute, Inc. - Version 2.1 Published September 30, 2014

Lesson 6: Planning for Project Time Management | Topic C

TOPIC D

Estimate Activity Resources

With the activities defined and sequenced for your project, you can start estimating the resources needed to complete those activities. Estimating the resources needed to carry out the project's activities is key in proper project execution. Without the resources, the project activities would not get done and therefore the project would be at a loss before it even started.

A Guide to the Project Management Body of Knowledge (PMBOK® Guide) – Fifth Edition, Project Management Institute, Inc., 2013, pg. 160-162

The following data flow diagram illustrates how the Estimate Activity Resources process relates to the other project management processes.

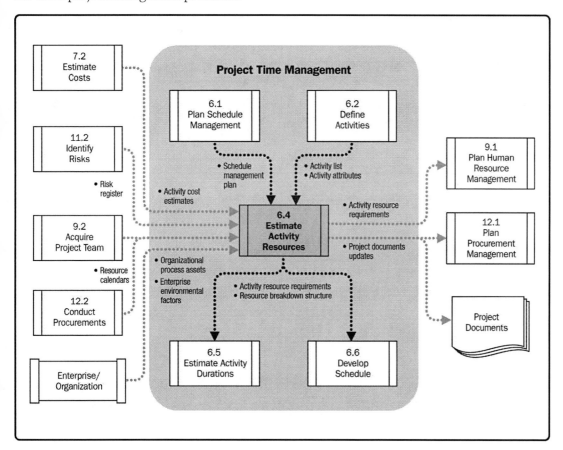

Figure 6-10: Estimate Activity Resources data flow diagram.

A Guide to the Project Management Body of Knowledge (PMBOK® Guide) – Fifth Edition, Project Management Institute, Inc., 2013, p. 161

What Are Activity Resources?

Activity resources refer to any useful material object or any individual needed for the project work to be completed. Project resources will vary greatly in size, cost, and function. They typically fall into one of the following categories: labor, materials, facilities, equipment, consultants, services, supplies, or utilities. Project resources are almost always limited in quantity, and therefore require thoughtful allocation.

A Guide to the Project Management Body of Knowledge (PMBOK® Guide) – Fifth Edition, Project Management Institute (PMI)®, Project Management Professional (PMP)®, and Certified Associate in Project Management (CAPM)® are registered trademarks of Project Management Institute, Inc. - Version 2.1 Published September 30, 2014

Lesson 6: Planning for Project Time Management | *Topic D*

For example, a project for a human resources team could be to present an annual employee health and wellness seminar. Resources would include: the conference room, which would be used for the seminar; the tangible information materials, such as brochures and pamphlets that would be given to employees; the visiting consultants, who would be hired to make presentations and answer employees' questions; and the vendors, who would participate in the seminar and offer their services.

A Guide to the Project Management Body of Knowledge (PMBOK® Guide) – Fifth Edition, Project Management Institute, Inc., 2013, p. 162

The Estimate Activity Resources Process

The *Estimate Activity Resources* process facilitates the estimation of the type and quantity of resources needed for each project activity. These resources can include people, materials, supplies and equipment. Once we know what resources are needed, we can estimate the cost and duration necessary to complete the activity.

A Guide to the Project Management Body of Knowledge (PMBOK® Guide) – Fifth Edition, Project Management Institute, Inc., 2013, pg. 160-162

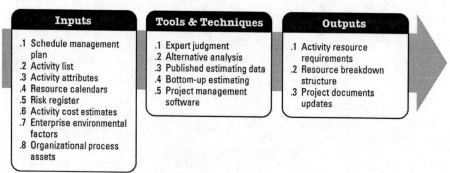

Figure 6–11: The Estimate Activity Resources process.

A Guide to the Project Management Body of Knowledge (PMBOK® Guide) – Fifth Edition, Project Management Institute, Inc., 2013, p. 161

Estimate Activity Resources Inputs

Various components provide input to the Estimate Activity Resources process.

Input	Description
Schedule management plan	Provides the level of accuracy and units of measure for the resources that need to be estimated.
Activity list	Provides the list of activities that need resource estimates.
Activity attributes	Provides the attribute data for the activities that need resource estimates.
Resource calendars (an output of 9.2)	The resource calendar includes availability of resources for each activity. Composite calendars will list additional information, such as the available list of resources and the skills and capabilities of human resources. Resource calendars are used to estimate resource utilization.
Risk register	Provides the list of risks that may influence the activity resource estimates.

Input	Description
Activity cost estimates (an output of 7.2)	Activity cost estimates are the outputs of the estimate cost process. They provide estimates on probable costs necessary to finish project work. This includes costs on direct labor, materials, equipment, facilities, services, information technology, contingency reserves, or indirect costs, if any.
Enterprise environmental factors	Enterprise environmental factors that can influence this process include resource location, availability, and skill set.
Organizational process assets	Organizational process assets that can influence this process include policies and procedures for staffing, rental and purchase of materials, and historical information from similar projects.

A Guide to the Project Management Body of Knowledge (PMBOK® Guide) – Fifth Edition, Project Management Institute, Inc., 2013, pg. 162-163

Estimate Activity Resources Tools and Techniques

There are five tools and techniques used in the Estimate Activity Resources process.

Tools & Techniques	Description
Expert judgment	Expert judgment is used to assess the resource related inputs to this process from people with resource planning and estimating knowledge and skills.
Alternative analysis	*Alternative analysis* is a technique used to identify different ways of accomplishing activities and the different resources required by each method. For example, thinking about individual skill sets, abilities and experience, size or type of machine, and make-rent-or-buy decisions are all alternatives to fulfill the project resource need.
Published estimating data	Professional organizations regularly publish data on production rates, costs, and more for many resources such as labor, materials, equipment, and so on for different countries and specific locations within countries that can be used as a reference for activity estimation.
Bottom-up estimating	*Bottom-up estimating* is used to decompose work in an activity to the last executable level and generates activity resource estimates by adding the resources required by each activity. This technique is used when a detailed understanding of the project or part of the project is available to decompose the activities into more depth. The accuracy of the estimates received by using this technique is generally very high.
Project management software	*Project management software* helps plan, organize, and manage project resources and develop resource estimates for activities. A scheduling software tool such as Microsoft Project is a tool that can facilitate resource estimation by managing resource availability, rates, calendars, etc.

A Guide to the Project Management Body of Knowledge (PMBOK® Guide) – Fifth Edition, Project Management Institute, Inc., 2013, p. 164

A Guide to the Project Management Body of Knowledge (PMBOK® Guide) – Fifth Edition, Project Management Institute (PMI)®, Project Management Professional (PMP)®, and Certified Associate in Project Management (CAPM)® are registered trademarks of Project Management Institute, Inc. - Version 2.1 Published September 30, 2014

Lesson 6: Planning for Project Time Management | *Topic D*

Estimate Activity Resources Outputs

There are three outputs from the Estimate Activity Resources process.

Output	Description
Activity resource requirements	*Activity resource requirements* determine the types and quantities of the resources that are needed for each project activity. These estimates are aggregated for each work package and work period. The basis of estimate for each activity and any assumptions should also be documented.
Resource breakdown structure	The *resource breakdown structure* represents the hierarchy of resources including their category and type. Categories of resources include labor skill level or grade level, materials, equipment, etc. It helps to organize the resource use information and project schedule data.
Project documents updates	Project documents that may be updated include activity list, attributes, and resource calendars.

A Guide to the Project Management Body of Knowledge (PMBOK® Guide) – Fifth Edition, Project Management Institute, Inc., 2013, p. 165

Guidelines to Estimate Activity Resources

To estimate activity resources, use the following guidelines:

- Review the schedule management plan for the level of accuracy and units of measure for the resources that need to be estimated.
- Review the activity list and activity attributes for all of the project activities that need to be estimated.
- Check the resource calendars for when resources are available.
- Review the risk register to consider any risks that may impact resource estimation.
- Review the activity cost estimates for the cost information.
- Use tools and techniques such as expert judgment, alternative analysis, published estimating data, bottom-up estimating, and project management software to determine good resource estimates for each activity.
- Document the activity estimates in the activity resource requirements and the resource breakdown structure.

A Guide to the Project Management Body of Knowledge (PMBOK® Guide) – Fifth Edition, Project Management Institute, Inc., 2013, pg. 160-165

A Guide to the Project Management Body of Knowledge (PMBOK® Guide) – Fifth Edition, Project Management Institute (PMI)®, Project Management Professional (PMP)®, and Certified Associate in Project Management (CAPM)® are registered trademarks of Project Management Institute, Inc. - Version 2.1 Published September 30, 2014

Lesson 6: Planning for Project Time Management | Topic D

ACTIVITY 6-4
Estimating Activity Resources

Data Files

C:\095001Data\Planning for Project Time Management\My Activity List.doc

Scenario

It is time to start estimating what resources you will need to complete the project activities for the 122 East Main project. Based on the activity list and attributes, you can start determining resource estimates for the framing portion of the build project. The framing work package activities will need resources assigned for each activity included in the package. For example, to install plywood flooring you will need plywood, nails, nail gun, hammers, and people with basic carpentry skills. By using the activity list you created in a previous activity, document the activity resource requirements for each activity, including labor and materials.

---

1. Brainstorm the possible resources for each activity in the list.

2. Open the **My Activity List.doc** file.

3. Enter the resources needed for each activity recorded in the list and provide the resource requirements.

4. Save the file and close it.

TOPIC E

Estimate Activity Durations

With your project activities identified and sequenced in a logical format, you can start estimating the duration of each activity. This process enables you to apply a rough duration to each project activity so you can eventually assemble them into a schedule. Without accurate activity duration estimates, you cannot create a meaningful, realistic, and useful schedule. In this topic, you will estimate activity durations.

A Guide to the Project Management Body of Knowledge (PMBOK® Guide) – Fifth Edition, Project Management Institute, Inc., 2013, pg. 165-167

The following data flow diagram illustrates how the Estimate Activity Durations process relates to the other project management processes.

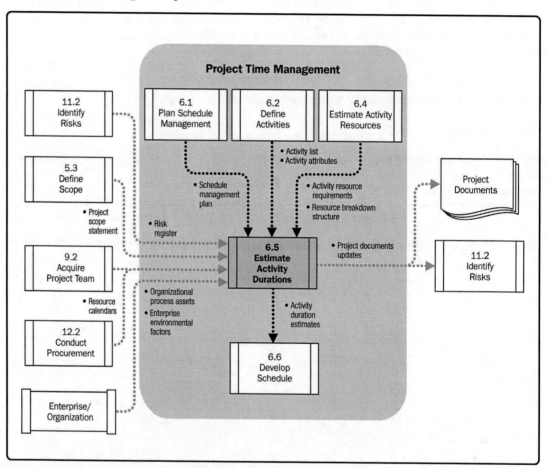

Figure 6-12: Estimate Activity Durations data flow diagram.

A Guide to the Project Management Body of Knowledge (PMBOK® Guide) – Fifth Edition, Project Management Institute, Inc., 2013, p. 166

The Estimate Activity Durations Process

The *Estimate Activity Durations process* involves the act of estimating the duration of work that will be needed to complete individual project activities using the available resources. It uses information on factors such as activity scope of work and resource calendars. The inputs for estimating activity durations are collected from people or groups who are familiar with the work an activity involves.

The resulting activity duration estimates will shape the preliminary project schedule. They contain assumptions made when making the estimate—for example, the availability of required resources— and a range of variance for the provided estimate, such as plus or minus 10 percent, or plus or minus two days.

A Guide to the Project Management Body of Knowledge (PMBOK® Guide) – Fifth Edition, Project Management Institute, Inc., 2013, pg. 165-167

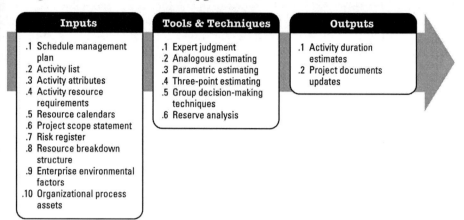

Figure 6–13: The Estimate Activity Durations process.

A Guide to the Project Management Body of Knowledge (PMBOK® Guide) – Fifth Edition, Project Management Institute, Inc., 2013, p. 166

Activity Duration Estimates

Activity duration estimates are the likely number of time periods that are needed to complete an activity. These estimates do not include any lags. They can be represented by a range such as four weeks +– four days (range of 16–24 business days) or 10 percent probability of exceeding four weeks (90 percent probability that the activity will take four or less weeks to complete).

A Guide to the Project Management Body of Knowledge (PMBOK® Guide) – Fifth Edition, Project Management Institute, Inc., 2013, p. 170

Elapsed Time and Effort

Elapsed time is the actual calendar time required for an activity from start to finish. An activity that requires two weeks to complete would take four calendar weeks of elapsed time if there's a two-week plant shutdown in the middle.

Effort is the number of person-hours or person-days required for completion of an activity. The estimates of effort provide the basis for cost estimating and resource allocation.

A Guide to the Project Management Body of Knowledge (PMBOK® Guide) – Fifth Edition, Project Management Institute, Inc., 2013, p. 167

Estimate Activity Durations Inputs

Various components provide input to the Estimate Activity Durations process.

Input	Description
Schedule management plan	Provides the method to use and the level of accuracy needed to estimate activity durations.
Activity list	Provides the list of activities that need duration estimates.
Activity attributes	Provides the attribute data for the activities that need duration estimates.

Input	Description
Activity resource requirements	Provides the resource required for an activity. The level of that resource can affect the time it will take to complete that activity.
Resource calendars	Provides availability of resources needed for project activities.
Project scope statement	Provides assumptions and constraints for project scope. Assumptions could include existing conditions, availability of information, and length of reporting periods. Constraints could include availability of skilled resources and contract terms and requirements.
Risk register	Provides the list of risks that may influence the activity duration estimates.
Resource breakdown structure	Provides hierarchical structure of resources by category and type.
Enterprise environmental factors	Enterprise environmental factors that influence this process include duration estimating databases, productivity metrics, published commercial information, and location of team members.
Organizational process assets	Organizational process assets that can influence this process include historical duration information, project calendars, scheduling methodology, and lessons learned.

A Guide to the Project Management Body of Knowledge (PMBOK® Guide) – Fifth Edition, Project Management Institute, Inc., 2013, pg. 167-169

Estimate Activity Durations Tools and Techniques

There are six tools and techniques used in the Estimate Activity Durations process.

Tools & Techniques	Description
Expert judgment	Expert judgment is used to review historical information for insight in estimating activity duration.
Analogous estimating	*Analogous estimation* uses historical data from similar projects to estimate duration for the current project activities. Parameters such as activity duration and cost, size, weight, and so on from actual results of similar activities on completed projects help generate good estimates for new activities. For example, if it took one hour to pour 3 square yards of concrete on a previous project, a good estimate to pour 3 square yards of concrete on a subsequent project would be one hour.
Parametric estimating	*Parametric estimation* uses an algorithm to calculate duration, budget, or cost based on historical data and project parameters. For example, if it previously took an average of 4 hours to fix a software defect and the project estimates 50 defects, then 200 hours should be allocated for defect correction.
Three-point estimating	*Three-point estimating* takes estimation uncertainty and risk into consideration by providing three estimates instead of a single point. This concept is from the program evaluation and review technique (PERT).

Tools & Techniques	Description
Group decision-making techniques	Techniques such as brainstorming, the Delphi, or nominal group can be used to assist teams in making decisions about activity duration estimates.
Reserve analysis	The reserve analysis looks at adding some contingency reserve time to a project schedule to account for uncertainties such as project risks. This contingency reserve time could be a percent of the full schedule, a fixed amount of time, or an amount determined by a Monte Carlo simulation. These are the "known-unknowns," which are identified risks.

A Guide to the Project Management Body of Knowledge (PMBOK® Guide) – Fifth Edition, Project Management Institute, Inc., 2013, pg. 169-171

Three-Point Estimating and PERT Analysis

The three-point estimating technique is based on PERT (program evaluation and review technique) analysis, which uses a weighted average of the three estimate types (most likely, optimistic, and pessimistic) to calculate the expected activity duration. The formula is as follows: [optimistic time + 4(most likely time) + pessimistic time]/6.

For example, to install plywood flooring, it takes 20 minutes to install one sheet of plywood and the first floor of the house will require 22 sheets of plywood. But, if everything goes right, it may be possible to get the plywood installed at 15 minutes per sheet. However, events may occur that will delay the installation, so it could take as long as 30 minutes per sheet. Realistically, the actual time required will likely fall somewhere between 15 minutes per sheet and 30 minutes per sheet. Therefore, a three point estimate will be as follows:

- Most likely (tM) = 22 sheets*20 minutes = 440 minutes.
- Optimistic (tO) = 22 sheets*15 minutes = 330 minutes.
- Pessimistic (tP) = 22 sheets*30 minutes = 660 minutes.

Triangular Distribution: Time Estimate is tE=(tO+tM+tP)/3 =(330+440+660)/3=477 minutes.

Beta Distribution (from PERT): Time Estimate is tE=(tO+4tM+tP)/6=(330+(4*440)+660)/6=458 minutes.

A Guide to the Project Management Body of Knowledge (PMBOK® Guide) – Fifth Edition, Project Management Institute, Inc., 2013, pg. 170-171

Monte Carlo Simulation

A *Monte Carlo simulation* is a computerized, statistical probability analysis software application that allows project managers to account for risk in quantitative analysis and decision making. Monte Carlo simulation provides the decision-maker with a range of possible outcomes and the probabilities that they will occur for any choice of action, with all possible consequences for middle-of-the-road decisions.

A Guide to the Project Management Body of Knowledge (PMBOK® Guide) – Fifth Edition, Project Management Institute, Inc., 2013, pg. 171, 340

Estimate Activity Durations Outputs

There are two outputs from the Estimate Activity Durations process.

Output	Description
Activity duration estimates	Approximate number of work units required to complete project activities. Lags are not considered when estimating activity durations.

A Guide to the Project Management Body of Knowledge (PMBOK® Guide) – Fifth Edition, Project Management Institute (PMI)®, Project Management Professional (PMP)®, and Certified Associate in Project Management (CAPM)® are registered trademarks of Project Management Institute, Inc. - Version 2.1 Published September 30, 2014

Lesson 6: Planning for Project Time Management | *Topic E*

Output	Description
Project documents updates	New activity attributes and assumptions may be added as a result of duration estimation.

A Guide to the Project Management Body of Knowledge (PMBOK® Guide) – Fifth Edition, Project Management Institute, Inc., 2013, p. 172

Guidelines to Estimate Activity Durations

Accurate activity duration estimates form the basis of an accurate project schedule. To ensure your estimates are as accurate and realistic as possible, follow these guidelines:

- Involve the work package owners or others who are very familiar with the work of the activity.
- Consult historical information.

  - Are there any detailed records from previous, similar projects that you could use to derive your estimates?
  - Are there any relevant commercial duration estimating databases?
  - Do any project team members have experience with similar activities?

- Review the schedule management plan to determine the appropriate estimation method to use and the level of accuracy needed to estimate activity durations.
- Determine how you want to quantify the work that needs to be done, in terms of the estimated hours of labor that will be needed, the number of units to be produced, and the number of customers to be served.

  - If it is early in the planning phase or if there is good historical data, consider using analogous estimating.
  - If there is inadequate historical data, consult subject matter experts.
  - Use quantitatively based durations to estimate activities when quantities of work units can be multiplied by the productivity rate.
  - If you are using the three-point estimating technique, ask the estimators for the best-case, most likely, and worst-case estimates.

- Consider resource requirements and capabilities.

  - Which people will be assigned to this activity?
  - How will the skills of the assigned staff affect the duration estimates?

- Review the resource requirements for each activity, as the level of that resource can affect the time it will take to complete that activity.
- Check the resource calendars for when resources are available.
- Review the project scope statement for assumptions and constraints.
- Review the risk register to consider any risks that may impact resource estimation.
- Review the resource breakdown structure of resources listed by category and type.
- Use tools and techniques such as expert judgment, analogous estimating, parametric estimating, three-point estimating, group decision-making techniques, and reserve analysis to determine good duration estimates for each activity.
- Document the activity duration estimates.

A Guide to the Project Management Body of Knowledge (PMBOK® Guide) – Fifth Edition, Project Management Institute, Inc., 2013, pg. 165-172

ACTIVITY 6-5
Estimating Activity Durations

Scenario

Now that you have determined your activities and resources to perform those activities, you can start applying duration estimates to those activities. By using the activity list, attributes, and resource estimates created previously, you will estimate the duration of the window installation activity for the build project. According to historical data, you know that each window most likely takes a volunteer two hours to complete, optimistically one hour, and pessimistically three hours. The house has 12 windows. You have been asked to provide a three-point estimate for the window installation activity:

- Most likely (tM) — 2
- Optimistic (tO) — 1
- Pessimistic (tP) — 3

Depending on the assumed values within the range, two formulas can be used to calculate the expected duration:

- Triangular Distribution: Time Estimate is $tE=(tO+tM+tP)/3$ $= 2$
- Beta Distribution (from PERT): Time Estimate is $tE=(tO+4tM+tP)/6$ $= 1.8 \approx 2$

---

1. Use the formulas and the historical data provided in the scenario to determine the most likely, optimistic, and pessimistic times. Then calculate the triangular distribution and the beta distribution for the window installation.

2. Why do you think it is a good practice to use a three-point estimate for activities?

A Guide to the Project Management Body of Knowledge (PMBOK® Guide) – Fifth Edition, Project Management Institute (PMI)®, Project Management Professional (PMP)®, and Certified Associate in Project Management (CAPM)® are registered trademarks of Project Management Institute, Inc. - Version 2.1 Published September 30, 2014

Lesson 6: Planning for Project Time Management | Topic E

TOPIC F

Develop a Project Schedule

With your activities in hand and sequenced in a logical format, you can start thinking about creating an official project schedule. The project schedule is a key component in scheduling tasks and resources to complete those tasks within a given time frame. In this topic, you will develop a project schedule.

A Guide to the Project Management Body of Knowledge (PMBOK® Guide) – Fifth Edition, Project Management Institute, Inc., 2013, pg. 172-174

The following data flow diagram illustrates how the Develop Schedule process relates to the other project management processes.

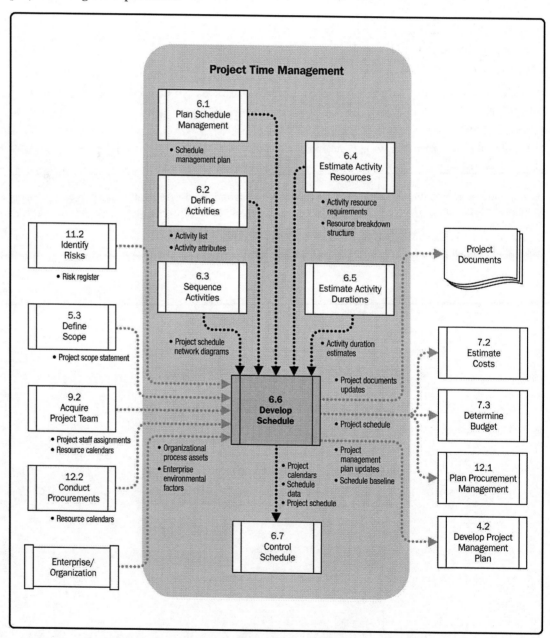

Figure 6-14: Develop Schedule data flow diagram.

A Guide to the Project Management Body of Knowledge (PMBOK® Guide) – Fifth Edition, Project Management Institute, Inc., 2013, p. 173

The Project Schedule

The *project schedule* is the visual presentation of the project team's plan for starting and finishing activities on specific dates and in a certain sequence. The schedule also specifies planned dates for meeting project milestones. With its supporting detail, the schedule is the main output of the develop schedule process. The purpose of the project schedule is to coordinate activities into a master plan in order to complete the project objectives on time. It is also used to track schedule performance and to keep upper management and project stakeholders informed about project status.

A Guide to the Project Management Body of Knowledge (PMBOK® Guide) – Fifth Edition, Project Management Institute, Inc., 2013, pg. 174, 182

Project Schedule Presentation Types

A project schedule can be presented in one of three graphical depictions:

A Guide to the Project Management Body of Knowledge (PMBOK® Guide) – Fifth Edition, Project Management Institute (PMI)®, Project Management Professional (PMP)®, and Certified Associate in Project Management (CAPM)® are registered trademarks of Project Management Institute, Inc. - Version 2.1 Published September 30, 2014

Lesson 6: Planning for Project Time Management | Topic F

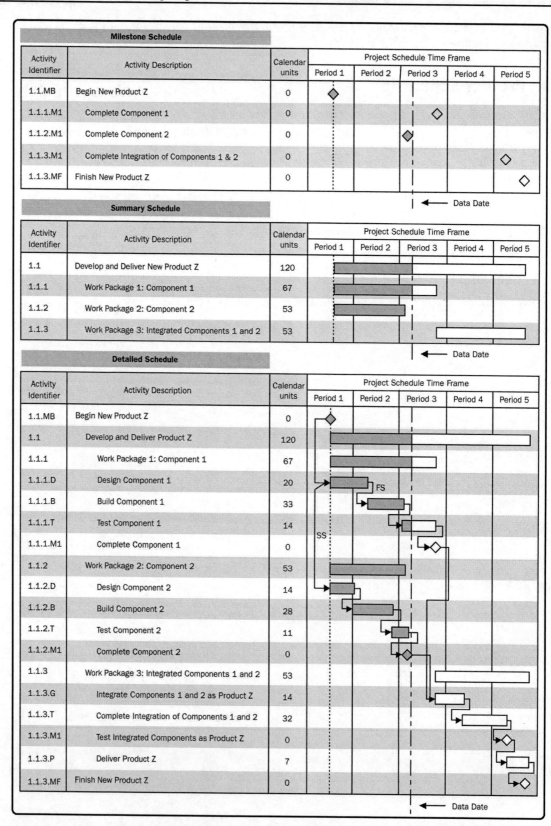

Figure 6–15: Project schedule presentation type examples.

A Guide to the Project Management Body of Knowledge (PMBOK® Guide) – Fifth Edition, Project Management Institute, Inc., 2013, p. 183

- *Bar charts* or Gantt charts show activities on the vertical axis and dates on the horizontal axis with durations shown as bars with start and end dates.

- *Milestone charts* are bar charts but include only milestone or major deliverables as a point in time.
- *Project schedule network diagrams* are activity-on-node diagrams that show activities and relationships but not the date detail, as we don't know what date the project is going to start. They represent the logic and relationship of the schedule activities.

A Guide to the Project Management Body of Knowledge (PMBOK® Guide) – Fifth Edition, Project Management Institute, Inc., 2013, p. 182

The Develop Schedule Process

The *Develop Schedule process* includes analyzing the activity sequences, durations, resource requirements and time constraints to develop the project schedule. The schedule then provides start and finish dates for completing the project activities. The project manager analyzes the activity sequences, durations, resource requirements, and schedule constraints to create the schedule. As the project progresses, the project schedule is revised or modified continuously to accommodate the changes in the project work.

A Guide to the Project Management Body of Knowledge (PMBOK® Guide) – Fifth Edition, Project Management Institute, Inc., 2013, pg. 172-174

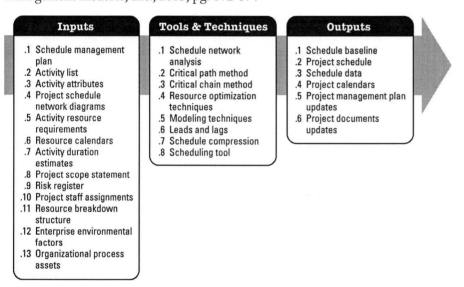

Inputs	Tools & Techniques	Outputs
.1 Schedule management plan .2 Activity list .3 Activity attributes .4 Project schedule network diagrams .5 Activity resource requirements .6 Resource calendars .7 Activity duration estimates .8 Project scope statement .9 Risk register .10 Project staff assignments .11 Resource breakdown structure .12 Enterprise environmental factors .13 Organizational process assets	.1 Schedule network analysis .2 Critical path method .3 Critical chain method .4 Resource optimization techniques .5 Modeling techniques .6 Leads and lags .7 Schedule compression .8 Scheduling tool	.1 Schedule baseline .2 Project schedule .3 Schedule data .4 Project calendars .5 Project management plan updates .6 Project documents updates

Figure 6–16: The Develop Schedule process.

A Guide to the Project Management Body of Knowledge (PMBOK® Guide) – Fifth Edition, Project Management Institute, Inc., 2013, p. 173

Develop Schedule Inputs

To develop a well-constructed project schedule, several elements should be included.

Input	*Description*
Schedule management plan	Provides the scheduling method and tool to be used and how the schedule is to be calculated.
Activity list	Provides the activities that will be included in the schedule model.
Activity attributes	Provides the details of the activities that will be used to build the schedule model.
Project schedule network diagrams	Provides the logical relationships of the predecessors and successors that will be used to build the schedule.

Input	Description
Activity resource requirements	Provides the types and quantities of resources required for each activity.
Resource calendars	Provides the availability for each resource.
Activity duration estimates	Provides the likely amount of time needed to complete each activity.
Project scope statement	Provides assumptions and constraints that could impact the schedule.
Risk register	Provides the details of the risks and any characteristics that may impact the schedule.
Project staff assignments (an output from 9.2)	The project staff assignments specify exactly which resources are assigned to each activity.
Resource breakdown structure	Provides the resource analysis and organizational reporting details.
Enterprise environmental factors	Enterprise environmental factors that influence this process include standards, communication channels, and the scheduling tool.
Organizational process assets	Organizational process assets that can influence this process include the scheduling methodology and project calendar(s).

A Guide to the Project Management Body of Knowledge (PMBOK® Guide) – Fifth Edition, Project Management Institute, Inc., 2013, pg. 174-176

Develop Schedule Tools and Techniques

There are various tools and techniques used in the Develop Schedule process.

Tools & Techniques	Description
Schedule network analysis	Produces the project schedule through a mix of analysis methods.
Critical path method	Analysis that calculates early and late start and finish dates for all activities in the project.
Critical chain method	Alters the project schedule to accommodate limits on resources. Involves adding buffer activities to keep focus on activity durations.
Resource optimization techniques	Assists in making scheduling decisions when there are resource management concerns.
Modeling techniques	Analysis that involves creating a scenario ("What if X happens?"), and then calculating various possible project durations. This analysis is helpful in assessing different schedules under adverse conditions.
Leads and lags	Provides a way to refine the schedule by adjusting the start time of successor activities.
Schedule compression	Involves shortening the schedule without affecting the scope of the project.
Scheduling tool	Automates or accelerates the schedule development process. May be used along with commercial project management software or in-house, custom-built applications

A Guide to the Project Management Body of Knowledge (PMBOK® Guide) – Fifth Edition, Project Management Institute (PMI)®, Project Management Professional (PMP)®, and Certified Associate in Project Management (CAPM)® are registered trademarks of Project Management Institute, Inc. - Version 2.1 Published September 30, 2014

Lesson 6: Planning for Project Time Management | Topic F

A Guide to the Project Management Body of Knowledge (PMBOK® Guide) – Fifth Edition, Project Management Institute, Inc., 2013, pg. 176-181

Standard Schedule Diagramming Notations

Project network diagrams use standard diagramming nomenclature.

Network Notations	Description
ES	Early start. The earliest time an activity can start. Usually, the ES of the first activity in a network diagram is zero. The ES of all other activities is the latest Early Finish (EF) of any predecessor activities (assuming that any successor activity starts as soon as all its predecessor activities are finished). *A Guide to the Project Management Body of Knowledge (PMBOK® Guide) – Fifth Edition,* Project Management Institute, Inc., 2013, p. 538
EF	Early finish. The earliest time an activity can finish. The EF for the first activity is the same as its duration. For all other activities, EF is the latest EF of all of an activity's predecessor activities plus its duration. *A Guide to the Project Management Body of Knowledge (PMBOK® Guide) – Fifth Edition,* Project Management Institute, Inc., 2013, p. 538
LF	Late finish. The latest time an activity can finish. The LF for the last activity is the same as its EF time. The LF for any predecessor activity is the earliest LS of any of its successor activities. *A Guide to the Project Management Body of Knowledge (PMBOK® Guide) – Fifth Edition,* Project Management Institute, Inc., 2013, p. 544
LS	Late start. The latest time an activity can start. The LS for the last activity is its EF minus its duration. The LS for any predecessor activity is its LF minus its duration. *A Guide to the Project Management Body of Knowledge (PMBOK® Guide) – Fifth Edition,* Project Management Institute, Inc., 2013, p. 544
DU	Duration. The number of work periods required for completion of an activity. *A Guide to the Project Management Body of Knowledge (PMBOK® Guide) – Fifth Edition,* Project Management Institute, Inc., 2013, p. 538

Schedule Network Analysis

Schedule network analysis is a technique used to calculate the theoretical early and late start and finish dates for all project activities. In other words, it helps create a project schedule. This method also generates float. Schedule network analysis may be achieved by using one of four methods:

- Critical Path Method (CPM)
- Critical chain method
- Modeling techniques
- Resource optimization

A Guide to the Project Management Body of Knowledge (PMBOK® Guide) – Fifth Edition, Project Management Institute, Inc., 2013, p. 176

The Critical Path Method

The *critical path method (CPM)* is a schedule network analysis method that uses a sequential finish-to-start network logic and calculates one early and late start and finish date for each activity by using a single duration estimate. The longest path through the network—the critical path—is identified. Then float is calculated to identify activities in which there is some scheduling flexibility. CPM is the mathematical analysis technique used in most types of project management software.

A Guide to the Project Management Body of Knowledge (PMBOK® Guide) – Fifth Edition, Project Management Institute, Inc., 2013, pg. 176-177

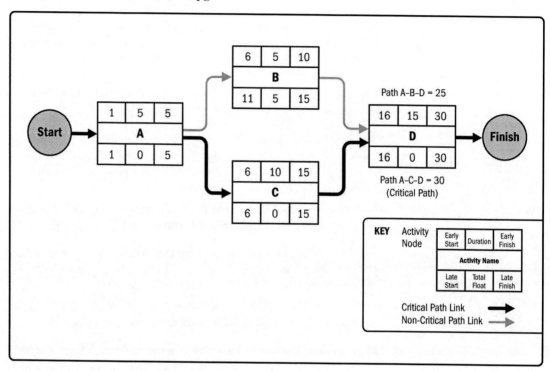

Figure 6-17: Critical Path method example.

A Guide to the Project Management Body of Knowledge (PMBOK® Guide) – Fifth Edition, Project Management Institute, Inc., 2013, p. 177

The Critical Path

The *critical path* is the network path that has the longest total duration. Activities on the critical path cannot be delayed, or the whole project will be delayed unless subsequent activities are shortened. The longest path in the project schedule represents the shortest project duration. The activities on this path must be monitored closely throughout the project. The critical path is calculated by doing a forward pass to calculate the ES and EF for each activity and then a backward pass to calculate the LS and LF for each activity. The path with the longest total duration and no scheduling flexibility is the critical path.

A Guide to the Project Management Body of Knowledge (PMBOK® Guide) – Fifth Edition, Project Management Institute, Inc., 2013, p. 176

Critical Activities

Critical activities are the activities that are on the critical path. Generally, for all activities along the critical path, ES = LS and EF = LF. There can be no flexibility in the start time or the finish time for these activities. Activities that are not on the critical path usually have some flexibility in their start and finish times.

A Guide to the Project Management Body of Knowledge (PMBOK® Guide) – Fifth Edition, Project Management Institute, Inc., 2013, p. 177

Float

Float is the amount of time an activity can be delayed from its ES without delaying the project finish date or the consecutive activities. Float occurs only in activities that are not on the critical path. Float used to be referred to as "slack." There are two types: total float and free float.

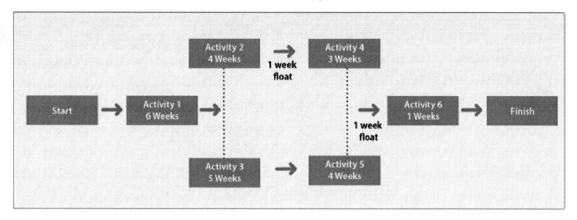

Figure 6-18: A schedule network diagram showing float.

A Guide to the Project Management Body of Knowledge (PMBOK® Guide) – Fifth Edition, Project Management Institute, Inc., 2013, p. 177

Total Float

Total float is a type of float in which the total amount of time an activity requires can be delayed without delaying the project finish date. Total float for an activity can be calculated by subtracting its EF from its LF or its ES from its LS.

In this diagram, Activity C has an ES of 25 days. However, should it begin on its Late Start (LS) date, the value is 36. Therefore, the amount of time the start date can be delayed without affecting the finish date is 11 days. The Total Float (TF) value is 11 (36 — 25 = 11).

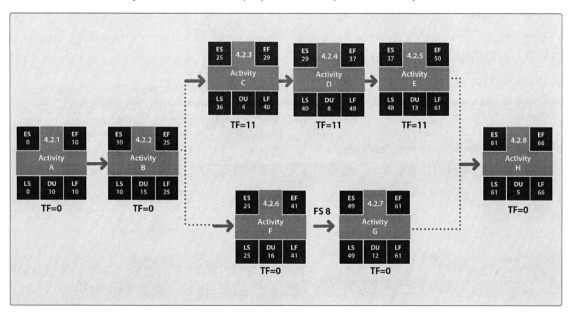

Figure 6-19: A network diagram with total float.

A Guide to the Project Management Body of Knowledge (PMBOK® Guide) – Fifth Edition, Project Management Institute, Inc., 2013, p. 177

Free Float

Free float is the amount of time an activity can be delayed without delaying the ES of any activity that immediately follows it. It allows flexibility of the start or finish time within that activity only. If there is a string of activities with float, free float will be available for the activity only at the end of the string. Free float on the activity is calculated by subtracting the EF of an activity from the ES of its successor activity.

In the diagram, the free float for activity E can be calculated by subtracting the EF from the ES of the successor activity, which in this case is Activity H. The free float value is Activity H's ES (61) — Activity E's EF (50), or 61 — 50. The free float is 11.

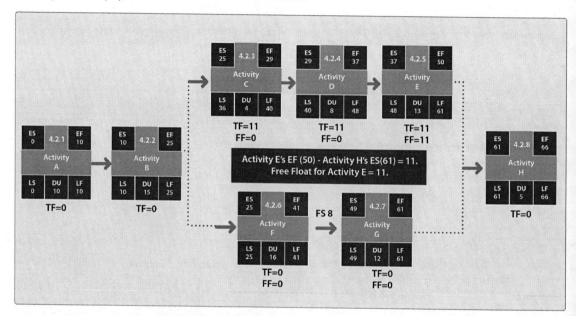

Figure 6-20: A network diagram with free float.

A Guide to the Project Management Body of Knowledge (PMBOK® Guide) – Fifth Edition, Project Management Institute, Inc., 2013, p. 177

The Critical Chain Method

The *critical chain method (CCM)* is a schedule network analysis method that allows you to consider resource limitations and adjust the schedule as appropriate to work within those limitations. The *critical chain* is established by analyzing the critical path alongside the resources that are actually available. The critical chain method is also used to plan and manage reserves or buffers and helps mitigate possible cost and schedule risks.

 Note: To further explore the critical path, you can access the LearnTO **Working with the Critical Path** presentation from the **LearnTO** tile on the LogicalCHOICE Course screen.

A Guide to the Project Management Body of Knowledge (PMBOK® Guide) – Fifth Edition, Project Management Institute (PMI)®, Project Management Professional (PMP)®, and Certified Associate in Project Management (CAPM)® are registered trademarks of Project Management Institute, Inc. - Version 2.1 Published September 30, 2014

Lesson 6: Planning for Project Time Management | Topic F

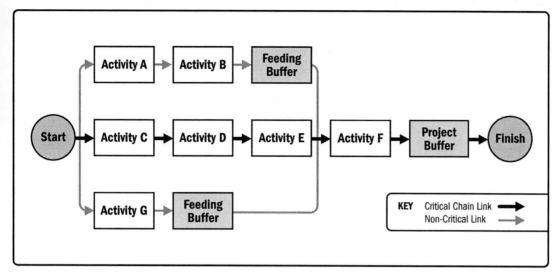

Figure 6-21: A critical chain method example.

A Guide to the Project Management Body of Knowledge (PMBOK® Guide) – Fifth Edition, Project Management Institute, Inc., 2013, p. 178

Resource Optimization Techniques

Resource optimization techniques are used to analyze the schedule model. It allows you to readjust the work as appropriate so that people are not overly allocated. It is also used to address scheduling activities when critical resources are available only at certain times. Optimization techniques are generally done after the critical path has been initially identified. The critical path frequently changes as a result of resource optimization results. There are two resource optimization techniques that we can use to optimize the project schedule.

- *Resource leveling* is a technique used to even out the resource demand for critical or shared resources in the schedule. This technique looks at the usage of each resource, when it is available, if it is over-allocated (for example, more than 40 hours a week), if it is assigned to two or more tasks that need their full time, and so on, and adjusts the schedule to accommodate resource modifications. This often extends the critical path.
- *Resource smoothing* adjusts the schedule so that resources do not exceed predefined resource limits. This does not affect the critical path, as float is used to accommodate these changes.

A Guide to the Project Management Body of Knowledge (PMBOK® Guide) – Fifth Edition, Project Management Institute, Inc., 2013, pg. 179-180

Automatic Resource Optimization Tools

Most project management software packages have resource optimization capabilities. However, make sure that you analyze the results before accepting them. Automated leveling or smoothing often pushes out the project's completion date. And, when you run the automated tool, resources may be reallocated to work at times that are inappropriate due to other constraints. Because of this, it is important that a human being review the changes before they are accepted.

A Guide to the Project Management Body of Knowledge (PMBOK® Guide) – Fifth Edition, Project Management Institute, Inc., 2013, pg. 179-180

Modeling Techniques

There are two modeling techniques we can use on complex projects to model various situations within the project schedule.

A Guide to the Project Management Body of Knowledge (PMBOK® Guide) – Fifth Edition, Project Management Institute (PMI)®, Project Management Professional (PMP)®, and Certified Associate in Project Management (CAPM)® are registered trademarks of Project Management Institute, Inc. - Version 2.1 Published September 30, 2014

Lesson 6: Planning for Project Time Management | Topic F

- The *what-if scenario analysis* method allows you to consider different situations that might occur and influence the schedule; it assesses the feasibility of the schedule under various adverse conditions. It allows you to compute different schedules based on potential delays, or the unplanned events that are a normal part of business life, such as key employees resigning during a project. The outcomes are also used to mitigate the impact of unexpected situations when preparing risk response plans. This method helps in selecting the optimum plan.
- The *simulation technique* enables you to calculate different schedules based on different assumptions that you are considering for the project. An example of this is a Monte Carlo simulation where a statistical distribution is defined for possible activity durations and a distribution of possible outcomes is calculated for the project.

A Guide to the Project Management Body of Knowledge (PMBOK® Guide) – Fifth Edition, Project Management Institute, Inc., 2013, p. 180

Schedule Compression

Schedule compression is the shortening of the project schedule without affecting the project scope. Setbacks or revised deadlines can cause production problems in which there is little time to do a lot of work. When these issues occur, product quality is often sacrificed. Schedule compression alleviates the pressure of completing too many activities in too little time without negatively affecting the project scope. Only critical path activities are compressed. Compression may be achieved in one of two ways: crashing and fast-tracking.

Crashing is a schedule compression method that analyzes cost and schedule trade-offs to determine how to obtain the greatest schedule compression for the least incremental cost. Crashing typically involves allocating more resources to activities on the critical path in an effort to shorten their duration and thereby increases project costs. To crash a schedule, analyze:

- Duration estimate under normal (for example, not compressed) conditions.
- Cost associated with the normal condition.
- Duration estimate under the crash condition.
- Cost associated with the crash condition.

The formula for calculating crash costs per week is **(Crash Cost – Normal Cost) / (Normal Time – Crash Time)**.

Fast-tracking is the process of compressing total project duration by performing some activities concurrently that were originally scheduled sequentially. Typically, fast-tracking involves identifying FS relationships that could be done in parallel, either as FF, SF, or SS relationships, or by simply adding some leads to FS activities. Some fast-tracking may entail looking very creatively at the network diagram to see if some discretionary dependencies could be done completely independently. Usually no added costs are incurred from fast-tracking; however, it can result in increased risk and rework.

A Guide to the Project Management Body of Knowledge (PMBOK® Guide) – Fifth Edition, Project Management Institute, Inc., 2013, p. 181

Crash Cost Plotting Methods

Crash cost plotting methods are techniques for analyzing the crash costs by creating a graph or a visual representation that clearly illustrates those costs. With the X axis showing the duration and the Y axis showing the cost, the activities are plotted on the grid from right to left, starting with the activity with the lowest crash cost per week. Activities with flatter slopes are the activities with relatively larger time savings for the associated cost. Crashing may result in increased risk and rework; the project team needs to identify the point at which it becomes impractical to crash the schedule any further.

A Guide to the Project Management Body of Knowledge (PMBOK® Guide) – Fifth Edition, Project Management Institute, Inc., 2013, p. 181

A Guide to the Project Management Body of Knowledge (PMBOK® Guide) – Fifth Edition, Project Management Institute (PMI)®, Project Management Professional (PMP)®, and Certified Associate in Project Management (CAPM)® are registered trademarks of Project Management Institute, Inc. - Version 2.1 Published September 30, 2014

Lesson 6: Planning for Project Time Management | Topic F

Scheduling Tools

A *scheduling tool* is an automatic scheduling program that generates the project schedule from the submitted start and finish dates. Tools can be helpful in creating project schedules quickly and efficiently because most of the calculating is done automatically. For example, Microsoft Project is commonly used by project managers to develop and build project schedules.

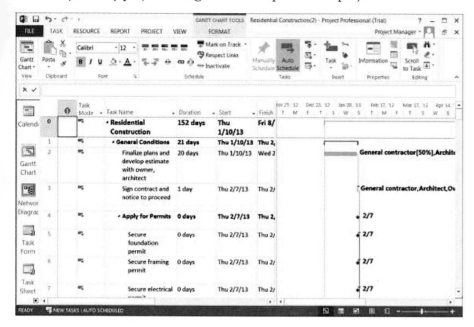

Figure 6-22: A Microsoft Project screen.

A Guide to the Project Management Body of Knowledge (PMBOK® Guide) – Fifth Edition, Project Management Institute, Inc., 2013, p. 181

Develop Schedule Outputs

There are six outputs from the Develop Schedule process.

Output	Description
Schedule baseline	May need to be updated by using a change request as this is the baseline schedule for the project.
Project schedule	As stated in the *PMBOK® Guide,* the project schedule is an output of the schedule model that presents lined activities with planned dates, durations, milestones, and resources.
Schedule data	*Schedule data* is the information that describes and controls the schedule. It includes milestones, activities, activity attributes, assumptions and constraints. It can also include resource requirements by time periods, alternative schedules, and scheduling of contingency reserves.
Project calendars	*Project calendars* show work days and shifts that are available for scheduling activities. These are used to avoid resource conflicts when developing a schedule model.
Project management plan updates	Project management plans that may need updating include the schedule baseline and the schedule management plan.

A Guide to the Project Management Body of Knowledge (PMBOK® Guide) – Fifth Edition, Project Management Institute (PMI)®, Project Management Professional (PMP)®, and Certified Associate in Project Management (CAPM)® are registered trademarks of Project Management Institute, Inc. - Version 2.1 Published September 30, 2014

Lesson 6: Planning for Project Time Management | Topic F

Output	Description
Project documents updates	Project documents that may need updating include: • Activity resource requirements: may be affected and require updates if resource leveling is used to develop the schedule. • Activity attributes: may be altered, especially if resource requirements are updated. • Calendar: used as a basis for project scheduling. The calendar units may change for each project. • Risk register: updated with opportunities and threats that arise while scheduling assumptions.

A Guide to the Project Management Body of Knowledge (PMBOK® Guide) – Fifth Edition, Project Management Institute, Inc., 2013, pg. 181-185

Guidelines to Develop a Project Schedule

To develop a project schedule:

- Perform a mathematical analysis to determine the time periods within which activities could be scheduled once resource limits and other known constraints are applied.
- Evaluate the possible impact of any constraints and assumptions on schedule development.
- Consider the availability of your resources.
  - Will you have the staff you need to perform the work when it is scheduled to be done?
  - Will you have access to the materials, facilities, and equipment you need to perform the work when it is scheduled to be done?
- Consult project calendars and assign dates to activities.
  - Are there any holidays during which your project team will not conduct work activities?
  - Will your project team conduct work activities on weekends or alternate work shifts?
  - When will your key project team members be taking vacations?
  - Are there any unmovable milestone dates that must be met?
- Assess the feasibility of the schedule under adverse conditions by conducting what-if scenario analysis.
- Consider external resource date constraints, if applicable.
  - Are there any regional or national holidays not previously accounted for?
  - Do you need to make considerations for travel time for meetings?
- Select project management software that best meets the needs and budget of your project. If your organization does not require the use of a particular software program, ask yourself the following questions to make the selection:
  - How complex is the project?
  - Do I need to manage more than one project at a time?
  - How easy will the software be to learn and to use?
  - How well will the software adapt to projects that vary greatly?
  - What type and depth of analyses do I need to perform?
  - What is the reputation of the software company?
  - What do other project managers in the field use and what do they recommend?
- Review rough drafts of the schedule with the project team, sponsor, and customer. You may also need to review the rough drafts with functional managers to ensure that there are no conflicts with functional resources.
- Choose the format in which you will publish the schedule.
  - If your audience requires only a summary-level view of the project's progress in terms of milestones, consider using a milestone chart.

A Guide to the Project Management Body of Knowledge (PMBOK® Guide) – Fifth Edition, Project Management Institute (PMI)®, Project Management Professional (PMP)®, and Certified Associate in Project Management (CAPM)® are registered trademarks of Project Management Institute, Inc. - Version 2.1 Published September 30, 2014

Lesson 6: Planning for Project Time Management | Topic F

- If you are reviewing the schedule with your project team, consider publishing a detailed bar chart or a network diagram with dates.
  - If you are preparing a presentation for key project stakeholders or upper management, consider printing the schedule in several different formats to show various views of the project's progress versus planned progress.
- Distribute the preliminary schedule to all program office personnel, functional team members, functional management, and the customer or sponsor to obtain approval.
- Following approval, baseline the schedule and distribute to the team.

A Guide to the Project Management Body of Knowledge (PMBOK® Guide) – Fifth Edition, Project Management Institute, Inc., 2013, pg. 172-185

Guidelines to Identify the Critical Path

To identify the critical path for a project with finish-to-start precedence relationships:

1. Conduct a forward pass to determine ES and EF times for each activity.

   a. Use zero (0) for the first activity's ES.
   b. Enter the first activity's duration as its EF.
   c. Calculate the ES for each successor activity by using the latest EF from any of its predecessor activities plus or minus any leads or lags.
   d. Calculate the EF for each successor activity by adding its duration to its ES.
   e. Move through all the activities until you have an ES and EF for each one.

2. Perform a backward pass to determine LS and LF times for each.

   a. Enter the last activity's EF for its LF time.
   b. Subtract the last activity's duration from its EF to determine its LS.
   c. Calculate the LF for each predecessor activity by using the earliest LS from any of its successor activities plus or minus any leads or lags.
   d. Calculate the LS for each predecessor activity by subtracting its duration from its LF.
   e. Move backward through all the activities until you have the LF and LS for each one.

3. Calculate float.

   a. For each activity, subtract its EF from its LF to determine total float.
   b. For each string of activities with float, calculate the free float for the last activity in the string by subtracting its EF from its successor activity ES.

4. Identify the critical path as the path with the longest duration and least amount of float.

A Guide to the Project Management Body of Knowledge (PMBOK® Guide) – Fifth Edition, Project Management Institute, Inc., 2013, pg. 176-178

A Guide to the Project Management Body of Knowledge (PMBOK® Guide) – Fifth Edition, Project Management Institute (PMI)®, Project Management Professional (PMP)®, and Certified Associate in Project Management (CAPM)® are registered trademarks of Project Management Institute, Inc. - Version 2.1 Published September 30, 2014

Lesson 6: Planning for Project Time Management | *Topic F*

ACTIVITY 6-6
Creating a Project Schedule

Data Files

C:\095001Data\Planning for Project Time Management\May and June 2013 Calendar.doc

C:\095001Data\Planning for Project Time Management\Project Schedule.doc

Scenario

Now that you have the list of activities, estimated durations, and estimated resources, it is time to draft the project schedule to determine the start and finish dates for the project activities. The project is scheduled to start on May 6 and must finish no later than the end of the June. In this activity, you will develop the project schedule for a single work package, and not the entire project. To draft a schedule, refer to the **May and June 2013 Calendar.doc** file.

---

1. What other inputs will you need to have available before developing the project schedule?

   ☑ Resource calendars

   ☐ Project scope statement

   ☑ Specific milestone dates that must be met

   ☑ Schedule baseline

2. Navigate to and open **C:\095001Data\Planning for Project Time Management\Project Schedule.doc**

3. Use the information provided to complete the project schedule for the Framing work package.

4. Once the schedule has been completed, save the file as *My Project Schedule.doc* and close the file.

A Guide to the Project Management Body of Knowledge (PMBOK® Guide) – Fifth Edition, Project Management Institute (PMI)®, Project Management Professional (PMP)®, and Certified Associate in Project Management (CAPM)® are registered trademarks of Project Management Institute, Inc. - Version 2.1 Published September 30, 2014

Summary

In this lesson, you identified the major elements of project schedules, which include activity lists, project network schedule diagrams, estimates of activity duration, and techniques for responding to organizational constraints by adjusting flexibility within schedules. You will now be able to develop effective project schedules and manage schedules in response to organizational constraints on time and resources so that you can bring your projects in on time and on budget.

Why is it important to do a thorough job at estimating the time it will take to complete each activity in a project?

Consider the importance of creating an activity list. How do you think that creating an activity list for your projects will help ensure that your project activities are tied to the project scope?

Note: Check your LogicalCHOICE Course screen for opportunities to interact with your classmates, peers, and the larger LogicalCHOICE online community about the topics covered in this course or other topics you are interested in. From the Course screen you can also access available resources for a more continuous learning experience.

A Guide to the Project Management Body of Knowledge (PMBOK® Guide) – Fifth Edition, Project Management Institute (PMI)®, Project Management Professional (PMP)®, and Certified Associate in Project Management (CAPM)® are registered trademarks of Project Management Institute, Inc. - Version 2.1 Published September 30, 2014

Lesson 6: Planning for Project Time Management |

7 | Planning Project Budget, Quality, and Communications

Lesson Time: 3 hours

Lesson Objectives

In this lesson, you will:

- Plan cost management.

- Estimate project costs.

- Determine a project budget.

- Plan for quality management.

- Plan for human resource management.

- Plan for communications management.

Lesson Introduction

Now that you have identified the project resources, estimated the activity durations, and drafted a project schedule, you can start focusing on how to manage the costs of project work and how to effectively manage the communication among team members. The ability to deliver projects on time and on budget is a key element of good project management. You want to be able to create accurate estimates regarding the work that must be done and the costs that will be incurred, as well as monitor progress against expectations while ensuring the quality is on target.

The following diagram highlights the next process group and knowledge areas covered in this lesson.

A Guide to the Project Management Body of Knowledge (PMBOK® Guide) – Fifth Edition, Project Management Institute (PMI)®, Project Management Professional (PMP)®, and Certified Associate in Project Management (CAPM)® are registered trademarks of Project Management Institute, Inc. - Version 2.1 Published September 30, 2014

	Project Management Process Groups				
Knowledge Areas	**Initiating Process Group**	**Planning Process Group**	**Executing Process Group**	**Monitoring and Controlling Process Group**	**Closing Process Group**
4. Project Integration Management	4.1 Develop Project Charter	4.2 Develop Project Management Plan	4.3 Direct and Manage Project Work	4.4 Monitor and Control Project Work 4.5 Perform Integrated Change Control	4.6 Close Project or Phase
5. Project Scope Management		5.1 Plan Scope Management 5.2 Collect Requirements 5.3 Define Scope 5.4 Create WBS		5.5 Validate Scope 5.6 Control Scope	
6. Project Time Management		6.1 Plan Schedule Management 6.2 Define Activities 6.3 Sequence Activites 6.4 Estimate Activity Resources 6.5 Estimate Activity Durations 6.6 Develop Schedule		6.7 Control Schedule	
7. Project Cost Management		7.1 Plan Cost Management 7.2 Estimate Cost 7.3 Determine Budget		7.4 Control Costs	
8. Project Quality Management		8.1 Plan Quality Management	8.2 Perform Quality Assurance	8.3 Control Quality	
9. Project Human Resource Management		9.1 Plan Human Resource Management	9.2 Acquire Project Team 9.3 Develop Project Team 9.4 Manage Project Team		
10. Project Communication Management		10.1 Plan Communications Management	10.2 Manage Communications	10.3 Control Communications	
11. Project Risk Management		11.1 Plan Risk Management 11.2 Identify Risks 11.3 Perform Qualitative Risk Analysis 11.4 Perform Quantitative Risk Analysis 11.5 Plan Risk Responses		11.6 Control Risks	
12. Project Procurement Management		12.1 Plan Procurement Management	12.2 Conduct Procurements	12.3 Control Procurements	12.4 Close Procurements
13. Project Stakeholder Management	13.1 Identify Stakeholders	13.2 Plan Stakeholder Management	13.3 Manage Stakeholder Engagement	13.4 Control Stakeholder Engagement	

TOPIC A

Plan Project Cost Management

With your schedule management plan in hand, you are ready to tackle the next area of the project, which involves planning how to effectively manage the project costs. Without proper management of project costs, expenses can get out of control quickly! You must be prepared to make adjustments and apply the correct costs to resources, activities, and services that align with your budget. The cost management plan helps you to plan, react to, and update project costs when issues or changes arise throughout the life cycle of a project.

A Guide to the Project Management Body of Knowledge (PMBOK® Guide) – Fifth Edition, Project Management Institute, Inc., 2013, pg. 195-196

The following data flow diagram illustrates how the Plan Cost Management process relates to the other knowledge areas within the Planning Process Group.

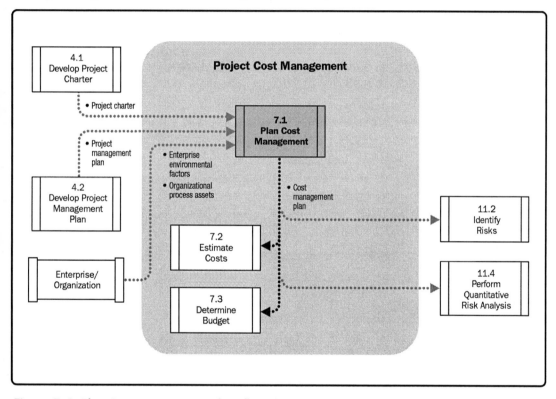

Figure 7-1: Plan Cost Management data flow diagram.

A Guide to the Project Management Body of Knowledge (PMBOK® Guide) – Fifth Edition, Project Management Institute, Inc., 2013, p. 196

What Is a Cost Management Plan?

The *Cost Management plan* is a subsidiary plan of the project management plan that defines the processes, procedures, tools, and techniques to effectively manage the cost of a project. It documents the policies, procedures, and documentation for planning, managing, expending, and controlling the costs of a project throughout the life of the project. Having a good cost estimate at the beginning of a project is critical to the project success in delivering the project objectives within the planned budget.

A Guide to the Project Management Body of Knowledge (PMBOK® Guide) – Fifth Edition, Project Management Institute (PMI)®, Project Management Professional (PMP)®, and Certified Associate in Project Management (CAPM)® are registered trademarks of Project Management Institute, Inc. - Version 2.1 Published September 30, 2014

Lesson 7: Planning Project Budget, Quality, and Communications | Topic A

A Guide to the Project Management Body of Knowledge (PMBOK® Guide) – Fifth Edition, Project Management Institute, Inc., 2013, pg. 193-194

Cost Management Plan Components

A cost management plan can contain the following information.

Component	Description
Units	Units defines the unit of measure for each resource (labor hours and labor days for time measures, and meters, cubic yards, and tons for quantity resources).
Precision	Precision is the degree to which activity cost estimates will be rounded up or down, for example, rounding $995.50 to $1,000.
Accuracy	Level of accuracy is the acceptable range used for dollar estimates (for example, +–10 percent).
Organizational procedures links	The WBS is used as the framework of the control account for project cost accounting so that there is consistency with the cost estimates.
Control thresholds	The acceptable variance for monitoring cost performance, usually represented as percentage deviations from the baseline plan, for example, 15 percent over plan.
Rules	Rules of performance measurement, such as Earned Value Management (EVM) rules for performance: • Defines points in the WBS where control account measurements will be reviewed. • Determines EVM techniques to be used (weighted milestones, fixed-formula, percent complete, etc.) • Documents computation equations for calculating estimate at completion (EAC) forecasts.
Reporting	Reporting formats define frequency and formats of the cost reports.
Process descriptions	Process descriptions documents other cost management processes that may be used.
Additional information	Additional details describe strategic funding choices, how to manage fluctuations in currency exchange rates, and the procedure for project cost recording.

A Guide to the Project Management Body of Knowledge (PMBOK® Guide) – Fifth Edition, Project Management Institute, Inc., 2013, pg. 198-199

The Plan Cost Management Process

The Plan Cost Management process documents the cost management strategies that will be used to effectively manage the project cost throughout the project life cycle, based on the scope definition of the project.

A Guide to the Project Management Body of Knowledge (PMBOK® Guide) – Fifth Edition, Project Management Institute, Inc., 2013, pg. 195-196

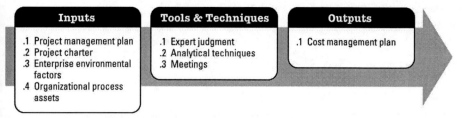

Figure 7–2: The Plan Cost Management process.

A Guide to the Project Management Body of Knowledge (PMBOK® Guide) – Fifth Edition, Project Management Institute, Inc., 2013, p. 195

Plan Cost Management Inputs

Various documents and factors provide input into the Plan Cost Management process.

Input	Description
Project management plan	Provides information such as the scope baseline, which contains the project scope statement and WBS for cost estimation; the schedule baseline, which defines when project costs will be incurred; and other cost-related scheduling, risk, and communications decisions.
Project charter	Contains summary budget information and defines who approves the project cost.
Enterprise environmental factors	Enterprise environmental factors that may influence this process include organizational culture and structure, market conditions, currency exchange rates, published commercial information, and the project management system.
Organizational process assets	Organizational process assets that can influence this process include financial controls procedures, historical information and lessons learned, financial databases and existing cost estimating, and budget-related policies, procedures, and guidelines.

A Guide to the Project Management Body of Knowledge (PMBOK® Guide) – Fifth Edition, Project Management Institute, Inc., 2013, pg. 196-198

Plan Cost Management Tools and Techniques

There are three tools and techniques used in the Plan Cost Management process.

Tools & Techniques	Description
Expert judgment	Expert judgment provides valuable insight about the cost estimation and management from prior projects.
Analytical techniques	The plan contains decisions on (1) how the project will be funded: such as self-funding, funding with equity, or funding with debt; and (2) ways to finance project resources such as equipment, which includes making, purchasing, renting, or leasing. Other techniques that could be chosen include payback period, return on investment, internal rate of return, discounted cash flow, and net present value.
Meetings	Meetings are held to develop the cost management plan and may include the project manager, project sponsor, selected project team members, and selected stakeholders.

A Guide to the Project Management Body of Knowledge (PMBOK® Guide) – Fifth Edition, Project Management Institute, Inc., 2013, p. 198

Plan Cost Management Outputs

There is one output from the Plan Cost Management process.

Output	Description
The cost management plan	As stated in the *PMBOK® Guide*, the cost management plan is a subsidiary plan of the project management plan that describes how costs will be planned, structured, and controlled.

A Guide to the Project Management Body of Knowledge (PMBOK® Guide) – Fifth Edition, Project Management Institute, Inc., 2013, pg. 198-199

Guidelines to Develop a Cost Management Plan

Guidelines to developing a cost management plan are as follows:

- Review the project management plan for information such as the scope baseline (which contains the project scope statement and WBS for cost estimation), the schedule baseline (which defines when project costs will be incurred and other cost-related scheduling), risk, and communications decisions.
- Review the project charter for summary budget information and who approves the project cost.
- Review the enterprise environmental factors such as organizational culture and structure, market conditions, currency exchange rates, published commercial information, and the project management system.
- Review the organizational process assets such as financial controls procedures, historical information and lessons learned, financial databases and existing cost estimating, and budget-related policies, procedures, and guidelines.
- Use tools and techniques such as expert judgment for valuable insight about the cost estimation and management from prior projects.
- Use analytical techniques for decisions on how the project will be funded such as self-funding, funding with equity, or funding with debt, and ways to finance project resources such as equipment, which includes making, purchasing, renting, or leasing. Other techniques include payback period, return on investment, internal rate of return, discounted cash flow, and net present value.
- Hold meetings to develop the cost management plan; this may include the project manager, project sponsor, selected project team members, and selected stakeholders.
- Document the cost management plan for the project.

A Guide to the Project Management Body of Knowledge (PMBOK® Guide) – Fifth Edition, Project Management Institute, Inc., 2013, pg. 195-199

A Guide to the Project Management Body of Knowledge (PMBOK® Guide) – Fifth Edition, Project Management Institute (PMI)®, Project Management Professional (PMP)®, and Certified Associate in Project Management (CAPM)® are registered trademarks of Project Management Institute, Inc. - Version 2.1 Published September 30, 2014

Lesson 7: Planning Project Budget, Quality, and Communications | *Topic A*

TOPIC B

Estimate Project Costs

You have developed your project schedules and determined the activities and resource requirements for your project. But how much will those resources cost? Estimating project costs will provide the answer. In this topic, you will estimate project costs.

A Guide to the Project Management Body of Knowledge (PMBOK® Guide) – Fifth Edition, Project Management Institute, Inc., 2013, pg. 200-201

The following data flow diagram illustrates how the Estimate Costs process relates to the other project management processes.

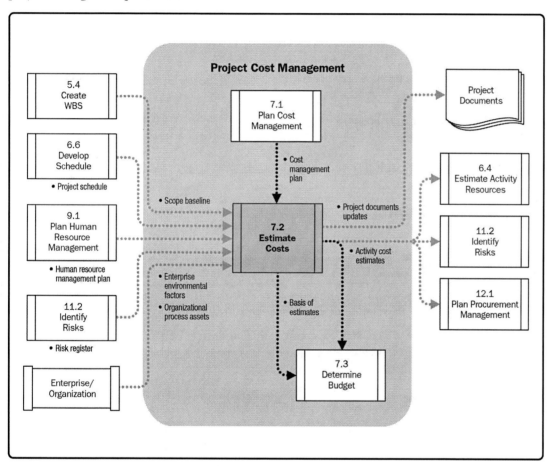

Figure 7–3: Estimate Costs data flow diagram.

A Guide to the Project Management Body of Knowledge (PMBOK® Guide) – Fifth Edition, Project Management Institute, Inc., 2013, p. 201

The Estimate Costs Process

Estimate Costs is the process of projecting the total expenditures necessary for the completion of your project. Logical estimates provide a basis for making sound decisions about projects and they establish baselines against which the success of the projects can later be measured. Cost estimating also involves identifying and considering cost alternatives. A different type of cost estimate and level of accuracy may be required for different phases of the project life cycle. A cost estimating method might be chosen due to:

A Guide to the Project Management Body of Knowledge (PMBOK® Guide) – Fifth Edition, Project Management Institute (PMI)®, Project Management Professional (PMP)®, and Certified Associate in Project Management (CAPM)® are registered trademarks of Project Management Institute, Inc. - Version 2.1 Published September 30, 2014

Lesson 7: Planning Project Budget, Quality, and Communications | *Topic B*

- Software availability
- Team member experience
- Project life cycle phase
- Time constraints
- Project definition
- Personal preference

A Guide to the Project Management Body of Knowledge (PMBOK® Guide) – Fifth Edition, Project Management Institute, Inc., 2013, pg. 200-202

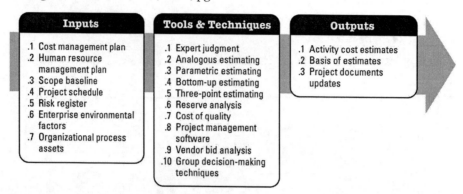

Figure 7–4: The Estimate Costs process.

A Guide to the Project Management Body of Knowledge (PMBOK® Guide) – Fifth Edition, Project Management Institute, Inc., 2013, p. 200

Estimate Costs Inputs

Accurate cost estimating requires numerous inputs.

Input	Description
The cost management plan	Indicates how project costs will be managed and controlled, and the method used and level of accuracy for estimating activity cost.
The human resources management plan	Includes the components necessary for developing cost estimates such as the project staffing attributes, personnel rates, and related rewards and recognitions.
Scope baseline	The scope baseline includes the approved detailed project scope statement along with its associated WBS and WBS dictionary. • Project scope statement: contains relevant information, such as project requirements, constraints, assumptions, and deliverables. • WBS: provides the relationship between individual project components and deliverables. • WBS dictionary: the WBS dictionary along with the statements of work provide specific details of work activities and deliverables.
Project schedule	The project schedule includes start and finish dates for each activity, and details of resources along with the time needed for them to complete project work that will incur project cost.
Risk register	Provides risks for estimating risk response costs.
Enterprise environmental factors	External factors, such as market trends, unavoidable budget restructuring, or commercial financial analysis may affect cost estimation.

Input	Description
Organizational process assets	Intra-organizational cost estimating policies or templates, team experience, or data from old projects.

A Guide to the Project Management Body of Knowledge (PMBOK® Guide) – Fifth Edition, Project Management Institute, Inc., 2013, pg. 202-204

Estimate Costs Tools and Techniques

There are many tools and techniques that can be used to estimate cost.

 Note: Most of these tools and techniques were discussed in detail in the previous Estimate Activity Duration process section and can be applied to the cost estimates.

Tools & Techniques	Description
Expert judgment	Variables such as labor costs, material costs, inflation, and risk factors can influence cost estimates. Expert judgment along with historical information will provide an insight on the information related to prior similar projects.
Analogous estimating	Uses the cost of a previous project with similar scope or activities to predict the cost of future activities.
Parametric estimating	Relies on the statistical relationship that exists between historical information and variables so as to arrive at an estimate for parameters such as duration and cost.
Bottom-up estimating	Estimates the cost of individual activities then "rolls up" to higher levels.
Three-point estimating	Incorporates three types of estimates into a singular cost estimate scenario: most likely, optimistic, and pessimistic.] PERT Formula
Reserve analysis	Contingency funds that are built into a cost estimate for as-yet unknown costs. Reserve analyses may increase a cost estimate.
Cost of Quality (COQ)	A technique that focuses on the cost of ensured quality. Costs include quality planning, control, and assurance.
Project management software	Project management cost estimating software simplifies the cost estimation process, can accelerate estimation time, and is applicable to most projects, regardless of scale or scope.
Vendor bid analysis	Cost estimation is based on the responsive bids obtained from vendors. Results must often be revisited once contract approval has been gained.
Group decision-making techniques	Techniques such as brainstorming, the Delphi, or nominal group can be used to assist teams in making decisions about activity duration estimates.

A Guide to the Project Management Body of Knowledge (PMBOK® Guide) – Fifth Edition, Project Management Institute, Inc., 2013, pg. 204-207

Estimate Costs Outputs

In addition to cost estimates, there are several possible outputs from the Estimate Cost process.

A Guide to the Project Management Body of Knowledge (PMBOK® Guide) – Fifth Edition, Project Management Institute (PMI)®, Project Management Professional (PMP)®, and Certified Associate in Project Management (CAPM)® are registered trademarks of Project Management Institute, Inc. - Version 2.1 Published September 30, 2014

Lesson 7: Planning Project Budget, Quality, and Communications | Topic B

Output	Description
Activity cost estimates	Provide estimates on probable costs necessary to finish project work. This includes costs on direct labor, materials, equipment, facilities, services, information technology, contingency reserves, or indirect costs, if any.
Basis of estimates	Supporting or additional information needed to justify the cost estimates. Details can include project scope, justification for the estimate, range of estimates, the assumptions, constraints, confidence level on the estimate, and expected range of estimates.
Project document updates	Updated project documents may include the risk register, human resource plan, activity list, project schedule, and training plans.

A Guide to the Project Management Body of Knowledge (PMBOK® Guide) – Fifth Edition, Project Management Institute, Inc., 2013, pg. 207-208

Common Estimate Types

This table describes some common estimate types and their associated degrees of accuracy.

Estimate Type	Degree of Accuracy
Rough Order of Magnitude (ROM)	Generally made early in the project. Developed without basis of detailed data and often based on very high-level historical data, expert judgment, or a costing model. Accuracy: –50 percent to +100 percent.
Budgetary	Often used for appropriation purposes. Accuracy: –10 to +25 percent.
Range of estimate	Often used as an alternative to ROM, in which the accuracy of the estimate is not well known. So, rather than $10M ±30 percent, the estimate could be stated as $7M to $13M. Accuracy: ±35 percent.
Approximate estimate	Based on more information than ROM estimates, but still lacks the detail required for high accuracy. May be possible if the project is similar to previous ones with reliable historical data for costing or where a proven costing model is applicable. Accuracy: ± 15 percent.
Definitive estimate (or "control" or "detailed")	Based on detailed information about the project work. Developed by estimating the cost for each work package in the WBS. Accuracy: –5 percent to +10 percent.
Phased estimate (or "rolling wave" or "moving window")	Allows the use of ROM or approximate estimates for some later parts of the work, whereas work that must be done earlier in the project life cycle is estimated at the definitive level. Accuracy: ±5 percent to ±15 percent in the window closest to present time; ±35 percent farther in the future.

A Guide to the Project Management Body of Knowledge (PMBOK® Guide) – Fifth Edition, Project Management Institute, Inc., 2013, p. 560

Estimating Techniques Advantages and Disadvantages

There are benefits and drawbacks to using different estimating techniques.

Estimating Technique	Advantages	Disadvantages
Analogous estimating	Can ensure no work is inadvertently omitted from work estimates.	Can sometimes be difficult for lower-level managers to apportion cost estimates.
Bottom-up estimating	Is very accurate and gives lower-level managers more responsibility.	May be very time consuming and can be used only after the WBS has been well-defined.
Parametric estimating	Is not time consuming.	May be inaccurate, depending on the integrity of the historical information used.

A Guide to the Project Management Body of Knowledge (PMBOK® Guide) – Fifth Edition, Project Management Institute, Inc., 2013, pg. 164, 169-170

Guidelines to Estimate Costs

Accurately estimating project costs will avoid overruns and unforeseen expenditures. Making good cost estimates will help you to create a strong cost baseline, which will ultimately be used for measuring project cost performance. Here are some guidelines for estimating costs:

- When possible, the cost figures that go into the cost estimates for individual work packages should be provided by those who will actually provide the resources. As always, it is the people who will do the work, provide the service, or supply the material that can best estimate what the associated costs will be. It is the project manager's responsibility to compile these cost figures into realistic estimates.
- For some projects, though, the project manager will be solely responsible for generating the cost estimates.
- Even in such cases, the project manager may want to do a reality check with the resource supplier to make sure no incorrect assumptions have been made.
- Gather any relevant input information that may help you prepare the estimates, such as estimating publications and resource rates.
- Determine which estimating technique to use.
- Look for alternative costing options, such as using stock components versus custom-made, stretching the duration of an activity to eliminate overtime charges, leasing versus purchasing of capital equipment, and outsourcing as opposed to handling the work in-house.
- Determine the units of measure that will be used.
- Consider possible risks that may impact cost.
- Ensure that all cost estimates are assigned to the appropriate account, according to the chart of accounts.
- Make sure your cost estimates include the following key elements:
  - Estimated costs for all resources that will be charged to the project. Use the WBS and resource requirements document to develop the estimates.
  - The level of estimate (degree of certainty).
  - A list of assumptions made when developing the estimates.

A Guide to the Project Management Body of Knowledge (PMBOK® Guide) – Fifth Edition, Project Management Institute, Inc., 2013, pg. 200-208

A Guide to the Project Management Body of Knowledge (PMBOK® Guide) – Fifth Edition, Project Management Institute (PMI)®, Project Management Professional (PMP)®, and Certified Associate in Project Management (CAPM)® are registered trademarks of Project Management Institute, Inc. - Version 2.1 Published September 30, 2014

Lesson 7: Planning Project Budget, Quality, and Communications | *Topic B*

ACTIVITY 7-1
Estimating Project Costs

Scenario

As the project manager for the home build project, your next task is to order doors for the house. On previous projects, an external door cost $200 and an internal door cost $100. There are two external doors on the house and eight internal doors. The two external doors have been donated. Estimate the costs for the doors for the home build project.

---

1. Use analogous estimating to calculate the cost of the doors for this house.

2. What basis of estimate documentation would you provide to show how you obtained your cost estimate for all the doors?

3. How does the project WBS help you when estimating costs for your project?

4. What are the benefits of the parametric modeling technique?

TOPIC C

Determine the Project Budget

After estimating project costs, you need to consolidate the costs into a project budget and prepare the project cost baseline. In this topic, you will determine the budget for your project.

A Guide to the Project Management Body of Knowledge (PMBOK® Guide) – Fifth Edition, Project Management Institute, Inc., 2013, pg. 208-209

The following data flow diagram illustrates how the Determine a Budget process relates to the other knowledge areas within the Planning Process Group.

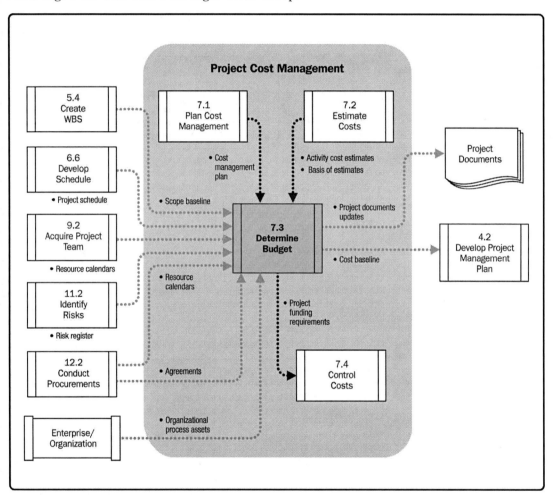

Figure 7–5: The Determine a Budget data flow diagram.

A Guide to the Project Management Body of Knowledge (PMBOK® Guide) – Fifth Edition, Project Management Institute, Inc., 2013, p. 209

Cost Baselines

A *cost baseline* is a time-phased budget that will be used to monitor and measure cost performance throughout the project life cycle. It is developed by adding the estimated costs of project components by period. The cost baseline typically includes a budget contingency to accommodate the risk of incurring identifiable, but not normally occurring, costs within the defined scope. Cost baselines will vary from project to project, depending on each project's unique budget and schedule.

Note: Once the baseline is established, the cost becomes a commitment from the project manager's perspective. The project manager should try to closely match the project's committed funds to the baseline, from a timing perspective.

A Guide to the Project Management Body of Knowledge (PMBOK® Guide) – Fifth Edition, Project Management Institute, Inc., 2013, p. 212

The Determine a Budget Process

To create a budget, we take all the individual activity cost estimates and aggregate them for the entire project to produce a baseline for cost for our project. This budget contains all the funding needed to complete the project as scoped and within the schedule. The project cost performance is then measured against this baseline.

A Guide to the Project Management Body of Knowledge (PMBOK® Guide) – Fifth Edition, Project Management Institute, Inc., 2013, pg. 208-209

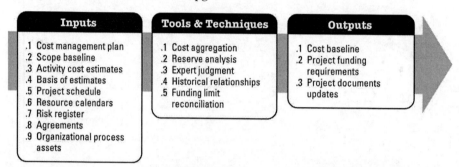

Figure 7-6: Determine a Budget process.

A Guide to the Project Management Body of Knowledge (PMBOK® Guide) – Fifth Edition, Project Management Institute, Inc., 2013, p. 208

Determine a Budget Inputs

Various components provide input to the Determine a Budget process.

Input	Description
Cost management plan	Provides information on how the costs will be managed and controlled.
Scope baseline	Provides the project scope statement, WBS, and WBS dictionary.
Activity cost estimates	Provides cost estimates for each activity or work package.
Basis of estimates	Provides supporting detail and assumptions for the cost estimates.
Project schedule	Provides planned start and finish dates for activities.
Resource calendars	Provides resource assignment and time frame for that assignment.
Risk register	Provides risks with risk response costs.
Agreements	Provides costs for purchasing products, services, or results.
Organizational process assets	Organizational process assets that influence this process include cost budgeting policies, procedures and guidelines, cost budgeting tools and reporting methods.

A Guide to the Project Management Body of Knowledge (PMBOK® Guide) – Fifth Edition, Project Management Institute (PMI)®, Project Management Professional (PMP)®, and Certified Associate in Project Management (CAPM)® are registered trademarks of Project Management Institute, Inc. - Version 2.1 Published September 30, 2014

Lesson 7: Planning Project Budget, Quality, and Communications | Topic C

A Guide to the Project Management Body of Knowledge (PMBOK® Guide) – Fifth Edition, Project Management Institute, Inc., 2013, pg. 209-211

Determine a Budget Tools and Techniques

There are five tools and techniques used in the Determine a Budget process.

Tools & Techniques	Description
Cost aggregation	*Cost aggregation* combines each activity cost within a work package, which are then aggregated up the WBS until a single project cost is produced.
Reserve analysis	Provides analysis to determine the contingency reserves and the management reserve estimates for risks.
Expert judgment	Expert judgment, along with cost estimate and budgeting experience, can be used to guide cost estimates.
Historical relationships	Involves relationships that result in parametric or analogous estimates, which use project parameters to develop simple or complex mathematical models to calculate project costs. The cost and accuracy of the parametric and analogous estimates will vary widely. They can be relied upon when the historical information used is accurate, parameters used are quantifiable, and when the models are scalable to be used for big or small projects or even in phases of a project.
Funding limit reconciliation	Perform funding limit reconciliation if there are existing funding limits set by the organization or customer as the budget must be mapped accordingly.

A Guide to the Project Management Body of Knowledge (PMBOK® Guide) – Fifth Edition, Project Management Institute, Inc., 2013, pg. 211-212

Funding Limit Reconciliation

Funding limit reconciliation is a method of adjusting, spending, scheduling, and resource allocation in order to bring expenditures into alignment with budgetary constraints. Most budgets are created on the premise of steady incoming and outgoing flows. Large, sporadic expenditures are usually incompatible with organizational operations. Therefore, funding limits are often in place to regulate the outgoing capital flow and to protect against over-spending. Budgets must be reconciled with such limits. This will affect the scheduling of project work and possibly reshuffle WBS work packages entirely. The schedule, in turn, can affect the distribution or acquisition of resources.

For example, customers set funding limits for large projects based on internal considerations such as when their fiscal years begin and end, and how healthy their cash flows are. A customer who wants to spread the costs of a project over two quarters might authorize $250,000 in spending during Quarter 1 and $350,000 during Quarter 2. In response, the project manager would need to align the resources, schedules, and activities so that the project work does not exceed those limits on funding.

A Guide to the Project Management Body of Knowledge (PMBOK® Guide) – Fifth Edition, Project Management Institute, Inc., 2013, p. 212

Determine a Budget Outputs

There are three outputs from the Determine a Budget process.

Output	Description
Cost baseline	The cost baseline is the approved cost for the project, excluding management reserves. This can be changed only through the change control process.
Project funding requirements	*Project funding requirements* state how a project will be funded. Created from the cost baseline, these are built-in cost increments that will allow for overruns and/or rapid progress on the project. It includes the cost baseline and the management reserves. It defines how funds will be allocated to the project over time, such as quarterly, annually, and so on, to show the cash flow to enable the project to progress.
Project documents updates	Project documents that may need updating include the risk register, activity cost estimates, and the project schedule.

A Guide to the Project Management Body of Knowledge (PMBOK® Guide) – Fifth Edition, Project Management Institute, Inc., 2013, pg. 212-214

Guidelines to Determine a Budget

To determine a project budget effectively:

- Review the cost management plan for information on how project costs will be managed and controlled, and the method used and level of accuracy for estimating activity cost.
- Review the human resource management plan for staffing attributes, personnel rates, and reward and recognition information.
- Review the scope baseline for the project scope statement, WBS, and WBS dictionary.
- Check the project schedule for type, quantity, and duration of resources needed for project activities.
- Review the risk register to consider any risks that may impact cost estimation.
- Review the organizational process assets that can influence this process such as cost estimating policies, cost estimating template, historical information, and lessons learned.
- Use tools and techniques such as cost aggregation, reserve analysis, expert judgment, historical relationships, and funding limit reconciliation to determine a budget for the project.
- Document the project budget, creating a cost baseline.
- Understand project funding requirements. This includes ensuring that project expenses are not incurred faster than project income is received.
- Update project documents, as needed.

A Guide to the Project Management Body of Knowledge (PMBOK® Guide) – Fifth Edition, Project Management Institute, Inc., 2013, pg. 208-214

ACTIVITY 7-2
Creating a Partial Budget

Scenario

You have been asked to create part of a budget for the framing work package by using the costs that you estimated in the previous process. Because the materials need to be ordered a few weeks ahead of time, the project sponsor needs to know what the budget will be for this work package before the materials are ordered. You already have the following information gathered to determine the budget:

- Framing takes 10 days and site supervisor rate is $20/hour
- Plywood: 66 sheets at $15 per sheet
- 2×4 lumber: 150 boards at $6.50 per board
- 30 pounds of nails at $5 per pound

900

990 9

Use information provided for the framing work package to determine the actual costs of the materials and the supervisor resource.

1600
990
975
150

3715

TOPIC D

Plan Quality Management

You developed your project schedule and planned the project costs; you have two of the project constraints for success, and quality is the next. In this topic, you'll focus on quality. You will create a quality management plan. It is important to plan for the quality aspect up front so that the deliverables of the project meet the stakeholders' quality expectations.

A Guide to the Project Management Body of Knowledge (PMBOK® Guide) – Fifth Edition, Project Management Institute, Inc., 2013, pg. 231-233

The following data flow diagram illustrates how the Plan Quality Management process relates to the other project management processes.

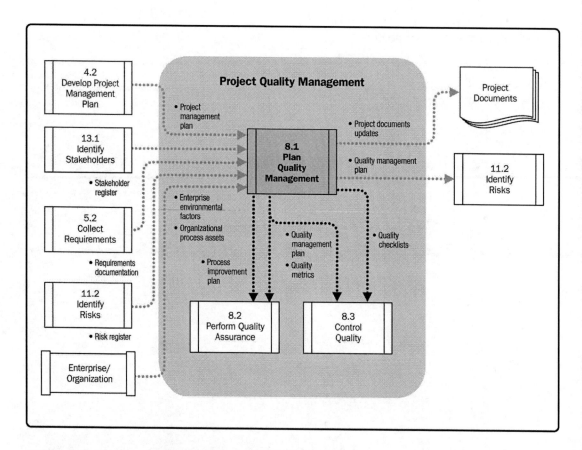

Figure 7-7: The Plan Quality Management data flow diagram.

A Guide to the Project Management Body of Knowledge (PMBOK® Guide) – Fifth Edition, Project Management Institute, Inc., 2013, p. 232

What Is Quality?

Quality is defined as the "totality of features and characteristics of a product or services that bear on its ability to satisfy stated or implied needs," in the *PMBOK® Guide.* In business, quality should be feasible, modifiable, and measurable. In order for a project to meet expectations on the quality of its project work and deliverables, the quality standards that need to be met must be managed throughout the life of the project. Quality policies and procedures that will be used on the project need to be planned at the beginning of the project and managed and controlled throughout the

A Guide to the Project Management Body of Knowledge (PMBOK® Guide) – Fifth Edition, Project Management Institute (PMI)®, Project Management Professional (PMP)®, and Certified Associate in Project Management (CAPM)® are registered trademarks of Project Management Institute, Inc. - Version 2.1 Published September 30, 2014

Lesson 7: Planning Project Budget, Quality, and Communications | Topic D

project by using the organization's quality management system. Continuous process improvement activities also need to be considered for the benefit of the project.

 Note: This definition is provided by the International Organization for Standardization, ISO Standard 8402: Terms and Definitions.

The *PMBOK® Guide* quality management guidelines are compatible with International Organization for Standards (ISO). Important aspects of ISO include:

- Customer satisfaction
- Prevention over inspection
- Continuous improvement
- Management responsibility
- Cost of Quality (COQ)

A Guide to the Project Management Body of Knowledge (PMBOK® Guide) – Fifth Edition, Project Management Institute, Inc., 2013, pg. 227-229

Standards and Regulations

Standards are voluntary guidelines or characteristics that have been approved by a recognized body of experts such as the International Organization for Standardization (ISO). In some cases, the standards body will provide certification that suppliers conform to the requirements of their standards. Often, the conformance to standards is a customer requirement.

Regulations are compliance-mandatory characteristics for specific products, services, or processes. Standards often start out as accepted or de facto best practices describing a preferred approach, and may later become de jure regulations, such as using the critical path method in scheduling major construction projects.

A Guide to the Project Management Body of Knowledge (PMBOK® Guide) – Fifth Edition, Project Management Institute, Inc., 2013, pg. 557, 563

The ISO 9000 Series

The *ISO 9000 Series* is a quality system standard that is applicable to any product, service, or process in the world. It was developed by ISO, which is a consortium of approximately 100 of the world's industrial nations. There are limits to the certification, which does not guarantee that an organization will produce high-quality products or services; it simply confirms that appropriate systems are in place. Subsections of the standard address particular industries or products.

A Guide to the Project Management Body of Knowledge (PMBOK® Guide) – Fifth Edition, Project Management Institute, Inc., 2013, pg. 228, 418

What Is a Quality Management Plan?

A *quality management plan* is another subsidiary plan of the project management plan. It documents and defines how the organization's quality policies and processes will be implemented for the project, how the project's quality requirements will be met, and how the quality aspect of the project will be managed. Quality requirements and standards need to be gathered and documented for both the project and its deliverables. How the project will demonstrate that the quality requirements and standards have been met and how that will be validated will also need to be determined and documented.

A Guide to the Project Management Body of Knowledge (PMBOK® Guide) – Fifth Edition, Project Management Institute (PMI)®, Project Management Professional (PMP)®, and Certified Associate in Project Management (CAPM)® are registered trademarks of Project Management Institute, Inc. - Version 2.1 Published September 30, 2014

Lesson 7: Planning Project Budget, Quality, and Communications | Topic D

QUALITY MANAGEMENT PLAN
HOMES R US SMITH FAMILY HOUSE PROJECT

INTRODUCTION

The Quality Management Plan for the Smith Family House project will establish the activities, processes, and procedures for ensuring a quality product upon the conclusion of the project.

QUALITY MANAGEMENT APPROACH

This section describes the approach the organization will use for managing quality throughout the project's life cycle.

QUALITY REQUIREMENTS / STANDARDS

This section should describe how the project team and/or quality group will identify and document the quality requirements and standards. Additionally, there should also be an explanation of how the project will demonstrate compliance with those identified quality standards. The quality standards and requirements should include both the product and processes.

QUALITY ASSURANCE

This section should explain how you will define and document the process for auditing the quality requirements and results from quality control measurements in order to ensure that quality standards and operational definitions are used. This section should also document the actual quality assurance metrics used for this project.

Figure 7–8: A sample quality management plan.

A Guide to the Project Management Body of Knowledge (PMBOK® Guide) – Fifth Edition, Project Management Institute, Inc., 2013, p. 241

The Plan Quality Management Process

The *Plan Quality Management process* involves developing a quality management plan to identify the quality requirements for the project process and its deliverables and to plan how to achieve compliance of these requirements. Quality needs to be managed and validated throughout the life of a project. Quality is a very broad topic that covers all aspects of a project and product.

A Guide to the Project Management Body of Knowledge (PMBOK® Guide) – Fifth Edition, Project Management Institute, Inc., 2013, pg. 231-233

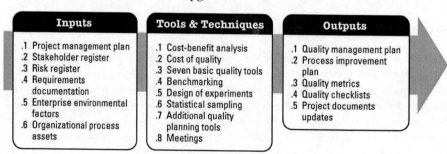

Figure 7–9: The Plan Quality Management process.

A Guide to the Project Management Body of Knowledge (PMBOK® Guide) – Fifth Edition, Project Management Institute, Inc., 2013, p. 232

Plan Quality Management Inputs

Various components provide input to the Plan Quality Management process.

Input	Description
Project management plan	Provides the scope, cost, and schedule baseline information and subsidiary plans on which the project is based.
Stakeholder register	Documents the stakeholders who may have an interest in or impact on the quality of the project.
Risk register	Documents the risks that may have an impact on the quality requirements.
Requirements documentation	Documents the project requirements, including the quality requirements or expectations.
Enterprise environmental factors	Enterprise environmental factors that can influence this process include governmental agency regulations, application-specific rules, standards and guidelines, working or operating conditions, and cultural perceptions.
Organizational process assets	Organizational process assets that can influence this process include organizational quality policies, procedures and guidelines, historical information, and lessons learned.

A Guide to the Project Management Body of Knowledge (PMBOK® Guide) – Fifth Edition, Project Management Institute, Inc., 2013, pg. 233-234

Plan Quality Management Tools and Techniques

There are numerous tools and techniques used in the Plan Quality Management process.

Tools & Techniques	Description
Cost-benefit analysis	*Cost-benefit analysis* considers the trade-offs and the benefit of meeting quality requirements of higher productivity and lower costs while increasing stakeholder satisfaction. The business case of each activity is used to compare the cost of each step with its expected benefits.
Cost of Quality (COQ)	Costs incurred by preventing non-conformance to requirements, appraising for conformance to requirements, and failing to meet requirements (rework), internal or external.
Seven basic quality tools	A standardized toolkit that can be used to plan, monitor, control, and manage quality of a project.
Benchmarking	Benchmarking evaluates the project practices against other projects to determine best practices, areas of improvement, and a basis for measuring performance.
Design of Experiments	*Design of Experiments (DOE)* is a statistical method of identifying the factors that may influence certain product or process variables. During quality planning, DOE determines the number and type of tests to be used and their influence on the cost of quality.
Statistical sampling	*Statistical sampling* is a tool that selects a subset of a population for inspection that is representative of the whole population. Used to measure an entire population by studying a randomly selected part of the population.

Tools & Techniques	Description
Additional quality planning tools	Additional quality planning tools include: • Brainstorming to generate ideas • Force field analysis, which diagrams the forces for and against change • Nominal group technique, where ideas brainstormed in small groups are reviewed by a larger group • Quality management and control tools used to link and sequence activities
Meetings	Meetings are held to develop the quality management plan and can include the project manager, and selected team members and stakeholders.

A Guide to the Project Management Body of Knowledge (PMBOK® Guide) – Fifth Edition, Project Management Institute, Inc., 2013, pg. 235-241

COQ

Cost of quality (COQ) refers to the total cost of effort needed to achieve an acceptable level of quality in the project's product or service. Those costs include all the work necessary to ensure conformance and all the work performed as a result of non-conformance to requirements.

Cost of conformance is the money spent during a project to avoid failures and includes prevention costs that build a high-quality product, and appraisal costs that assess the quality. Examples of prevention costs include training, doing things right the first time, and following documented processes. Appraisal costs include testing and inspection.

Cost of non-conformance is the money spent after a project is complete because of failures and includes internal and external failure costs. Internal failures found during the project include rework and scrap. External failures found by the customer include liabilities, warranty work, and lost business due to a poor-quality product or damaged reputation.

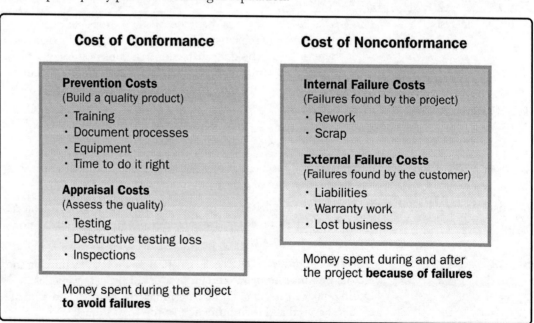

Figure 7-10: COQ areas of consideration.

A Guide to the Project Management Body of Knowledge (PMBOK® Guide) – Fifth Edition, Project Management Institute (PMI)®, Project Management Professional (PMP)®, and Certified Associate in Project Management (CAPM)® are registered trademarks of Project Management Institute, Inc. - Version 2.1 Published September 30, 2014

Lesson 7: Planning Project Budget, Quality, and Communications | Topic D

A Guide to the Project Management Body of Knowledge (PMBOK® Guide) – Fifth Edition, Project Management Institute, Inc., 2013, pg. 229, 235

Types of Cost

The four types of cost associated with quality are prevention costs, appraisal costs, internal failure costs, and external failure costs. Prevention and appraisal costs are called conformance costs—amount spent to avoid failures. Internal and external failure costs are called non-conformance costs—amount spent to rectify errors.

Type of Cost	Description	Example
Prevention costs	The up-front costs of programs or processes needed to meet customer requirements, or to design in quality.	• Design plans • Quality plans • Employee and customer training • Process evaluations and improvements • Vendor surveys • Other related preventive activities
Appraisal costs	The costs associated with evaluating whether the programs or processes meet requirements.	• Inspections • Testing • Design reviews • Destructive testing loss
Internal failure costs	The costs associated with making the product or service acceptable to the customer after it fails internal testing and before it's delivered to the customer.	• Scrap or rejects • Design flaws • Rework or repair • Defect evaluation
External failure costs	The costs resulting from rejection of the product or service by the customer.	• Product returns • Liabilities • Evaluation of customer complaints • Maintenance costs • Corrective action • Loss of contract

The Seven Basic Quality Tools

The seven basic quality tools, also known as 7QC in the industry, can be used to troubleshoot and resolve issues that arise with a project's quality management.

Tool	Description
Cause and effect diagrams	Also known as Ishikawa or fishbone diagrams, is a diagramming method that places the potential problem to be worked out at the "head of the fish" as a starting point. Then, the "fish bones" are used to work back to the source of the problem until the root cause is clearly identified.
Flowcharts	Also referred to as process maps, flowcharts display the sequence of steps and branching options for a process that transforms a project's inputs to outputs. It is used to document the flow of the process.

A Guide to the Project Management Body of Knowledge (PMBOK® Guide) – Fifth Edition, Project Management Institute (PMI)®, Project Management Professional (PMP)®, and Certified Associate in Project Management (CAPM)® are registered trademarks of Project Management Institute, Inc. - Version 2.1 Published September 30, 2014

Lesson 7: Planning Project Budget, Quality, and Communications | Topic D

Tool	Description
Checksheets	Also known as tally sheets, can be used as a checklist to organize information to collect attribute data while performing inspections. For example, data about the root cause of defects could be collected for analysis.
Pareto diagrams	Vertical bar charts that are used to display the frequency of observations, for example, the frequency of root causes of defects.
Histograms	Bar charts that describe the central tendency, dispersion, and shape of a statistical distribution.
Control charts	Used to determine if a process is stable or predictable by using upper and lower specification limits and control limits.
Scatter diagrams	Also referred to as correlation charts, are used to plot pairs (x,y) to evaluate the correlation between these two variables. A regression line can estimate how the change in one value will influence the value of the other variable.

A Guide to the Project Management Body236 of Knowledge (PMBOK® Guide) – Fifth Edition, Project Management Institute, Inc., 2013, pg. 235-238

DOE

Design of experiments (DOE) is a statistical tool for determining which factors influence a specific variable in a process or product. For example, engineers use this tool to evaluate which combination of times and suspension provides the smoothest ride within a reasonable cost.

DOE can determine:

- Which variable has the greatest effect.
- What the relationship is between each variable and the customer-focused quality specifications.
- What the best value is for each variable, ensuring optimal quality or value.

When done properly, DOE can result in significant improvements to products and processes, including shorter development cycles, more robust products, and cost reductions.

A Guide to the Project Management Body of Knowledge (PMBOK® Guide) – Fifth Edition, Project Management Institute, Inc., 2013, pg. 239-240

Additional Quality Planning Tools

There are also some additional quality planning tools that can be helpful when planning for quality management. These include:

- Brainstorming to generate ideas
- Force field analysis, which diagrams the forces for and against change
- Nominal group technique, where ideas brainstormed in small groups are reviewed by a larger group
- Quality management and control tools used to link and sequence activities

A Guide to the Project Management Body of Knowledge (PMBOK® Guide) – Fifth Edition, Project Management Institute, Inc., 2013, p. 240

Plan Quality Management Outputs

There are four outputs from the Plan Quality Management process.

Output	Description
Quality management plan	Describes the project management team's approach to implementing the quality policy.
Process improvement plan	Describes the project management team's approach to identify unnecessary activity, including process boundaries indicating all aspects of a process, process configuration flowcharting, process interfaces, metrics for process control, and improvement guidelines.
Quality metrics	Specifically describes what something is and how the quality control process measures it.
Quality checklists	Job aids that prompt employees to perform activities according to a consistent standard.
Project documents updates	Documents that may be updated include quality standards, agreements, quality audit logs and change reports, training plans, and process documentation.

A Guide to the Project Management Body of Knowledge (PMBOK® Guide) – Fifth Edition, Project Management Institute, Inc., 2013, pg. 241-242

Process Improvement Plan

The *process improvement plan* is also a subsidiary plan of the project management plan. It documents the steps to take a look at the project management processes and the product development processes in order to identify ways to enhance their value to the project and the organization.

Initiation	Assessment	Design			Implementation	
(1) Select the Process	**(2) Understand** Current Process	**(3)** Create Process Vision	**(4)** Design the New Process	**(5)** Determine Organizational Changes to Support New Process	**(6)** Plan Implemen- tation	**(7)** Implement
• Importance • Scope	• Process Mapping • Process Outcomes - Time - Quality - Costs - Service • Process Rules • Case for Action	• Performance Targets • Design Criteria • Benchmarks /Best Practice	• Process Redesign • Scenarios	• Structure & Jobs • Rewards & Measures • Technology • Organizational Culture • HR Processes • Renewal	• Timing • Get Ready • Resources	• Prototype • Pilot • Rollout

Figure 7-11: A sample process improvement plan.

Areas to consider for process improvement include:

- Process boundaries describing the purpose of the process, the beginning and end of a process, the inputs and outputs, and the owner and stakeholders of a process.
- Process configuration, which is a picture of the process and its interfaces.
- Process metrics such as control limits to analyze process efficiency.
- Targets for improved performance to guide process improvement activities.

A Guide to the Project Management Body of Knowledge (PMBOK® Guide) – Fifth Edition, Project Management Institute, Inc., 2013, p. 241

Process Improvement Planning

Process improvement planning is the process of analyzing and identifying areas of improvement in project processes and enumerating an action plan based on the project goals and identified issues. The process involves:

- Describing operational theories and project roles and responsibilities
- Identifying long- and short-term goals
- Describing process improvement objectives and activities
- Identifying risks and resource requirements
- Determining process improvement activities
- Creating a process improvement plan
- Receiving approval from stakeholders and senior managers
- Executing the process improvement plan

A Guide to the Project Management Body of Knowledge (PMBOK® Guide) – Fifth Edition, Project Management Institute, Inc., 2013, pg. 241, 244, 552

Quality Metrics and Checklists

A *quality metric* describes a project attribute and how it will be measured. The tolerance is the allowable variation in this measurement. For example, a quality metric on the schedule could say that the schedule is to stay within +10 percent and –10 percent of the actual schedule. When the measurement falls outside this range, action needs to be taken. Other examples of quality metrics include budget variance, defect count, requirements coverage, and failure rate.

Quality checklists are used to confirm that a set of steps has been performed. An organization may have standard checklists that could be simple or complex depending on their purpose. Checklists can be simple or complex and may range in detail depending on the experience and skill level of the employees and the complexity of the situation.

A Guide to the Project Management Body of Knowledge (PMBOK® Guide) – Fifth Edition, Project Management Institute, Inc., 2013, p. 242

Guidelines to Plan Quality Management

Creating a quality management plan will ensure that the organizational structure, responsibilities, procedures, processes, and resources are in place to implement quality management. Guidelines to developing a quality management plan are as follows:

- Review the organization's quality policy and determine how your project team will implement the policy.
  - How will your team identify potential quality problems and their potential impact on the quality of the project's product, service, systems, or processes? Will you use particular flowcharting methods, benchmarking, design of experiments, or other techniques?
  - Are there any standards and regulations that are applicable to your project?
  - Are there any activities or components that require the development of operational definitions to provide a common understanding of the project's quality standards? If so, who is responsible for developing them?
  - Does your organization have any standard checklists that can be modified, or used as is, to prompt employees to perform certain activities according to a specific quality standard? If not, should checklists be developed? Who is responsible for developing them? What are the conditions under which they should be developed?
- Review the product description to identify customer/stakeholder quality requirements.
- Determine the cost of quality trade-offs.
  - How will your team "design in" quality to avoid expensive rework to bring the quality back into conformance?

- Are the proposed processes and systems worth the cost of implementing them?
- Use these tools and techniques to develop the quality management plan:
  - Cost-benefit analysis
  - Cost of quality
  - The seven basic quality tools
  - Benchmarking
  - Design of experiments
  - Statistical sampling
  - Meetings
- Document the outputs of this process:
  - Quality management plan
  - Process improvement plan
  - Quality metrics
  - Quality checklists
  - Updates to other project documents as needed.
- Review the quality management plan and make sure it:
  - Describes the project management team's approach to implementing its quality policy (quality assurance, quality control, and quality improvement approaches).
  - Describes the resources required to implement quality management.
  - Includes quality management roles and responsibilities for the project.
  - Is as detailed and formal as required, based on the quality needs of the project.
  - Includes how customer satisfaction will be measured and managed.

A Guide to the Project Management Body of Knowledge (PMBOK® Guide) – Fifth Edition, Project Management Institute, Inc., 2013, pg. 231-242

A Guide to the Project Management Body of Knowledge (PMBOK® Guide) – Fifth Edition, Project Management Institute (PMI)®, Project Management Professional (PMP)®, and Certified Associate in Project Management (CAPM)® are registered trademarks of Project Management Institute, Inc. - Version 2.1 Published September 30, 2014

Lesson 7: Planning Project Budget, Quality, and Communications | *Topic D*

ACTIVITY 7-3
Examining Quality Management

Scenario

Every project for Building with Heart must comply with the Greene City building regulations including:

- Building code inspection
- Plumbing inspection
- Certificate of occupancy
- Grounds inspection for contaminants
- Electrical inspection

Dave Fullerton is the city building inspector and he will be scheduled to come to the site to conduct a full inspection.

---

1. What are some of the costs of quality?

2. How can you prevent some of these costs to avoid exceeding your budget?

3. Which of the following seven basic quality tools should you use to identify a root cause of a quality issue?

- ⊘ Fishbone diagram
- ○ Checksheet
- ○ Histogram
- ○ Pareto diagram

4. Which two of the following are costs of conformance to ensure quality?

- ☑ Prevention costs
- ☑ Appraisal costs
- ☐ Failure costs
- ☐ Warranties

TOPIC E

Plan Human Resource Management

Now that you have created a quality management plan for your project and put plans into place to ensure that standards for quality will be met and measured, you are ready to move forward with the next element of good planning, which is documenting how people on your project will be managed. In this topic, you will plan for the management of the people who work on a project team.

A Guide to the Project Management Body of Knowledge (PMBOK® Guide) – Fifth Edition, Project Management Institute, Inc., 2013, pg. 258-259

The following data flow diagram illustrates how the Plan Human Resource Management process relates to the other project management processes.

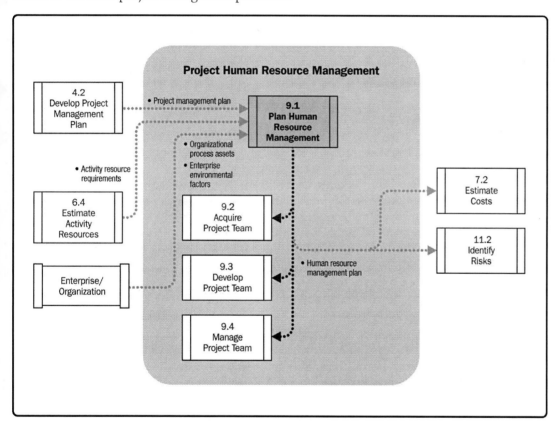

Figure 7-12: The Plan Human Resource Management data flow diagram.

A Guide to the Project Management Body of Knowledge (PMBOK® Guide) – Fifth Edition, Project Management Institute, Inc., 2013, p. 258

What Is Human Resource Management?

Human resource management contains the processes to organize, manage, and lead the people on the project team. These people have skills and may be assigned to the project part or full-time at different times in the project life cycle. They have specific assigned roles and responsibilities on the project. By carefully orchestrating the roles and responsibilities of everyone involved on your project, and making sure that those relationships are documented, you will effectively ensure that everyone on the project has a clear understanding of their duties. This will help eliminate confusion and misunderstandings throughout the life cycle of the project, and will help everyone feel that they are part of a smoothly running operation.

A Guide to the Project Management Body of Knowledge (PMBOK® Guide) – Fifth Edition, Project Management Institute, Inc., 2013, pg. 255-259

What Is a Human Resource Management Plan?

The *human resource management plan* is a subsidiary plan of the project management plan that defines project roles, responsibilities, required skills, reporting relationships, and a staff management plan for the project.

A Guide to the Project Management Body of Knowledge (PMBOK® Guide) – Fifth Edition, Project Management Institute, Inc., 2013, pg. 258-259

Staff Management Plan

A *staff management plan* is a component of the human resource management plan and forecasts what types of staff will work on the project, when they will be needed, how they will be recruited onto the project, and when they will be released from the project. Depending upon the project requirements, the staffing management plan may be formal or informal, exhaustive or brief. The plan is a subsidiary plan to the human resource plan and is an important input to the develop human resource plan process.

There are several components of the staffing management plan that will continue to evolve as you develop the project plan.

- **Staff acquisition:** when planning resources, consider whether you will use team members from within the organization or from external sources, the costs associated with the level of expertise required for the project, physical location of resources, and the amount of assistance that can be provided by other departments for the project management team.
- **Resource calendars:** the staffing management plan details the time frame required for a project and for each project team member. Optimizing the use of people on a project will help finish the project on time and within budget. Use of human resource charting tools, such as resource histograms, can help illustrate the number of hours that a person, department, or entire project team will be needed for each week or month over the course of the project.
- **Staff release plan:** developing a plan for releasing resources helps control project costs by using team members' expertise or skills as and when they are needed. Planning for release also allows for a smooth transition to other projects and mitigation of human resource risks that may occur during the final phases of the project.
- **Training needs:** a training plan can be developed for team members who need to improve their competency levels or who may need to obtain certifications that will benefit the project.
- **Recognition and rewards:** creating incentives for meeting milestones or other project deliverables can have a positive effect on morale. An effective recognition plan rewards team members for meeting goals that are under their control.
- **Compliance:** if the contract requires compliance with government regulation, contracts, or other standards, this should be stipulated in the staffing management plan.
- **Safety Projects:** performed where specific safety precautions must be taken, for example, construction sites or nuclear power plants can have documented policies and procedures for the protection of team members. These procedures should also be documented in the risk register.

A Guide to the Project Management Body of Knowledge (PMBOK® Guide) – Fifth Edition, Project Management Institute, Inc., 2013, pg. 265-267

The Plan Human Resource Management Process

The *plan human resource management process* identifies and documents the peoples' roles, responsibilities, necessary skills, and reporting relationships, and creates a staffing plan for the project. The staffing plan includes the schedule for each person's start and end time on the project.

A Guide to the Project Management Body of Knowledge (PMBOK® Guide) – Fifth Edition, Project Management Institute, Inc., 2013, pg. 258-259

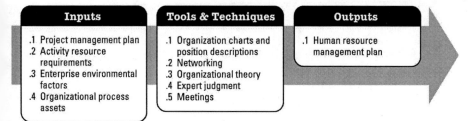

Figure 7-13: The Plan Human Resource Management process.

A Guide to the Project Management Body of Knowledge (PMBOK® Guide) – Fifth Edition, Project Management Institute, Inc., 2013, p. 258

Plan Human Resource Management Inputs

Various components provide input to the Plan Human Resource Management process.

Input	Description
Project management plan	Provides information on the project life cycle, how work will be executed, how changes will be monitored and controlled, how configuration will be performed, how integrity of the project baselines will be maintained, and how stakeholders communication needs will be met.
Activity resource requirements (an output of 6.4)	Activity resource requirements will provide a list of the required people and competencies necessary for each activity, which will be progressively elaborated when developing the human resource plan.
Enterprise environmental factors	Enterprise environmental factors that can influence this process include organizational culture and structure, existing human resources and their locations, personnel administration policies, and marketplace conditions.
Organizational process assets	Organizational process assets that can influence this process include organizational processes, policies, and role descriptions, templates, lessons learned, and escalation procedures for team issues.

A Guide to the Project Management Body of Knowledge (PMBOK® Guide) – Fifth Edition, Project Management Institute, Inc., 2013, pg. 259-260

Plan Human Resource Management Tools and Techniques

There are five tools and techniques used in the Plan Human Resource Management process.

Tools & Techniques	Description
Organization charts and position descriptions	Document team members' roles and responsibilities by using hierarchical, matrix, and text-oriented formats so each work package has a clear owner and each team member understands his or her role. Subsidiary project plans may list resource roles as well.
Networking	Networking involves formal and informal interactions, such as correspondence, meetings, and conversations. Networking tools are used to understand how interpersonal factors affect staffing options. Networking also enhances the professional project management practices of a project manager at different phases of a project.

A Guide to the Project Management Body of Knowledge (PMBOK® Guide) – Fifth Edition, Project Management Institute (PMI)®, Project Management Professional (PMP)®, and Certified Associate in Project Management (CAPM)® are registered trademarks of Project Management Institute, Inc. - Version 2.1 Published September 30, 2014

Lesson 7: Planning Project Budget, Quality, and Communications | Topic E

Tools & Techniques	Description
Organizational theory	Organizational theory provides information on the organization of work processes through, among other things, organizational structure, power, culture, and behavior of people. The project manager must understand how different organizational structures influence human resources differently.
Expert judgment	Expert judgment is used to list requirements for skills; assess required roles; determine effort level, number of resources, reporting relationships, and guidelines for staffing lead time; identify risks; and identify any compliance requirements for the project.
Meetings	Meetings are held to plan the management of the human resources for the project.

A Guide to the Project Management Body of Knowledge (PMBOK® Guide) – Fifth Edition, Project Management Institute, Inc., 2013, pg. 261-264

Organization Charts and Position Descriptions

Organization charts and position descriptions are used to document the team members' roles and responsibilities on the project. There are three types of charts: hierarchical, matrix, and text-oriented. The goal is to ensure that each work package has a specific owner and that the team members clearly understand their roles and responsibilities.

A Guide to the Project Management Body of Knowledge (PMBOK® Guide) – Fifth Edition, Project Management Institute, Inc., 2013, p. 261

Hierarchical-Type Charts

Hierarchical charts are a top-down format. They use the WBS as the structure for the work assignments and the organizational breakdown structure (OBS) to coordinate the work assignments to people.

A Guide to the Project Management Body of Knowledge (PMBOK® Guide) – Fifth Edition, Project Management Institute, Inc., 2013, p. 261

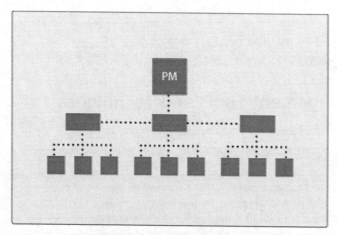

Organization Chart (Hierarchical)

Figure 7-14: A sample hierarchical chart.

A Guide to the Project Management Body of Knowledge (PMBOK® Guide) – Fifth Edition, Project Management Institute, Inc., 2013, p. 261

Matrix Charts

A matrix chart, or responsibility assignment matrix (RAM), is a grid format that shows the connection between each work package or activity and the project team member who is assigned to that work.

A Guide to the Project Management Body of Knowledge (PMBOK® Guide) – Fifth Edition, Project Management Institute, Inc., 2013, p. 262

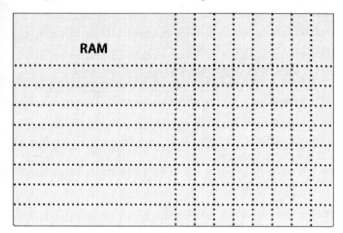

Responsibility Chart (matrix)

Figure 7-15: A sample matrix chart.

A Guide to the Project Management Body of Knowledge (PMBOK® Guide) – Fifth Edition, Project Management Institute, Inc., 2013, p. 261

Text Formats

Text formats are written in an outline form and are also called position descriptions. They are in paragraph form.

A Guide to the Project Management Body of Knowledge (PMBOK® Guide) – Fifth Edition, Project Management Institute, Inc., 2013, p. 262

Role ....

Responsibilities ....

Authority ....

Role Description (text)

Figure 7-16: A sample text format.

A Guide to the Project Management Body of Knowledge (PMBOK® Guide) – Fifth Edition, Project Management Institute, Inc., 2013, p. 261

A Guide to the Project Management Body of Knowledge (PMBOK® Guide) – Fifth Edition, Project Management Institute (PMI)®, Project Management Professional (PMP)®, and Certified Associate in Project Management (CAPM)® are registered trademarks of Project Management Institute, Inc. - Version 2.1 Published September 30, 2014

Lesson 7: Planning Project Budget, Quality, and Communications | Topic E

Networking

Networking is the interaction between people to expand their knowledge about business topics. It can take place in an organization, industry, or professional environment. Networking activities include professional organization events, such as PMI conferences, symposiums, lunch meetings, and more.

A Guide to the Project Management Body of Knowledge (PMBOK® Guide) – Fifth Edition, Project Management Institute, Inc., 2013, p. 263

Organizational Theory

Organizational theory is the study of how people, teams, and organizations behave. It is used to look for common themes for the purpose of maximizing efficiency and productivity, problem solving, and meeting the stakeholder requirements of a project.

A Guide to the Project Management Body of Knowledge (PMBOK® Guide) – Fifth Edition, Project Management Institute, Inc., 2013, p. 263

Plan Human Resource Management Outputs

There is one output from the Plan Human Resource Management process.

Output	Description
Human resource management plan	As stated in the *PMBOK® Guide*, the human resource management plan is a component of the project management plan that describes how the roles and responsibilities, reporting relationships, and staff management will be addressed and structured.

A Guide to the Project Management Body of Knowledge (PMBOK® Guide) – Fifth Edition, Project Management Institute, Inc., 2013, pg. 264-267

Guidelines to Plan Human Resource Management

Guidelines to developing a human resource management plan are as follows:

- Review the project management plan for information on the project life cycle, how work will be executed, how changes will be monitored and controlled, how configuration will be performed, how integrity of the project baselines will be maintained and stakeholders communication needs will be met.
- Review the activity resource requirements for the types and quantities of resources required for each activity in a work package.
- Review the enterprise environmental factors, such as organizational culture and structure, existing human resources and their locations, personnel administration policies, and marketplace conditions.
- Review the organizational process assets such as organizational processes, policies, and role descriptions; templates; lessons learned; and escalation procedures for team issues.
- Use these tools and techniques to develop the human resource management plan:
  - Organization charts and position descriptions
  - Networking
  - Organization theory
  - Expert judgment
  - Meetings
- Create a human resource management plan.

A Guide to the Project Management Body of Knowledge (PMBOK® Guide) – Fifth Edition, Project Management Institute, Inc., 2013, pg. 258-267

A Guide to the Project Management Body of Knowledge (PMBOK® Guide) – Fifth Edition, Project Management Institute (PMI)®, Project Management Professional (PMP)®, and Certified Associate in Project Management (CAPM)® are registered trademarks of Frjěct Management Institute, Inc. - Version 2.1 Published September 30, 2014

Lesson 7: Planning Project Budget, Quality, and Communications | Topic E

ACTIVITY 7–4
Examining Human Resource Management

Scenario

As the project manager for the 122 East Main project, you must plan for managing the various roles that will be working on the project. For the house build, the work packages will include:

- Water and plumbing
- Foundation
- Landscaping
- Quality control inspections
- Electrical wiring
- Windows, doors, siding, and roof

1. Determine what skills are needed for each work package.

2. What method could you use to attain volunteers for the build project?

3. You have reviewed the staffing management plan, and to your surprise, it appears that there are now staffing gaps due to resource reassignments. What could you do to address this problem?

A Guide to the Project Management Body of Knowledge (PMBOK® Guide) – Fifth Edition, Project Management Institute (PMI)®, Project Management Professional (PMP)®, and Certified Associate in Project Management (CAPM)® are registered trademarks of Project Management Institute, Inc. - Version 2.1 Published September 30, 2014

Lesson 7: Planning Project Budget, Quality, and Communications | Topic E

TOPIC F

Plan Communications Management

You determined the roles, responsibilities, and reporting relationships for your project. Now you need to define how you and your project team will communicate with each other. In this topic, you'll put strategies in place to ensure effective communication by creating a communications management plan.

A Guide to the Project Management Body of Knowledge (PMBOK® Guide) – Fifth Edition, Project Management Institute, Inc., 2013, pg. 289-290

The following data flow diagram illustrates how the Plan Communications Management process relates to the other project management processes.

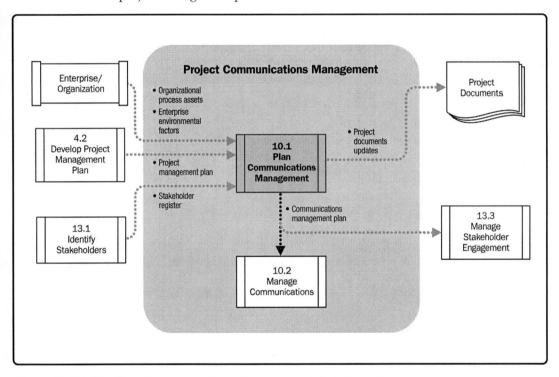

Figure 7–17: The Plan Communications Management data flow diagram.

A Guide to the Project Management Body of Knowledge (PMBOK® Guide) – Fifth Edition, Project Management Institute, Inc., 2013, p. 289

What Is Project Communications Management?

Project managers spend a great deal of their time communicating with the project team members and the project stakeholders. These communications can be internal (project team) and external (customers), formal (memos) or informal (emails and phone calls), vertical and horizontal within the organization, official or unofficial, written, and oral, verbal (tone or inflection) or nonverbal (body language).

Other skills that a project manager needs include:

*   Listening
*   Questioning and probing
*   Educating
*   Fact finding

A Guide to the Project Management Body of Knowledge (PMBOK® Guide) – Fifth Edition, Project Management Institute (PMI)®, Project Management Professional (PMP)®, and Certified Associate in Project Management (CAPM)® are registered trademarks of Project Management Institute, Inc. - Version 2.1 Published September 30, 2014

Lesson 7: Planning Project Budget, Quality, and Communications | Topic F

- Setting and managing expectations
- Persuading
- Coaching
- Negotiating
- Resolving conflict
- Summarizing and recapping

A Guide to the Project Management Body of Knowledge (PMBOK® Guide) – Fifth Edition, Project Management Institute, Inc., 2013, pg. 287-288

Communications Management Plan

A *communications management plan* is another component of the project management plan and it documents how project communications will be planned, structured, monitored, and controlled throughout the life of the project.

Stakeholder	Communication Method	Frequency	Responsibility	Notes
Key Stakeholders	Project Kickoff Meeting	Start of project	Project Management Office	Both team and client kickoff meetings recommended
	Extranet	Ongoing	Project Management Office	Includes project schedule, key project deliverables, meeting minutes, change request log, issues log
Client Executive	Executive Steering Committee	Monthly – first Wednesday of each month	Account Manager	Review, status, milestones met, earned value indicators, key issues
Client Sponsor	Status Meetings Status Report (Email)	Weekly – Friday 2 p.m.	Project Manager	Review project status, schedule, change requests, issues
Development Team	Status Meetings	Weekly – Friday 11 a.m.	Project Manager	Provides input for subsequent meetings with client sponsor
Client Managers	Newsletter (Email)	Weekly – Friday	Project Management Office	
Client Sponsor/Key Client Stakeholders	Client Satisfaction Survey	Monthly/end of each phase	Account Manager/Project Manager	Informal (Monthly) Formal (End of each phase)

Figure 7-18: A sample communications management plan.

A Guide to the Project Management Body of Knowledge (PMBOK® Guide) – Fifth Edition, Project Management Institute, Inc., 2013, p. 296

Components of the Communications Management Plan

As stated in the *PMBOK® Guide,* the communications management plan contains the following information:

- Stakeholder communications requirements
- Information to be communicated, including language to be used
- Reason for the distribution of the information
- Time frame and frequency of information distribution
- Person responsible for the communication
- Person responsible for the release of confidential information
- People who will receive the information
- Methods or technologies that will be used to convey the information
- Time and budget allocated for communication
- Escalation process for issues that need visibility

- Method for updating the communications management plan
- Glossary of common terminology
- Flowcharts of information flow
- Any communication constraints due to regulation or policies

A Guide to the Project Management Body of Knowledge (PMBOK® Guide) – Fifth Edition, Project Management Institute, Inc., 2013, p. 296

The Plan Communications Management Process

The *Plan Communications Management process* identifies and documents the way the project team will communicate efficiently and effectively with the stakeholders. Information needs to be provided at the right time, in the right format, to the right people to achieve the intended impact.

A Guide to the Project Management Body of Knowledge (PMBOK® Guide) – Fifth Edition, Project Management Institute, Inc., 2013, pg. 289-290

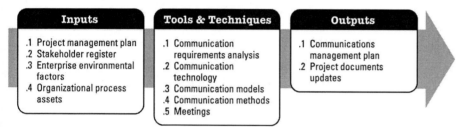

Figure 7-19: The Plan Communications Management process.

A Guide to the Project Management Body of Knowledge (PMBOK® Guide) – Fifth Edition, Project Management Institute, Inc., 2013, p. 289

Communication Considerations

This process develops the approach and the plan to ensure that project communication is successful. Other considerations for communication include:

- Who needs what information and who can access information?
- When is the information needed and who can retrieve the information?
- Where and in what format will project information be stored?
- What language, time zone, or other cross cultural requirements need to be considered?

A Guide to the Project Management Body of Knowledge (PMBOK® Guide) – Fifth Edition, Project Management Institute, Inc., 2013, pg. 287-288

Plan Communications Management Inputs

Various components provide input to the Plan Communications Management process.

Input	Description
Project management plan	Provides information on how the project will be executed, monitored, controlled, and closed.
Stakeholder register	Provides information on stakeholders' communication requirements and needs.
Enterprise environmental factors	All enterprise environmental factors can influence the communications management process, as it is central to the project management process.

A Guide to the Project Management Body of Knowledge (PMBOK® Guide) – Fifth Edition, Project Management Institute (PMI)®, Project Management Professional (PMP)®, and Certified Associate in Project Management (CAPM)® are registered trademarks of Project Management Institute, Inc. - Version 2.1 Published September 30, 2014

Lesson 7: Planning Project Budget, Quality, and Communications | Topic F

Input	Description
Organizational process assets	All organizational process assets can influence the communications management process, as it is central to the project management process, with historical information and lessons learned being especially important.

A Guide to the Project Management Body of Knowledge (PMBOK® Guide) – Fifth Edition, Project Management Institute, Inc., 2013, pg. 290-291

Plan Communications Management Tools and Techniques

There are five tools and techniques used in the Plan Communications Management process.

Tools & Techniques	Description
Communication requirements analysis	As stated in the *PMBOK® Guide,* communication requirements analysis is an analytical technique used to determine the information needs of the project stakeholders through interviews, workshops, and study of lessons learned from previous projects.
Communication technology	As stated in the *PMBOK® Guide,* communication technology is specific tools, systems, and computer programs used to transfer information among project stakeholders.
Communication models	As stated in the *PMBOK® Guide,* communication models are a description, analogy, or schematic used to represent how the communication process will be performed for the project.
Communication methods	As stated in the *PMBOK® Guide,* communication methods are a systematic procedure, technique, or process used to transfer information among project stakeholders.
Meetings	Meetings can be held to discuss how to update and communicate project information.

A Guide to the Project Management Body of Knowledge (PMBOK® Guide) – Fifth Edition, Project Management Institute, Inc., 2013, pg. 290-295

Communication Requirements Analysis

Communications requirements are the project stakeholders' documented communications needs. They include relevant information that contributes to the success of a project, as well as an analysis of cost, time, and logistics. Not all stakeholders will require the same amount, level, or timeliness of communication. The variances must be factored into the communications requirements. *Communication requirements analysis* is an investigation that leads to a clear articulation of the stakeholders' communications needs and helps the project manager make effective choices regarding the technologies to be recommended in the communications management plan. This analysis should take the form of a grid, questionnaire, or survey that documents the communications and technology requirements for each stakeholder. It will also enable the project manager to obtain buy-in from stakeholders and to shape their perceptions by providing the right information at the right time.

A Guide to the Project Management Body of Knowledge (PMBOK® Guide) – Fifth Edition, Project Management Institute, Inc., 2013, pg. 291-292

Identifying Communication Channels

Communication complexity in a project can be calculated by the total number of communication paths is $n (n - 1) / 2$, where n is the number of stakeholders. The more stakeholders, the more complex the communication becomes. If there are 20 stakeholders, then $20 (20 - 1) / 2 = 190$ communications paths.

A Guide to the Project Management Body of Knowledge (PMBOK® Guide) – Fifth Edition, Project Management Institute, Inc., 2013, pg. 291-292

Communication Technologies

Communication technology includes various methods to transfer information. Examples include brief conversations to long meetings, and quick emails to extensive documents. The choice of what communication technology to use depends on:

- The urgency of the need for information.
- The availability to technology that is accessible to all stakeholders.
- The ease of use; all stakeholders need to be trained to use various technologies.
- The project environment, which includes languages and time zones for stakeholders. Can the stakeholders meet face-to-face or are they a virtual team? Culture can be a factor in the project environment.
- The sensitivity and confidentiality of the information, which may require additional security measures.

A Guide to the Project Management Body of Knowledge (PMBOK® Guide) – Fifth Edition, Project Management Institute, Inc., 2013, pg. 292-293

Communication Models

Communication models are used to facilitate communications and information exchange. There are five steps to a standard communications model:

1. Encode—ideas are translated into language used by the sender to convey information.
2. Transmit message—the information is actually sent to the receiver by the sender.
3. Decode—the receiver translates the message into meaningful ideas.
4. Acknowledge—the receiver signals that he or she has received the information.
5. Feedback/response—the receiver encodes a message and transmits it back to the sender.

A Guide to the Project Management Body of Knowledge (PMBOK® Guide) – Fifth Edition, Project Management Institute, Inc., 2013, p. 293

Communication Methods

There are three communications methods that can be used to share information with stakeholders.

- *Interactive communications* is an exchange of information between two or more people that ensures common understanding for everyone participating in that exchange. Examples include meetings, phone conversations, and video conferences.
- *Push communications* are sent out to people who need to receive this information. Examples include emails with attached notes, voice mails, and so on.
- *Pull communications* require the interested people to access the information based on their own initiative. Examples include websites, Microsoft SharePoint®, and lessons-learned databases.

A Guide to the Project Management Body of Knowledge (PMBOK® Guide) – Fifth Edition, Project Management Institute, Inc., 2013, pg. 294-295

A Guide to the Project Management Body of Knowledge (PMBOK® Guide) – Fifth Edition, Project Management Institute (PMI)®, Project Management Professional (PMP)®, and Certified Associate in Project Management (CAPM)® are registered trademarks of Project Management Institute, Inc. - Version 2.1 Published September 30, 2014

Lesson 7: Planning Project Budget, Quality, and Communications | Topic F

Plan Communications Management Outputs

There are two outputs from the Plan Communications Management process.

Output	Description
Communications management plan	Documents the project team's approach to communicating project information.
Project document updates	Project documents that could be updated include the project schedule and the stakeholder register.

A Guide to the Project Management Body of Knowledge (PMBOK® Guide) – Fifth Edition, Project Management Institute, Inc., 2013, pg. 296-297

Guidelines to Plan Communications Management

To create an effective communications management plan, follow these guidelines:

- Gather and distribute contact information for all involved parties.
- Determine the communication needs of project stakeholders.
    - Work from an organization chart to avoid omitting a key stakeholder.
    - Ask for your project sponsor's input.
    - Ask open-ended questions.
- As a rule of thumb, project team members require more detail on a more frequent basis. Senior management typically requires summary information on a less frequent basis.
- Analyze the value to the project of providing the information.
- Evaluate any constraints and assumptions to determine their possible impact on communication planning.
- Determine the appropriate communication technologies to use for communicating project information.
    - Determine the immediacy of the need for information.
    - Analyze the availability of technology systems.
    - Evaluate the expected project staff to identify their knowledge of and access to proposed technology.
    - Conduct research to determine the likelihood that there will be changes to the proposed technology before the project is over.
- Make sure your communications management plan includes all key elements:
    - A description of the types of information required for each project stakeholder.
    - A collection and filing structure that describes the methods the project team will use to collect and file project information.
    - A distribution structure describing to whom and by whom project information, such as status reports, data schedules, and meeting minutes should be provided.
    - The methods that will be used to distribute the various types of information.
    - Schedules for the production of each type of communication.
    - Methods for accessing information between scheduled communications.
    - A method for updating and refining the communications management plan throughout the project life cycle.
- Integrate the communications management plan into the overall project plan.
- Distribute the plan to project stakeholders.

A Guide to the Project Management Body of Knowledge (PMBOK® Guide) – Fifth Edition, Project Management Institute, Inc., 2013, pg. 289-297

ACTIVITY 7-5
Discussing Communications Management

Scenario

You have assigned roles and responsibilities to your project team members and now you need to define in your communications management plan how you and your project team will communicate with each other. Although most of your team is local, there are a few key members that are dispersed across several states.

1. **What communication skills can be used when working with the various people and volunteers on the build project?**

2. **Which item should you use to determine the communications needs of your project stakeholders?**
   - ✓ Stakeholder analysis data
   - ○ Research material
   - ○ Project report deadlines
   - ○ Executive board schedule

3. **Given the scenario, what would be a good technology for enhancing team member interactions and building relationships throughout the life of the project?**
   - ○ Team building event at project kick-off
   - ○ Project team threaded discussion board
   - ○ Use email and databases to collect and store information
   - ○ High-quality virtual teleconferencing on a semi-weekly or weekly basis

4. **After integrating the communications management plan into the overall project plan, what would be the next logical step?**
   - ○ Determining whether there will be changes to the proposed technology before the project is over
   - ○ Creating a schedule for the production of each type of communication
   - ○ Creating a description of stakeholder communication requirements
   - ○ Distributing the plan to all the stakeholders

5. **Today, at the new build site, there are 10 volunteers working, and you as the site coordinator need to communicate with all these volunteers a number of times throughout the day. How many communication paths exist today? Use the communications requirements analysis [$n(n-1)/2$] to determine the number of communication paths.**

   $[11(11-1)/2] = 55$

   You a site co-ordinator

A Guide to the Project Management Body of Knowledge (PMBOK® Guide) – Fifth Edition, Project Management Institute (PMI)®, Project Management Professional (PMP)®, and Certified Associate in Project Management (CAPM)® are registered trademarks of Project Management Institute, Inc. - Version 2.1 Published September 30, 2014

Lesson 7: Planning Project Budget, Quality, and Communications | Topic F

Summary

In this lesson, you examined a number of different processes that can be used to plan, estimate, and manage the project budget, as well as plan for quality and communications within the project. These tools provide you with the necessary framework to effectively plan project cost, quality, staffing, and communications.

How do you think the ability to estimate costs effectively will improve your performance on the job?

Why is communication such an important and central knowledge area for project management?

 Note: Check your LogicalCHOICE Course screen for opportunities to interact with your classmates, peers, and the larger LogicalCHOICE online community about the topics covered in this course or other topics you are interested in. From the Course screen you can also access available resources for a more continuous learning experience.

A Guide to the Project Management Body of Knowledge (PMBOK® Guide) – Fifth Edition, Project Management Institute (PMI)®, Project Management Professional (PMP)®, and Certified Associate in Project Management (CAPM)® are registered trademarks of Project Management Institute, Inc. - Version 2.1 Published September 30, 2014

Lesson 7: Planning Project Budget, Quality, and Communications |

8 | Planning for Risk, Procurements, and Stakeholder Management

Lesson Time: 4 hours

Lesson Objectives

In this lesson, you will:

- Plan for risk management.

- Identify risks for a project.

- Perform qualitative risk analysis.

- Perform quantitative risk analysis.

- Plan for risk response.

- Plan project procurements.

- Plan stakeholder management.

Lesson Introduction

So far you have planned for most aspects of your project. At this point in the planning process group, you can start looking at how to plan for risk, procurements, and stakeholders. Each of these areas play an important role to a project's success. In this lesson, you will examine risk management, procurement management, and stakeholder management. Once the plans are in place for these processes, you can start executing project work!

The following diagram highlights the next process group and knowledge areas covered in this lesson.

Project Management Process Groups					
Knowledge Areas	Initating Process Group	Planning Process Group	Executing Process Group	Monitoring and Controlling Process Group	Closing Process Group
4. Project Integration Management	4.1 Develop Project Charter	4.2 Develop Project Management Plan	4.3 Direct and Manage Project Work	4.4 Monitor and Control Project Work 4.5 Perform Integrated Change Control	4.6 Close Project or Phase
5. Project Scope Management		5.1 Plan Scope Management 5.2 Collect Requirements 5.3 Define Scope 5.4 Create WBS		5.5 Validate Scope 5.6 Control Scope	
6. Project Time Management		6.1 Plan Schedule Management 6.2 Define Activities 6.3 Sequence Activites 6.4 Estimate Activity Resources 6.5 Estimate Activity Durations 6.6 Develop Schedule		6.7 Control Schedule	
7. Project Cost Management		7.1 Plan Cost Management 7.2 Estimate Cost 7.3 Determine Budget		7.4 Control Costs	
8. Project Quality Management		8.1 Plan Quality Management	8.2 Perform Quality Assurance	8.3 Control Quality	
9. Project Human Resource Management		9.1 Plan Human Resource Management	9.2 Acquire Project Team 9.3 Develop Project Team 9.4 Manage Project Team		
10. Project Communication Management		10.1 Plan Communications Management	10.2 Manage Communications	10.3 Control Communications	
11. Project Risk Management		11.1 Plan Risk Management 11.2 Identify Risks 11.3 Perform Qualitative Risk Analysis 11.4 Perform Quantitative Risk Analysis 11.5 Plan Risk Responses		11.6 Control Risks	
12. Project Procurement Management		12.1 Plan Procurement Management	12.2 Conduct Procurements	12.3 Control Procurements	12.4 Close Procurements
13. Project Stakeholder Management	13.1 Identify Stakeholders	13.2 Plan Stakeholder Management	13.3 Manage Stakeholder Engagement	13.4 Control Stakeholder Engagement	

A Guide to the Project Management Body of Knowledge (PMBOK® Guide) – Fifth Edition, Project Management Institute (PMI)®, Project Management Professional (PMP)®, and Certified Associate in Project Management (CAPM)® are registered trademarks of Project Management Institute, Inc. - Version 2.1 Published September 30, 2014

TOPIC A

Plan Risk Management

Up to this point, you have laid out all your project activities, developed a schedule, and planned a project budget. That is all well and good until something unforeseen happens that affects all the plans you have made. How will you react? With a proper risk management plan, you will have specific actions to take and will already have plans for responding to potential project risks. In this topic, you will develop a proper risk management plan.

A Guide to the Project Management Body of Knowledge (PMBOK® Guide) – Fifth Edition, Project Management Institute, Inc., 2013, pg. 313-314

The following data flow diagram illustrates how the Plan Risk Management process relates to the other knowledge areas within the Planning Process Group.

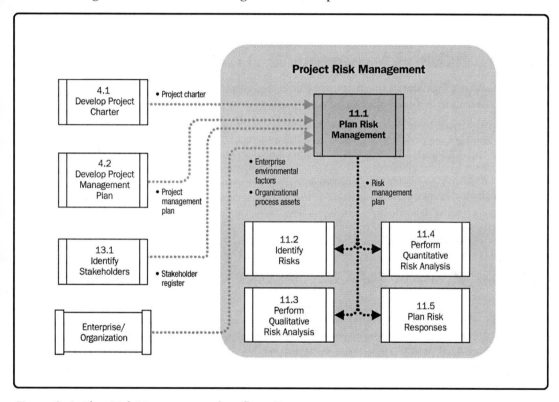

Figure 8–1: Plan Risk Management data flow diagram.

A Guide to the Project Management Body of Knowledge (PMBOK® Guide) – Fifth Edition, Project Management Institute, Inc., 2013, p. 313

Risk

Risk is an uncertain event that may have either a positive or negative effect on the project. Its primary components are a measure of probability that a risk will occur, and the impact of the risk on a project. Some common ways to classify risk are effect-based classification, source-based classification, and level of uncertainty. The level of uncertainty describes how much is known about the risks, which are often described as knowns (which means something has actually occurred), known-unknowns, and unknown-unknowns. *Known risks* are those that have been identified and analyzed so that they can have a planned risk response. These can be managed proactively and have a contingency reserve to pay for the risk if it occurs. *Unknown risks* cannot be identified and so they

A Guide to the Project Management Body of Knowledge (PMBOK® Guide) – Fifth Edition, Project Management Institute (PMI)®, Project Management Professional (PMP)®, and Certified Associate in Project Management (CAPM)® are registered trademarks of Project Management Institute, Inc. - Version 2.1 Published September 30, 2014

Lesson 8: Planning for Risk, Procurements, and Stakeholder Management | Topic A

cannot be managed proactively and may have a management reserve. *Risk attitude* describes the willingness of organizations and stakeholders to accept varying degrees of risk. Risk attitude is influenced by:

- *Risk appetite,* which is the degree of uncertainty a person or group is willing to take on in anticipation of a benefit.
- *Risk tolerance* is the amount of risk an organization or individual will endure.
- *Risk threshold* is the level of uncertainty or impact that a stakeholder can accept. Below that threshold, the organization will accept the risk, above that threshold, the organization will not tolerate the risk.

A Guide to the Project Management Body of Knowledge (PMBOK® Guide) – Fifth Edition, Project Management Institute, Inc., 2013, pg. 310-311

Residual Risk

Residual risks are risks that remain after risk responses have been taken.

A Guide to the Project Management Body of Knowledge (PMBOK® Guide) – Fifth Edition, Project Management Institute, Inc., 2013, p. 589

What Is Project Risk Management?

Project risk management includes conducting risk management planning, identification, and analysis; risk response planning; and controlling risk on a project.

Risk management must be addressed proactively and consistently throughout the project in order to reduce the potential for unmanaged threats to negatively impact the project. The following diagram displays the Project Risk Management Overview knowledge area.

A Guide to the Project Management Body of Knowledge (PMBOK® Guide) – Fifth Edition, Project Management Institute, Inc., 2013, p. 313

The Risk Management Plan

A *risk management plan* is a component of the project management plan that describes the team's approach to identifying risks. It identifies the methodology, approaches, and tools that will be used, documents the roles and responsibilities of those involved, identifies the budgeting and the scheduling for risk management activities, and identifies risk categories.

Plan Component	Description
Methodology	Describes and defines what specific tools, approaches, and data sources will be used to perform risk management for a project.
Roles and responsibilities	Defines the lead, support, and risk management team membership for each type of action in the risk management plan.
Budget	This component includes budgeting information that estimates and identifies risk funds that will need to be included in the cost baseline and how the contingency and management reserves will be estimated.
Timeline	Defines at what points the risk management process will be performed on the project and determines guidelines for use of schedule contingency reserves. Determines what risk management activities will be in the project schedule.
Risk categories	Categories can be used to group potential causes of risk. A Risk Breakdown Structure (RBS) documents what sources a project risk may come from in a risk identification exercise. The categories could be technical, external, financial, organizational, and project management risk.

Plan Component	Description
Definition of risk probability and impact	Defines the levels of probability and impact for the project. The following table is an example of definitions of an impact scale used in evaluating risk impacts related to four project objectives of cost, time, scope, and quality.

Defined Conditions for Impact Scales of a Risk on Major Project Objectives
(Examples are shown for negative impacts only)

Project Objective	Relative or numerical scales are shown				
	Very low /0.05	Low /0.10	Moderate /0.20	High /0.40	Very high /0.80
Cost	Insignificant cost increase	< 10% cost increase	10 – 20% cost increase	20 – 40% cost increase	> 40% cost increase
Time	Insignificant time increase	< 5% time increase	5 – 10% time increase	10 – 20% time increase	> 20% time increase
Scope	Scope decrease barely noticeable	Minor areas of scope affected	Major areas of scope affected	Scope reduction unacceptable to sponsor	Project end item is effectively useless
Quality	Quality degradation barely noticeable	Only very demanding applications are affected	Quality reduction requires sponsor approval	Quality reduction unacceptable to sponsor	Project end item is effectively useless

This table presents examples of risk impact definitions for four different project objectives. They should be tailored in the Risk Management Planning process to the individual project and to the organization's risk thresholds. Impact definitions can be developed for opportunities in a similar way.

A Guide to the Project Management Body of Knowledge (PMBOK® Guide) – Fifth Edition, Project Management Institute, Inc., 2013, p. 318

Probability and impact matrix	This section maps the probability of occurrence for each risk and the impact on the project if that risk occurs. Risks need to be prioritized based on their impact by using a probability and impact matrix. The organization determines the specific combinations of probability and impact that lead a risk to be rated as high, medium, or low importance, or rated according to other similar rating scales.
Revised stakeholders' tolerances	This section may be reviewed and updated for a project during the risk management planning process.
Reporting formats	Defines how project risk information will be documented, analyzed, and communicated to the stakeholders. This section also describes the format of the risk register and other risk reports.
Tracking documents	Documents how risk activities will be recorded and how the risk management processes will be audited during the course of a project.

A Guide to the Project Management Body of Knowledge (PMBOK® Guide) – Fifth Edition, Project Management Institute, Inc., 2013, pg. 316-317

RBS

A *Risk Breakdown Structure (RBS)* is a documented breakdown of identified project risks. The risks are represented in a hierarchy according to the category assigned. The RBS is similar to a WBS in that the risks are categorized and arranged within a hierarchy to help project managers manage risk at a more detailed level.

A Guide to the Project Management Body of Knowledge (PMBOK® Guide) – Fifth Edition, Project Management Institute (PMI)®, Project Management Professional (PMP)®, and Certified Associate in Project Management (CAPM)® are registered trademarks of Project Management Institute, Inc. - Version 2.1 Published September 30, 2014

Lesson 8: Planning for Risk, Procurements, and Stakeholder Management | Topic A

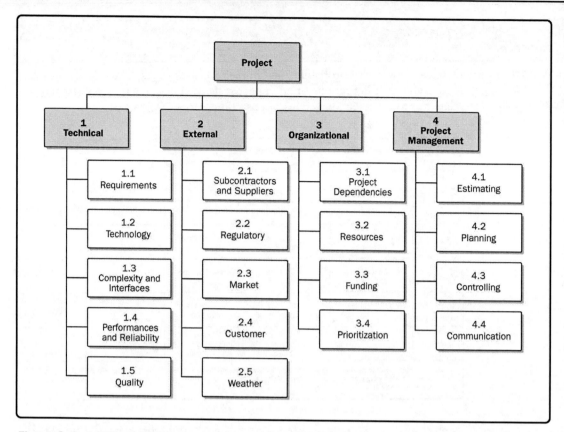

Figure 8-2: A RBS example.

A Guide to the Project Management Body of Knowledge (PMBOK® Guide) – Fifth Edition, Project Management Institute, Inc., 2013, pg. 245, 317, 332

Effect- and Source-Based Risk Classification

Effect-based risk classification is a way of analyzing the major risks that are inherent to a project that could have an impact on its success. These major risks include time, cost, quality, and scope. All these risks are interrelated such that changes to one will affect all of the others.

Source-based risk classification is a method of analyzing risk in terms of its origins. Sources may be internal or external to the project, as well as technical, non-technical, industry-specific, or generic.

A Guide to the Project Management Body of Knowledge (PMBOK® Guide) – Fifth Edition, Project Management Institute, Inc., 2013, pg. 316-318

Probability and Impact Scales

A probability scale is a graph showing the assignment of value to the likelihood of a risk occurring. Probability scales are designed using a variety of values, such as linear, non-linear, or an ordinal scale using relative probability values ranging from very unlikely to almost certain. A risk's probability score can range in value from 0.0 (no probability) to 1.0 (certainty).

An impact scale is a rating system showing the assignment of a value that reflects the magnitude of the impact of a risk event on project objectives. They can be ordinal scales using values of very low, low, moderate, high, and very high. They can also be ordinal scales using linear or non-linear numeric values. Often, impact scales use both methods. To improve the integrity and quality of the data and make the processes consistent and repeatable, organizations typically develop definitions for each value to help the risk management team assign each risk's impact score consistently.

A Guide to the Project Management Body of Knowledge (PMBOK® Guide) – Fifth Edition, Project Management Institute, Inc., 2013, pg. 316-318

The Plan Risk Management Process

The *Plan Risk Management process* defines how to conduct risk management activities for a project. It makes sure that the degree, type, and visibility of the risk management is at an appropriate level for the importance of the project to the organization. All stakeholders need to agree with and support the risk management plan. This planning process should begin at the very start of the project and may be updated through the life of the project as necessary.

A Guide to the Project Management Body of Knowledge (PMBOK® Guide) – Fifth Edition, Project Management Institute, Inc., 2013, pg. 313-314

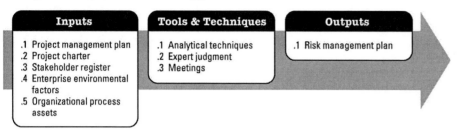

Figure 8-3: The Plan Risk Management process.

A Guide to the Project Management Body of Knowledge (PMBOK® Guide) – Fifth Edition, Project Management Institute, Inc., 2013, p. 313

Plan Risk Management Inputs

Various components provide input to the Plan Risk Management process.

Input	Description
Project management plan	Contains all approved subsidiary plans of the project management plan and all baselines (scope, schedule, and cost) that should be taken into consideration for planning risk management.
Project charter	Provides high-level risks, high-level project descriptions, and high-level requirements.
Stakeholder register	Provides an overview of each stakeholder's role on the project.
Enterprise environmental factors	The enterprise environmental factors that influence this process can include risk attitudes, risk thresholds, and tolerances that an organization will withstand.
Organizational process assets	Organizational process assets that can influence this process can include risk categories, common definitions of concepts and terms, risk statement formats, templates, roles and responsibilities, authority levels for decision making, and lessons learned.

A Guide to the Project Management Body of Knowledge (PMBOK® Guide) – Fifth Edition, Project Management Institute, Inc., 2013, pg. 314-315

Plan Risk Management Tools and Techniques

There are three tools and techniques used in the Plan Risk Management process.

 Note: Analytical techniques are described in more detail in the following section on risk management processes.

A Guide to the Project Management Body of Knowledge (PMBOK® Guide) – Fifth Edition, Project Management Institute (PMI)®, Project Management Professional (PMP)®, and Certified Associate in Project Management (CAPM)® are registered trademarks of Project Management Institute, Inc. - Version 2.1 Published September 30, 2014

Lesson 8: Planning for Risk, Procurements, and Stakeholder Management | Topic A

Tools & Techniques	Description
Analytical techniques	Analytical techniques that can be used include stakeholder risk profile analysis or strategic risk scoring sheets.
Expert judgment	Expert judgment about risks may be obtained from senior management, project stakeholders, project managers, subject matter experts, industry groups, and professional and technical associations.
Meetings	Meetings are held with the project manager, selected team members, and stakeholders to develop the risk management plan.

A Guide to the Project Management Body of Knowledge (PMBOK® Guide) – Fifth Edition, Project Management Institute, Inc., 2013, pg. 315-316

Plan Risk Management Outputs

There is one output from the Plan Risk Management process.

Output	Description
Risk management plan	As stated in the *PMBOK® Guide,* a risk management plan is a component of the project, program, or portfolio management plan that describes how risk management activities will be structured and performed.

A Guide to the Project Management Body of Knowledge (PMBOK® Guide) – Fifth Edition, Project Management Institute, Inc., 2013, pg. 316-318

Guidelines to Develop a Risk Management Plan

Guidelines to developing a risk management plan are as follows:

- Review the project management plan for all approved subsidiary plans of the project management plan and all baselines (scope, schedule, and cost) that should be considered for planning risk management.
- Review the project charter for the high-level risks, high-level project descriptions, and high-level requirements.
- Review the stakeholder register for an overview of each stakeholder's role on the project.
- Review the enterprise environmental factors such as risk attitudes, risk thresholds, and tolerances that an organization will withstand.
- Review the organizational process assets such as risk categories, common definitions of concepts and terms, risk statement formats, templates, roles and responsibilities, authority levels for decision making, and lessons learned.
- Use tools and techniques such as expert judgment about risks from senior management, project stakeholders, project managers, subject matter experts, industry groups, and professional and technical associations.
- Use analytical techniques such as stakeholder risk profile analysis or strategic risk scoring sheets.
- Hold meetings with selected team members and stakeholders to develop the risk management plan.
- Document the risk management plan for the project.

A Guide to the Project Management Body of Knowledge (PMBOK® Guide) – Fifth Edition, Project Management Institute, Inc., 2013, pg. 313-318

ACTIVITY 8–1
Researching Risk Management Plans

Data Files

C:\095001Data\Planning for Risk, Procurements, and Stakeholder Management\Sample Risk Management Plan.doc

Scenario

Before you put together a risk management plan for Building with Heart's 122 East Main project, you decide to review a project management plan used for a previous build to give you some ideas for potential risk planning on your project.

---

1. Review project management plans available on the Internet.
   a) From the desktop, launch Internet Explorer.
   b) In the search engine text box, enter *Risk Management Plan Template*
      Review the results of the search.
   c) In the address bar, enter *projectmanagementdocs.com*
   d) Select the **Project Planning** tab, and scroll down to the **Risk Management Plan.** Select the link and review the information on the page.

2. Review an existing risk management plan.
   a) Launch Windows Explorer and navigate to **C:\095001Data\Planning for Risk, Procurements, and Stakeholder Management\Sample Risk Management Plan.doc**
   b) Review the previous project's risk management plan to determine how risk was managed.

3. After reviewing the risk management plan for a previous project, what changes, if any, would you make in your new plan?

4. Why do you think the roles and responsibilities section is important to include in a risk management plan?

5. Close all open files and windows.

A Guide to the Project Management Body of Knowledge (PMBOK® Guide) – Fifth Edition, Project Management Institute (PMI)®, Project Management Professional (PMP)®, and Certified Associate in Project Management (CAPM)® are registered trademarks of Project Management Institute, Inc. - Version 2.1 Published September 30, 2014

Lesson 8: Planning for Risk, Procurements, and Stakeholder Management | Topic A

TOPIC B

Identify Risks

After planning how to manage the project risks, the next step is to identify the risks, both positive and negative, that may occur during the course of a project.

A Guide to the Project Management Body of Knowledge (PMBOK® Guide) – Fifth Edition, Project Management Institute, Inc., 2013, pg. 319-321

The following data flow diagram illustrates how the Identify Risks process relates to the other knowledge areas within the Planning Process Group.

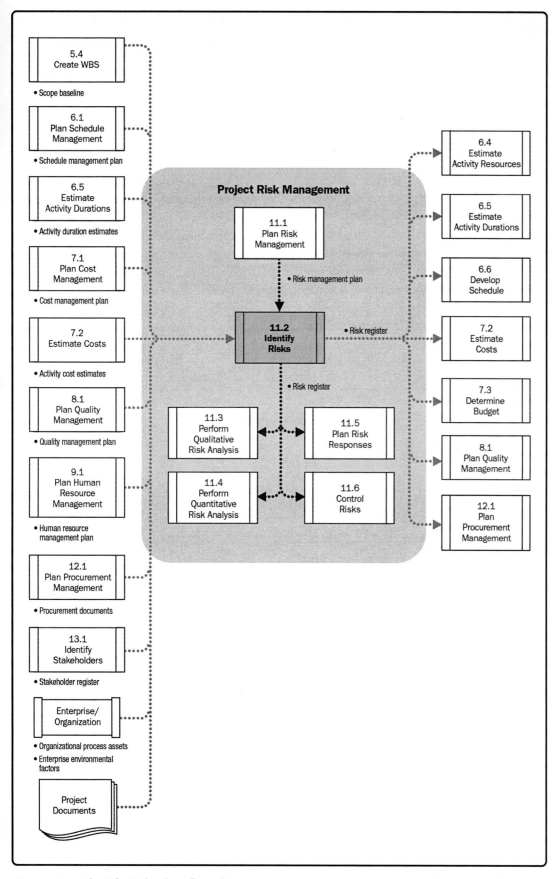

Figure 8–4: Identify Risks data flow diagram.

A Guide to the Project Management Body of Knowledge (PMBOK® Guide) – Fifth Edition, Project Management Institute, Inc., 2013, p. 320

Project Risks

Project risks are uncertain events that may or may not occur within a project. Project risks can have either a positive or negative effect on a project. Positive risks are referred to as *opportunities* and can have a positive impact on the overall project. For example, if a project team member has given notice and left the organization, the hiring manager might hire a replacement that not only fulfills the job requirements, but also comes with extraneous skills that can have a positive impact on the project. This risk would be categorized as an opportunity. For an organization that is developing a new product that is competitive in the marketplace, the possibility that a competitor could beat you to market is a risk. This risk would be categorized as a negative risk.

Risks, whether positive or negative should be identified and documented as early as possible in the project life cycle. Anticipating a potential risk reduces the chance of a surprise that could dramatically affect the project schedule, cost, scope, or quality.

A Guide to the Project Management Body of Knowledge (PMBOK® Guide) – Fifth Edition, Project Management Institute, Inc., 2013, pg. 310-311

Risk Teams

Risk management can be a very tedious and time-consuming task. In many organizations, when there are numerous large projects going on at the same time, there might be a designated team appointed whose purpose it is to identify, manage, handle, and monitor risks throughout the project life cycle.

A Guide to the Project Management Body of Knowledge (PMBOK® Guide) – Fifth Edition, Project Management Institute, Inc., 2013, p. 321

Risk Categories

Risk categories divide project risks into areas reflecting common sources of the risk.

Category	Examples
Technical, quality, or performance risks	Technical changes, changes to industry standards during the project, reliance on unproven or complex technology, and unrealistic performance goals.
Project management risks	Inadequate time and resource allocation, ineffective project plan development, and poor cost estimates.
Organizational risks	Resource conflicts with other projects, inadequate project funding, and inconsistent management support.
External risks	Union issues, change of management in customer's organization, and regional security issues.

A Guide to the Project Management Body of Knowledge (PMBOK® Guide) – Fifth Edition, Project Management Institute, Inc., 2013, p. 317

Triggers

Triggers are the early warning signs or indications that a project risk is likely to occur. Triggers can come from external sources or can be internal organizational events. Triggers can have both negative and positive effects on a project. For example, a trigger that could cause negative effects would be unexpected changes to governmental regulations, which can have a big impact on project timelines and budget. Known triggers can be identified during the Identify Risks process and documented within the risk management plan and the risk register.

A Guide to the Project Management Body of Knowledge (PMBOK® Guide) – Fifth Edition, Project Management Institute (PMI)®, Project Management Professional (PMP)®, and Certified Associate in Project Management (CAPM)® are registered trademarks of Project Management Institute, Inc. - Version 2.1 Published September 30, 2014

Lesson 8: Planning for Risk, Procurements, and Stakeholder Management | Topic B

A Guide to the Project Management Body of Knowledge (PMBOK® Guide) – Fifth Edition, Project
Management Institute, Inc., 2013, p. 566

The Identify Risks Process

The *Identify Risks process* is used to evaluate and determine what risks may affect the project so you
can understand them and document their signs and attributes. This process allows you to anticipate
risk events for the project and not be surprised by and unprepared for them during the project
execution.

A Guide to the Project Management Body of Knowledge (PMBOK® Guide) – Fifth Edition, Project
Management Institute, Inc., 2013, pg. 319-321

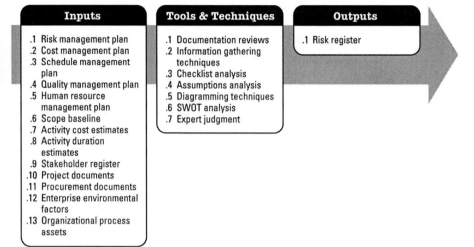

Inputs	Tools & Techniques	Outputs
.1 Risk management plan .2 Cost management plan .3 Schedule management plan .4 Quality management plan .5 Human resource management plan .6 Scope baseline .7 Activity cost estimates .8 Activity duration estimates .9 Stakeholder register .10 Project documents .11 Procurement documents .12 Enterprise environmental factors .13 Organizational process assets	.1 Documentation reviews .2 Information gathering techniques .3 Checklist analysis .4 Assumptions analysis .5 Diagramming techniques .6 SWOT analysis .7 Expert judgment	.1 Risk register

Figure 8-5: The Identify Risks process.

A Guide to the Project Management Body of Knowledge (PMBOK® Guide) – Fifth Edition, Project
Management Institute, Inc., 2013, p. 319

Identify Risks Inputs

Various components provide input to the Identify Risks process.

Input	Description
Risk management plan	Provides assignments of roles and responsibilities, provisions for risk management activities in the budget and schedule, and categories of risk.
Cost management plan	Provides processes and controls that can be used to help identify risks across the project.
Schedule management plan	Provides insight to project time/schedule objectives and expectations, which may be affected by risks.
Quality management plan	Describes the project management team's approach to implementing the quality policy. It is reviewed to identify risks related to quality and those that might be generated by the quality management plan.
Human resource management plan	Describes how the roles and responsibilities, reporting relationships, and staff management will be addressed and structured within the project. It is reviewed to ensure that all roles and responsibilities are accounted for and to identify any potential risks.

Input	Description
Scope baseline	Provides project assumptions. Uncertainty in these assumptions should be evaluated as potential causes of risk.
Activity cost estimates	Provide a quantitative assessment of the costs involved in completing each scheduled activity, with range of estimates indicating risk range. They also indicate whether the cost estimates are sufficient or insufficient to complete the activities.
Activity duration estimates	Indicate the time allotted for each activity or for the whole project. They are reviewed periodically for identifying the risk involved in the estimated durations.
Stakeholder register	Provides information about the stakeholders that is useful for gathering inputs to identifying risks and ensures that key stakeholders participate in the identify risks process.
Project documents	Documents that help to better identify risks include the project charter, project schedule, WBS, schedule network diagrams, issues log, quality checklist, and other information to identify risks.
Procurement documents	The complexity and level of detail of these documents should be consistent with the values of, and risks associated with, the planned procurement for the project.
Enterprise environmental factors	Enterprise environmental factors that can influence this process can include published information, academic studies, published checklists, benchmarking, industry studies, and risk attitudes.
Organizational process assets	Organizational process assets that can influence this process can include project files, organizational and project process controls, risk statement formats, templates, and lessons learned.

A Guide to the Project Management Body of Knowledge (PMBOK® Guide) – Fifth Edition, Project Management Institute, Inc., 2013, pg. 321-324

Identify Risks Tools and Techniques

There are numerous tools and techniques used in the Identify Risks process.

Tools & Techniques	Description
Documentation reviews	*Documentation reviews* are structured reviews of project plans and related documents to identify previously identified risks that might apply to your existing project. These reviews can be performed on project documentation such as project plans, assumptions, previous project files, agreements, and other information. Quality of and consistency between plans and project requirements and assumptions may be areas of risks that should be considered.
Information gathering techniques	Data collection methods such as brainstorming, the Delphi technique, interviewing, and root cause analysis that the project team can use to assist in identifying risks.
Checklist analysis	Developed based on historical information as a standardized way to identify risks. Be careful to look for items that do not appear on the existing checklist, as each project is unique.

A Guide to the Project Management Body of Knowledge (PMBOK® Guide) – Fifth Edition, Project Management Institute (PMI)®, Project Management Professional (PMP)®, and Certified Associate in Project Management (CAPM)® are registered trademarks of Project Management Institute, Inc. - Version 2.1 Published September 30, 2014

Lesson 8: Planning for Risk, Procurements, and Stakeholder Management | Topic B

Tools & Techniques	Description
Assumptions analysis	*Assumptions analysis* explores the validity of the project assumptions and identifies risks from any incompleteness or inaccuracy of these project assumptions. Technique used to explore the validity of project assumptions.
Diagramming techniques	Cause-and-effect diagrams, process flowcharts, and influence diagrams are used to identify risk causes.
SWOT analysis	Analysis that examines the project from the perspective of strengths, weaknesses, opportunities, and threats.
Expert judgement	Individuals with the proper experience in risk analysis provide appropriate feedback.

A Guide to the Project Management Body of Knowledge (PMBOK® Guide) – Fifth Edition, Project Management Institute, Inc., 2013, pg. 324-327

Information Gathering Techniques

Information gathering can be useful when you need to determine what areas of the project will be most susceptible for risk. There are a number of techniques used to gather useful information:

- A *brainstorm session* is a meeting during which a facilitator helps the group identify project risks in a free-form session where ideas are generated, built on, and recorded.
- The *Delphi technique* can be used to reach consensus of a group of experts. A facilitator uses a questionnaire to anonymously solicit ideas about important project risks. The responses are summarized and recirculated for further comment. Consensus may be reached after a few rounds of this process. The process reduces bias and levels influence.
- *Interviewing* experienced project participants, stakeholders, and subject matter experts helps identify risks.
- *Root cause analysis* is used to identify a problem, determine the underlying causes that led to that problem, and determine actions to prevent the risk.

A Guide to the Project Management Body of Knowledge (PMBOK® Guide) – Fifth Edition, Project Management Institute, Inc., 2013, pg. 324-325

Types of Interviewing Methods

There are two interviewing methods used for generating risk probabilities.

- The direct method asks an expert to assign subjective probabilities to a given range of values, providing a lowest possible value, most likely value, and highest possible value.
- The diagrammatic method uses diagrams for an expert to assign subjective probabilities to a given range of values, providing a lowest possible value, most likely value, and highest possible value.

A Guide to the Project Management Body of Knowledge (PMBOK® Guide) – Fifth Edition, Project Management Institute, Inc., 2013, pg. 325-326, 336-337

Checklist Analysis

Risk identification checklists are generally created from historical information, knowledge, and lessons learned from previous projects. *Checklist analysis* involves reviewing and analyzing previous project documents and checklists. The lowest level of an RBS can be used as a risk checklist. A checklist is not an exhaustive list and it should be updated occasionally to remove out-of-date items and add lessons learned when a project ends.

A Guide to the Project Management Body of Knowledge (PMBOK® Guide) – Fifth Edition, Project Management Institute (PMI)®, Project Management Professional (PMP)®, and Certified Associate in Project Management (CAPM)® are registered trademarks of Project Management Institute, Inc. - Version 2.1 Published September 30, 2014

Lesson 8: Planning for Risk, Procurements, and Stakeholder Management | *Topic B*

A Guide to the Project Management Body of Knowledge (PMBOK® Guide) – Fifth Edition, Project Management Institute, Inc., 2013, p. 325

Diagramming Techniques

When identifying risks, there are three diagramming techniques that can be used for risk management:

- Cause-and-effect diagrams, also known as *Ishikawa* or *fishbone* diagrams, can help identify causes of risks.
- System or process flowcharts show how parts of a system interrelate and where areas of risk may be located.
- *Influence diagrams* are graphical representations of decision situations that show causal influences, time ordering of events, and other relationships among variables and outcomes that support team decision analysis.

A Guide to the Project Management Body of Knowledge (PMBOK® Guide) – Fifth Edition, Project Management Institute, Inc., 2013, pg. 325-326

SWOT Analysis

The *SWOT analysis* technique examines the project by its strengths, weaknesses, opportunities, and threats (SWOT) to uncover any internally generated risks. First strengths and weaknesses of the organization, project, or business area are identified. Strengths are characteristics of the project that give it an advantage and weaknesses are characteristics that put the project at a disadvantage. Then opportunities that arise from any strengths and threats from any weaknesses are identified. Opportunities are areas that the project could exploit to its advantage, and threats are areas that could cause risks for the project. Finally, the degree to which strengths offset threats, as well as opportunities that may overcome weaknesses are then identified and documented.

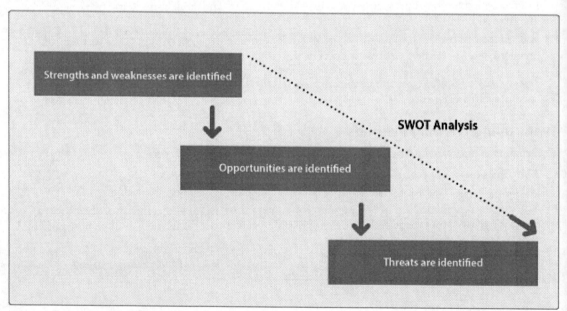

Figure 8–6: SWOT analysis.

A Guide to the Project Management Body of Knowledge (PMBOK® Guide) – Fifth Edition, Project Management Institute, Inc., 2013, p. 326

Identify Risks Outputs

There is one output from the Identify Risks process.

Output	Description
Risk register	The risk register contains the list of identified risks and the potential responses. When complete, the risk register will ultimately contain the outcomes of the other risk management processes, including the results of the qualitative risk analysis, quantitative risk analysis, and risk response planning.

A Guide to the Project Management Body of Knowledge (PMBOK® Guide) – Fifth Edition, Project Management Institute, Inc., 2013, p. 327

Risk Register

A *risk register* is a document that identifies and categorizes risks, potential risk responses, and their triggers, or warning signs. If risk categories are changed, the risk register must be updated. Any possible risk responses included in the risk register are forwarded for use in the risk response planning process. The risk register will be updated with the results of other risk management processes and provided to any project team members involved in project risk management.

ID	Risk	Consequence		Likelihood		Rating
		Current	Target	Current	Target	Level of Risk
1	Loss of IT (data)	Major	Insignificant	Moderate	Unlikely	Extreme
2	Loss of precinct	Major	Minor	Rare	Rare	High
3	Loss of building	Major	Minor	Unlikely	Unlikely	High
4	Denial of access to building	Major	Minor	Unlikely	Unlikely	High
5	Loss of key dependencies	Major	Minor	Unlikely	Unlikely	High
6	Loss of vital records	Major	Insignificant	Unlikely	Rare	High
7	Loss of key staff	Moderate	Minor	Unlikely	Unlikely	Low
8	Loss of IT (voice)	Minor	Insignificant	Unlikely	Unlikely	Low

Figure 8–7: A sample risk register.

The register typically includes:

- A list of identified risks which documents details of identified risks and their root causes, and the conditions or events that may cause the risk to happen.
- A list of potential responses that documents a possible response. The register may also be used as an input to the plan risk response process.

 Note: The risk register will ultimately contain the outcomes of the other risk management processes, including the results of the qualitative risk analysis, quantitative risk analysis, and risk response planning. In its initial stage, the risk register does not necessarily contain information regarding planned responses to deal with the effects of risk.

A Guide to the Project Management Body of Knowledge (PMBOK® Guide) – Fifth Edition, Project Management Institute, Inc., 2013, p. 327

A Guide to the Project Management Body of Knowledge (PMBOK® Guide) – Fifth Edition, Project Management Institute (PMI)®, Project Management Professional (PMP)®, and Certified Associate in Project Management (CAPM)® are registered trademarks of Project Management Institute, Inc. - Version 2.1 Published September 30, 2014

Lesson 8: Planning for Risk, Procurements, and Stakeholder Management | *Topic B*

Guidelines to Identify Project Risks

It is important to identify and document the characteristics of risks that might affect the project so that the project team can determine the most effective action to take for each risk. The project risks and triggers identified will determine the type of risk analysis to be performed. To identify project risks and triggers, follow these guidelines:

- Perform a structured review of appropriate documentation from other planning processes with key project stakeholders to ensure an understanding of each. These documents are a valuable source for risk identification and they may include:
  - Project charter
  - WBS
  - Product description
  - Schedule and cost estimates
  - The network diagram
  - Estimates of duration
  - Resource plan
  - Procurement plan
  - List of constraints and assumptions

- Use one or more risk identification techniques to identify risks and their possible triggers. Techniques may include:
  - Information-gathering techniques, such as brainstorming, interviewing, the Delphi technique, and SWOT analysis, among others.
  - Risk identification checklists (make every effort to itemize all types of possible risks to the project on the checklist).
  - Assumptions analysis.
  - Diagramming techniques such as cause-and-effect diagrams and system flowcharts. You can also use influence diagrams, which provide a graphical representation of a problem showing causal influences, time ordering of events, and other relationships among variables and outcomes.

- Be consistent. Whatever method you adopt, apply it systematically across your project. Before the project begins, identify risks in every project segment and work package. At the start of each project milestone, segment, or phase, re-examine the risks for that segment. Update your list of risks at the close of each project segment.

- Apply your method consistently, but be on the lookout for special circumstances that might arise in any project segment. Those checklists and templates are in place to help get the risk identification process going, but they are far from complete. As the project progresses, circumstances change. Be on the lookout for changed assumptions, new risks, or additional impacts from previously identified risks.

- Consult relevant historical information, such as risk response plans and final reports from previous, similar projects that may include lessons learned describing problems and their resolutions. Another source of historical information for risk identification is published information, such as commercial databases, academic studies, and benchmarking results.

- Once risks have been identified, group them into categories that reflect common sources of risk for your industry or application area. Examine each identified risk to determine what triggers will indicate that a risk has occurred or is about to occur.

- Use the results of your analysis to initiate the risk register.
  - Consider implementing any risk-register software that may be in common usage at your company. You can also create a risk register without specialized software by using a spreadsheet or table.
  - Include the project's name, sponsor, key stakeholders, and objectives.
  - Identify the risks inherent in your project with a description of each.

A Guide to the Project Management Body of Knowledge (PMBOK® Guide) – Fifth Edition, Project Management Institute, Inc., 2013, pg. 319-327

A Guide to the Project Management Body of Knowledge (PMBOK® Guide) – Fifth Edition, Project Management Institute (PMI)®, Project Management Professional (PMP)®, and Certified Associate in Project Management (CAPM)® are registered trademarks of Project Management Institute, Inc. - Version 2.1 Published September 30, 2014

Lesson 8: Planning for Risk, Procurements, and Stakeholder Management | Topic B

ACTIVITY 8–2
Populating the Risk Register

Data Files

C:\095001Data\Planning for Risk, Procurements, and Stakeholder Management\Risk Register.doc

Scenario

For the 122 East Main project, there will be a number of different volunteers working on site throughout the project. This scheduling will need to be managed around the delivery of products and materials. As the project manager, you may not have oversight of the volunteer recruitment and assignments. However, the marketing team has reached out to past experienced volunteers to try and get more help and assistance to get this build completed on time. You will also need to manage the procurement of the building materials if they are not donated by a local business. The costs of these materials have been known to fluctuate lately due to rising oil prices. Occasionally, Building with Heart projects are vandalized during construction. Again, you must also be mindful of the weather when the project starts. The weather is unpredictable, and as far as you know, the forecast is looking clear for the next few weeks.

Now that you have identified how to manage the project and what the costs are, you can take the next step and determine what the project risks are for the house build project. Your organization would like to review the potential project risks in a risk register.

---

1. Open the risk register template.
   a) Launch Windows Explorer and navigate to **C:\095001Data\Planning for Risk, Procurements, and Stakeholder Management\Risk Register.doc**.
   b) Using the information known for the 122 East Main Building with Heart project, identify possible risks and opportunities.

2. Populate the risk register for the project.
   a) In the **Risk/Opportunity** column, enter the risks and fill in the details for each risk in the **R/O Details** column.
   b) In the **Root Cause** column, fill in the possible causes for each risk and then the trigger for each risk in the **Event/Cause for R/O to Happen (Trigger)**.

3. Save the file as *My Risk Register.doc* and leave it open.

TOPIC C

Perform Qualitative Risk Analysis

After identifying the project risks, the next step is to perform qualitative risk analysis on each of those risks to prioritize the risks for further analysis or action. This step qualifies the risks so that the most important ones move forward in the risk process.

A Guide to the Project Management Body of Knowledge (PMBOK® Guide) – Fifth Edition, Project Management Institute, Inc., 2013, pg. 328-329

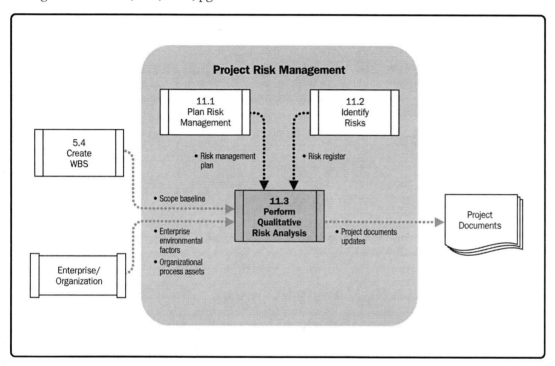

Figure 8-8: Perform Qualitative Risk Analysis data flow diagram.

A Guide to the Project Management Body of Knowledge (PMBOK® Guide) – Fifth Edition, Project Management Institute, Inc., 2013, p. 328

Qualitative Risk Analysis

Qualitative risk analysis is a technique used to determine the probability of occurrence and the impact of identified risk. To determine the risk exposure to the project of a particular risk, multiply its probability and impact. To get an overall risk figure for the entire project, you can either sum the risk figures for each risk, or sum those figures and then divide by the total number of risks. The qualitative risk analysis process ultimately provides the list of prioritized risks for further actions.

A Guide to the Project Management Body of Knowledge (PMBOK® Guide) – Fifth Edition, Project Management Institute, Inc., 2013, pg. 328-329

The Perform Qualitative Risk Analysis Process

The *Perform Qualitative Risk Analysis process* is used to assess each risk for the probability of occurrence and its potential impact on the project. We do this to reduce the level of uncertainty on the project and it allows us to focus on the high priority risks. To prioritize the risks, we look at the probability of occurrence, the impact on the project if it does occur, the time frame for response to

A Guide to the Project Management Body of Knowledge (PMBOK® Guide) – Fifth Edition, Project Management Institute (PMI)®, Project Management Professional (PMP)®, and Certified Associate in Project Management (CAPM)® are registered trademarks of Project Management Institute, Inc. - Version 2.1 Published September 30, 2014

Lesson 8: Planning for Risk, Procurements, and Stakeholder Management | *Topic C*

the risk, and the organization's risk tolerance on the project constraints with respect to cost, schedule, scope, and quality. Prioritizing the risks prepares them for the next step of quantifying the project risks.

A Guide to the Project Management Body of Knowledge (PMBOK® Guide) – Fifth Edition, Project Management Institute, Inc., 2013, pg. 328-329

Figure 8–9: Perform Qualitative Risk Analysis process.

A Guide to the Project Management Body of Knowledge (PMBOK® Guide) – Fifth Edition, Project Management Institute, Inc., 2013, p. 328

Risk Tolerance

Risk tolerance refers to the amount of risk, and potential impact of that risk occurring, that a project manager or key stakeholder is willing to accept. When analyzing project risks, the risk tolerance must be known and understood by the project risk team so that identified risks can be evaluated against the accepted risk tolerance for the project.

A Guide to the Project Management Body of Knowledge (PMBOK® Guide) – Fifth Edition, Project Management Institute, Inc., 2013, pg. 311, 329

Perform Qualitative Risk Analysis Inputs

Various components provide input to the Perform Qualitative Risk Analysis process.

Input	Description
Risk management plan	Provides information on roles and responsibilities for conducting risk management, budgets, schedule activities for risk management, risk categories, definitions of probability and impact, the probability and impact matrix, and revised stakeholders' risk tolerances.
Scope baseline	The scope baseline is evaluated to determine if the project is ordinary and has well-understood risks, or if it is state-of-the-art or more complex and has greater uncertainty.
Risk register	Contains information about the identified risks that will be used to assess and prioritize these risks.
Enterprise environmental factors	Enterprise environmental factors that may provide insight include industry studies of similar projects by risk specialists and risk databases from industry or proprietary sources.
Organizational process assets	Organizational process assets that can influence this process include information on prior, similar completed projects.

A Guide to the Project Management Body of Knowledge (PMBOK® Guide) – Fifth Edition, Project Management Institute, Inc., 2013, pg. 329-330

Perform Qualitative Risk Analysis Tools and Techniques

Various tools and techniques are used in the Perform Qualitative Risk Analysis process.

Tools & Techniques	Description
Risk probability and impact assessment	*Risk probability* is the likelihood that a risk event will occur or prove true during the project. In risk analysis, each risk is assigned a value to represent its probability or degree of uncertainty. *Risk impact* is the likely effect on project objectives if the risk event occurs. In risk analysis, each risk is assigned a value representing the likely consequences of the risk event occurring. These factors are often described in terms of being very high, high, moderate, low, and very low; or are rated on a similar appropriate scale, such as 1-10. These are both assessed for each risk by interviews or meetings with participants familiar with the risk categories, such as sources of risk or root cause. Details about the risk and any assumptions are also documented. Risks with low ratings are included on the risk register as part of the watch list for future monitoring. The assessment information is put into a probability and impact matrix for further evaluation.
Probability and impact matrix	Illustrates a risk rating assignment for identified risks. The matrix specifies the probability and impact of the risks identified and rates them as high, medium, or low priority.
Risk data quality assessment	The *risk data quality assessment* is a technique used to examine how well each risk is understood and assesses the accuracy, quality, reliability, and integrity of the data about the risk. If the quality of the data about a risk is low, then the qualitative risk analysis may be of little value and it may be necessary to collect better data to understand the risk.
Risk categorization	*Risk categorization* is used to group and organize risks into specific categories so you can evaluate them by urgency, or other designated values. Risks can be categorized by the source of the risk by using the RBS, the WBS, and the specific project phase to determine the area of the project with the most uncertainty. Risks can also be categorized by root cause. This categorization helps develop effective risk responses.
Risk urgency assessment	*Risk urgency* assessment is used to determine the urgency of project risks. It indicates priority and can include specific information on timing for response.
Expert judgment	Information provided by a group or individual with expertise based on relevant experience on similar projects, and through risk facilitation interviews or workshops. Helps assess the impact and probability of each risk.

A Guide to the Project Management Body of Knowledge (PMBOK® Guide) – Fifth Edition, Project Management Institute, Inc., 2013, pg. 330-333

Probability and Impact Matrix

The *probability and impact matrix* is used to assign a numerical value or risk score to each risk from the risk assessment. The matrix combines the probability and impact scales to prioritize risks and identify risks that are likely to require further analysis. The risk rating is calculated by multiplying the risk's impact score by its probability score. The risks can then be ordered in priority order, highest

A Guide to the Project Management Body of Knowledge (PMBOK® Guide) – Fifth Edition, Project Management Institute (PMI)®, Project Management Professional (PMP)®, and Certified Associate in Project Management (CAPM)® are registered trademarks of Project Management Institute, Inc. - Version 2.1 Published September 30, 2014

Lesson 8: Planning for Risk, Procurements, and Stakeholder Management | Topic C

score at the top of the list. The higher rating indicates a higher risk to the project. This ranking allows you to focus on the higher value risks as you develop the risk responses. The probability and impact risk rating matrix will guide the response plans.

Probability and Impact Matrix

Probability	Threats					Opportunities				
0.90	0.05	0.09	0.18	0.36	0.72	0.72	0.36	0.18	0.09	0.05
0.70	0.04	0.07	0.14	0.28	0.56	0.56	0.28	0.14	0.07	0.04
0.50	0.03	0.05	0.10	0.20	0.40	0.40	0.20	0.10	0.05	0.03
0.30	0.02	0.03	0.06	0.12	0.24	0.24	0.12	0.06	0.03	0.02
0.10	0.01	0.01	0.02	0.04	0.08	0.08	0.04	0.02	0.01	0.01
	0.05/ Very Low	0.10/ Low	0.20/ Moderate	0.40/ High	0.80/ Very High	0.80/ Very High	0.40/ High	0.20/ Moderate	0.10/ Low	0.05/ Very Low

Impact (numerical scale) on an objective (e.g., cost, time, scope or quality)

Each risk is rated on its probability of occurring and impact on an objective if it does occur. The organization's thresholds for low, moderate or high risks are shown in the matrix and determine whether the risk is scored as high, moderate or low for that objective.

Figure 8-10: Probability and impact matrix.

A Guide to the Project Management Body of Knowledge (PMBOK® Guide) – Fifth Edition, Project Management Institute, Inc., 2013, p. 331

Perform Qualitative Risk Analysis Outputs

There is one output from the Perform Qualitative Risk Analysis process.

Output	Description
Project document updates	Project documents that could be updated include the risk register, which is updated with assessments of probability and impact for each risk, risk scores, risk urgency, risk categorization, the watch list or risks requiring further analysis, and the assumptions log can be updated to include any assumption changes.

A Guide to the Project Management Body of Knowledge (PMBOK® Guide) – Fifth Edition, Project Management Institute, Inc., 2013, p. 333

Guidelines to Perform Qualitative Risk Analysis

Guidelines to perform qualitative risk analysis are as follows:

• Review the risk management plan for information on roles and responsibilities for conducting risk management, budgets, schedule activities for risk management, risk categories, definitions of probability and impact, the probability and impact matrix, and revised stakeholders' risk tolerances.
• Review the scope baseline to determine if the project is ordinary and has well-understood risks, or if it is state-of-the-art or more complex and has greater uncertainty.
• Examine the list of identified risks.

A Guide to the Project Management Body of Knowledge (PMBOK® Guide) – Fifth Edition, Project Management Institute (PMI)®, Project Management Professional (PMP)®, and Certified Associate in Project Management (CAPM)® are registered trademarks of Project Management Institute, Inc. - Version 2.1 Published September 30, 2014

Lesson 8: Planning for Risk, Procurements, and Stakeholder Management | Topic C

- Are all the risks identified?
- Are all the risks completely documented?
- Analyze the data available for each risk to assign a data precision ranking score.

    - Does the source of the data fully understand the risk?
    - Is the source reliable and trustworthy?
    - Is the amount of data sufficient to adequately analyze the risk?
    - What is the accuracy and quality of the data?
    - Are there risks that require further monitoring? Should they be placed in the risk register for watching?
- Determine the organization's risk threshold for this project.
- Analyze the assumptions identified during risk identification as potential risks against the validity of the assumption and the impact on the project if false.
- Analyze the probability and impact of each identified risk by using well-defined probability and impact scales.
- Determine the risk factor scores by using a probability and impact risk matrix.
- Prioritize the risks according to the risk management plan. Identify risks that require further analysis. Determine the overall risk for the project and compare with the organization risk threshold.
- Update the risk register and other project documents for the project.

A Guide to the Project Management Body of Knowledge (PMBOK® Guide) – Fifth Edition, Project Management Institute, Inc., 2013, pg. 328-333

ACTIVITY 8-3
Performing Qualitative Risk Analysis

Data Files
My Risk Register.doc

Before You Begin
My Risk Register.doc is open.

Scenario
Now that you have identified the possible risks and opportunities for your build project, you will analyze each one and assess the probability of it occurring and the impact it would have on the project.

- Bad weather has a 30 percent probability, with very high impact on basement construction.
- Good weather has a 70 percent probability, with a high impact on outside construction.

---

1. Use the matrix to assign each risk a probability and value and record it in the **Probability** column of the risk register.

2. Assign each risk an impact value and record it in the **Impact** column of the risk register.

3. Save **My Risk Register.doc** and leave it open.

A Guide to the Project Management Body of Knowledge (PMBOK® Guide) – Fifth Edition, Project Management Institute (PMI)®, Project Management Professional (PMP)®, and Certified Associate in Project Management (CAPM)® are registered trademarks of Project Management Institute, Inc. - Version 2.1 Published September 30, 2014

TOPIC D

Perform Quantitative Risk Analysis

Now that you are familiar with qualitative risk analysis and how it can be used on each risk, the next step is to take a look at quantitative risk analysis and how it can used to analyze project risks.

A Guide to the Project Management Body of Knowledge (PMBOK® Guide) – Fifth Edition, Project Management Institute, Inc., 2013, pg. 333-335

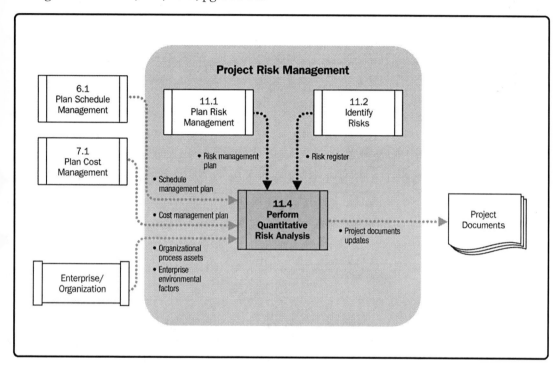

Figure 8-11: The Perform Quantitative Risk Analysis data flow diagram.

A Guide to the Project Management Body of Knowledge (PMBOK® Guide) – Fifth Edition, Project Management Institute, Inc., 2013, p. 334

Quantitative Risk Analysis

Quantitative risk analysis is a technique used to assess the risk exposure events to overall project objectives and determine the confidence levels of achieving the project objectives. Quantifying risk can help you to identify time and cost contingencies of a project. It further refines and enhances the prioritization and scoring of risks produced during qualitative analysis.

A Guide to the Project Management Body of Knowledge (PMBOK® Guide) – Fifth Edition, Project Management Institute, Inc., 2013, pg. 333-335

The Perform Quantitative Risk Analysis Process

The *Perform Quantitative Risk Analysis process* numerically analyzes the effect for each identified risk against the project objectives. It produces quantitative risk information for decision making so that the uncertainty on the project is reduced. This process is performed on the risks that were qualified in the previous process as risks that could substantially impact the project's objectives. Not all risks will need to be quantitatively analyzed, just the ones with the greatest impact.

A Guide to the Project Management Body of Knowledge (PMBOK® Guide) – Fifth Edition, Project Management Institute, Inc., 2013, pg. 333-335

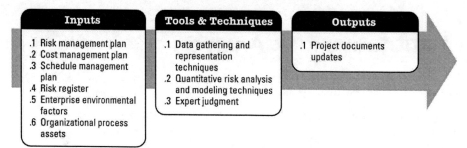

Figure 8-12: The Perform Quantitative Risk Analysis process.

A Guide to the Project Management Body of Knowledge (PMBOK® Guide) – Fifth Edition, Project Management Institute, Inc., 2013, p. 334

Perform Quantitative Risk Analysis Inputs

Various components provide input to the Perform Quantitative Risk Analysis process.

Input	Description
Risk management plan	Contains roles and responsibilities, budgets and schedule for risk management activities, RBS, risk categories, the probability and impact matrix, and risk tolerances.
Cost management plan	Sets the criteria for planning, estimating, budgeting, and controlling project costs.
Schedule management plan	Sets the criteria for developing and controlling the project schedule.
Enterprise environmental factors	Enterprise environmental factors that may provide insight include industry studies of similar projects by risk specialists and risk databases from industry or proprietary sources.
Organizational process assets	Contains information on completed projects, studies from risk specialists, and risk databases.

A Guide to the Project Management Body of Knowledge (PMBOK® Guide) – Fifth Edition, Project Management Institute, Inc., 2013, pg. 335-336

Perform Quantitative Risk Analysis Tools and Techniques

There are three tools and techniques used in the Perform Quantitative Risk Analysis process.

Tools & Techniques	Description
Data gathering and representation techniques	There are two techniques used in data gathering and representation: • Interviewing: Taking subjective probability and representing that data objectively. • Probability distributions: Visually represent risk probability.

Tools & Techniques	Description
Quantitative risk analysis and modeling techniques	There are three techniques used in risk analysis and modeling: • Sensitivity analysis: Examines how the uncertainty of a project element affects the objective in question if the other uncertain elements remain unchanged. • Expected monetary value analysis: Calculates the average outcome under uncertainty. • Modeling and simulation: Includes cost and schedule risk analysis, which, when performed al all, is most commonly performed using the Monte Carlo method.
Expert judgment	Utilizes subject matter expertise to analyze potential cost, identify schedule impacts, and validate risks. Also, utilized for interpretation of data and to identify the strength and weakness of the tools used.

A Guide to the Project Management Body of Knowledge (PMBOK® Guide) – Fifth Edition, Project Management Institute, Inc., 2013, pg. 336-341

Data Gathering and Representation Techniques

There are two data gathering and representation techniques:

• Interviewing is used to determine the probability and impact of risks on project objectives. Information should be gathered on the optimistic (low), pessimistic (high), or most likely scenario for each risk. This gives a range for the cost estimates for different sections of the project. An example of three-point estimates for cost is shown in the following table.

Range of Project Cost Estimates

WBS Element	Low	Most Likely	High
Design	$4M	$6M	$10M
Build	$16M	$20M	$35M
Test	$11M	$15M	$23M
Total Project	$31M	$41M	$68M

Interviewing relevant stakeholders helps determine the three-point estimates for each WBS element for triangular, beta or other distributions.

Figure 8–13: The interviewing technique.

A Guide to the Project Management Body of Knowledge (PMBOK® Guide) – Fifth Edition, Project Management Institute, Inc., 2013, p. 336

• *Probability distribution* is used for modeling and simulation, and represents the uncertainty in values such as durations of schedule activities and costs of project components. These distributions can represent uncertain events using data developed during quantitative analysis. The following figure shows two common probability distributions:

A Guide to the Project Management Body of Knowledge (PMBOK® Guide) – Fifth Edition, Project Management Institute (PMI)®, Project Management Professional (PMP)®, and Certified Associate in Project Management (CAPM)® are registered trademarks of Project Management Institute, Inc. - Version 2.1 Published September 30, 2014

Lesson 8: Planning for Risk, Procurements, and Stakeholder Management | *Topic D*

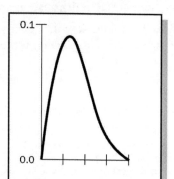
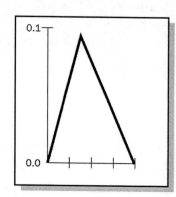

Beta and triangular distributions are frequently used in quantitative risk analysis. The data shown in the figure on the left (Beta Distribution) is one example of a family of such distributions determined by two "shape parameters". Other commonly used distributions include the uniform, normal and lognormal. In these charts the horizontal (X) axes represent possible values of time or cost and the vertical (Y) axes represent relative likelihood.

Figure 8–14: The probability distribution technique.

A Guide to the Project Management Body of Knowledge (PMBOK® Guide) – Fifth Edition, Project Management Institute, Inc., 2013, p. 337

The beta distribution estimate (E) is a weighted average of the optimistic estimate (O), plus four times the most likely estimate (M), plus the pessimistic estimate (P), divided by six.

$$E = \frac{O + 4M + P}{6}$$

The triangular distribution estimate (E) is a flat average of the optimistic estimate (O), plus the most likely estimate (M), plus the pessimistic estimate (P), divided by three.

$$E = \frac{O + M + P}{3}$$

When you are estimating the likely duration or cost of an activity, these are the two ways to build in the probability factor. During project execution, it is very unlikely that the actual durations and costs of all the activities will meet planned durations and costs. Some activities will take more time and money than planned, while others will take less time and money. Probability distributions help you understand and build in the potential variance.

A Guide to the Project Management Body of Knowledge (PMBOK® Guide) – Fifth Edition, Project Management Institute, Inc., 2013, pg. 336-337

Project Risk Ranking

Project risk ranking is the overall risk ranking for producing the final deliverable of the product or service of the project. It allows for comparisons among other projects, assisting in project initiation, budget and resource allocation, and other decisions.

Basics of Probability

When you perform probabilistic analysis, you will need to apply some of the basic principles of probability.

Principle of Probability	Description
Sum of probabilities	The sum of the probabilities of all possible events must equal 1 (100 percent).
Probability of single event	The probability of any single event must be greater than or equal to 0 and less than or equal to 1.
Dependent joint events	The probability of joint events is the product of the probability that one event occurs and the probability that another event occurs, given that the first event has occurred. Under these circumstances, the events are considered to be dependent (connected in some way with each other).
Independent joint events	When the probability of joint events occurring is the product of the probabilities of each, the events are considered to be independent (the two events have nothing in common and may occur simultaneously).
Mean	The sum of the events divided by the number of occurrences.
Median	The number that separates the higher half of a probability distribution from the lower half. It is not the same as the average, although the two terms are often confused.
Average	The number that typifies the data in a set. It is calculated by adding the values of a group of numbers and dividing that total by the number of objects included.
Standard deviation	This is the measure of the spread of the data, or the statistical dispersion of the values in your data set.

Probability Distribution

Probability distribution is the scattering of values assigned to likelihood in a sample population. It can be visually depicted in the form of a Probability Density Function (PDF). In a PDF, the vertical axis refers to the probability of the risk event and the horizontal axis refers to the impact that the risk event will have on the project objectives.

A Guide to the Project Management Body of Knowledge (PMBOK® Guide) – Fifth Edition, Project Management Institute, Inc., 2013, p. 337

Uniform Distribution PDF

A *uniform distribution PDF* results when all outcomes are equally likely to occur, so the data is shown in a straight line.

A Guide to the Project Management Body of Knowledge (PMBOK® Guide) – Fifth Edition, Project Management Institute, Inc., 2013, p. 337

A Guide to the Project Management Body of Knowledge (PMBOK® Guide) – Fifth Edition, Project Management Institute (PMI)®, Project Management Professional (PMP)®, and Certified Associate in Project Management (CAPM)® are registered trademarks of Project Management Institute, Inc. - Version 2.1 Published September 30, 2014

Lesson 8: Planning for Risk, Procurements, and Stakeholder Management | *Topic D*

Normal Distribution PDF

A *normal distribution PDF* results when there is a symmetrical range or variation in the probabilities of each outcome. Visually, the data is distributed symmetrically in the shape of a bell with a single peak, resulting in the common term "bell curve." The peak represents the mean; the symmetry indicates that there is an equal number of occurrences above and below the mean.

A Guide to the Project Management Body of Knowledge (PMBOK® Guide) – Fifth Edition, Project Management Institute, Inc., 2013, p. 337

Triangular Distribution PDF

A *triangular distribution PDF* results when there is an asymmetrical distribution of probabilities. Visually, the data is skewed to one side, indicating that an activity or element presents relatively little risk to project objectives. Note that if either the probability of occurrence is low or the impact is low, then this necessarily indicates there is little risk.

A Guide to the Project Management Body of Knowledge (PMBOK® Guide) – Fifth Edition, Project Management Institute, Inc., 2013, p. 337

Quantitative Analysis Methods

Quantitative analysis methods allow project managers to consistently determine the probability and impact of each risk. There are three techniques that can be used to analyze and model risks on a project.

- Sensitivity analysis
- Expected Monetary Value (EMV)
- Modeling and simulation

A Guide to the Project Management Body of Knowledge (PMBOK® Guide) – Fifth Edition, Project Management Institute, Inc., 2013, pg. 338-340

Sensitivity Analysis

Sensitivity analysis is a method of assessing the relative impact of changing a variable in the project to gain insight into possible outcomes of one or more potential courses of action. Sensitivity analysis places a value on the effect of changing a single variable within a project by analyzing that effect on the project plan. Sensitivity analysis is probably the simplest method of analyzing the impact of a potential risk and its results are easy for project stakeholders to understand. However, it does not lend itself well to assessing combinations of risks and how they might affect a project. Furthermore, the sensitivity diagram does not provide an indication of anticipated probability of occurrence of the risk event. A tornado diagram is an example of a display of sensitivity analysis.

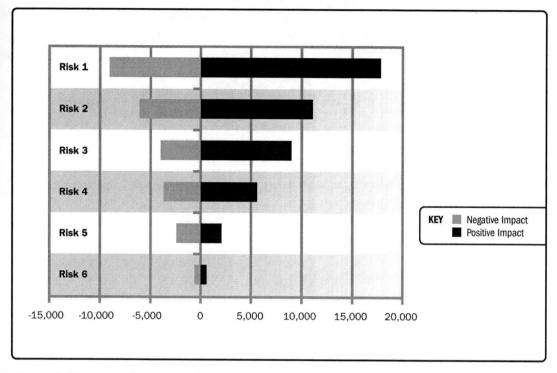

Figure 8-15: A sample tornado diagram.

A Guide to the Project Management Body of Knowledge (PMBOK® Guide) – Fifth Edition, Project Management Institute, Inc., 2013, p. 338

EMV

EMV is a method of calculating the average outcome when the future is uncertain. Opportunities will have positive values and threats will have negative values. EMV is found by multiplying the monetary value of a possible outcome by the probability it will occur. This is done for all possible outcomes and their figures are added together. The sum is the EMV for that scenario. This technique is used in decision tree analysis; EMV must be calculated in order for the analysis to find the best outcome. The best outcome is the one resulting in the greatest amount of net gain or the least amount of net loss.

A Guide to the Project Management Body of Knowledge (PMBOK® Guide) – Fifth Edition, Project Management Institute, Inc., 2013, p. 339

Modeling and Simulation

Simulation is a technique that uses computer models and estimates of risk to translate uncertainties at a detailed level into their potential impact on project objectives. Simulations involve calculating multiple project durations with different sets of activity assumptions. A project simulation uses a model that translates project uncertainties into their potential impact on project objectives. The project model is created many times with different variables to calculate a probability distribution.

A Guide to the Project Management Body of Knowledge (PMBOK® Guide) – Fifth Edition, Project Management Institute, Inc., 2013, p. 340

Monte Carlo Analysis

Monte Carlo analysis is a technique used by project managers to make predictions about the optimistic, most likely, and pessimistic estimates for variables in the model and simulates various outcomes of the project schedule to provide a statistical distribution of the calculated results. In addition to the what-if scenario analysis method, this is the other most common simulation type. A Monte Carlo analysis does not produce a single result, but calculates a range of possible results.

In more general business terms, "Monte Carlo" refers to not one single analysis method, but to a wide class of techniques, mostly making use of sophisticated computers and inputs of random numbers, probabilities, and algorithms. It has a wide range of applications in many fields, including finance and engineering. Because it works effectively with large inputs of numbers, it is well suited to complex project management problems in which more than a few inputs, such as costs, activity, and durations, are unknown.

A Guide to the Project Management Body of Knowledge (PMBOK® Guide) – Fifth Edition, Project Management Institute, Inc., 2013, pg. 338, 340

Perform Quantitative Risk Analysis Outputs

There is one output from the Perform Quantitative Risk Analysis process.

Output	Description
Project documents updates	Documents that could be updated as a result of this process include: • Probabilistic analysis of the project provides estimates of possible project schedule and cost outcomes and quantifies cost and time contingency reserves. • Probability of achieving cost and time objectives are estimates of the probability or achieving project objectives under the current plan. • Prioritized list of quantified risks is a list of risks that present the greatest threat or opportunity for the project and may affect the cost contingency or critical path. • Trends in quantitative risk analysis results should be noted and documented. Repeating the quantitative risk analysis allows the project's risk management team to analyze the trends and make adjustments as necessary. Information on project schedule, cost, quality, and performance gained through the perform quantitative risk analysis process will help the team to prepare a quantitative risk analysis report.

A Guide to the Project Management Body of Knowledge (PMBOK® Guide) – Fifth Edition, Project Management Institute, Inc., 2013, p. 341

Guidelines to Perform Quantitative Risk Analysis

Performing quantitative risk analysis enables the project's risk management team to prioritize risks according to the threat they pose or the opportunity they present to the project. The prioritized list can be used to develop an effective response plan for each risk. To effectively perform quantitative risk analysis, follow these guidelines:

• Begin with your original estimate of time or cost and break out the various components of the estimate into manageable chunks.
• Determine the variable that you wish to investigate and identify its likely range of variation.
• Calculate and assess the impact of changing the range of results on the overall project estimate for each value in the range.
• Consult historical information, such as similar completed projects, studies of similar projects by risk specialists, and risk databases for information that may be useful for quantitative risk analysis on your project.
• Use the appropriate interviewing technique and obtain probability distributions from stakeholders and subject matter experts.
• Depict the distributions in a PDF.

- Perform a sensitivity analysis to determine which risks have the most potential impact on the project by examining the extent to which the uncertainty of each element affects the objective being examined (if all other uncertain elements are held at their baseline values).
- Conduct a project simulation by using a model to translate uncertainties at a detailed level into their potential impact on project objectives at the total project level.

A Guide to the Project Management Body of Knowledge (PMBOK® Guide) – Fifth Edition, Project Management Institute, Inc., 2013, pg. 333-341

ACTIVITY 8-4
Performing Quantitative Risk Analysis

Data Files

C:\095001Data\Planning for Risk, Procurements and Stakeholder Management\Sample Risk Management Plan.doc

My Risk Register.doc

Before You Begin

My Risk Register.doc is open.

Scenario

With the qualitative risk values added to the risk register, you can go ahead and apply the quantitative risk values to each risk in your project. You are expected to report back to the stakeholders when the cost or time frame of the project slips. Quantitative risk values will help you in determining when this is likely to happen and what the impact will be on the project. Calculate EMV for each risk in the risk register.

1. Launch Windows Explorer and navigate to **C:\095001Data\Planning for Risk, Procurements, and Stakeholder Management\Sample Risk Management Plan.doc.**

2. Use the probability and impact matrix included in the Sample Risk Management Plan.doc file to determine the potential cost and/or time impact to the project if the risk occurs.

3. Complete the EMV value for each risk in the **EMV** column of the risk register.

4. When you have calculated the EMV values for each risk, save the **My Risk Register.doc** file and close the **Sample Risk Management Plan.doc** file.

A Guide to the Project Management Body of Knowledge (PMBOK® Guide) – Fifth Edition, Project Management Institute (PMI)®, Project Management Professional (PMP)®, and Certified Associate in Project Management (CAPM)® are registered trademarks of Project Management Institute, Inc. - Version 2.1 Published September 30, 2014

Lesson 8: Planning for Risk, Procurements, and Stakeholder Management | Topic D

TOPIC E

Plan for Risk Response

After performing both qualitative and quantitative risk analysis on the risks, we can take a closer look at how to plan for responding to potential risks.

A Guide to the Project Management Body of Knowledge (PMBOK® Guide) – Fifth Edition, Project Management Institute, Inc., 2013, pg. 342-343

The following data flow diagram illustrates how the Plan Risk Responses process relates to the other project management processes.

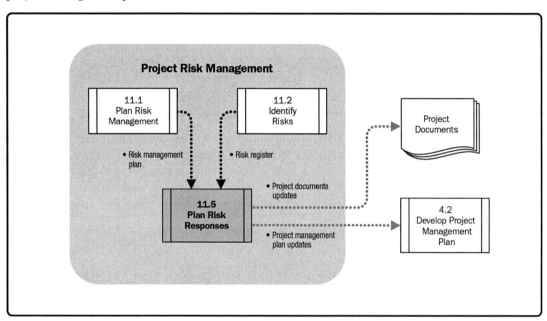

Figure 8–16: The Plan Risk Responses data flow diagram.

A Guide to the Project Management Body of Knowledge (PMBOK® Guide) – Fifth Edition, Project Management Institute, Inc., 2013, p. 342

The Plan Risk Responses Process

The *plan risk responses* process determines and documents options and specific actions to take to reduce the threats and enhance the opportunities to project objectives. Risks are addressed by priority, and resources and activities can be added to the budget, schedule, and project management plan to support the risks. Each risk is assigned a risk response, which is an action to address that risk and a person to implement that action, if the risk occurs.

There are various risk response strategies to choose from to determine a risk response for each risk. Both a primary and a backup strategy may be developed, and a fallback plan can also be developed in case the primary and backup strategies are not effective. Secondary risks should also be reviewed. These are risks that could occur as a result of implementing a risk response. These strategies are discussed in more detail in the "Plan Risk Responses Tools and Techniques" section.

A Guide to the Project Management Body of Knowledge (PMBOK® Guide) – Fifth Edition, Project Management Institute, Inc., 2013, pg. 342-343

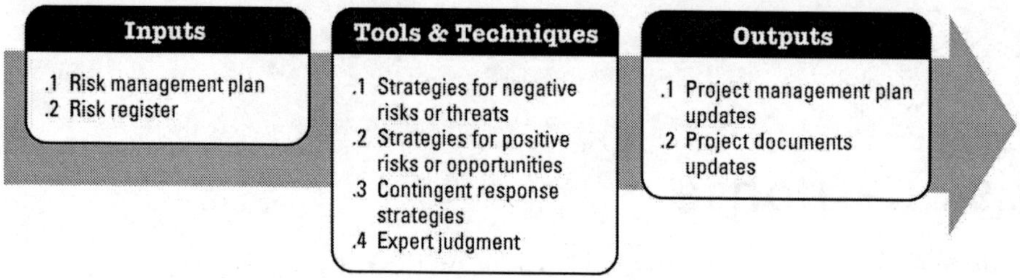

Inputs	Tools & Techniques	Outputs
.1 Risk management plan .2 Risk register	.1 Strategies for negative risks or threats .2 Strategies for positive risks or opportunities .3 Contingent response strategies .4 Expert judgment	.1 Project management plan updates .2 Project documents updates

Figure 8-17: The Plan Risk Responses process.

A Guide to the Project Management Body of Knowledge (PMBOK® Guide) – Fifth Edition, Project Management Institute, Inc., 2013, p. 342

Plan Risk Responses Inputs

Various components provide input to the Plan Risk Responses process.

Input	Description
Risk management plan	Provides roles and responsibilities, risk analysis definitions, timing of reviews, and risk thresholds for low, moderate, and high risks.
Risk register	Provides identified risks, root causes of risks, list of potential responses, risk owners, symptoms and warning signs, the relative rating or priority list of risks, risks requiring responses in the near term, risk for additional analysis and response, trends in qualitative analysis results, and a watch list.

A Guide to the Project Management Body of Knowledge (PMBOK® Guide) – Fifth Edition, Project Management Institute, Inc., 2013, p. 343

Plan Risk Responses Tools and Techniques

There are four tools and techniques used in the Plan Risk Responses process.

Tools & Techniques	Description
Strategies for negative risks or threats	The common strategies for threats are: avoid, transfer, mitigate, and accept.
Strategies for positive risks or opportunities	The common strategies for opportunities are: exploit, share, enhance, and accept.
Contingent response strategies	Strategies to use so that if a risk is about to happen, the contingency plans can be invoked.
Expert judgment	Expertise provided by a group or individual with relevant experience and skill to take action on identified risks and establish risk responses.

A Guide to the Project Management Body of Knowledge (PMBOK® Guide) – Fifth Edition, Project Management Institute, Inc., 2013, pg. 343-346

Negative Risks Strategies (Threats)

There are four strategies for managing negative risks or threats. These strategies are selected based on the risk's probability and impact on the project. Critical risks with high impact should be avoided or mitigated, whereas less critical risks can be transferred or accepted. You may also outsource critical risks and avoid less critical risks without having to accept them.

- *Avoid*: Changing the project management plan to remove the risk entirely by extending the schedule, changing the strategy, increasing the funding, or reducing scope. Some risks can be avoided entirely by clarifying requirements, obtaining more information, improving communication, or acquiring expertise in that area of risk.
- *Transfer*: Shifting the impact and ownership of the risk to a third party and paying a risk premium to the party taking on the liability of the risk. This can be done with insurance, performance bonds, warranties, guarantees, contracts or agreements, and so on. An example of when you may want to transfer risk is in the case of having little internal experience performing a particular type of work on a project. In this case, you may want to outsource that work to a vendor that is more capable of performing it.
- *Mitigate*: Taking action to reduce the probability of occurrence or the impact of a risk. Adopting less complex processes, increasing the duration of an activity, conducting more testing, and choosing a more stable supplier are examples of mitigating a risk.
- *Accept*: Acknowledging a risk and not taking any action until the risk occurs. Acceptance can be either a passive or an active strategy. An example of passive acceptance would be simply acknowledging and documenting the risks. Then, the risk management team can periodically review the threat and determine what, if any, action to take with risks as they occur. A common active acceptance strategy involves creating a contingency reserve with amounts of time, money, or resources to address the risk if it happens.

A Guide to the Project Management Body of Knowledge (PMBOK® Guide) – Fifth Edition, Project Management Institute, Inc., 2013, pg. 344-345

Positive Risks Strategies (Opportunities)

There are four strategies for managing positive risks or opportunities. These strategies are selected based on the risk's probability and impact on the project.

- *Exploit*: Attempting to make sure that the opportunity happens. Examples include assigning the best resources to the project, hiring an expert consultant, or using new technology to reduce project cost and duration.
- *Enhance*: Increasing the probability that the opportunity will happen or the impact it will have by identifying and maximizing enablers of these opportunities. An example is to add more resources to an activity so it finishes early.
- *Share*: Allocating some or all of the ownership of the opportunity to a third party. Examples include risk-sharing partnerships, teams, special purpose companies, or joint ventures.
- *Accept*: Be willing to take advantage of an opportunity if it happens, but not actively pursuing it.

A Guide to the Project Management Body of Knowledge (PMBOK® Guide) – Fifth Edition, Project Management Institute, Inc., 2013, pg. 345-346

Contingency Plans

A *contingency plan* is a risk response strategy developed in advance, before risks occur; it is meant to be used if and when identified risks become reality. An effective contingency plan allows a project manager to react quickly and appropriately to the risk event, mitigating its negative impact or increasing its potential benefits. A contingency plan may include a fallback plan for risks with high impact. The fallback plan is implemented if the initial contingency plan is ineffective in responding to the risk event.

A Guide to the Project Management Body of Knowledge (PMBOK® Guide) – Fifth Edition, Project Management Institute, Inc., 2013, pg. 346, 348

A Guide to the Project Management Body of Knowledge (PMBOK® Guide) – Fifth Edition, Project Management Institute (PMI)®, Project Management Professional (PMP)®, and Certified Associate in Project Management (CAPM)® are registered trademarks of Project Management Institute, Inc. - Version 2.1 Published September 30, 2014

Lesson 8: Planning for Risk, Procurements, and Stakeholder Management | *Topic E*

Contingency Reserves

A *contingency reserve* is a predetermined amount of time in the schedule baseline that is allocated for known risks that are accepted. The amount of the reserve is estimated to account for the rework amount.

A Guide to the Project Management Body of Knowledge (PMBOK® Guide) – Fifth Edition, Project Management Institute, Inc., 2013, pg. 348, 533

Plan Risk Responses Outputs

There are two outputs from the Plan Risk Responses process.

Output	Description
Project management plan updates	Subsidiary management plans and their various requirements needed for the plan risk responses process. Elements that need to be updated include: • Schedule management plan • Cost management plan • Quality management plan • Procurement management plan • Human resource management plan • Work breakdown structure • Schedule baseline • Cost performance baseline
Project documents updates	Project documents that are updated could include the risk register information, such as: • Risk owners and assigned responsibilities • Agreed upon risk strategies • Specific actions to implement chosen response strategy • Trigger conditions, symptoms and warning signs of a risk occurrence • Budget and schedule activities to support risk responses • Contingency plans • Fallback plans • Residual risks • Secondary risks • Contingency reserves Additional documents that could be updated as a result of this process include: • Assumption log updates, includes new information on assumptions. • Technical documentation updates, includes technical approaches and physical deliverables. • Change requests that are generated for changes to resources, activities, cost estimates, and more.

A Guide to the Project Management Body of Knowledge (PMBOK® Guide) – Fifth Edition, Project Management Institute, Inc., 2013, pg. 346-348

Guidelines to Plan Risk Responses

An effective risk response plan describes the response strategies for each identified risk. The selected response strategies should take advantage of opportunities and reduce the probability and/or impact of threats to project objectives. To develop an effective risk response plan, follow these guidelines:

- Examine each identified risk to determine its causes and how it may affect project objectives. Brainstorm possible strategies for each risk.

  - Identify which project stakeholders can be assigned responsibility of a risk. Involve those people in your risk response planning.
  - Write down every idea mentioned regardless of feasibility or cost.

- Choose the response strategy that is most likely to be effective for each identified risk. Ensure that the chosen risk response strategies are:

  - Enough to bring the risk threshold below the organization's limit.
  - Appropriate to the severity of the risk.
  - Cost effective.
  - Timely enough to be successful.
  - Realistic within the context of the project.
  - Agreed to by all parties involved.
  - Owned by a responsible person.

- If you are unable to bring a risk's rating below the organization's risk threshold, ask your sponsor for help. Develop specific actions for implementing the chosen strategy.
- Identify backup strategies for risks with high risk factor scores.
- Determine the amount of contingency reserves necessary to deal with identified risks.

  - How much will your contingency plans cost?
  - How much time will your contingency plans add to the schedule?

- Consult the risk management plan for the description of the content and format of the risk response plan. Include the following elements in your risk response plan:

  - A description of the identified risks along with the area of the project affected (that is, the WBS element)
  - Risk owners and assigned responsibilities
  - Qualitative and/or quantitative risk analysis results
  - Response strategies selected and the specific actions for implementing the strategies
  - Level of residual risk expected to remain after the response strategies are implemented
  - Budget and schedule for responses
  - Contingency plans and fallback plans for all accepted risks with high impact

- Incorporate the risk response plan into the overall project plan so the strategies can be implemented and monitored. As the project progresses through the life cycle, examine trends in qualitative and quantitative analysis results that may guide your response strategies.

A Guide to the Project Management Body of Knowledge (PMBOK® Guide) – Fifth Edition, Project Management Institute, Inc., 2013, pg. 342-348

A Guide to the Project Management Body of Knowledge (PMBOK® Guide) – Fifth Edition, Project Management Institute (PMI)®, Project Management Professional (PMP)®, and Certified Associate in Project Management (CAPM)® are registered trademarks of Project Management Institute, Inc. - Version 2.1 Published September 30, 2014

Lesson 8: Planning for Risk, Procurements, and Stakeholder Management | Topic E

ACTIVITY 8-5
Planning for Risk Response

Data Files
My Risk Register.doc

Before You Begin
The My Risk Register.doc is open

Scenario
As part of the full risk analysis for the build project, you must plan for how to respond to the risks if they occur. The next step in developing the risk register is to develop response strategies for each risk identified.

---

1. Examine each opportunity (positive risk) in the risk register. Determine an appropriate response and complete the **R/O Strategy** column with **exploit**, **enhance**, **share**, or **accept**.

2. Examine each threat (negative risk) in the risk register. Determine an appropriate response and complete the **R/O Strategy** column with **avoid**, **transfer**, **mitigate**, or **accept**.

3. Save the **My Risk Register.doc** file and close it.

TOPIC F

Plan Project Procurements

You have planned for project risk and you are almost ready to transition your project into the executing process group. But before you can do that, you need to identify ways of securing external resources when necessary. In this topic, you will plan project procurements and create a procurement management plan.

A Guide to the Project Management Body of Knowledge (PMBOK® Guide) – Fifth Edition, Project Management Institute, Inc., 2013, pg. 357-360

The following data flow diagram illustrates how the Plan Procurement Management process relates to the other project management processes.

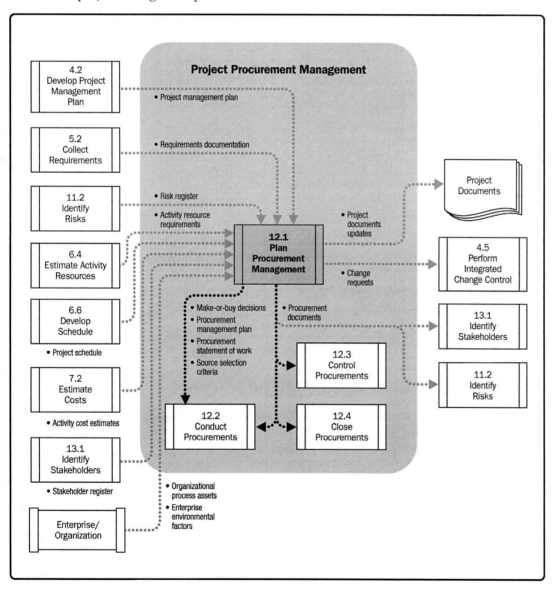

Figure 8–18: The Plan for Project Procurement Management data flow diagram.

A Guide to the Project Management Body of Knowledge (PMBOK® Guide) – Fifth Edition, Project Management Institute, Inc., 2013, p. 359

What Is a Procurement Management Plan?

The *procurement management plan* is a document that outlines the specifications for procuring work from outside sources; it specifies the types of contracts that will be used, describes the process for obtaining and evaluating bids, mandates the standardized procurement documents that must be used, and describes how multiple providers will be managed. The plan also states how procurement activities will be coordinated with other project management activities, such as scheduling and performance reporting. Depending on the needs of the project, the procurement management plan may be formal or informal; brief or highly detailed.

For example, a small advertising agency would procure contracts from external sources for some of the work considered necessary but beyond its core capabilities, such as specialized printing and professional photography services. The procurement management plan would outline the company's processes for soliciting and evaluating bids from competing service providers and would specify how management would schedule the contract work, schedule payments to providers for the work done, and evaluate the quality.

As stated in the *PMBOK® Guide,* the procurement management plan can include guidance for:

- Types of contracts to be used
- Risk management issues
- If independent estimates will be used and if they are needed as evaluation criteria
- Potential use of organization's procurement, contracting, or purchasing department
- Standardized procurement documents
- Managing multiple suppliers
- Coordinating procurement with scheduling and performance reporting
- Constraints and assumptions that affect procurement
- Handling any long lead times for purchases
- Handling make-or-buy decisions
- Setting dates for contracted deliverables
- Identifying requirements for performance bonds or insurance contracts
- Establishing direction to sellers to use a WBS
- Establishing the format for SOWs
- Identifying pre-qualified sellers to be used
- Procurement metrics for managing contracts and evaluating sellers

A Guide to the Project Management Body of Knowledge (PMBOK® Guide) – Fifth Edition, Project Management Institute, Inc., 2013, pg. 366-367

The Plan Procurement Management Process

The *Plan Procurement Management process* allows project managers to document project purchasing decisions, specify the approach to be followed for project procurements, and identify potential sellers to meet the purchase requirements of the project. It also determines whether the project needs will be met internally by the project team, or the required products, services, or results need to be acquired from outside the project organization.

When the project needs are to be procured from outside the project organization, the project management team needs to determine what to acquire, how to acquire, how much to acquire, and when to acquire the project resources. The buyer's involvement in the procurement process should also be considered when planning procurements. The process includes consideration of the risks inherent in making decisions in the planning phase of the project. In mitigating the risks, the project managers would consider the type of contract to be used for the procurement and may involve transference of the risks to the seller.

A Guide to the Project Management Body of Knowledge (PMBOK® Guide) – Fifth Edition, Project Management Institute, Inc., 2013, pg. 357-360

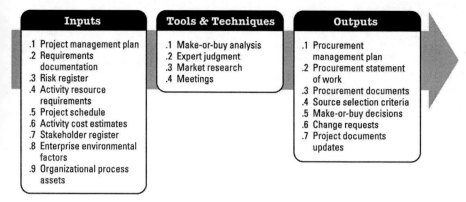

Figure 8-19: The Plan Procurement Management process.

A Guide to the Project Management Body of Knowledge (PMBOK® Guide) – Fifth Edition, Project
Management Institute, Inc., 2013, p. 358

Plan Procurement Management Inputs

Various components provide input to the Plan Procurement Management process.

Input	Description
Project management plan	Provides the project scope statement, WBS, and WBS dictionary.
Requirements documentation	Includes information about project requirements along with details of any contractual or legal implications that may apply to the requirements.
Risk register	Includes identified project risks, risk owners, and risk responses that may influence project procurements.
Activity resource requirements	Provides information on the specific activity resource needs of the project, namely people, equipment, or location.
Project schedule	Contains information on the required timelines or the mandated deliverable dates.
Activity cost estimates	Includes cost estimates developed for the procuring activity within the project that are used to evaluate bids or proposals received from the sellers.
Stakeholder register	Provides information on the project stakeholders and their interests in the project.
Enterprise environmental factors	Enterprise environmental factors that can influence this process include marketplace conditions, products, services and results that are available to buy, suppliers, terms and conditions, and unique local requirements.
Organizational process assets	Organizational process assets that can influence this process include procurement policies, procedures, and guidelines; management systems; and an established supplier system of pre-qualified suppliers.

A Guide to the Project Management Body of Knowledge (PMBOK® Guide) – Fifth Edition, Project
Management Institute, Inc., 2013, pg. 360-364

A Guide to the Project Management Body of Knowledge (PMBOK® Guide) – Fifth Edition, Project Management Institute (PMI)®, Project Management Professional
(PMP)®, and Certified Associate in Project Management (CAPM)® are registered trademarks of Project Management Institute, Inc. - Version 2.1 Published September 30, 2014

Lesson 8: Planning for Risk, Procurements, and Stakeholder Management | Topic F

Contracts

Contracts are mutually binding agreements that detail the obligations of both parties; in terms of procuring work, they relate to both the buyer and the seller. Although contracts are customized for each agreement, they tend to fall into a number of standard patterns, such as fixed-price, cost-reimbursable, or time-and-material (T&M) contracts.

A Guide to the Project Management Body of Knowledge (PMBOK® Guide) – Fifth Edition, Project Management Institute, Inc., 2013, pg. 362-364

Components of Contracts

In general, any contract must include these elements, at a minimum:

- Description of the work being procured for the project, its deliverables, and scope
- Delivery date or other schedule information
- Identification of authority, where appropriate
- Responsibilities of both parties
- Management of technical and business aspects
- Price and payment terms
- Provisions for termination
- Applicable guarantees and warranties

Types of Contracts

Three common types of contracts are used in the procurement of goods and services.

Lesson 8: Planning for Risk, Procurements, and Stakeholder Management | Topic F

Contract Type	Description
Fixed-price	Also called a lump sum contract, it establishes a total price for a product or service. The seller agrees to perform the work at the negotiated contract value. This value is based on anticipated costs and profit, as well as a premium to cover unforeseen problems. The contract may include incentives for meeting or exceeding requirements, such as schedule milestones. Fixed-price contracts provide maximum protection to the buyer but require a long time for preparation and bid evaluation. Because this type of contract is tied to a fixed cost, it is most suited to projects with a high degree of certainty about their parameters. Types of fixed-price contracts include: • *Firm Fixed Price (FFP) Contracts*: This is a commonly used contract type favored by most buying organizations because the price for products or services is set at the outset and not subject to change unless the scope of work changes. • *Fixed Price Incentive Fee (FPIF) Contracts*: This fixed-price contract is flexible in that it allows for deviation from performance. Financial incentives are tied to achieving metrics that are agreed to earlier. • *Fixed Price with Economic Price Adjustment (FPEPA) Contracts*: This is a fixed-price contract type with special provision to allow pre-defined final adjustments to the contract price due to changed conditions, such as inflation changes, or cost increases or decreases for specific commodities such as fuel, and for currency fluctuations. An FPEPA contract protects both buyer and seller from external conditions beyond their control. It is used whenever the seller's performance period spans a considerable period. The economic price adjustment (EPA) clause must relate to a reliable financial index, which is used to precisely adjust the final price.

A Guide to the Project Management Body of Knowledge (PMBOK® Guide) – Fifth Edition, Project Management Institute (PMI)®, Project Management Professional (PMP)®, and Certified Associate in Project Management (CAPM)® are registered trademarks of Project Management Institute, Inc. - Version 2.1 Published September 30, 2014

Lesson 8: Planning for Risk, Procurements, and Stakeholder Management | Topic F

Contract Type	Description
Cost-reimbursable	This contract provides sellers a refund of the expenses incurred while providing a service, plus a fee representing seller profit. Incurred costs are generally classified as direct costs (those incurred for the project), or indirect costs (costs allocated to the project by the organization as a cost of doing business). These contracts sometimes include incentives for meeting certain objectives, such as costs, schedule, or technical performance targets. This approach is tied to the actual cost to perform the contract, and therefore is most suitable if project parameters are uncertain. The cost-reimbursable contracts include: • *Cost Plus Fixed Fee (CPFF) Contracts*: This contract ensures that the seller is reimbursed for all allowable costs for performing the contract work. The seller receives a fixed fee payment calculated based on the initial estimated project costs. This fixed fee does not change due to seller performance. • *Cost Plus Incentive Fee (CPIF) Contracts*: This contract ensures that the seller is reimbursed for all allowable costs for performing the contract work. The seller also receives a predetermined target fee. In addition to this, there is a provision of an incentive fee payable to the seller, which is based on achieving certain performance objectives as set forth in the contract. In case the final costs are lesser or greater than the original estimated costs, then both the buyer and seller share the costs from the difference based on the pre-negotiated cost sharing formula; for example, an 80/20 split over or under target costs based on actual performance of the seller. • *Cost Plus Award Fee (CPAF) Contracts*: This contract ensures that the seller is reimbursed for all legitimate costs. The majority of the fee is earned based on the satisfaction of certain broad subjective performance criteria defined and incorporated into the contract. The determination of the fee is based on the buyer's subjective determination of seller performance and is generally not subject to appeals.
Time-and-material (T&M)	This type of contract includes aspects of both fixed-price and cost-reimbursable contracts. The buyer pays the seller a negotiated hourly rate and full reimbursement for materials used to complete the project. This contract is used for staff augmentation, acquisition of experts, and any outside support when a precise statement of work cannot be quickly prescribed. Many organizations include not-to-exceed values and time limits in T&M contracts to prevent unlimited cost growth.

A Guide to the Project Management Body of Knowledge (PMBOK® Guide) – Fifth Edition, Project Management Institute, Inc., 2013, pg. 362-364

Plan Procurement Management Tools and Techniques

There are four tools and techniques used in the Plan Procurement Management process.

Tools & Techniques	Description
Make-or-buy analysis	Assesses the cost-effectiveness of using in-house resources as opposed to outside sellers.

A Guide to the Project Management Body of Knowledge (PMBOK® Guide) – Fifth Edition, Project Management Institute (PMI)®, Project Management Professional (PMP)®, and Certified Associate in Project Management (CAPM)® are registered trademarks of Project Management Institute, Inc. - Version 2.1 Published September 30, 2014

Lesson 8: Planning for Risk, Procurements, and Stakeholder Management | Topic F

Tools & Techniques	Description
Expert judgment	Expert judgment is available from sources such as the organization's finance department, legal consultants, risk professionals, technical associations, and so on.
Market research	Market research is done to evaluate industry and specific vendor capabilities. It helps discover what options are out in the marketplace that meet the project's outside purchasing requirements.
Meetings	Meetings may be held to provide a two-way information exchange with potential bidders. This can be beneficial to both the buyer and the potential sellers.

A Guide to the Project Management Body of Knowledge (PMBOK® Guide) – Fifth Edition, Project Management Institute, Inc., 2013, pg. 365-366

Make-or-Buy Analysis

Make-or-buy analysis is a technique used to determine whether it would be more cost effective to produce a product or service in-house or to procure it from an outside seller. Make-or-buy decisions can significantly impact project time, cost, and quality. In the case of a buy decision, you must also consider if the product needs to be purchased, leased, or rented.

A Guide to the Project Management Body of Knowledge (PMBOK® Guide) – Fifth Edition, Project Management Institute, Inc., 2013, p. 365

Make-or-Buy Decisions

When considering a make-or-buy decision, it is important to consider several factors.

- Consider the impact on cost, time, or quality. For instance, if current personnel must be retrained for services requiring a new skill set, it may be less expensive to outsource those services.
- Consider the ongoing need of a specific skill set—even for future, unrelated projects—it may be a worthwhile investment to train current personnel to perform that service.
- Think about the learning curve. Although it may make financial sense to develop an in-house solution, there may not be enough time to train personnel and/or implement the necessary policies and equipment to produce that solution.
- If the required resources are readily available internally, organizations will usually use them. However, if the project involves technology, skills, materials, or resources that are beyond the organization's capabilities, it may be cost-effective to hire outside help.

A Guide to the Project Management Body of Knowledge (PMBOK® Guide) – Fifth Edition, Project Management Institute, Inc., 2013, p. 365

Plan Procurement Management Outputs

There are seven outputs from the Plan Procurement Management process.

Output	Description
Procurements management plan	Describes how the procurement processes will be handled. It includes the information on contract types to be used, standard procurement documents, procurement metrics, constraints and assumptions, and procurement-related risk management issues.
Procurement statement of work	Detailed, written description of a product or service being procured under contract.

A Guide to the Project Management Body of Knowledge (PMBOK® Guide) – Fifth Edition, Project Management Institute (PMI)®, Project Management Professional (PMP)®, and Certified Associate in Project Management (CAPM)® are registered trademarks of Project Management Institute, Inc. - Version 2.1 Published September 30, 2014

Lesson 8: Planning for Risk, Procurements, and Stakeholder Management | Topic F

Output	Description
Procurement documents	The documents that are submitted to prospective sellers and service providers to solicit their proposals for the work needed. These can include Request for Information (RFI), Invitation for Bid (IFB), Request for Proposal (RFP), and Request for Quotation (RFQ).
Source selection criteria	The metrics that are used to evaluate each seller's proposal and make comparisons among different proposals. The criteria can be objective or subjective and are used to rate or score seller proposals.
Make-or-buy decisions	Decisions about which resources, services, or products will be created or purchased by the organization.
Change requests	May apply to the subsidiary management plans in the project management plan, especially in light of new products or services being acquired.
Project documents updates	Project documents that may need to be updated include requirements documentation, requirements traceability matrix, and the risk register.

A Guide to the Project Management Body of Knowledge (PMBOK® Guide) – Fifth Edition, Project Management Institute, Inc., 2013, pg. 366-370

Procurement Statement of Work

A *procurement SOW* is a detailed narrative description of the resources, goods, or services that are being sought from external sources to fulfill a project's requirements. It is distributed to potential sellers, who will use it to evaluate their capability to perform the work or provide the services. In addition, the SOW will serve as a basis for developing the procurement documents during the solicitation process. Information in the project scope baseline is used to create the procurement SOW. The procurement SOW goes through multiple rounds of reviews and fixes until the contract award is signed.

A Guide to the Project Management Body of Knowledge (PMBOK® Guide) – Fifth Edition, Project Management Institute, Inc., 2013, p. 367

Procurement Documents

Procurement documents are the documents that are submitted to prospective sellers and service providers to solicit their proposals for the work needed. There are different types of procurement documents. The type of document used will depend on the type of project and the product or service being procured.

A Guide to the Project Management Body of Knowledge (PMBOK® Guide) – Fifth Edition, Project Management Institute, Inc., 2013, p. 368

Procurement Document Types

Many organizations use procurement document terms interchangeably. It is important to be sure that you understand the terms and definitions used by your organization.

Type	Description
Request for Information (RFI)	Commonly used to develop lists of qualified sellers and to gain more input for resource availability. *A Guide to the Project Management Body of Knowledge (PMBOK® Guide) – Fifth Edition,* Project Management Institute, Inc., 2013, pg. 368, 557

Type	Description
Invitation for Bid (IFB)	Sometimes used interchangeably with RFP, an IFB is most commonly used when deliverables are commodities for which there are clear specifications and when the quantities are very large. The invitation is usually advertised and any seller may submit a bid. Negotiation is typically not anticipated. *A Guide to the Project Management Body of Knowledge (PMBOK® Guide) – Fifth Edition,* Project Management Institute, Inc., 2013, pg. 368, 544
Request for Proposal (RFP)	Commonly used when deliverables are not well-defined or when other selection criteria will be used in addition to price. Sellers are often encouraged to offer suggestions and alternative approaches to meet the project goals. Preparing the RFP is time consuming and costly for the seller. Negotiation is expected. Because it is time-consuming and expensive to create a proposal in response to an RFP, it is typical that not all the sellers solicited will respond. *A Guide to the Project Management Body of Knowledge (PMBOK® Guide) – Fifth Edition,* Project Management Institute, Inc., 2013, pg. 368, 558
Request for Quotation (RFQ)	Commonly used when deliverables are commodities for which there are clear specifications, and when price will be the primary determining factor. Unlike an RFB, this solicited price quote is used for comparison purposes and is not a formal bid for work. This may allow for some negotiation of price. *A Guide to the Project Management Body of Knowledge (PMBOK® Guide) – Fifth Edition,* Project Management Institute, Inc., 2013, pg. 368, 558
Invitation for negotiation	Commonly used to verify all interested parties are involved. A documented attempt to make sure that everyone who may have an interest in contracting with the offering party has a chance to do so. *A Guide to the Project Management Body of Knowledge (PMBOK® Guide) – Fifth Edition,* Project Management Institute, Inc., 2013, p. 368

Source Selection Criteria

Source selection criteria are the standards used to rate or score proposals, quotes, or bids and form a part of the procurement solicitation documents. Some criteria are objective and can be readily demonstrated and measured. Other criteria are subjective and open to different interpretations. Objective criteria tend to be much more specific than subjective criteria.

A Guide to the Project Management Body of Knowledge (PMBOK® Guide) – Fifth Edition, Project Management Institute, Inc., 2013, pg. 368-369

Sample Source Selection Criteria

Sample source selection criteria include the following

Source Selection Criteria	Description
Overall or life-cycle cost	Does the selected seller produce the lowest total cost of ownership, which includes the purchase cost plus operating cost?
Understanding of need	How well does the seller's proposal address the procurement statement of work?

Source Selection Criteria	Description
Technical capability	Does the seller have or is the seller expected to acquire the technical skills and knowledge needed for the project?
Management approach	Does the seller have or can the seller reasonably develop the management processes and procedures to ensure a successful project?
Technical approach	Do the seller's proposed technical methodologies, techniques, solutions, and services meet the project requirements?
Warranty	Does the seller provide warranty for the final product and for what duration?
Financial capacity	Does the seller have or is the seller expected to obtain the necessary financial production capacity and interest resources?
Production capacity and interest	Does the seller have the capacity and interest to meet the project requirements?
Business size and type	Does the seller's company meet a specific category of business defined by the buyer, or established by a governmental agency, and included as a condition in the contract? Categories could include small, women-owned, or disadvantaged small businesses.
Past performance of sellers	Does the company have past experience with selected sellers?
References	Does the seller provide references from previous customers verifying the seller's work experience and compliance with contractual requirements?
Intellectual property rights	Are intellectual property rights established by the seller in work processes or services to be used for the project?
Proprietary rights	Are proprietary rights ensured by the seller in the work processes or services to be used for the project?

A Guide to the Project Management Body of Knowledge (PMBOK® Guide) – Fifth Edition, Project Management Institute, Inc., 2013, pg. 368-369

Guidelines to Develop a Procurement Management Plan

Effective planning of project procurements documents the project purchasing decisions, specifies the approach to be used in project procurements, and identifies potential sellers for the project and documents these in the procurement management plan. To generate an effective procurement management plan, follow these guidelines:

- Identify the project needs that can be fulfilled by acquiring products, services, or results. Determine what is to be acquired, how to acquire, how much to acquire, and when to acquire.
- Study the various plan procurement input documents to determine information related to the procurement requirements. The input documents could include:
  - Project scope baseline
  - Requirements documentation
  - Existing teaming agreements
  - Project risk registers
  - Risk-related contract decisions
  - Activity resource requirements
  - The project schedule
  - Activity cost estimates

A Guide to the Project Management Body of Knowledge (PMBOK® Guide) – Fifth Edition, Project Management Institute (PMI)®, Project Management Professional (PMP)®, and Certified Associate in Project Management (CAPM)® are registered trademarks of Project Management Institute, Inc. - Version 2.1 Published September 30, 2014

Lesson 8: Planning for Risk, Procurements, and Stakeholder Management | Topic F

- The cost performance baseline
- Appropriate enterprise environmental factors
- Existing organizational process assets
- Consult technical experts to define specifications for the project needs clearly, concisely, and completely.
- Perform a make-or-buy analysis to determine whether particular work can be accomplished by the project team or must be procured from outside the organization.
- Determine the contract types to be used for the specific procurement needs of the project.
- Document the plan procurement information you have identified so far in the procurement management plan.
- After the procurement management plan is created, you will also generate other relevant plan procurement outputs, including:
  - Procurement statements of work
  - Make-or-buy decisions
  - Procurement documents
  - Source selection criteria
  - Change requests
- Some of the information developed in generating these outputs will be used to finalize the procurement management plan.

A Guide to the Project Management Body of Knowledge (PMBOK® Guide) – Fifth Edition, Project Management Institute, Inc., 2013, pg. 358-370

ACTIVITY 8-6
Planning Project Procurements

Scenario

In this activity, you will consider how to plan for procurements.

1. When planning procurement management, what should you do first?

2. What are the three contract types and when would you use each one?

3. What do you need to create a procurement statement of work document?

4. Why can change requests be generated from procurement planning?

A Guide to the Project Management Body of Knowledge (PMBOK® Guide) – Fifth Edition, Project Management Institute (PMI)®, Project Management Professional (PMP)®, and Certified Associate in Project Management (CAPM)® are registered trademarks of Project Management Institute, Inc. - Version 2.1 Published September 30, 2014

Lesson 8: Planning for Risk, Procurements, and Stakeholder Management | Topic F

TOPIC G

Plan Stakeholder Management

Now that you have established a project management plan, you are ready to dive in a little further and start planning how stakeholders will be managed during the course of a project. As project managers, it is in our best interest to keep project stakeholders interested in the project and the outcomes. We rely on their knowledge and expertise in specific areas. Because stakeholders have a vested interest in the project as a whole, they may request updates, changes, or project outcome status.

By developing good planning techniques at the start of project, you will be able to react quickly and seamlessly to any requests made by project stakeholders during the course of your project.

A Guide to the Project Management Body of Knowledge (PMBOK® Guide) – Fifth Edition, Project Management Institute, Inc., 2013, pg. 399-400

The following data flow diagram illustrates how the Plan Stakeholder Management process relates to the other knowledge areas within the Planning Process Group.

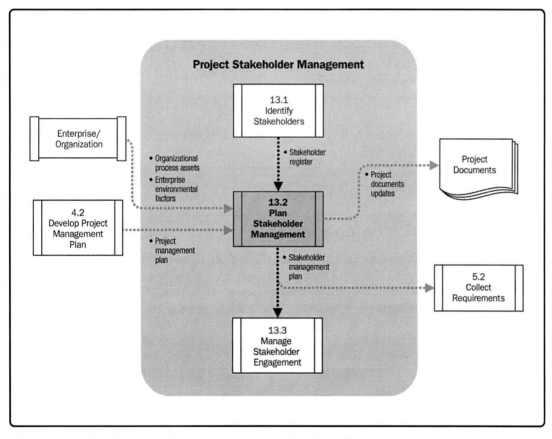

Figure 8–20: The Plan Stakeholder Management data flow diagram.

A Guide to the Project Management Body of Knowledge (PMBOK® Guide) – Fifth Edition, Project Management Institute, Inc., 2013, p. 399

What Is a Stakeholder Management Plan?

The *stakeholder management plan* is a subsidiary plan of the project management plan that defines the processes, procedures, tools, and techniques to effectively engage stakeholders in project decisions

A Guide to the Project Management Body of Knowledge (PMBOK® Guide) – Fifth Edition, Project Management Institute (PMI)®, Project Management Professional (PMP)®, and Certified Associate in Project Management (CAPM)® are registered trademarks of Project Management Institute, Inc. - Version 2.1 Published September 30, 2014

Lesson 8: Planning for Risk, Procurements, and Stakeholder Management | Topic G

and execution based on the analysis of their needs, interests, and potential impact. Keeping stakeholders engaged is crucial to the success of your project. With their support, you can determine a project's requirements quicker and know that they are accurate.

Documenting a stakeholder management plan provides a clear, actionable plan that will be used when interacting with project stakeholders to support the project's interests. A stakeholder management plan documents how the project will interact with the identified project stakeholders for the life of the project.

A stakeholder management plan identifies the management strategies required to effectively engage stakeholders. Project managers should be aware of the sensitive nature of the stakeholder management plan and take appropriate precautions when distributing the plan to other team members.

A Guide to the Project Management Body of Knowledge (PMBOK® Guide) – Fifth Edition, Project Management Institute, Inc., 2013, pg. 403-404

Contents of the Stakeholder Management Plan

In addition to the data gathered in the stakeholder register, the stakeholder management plan often provides additional stakeholder information such as:

- Desired and current engagement level of key stakeholders
- Scope and impact of change to stakeholders
- Identified interrelationships and potential overlap between stakeholders
- Stakeholder communication requirements
- Information to be distributed to stakeholders
- Reason for the distribution of that information and the expected impact to stakeholder engagement
- Time frame and frequency for the distribution of required information
- Method for updating and refining the stakeholder management plan

A Guide to the Project Management Body of Knowledge (PMBOK® Guide) – Fifth Edition, Project Management Institute, Inc., 2013, p. 399

The Plan Stakeholder Management Process

The *plan stakeholder management process* is used to guide project managers in effectively managing and engaging the stakeholders throughout the life cycle of a project. This process enables you to provide the right level of management to the number of stakeholders you have on a specific project. The process enables you to develop appropriate management strategies to effectively engage stakeholders throughout the project life cycle, based on the analysis of their needs, interests, and potential impact on the project success. This process is about the creation and maintenance of relationships between the project team and stakeholders, while satisfying their respective needs and requirements within project boundaries.

A Guide to the Project Management Body of Knowledge (PMBOK® Guide) – Fifth Edition, Project Management Institute, Inc., 2013, pg. 399-400

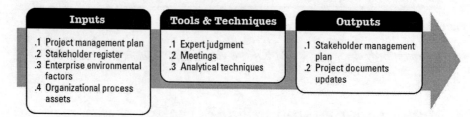

Inputs	Tools & Techniques	Outputs
.1 Project management plan .2 Stakeholder register .3 Enterprise environmental factors .4 Organizational process assets	.1 Expert judgment .2 Meetings .3 Analytical techniques	.1 Stakeholder management plan .2 Project documents updates

Figure 8-21: The Plan Stakeholder Management process.

A Guide to the Project Management Body of Knowledge (PMBOK® Guide) – Fifth Edition, Project Management Institute (PMI)®, Project Management Professional (PMP)®, and Certified Associate in Project Management (CAPM)® are registered trademarks of Project Management Institute, Inc. - Version 2.1 Published September 30, 2014

Lesson 8: Planning for Risk, Procurements, and Stakeholder Management | Topic G

A Guide to the Project Management Body of Knowledge (PMBOK® Guide) – Fifth Edition, Project
Management Institute, Inc., 2013, p. 399

Plan Stakeholder Management Inputs

Various components provide input to creating a well defined stakeholder management plan.

Input	Description
Project management plan	Provides information such as life cycle selected for the project, description of how work will be executed, description of how human resources requirements will be met, how changes will be monitored and controlled, and the need and techniques for communication among stakeholders.
Stakeholder register	Provides information needed to plan appropriate ways to engage project stakeholders.
Enterprise environmental factors	Enterprise environmental factors are reviewed because the management of stakeholders should be adapted to the project environment. Organizational culture, structure, and political climate can help in determining the best options to support a better adaptive process for managing stakeholders.
Organizational process assets	Organizational process assets that can influence this process include lessons learned database and historical information, as they provide insight on previous stakeholder management plans and their effectiveness.

A Guide to the Project Management Body of Knowledge (PMBOK® Guide) – Fifth Edition, Project
Management Institute, Inc., 2013, pg. 400-401

Plan Stakeholder Management Tools and Techniques

The following tools and techniques are used to engage with stakeholders to make sure that their
needs are met and that the stakeholder management plan is comprehensive and includes all the
needed information.

Tools & Techniques	Description
Expert judgment	Expert judgment is used to decide upon the level of engagement required at each stage of the project from each stakeholder.
Meetings	Meetings should be held with experts and the project team to define the required engagement levels of all stakeholders.
Analytical techniques	Analytical techniques can be a great tool to assess and classify the level of involvement stakeholders will have in a project.

A Guide to the Project Management Body of Knowledge (PMBOK® Guide) – Fifth Edition, Project
Management Institute, Inc., 2013, pg. 401-403

Stakeholder Classification

Stakeholder classification is a technique used to classify project stakeholders into smaller groups that are
rated based on a classification level. Stakeholder engagement and involvement will vary with every
project. Classification levels can include:

A Guide to the Project Management Body of Knowledge (PMBOK® Guide) – Fifth Edition, Project Management Institute (PMI)®, Project Management Professional
(PMP)®, and Certified Associate in Project Management (CAPM)® are registered trademarks of Project Management Institute, Inc. - Version 2.1 Published September 30, 2014

Lesson 8: Planning for Risk, Procurements, and Stakeholder Management | *Topic G*

- Unaware—Unaware of project and potential impacts
- Resistant—Aware of project and potential impacts and resistant to change
- Neutral—Aware of project yet neither supportive nor resistant
- Supportive—Aware of project and potential impacts and supportive to change
- Leading—Aware of project and potential impacts and actively engaged in ensuring the project is a success

You can use the Stakeholders Engagement Assessment Matrix to document stakeholder engagement. Current engagement level is indicated by a C and desired engagement level is indicated by a D.

A Guide to the Project Management Body of Knowledge (PMBOK® Guide) – Fifth Edition, Project Management Institute, Inc., 2013, pg. 402-403

Stakeholder	Unaware	Resistant	Neutral	Supportive	Leading
Stakeholder 1	C			D	
Stakeholder 2			C	D	
Stakeholder 3				D C	

Figure 8–22: The stakeholders engagement assessment matrix.

A Guide to the Project Management Body of Knowledge (PMBOK® Guide) – Fifth Edition, Project Management Institute, Inc., 2013, p. 403

Plan Stakeholder Management Outputs

There are two outputs from the Plan Stakeholder Management process.

Output	Description
Stakeholder management plan	As stated in the *PMBOK® Guide,* this plan is a subsidiary plan of the project management plan that defines the processes, procedures, tools, and techniques to effectively engage stakeholders in project decisions and execution based on the analysis of their needs, interests, and potential impact.
Project documents	In this process, project documents that may be updated include the project schedule and the stakeholder register.

A Guide to the Project Management Body of Knowledge (PMBOK® Guide) – Fifth Edition, Project Management Institute, Inc., 2013, pg. 403-404

Guidelines to Develop a Stakeholder Management Plan

Guidelines to developing a stakeholder management plan are as follows:

- Review the project management plan for information such as life cycle selected for the project, description of how work will be executed, description of how human resources requirements will be met, how changes will be monitored and controlled, and the need and techniques for communication among stakeholders.
- Review the stakeholder register for information needed to plan appropriate ways to engage project stakeholders.
- Review enterprise environmental factors such as organizational culture, structure, and political climate that can help in determining the best options to support a better adaptive process for managing stakeholders.

- Review organizational process assets such as the lessons learned database and historical information, as they provide insight on previous stakeholder management plans and their effectiveness.
- Use tools and techniques, such as expert judgment, to decide upon the level of engagement required at each stage of the project from each stakeholder.
- Hold meetings with experts and the project team to define the required engagement levels of all stakeholders.
- Use analytical techniques to classify the level of engagement for stakeholders.
- Document the stakeholder management plan.

A Guide to the Project Management Body of Knowledge (PMBOK® Guide) – Fifth Edition, Project Management Institute, Inc., 2013, pg. 399-404

A Guide to the Project Management Body of Knowledge (PMBOK® Guide) – Fifth Edition, Project Management Institute (PMI)®, Project Management Professional (PMP)®, and Certified Associate in Project Management (CAPM)® are registered trademarks of Project Management Institute, Inc. - Version 2.1 Published September 30, 2014

Lesson 8: Planning for Risk, Procurements, and Stakeholder Management | Topic G

ACTIVITY 8-7
Researching Stakeholder Management Plans

Scenario

With your stakeholder register completed for the 122 East Main project, you can start planning how to manage those stakeholders. Before you put the plan together, you need to research the different types of stakeholder management plans that are available.

---

1. Review stakeholder management plans available on the Internet.
   a) From the desktop, launch Internet Explorer.
   b) In the search engine text box, enter *Stakeholder Management Plan Template* Review the results of the search.
   c) In the address bar, enter *projectmanagementdocs.com*
   d) Select the **Project Planning** tab and scroll down to the **Stakeholder Management Plan**. Select the link and review the information on the page.

2. Why is it important to plan for stakeholder management?

3. Bob Jones is the manager of the accounting department of a large manufacturing firm. The organization's Information Technology department has a new initiative to upgrade and improve the existing accounting system due to new tax regulations. Bob likes the older system he's been using for more than 10 years and is questioning whether the new system will produce the same results as the old one. What classification would you use for Bob's level of involvement in this project?

   ○ Resistant

   ○ Unaware

   ○ Leading

   ○ Supportive

   ○ Neutral

4. Close all open files and windows.

A Guide to the Project Management Body of Knowledge (PMBOK® Guide) – Fifth Edition, Project Management Institute (PMI)®, Project Management Professional (PMP)®, and Certified Associate in Project Management (CAPM)® are registered trademarks of Project Management Institute, Inc. - Version 2.1 Published September 30, 2014

Lesson 8: Planning for Risk, Procurements, and Stakeholder Management | Topic G

Summary

In this lesson, you analyzed risks, planned for risk responses, planned for procurements and stakeholder management. You created a risk register that describes how project risk management activities are structured and performed throughout the project. By taking a proactive approach during risk, procurement, and stakeholder planning, you arm yourself with the necessary information to manage potential risks and procurements issues that may arise during the course of your project and ensure the best possible environment for success.

How could your organization benefit from comprehensive risk planning?

How could your organization benefit from more effective procurement planning?

Note: Check your LogicalCHOICE Course screen for opportunities to interact with your classmates, peers, and the larger LogicalCHOICE online community about the topics covered in this course or other topics you are interested in. From the Course screen you can also access available resources for a more continuous learning experience.

A Guide to the Project Management Body of Knowledge (PMBOK® Guide) – Fifth Edition, Project Management Institute (PMI)®, Project Management Professional (PMP)®, and Certified Associate in Project Management (CAPM)® are registered trademarks of Project Management Institute, Inc. - Version 2.1 Published September 30, 2014

Lesson 8: Planning for Risk, Procurements, and Stakeholder Management |

9 | Executing a Project

Lesson Time: 4 hours, 30 minutes

Lesson Objectives

In this lesson, you will:

- Direct and manage project work.
- Perform quality assurance.
- Acquire a project team.
- Develop a project team.
- Manage the project team.
- Manage project communications.
- Conduct project procurements.
- Manage project stakeholder engagement.

Lesson Introduction

You finished your project planning and integrated the outputs from each of the planning processes into a comprehensive project management plan. Now your project transitions from planning to executing. Project execution is the third of five project management process groups that you will perform on most projects you manage. In this lesson, you will execute project work.

The following diagram highlights the next process group and knowledge areas covered in this lesson.

Knowledge Areas	Initiating Process Group	Planning Process Group	Executing Process Group	Monitoring and Controlling Process Group	Closing Process Group
4. Project Integration Management	4.1 Develop Project Charter	4.2 Develop Project Management Plan	4.3 Direct and Manage Project Work	4.4 Monitor and Control Project Work 4.5 Perform Integrated Change Control	4.6 Close Project or Phase
5. Project Scope Management		5.1 Plan Scope Management 5.2 Collect Requirements 5.3 Define Scope 5.4 Create WBS		5.5 Validate Scope 5.6 Control Scope	
6. Project Time Management		6.1 Plan Schedule Management 6.2 Define Activities 6.3 Sequence Activities 6.4 Estimate Activity Resources 6.5 Estimate Activity Durations 6.6 Develop Schedule		6.7 Control Schedule	
7. Project Cost Management		7.1 Plan Cost Management 7.2 Estimate Cost 7.3 Determine Budget		7.4 Control Costs	
8. Project Quality Management		8.1 Plan Quality Management	8.2 Perform Quality Assurance	8.3 Control Quality	
9. Project Human Resource Management		9.1 Plan Human Resource Management	9.2 Acquire Project Team 9.3 Develop Project Team 9.4 Manage Project Team		
10. Project Communication Management		10.1 Plan Communications Management	10.2 Manage Communications	10.3 Control Communications	
11. Project Risk Management		11.1 Plan Risk Management 11.2 Identify Risks 11.3 Perform Qualitative Risk Analysis 11.4 Perform Quantitative Risk Analysis 11.5 Plan Risk Responses		11.6 Control Risks	
12. Project Procurement Management		12.1 Plan Procurement Management	12.2 Conduct Procurements	12.3 Control Procurements	12.4 Close Procurements
13. Project Stakeholder Management	13.1 Identify Stakeholders	13.2 Plan Stakeholder Management	13.3 Manage Stakeholder Engagement	13.4 Control Stakeholder Engagement	

TOPIC A

Direct and Manage Project Work

Your project has officially advanced from planning to executing. Now it is finally time to start leveraging the plan. In this topic, you will identify the components and purpose of the direct and manage project execution phase of the project.

A Guide to the Project Management Body of Knowledge (PMBOK® Guide) – Fifth Edition, Project Management Institute, Inc., 2013, pg. 79-81

The following data flow diagram illustrates how the Direct and Manage Project Work process relates to the other knowledge areas within the Process Groups.

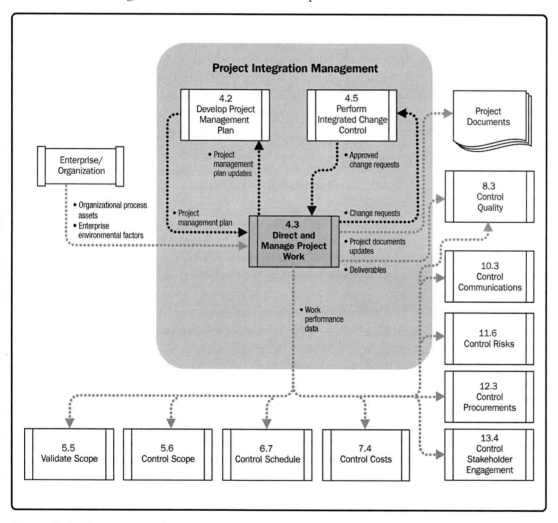

Figure 9–1: Plan Direct and Manage Project Work work flow diagram.

A Guide to the Project Management Body of Knowledge (PMBOK® Guide) – Fifth Edition, Project Management Institute, Inc., 2013, p. 80

The Direct and Manage Project Work Process

The *Direct and Manage Project Work process* involves carrying out the project management plan to produce a product or provide a service so as to meet the project objectives. It requires the project team to build on the foundation laid during project plan development, as they coordinate and direct

A Guide to the Project Management Body of Knowledge (PMBOK® Guide) – Fifth Edition, Project Management Institute (PMI)®, Project Management Professional (PMP)®, and Certified Associate in Project Management (CAPM)® are registered trademarks of Project Management Institute, Inc. - Version 2.1 Published September 30, 2014

Lesson 9: Executing a Project | Topic A

the technical and organizational project interfaces. This is not just one coherent task, but is a lengthy and complex iterative process.

A Guide to the Project Management Body of Knowledge (PMBOK® Guide) – Fifth Edition, Project Management Institute, Inc., 2013, pg. 79-81

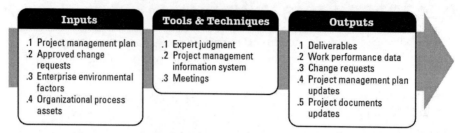

Figure 9-2: The Direct and Manage Project Work process.

A Guide to the Project Management Body of Knowledge (PMBOK® Guide) – Fifth Edition, Project Management Institute, Inc., 2013, p. 79

Direct and Manage Project Work Inputs

Various components provide input to the Direct and Manage Project Work process.

Input	Description
Project management plan	Describes each step of the project, including the way it is executed, monitored, controlled, and closed.
Approved change requests	Includes approved changes, which are ready for implementation by the project team. These change requests are recorded and can either increase or decrease the project scope. They may also be used for revising policies, project management plans, procedures, costs and budgets, and adjusting schedules.
Enterprise environmental factors	Includes factors such as organizational culture and structure, infrastructure, personnel administration, stakeholder tolerances, and Project Management Information System (PMIS) that can influence the direct and manage project execution process.
Organizational process assets	Includes existing documents and databases such as standard guidelines, communication requirements, defect management processes, and process measurement databases that can influence the direct and manage project execution process.

A Guide to the Project Management Body of Knowledge (PMBOK® Guide) – Fifth Edition, Project Management Institute, Inc., 2013, pg. 82-83

Approved Change Requests

Approved change requests are requests that have been reviewed and approved by the change control board (CCB) and are ready to be scheduled for implementation. These changes can affect costs, scope, schedule, quality, procedures, plans or policies. Approved changes can include:

- Corrective action, which is an activity that adjusts the performance of the project work with the project management plan.
- Preventive action, which is an activity that ensures future performance of the project work with the project management plan.
- Defect repair, which is an activity that modifies a non-conformance within the project.

- Update, which is a modification to a project document or plan.

A Guide to the Project Management Body of Knowledge (PMBOK® Guide) – Fifth Edition, Project Management Institute, Inc., 2013, p. 82

Direct and Manage Project Work Tools and Techniques

There are three tools and techniques used in the Direct and Manage Project Work process.

Tools & Techniques	Description
Expert judgment	Used to provide direction to effectively execute the project management plan. The expertise provided by the project manager, project management team, consultants, other departments in the organization, or other stakeholders will be applied to both technical and management details.
Project Management Information System (PMIS)	An automated or manual system, which is a part of the enterprise environmental factors, helps with directing and managing project execution. PMIS includes systems such as scheduling software and configuration management system.
Meetings	Used to discuss the direction and management of the project work. They can be information exchange, brainstorming, option evaluation or design, or decision making meetings.

A Guide to the Project Management Body of Knowledge (PMBOK® Guide) – Fifth Edition, Project Management Institute, Inc., 2013, pg. 83-84

PMIS

A *PMIS* is an automated or manual system used by a project team to gather, analyze, communicate, and store project information. The PMIS collects information on the work that has and has not been accomplished in each work package, and how that work result compares to the planned schedule, cost, quality, and scope. A PMIS can utilize sophisticated software tools, either those purchased off-the-shelf or custom-built by an internal IT group, to manage some of its components. There is some overlap between a communication plan and a PMIS; the PMIS has a calendar associated with it and includes a lot of communication between the project manager and the team.

> **Note:** A common pitfall associated with using a PMIS is creating a system in which the various pieces of data are incompatible with one another. For example, the financial data may be created in one application and the reporting in a different application and there is no way to get these two systems to talk to each other.

A Guide to the Project Management Body of Knowledge (PMBOK® Guide) – Fifth Edition, Project Management Institute, Inc., 2013, p. 84

Common PMIS Issues

Several common PMIS issues arise when directing and managing project execution.

Issue	Description
Reacting to lagging indicators	PMIS reports show problems after the fact. Good project management requires proactive problem prevention.

A Guide to the Project Management Body of Knowledge (PMBOK® Guide) – Fifth Edition, Project Management Institute (PMI)®, Project Management Professional (PMP)®, and Certified Associate in Project Management (CAPM)® are registered trademarks of Project Management Institute, Inc. - Version 2.1 Published September 30, 2014

Lesson 9: Executing a Project | *Topic A*

Issue	Description
Managing symptoms rather than problems	Although the PMIS reports exceptions and overruns, it can't explain the reason for the problem. It is important to focus on finding the cause and solving the problem, rather than making the exception or overrun go away.
Over-reliance on PMIS communication	Project managers need to communicate frequently with team members and other stakeholders. Sending PMIS reports is important, but shouldn't take the place of other types of communication.
Invalid data in the PMIS	PMIS reports can be wrong, either making problems look greater or smaller than they are. Some very real problems may not show up in the PMIS at all. The project manager must look beyond the PMIS to verify information about the problems, and then concentrate on getting the problems solved.
Too much information	Too much information is counterproductive, forcing people to cope by ignoring some of the messages. It is important to make sure that the right people get the information they need at the right time, but it is equally important not to swamp people with irrelevant or untimely information. Someone has to control the scope of the information in the PMIS, or it will overload the team and the project manager.

A Guide to the Project Management Body of Knowledge (PMBOK® Guide) – Fifth Edition, Project Management Institute, Inc., 2013, p. 84

Work Authorization Systems

A *work authorization system* is a tool used to communicate official permission to begin working on an activity or work package. It is a function, or component, of the PMIS. Its purpose is to ensure that work is done at the appropriate time, by the appropriate individual or group, by a specific time, and in the proper sequence. Work authorization systems include the necessary processes, documents, tracking systems, and approval levels required to provide work authorizations. Depending on the project, your work authorization mechanism may be a simple email or a formal, written notice to begin work. Smaller projects may require only verbal authorization. The work authorization system is integrated with the communications plan.

A Guide to the Project Management Body of Knowledge (PMBOK® Guide) – Fifth Edition, Project Management Institute, Inc., 2013, p. 567

Direct and Manage Project Work Outputs

There are several outputs from the Direct and Manage Project Work process.

Output	Description
Deliverables	A *deliverable* is the product, result, or capability produced as a result of completed work packages that were determined in the WBS creation process. Some deliverables may have been affected by approved change requests. They include a unique and verifiable product, result, or service that is required to complete a process, phase, or project.

A Guide to the Project Management Body of Knowledge (PMBOK® Guide) – Fifth Edition, Project Management Institute (PMI)®, Project Management Professional (PMP)®, and Certified Associate in Project Management (CAPM)® are registered trademarks of Project Management Institute, Inc. - Version 2.1 Published September 30, 2014

Lesson 9: Executing a Project | Topic A

Output	Description
Work performance data	Periodically collected information about project activities being performed to accomplish the project work, including deliverable status and costs incurred. This data would reside in your PMIS, if you have one. Information can include: • Schedule progress with status information • Deliverables that have been completed and not completed • All schedule activities and their start and finish dates • The degree to which quality standards are being accomplished • Expenses authorized and incurred • Estimates to complete the schedule activities already in progress • Percent of schedule activities that have been completed • Lessons learned that are posted to the lessons learned knowledge base • Details on resource utilization • Status for implementation of change requests • Details on corrective and preventive actions and defect repairs
Change requests	Changes requested by the stakeholders that may impact the project scope, policies, procedures, cost, and budgets, or lead to reworking of project schedules. Changes may be categorized as preventive and corrective actions, defect repairs, and updates.
Project management plan updates	Project management plan components that may be updated when directing and managing project execution include: • Requirements management plan • Schedule management plan • Cost management plan • Quality management plan • Human resource management plan • Communications management plan • Risk management plan • Procurement management plan • Project baselines
Project document updates	Project documents that may be updated include the requirements document, project logs, risk register, and stakeholder register.

A Guide to the Project Management Body of Knowledge (PMBOK® Guide) – Fifth Edition, Project Management Institute, Inc., 2013, pg. 84-86

Guidelines to Effectively Direct and Manage Project Work

Throughout the entire execution of a project, the project manager can employ various techniques to coordinate and direct the various technical and organizational aspects of a project. Tools, such as the PMIS and the work authorization system, are powerful work aids that an organization can use to ensure project success. To effectively execute the project plan, follow these guidelines:

• Comply with any organizational policies and procedures that the organization has in place regarding project execution to ensure predictable and consistent results. Make sure that all contractors are familiar with and comply with the procedures.

• Evaluate and select the work authorization system you will use to formally sanction work to begin on an activity or deliverable. The value of the control your system provides should be balanced with the cost (money and time) of designing, implementing, and using the system.

A Guide to the Project Management Body of Knowledge (PMBOK® Guide) – Fifth Edition, Project Management Institute (PMI)®, Project Management Professional (PMP)®, and Certified Associate in Project Management (CAPM)® are registered trademarks of Project Management Institute, Inc. - Version 2.1 Published September 30, 2014

Lesson 9: Executing a Project | Topic A

- In line with good project management practice, use the artifacts necessary to get the job done. Use the organization's project management infrastructure. If it is not there already, then invent it.
- If necessary, work with a systems analyst to create a PMIS that is workable for your project. Make sure the systems analyst understands the following:
    - Who needs to use the information?
    - What types of information will be needed by each user?
    - When and in what sequence will the information be used?
    - Who will generate the initial information to be incorporated into the system?
- Once the system is in place, determine who will be responsible for its day-to-day operation, whether it will be you or someone else. Specifically, you need to determine who will be responsible for:
    - Data entry of initial information
    - Analysis of information
    - Storage, archiving, and retrieval
    - Systems documentation
- Evaluate the effectiveness of the PMIS for your project.

A Guide to the Project Management Body of Knowledge (PMBOK® Guide) – Fifth Edition, Project Management Institute, Inc., 2013, pg. 79-86

A Guide to the Project Management Body of Knowledge (PMBOK® Guide) – Fifth Edition, Project Management Institute (PMI)®, Project Management Professional (PMP)®, and Certified Associate in Project Management (CAPM)® are registered trademarks of Project Management Institute, Inc. - Version 2.1 Published September 30, 2014

Lesson 9: Executing a Project | Topic A

ACTIVITY 9-1
Identifying Responsibilities for Project Execution

Scenario

In preparation for the project execution phase of the project, the PMO will implement a PMIS that all project teams will use to gather, analyze, communicate, and store project information. The project team will be the first team within the organization to use this system. You have completed your project planning and the project is ready to begin. You now have to coordinate and direct both the technical and organizational aspects of the project.

1. You need to assist the systems analyst in the creation of a PMIS that is workable for your project. In order to design an effective PMIS, what are the inputs that a systems analyst should know about the project that the PMIS will manage?

   ☑ What people will have access to the information?

   ☑ When will the information be needed?

   ☑ Who will incorporate the information into the system?

   ☐ Who is the customer?

2. As the project manager, you have made sure all organizational policies and procedures were followed, and the contract training vendor is familiar with their responsibilities. What would you do next?

   ○ Call a meeting with the project sponsor so she can commence work.

   ◉ Issue work authorization.

   ○ Work with a systems analyst to create a PMIS.

   ○ Collect work performance information.

3. An activity did not start on its scheduled date. The responsible team, Team 1, claimed that they could not start the activity because its predecessor activity did not show a completion date in the latest status report. Team 2 claimed that they had completed the activity on time and had followed the appropriate procedure for updating its completion status. What are some things you would do to investigate why the status report was not up to date?

TOPIC B

Perform Quality Assurance

Now that you know what is involved in creating a quality assurance plan, you are ready to move forward with this key element of ensuring that your project meets its stated goals. This is the action phase of your work, in which you will measure, verify, and quantify the progress achieved. In this topic, you'll execute quality assurance.

A Guide to the Project Management Body of Knowledge (PMBOK® Guide) – Fifth Edition, Project Management Institute, Inc., 2013, pg. 242-244

The following data flow diagram illustrates how the Perform Quality Assurance process relates to the other knowledge areas within the Process Groups.

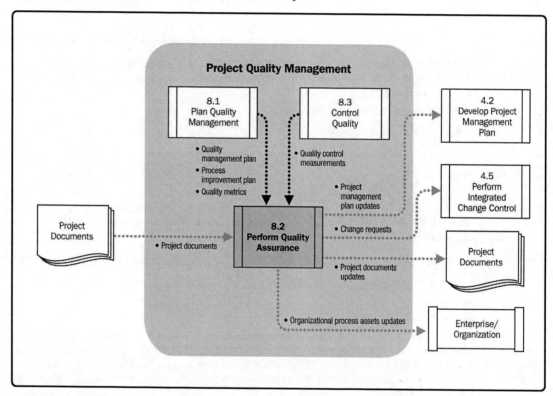

Figure 9–3: Perform Quality Assurance work flow diagram.

A Guide to the Project Management Body of Knowledge (PMBOK® Guide) – Fifth Edition, Project Management Institute, Inc., 2013, p. 243

Quality Assurance Plans

A *quality assurance plan* is a document that specifies a project's parameters and standards for quality, identifies how testing will be carried out, and describes how, when, in what manner, and to what degree the project will be reviewed and evaluated against quality criteria. It includes recommendations for the appropriate actions to be taken to improve quality, and it lists the quality assurance team members who are responsible for carrying out the quality reviews.

A Guide to the Project Management Body of Knowledge (PMBOK® Guide) – Fifth Edition, Project Management Institute, Inc., 2013, pg. 241-244

A Guide to the Project Management Body of Knowledge (PMBOK® Guide) – Fifth Edition, Project Management Institute (PMI)®, Project Management Professional (PMP)®, and Certified Associate in Project Management (CAPM)® are registered trademarks of Project Management Institute, Inc. - Version 2.1 Published September 30, 2014

Lesson 9: Executing a Project | Topic B

The Perform Quality Assurance Process

The *Perform Quality Assurance process* ensures that the project quality standards and operational definitions are being used, by auditing the quality requirements and results from quality control measurements. This facilitates the improvement of the quality processes. These audits are performed throughout the project life cycle and are considered part of the cost of quality. A quality assurance department may perform or oversee the activities in the process to provide an outside, unbiased perspective.

A Guide to the Project Management Body of Knowledge (PMBOK® Guide) – Fifth Edition, Project Management Institute, Inc., 2013, pg. 242-244

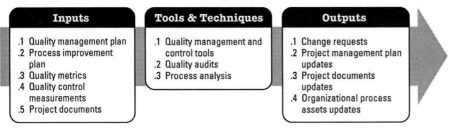

Figure 9-4: The Perform Quality Assurance process.

A Guide to the Project Management Body of Knowledge (PMBOK® Guide) – Fifth Edition, Project Management Institute, Inc., 2013, p. 243

Perform Quality Assurance Inputs

Various components provide input to the Perform Quality Assurance process.

Input	Description
Quality management plan	Details how project quality assurance should be conducted.
Process improvement plan	Provides detailed steps for analyzing processes and identifying ways to enhance the value of the processes.
Quality metrics	Describes what specific elements of the project are going to be measured, how they will be measured, and how they are factored into the project.
Quality control measurements (an output of 8.3)	Used to assess the organization's quality standards and processes. These measurements are the results of the control project quality process and are developed during the quality control processes. They are assessed and analyzed for determining the process reliability.
Project documents	Should be under configuration management to ensure timeliness and quality.

A Guide to the Project Management Body of Knowledge (PMBOK® Guide) – Fifth Edition, Project Management Institute, Inc., 2013, pg. 244-245

Perform Quality Assurance Tools and Techniques

There are three tools and techniques used in the Perform Quality Assurance process.

Tools & Techniques	Description
Quality management and control tools	All tools and techniques used for the plan quality and perform quality control processes such as the cause-and-effect diagrams, control charts, flowcharting, histogram, Pareto diagram, run chart, scatter diagram, statistical sampling, inspection, approved change requests review, cost-benefit analysis, cost of quality, control charts, benchmarking, design of experiments, proprietary quality management methodologies, and additional quality planning tools are used in the Perform the Quality Assurance process.
Quality audits	A quality audit is a review to determine if the activities comply with policies, processes, and procedures in an attempt to identify inefficient or ineffective procedures in use, resulting in lower cost of quality and higher percentage of output acceptance. Quality audits may be carried out by internal or external auditors at regular intervals or at random. It confirms that the approved changes have been implemented.
Process analysis	Process analysis uses the process improvement plan to identify needed improvements to processes. It looks at constraints and problems experienced, non-value added activities, and root causes for these issues. Root cause analysis identifies a problem, determines the underlying causes, and then develops preventive actions to keep it from reoccurring.

A Guide to the Project Management Body of Knowledge (PMBOK® Guide) – Fifth Edition, Project Management Institute, Inc., 2013, pg. 245-247

Types of Quality Tools

There are numerous quality tools that support the Perform Quality Assurance process.

Tool	Description
Affinity diagrams	Used to generate ideas that form patterns of thought about a problem.
Process decision program charts (PDPC)	Used to understand a goal in relation to the steps for getting to the goal.
Interrelationship digraphs	Used for creative problem solving of complex scenarios with intertwined logical relationships. It can use data from affinity diagrams, tree diagrams, and fishbone diagrams.
Tree diagrams	Also referred to as systematic diagrams, can be used to represent decomposition hierarchies such as the WBS, RBS, and organizational breakdown structure (OBS). This uses nested branches to show hierarchical relationships.
Prioritization matrices	Used to identify key issues and alternatives that are prioritized as a set of decisions for implementation. Prioritized and weighted criteria are applied to these alternatives to score and then rank the options
Activity network diagrams	Also referred to as arrow diagrams, includes activity-on-arrow (AOA) and activity-on-node (AON) formats of a network diagram. This diagram is used with PERT, CPM, and PDM for scheduling.

A Guide to the Project Management Body of Knowledge (PMBOK® Guide) – Fifth Edition, Project Management Institute (PMI)®, Project Management Professional (PMP)®, and Certified Associate in Project Management (CAPM)® are registered trademarks of Project Management Institute, Inc. - Version 2.1 Published September 30, 2014

Lesson 9: Executing a Project | Topic B

Tool	Description
Matrix diagrams	Uses a row-and-column format to show relationships between factors, causes, and objectives.

A Guide to the Project Management Body of Knowledge (PMBOK® Guide) – Fifth Edition, Project Management Institute, Inc., 2013, pg. 245-246

Quality Audits

A *quality audit* is an independent evaluation, inspection, or review of a project's quality assurance system to improve quality performance of a project. The audits can take place at scheduled or random intervals. The auditor may be a trained individual from within the performing organization or a qualified representative of a third-party organization. During a quality audit, the quality management plan is analyzed to make sure that it is still reflective of what has been learned in the project and to make sure the operational definitions are still adequate and valid. The results of a quality audit are important for the current project, as well as for later projects or other parts of the organization.

A Guide to the Project Management Body of Knowledge (PMBOK® Guide) – Fifth Edition, Project Management Institute, Inc., 2013, p. 247

Quality Audit Objectives

There are various objectives for performing quality audits. Some of them are:

- Identify the best practices that have been implemented.
- Identify the flaws or deficiencies in the project processes.
- Use the best practices followed in similar projects performed earlier.
- Help increase team productivity by providing assistance for process implementation improvements.
- Highlight the contributions of each quality audit in the organization's lessons learned library.

A Guide to the Project Management Body of Knowledge (PMBOK® Guide) – Fifth Edition, Project Management Institute, Inc., 2013, p. 247

Topics of Quality Audits

Several topics can be included in a quality audit.

Topic	Description
Quality management policy	May be evaluated to determine how well management uses quality data and how well others in the organization understand how the data is being used. The evaluation might include an analysis of management policies for collection, analysis, and use of data in decision-making or strategic planning.
Collection and use of information	May be evaluated to determine how well the project team is collecting, distributing, and using quality data. Items for analysis in this category might include consistency of data collection processes, speed of information distribution, and use of quality data in decision-making.
Analytical methods	May be evaluated to determine if the best analytical methods are being used consistently and how well their results are being used. Items for audit might include how analysis topics and analysis methods are selected, what technology is used, and how results are fed back to others in the process.

Topic	Description
Cost of quality	May be evaluated to determine the most effective proportion between prevention, inspection, and costs of repair or rework.
Quality process design	May be evaluated to determine how process design, process analysis, and statistical process control should be used to establish and improve the capability of a process.

A Guide to the Project Management Body of Knowledge (PMBOK® Guide) – Fifth Edition, Project Management Institute, Inc., 2013, p. 247

Perform Quality Assurance Outputs

There are four outputs from the Perform Quality Assurance process.

Output	Description
Change requests	Actions suggested to improve quality, effectiveness, and efficiency of policies, processes, and procedures in the organization. This results in enhanced stakeholder benefits. Change requests are used to analyze recommended improvements and take appropriate corrective or preventive actions.
Project management plan updates	Project management plans that may need updates include the quality, scope, schedule, and cost management plans.
Project documents updates	Project documents that may need updates include quality audit reports, training plans, and process documentation.
Organizational process assets updates	Include updates to components such as project quality standards.

A Guide to the Project Management Body of Knowledge (PMBOK® Guide) – Fifth Edition, Project Management Institute, Inc., 2013, pg. 247-248

Guidelines to Perform Quality Assurance

Effective quality assurance provides confidence that the project's product or service will satisfy relevant quality requirements and standards. To apply quality assurance to your project, follow these guidelines:

- Ensure that random and/or scheduled quality audits are conducted by qualified auditors to evaluate the quality management plan, quality testing procedures, and measurement criteria.
  - Are the quality parameters set forth in the quality assurance plan valid?
  - Are the operational definitions and checklists adequate and appropriate to achieving the desired final results?
  - Are the testing methods being implemented correctly?
  - Is data being interpreted, recorded, and fed back into the system properly?
- Use one or more of the quality assurance tools and techniques to determine the causes of quality problems of the project's product, service, systems, or processes.
- Identify and implement the appropriate actions to increase the effectiveness and efficiency of the project team's work results to improve quality in the product or service.

A Guide to the Project Management Body of Knowledge (PMBOK® Guide) – Fifth Edition, Project Management Institute, Inc., 2013, pg. 242-248

A Guide to the Project Management Body of Knowledge (PMBOK® Guide) – Fifth Edition, Project Management Institute (PMI)®, Project Management Professional (PMP)®, and Certified Associate in Project Management (CAPM)® are registered trademarks of Project Management Institute, Inc. - Version 2.1 Published September 30, 2014

Lesson 9: Executing a Project | *Topic B*

ACTIVITY 9-2
Performing Quality Assurance

Scenario

The framing phase is getting started on the new build site. Materials have been ordered and delivered and the foundation is almost complete. You have a quality management plan that was used for previous projects and you have made a few changes to meet the needs of your current project. The plan contains specific operational definitions for measuring the quality of the construction work. In addition, it states that scheduled and random quality inspections will occur. These inspections will be done by an internal Building with Heart quality assurance engineer and will be in addition to the inspections conducted by the city. Your company is ISO certified, so relevant ISO standards and regulations must be adhered to as well. You have selected a good team of workers and volunteers for the construction and you are confident in their ability to meet the quality standards.

---

1. **The manager of quality assurance has asked you about your quality management plan. Which feature might he find problematic?**

   ○ Any corrective actions that a project manager feels will improve the effectiveness or efficiency.

   ○ Scheduled and random quality inspections will take place, which will be conducted by an internal quality assurance engineer, as well as by the city.

   ○ Operational definitions were defined for measuring the quality of the construction work.

   ○ Occurrence of scheduled and random quality inspections during the course of the project.

2. **As construction gets under way, random inspection results of completed construction elements are unexpectedly negative. What sort of quality activities should be taking place?**

3. **The stakeholders are questioning the amount of resources dedicated to quality assurance. How can you demonstrate to them that the benefits of quality assurance outweigh the cost?**

   ○ Perform benchmarking to compare project practices to other projects to generate ideas for improvement.

   ○ Conduct an array of experiments to identify which factors may be influencing specific variables.

   ○ Use flowcharts to see how systems relate and how various factors might be linked to problems or effects.

   ○ Document the identified corrective actions so that their effect on project quality, cost, and schedule can be monitored during quality control.

A Guide to the Project Management Body of Knowledge (PMBOK® Guide) – Fifth Edition, Project Management Institute (PMI)®, Project Management Professional (PMP)®, and Certified Associate in Project Management (CAPM)® are registered trademarks of Project Management Institute, Inc. - Version 2.1 Published September 30, 2014

TOPIC C

Acquire Project Team

During project planning, you paved the way for effectively documenting the roles, responsibilities, and reporting relationships for your project. Now you're ready to begin appointing the individuals you need to fulfill these positions. In this topic, you will acquire your project team.

A Guide to the Project Management Body of Knowledge (PMBOK® Guide) – Fifth Edition, Project Management Institute, Inc., 2013, pg. 267-269

The following data flow diagram illustrates how the Acquire a Project Team process relates to the other knowledge areas within the Process Groups.

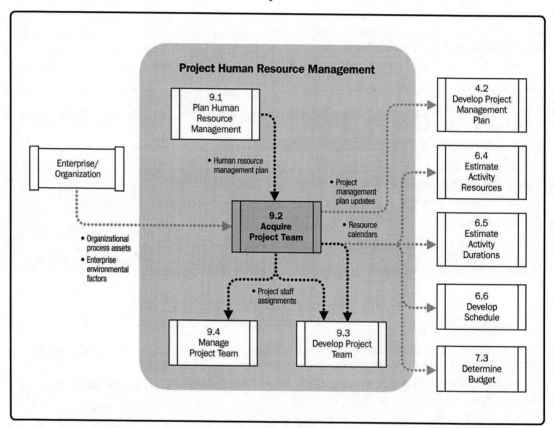

Figure 9–5: The Acquire a Project Team work flow diagram.

A Guide to the Project Management Body of Knowledge (PMBOK® Guide) – Fifth Edition, Project Management Institute, Inc., 2013, p. 268

The Acquire Project Team Process

The *acquire project team process* involves making the identified resources available to the project. The project manager needs to build a cohesive team, ensure effective communication, and clearly define people's roles and responsibilities. Resource selection may be driven by different factors such as collective bargaining agreements, or other internal or external reporting relationships. In such cases, the project management team may not be directly involved in the team member selection processes. Resources may be dictated by senior management, limiting a project manager's ability to negotiate.

A Guide to the Project Management Body of Knowledge (PMBOK® Guide) – Fifth Edition, Project Management Institute, Inc., 2013, pg. 267-269

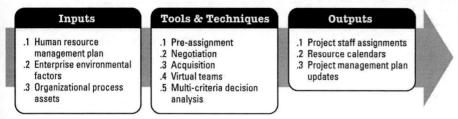

Figure 9-6: The Acquire Project Team process.

A Guide to the Project Management Body of Knowledge (PMBOK® Guide) – Fifth Edition, Project Management Institute, Inc., 2013, p. 267

Planning for Acquiring a Project Team

Factors to be considered when planning for acquiring the project team include:

- Project managers must effectively negotiate with the appropriate people for the needed project resources.
- Failure to acquire the appropriate resources may impact project performance and may ultimately result in the termination of the project.
- If human resources with the required skills and capabilities are not available at the appropriate time, alternate resources with lower competencies may be assigned without violating legal, regulatory, or other criteria.

The project team or the project management team must ensure that all project documents such as the project schedule, budget, risks, quality, training plans, and the project management plan components reflect the possible resource constraints and other problems in acquiring the required resources.

A Guide to the Project Management Body of Knowledge (PMBOK® Guide) – Fifth Edition, Project Management Institute, Inc., 2013, pg. 268-269

Acquire a Project Team Inputs

Various components provide input to the Acquire a Team process.

Input	Description
Human resource management plan	The human resources plan that provides information about how to identify, acquire, assign, manage, control, and later release the human resources. It also specifies: • The roles and responsibilities, the positions, skills, and competencies required for each project. • The project organization chart indicating the number of human resources required to work on the project. • The staffing management plan that provides information about acquiring the project team and the duration for which each team member will work on the project.
Enterprise environmental factors	Factors the project management team needs to take into consideration when acquiring their team include: • Information about human resources such as which resources are free during the required time frame, their experience, and their cost rate • Personnel administration policies • Organizational structure • Location(s) of the resources

Input	Description
Organizational process assets	Any kind of policies, guidelines, or procedures that organizations follow when delegating staff assignments and selecting resources for the project.

A Guide to the Project Management Body of Knowledge (PMBOK® Guide) – Fifth Edition, Project Management Institute, Inc., 2013, p. 269

Acquire Project Team Tools and Techniques

There are various tools and techniques used in the Acquire Project Team process.

Tools & Techniques	Description
Pre-assignment	When project team members know in advance what their assignment is before the project has its official kick-off.
Negotiation	Staff assignments can be negotiated with functional managers, vendors, or external organizations. This helps ensure that the appropriate staff is assigned within the time frame, when there is a need for scarce or specialized resources.
Acquisition	When there isn't enough staff to complete the project, outside sources such as consultants or contractors can be hired.
Virtual teams	Groups of people, hired for the same project, who never or rarely speak face-to-face. Using currently available communications technology such as collaborative software aids in communication. Virtual teams make it possible for people to: • Form teams where people live in widespread geographic areas, but work for the same company • Add expertise to projects from people who are not in the same geographical area • Include employees who work from home • Include employees who work different shifts • Include employees with disabilities • Avoid travel expenses Planning for effective communication among the virtual team members is an important consideration that needs to be considered when setting up a virtual team.
Multi-criteria decision analysis	*Multi-criteria decision analysis* uses multiple weighted criteria to rate or score potential team members to ensure the best selection to meet the project's objectives.

A Guide to the Project Management Body of Knowledge (PMBOK® Guide) – Fifth Edition, Project Management Institute, Inc., 2013, pg. 270-272

Virtual Teams

A *virtual team* is a team that is distributed across multiple locations. Some virtual teams have occasional physical meetings, while others may never meet face-to-face. Virtual team building is more difficult, for a number of reasons.

- Bonding and team identity can be hard to create when team members are geographically dispersed, because finding ways to provide a sense of team spirit and cooperation may be difficult.
- Communication and information sharing needs to rely on various forms of technology because teams cannot meet face-to-face. However, managing electronic collaboration so that everyone on the team can reliably transmit and access information from one another can be challenging.
- Because roles, reporting, and performance can be harder to track on a dispersed team, individual contributions may be overlooked.

A Guide to the Project Management Body of Knowledge (PMBOK® Guide) – Fifth Edition, Project Management Institute, Inc., 2013, p. 271

Criteria Types

There a few different types of criteria used when applying the multi-criteria decision analysis method:

- Availability—is the person available when needed?
- Cost—is the rate within the projected budget?
- Experience—does the person have the experience needed by the project?
- Ability—does the person have the competencies needed by the project?
- Knowledge—does the person have knowledge of the customer, similar project, or project environment?
- Skills—does the person have the skills to use a project tool or other needed skills?
- Attitude—does the person have the ability to work with other team members?
- International factors—what are the person's location, time zone, and communication capabilities?

A Guide to the Project Management Body of Knowledge (PMBOK® Guide) – Fifth Edition, Project Management Institute, Inc., 2013, pg. 271-272

Acquire a Project Team Outputs

There are three outputs from the Acquire a Project Team process.

Output	Description
Project staff assignments	The assignment of the people who will work on the project, whether full-time, part-time, or as needed. This includes members of the project office, as well as all other members of the project team, and usually includes a team directory, memos to/from team members, and project organization charts and schedules.
Resource calendars	Provides information on the schedule and availability of the project resources. It also prevents resource scheduling conflicts and factors in details such as vacation time and other project commitments.
Project management plan updates	As people are assigned to project roles and responsibilities, changes may need to be made to the human resources management plan due to promotions, retirements, illnesses, performance issues, workloads, and expertise.

A Guide to the Project Management Body of Knowledge (PMBOK® Guide) – Fifth Edition, Project Management Institute, Inc., 2013, p. 272

A Guide to the Project Management Body of Knowledge (PMBOK® Guide) – Fifth Edition, Project Management Institute (PMI)®, Project Management Professional (PMP)®, and Certified Associate in Project Management (CAPM)® are registered trademarks of Project Management Institute, Inc. - Version 2.1 Published September 30, 2014

Lesson 9: Executing a Project | Topic C

Guidelines to Acquire a Project Team

Acquiring well-formed project teams will result in meeting the resource needs of the project to fulfill project requirements. To acquire a project team, follow these guidelines:

- Form good relationships with functional managers.
- Know when you need specific resources.
- Negotiate with the appropriate organizations or parties for critical resources timed with project need.
- Look for synergy and diversity among team members.
- Look outside to competent suppliers where in-house resources are not available.
- Make sure that roles and responsibilities are clearly understood by the team and other stakeholders.
- Publish an organization chart to all stakeholders.

A Guide to the Project Management Body of Knowledge (PMBOK® Guide) – Fifth Edition, Project Management Institute, Inc., 2013, pg. 267-272

A Guide to the Project Management Body of Knowledge (PMBOK® Guide) – Fifth Edition, Project Management Institute (PMI)®, Project Management Professional (PMP)®, and Certified Associate in Project Management (CAPM)® are registered trademarks of Project Management Institute, Inc. - Version 2.1 Published September 30, 2014

Lesson 9: Executing a Project | Topic C

ACTIVITY 9-3
Acquiring a Project Team

Scenario

During project planning, you have documented the roles, responsibilities, and reporting relationships for your project. Now you're ready to determine the individuals you will need to fulfill these positions.

1. Three members of your project team have to be allocated to you on a part-time, 50 percent basis. What would be your first step in acquiring these resources for the project team?

2. The functional manager of the department informs you that, based on the time frame for your project, two of the resources that are available are new volunteers who have not yet worked in a project on their own. What should you do?

3. Why is negotiation so important when acquiring your project team?

4. During the first meeting of the new project team, some confusion arises between two team members about their roles and responsibilities. Because this conversation is not appropriate in this forum, how might you respond?

A Guide to the Project Management Body of Knowledge (PMBOK® Guide) – Fifth Edition, Project Management Institute (PMI)®, Project Management Professional (PMP)®, and Certified Associate in Project Management (CAPM)® are registered trademarks of Project Management Institute, Inc. - Version 2.1 Published September 30, 2014

TOPIC D

Develop Project Team

Now that you have acquired your project team, you need to help them achieve peak performance. Team building ensures that you build an atmosphere of trust and open communication. In this topic, you will develop the project team.

A Guide to the Project Management Body of Knowledge (PMBOK® Guide) – Fifth Edition, Project Management Institute, Inc., 2013, pg. 273-274

The following data flow diagram illustrates how the Develop Project Team process relates to the other knowledge areas within the Process Groups.

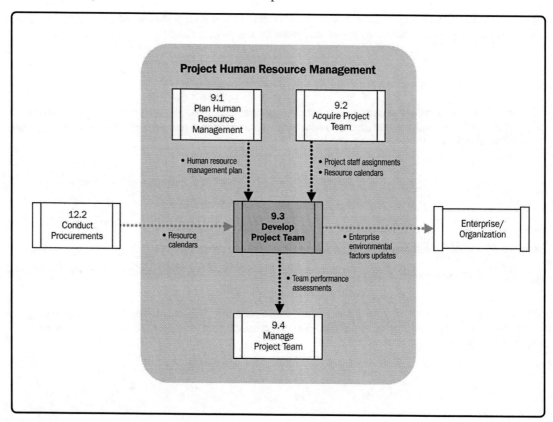

Figure 9–7: The Develop Project Team work flow diagram.

A Guide to the Project Management Body of Knowledge (PMBOK® Guide) – Fifth Edition, Project Management Institute, Inc., 2013, p. 273

The Develop Project Team Process

The *develop project team process* is an ongoing effort to build a cohesive team that benefits from good communication and a foundation of trust. Its goal is to enhance the team's collective performance and improve their skills so that you increase the likelihood of meeting project objectives. It includes good general management practices including providing training and coaching to the team, building trust, encouraging good communication and the sharing of resources, and recognizing and rewarding desirable behavior. Project managers use the develop project team process to enhance the performance of the project and the project team in an effort to increase the likelihood of meeting project objectives.

A Guide to the Project Management Body of Knowledge (PMBOK® Guide) – Fifth Edition, Project Management Institute, Inc., 2013, pg. 273-274

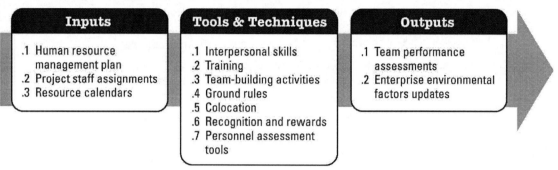

Figure 9-8: The Develop Project Team process.

A Guide to the Project Management Body of Knowledge (PMBOK® Guide) – Fifth Edition, Project Management Institute, Inc., 2013, p. 273

Foster Team Building

To foster team building within a project team, a project manager might ask each of the veteran employees on the team to partner with a less experienced team member, offering coaching as needed and sharing knowledge, information, and expertise. Working collaboratively toward a shared goal is a great way for team members to help each other reach a higher level of performance.

A Guide to the Project Management Body of Knowledge (PMBOK® Guide) – Fifth Edition, Project Management Institute, Inc., 2013, p. 273

Effective Project Teams

The team members should work in a collaborative way to ensure project success. It is the responsibility of the project manager to build an effective project team and foster teamwork. Managers should give opportunities that challenge the team members' abilities, provide support and timely feedback, and recognize and reward good performance. To achieve the best team performance, managers should use effective communication methods, develop trust among team members, manage conflicts, and promote collaborative decision making and problem solving.

Project managers should seek support from the management or the appropriate stakeholders to effectively build project teams. This will help improve people skills, advance technical competencies, build good team environment, and increase project performance.

A Guide to the Project Management Body of Knowledge (PMBOK® Guide) – Fifth Edition, Project Management Institute, Inc., 2013, p. 273

Team Development Stages

The development of the project team generally proceeds in five stages.

Stage	Description
Forming	Team members are wondering whether the decision to join the team was a wise one. They are making initial judgments about the skills and personal qualities of their teammates, as well as worrying about how they personally will be viewed by the rest of the team. During this stage, conversations tend to be polite and noncommittal, as people hesitate to reveal too much about their personal views. In addition, team meetings tend to be confusing, as the team tries to figure out who is in charge.

A Guide to the Project Management Body of Knowledge (PMBOK® Guide) – Fifth Edition, Project Management Institute (PMI)®, Project Management Professional (PMP)®, and Certified Associate in Project Management (CAPM)® are registered trademarks of Project Management Institute, Inc. - Version 2.1 Published September 30, 2014

Lesson 9: Executing a Project | Topic D

Stage	Description
Storming	Team members begin to assert themselves and control issues as they emerge. Personality differences begin to arise. Conflicts result as team members differ on the way they want to do the project work, or the way they want to make decisions.
Norming	The team begins to work productively, without worrying about personal acceptance or control issues. There are still conflicts; however, they tend to be focused on process issues rather than personality differences. The team begins to operate off mutual dependence and trust.
Performing	The team is working at optimum productivity. It is collaborating easily, communicating freely, and solving its own conflict problems. Team members feel safe in reporting problems, trusting their fellow team members to help them create the best solution for the team as a whole.
Adjourning	The team members complete their assigned work and shift to the next project or assigned work. This phase is sometimes known as "mourning."

A Guide to the Project Management Body of Knowledge (PMBOK® Guide) – Fifth Edition, Project Management Institute, Inc., 2013, p. 276

Develop Project Team Inputs

Various components provide input to the Develop Project Team process.

Input	Description
Human resource management plan	Identifies training strategies and plans for developing the project team through rewards, feedback, and disciplinary actions.
Project staff assignments	The assignment of the people who will work on the project, whether full-time, part-time, or as needed. This includes members of the project office as well as all other members of the project team.
Resource calendars	Helps identify the schedules of team members and the time when they can participate in team development tasks.

A Guide to the Project Management Body of Knowledge (PMBOK® Guide) – Fifth Edition, Project Management Institute, Inc., 2013, pg. 274-275

Develop Project Team Tools and Techniques

There are various tools and techniques used in the Develop Project Team process.

Tools & Techniques	Description
Interpersonal skills	Interpersonal skills, often referred to as "soft skills," can help a project manager prevent or resolve team issues that hinder successful completion of the project. Leadership, influencing, communicating, delegating, and empowerment skills are particularly relevant to team development.

Tools & Techniques	Description
Training	Project team members can acquire new or enhanced management or technical skills, knowledge, or attitudes through training. Training may be provided to teams, small groups, or individuals through a variety of methods such as classroom, online, computer-based, on-the-job training, mentoring, and coaching.
Team-building activities	Exercises that help the team develop into a mature, productive team. Effective project teams can be realized through factors such as: • Gaining support from top management • Obtaining commitment from team members • Encouraging team members through awards and recognition • Creating a team identity • Managing conflicts effectively • Building trust among team members • Promoting effective communication methods • Providing good team leadership
Ground rules	Rules setting clear expectations as to the expected code of conduct from team members so as to increase productivity and decrease misunderstandings.
Co-location	The establishment of a common physical location for a project team to enhance overall team performance. Co-location can be done on a temporary or permanent basis for a given project.
Recognition and rewards	A formal method used to reinforce behaviors or performance, which will make individuals feel that they are valued in the organization.
Personnel assessment tools	Used to give the project team members insight into their areas of strengths and weaknesses. They highlight peoples' preferences, aspirations, decision making process, and more. These tools provide opportunities for improving trust, commitment, understanding and communications between the team members. Examples are the Myers-Briggs Type Indicator® and DiSC®.

A Guide to the Project Management Body of Knowledge (PMBOK® Guide) – Fifth Edition, Project Management Institute, Inc., 2013, pg. 275-278

Training

Training is an activity in which team members acquire new or enhanced skills, knowledge, or attitudes. Training may be provided to teams, small groups, or individuals and can cover management, technical, or administrative topics. It can range from a multi-day, formal workshop in a classroom to a five-minute, informal on-the-job training demonstration at the employee's desk. It may be formulated to provide generic skills, or customized to provide a specific skill set that is unique to the project. Training should be made available to team members as soon as the need becomes apparent.

A Guide to the Project Management Body of Knowledge (PMBOK® Guide) – Fifth Edition, Project Management Institute, Inc., 2013, p. 275

Team-Building Activities

Team-building activities are the specific functions or actions taken to help the team to develop into a mature, productive team. They can be formal or informal, brief or extended, and facilitated by the project manager or a group facilitator.

For example, the new project manager for a line of youth-oriented sportswear decided that a good way to get to know her team was to plan an outdoor team-building activity. Two of the designers were located on the east coast and would be working very closely with the manufacturing team at the company's San Diego facility. Robin arranged to fly the two designers to San Diego to participate in the all-day, off-site ropes course. Robin participated in the rope climbing exercise as well, and an experienced team-building coach facilitated the activity.

A Guide to the Project Management Body of Knowledge (PMBOK® Guide) – Fifth Edition, Project Management Institute, Inc., 2013, p. 276

Co-location

Co-location refers to positioning most or all key team members in the same physical location to make communication easier and enhance team performance and team spirit. Although most commonly used on large projects, smaller project teams may also benefit from co-location. There are different degrees of co-location. On some projects, some of the team may be co-located, whereas others are not.

For example, a political candidate announcing a run for the presidency of the United States would establish a national campaign headquarters office, at which the key members of the campaign's project team would be co-located. The headquarters would serve as a base for national operations and centralize the efforts of the candidate's political machine. The co-location of the project team would last for only the duration of the campaign.

A Guide to the Project Management Body of Knowledge (PMBOK® Guide) – Fifth Edition, Project Management Institute, Inc., 2013, p. 277

Rewards and Recognition Systems

A *reward and recognition system* is a formal system used to reinforce performance or behavior. The purpose is to motivate the team to perform well. Rewards could include monetary gifts, additional vacation time or other perks, company plaques or trophies, or small gifts. Reward and recognition systems are generally standardized throughout an organization and approved through corporate channels.

For example, Tim is an art director assigned to the company website. Often, Tim helps new team members and provides coaching and mentoring. Carrie, the project manager, recognized Tim's extra efforts at the weekly project team meeting. She presented Tim with a gift certificate to a new restaurant as a reward and incentive for his outstanding performance.

A Guide to the Project Management Body of Knowledge (PMBOK® Guide) – Fifth Edition, Project Management Institute, Inc., 2013, p. 277

Rewarding Individual Performance

In traditional U.S. organizations, rewarding individual performance refers to giving pay increases or promotions to individuals based on merit. In a team environment, it is difficult to tie merit increases to individual performance because of the mutual interdependence of the team members.

A Guide to the Project Management Body of Knowledge (PMBOK® Guide) – Fifth Edition, Project Management Institute, Inc., 2013, pg. 277-278

A Guide to the Project Management Body of Knowledge (PMBOK® Guide) – Fifth Edition, Project Management Institute (PMI)®, Project Management Professional (PMP)®, and Certified Associate in Project Management (CAPM)® are registered trademarks of Project Management Institute, Inc. - Version 2.1 Published September 30, 2014

Lesson 9: Executing a Project | Topic D

Develop Project Team Outputs

There are two outputs from the Develop Project Team process.

Output	Description
Team performance assessments	Formal or informal evaluations of the team's performance are done periodically in order to help improve interaction between team members, solve issues, and deal with conflicts. A team's technical success is measured on the basis of meeting the project objectives, and finishing the project on time and within the decided budget. An effective team will show improvements in skills, competencies, and team cohesiveness.
Enterprise environmental factors updates	Includes updates on employee training records and skills assessments.

A Guide to the Project Management Body of Knowledge (PMBOK® Guide) – Fifth Edition, Project Management Institute, Inc., 2013, pg. 278-279

Guidelines to Develop a Team

Effective team development results in improved individual and team performance, which increases the team's ability to achieve project objectives. To effectively develop your project team, follow these guidelines:

- Recognize the project team's current stage of development and be proactive in helping the team be as productive as possible.
  - During the forming stage, conduct activities that will help the team get to know one another and develop a sense of mutual respect. The following is a list of activities for the forming stage:
    - A kick-off meeting that includes time for introductions.
    - Creation of a team handbook documenting the team's goal, the major tasks required to achieve the goal, and any constraints under which the team must operate.
    - Publication of a team directory.
    - Development of a team charter that sets forth guidelines on how team members will behave toward one another, how they will communicate, when they will meet, how they will make decisions, and how they will escalate problems.
    - Selection of a team name or emblem.
    - Initial social events to allow time to get to know one another on a personal level.
  - During the storming stage, use conflict management approaches to help the team work through problems.
  - In the norming stage, concentrate on issues of project performance.
    - Focus on the team's productivity towards meeting the project goals.
    - If the team is bogged down on certain problems, help to create cross-functional sub-teams to work on the problems.
    - Eliminate barriers that may be hampering team performance.
    - Provide opportunities for recognition for the team's performance from management, customers, or peers.
  - In the performing stage, provide recognition for team performance, but stay out of the way as the team manages its own problems. However, if project progress is sluggish, this is a good stage in which to challenge the team with more stringent performance goals.
  - In the adjourning stage, team members complete project work and shift to the next project or assigned task.
    - This phase indicates the transformational phase of achievement through synergy.

- In this phase, ensure that formal closure and completion of the tasks happens. Also, facilitate the smooth transition of the project team members to the next project.
- Develop and implement a formal reward and recognition system.
- Consider co-location to enhance the team's ability to perform as a team and improve communication. When co-location is not feasible, it becomes especially important to encourage and enhance interaction among team members.
- Provide appropriate training and coaching to help team members acquire new or enhanced skills, knowledge, or behaviors.

A Guide to the Project Management Body of Knowledge (PMBOK® Guide) – Fifth Edition, Project Management Institute, Inc., 2013, pg. 273-279

A Guide to the Project Management Body of Knowledge (PMBOK® Guide) – Fifth Edition, Project Management Institute (PMI)®, Project Management Professional (PMP)®, and Certified Associate in Project Management (CAPM)® are registered trademarks of Project Management Institute, Inc. - Version 2.1 Published September 30, 2014

Lesson 9: Executing a Project | Topic D

ACTIVITY 9-4
Developing Your Project Team

Scenario

As your project team continues executing the project plan, you are learning more about the team members and their interpersonal skills and relationships.

1. You notice that Rachel, a team member, has consistently met her deliverable deadlines and is always on time with her status reports. She actively participates in brainstorming sessions and makes valuable contributions to the discussions. When required, she has gone beyond her responsibilities and has helped her project manager facilitate brainstorming meetings and discussion sessions. How should you respond?

2. One of your junior team members, who is assigned to gather information from supervisors through an interview process, has confided in you that he is not comfortable during the interviews. He feels that the supervisors seem impatient with the questions he is asking. The other junior team members assigned to interviews have not had any problems. What are some things you would do to address this issue?

3. What specific Develop Project Team tools and techniques could you use with the Building with Heart 122 East Main Street volunteer team?

TOPIC E

Manage a Project Team

Your staffing management plan describes when and how you will meet your project team requirements. Now that your project is well under way, you need to monitor individual and team performance and provide relevant feedback and appraisals. In this topic, you will manage your project team.

A Guide to the Project Management Body of Knowledge (PMBOK® Guide) – Fifth Edition, Project Management Institute, Inc., 2013, pg. 279-280

The following data flow diagram illustrates how the Manage Project Team process relates to the other knowledge areas within the Process Groups.

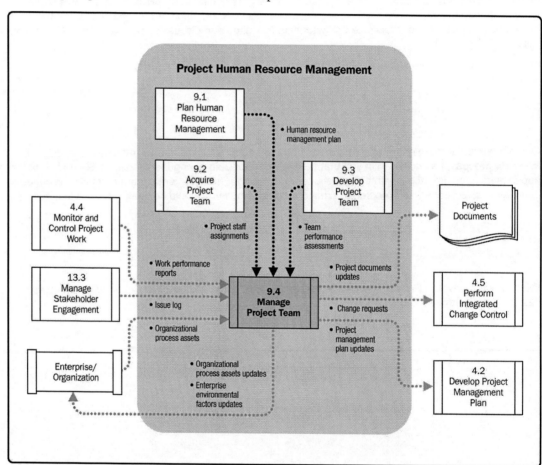

Figure 9-9: Manage Project Team work flow diagram.

A Guide to the Project Management Body of Knowledge (PMBOK® Guide) – Fifth Edition, Project Management Institute, Inc., 2013, p. 280

The Manage Project Team Process

The *Manage Project Team process* monitors individual performance, gives feedback, solves issues, and organizes changes to improve project performance. This results in updates to the human resource plan, submission of change requests, resolved issues, input given for performance appraisals, and

A Guide to the Project Management Body of Knowledge (PMBOK® Guide) – Fifth Edition, Project Management Institute (PMI)®, Project Management Professional
(PMP)®, and Certified Associate in Project Management (CAPM)® are registered trademarks of Project Management Institute, Inc. - Version 2.1 Published September 30, 2014

Lesson 9: Executing a Project | Topic E

documentation of lessons learned. Efficiently managing a project team requires a combination of project management and interpersonal skills to foster teamwork and enhance the team performance.

A Guide to the Project Management Body of Knowledge (PMBOK® Guide) – Fifth Edition, Project Management Institute, Inc., 2013, pg. 279-280

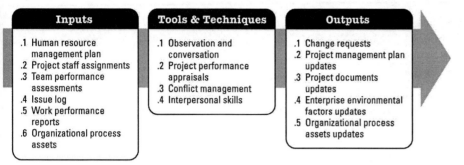

Figure 9-10: The Manage Project Team process.

A Guide to the Project Management Body of Knowledge (PMBOK® Guide) – Fifth Edition, Project Management Institute, Inc., 2013, p. 279

Dual Reporting

Managing the project team can become more complicated when team members are required to report to both a functional manager and a project manager. Coordination of this dual reporting relationship can be very important for the success of the project; it is the project manager's responsibility to make sure that team members are reporting appropriately.

Manage Project Team Inputs

Various components provide input to the Manage Project Team process.

Input	Description
Human resource management plan	Includes the roles and responsibilities of project team members and the staffing management plan.
Project staff assignments	Documentation on the list of project team members, project organization charts, and schedules.
Team performance assessments	During the project, the project management team makes formal and informal judgments on team performance. Continual assessment can result in resolving issues, improving communication, recognizing conflict, and improving team interaction.
Issue log (an output of 13.3)	An issue log is used to document individuals responsible for resolving certain issues by a specific date, whereas issue resolution addresses obstacles that hinder the team from achieving its goals. As stated in the *PMBOK® Guide,* an issue is a point or matter in question or in dispute, or a point or matter that is not settled and is under discussion or over which there are opposing views or disagreements.
Work performance reports (an output of 4.4)	Give documented performance information on the status of the project with regards to the forecasts made. Performance areas that are documented include schedule control, cost control, quality control, and scope verification. This information can be helpful when determining corrections or updates required in future human resource requirements, awards and recognition, and modifications to the staffing management plan.

A Guide to the Project Management Body of Knowledge (PMBOK® Guide) – Fifth Edition, Project Management Institute (PMI)®, Project Management Professional (PMP)®, and Certified Associate in Project Management (CAPM)® are registered trademarks of Project Management Institute, Inc. - Version 2.1 Published September 30, 2014

Lesson 9: Executing a Project | Topic E

Input	Description
Organizational process assets	Inputs that can influence the manage project team process include certificates of appreciation, websites, newsletters, bonus structures, corporate apparel, and organizational prerequisites.

A Guide to the Project Management Body of Knowledge (PMBOK® Guide) – Fifth Edition, Project Management Institute, Inc., 2013, pg. 281-282

360-Degree Feedback

360-degree feedback is the collection of performance data from several key sources, including peers, managers, and subordinates. Confidentiality is crucial to employing 360-degree feedback as it is implemented in most organizations. Many project practices do not have the sophistication or resources to manage employee relations in a manner that makes implementation of 360-degree feedback practical. The consensus within the human resources field that 360-degree feedback is best used only for developmental purposes, and not for performance management.

Manage Project Team Tools and Techniques

There are various tools and techniques used in the Manage Project Team process.

Tools & Techniques	Description
Observation and conversation	Used to stay in constant communication with the work and attitudes of the team. Measurements include progress toward deliverables, interpersonal issues, and accomplishments resulting in pride for team members.
Project performance appraisals	The need for formal or informal appraisals often relies on project length, project complexity, organizational policy, labor contract requirements, and amount and quality of communication. Evaluation can come from supervisors and people who interact with the team. Some of the main objectives to conduct performance appraisals are to clarify the roles and responsibilities of project team members, provide constructive feedback, identify unknown or unresolved issues, develop individual training plans, and establish futuristic goals.
Conflict management	Proper conflict management will result in improved productivity and good relationships. To reduce the amount of conflict, establish team rules, group norms, and stable project management practices. If the team is managed properly, disagreements will be healthy and can lead to increased productivity and good decision making. Care should be taken that conflicts are handled early and in private using a direct, collaborative approach.
Interpersonal skills	Skills that capitalize on the strengths of team members include leadership, influencing, and effective decision making.

A Guide to the Project Management Body of Knowledge (PMBOK® Guide) – Fifth Edition, Project Management Institute, Inc., 2013, pg. 282-284

Causes of Conflict

Conflict arises in most groups and working situations. Causes of conflict include:

*   Competition
*   Differences in objectives, values, and perceptions

- Disagreements about role requirements, work activities, and individual approaches
- Communication breakdowns

Project managers should be aware of certain characteristics of conflict that will help them effectively handle conflicts when they arise. Conflict is natural and forces the need for exploring alternatives. It is a team aspect and openness about the situation or opinions can resolve conflicts. While resolving conflicts, focus should be on the issues and not on individuals—on the present situation and not the past.

A Guide to the Project Management Body of Knowledge (PMBOK® Guide) – Fifth Edition, Project Management Institute, Inc., 2013, pg. 282-283

Conflict Management

Conflict management is the application of one or more strategies for dealing with disagreements that may be detrimental to team performance. Effective conflict management can lead to improved understanding, performance, and productivity. Conversely, ineffective or nonexistent conflict management can lead to destructive behavior, animosity, poor performance, and reduced productivity—all of which threaten successful completion of the project's deliverables. There are certain conflict resolution methods and the need to follow a particular method includes the intensity and importance of the conflict, the time given to resolve the conflict, the positions of the conflicting parties, and the motivation to resolve conflicts on a short-term or long-term basis.

 Note: To further explore how to manage conflicts, you can access the LearnTO **Manage Conflicts** presentation from the **LearnTO** tile on the LogicalCHOICE Course screen.

A Guide to the Project Management Body of Knowledge (PMBOK® Guide) – Fifth Edition, Project Management Institute, Inc., 2013, pg. 282-283

Conflict Management Approaches

According to the *PMBOK® Guide Fifth Edition*, there are five basic approaches for handling conflicts; each is effective in different circumstances.

Approach	Description
Withdraw/Avoid	• Retreating from an actual or potential conflict situation. • Postponing the issue to be better prepared or to be resolved by others.
Smooth/Accommodate	• Emphasising areas of agreement rather than areas of difference. • Conceding your position to the needs of others to maintain harmony and relationships.
Compromise/Reconcile	• Searching for solutions that bring some degree of satisfaction to all parties in the order to temporarily or partially resolve the conflict.
Force/Direct	• Pursuing your viewpoint at the expense of others. • Offering only win/lose solutions, usually enforce through a power position to resolve an emergency.
Collaborate/Problem Solve	• Incorporating multiple viewpoints and insight from differing perspectives. • Requires a cooperative attitude an open dialogue that typically leads to consensus and commitment.

A Guide to the Project Management Body of Knowledge (PMBOK® Guide) – Fifth Edition, Project Management Institute (PMI)®, Project Management Professional (PMP)®, and Certified Associate in Project Management (CAPM)® are registered trademarks of Project Management Institute, Inc. - Version 2.1 Published September 30, 2014

Lesson 9: Executing a Project | Topic E

A Guide to the Project Management Body of Knowledge (PMBOK® Guide) – Fifth Edition, Project Management Institute, Inc., 2013, p. 283

Performance Appraisal Tasks

You can use performance appraisal to accomplish a number of tasks, including:

- Comparing performance to goals
- Re-clarifying roles and responsibilities
- Delivering positive as well as negative feedback
- Discovering unknown or unresolved issues
- Creating and monitoring individual training plans
- Establishing future goals

A Guide to the Project Management Body of Knowledge (PMBOK® Guide) – Fifth Edition, Project Management Institute, Inc., 2013, p. 282

Manage Project Team Outputs

There are five outputs from the Manage Project Team process.

Output	Description
Change requests	Staffing changes can affect the project plan. This results in a request to be processed through the perform integrated change control process. These changes include moving people to different tasks, outsourcing work, and replacing team members during absence or when they leave the company. Preventive methods can be adopted to avoid such situations.
Project management plan updates	Any approved change requests and corrective actions should result in updates to the staffing management plan, a subset of the project management plan.
Project documents updates	Updates to project documents including the issue log, roles description, and project staff assignments.
Enterprise environmental factors updates	Updates include inputs to organizational performance appraisals and on personnel skills.
Organizational process assets updates	Updates include historical information, lessons learned documents, templates, and organizational standard processes.

A Guide to the Project Management Body of Knowledge (PMBOK® Guide) – Fifth Edition, Project Management Institute, Inc., 2013, pg. 284-285

Guidelines to Manage a Project Team

Using good management skills to manage your project team results in a solid staffing management plan, updated and submitted change requests, resolution of issues, and good lessons learned documentation, as well as productive team members. To effectively manage a project team, follow these guidelines:

- Establish good communication among team members, internally and externally.
- Monitor performance of team members on an ongoing basis.
  - Monitor progress of team members by speaking with them one-on-one. Don't wait for the emails or monthly reports. Get out there and see for yourself what progress is being made by the team, and what intangibles (such as morale, engagement, or cynicism) are at play.

A Guide to the Project Management Body of Knowledge (PMBOK® Guide) – Fifth Edition, Project Management Institute (PMI)®, Project Management Professional (PMP)®, and Certified Associate in Project Management (CAPM)® are registered trademarks of Project Management Institute, Inc. - Version 2.1 Published September 30, 2014

Lesson 9: Executing a Project | *Topic E*

- Develop a set of metrics for each project to measure team performance. Establish tolerances for each so that corrective actions can be taken when needed. Use a management by exception approach to avoid micromanaging the team.
- Provide constructive feedback to team members on a frequent basis. Team members need to know they are either on track or need to take steps to get back on track. Performance reviews can be formal or informal. If disciplinary actions are taken, these must be in writing to avoid any misunderstanding.
- Consider additional training for those team members who need to improve their performance.
- Manage conflict by using the appropriate approach based on the circumstances and the individuals involved. Regardless of the approach, apply the following principles:
  - Allow people to have their say. Make sure you give both sides a chance to state their case. Demonstrating respect and acknowledging people's different positions is necessary to address conflicts effectively.
  - Listen hard to what people are telling you. Paraphrase or ask questions to be sure everyone understands what is being said.
  - Find those areas at issue where both sides are in agreement.
  - Encourage both sides to find a win-win resolution to the problem. Restate the resolution and get agreement from both parties.
  - Focus on the reasons that the group has come together: to find a resolution to the problem.
  - To help avoid unnecessary conflict, set expected ground rules in the beginning for the team to operate with based on the communications management plan.
  - During the project life cycle, follow established project management practices. Refer to your communications management plan for guidance.
  - When conflict occurs among team members or between the team and other organizational entities, it may be effective to implement the conflict management approach of confrontation—focusing on the problem. It may be advantageous to try to defuse conflicts early to avoid escalation.
- As results are being obtained during the implementation phase, establish an issues log to track and assign project issues. This log is useful for regular follow-up with the project team. Hold specific team members accountable for resolution of issues.

A Guide to the Project Management Body of Knowledge (PMBOK® Guide) – Fifth Edition, Project Management Institute, Inc., 2013, pg. 279-285

A Guide to the Project Management Body of Knowledge (PMBOK® Guide) – Fifth Edition, Project Management Institute (PMI)®, Project Management Professional (PMP)®, and Certified Associate in Project Management (CAPM)® are registered trademarks of Project Management Institute, Inc. - Version 2.1 Published September 30, 2014

Lesson 9: Executing a Project | *Topic E*

TOPIC F

Manage Communications

During project planning, you developed a communications management plan describing the team's approach to project communications. Now that work results are being accomplished, you need to let project stakeholders know how the project is progressing. In this topic, you will identify the process involved in communicating project information.

A Guide to the Project Management Body of Knowledge (PMBOK® Guide) – Fifth Edition, Project Management Institute, Inc., 2013, pg. 297-299

The following data flow diagram illustrates how the Manage Communications process relates to the other knowledge areas within the Process Groups.

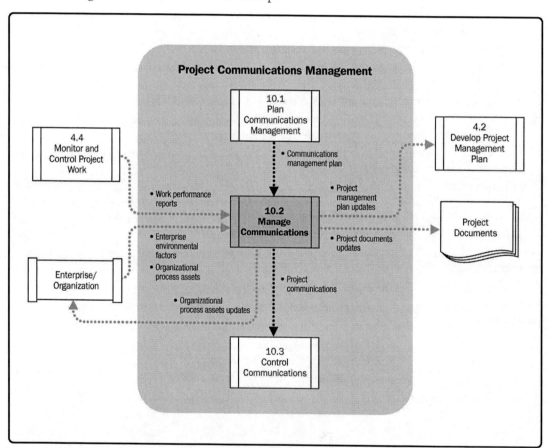

Figure 9–11: Manage Communications work flow diagram.

A Guide to the Project Management Body of Knowledge (PMBOK® Guide) – Fifth Edition, Project Management Institute, Inc., 2013, p. 298

The Manage Communications Process

The *Manage Communications process* involves getting the right information to the right people, both internally and externally, at the right time. During the Manage Communications process, the project team implements the communications management plan. This plan documents what information will be communicated, to whom, by whom, when, and in what manner, as well as how information is collected, archived, and accessed.

A Guide to the Project Management Body of Knowledge (PMBOK® Guide) – Fifth Edition, Project Management Institute (PMI)®, Project Management Professional (PMP)®, and Certified Associate in Project Management (CAPM)® are registered trademarks of Project Management Institute, Inc. - Version 2.1 Published September 30, 2014

A Guide to the Project Management Body of Knowledge (PMBOK® Guide) – Fifth Edition, Project Management Institute, Inc., 2013, pg. 297-299

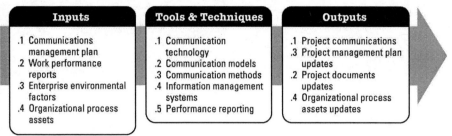

Figure 9-12: The Manage Communications process.

A Guide to the Project Management Body of Knowledge (PMBOK® Guide) – Fifth Edition, Project Management Institute, Inc., 2013, p. 297

Effective Manage Communications Techniques

While you manage communications, you must distribute information to stakeholders using a variety of techniques.

Technique	Description
Sender-receiver models	Includes setting up appropriate feedback loop and avoiding communication barriers.
Choice of media	Includes specifying when to communicate in writing or in oral form, and which communication media should be used such as verbal, written, email, and phone.
Writing style	Includes choosing the right tone and word choice.
Meeting management techniques	Includes identifying the meeting agenda and managing conflicts.
Presentation techniques	Includes using appropriate design of visual aids and body language.
Facilitation techniques	Includes building harmony within the team.
Listening techniques	Includes removing barriers and active listening (acknowledging, clarifying, and confirming understanding).

A Guide to the Project Management Body of Knowledge (PMBOK® Guide) – Fifth Edition, Project Management Institute, Inc., 2013, pg. 298-299

Manage Communications Inputs

Various components provide input to the Manage Communications process.

Input	Description
Communications management plan	Describes the details for distributing information to various concerned parties in the form of how to distribute the info, such as whom to, when to, and what to.
Work performance reports	Describes the current performance status of a project. These reports are distributed to the relevant stakeholders prior to project meetings. Based on the performance reports, the management and the stakeholders assess the project progress and can forecast future course of action, if any.

A Guide to the Project Management Body of Knowledge (PMBOK® Guide) – Fifth Edition, Project Management Institute (PMI)®, Project Management Professional (PMP)®, and Certified Associate in Project Management (CAPM)® are registered trademarks of Project Management Institute, Inc. - Version 2.1 Published September 30, 2014

Lesson 9: Executing a Project | *Topic F*

Input	Description
Enterprise environmental factors	Enterprise environmental factors that may influence this process include organizational culture and structure, government or industry standards and regulations, and the Project Management Information System.
Organizational process assets	Factors that can have an impact on the distribute information process could include: • Past lessons learned and historical project information • Guidelines, policies, and procedures regarding information distribution • Templates

A Guide to the Project Management Body of Knowledge (PMBOK® Guide) – Fifth Edition, Project Management Institute, Inc., 2013, pg. 299-300

Manage Communications Tools and Techniques

There are numerous tools and techniques used in the Manage Communications process.

Tools & Techniques	Description
Communication technology	The technology that can be used to communicate with team members and stakeholders. The technology could include email, presentation applications, and video conferencing software.
Communication models	Includes various communication models that can be used to communicate with project team members.
Communication methods	The communication methods could include video and audio conferences, computer chats, individual group meetings, and other remote communication methods.
Information management systems	Systems that facilitate the storing, transferring, and sharing of information.
Performance reporting	Includes collecting and distributing project performance information such as status reports, forecasts, and progress measurements. It looks at baseline versus actual data to measure the progress of the project and could include status of risks and issues, work completed in a time period, analysis of cost and schedule forecasts, and more.

A Guide to the Project Management Body of Knowledge (PMBOK® Guide) – Fifth Edition, Project Management Institute, Inc., 2013, pg. 300-301

Manage Communications Outputs

There are four outputs from the Manage Communications process.

Output	Description
Project communications	Project communications are activities required for information to be created, distributed, received, acknowledged, and understood. They include schedule and cost status, performance reports, deliverables status, and so on.

A Guide to the Project Management Body of Knowledge (PMBOK® Guide) – Fifth Edition, Project Management Institute (PMI)®, Project Management Professional (PMP)®, and Certified Associate in Project Management (CAPM)® are registered trademarks of Project Management Institute, Inc. - Version 2.1 Published September 30, 2014

Lesson 9: Executing a Project | Topic F

Output	Description
Project management plan updates	Documents that may need updates include project baselines, communications management plan, and stakeholder management plan. Updates may include current performance tracking against the baselines.
Project documents updates	Project documents that may need updates include the issues log, project schedule, and project funding requirements.
Organizational process assets updates	Organizational process assets that may need updates can include stakeholder notifications, project reports, project presentations, project records, feedback from stakeholders, and lessons learned.

A Guide to the Project Management Body of Knowledge (PMBOK® Guide) – Fifth Edition, Project Management Institute, Inc., 2013, pg. 301-303

Guidelines to Manage Project Communications

Effective communication management ensures that project information is appropriately dispensed to project stakeholders. Getting the necessary information in a timely manner enables the stakeholders to make decisions regarding the project in time to make a difference. To distribute project information effectively, follow these guidelines:

- Create and distribute requests for project information, such as project records, reports, and presentations, in accordance with the communications management plan.
- Use effective communication skills to exchange information.
- Use an information retrieval system to provide stakeholders access to project information. Everyone should have access to the information needed. Whether manual, computerized, or a combination of both, make sure your system complies with the following standards:

  - The system has sufficient storage capacity to hold the necessary project information.
  - The system follows any security protection protocols established in the communications management plan so that sensitive information can be accessed only by appropriate stakeholders.
  - The system provides a method of version control to protect data and to ensure that everyone is working off the same, most recent document.
  - The system is organized to meet the needs of the project and the stakeholders.

- Select the appropriate information distribution method for distributing project information.

  - Sending an email announcing that a report is posted on the intranet site.
  - Making a telephone call to schedule a one-on-one meeting.
  - Taking notes of phone calls to provide a written record of the communication.
  - Making a presentation to highlight the important points in a report.

- Monitor the communications system for feedback to make sure that messages are getting through as planned. If individuals, locations, or organizations are not able to send or receive messages adequately, identify the problem and adjust the communications management plan, information distribution method, or retrieval system accordingly.

A Guide to the Project Management Body of Knowledge (PMBOK® Guide) – Fifth Edition, Project Management Institute, Inc., 2013, pg. 297-303

ACTIVITY 9-5
Managing Project Communications

Scenario

A primary PMO goal for all Building with Heart programs is consistent and timely reporting of project information. The project managers are now concerned that they will be spending more time creating reports for senior management than actually managing their projects. You are meeting with the new PMO Director to discuss these concerns.

---

1. An automated information retrieval system will provide stakeholders with access to project information via the intranet. What, if any, concerns do you have with relying on this type of distribution of project information to stakeholders?

2. As people strive to meet their deadlines, reporting the status of activities can become a low priority. This is a problem when you are trying to distribute up-to-date information on the status of the project. What are some things that you could do to make sure that people report accurate and timely information to you?

3. How could poor communication between project team members affect the overall project?

4. You are asked by your manager to provide the senior executives your project's progress to-date. Which information distribution methods would be most appropriate in this situation?

    ○   Send an email announcing that a report is posted on the intranet site.

    ○   Make a telephone call to schedule one-on-one meetings with each executive.

    ○   Send an email based on status notes that you took over the phone while communicating with team members.

    ○   Make a presentation to the senior executives and highlight the important points in the report.

A Guide to the Project Management Body of Knowledge (PMBOK® Guide) – Fifth Edition, Project Management Institute (PMI)®, Project Management Professional (PMP)®, and Certified Associate in Project Management (CAPM)® are registered trademarks of Project Management Institute, Inc. - Version 2.1 Published September 30, 2014

Lesson 9: Executing a Project | Topic F

TOPIC G

Conduct Procurements

Your project is now in the executing process group and you need to procure the external resources that are required by your project. Procuring products and services from external suppliers requires identifying suppliers, obtaining bids or proposals from them, and awarding contracts based on their evaluation. All procurements for the project must be done within the specified parameters of time, cost, and quality so as to ensure that the project meets the stakeholder's requirements. In this topic, you will conduct project procurements.

A Guide to the Project Management Body of Knowledge (PMBOK® Guide) – Fifth Edition, Project Management Institute, Inc., 2013, pg. 371-373

The following data flow diagram illustrates how the Conduct Procurements process relates to the other knowledge areas within the Process Groups.

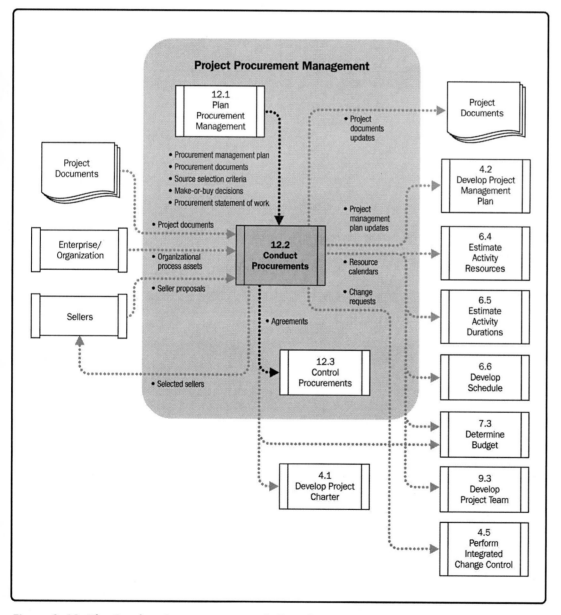

Figure 9–13: The Conduct Procurements work flow diagram.

A Guide to the Project Management Body of Knowledge (PMBOK® Guide) – Fifth Edition, Project Management Institute, Inc., 2013, p. 372

The Conduct Procurements Process

In the *Conduct Procurements process*, project managers will obtain seller responses, select a seller, and award contracts to the identified seller for the procurement of the required product, service, or result from the seller. In this process, the project management team will receive bids or proposals from sellers, apply predefined selection criteria to select sellers who are qualified to perform the work, rank all proposals by using weighted evaluation scores and conduct negotiations with the selected sellers, and finally select a single seller who is required to sign a standard contract that will meet the procurement requirements of the project.

A Guide to the Project Management Body of Knowledge (PMBOK® Guide) – Fifth Edition, Project Management Institute, Inc., 2013, pg. 371-373

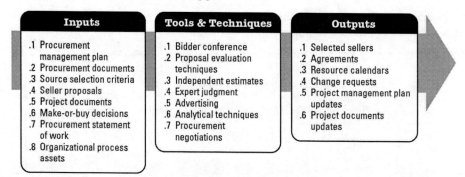

Inputs	Tools & Techniques	Outputs
.1 Procurement management plan .2 Procurement documents .3 Source selection criteria .4 Seller proposals .5 Project documents .6 Make-or-buy decisions .7 Procurement statement of work .8 Organizational process assets	.1 Bidder conference .2 Proposal evaluation techniques .3 Independent estimates .4 Expert judgment .5 Advertising .6 Analytical techniques .7 Procurement negotiations	.1 Selected sellers .2 Agreements .3 Resource calendars .4 Change requests .5 Project management plan updates .6 Project documents updates

Figure 9-14: The Conduct Procurements process.

A Guide to the Project Management Body of Knowledge (PMBOK® Guide) – Fifth Edition, Project Management Institute, Inc., 2013, p. 371

Conduct Procurements Inputs

Various components provide input to the Conduct Procurements process.

Input	Description
Procurement management plan	Describes every management step of the procurement process starting with development and ending with closing the contract.
Procurement documents	Contain information that you provide to prospective sellers so that they can completely and accurately respond to your request.
Source selection criteria	Can include examples of existing products from the supplier, services, the supplier's history with the organization and other organizations, or results from the evaluation of the supplier's capabilities and quality of their products.
Seller proposals	A response submitted by a potential seller that is prepared in accordance with the requirements stated in the procurement documents. The proposal should demonstrate an understanding of the procurement need, describe the sellers' ability to provide the service or product, and detail the price for delivering the desired goods and/or services.
Project documents	Project documents used in conducting the project procurement include the risk register and the risk-related contract decisions document.

Input	Description
Make-or-buy decisions	Decisions about which resources, services, or products will be procured in-house or purchased by the organization.
Procurement statement of work	Describes the requirements for the item to be procured in order for potential vendors to determine if they are able to provide it.
Organizational process assets	A list of sellers (or sometimes called bidders) who can be asked to bid, quote, or propose work. These lists give information about sellers' past experience. These may be previously qualified sellers or a preferred sellers list.

A Guide to the Project Management Body of Knowledge (PMBOK® Guide) – Fifth Edition, Project Management Institute, Inc., 2013, pg. 373-375

Conduct Procurements Tools and Techniques

There are numerous tools and techniques used in the Conduct Procurements process.

Tools & Techniques	Description
Bidder conference	These conferences are conducted by the buyer prior to submissions of a bid or proposal by the sellers. The buyer explains the requirements, proposed terms, and conditions. Sellers clarify their queries during this meeting. The buyer facilitates the conference to ensure that all prospective sellers have a clear and common understanding of the technical and contractual requirements of the procurement. Bidder conferences are also called vendor conferences, pre-bid conferences, or contractor conferences.
Proposal evaluation techniques	A set of methods to evaluate, shortlist, and then select the seller. The fundamental part of any evaluation technique is the set of evaluation criteria. The evaluation techniques may suggest subjective or objective criteria or a combination of both. Although a weighting system is the most commonly used evaluation technique, short-listing (screening) or independent estimating are also used in combination.
Independent estimates	Usually, you'll have at least a general idea of what you expect the price to be. If a proposal comes in at an unexpectedly high or low price, you may want to obtain an independent estimate to verify that the proposed price is reasonable and responsible. The purchasing department is a good source for independent estimates. For large projects, they will usually prepare an independent estimate before the procurement documents go out, so they will have sound current data against which to evaluate the proposals received.
Expert judgment	Used by a multi-discipline review team to evaluate seller proposals. The review team has expertise in the topics covered in the procurement documents and the proposed contract.
Advertising	Companies regularly post advertisements in newspapers, magazines, business journals, television, and other media, requesting sellers for bids and proposals. Advertising is a mass method for seeking responses from prospective sellers.
Analytical techniques	Used to analyze seller proposals to determine which proposals are valid.

A Guide to the Project Management Body of Knowledge (PMBOK® Guide) – Fifth Edition, Project Management Institute (PMI)®, Project Management Professional (PMP)®, and Certified Associate in Project Management (CAPM)® are registered trademarks of Project Management Institute, Inc. - Version 2.1 Published September 30, 2014

Lesson 9: Executing a Project | Topic G

Tools & Techniques	Description
Procurement negotiations	Procurement negotiation is the process of bargaining to come to a mutual agreement regarding the terms and conditions of a contract.

A Guide to the Project Management Body of Knowledge (PMBOK® Guide) – Fifth Edition, Project Management Institute, Inc., 2013, pg. 375-377

Weighting Systems

A *weighting system* is a method for quantifying qualitative data to minimize the influence of personal bias on source selection. By assigning numerical weights to evaluation criteria, you can objectively prioritize the criteria that best meet the needs of your project.

A Guide to the Project Management Body of Knowledge (PMBOK® Guide) – Fifth Edition, Project Management Institute, Inc., 2013, p. 376

Procurement Negotiations

Procurement negotiation is the process of bargaining to come to a mutual agreement regarding the terms and conditions of a contract. Before a contract is signed by both parties, several procurement negotiation are conducted between the concerned parties to arrive at a consensus on the terms and conditions of the contract.

There are five different stages for contract negotiation.

1. Introduction: All parties become acquainted and the overall attitude of the negotiation is established; this tone is largely set by the buyer's team leader—normally, the person with authority to sign the contract will lead the contract negotiation team.
2. Probing: Each side attempts to learn more about the other's real position.
3. Bargaining: Give-and-take discussions take place to arrive at the best possible agreement for all.
4. Closure: The tentative agreement is revised and everyone has an opportunity to tweak the results.
5. Agreement: The team tries to ensure that all parties clearly understand and agree to all terms and conditions of the contract.

A Guide to the Project Management Body of Knowledge (PMBOK® Guide) – Fifth Edition, Project Management Institute, Inc., 2013, p. 377

Conduct Procurements Outputs

There are six outputs from the Conduct Procurements process.

Output	Description
Selected sellers	Sellers who have been judged based on the outcome of the proposal or bid evaluation. These sellers include those who have negotiated an outline of a contract, which will turn into the actual contract when the deal is made.
Agreements	Agreements detail the obligations of the buyer and seller. One is given to each selected seller.
Resource calendars	The quantity and availability of resources and documented dates on when each resource can be active or idle.
Change requests	Certain changes to the project management plan, its sub-plans, and other components may result from the conduct procurements process. Any requested changes are sent for review and disposition in the integrated change control process.

A Guide to the Project Management Body of Knowledge (PMBOK® Guide) – Fifth Edition, Project Management Institute (PMI)®, Project Management Professional (PMP)®, and Certified Associate in Project Management (CAPM)® are registered trademarks of Project Management Institute, Inc. - Version 2.1 Published September 30, 2014

Lesson 9: Executing a Project | Topic G

Output	Description
Project management plan updates	Elements of the plan updates include the cost baseline, scope baseline, schedule baseline, and the procurement management plan.
Project documents updates	Various documents that require updates include the requirements documentation, the requirements traceability documentation, and the risk register.

A Guide to the Project Management Body of Knowledge (PMBOK® Guide) – Fifth Edition, Project Management Institute, Inc., 2013, pg. 377-379

Qualified Sellers

Qualified sellers are sellers who are approved to deliver the products, services, or results based on the procurement requirements identified for a project. The list of qualified sellers can be obtained from historical information about different sellers who delivered the resources required for prior projects executed in your organization. If the resources you require are new to the organization, you may need to do some research in collaboration with your purchasing department to identify qualified sellers for each resource. This research will generate a list of possible sellers, and you would need to interview the prospective sellers, visit their work sites, review work samples, interview their references, check with certification boards, or use other approaches to validate whether or not they qualify as sellers for the procurement requirements.

A Guide to the Project Management Body of Knowledge (PMBOK® Guide) – Fifth Edition, Project Management Institute, Inc., 2013, pg. 377, 386

Term vs. Completion Contracts

A term contract engages the seller to deliver a set amount of service—measured in staff-hours or a similar unit—over a set period of time. A completion contract stipulates that the work will not be considered complete until the seller delivers the product to the buyer and the buyer accepts the product.

A Guide to the Project Management Body of Knowledge (PMBOK® Guide) – Fifth Edition, Project Management Institute, Inc., 2013, pg. 362-364

Guidelines to Conduct Procurements

To conduct procurements effectively, follow these guidelines:

* Gather and review all of your procurement documents for accuracy and completeness.
* If necessary, obtain or develop a qualified sellers list.
* Determine how and from whom you will request seller responses.
* If necessary, hold a bidder conference to allow prospective sellers to ask questions and get clarification about the deliverables and the requirements for preparing their responses.
* Send the request for seller responses to the identified prospective sellers. The type of request sent to prospective sellers depends on the procurement criteria set for the project. The types of requests sent to obtain responses include: Request for Bid (RFB) and Request for Proposal (RFP).

A Guide to the Project Management Body of Knowledge (PMBOK® Guide) – Fifth Edition, Project Management Institute, Inc., 2013, pg. 371-379

Guidelines to Determine Project Sellers

To determine a project seller:

A Guide to the Project Management Body of Knowledge (PMBOK® Guide) – Fifth Edition, Project Management Institute (PMI)®, Project Management Professional (PMP)®, and Certified Associate in Project Management (CAPM)® are registered trademarks of Project Management Institute, Inc. - Version 2.1 Published September 30, 2014

1. Assign a numerical weighting factor to each evaluation criterion or category of criteria based on its relative importance to the success of the project.
2. Develop or obtain a rating scale for scoring the criteria.
3. Score each prospective seller on each criterion by using the rating scale.
4. Multiply the seller's score by the weighting factor for each criterion or sum of the criteria in a category.
5. Add the final scores.
6. Select the seller with the highest score.
7. If necessary, negotiate with the seller on the terms and conditions of the contract.
8. It is a good idea to identify the seller who would be your second choice in case negotiations fall through with your first choice.

A Guide to the Project Management Body of Knowledge (PMBOK® Guide) – Fifth Edition, Project Management Institute, Inc., 2013, pg. 371-379

A Guide to the Project Management Body of Knowledge (PMBOK® Guide) – Fifth Edition, Project Management Institute (PMI)®, Project Management Professional (PMP)®, and Certified Associate in Project Management (CAPM)® are registered trademarks of Project Management Institute, Inc. - Version 2.1 Published September 30, 2014

Lesson 9: Executing a Project | Topic G

ACTIVITY 9-6
Conducting Procurements

Scenario

Working with the Building with Heart's procurement manager, you have planned the 122 East Main project's external procurements and you are ready to manage this phase of work by soliciting proposals from prospective sellers. An RFP has been created and the procurement manager has approved it for release to potential building suppliers. The next step is to send the RFP to prospective suppliers.

1. What do you think would be the most appropriate method of finding qualified trained suppliers for the 122 East Main project?

2. There are only two local suppliers in a 20-mile radius of the build site. You decide to expand your supplier list outside of the local area. What methods would you use to do this?

3. Based on the scenario, would you conduct a bidder conference? Why or why not?

TOPIC H

Manage Stakeholder Engagement

You've informed project stakeholders about how project resources are being used to achieve project objectives. As project issues arise, you need to address and resolve them with the appropriate project stakeholders. In this topic, you will identify the process involved in actively managing stakeholder relationships and working within their expectations.

A Guide to the Project Management Body of Knowledge (PMBOK® Guide) – Fifth Edition, Project Management Institute, Inc., 2013, pg. 404-406

The following data flow diagram illustrates how the Manage Stakeholder Engagement process relates to the other knowledge areas within the Process Groups.

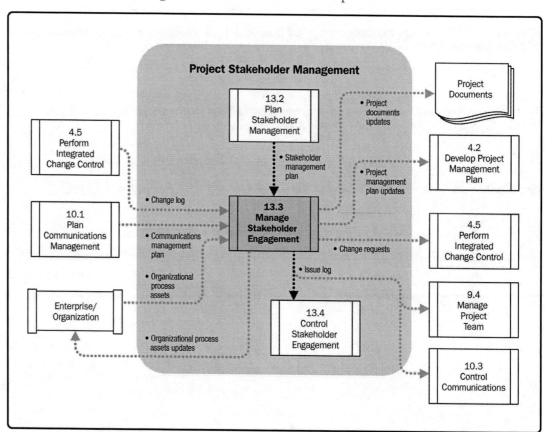

Figure 9-15: The Manage Stakeholder Engagement work flow diagram.

A Guide to the Project Management Body of Knowledge (PMBOK® Guide) – Fifth Edition, Project Management Institute, Inc., 2013, p. 405

The Manage Stakeholder Engagement Process

The Manage Stakeholder Engagement process aims at managing communications to meet the needs and expectations of the stakeholders. The project manager is responsible for managing stakeholder expectations. Actively managing stakeholder expectations will increase the chances of project acceptance and will address emerging issues and concerns before they manifest into a serious impediment. This includes clarifying and resolving issues that have already been identified.

A Guide to the Project Management Body of Knowledge (PMBOK® Guide) – Fifth Edition, Project Management Institute (PMI)®, Project Management Professional (PMP)®, and Certified Associate in Project Management (CAPM)® are registered trademarks of Project Management Institute, Inc. - Version 2.1 Published September 30, 2014

Lesson 9: Executing a Project | Topic H

A Guide to the Project Management Body of Knowledge (PMBOK® Guide) – Fifth Edition, Project Management Institute, Inc., 2013, pg. 404-406

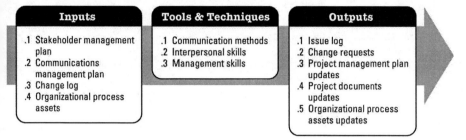

Figure 9-16: The Manage Stakeholder Engagement process.

A Guide to the Project Management Body of Knowledge (PMBOK® Guide) – Fifth Edition, Project Management Institute, Inc., 2013, p. 404

Manage Stakeholder Engagement Inputs

Various components provide input to the Manage Stakeholder Engagement process.

Input	Description
Stakeholder management plan	Contains the procedure for understanding the stakeholder goals and objectives, in order to manage their expectations.
Communications management plan	Provides stakeholder requirements, information to be communicated, reasons for information distribution, who will receive information, and the escalation process.
Change log (an output of 4.5)	A record of the changes that occur during project execution. Appropriate stakeholders are told of these changes in order to gain their consent.
Organizational process assets	Organizational process assets include: • Change control procedures • Past project information • Issue management procedures • Organizational communication

A Guide to the Project Management Body of Knowledge (PMBOK® Guide) – Fifth Edition, Project Management Institute, Inc., 2013, pg. 406-407

Manage Stakeholder Engagement Tools and Techniques

There are numerous tools and techniques used in the Manage Stakeholder Engagement process.

Tools & Techniques	Description
Communication methods	Each stakeholder's method of communication is documented in the communications management plan and applied during stakeholder management. Face-to-face meetings are the best way to communicate with stakeholders. When face-to-face meetings are not possible, phone calls, email, and other electronic tools are acceptable for exchanging information.

A Guide to the Project Management Body of Knowledge (PMBOK® Guide) – Fifth Edition, Project Management Institute (PMI)®, Project Management Professional (PMP)®, and Certified Associate in Project Management (CAPM)® are registered trademarks of Project Management Institute, Inc. - Version 2.1 Published September 30, 2014

Lesson 9: Executing a Project | *Topic H*

Tools & Techniques	Description
Interpersonal skills	A project manager should apply appropriate interpersonal skills to manage stakeholder expectations. These could include skills such as conflict resolution, building trust, active listening, and overcoming resistance to change.
Management skills	A project manager should apply his management skills of directing and controlling the team members, thus channeling their efforts towards achieving the project objectives. These skills could include presentation, writing, and negotiation skills.

A Guide to the Project Management Body of Knowledge (PMBOK® Guide) – Fifth Edition, Project Management Institute, Inc., 2013, pg. 407-408

Manage Stakeholder Engagement Outputs

There are five outputs from the Manage Stakeholder Engagement process.

Output	Description
Issue log	Includes updates to an issue that has been changed or resolved during the process.
Change requests	There may be changes that might take place to the product or project during the process of managing stakeholder expectations. These could also include preventive and corrective actions.
Project management plan updates	The project management plan is updated due to a change in the stakeholder communication management. This may occur as a result of the identification of a new communication requirement or method. The project management plan can also be updated in case a communication method is deemed redundant.
Project documents updates	Documents that may be updated include stakeholder management strategy, stakeholder register, and issues log.
Organizational process assets updates	Updates to the organizational process assets could include reasons for issues, and the motives behind why certain corrective actions are chosen. The updates could also include lessons learned from managing stakeholder expectations. Lessons learned are documented to be part of the historical database for the current project and future projects in the organization.

A Guide to the Project Management Body of Knowledge (PMBOK® Guide) – Fifth Edition, Project Management Institute, Inc., 2013, pg. 408-409

Guidelines to Manage Stakeholder Engagement

Actively managing stakeholder engagement ensures that your stakeholders understand the progress your project is making and that they are involved through the project life cycle. Managing stakeholder expectations will support your team's project schedule, enhance team performance, and decrease project interruption. To effectively manage stakeholder engagement, follow these guidelines:

- During the planning phase of the project, the communication plan for each stakeholder is developed. In managing stakeholders, the project manager needs to follow that plan and periodically obtain stakeholder feedback to make any required adjustments to the plan.

- Face-to-face meetings with stakeholders are most effective. Assessing body language provides the project manager with an opportunity to determine if the stakeholder is pleased or not with the project's progress. For example, if during a project update the stakeholder is frowning, has arms folded, and is looking at his shoes, it is essential that the project manager determine the stakeholder's concerns. By managing stakeholder expectations, the project will continue to have their buy-in.

- When face-to-face meetings are not practical, as in global projects, video/web conferencing, webinars, desktop sharing, net meeting, and video chat can be useful substitutes, if available to the project team.

- Be flexible in communications for the project sponsor or other members of senior management. Be prepared to provide a summary of project status in five minutes or less if the need arises. Flexible communication is the ability to meet the specific communication requirements of each stakeholder. For example, one might prefer extensive numerical data while some others might just prefer a synopsis.

- Use an issues log to assign, track, and resolve open issues that are of interest to stakeholders. Issues that remain unresolved can lead to project delays.

- Change requests need to be processed to update the communication plan reflecting changes in project staffing.

- Take corrective action as needed to bring project performance in line with customer expectations.

- Document lessons learned to reflect the causes of issues and changes made to rectify them.

A Guide to the Project Management Body of Knowledge (PMBOK® Guide) – Fifth Edition, Project Management Institute, Inc., 2013, pg. 404-409

A Guide to the Project Management Body of Knowledge (PMBOK® Guide) – Fifth Edition, Project Management Institute (PMI)®, Project Management Professional (PMP)®, and Certified Associate in Project Management (CAPM)® are registered trademarks of Project Management Institute, Inc. - Version 2.1 Published September 30, 2014

Lesson 9: Executing a Project | *Topic H*

ACTIVITY 9-7
Managing Stakeholder Engagement

Scenario

The Building with Heart 122 East Main project has faced several challenges, including staffing changes and construction problems. Although you have consistently informed stakeholders of all changes by using the protocols outlined in the communications plan, several stakeholders have expressed concern that the project has gotten off track.

---

1. Stakeholders are worried about the current state of the project. How should you handle their concerns?
   - ○ Follow processes outlined in the communications plan.
   - ○ Take corrective action.
   - ☑ Conduct a face-to-face meeting with a clear agenda targeting their specific concerns.
   - ○ Document lessons learned.

2. Two stakeholders are out of town on a business trip and are available sporadically. Another has an extremely busy schedule and can't squeeze another lengthy meeting into his day. You know it is important to have face-to-face interaction with each stakeholder. How can you accommodate their needs? (Select all that apply.)
   - ☑ Use video conferencing
   - ☐ Send a memo via email
   - ☐ Use an instant messaging service
   - ☑ Hold a brief summarization meeting

3. During the face-to-face meeting with project stakeholders, you offer a recap of some contractor changes that occurred. It became necessary to add another electrical contractor to the team, which resulted in changes to the project cost baseline. While you are talking about this issue, you notice that one of the project stakeholders continually looks down at the floor and rapidly taps her pen against the table. What does her behavior indicate?

Summary

In this lesson, you managed project execution. Executing project work according to your project management plan ensures that your project team is on the same page and that your project finishes on time, on budget, and with the required quality.

What aspects of executing the project plan have you found to be the most challenging? Why?

What tools and techniques will you use to more effectively execute projects in the future?

 Note: Check your LogicalCHOICE Course screen for opportunities to interact with your classmates, peers, and the larger LogicalCHOICE online community about the topics covered in this course or other topics you are interested in. From the Course screen you can also access available resources for a more continuous learning experience.

10 | Managing Project Work, Scope, Schedules, and Cost

Lesson Time: 3 hours

Lesson Objectives

In this lesson, you will:

- Monitor and control project work.

- Perform integrated change control.

- Validate project scope.

- Control project scope.

- Control the project schedule.

- Control the project costs.

Lesson Introduction

You have begun executing your project. As the project work accelerates, your focus will advance from execution to monitoring and controlling project work, scope, schedule, and cost, which is a key element in your overall goal of keeping a project on track. In this lesson, you will focus on the Monitoring and Controlling Process Group.

The following diagram highlights the next process group and knowledge areas covered in this lesson.

	Project Management Process Groups				
Knowledge Areas	Initiating Process Group	Planning Process Group	Executing Process Group	Monitoring and Controlling Process Group	Closing Process Group
4. Project Integration Management	4.1 Develop Project Charter	4.2 Develop Project Management Plan	4.3 Direct and Manage Project Work	4.4 Monitor and Control Project Work / 4.5 Perform Integrated Change Control	4.6 Close Project or Phase
5. Project Scope Management		5.1 Plan Scope Management / 5.2 Collect Requirements / 5.3 Define Scope / 5.4 Create WBS		5.5 Validate Scope / 5.6 Control Scope	
6. Project Time Management		6.1 Plan Schedule Management / 6.2 Define Activities / 6.3 Sequence Activities / 6.4 Estimate Activity Resources / 6.5 Estimate Activity Durations / 6.6 Develop Schedule		6.7 Control Schedule	
7. Project Cost Management		7.1 Plan Cost Management / 7.2 Estimate Cost / 7.3 Determine Budget		7.4 Control Costs	
8. Project Quality Management		8.1 Plan Quality Management	8.2 Perform Quality Assurance	8.3 Control Quality	
9. Project Human Resource Management		9.1 Plan Human Resource Management	9.2 Acquire Project Team / 9.3 Develop Project Team / 9.4 Manage Project Team		
10. Project Communication Management		10.1 Plan Communications Management	10.2 Manage Communications	10.3 Control Communications	
11. Project Risk Management		11.1 Plan Risk Management / 11.2 Identify Risks / 11.3 Perform Qualitative Risk Analysis / 11.4 Perform Quantitative Risk Analysis / 11.5 Plan Risk Responses		11.6 Control Risks	
12. Project Procurement Management		12.1 Plan Procurement Management	12.2 Conduct Procurements	12.3 Control Procurements	12.4 Close Procurements
13. Project Stakeholder Management	13.1 Identify Stakeholders	13.2 Plan Stakeholder Management	13.3 Manage Stakeholder Engagement	13.4 Control Stakeholder Engagement	

A Guide to the Project Management Body of Knowledge (PMBOK® Guide) – Fifth Edition, Project Management Institute (PMI)®, Project Management Professional (PMP)®, and Certified Associate in Project Management (CAPM)® are registered trademarks of Project Management Institute, Inc. - Version 2.1 Published September 30, 2014

TOPIC A

Monitor and Control Project Work

With your project execution well on its way, you need to control changes to the project's performance baseline so that you can best ensure that it meets expectations for schedule and cost. Change control and several other tasks are part of the Monitor and Control Project Work process. In this topic, you will identify best practices for the Monitor and Control Project Work process.

A Guide to the Project Management Body of Knowledge (PMBOK® Guide) – Fifth Edition, Project Management Institute, Inc., 2013, pg. 86-88

The following data flow diagram illustrates how the Monitor and Control Project Work process relates to the other knowledge areas within the Planning Process Group.

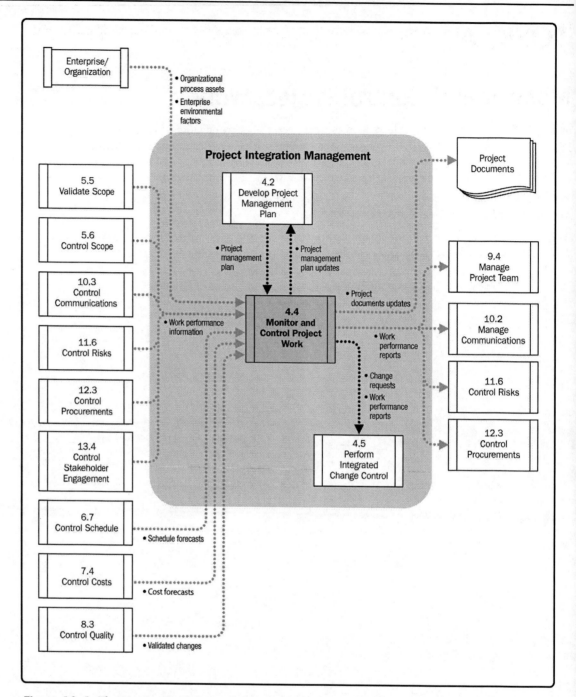

Figure 10-1: The Monitor and Control Project Work work data flow diagram.

A Guide to the Project Management Body of Knowledge (PMBOK® Guide) – Fifth Edition, Project Management Institute, Inc., 2013, p. 87

The Monitor and Control Project Work Process

The *Monitor and Control Project Work process* involves tracking, reviewing, and regulating the project processes to meet the project's performance objectives. Monitoring includes collecting, measuring, and distributing performance information, as well as reviewing trends to make process improvements. Controlling involves identifying corrective or preventive actions or replanning and tracking the execution of action plans. When executed regularly, the monitor and control project work process gives the project management team a closer look at the strengths of the project and identifies weaknesses. Monitoring and controlling occurs throughout the project from inception to close-out.

A Guide to the Project Management Body of Knowledge (PMBOK® Guide) – Fifth Edition, Project Management Institute, Inc., 2013, pg. 86-88

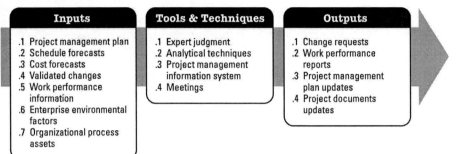

Figure 10-2: The Monitor and Control Project Work process.

A Guide to the Project Management Body of Knowledge (PMBOK® Guide) – Fifth Edition, Project Management Institute, Inc., 2013, p. 86

This process is concerned with:

- Comparing actual performance to the project management plan.
- Assessing performance to see if any corrective action is needed.
- Identifying new risks and monitoring previously documented risks.
- Maintaining an accurate and timely information base.
- Providing information to support status reporting, progress measurement, and forecasting.
- Providing forecasts to update current cost and schedule information.
- Monitoring implementation of approved changes.
- Providing reporting on project progress and status.

A Guide to the Project Management Body of Knowledge (PMBOK® Guide) – Fifth Edition, Project Management Institute, Inc., 2013, p. 88

Monitor and Control Project Work Inputs

Various components provide input to the Monitor and Control Project Work process.

Input	Description
Project management plan	Contains all subsidiary management plans and baselines that must be considered when performing the monitor and control project work process and describes each step of the project, including the way it is executed, monitored, and closed.
Schedule forecasts (an output of 6.7)	Contain estimates or predictions of conditions and events in the project's future based on information and knowledge available at the time the schedule is calculated.
Cost forecasts (an output of 7.4)	Contain estimates or predictions of conditions and events in the project's future based on information and knowledge available at the time the project cost is calculated.
Validated changes (an output of 8.3)	Provides confirmation that the approved changes to the project were implemented properly.

A Guide to the Project Management Body of Knowledge (PMBOK® Guide) – Fifth Edition, Project Management Institute (PMI)®, Project Management Professional (PMP)®, and Certified Associate in Project Management (CAPM)® are registered trademarks of Project Management Institute, Inc. - Version 2.1 Published September 30, 2014

Lesson 10: Managing Project Work, Scope, Schedules, and Cost | *Topic A*

Input	Description
Work performance information (an output of 5.5)	Provides key information such as current project status, significant accomplishments for the given period, scheduled activities (activities completed vs. those that should have been completed), issues, and forecasts.
Enterprise environmental factors	Includes governmental or industry standards, stakeholder risk tolerances, and Project Management Information Systems.
Organizational process assets	Includes organizational communication requirements, financial control procedures such as reporting time and accounting codes, and lessons learned databases.

A Guide to the Project Management Body of Knowledge (PMBOK® Guide) – Fifth Edition, Project Management Institute, Inc., 2013, pg. 88-91

Monitor and Control Project Work Tools and Techniques

There are four tools and techniques used in the Monitor and Control Project Work process.

Tools & Techniques	Description
Expert judgment	Used by the project management team to understand the data obtained from the monitor and control processes. Based on the interpretation, the project manager and the project team identify the necessary actions to make sure that the project performance is aligned with the project expectations.
Analytical techniques	Statistical techniques used to forecast potential outcomes based on possible variations of project variables and their relationships with other variables. Examples include regression analysis, grouping methods, causal analysis, root cause analysis, failure mode and defect analysis (FEMA), fault tree analysis (FTA), reserve analysis, earned value management (EVM), variance analysis, and forecasting methods.
Project Management Information Systems (PMIS)	Provide access to automated scheduling, cost and resourcing tools, performance indicators, databases, project records, and financials.
Meetings	Meetings supporting this process include user groups and review meetings.

A Guide to the Project Management Body of Knowledge (PMBOK® Guide) – Fifth Edition, Project Management Institute, Inc., 2013, pg. 91-92

Monitor and Control Project Work Outputs

There are four outputs from the Monitor and Control Project Work process.

Output	Description
Change requests	Issued as a result of comparison between actual and planned results. Change requests may result in modifying project scope, policies, procedures, cost and budgets, or a rework of project schedules. Documents such as the project management plan and product deliverables may also be impacted by change requests.

A Guide to the Project Management Body of Knowledge (PMBOK® Guide) – Fifth Edition, Project Management Institute (PMI)®, Project Management Professional (PMP)®, and Certified Associate in Project Management (CAPM)® are registered trademarks of Project Management Institute, Inc. - Version 2.1 Published September 30, 2014

Lesson 10: Managing Project Work, Scope, Schedules, and Cost | Topic A

Output	Description
Work performance reports	Include the project management plan components such as the schedule management plan, cost management plan, quality management plan, and scope, schedule, and cost performance baselines.
Project management plan updates	Approved changes can lead to project management plan and scope, schedule, and cost baseline updates.
Project documents updates	Include forecasts, performance reports, and issue log.

A Guide to the Project Management Body of Knowledge (PMBOK® Guide) – Fifth Edition, Project Management Institute, Inc., 2013, pg. 92-94

Guidelines to Monitor and Control Project Work

During the Monitor and Control Project Work process, the project manager tracks, reviews, and regulates the project processes to meet the project's performance objectives. Effective monitoring ensures that necessary preventative actions are taken in order to control project performance. To effectively monitor and control project work, follow these guidelines:

* Compare and evaluate project performance with the project plan. If necessary, recommend actions to take.
* Analyze, track, and monitor risks to make sure they are being recognized and reported, and that response plans are being executed.
* Maintain accurate information about the project as it unfolds.
* Maintain the integrity of baselines ensuring that only approved changes are incorporated.
* Provide information to support status reporting, progress, and forecasting.
* Provide forecasts to update recent cost and schedule information.
* Monitor the execution of approved changes when they occur.

A Guide to the Project Management Body of Knowledge (PMBOK® Guide) – Fifth Edition, Project Management Institute, Inc., 2013, pg. 86-94

ACTIVITY 10-1
Monitoring and Controlling Project Work

Scenario

The new build project has been running smoothly, thanks in large part to the efforts of the site manager, Sarah. She has been instrumental in getting all teams to work together to meet their tight deadlines. During a crucial phase in the project, Sarah falls ill. A less-experienced manager, Kevin, is brought in to replace her. For this project, it is more important to maintain the schedule than to maintain the cost baseline.

1. **What can you do, as the project manager, to mitigate the negative effects of a staffing change?**
   - ○ Put the project on hold until Sarah returns from sick leave.
   - ○ Rebuild the schedule to include additional time for Kevin to complete his tasks.
   - ○ Closely monitor Kevin's work to assess any possible risk.
   - ○ Discuss with the team the impending change and that the team can expect to go through the team development stages again.

2. **Kevin missed an important deadline. What action can you take to help Kevin get back on schedule?**

3. **After he has been given extra help, Kevin manages to meet his next important deadline. What should be your next action as project manager?**
   - ○ Keep a private log for your own reference, detailing changes that have been made to the project.
   - ○ Update recent cost and schedule changes that may have resulted from recent changes.
   - ○ Ask Kevin to closely monitor changes to the project's cost and schedule.
   - ○ Ask Kevin to let you know if he has any further problems as the project progresses.

A Guide to the Project Management Body of Knowledge (PMBOK® Guide) – Fifth Edition, Project Management Institute (PMI)®, Project Management Professional (PMP)®, and Certified Associate in Project Management (CAPM)® are registered trademarks of Project Management Institute, Inc. - Version 2.1 Published September 30, 2014

Lesson 10: Managing Project Work, Scope, Schedules, and Cost | *Topic A*

TOPIC B

Perform Integrated Change Control

Now that you have identified the best practices for monitoring and controlling project work, you understand the important steps you must take toward making sure that your project is conducted with the appropriate internal integrity and oversight. You will further this goal by developing an integrated change control system, which formally governs changes to the project work, schedule baseline, and budget. In this topic, you will develop an integrated change control system.

A Guide to the Project Management Body of Knowledge (PMBOK® Guide) – Fifth Edition, Project Management Institute, Inc., 2013, pg. 94-97

The following data flow diagram illustrates how the Perform Integrated Change Control process relates to the other knowledge areas within the Planning Process Group.

A Guide to the Project Management Body of Knowledge (PMBOK® Guide) – Fifth Edition, Project Management Institute (PMI)®, Project Management Professional (PMP)®, and Certified Associate in Project Management (CAPM)® are registered trademarks of Project Management Institute, Inc. - Version 2.1 Published September 30, 2014

Lesson 10: Managing Project Work, Scope, Schedules, and Cost | *Topic B*

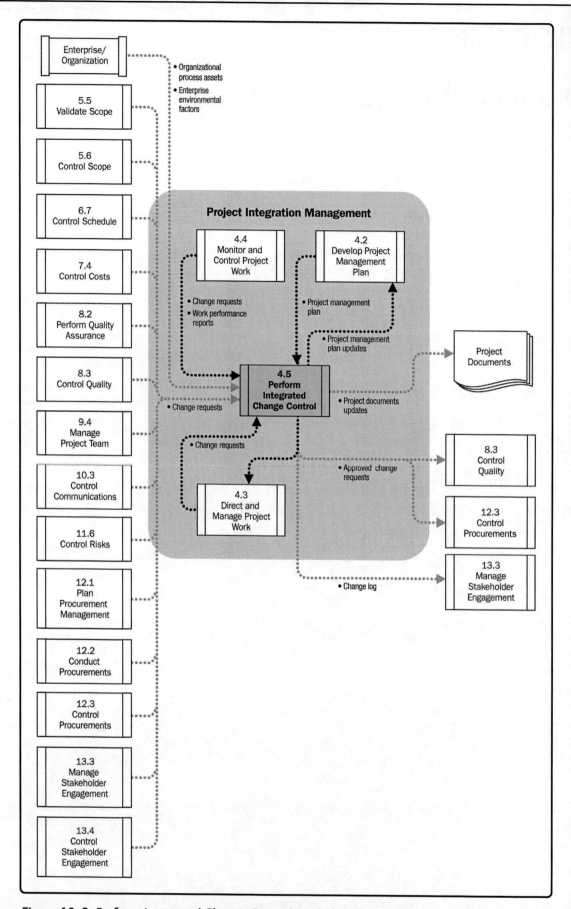

Figure 10-3: Perform Integrated Change Control work data flow diagram.

A Guide to the Project Management Body of Knowledge (PMBOK® Guide) – Fifth Edition, Project Management Institute (PMI)®, Project Management Professional (PMP)®, and Certified Associate in Project Management (CAPM)® are registered trademarks of Project Management Institute, Inc. - Version 2.1 Published September 30, 2014

A Guide to the Project Management Body of Knowledge (PMBOK® Guide) – Fifth Edition, Project Management Institute, Inc., 2013, p. 95

Integrated Change Control

Integrated change control is the process of identifying, documenting, approving or rejecting, and controlling any changes to the project baselines. Integrated change control reduces risk to your project by governing the execution of proposed changes that will affect schedule and cost or any other objectives of the project. It allows project managers to record the changes that are requested, makes sure that changes are implemented in a standardized and approved manner, minimizes their disruptive effect, and monitors their progression from initial request through completion.

A Guide to the Project Management Body of Knowledge (PMBOK® Guide) – Fifth Edition, Project Management Institute, Inc., 2013, pg. 96-97

Causes of Project Changes

Performance variation is an inevitable component of project work and can be caused by any of several common factors.

Cause	Description
Inaccurate initial estimates	There are many reasons why initial time and cost estimates for completing the project work prove to be inaccurate. These reasons may range from lack of experience, lack of information, or precedence to inaccurate data, excessive optimism, technological difficulties, and unreliable resources. Getting those original estimates to be as realistic and accurate as possible makes the control process more manageable.
Specification changes	Project work can open up new avenues of development and design that were not considered during the initial planning of the project work and scope. As new options for a product or service become apparent, customers, sponsors, or the project manager may broaden the project's scope to include new specifications and deliverables.
New regulations	As project work progresses, new governmental or industry-specific regulations may be enacted. This can be especially true for very lengthy projects. If the new regulations are related to the ongoing projects, project change becomes necessary. Accommodating new regulations or legislation can also mean revisiting the planning process to determine the effect the new regulations will have on resource needs, schedule durations, and quality specifications.
Missed requirements	Many times the requirements are understood by reviewing the documentation, and interviewing the end users and policy makers. However, there are times when complete and comprehensive understanding may not be possible. The interviewer feels that he/she has understood the point, and the interviewee feels that he has expressed all that matters. Although a Requirements Traceability Matrix (RTM) is prepared, the same confusion might arise in a written document. Prototyping is used where a demonstration of functional and/or technical requirements is done. Although all these techniques reduce the chances of missing any requirements, it cannot guarantee that every requirement is captured. There are often some slippages that surface at different phases in the project.

A Guide to the Project Management Body of Knowledge (PMBOK® Guide) – Fifth Edition, Project Management Institute (PMI)®, Project Management Professional (PMP)®, and Certified Associate in Project Management (CAPM)® are registered trademarks of Project Management Institute, Inc. - Version 2.1 Published September 30, 2014

Lesson 10: Managing Project Work, Scope, Schedules, and Cost | *Topic B*

A Guide to the Project Management Body of Knowledge (PMBOK® Guide) – Fifth Edition, Project Management Institute, Inc., 2013, pg. 96-97

Change Control Systems

A *change control system* is a collection of formal, documented procedures for changing official project documents; it specifies how project deliverables will be controlled, changed, and approved. An effective change control system includes the forms, tracking methods, processes, and approval levels required for authorizing or rejecting requested changes. Change control systems often specify that a Change Control Board (CCB) will address the issues that affect cost, time, and product quality.

A Guide to the Project Management Body of Knowledge (PMBOK® Guide) – Fifth Edition, Project Management Institute, Inc., 2013, pg. 96-97, 531

CCB

A CCB is an internal unit or department charged with not only monitoring, controlling, coordinating, and implementing changes to all elements of project work, but also with accepting or rejecting changes that have been requested by customers or any other stakeholders. Normally, the CCB operates closely with the project's sponsor, customers, and other key stakeholders.

The responsibilities of the CCB will have been delineated, documented, and agreed to by the stakeholders, customers, and project team. Decisions made during the change control board meetings are documented and communicated to the required stakeholders. Stakeholders can use this information to follow-up on the necessary actions.

A Guide to the Project Management Body of Knowledge (PMBOK® Guide) – Fifth Edition, Project Management Institute, Inc., 2013, pg. 96-97, 530

Configuration Management

Configuration management is a tool used to manage changes to a product or service being produced as well as changes to any of the project documents, such as schedule updates. These can include changes of a technical nature, and changes in administrative direction. Configuration management is used to:

- Control product iterations.
- Ensure that product specifications are current.
- Control the steps for reviewing and approving product prototypes, testing standards, and drawings or blueprints.

 Note: When dealing with government contracts or other large systems, a configuration management system is often required.

A Guide to the Project Management Body of Knowledge (PMBOK® Guide) – Fifth Edition, Project Management Institute, Inc., 2013, pg. 96-97

Configuration Management Systems

A *configuration management system* is a tool that contains procedures that help provide technical and administrative guidance for: identifying and recording the characteristics of a product or service; controlling changes made to the characteristics; documenting the changes and the status of implementation; and verifying the product's conformance to the requirements. One of the subsystems of the configuration management system is the change control system.

Configuration management systems, when combined with integrated change control, provide standardized and effective ways of managing approved changes and baselines within a project. Configuration control involves specifying the deliverables and processes, whereas change control involves identifying, recording, and supervising changes to project baselines.

A Guide to the Project Management Body of Knowledge (PMBOK® Guide) – Fifth Edition, Project Management Institute, Inc., 2013, pg. 96-97, 532

The Perform Integrated Change Control Process

The *Perform Integrated Change Control process* is the formal method of governing and organizing the manner in which changes will be requested, reviewed, approved or rejected, implemented, controlled, and coordinated. Its goal is to make sure that changes to the project's baselines are managed with the least amount of disruption to important project parameters such as cost, time, and quality. All change requests must be recorded in the change management or configuration management system. Change requests follow the processes specified in the configuration management system. These processes may need information about the estimated time and cost impacts for implementing the changes. The change control process also ensures that the appropriate parties such as stakeholders, project team members, and/or customers are aware of and approve of changes to the project that will affect time, cost, and quality.

A Guide to the Project Management Body of Knowledge (PMBOK® Guide) – Fifth Edition, Project Management Institute, Inc., 2013, pg. 94-97

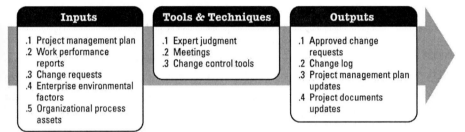

Figure 10-4: The Perform Integrated Change Control process.

A Guide to the Project Management Body of Knowledge (PMBOK® Guide) – Fifth Edition, Project Management Institute, Inc., 2013, p. 94

Perform Integrated Change Control Inputs

Various components provide input to the Perform Integrated Change Control process.

Input	Description
Project management plan	Describes each step of the project including the way it is executed, monitored, and closed.
Work performance reports	Periodically collected information about project activities being performed to accomplish the project work.
Change requests	Include corrective actions, preventive actions, and defect repairs. This may result in modifying project scope, policies, procedures, cost, and budgets, or a rework of project schedules. Corrective and preventive actions do not generally affect the project baselines, but the performance against baselines.
Enterprise environmental factors	Include Project Management Information Systems that can influence the integrated change control process. The PMIS includes automated tools such as scheduling software tools or information collection and distribution system.

Input	Description
Organizational process assets	Includes process assets such as:

- Change control procedures, which will also include steps used to modify official company standards, policies, and plans and to approve, validate, and implement changes.
- Procedures used to approve and issue change authorizations.
- Process measurement databases used to collect and create measurement data on products and processes.
- Project files such as scope, cost, schedule, and performance measurement baselines.
- A configuration management knowledge base that contains the versions of all documents such as the official standards and procedures of the company.

A Guide to the Project Management Body of Knowledge (PMBOK® Guide) – Fifth Edition, Project Management Institute, Inc., 2013, pg. 97-98

Perform Integrated Change Control Tools and Techniques

There are three tools and techniques used in the Perform Integrated Change Control process.

Tools & Techniques	Description
Expert judgment	Expert judgment is used to provide expertise on the project's CCB.
Meetings	CCB meetings are held to review and disposition all project change requests.
Change control tools	Manual or automated tools are used to manage both changes and configuration management. Change requests are logged in the tool and the resulting decisions and dispositions are recorded by the CCB.

A Guide to the Project Management Body of Knowledge (PMBOK® Guide) – Fifth Edition, Project Management Institute, Inc., 2013, pg. 98-99

Perform Integrated Change Control Outputs

There are four outputs from the Perform Integrated Change Control process.

Outputs	Description
Approved change requests	Status of all approved change requests should be updated in the change request log when updating the process documents. Rejected changes should also be documented in the change request log.
Change log	Updated to record all changes that occur during a project along with the disposition of each change request, including change requests that are rejected.
Project management plan updates	Any actions needed to define, integrate, and coordinate all sub-plans into a project management plan. Documents that may be updated during the process include subsidiary management plans and baselines that have been changed as a result of the change control process. Changes made to the baselines should not affect the past performance data.

Outputs	Description
Project documents updates	Documents such as change request logs and other documents that are affected by the change control process may be updated during the Perform Integrated Change Control process.

A Guide to the Project Management Body of Knowledge (PMBOK® Guide) – Fifth Edition, Project Management Institute, Inc., 2013, pg. 99-100

Guidelines to Perform Integrated Change Control

Managing changes to performance baselines ensures that the original project scope and the integrity of performance baselines are maintained. Ensuring that changes are agreed upon and continuously managing changes as they occur minimizes the impact changes may have on project time, cost, and quality concerns. To effectively perform integrated change control, follow these guidelines:

- Make sure your change control system is cost-effective. It should not cost more money to implement than it saves through controlling.
- Establish or make use of an existing CCB composed of project stakeholders to evaluate change requests.
- Document the effect the changes have on the project performance baseline.
- Obtain approval from the appropriate parties for all change requests before implementing the change.
- Use configuration management to document and control changes to original product characteristics.
- Coordinate changes across knowledge areas as appropriate. For example, does a proposed schedule change affect cost, risk, quality, and/or staffing?
- Use performance reports to measure project performance and assess whether planned variances require corrective action. Make sure performance reports are timely and accurate to increase the effectiveness of control decisions.
- Identify corrective action necessary to bring expected performance in line with the project plan.
    - Determine the source and severity of the problem.
    - Review the project plan and objectives.
    - Consider factors inside and outside the project that may influence corrective action decisions.
    - Identify alternative options available.
    - Choose from among the alternatives by evaluating the impact of each alternative on cost, schedule, quality, and risk.
- Update the project plan to reflect changes made that affect performance baselines.
- Document the causes of variances, the steps taken to correct performance problems, and the rationale behind the decision-making process to avoid similar problems on future projects.

A Guide to the Project Management Body of Knowledge (PMBOK® Guide) – Fifth Edition, Project Management Institute, Inc., 2013, pg. 94-100

A Guide to the Project Management Body of Knowledge (PMBOK® Guide) – Fifth Edition, Project Management Institute (PMI)®, Project Management Professional (PMP)®, and Certified Associate in Project Management (CAPM)® are registered trademarks of Project Management Institute, Inc. - Version 2.1 Published September 30, 2014

Lesson 10: Managing Project Work, Scope, Schedules, and Cost | *Topic B*

ACTIVITY 10-2
Performing Integrated Change Control

Scenario

The new build project has a very tight deadline, as well as a strict budget. You are concerned that any possible changes could negatively affect project performance baselines. You need to ensure that there is a standardized method for handling changes to project work.

---

1. Who will you involve in the change control process for the new build project and what is their role in the change control process?

2. The site manager informs you that the window and door installation will have a significant delay. In the risk register, you accounted for a delay due to the weather, but this delay is much longer than originally anticipated. What action should you take first?

   ○ Coordinate changes across knowledge areas.

   ⦿ Document the change request in a change control system.

   ○ Update the project plan to reflect changes.

   ○ Bring the information to the stakeholders for evaluation and approval.

3. The site manager contacted the window and door supplier and was able to secure half of the windows before the next shipment. Based on your change control process, what further action, if any, should you take?

TOPIC C

Validate Project Scope

Your project team has produced deliverables and work results. Before you can gain formal acceptance of deliverables from your stakeholders, you need to verify that they meet project requirements and stakeholders' expectations. In this topic, you'll validate project scope.

A Guide to the Project Management Body of Knowledge (PMBOK® Guide) – Fifth Edition, Project Management Institute, Inc., 2013, pg. 133-134

The following data flow diagram illustrates how the Validate Scope process relates to the other knowledge areas within the Planning Process Group.

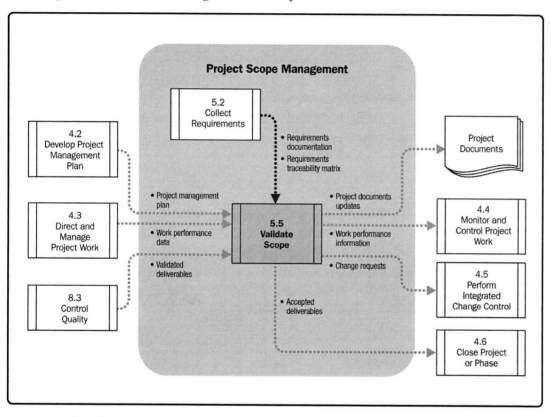

Figure 10–5: Validate Scope work data flow diagram.

A Guide to the Project Management Body of Knowledge (PMBOK® Guide) – Fifth Edition, Project Management Institute, Inc., 2013, p. 133

The Validate Scope Process

The *Validate Scope process* demonstrates to stakeholders that they have received what they have been promised in a given deliverable and formalizes their acceptance. The validate scope process usually involves reviewing the deliverables with the project customer or sponsor to ensure that they are satisfied with the final deliverable and securing their formal acceptance for the completeness of the deliverable. Scope verification is generally done after quality control to ensure that only the correct deliverables are validated for completeness based on criteria as described in the official project plans and product documentation.

A Guide to the Project Management Body of Knowledge (PMBOK® Guide) – Fifth Edition, Project Management Institute, Inc., 2013, pg. 133-134

Inputs	Tools & Techniques	Outputs
.1 Project management plan .2 Requirements documentation .3 Requirements traceability matrix .4 Verified deliverables .5 Work performance data	.1 Inspection .2 Group decision-making techniques	.1 Accepted deliverables .2 Change requests .3 Work performance information .4 Project documents updates

Figure 10-6: The Validate Scope process.

A Guide to the Project Management Body of Knowledge (PMBOK® Guide) – Fifth Edition, Project Management Institute, Inc., 2013, p. 133

Validate Scope Inputs

Various components provide input to the Validate Scope process.

Input	Description
Project management plan	Contains the project scope baseline of all planning processes. The scope baseline components include the project scope statement, WBS, and WBS dictionary.
Requirements documentation	Lists the project, product, technical, and other project requirements and their acceptance criteria.
Requirements traceability matrix	Links the identified requirements with their source and helps track them throughout the project. This also helps ensure that all approved requirements are delivered at the end of the project.
Verified deliverables	Deliverables that are completed and verified for correctness by the perform quality control process.
Work performance data	Includes number and severity of non-conformances, how many requirements have been met, and number of validation cycles performed during the project.

A Guide to the Project Management Body of Knowledge (PMBOK® Guide) – Fifth Edition, Project Management Institute, Inc., 2013, pg. 134-135

Validate Scope Tools and Techniques

There are various tools and techniques used in the Validate Scope process.

Tools & Techniques	Description
Inspection	Used for scope verification. Inspection refers to measuring, examining, and verifying to be sure that work and deliverables meet requirements and acceptance criteria. It is sometimes referred to as reviews, product reviews, audits, or walkthroughs. These terms have specific meanings in some application areas.
Group decision-making techniques	Technique used to reach a conclusion when validation is performed by the project team and stakeholders.

A Guide to the Project Management Body of Knowledge (PMBOK® Guide) – Fifth Edition, Project Management Institute, Inc., 2013, p. 135

Inspections

An *inspection* is an official examination of work results to verify that requirements are met. It is sometimes referred to as a review, product review, audit, or walkthrough. The inspection may be conducted by an internal or external inspection team. During scope verification, an inspection typically involves:

- Comparing the baseline specifications and any approved changes to the actual project results.
- Determining the likelihood that remaining deliverables will be completed as promised.
- Identifying actions that may be needed to ensure that the work results will meet specifications, scope, or schedule and budget goals.

A Guide to the Project Management Body of Knowledge (PMBOK® Guide) – Fifth Edition, Project Management Institute, Inc., 2013, p. 135

Inspectors

In some cases, your team will be asked to conduct the inspection. In other cases, stakeholders may decide to ask an outside entity to either conduct the inspection, or to participate with you in conducting it.

Inspection Report Components

Inspection reports are necessary and contain several components.

Component	Description
Project baseline and status comparison	This is the comparison of the baseline specifications, schedules, and budgets to the actual project results for the project phase or deliverable.
Overall project status	This is a discussion of whether the project as a whole is on track, or whether it is likely to deviate in some way from the project plans.
Change recommendations	Based on the inspection result, there may need to be recommended changes that will be needed in order to meet specifications, scope, or schedule and budget goals.
Scope and methodology of the inspection	This section should explain what the audit attempted to prove, how it went about proving it, what measurements were used to determine conformance to requirements, and what assumptions or limitations influenced the way that data was collected.

A Guide to the Project Management Body of Knowledge (PMBOK® Guide) – Fifth Edition, Project Management Institute, Inc., 2013, pg. 135, 252, 543

Validate Scope Outputs

There are four outputs from the Validate Scope process.

Output	Description
Accepted deliverables	The Verify Scope process keeps track of all deliverables that are completed, accepted, and formally signed off. The deliverables that have been formally signed-off or acknowledged by the sponsors or customers are moved to the close project or phase process. You should also document all rejected deliverables.

A Guide to the Project Management Body of Knowledge (PMBOK® Guide) – Fifth Edition, Project Management Institute (PMI)®, Project Management Professional (PMP)®, and Certified Associate in Project Management (CAPM)® are registered trademarks of Project Management Institute, Inc. - Version 2.1 Published September 30, 2014

Lesson 10: Managing Project Work, Scope, Schedules, and Cost | *Topic C*

Output	Description
Change requests	Any deliverable that has not been accepted formally is documented along with the reasons for rejection. These deliverables may undergo change requests for defect repairs. Change requests can be developed for review through the perform integrated change control process.
Work performance information	Includes the status of each deliverable (started, in progress, completed, accepted).
Project documents updates	Documents that define the product or report status on project completion may need to be updated as a result of project scope verification.

A Guide to the Project Management Body of Knowledge (PMBOK® Guide) – Fifth Edition, Project Management Institute, Inc., 2013, pg. 135-136

Guidelines to Validate Project Scope

To validate the scope of your project:

- Prepare for a scope verification inspection:
  1. Establish the scope and boundaries of the inspection.
  2. Establish and/or approve measurements to be used in the inspection.
  3. Establish and/or approve the methodology of the inspection, including a methodology for double-checking data or measurements.
  4. Gather all relevant scope documentation (for example, WBS, scope statement, and requirements documentation).
  5. Communicate with all team members in advance so they can prepare for the inspection in a timely fashion.
- Conduct an inspection to review deliverables and work results to ensure satisfactory completeness.
- Prepare an inspection report.
- Provide the inspection report to key stakeholders to obtain complete or conditional formal acceptance of the deliverables and work results.
- Distribute formal acceptance documentation to project stakeholders according to the communications management plan. If the project is terminated early, document the level and extent of deliverables completed and distribute the documentation to project stakeholders.

A Guide to the Project Management Body of Knowledge (PMBOK® Guide) – Fifth Edition, Project Management Institute, Inc., 2013, pg. 133-136

ACTIVITY 10-3
Validating Project Scope

Scenario

On the first Monday of every month, you are required to attend a meeting with the city officials and the homeowners to give a status on any Building with Heart projects in process. You have just been to the site and verified with the site manager that most of the initial build is complete. You need to verify that the house meets project requirements and stakeholders' expectations.

1. Your build team has decided to use a checklist and job aid in combination for the house build completed tasks. Before beginning the actual review, what else would you consider doing?

2. The initial build components have passed the inspection. What should be included in your review report and why?

3. You receive formal approval for the initial build components. How will you inform stakeholders?

4. What could happen if the project scope is not validated regularly for this project?

A Guide to the Project Management Body of Knowledge (PMBOK® Guide) – Fifth Edition, Project Management Institute (PMI)®, Project Management Professional (PMP)®, and Certified Associate in Project Management (CAPM)® are registered trademarks of Project Management Institute, Inc. - Version 2.1 Published September 30, 2014

Lesson 10: Managing Project Work, Scope, Schedules, and Cost | Topic C

TOPIC D

Control Project Scope

You defined your project's scope and developed a WBS as part of your project planning effort. Now that the project work is moving forward, you need to control changes to project scope using the control scope inputs and tools. In this topic, you'll control the scope of the project.

A Guide to the Project Management Body of Knowledge (PMBOK® Guide) – Fifth Edition, Project Management Institute, Inc., 2013, pg. 136-137

The following data flow diagram illustrates how the Control Scope process relates to the other knowledge areas within the Planning Process Group.

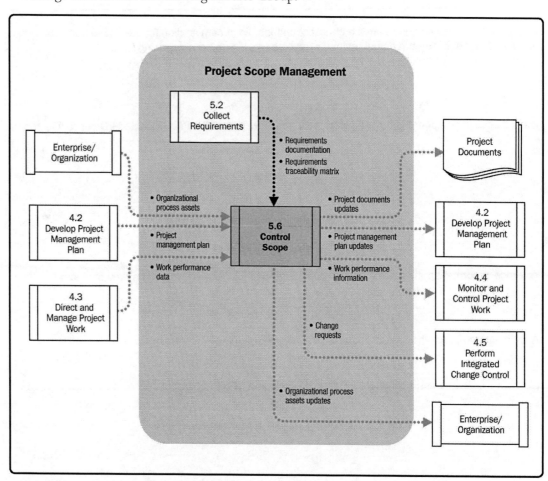

Figure 10-7: The Control Scope data flow diagram.

A Guide to the Project Management Body of Knowledge (PMBOK® Guide) – Fifth Edition, Project Management Institute, Inc., 2013, p. 137

The Control Scope Process

Control scope is the process of monitoring project scope and holding changes to the project scope baseline in check by:

- Evaluating change requests to determine the need and impact of the change to project objectives.
- Making sure changes are agreed upon.

A Guide to the Project Management Body of Knowledge (PMBOK® Guide) – Fifth Edition, Project Management Institute (PMI)®, Project Management Professional (PMP)®, and Certified Associate in Project Management (CAPM)® are registered trademarks of Project Management Institute, Inc. - Version 2.1 Published September 30, 2014

Lesson 10: Managing Project Work, Scope, Schedules, and Cost | Topic D

- Managing the actual changes to ensure that they are implemented correctly and that they are effective.

Scope change control must be integrated with the other controlling processes to prevent unauthorized changes that result in scope creep.

A Guide to the Project Management Body of Knowledge (PMBOK® Guide) – Fifth Edition, Project Management Institute, Inc., 2013, pg. 136-137

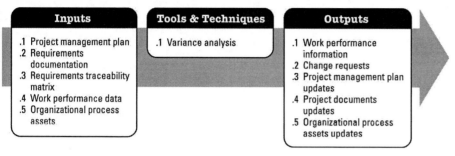

Figure 10–8: The Control Scope process.

A Guide to the Project Management Body of Knowledge (PMBOK® Guide) – Fifth Edition, Project Management Institute, Inc., 2013, p. 136

Control Scope Inputs

Various components provide input to the Control Scope process.

Input	Description
Project management plan	Includes several components such as: • Scope baseline: Used in determining if a change or if a corrective or preventive action is required by comparing the scope baseline with the actual results. • Scope management plan: Includes guidelines for managing and controlling the project scope. The project management team follows these guidelines when controlling the project scope. • Change management plan: Details the process of change management. • Configuration management plan: Provides information on elements that can be configured, those that need to undergo formal change control, and the process of controlling such changes. • Requirements management plan: Provides information about how requirements activities should be planned, tracked, and reported and how changes to the product requirements must be initiated.
Requirements documentation	Documents how each project requirement meets the overall business need of the project. Requirements documentation components include the project's business needs, functional requirements such as business processes and information, and non-functional requirements such as performance, safety, and supportability.

Input	Description
Requirements traceability matrix	Links project requirements to the business and project objectives and ensures that the requirements add business value to the project. It also helps track requirements throughout the project life cycle and ensures that the approved requirements are delivered when the project ends.
Work performance data	Periodically collected information about project activities that are being performed to accomplish the project work.
Organizational process assets	Includes existing formal and informal policies, procedures, and guidelines that are related to scope control and the necessary monitoring and reporting methods.

A Guide to the Project Management Body of Knowledge (PMBOK® Guide) – Fifth Edition, Project Management Institute, Inc., 2013, pg. 138-139

Control Scope Tools and Techniques

There is only one tool and technique used for controlling project scope.

Tools & Techniques	Description
Variance analysis	The analysis of variance from the original scope baseline or the quantification of departure from expected results. Scope control includes determining the cause of variance relative to the baseline, and deciding if corrective or preventive action is necessary.

A Guide to the Project Management Body of Knowledge (PMBOK® Guide) – Fifth Edition, Project Management Institute, Inc., 2013, p. 139

Control Scope Outputs

Several outputs result from the Control Scope process.

Output	Description
Work performance information	Includes measuring the variance between the planned and actual, technical or other scope performance measurements. The results are documented and communicated to the project stakeholders.
Change requests	Project scope performance analysis may cause changes such as defect repairs or preventive or corrective actions, which are then processed for review and disposition in compliance with the integrated change control process.
Project management plan updates	If any change requests impact the project scope or project baselines, then the project scope, the scope statement, the WBS, the WBS dictionary, and any corresponding cost baseline and schedule baselines of the project management plan need to be updated and reissued to accommodate the approved changes.
Project documents updates	Project documents such as requirements documentation and the requirements traceability matrix may need to be updated when controlling project scope.

A Guide to the Project Management Body of Knowledge (PMBOK® Guide) – Fifth Edition, Project Management Institute (PMI)®, Project Management Professional (PMP)®, and Certified Associate in Project Management (CAPM)® are registered trademarks of Project Management Institute, Inc. - Version 2.1 Published September 30, 2014

Lesson 10: Managing Project Work, Scope, Schedules, and Cost | Topic D

Output	Description
Organizational process assets updates	Any causes of variances, reasons for corrective actions, and any other types of lessons learned from project scope control are documented in the organizational process assets database.

A Guide to the Project Management Body of Knowledge (PMBOK® Guide) – Fifth Edition, Project Management Institute, Inc., 2013, pg. 139-140

Guidelines to Control Project Scope

Continually monitoring and controlling changes to the project scope enables you to maintain the original project scope definition. In addition, controlling project scope changes ensures that cost, schedule, and quality performance baselines are maintained. To effectively control project scope, follow these guidelines:

- Develop and implement a scope change control system. Make sure that your system:
  - Is integrated with the project's integrated change control system.
  - Includes the paperwork, tracking systems, and approval levels necessary for authorizing scope changes.
  - Complies with any relevant contractual provisions when the project is done under contract.
  - Complies with the guidelines specified in the scope management plan.
- Identify and document corrective action to take to bring expected future project performance in line with planned performance.
- Make sure that formal agreements are reached and new specifications detailed when project scope is expanded to include either additional work that is clearly outside the original scope, or additional work that is required as a result of scope boundary clarifications.
- Depending upon the nature of the change, you may need to revise the cost, schedule, or quality performance baselines to reflect the changes and to form a new baseline against which future performance can be measured. Notify project stakeholders of any changes made to project baselines.
- Use performance measurement techniques to monitor the changes.
  - Are the changes being properly implemented?
  - Do the changes bring about the desired results?
  - Are new risks being introduced as a result of implementing the changes? It would be very unusual for additional risks to not appear or for the nature of existing risks to not change significantly. Structuring a risk review after any change in scope is considered prudent practice.
- Document lessons learned during scope change control for use on future projects. The documentation should include:
  - Causes of variances
  - Performance baselines affected by the changes
  - Rationale behind the recommended corrective action
  - Any other lessons learned during scope change control

A Guide to the Project Management Body of Knowledge (PMBOK® Guide) – Fifth Edition, Project Management Institute, Inc., 2013, pg. 136-140

ACTIVITY 10-4
Controlling the Project Scope

Scenario

The Building with Heart's new PMO director has spent several weeks reviewing the business transformation project. Due to the complexity of such a large company-wide initiative, the director has received authorization for all project managers to attend a one-week comprehensive project management workshop. Although the departure of a site supervisor and possible organizational changes were included in the risk management plan, no cost or schedule contingency was allocated for such a change to the project scope.

---

1. A scope change request recommending additional work site documentation has been submitted to the CCB for analysis. This change might impact the project finish date. What should be done first with this request?

   - ☑ Evaluate the request
   - ○ Ensure that new specifications are detailed
   - ○ Monitor changes
   - ○ Identify corrective action to take

2. What controlling scope input provides information on elements that can be configured, those that undergo formal change control, and the process of controlling such changes?

   - ☑ Configuration management plan
   - ○ Work performance information
   - ○ Requirements documentation
   - ○ Requirements traceability matrix

3. What controlling scope input documents how each project requirement meets the overall business need of the project?

   - ○ Configuration management plan
   - ○ Work performance information
   - ☑ Requirements documentation
   - ○ Requirements traceability matrix

4. The CCB informs you that the additional costs for the work site requests will be adjusted in the project budget. However, the project finish date must remain the same. As the project manager, what could you do to ensure that the project finishes on time?

TOPIC E

Control the Project Schedule

When you planned your project, you developed a schedule to serve as a baseline during project execution, monitoring, and controlling. Now you need to determine how much variance exists between the actual work completed and the work scheduled. In this topic, you will examine the Control Schedule process and control the project schedule.

A Guide to the Project Management Body of Knowledge (PMBOK® Guide) – Fifth Edition, Project Management Institute, Inc., 2013, pg. 185-187

The following data flow diagram illustrates how the Control Schedule process relates to the other knowledge areas within the Planning Process Group.

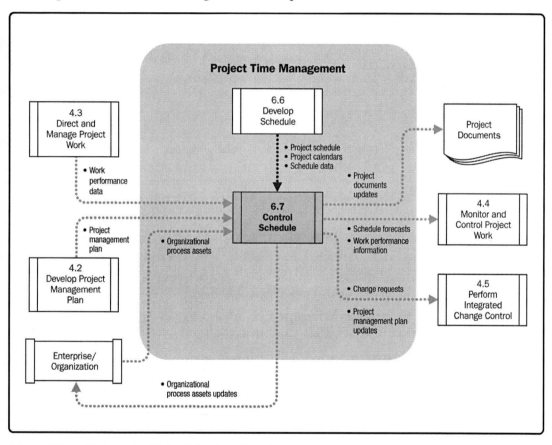

Figure 10-9: The Control Schedule data flow diagram.

A Guide to the Project Management Body of Knowledge (PMBOK® Guide) – Fifth Edition, Project Management Institute, Inc., 2013, p. 186

The Control Schedule Process

Control schedule is a process of monitoring schedule performance and controlling changes to the schedule baseline. During this process, the project manager continually monitors schedule performance by comparing actual work completed to the amount of work that was planned to be completed. In addition, the project manager, along with a CCB, monitors, coordinates, and implements changes to the project schedule and evaluates the impact of those changes on other performance baselines and the original scope definition.

A Guide to the Project Management Body of Knowledge (PMBOK® Guide) – Fifth Edition, Project Management Institute (PMI)®, Project Management Professional (PMP)®, and Certified Associate in Project Management (CAPM)® are registered trademarks of Project Management Institute, Inc. - Version 2.1 Published September 30, 2014

Lesson 10: Managing Project Work, Scope, Schedules, and Cost | *Topic E*

A Guide to the Project Management Body of Knowledge (PMBOK® Guide) – Fifth Edition, Project Management Institute, Inc., 2013, pg. 185-187

Inputs	Tools & Techniques	Outputs
.1 Project management plan .2 Project schedule .3 Work performance data .4 Project calendars .5 Schedule data .6 Organizational process assets	.1 Performance reviews .2 Project management software .3 Resource optimization techniques .4 Modeling techniques .5 Leads and lags .6 Schedule compression .7 Scheduling tool	.1 Work performance information .2 Schedule forecasts .3 Change requests .4 Project management plan updates .5 Project documents updates .6 Organizational process assets updates

Figure 10-10: The Control Schedule process.

A Guide to the Project Management Body of Knowledge (PMBOK® Guide) – Fifth Edition, Project Management Institute, Inc., 2013, p. 185

Control Schedule Inputs

Various components provide input to the Control Schedule process.

Input	Description
Project management plan	Contains the schedule management plan, which sets up guidelines on how the project schedule will be administered and directed. It also contains the schedule baseline that is used for comparing actual results and determining the type of corrective action that is needed.
Project schedule	Contains the up-to-date version of the project schedule with details on completed activities and activities that are yet to commence, with their respective start and end dates.
Work performance data	Provides information on project progression, such as activities that are started, in progress, or finished.
Project calendars	Includes different work periods for activities so that schedule forecasts can be calculated.
Schedule data	Includes any data that has been tracked in the schedule and can ultimately affect the project scope.
Organizational process assets	Include schedule control related policies, procedures, and guidelines, schedule control tools, and monitoring and reporting methods that are to be followed.

A Guide to the Project Management Body of Knowledge (PMBOK® Guide) – Fifth Edition, Project Management Institute, Inc., 2013, pg. 187-188

Control Schedule Tools and Techniques

There are various tools and techniques used in the Control Schedule process.

Tools & Techniques	Description
Performance reviews	Reviews to measure, analyze, and compare schedule performance. This includes comparing the actual start and finish dates, percent complete, and the time needed to complete the work in progress.

A Guide to the Project Management Body of Knowledge (PMBOK® Guide) – Fifth Edition, Project Management Institute (PMI)®, Project Management Professional (PMP)®, and Certified Associate in Project Management (CAPM)® are registered trademarks of Project Management Institute, Inc. - Version 2.1 Published September 30, 2014

Lesson 10: Managing Project Work, Scope, Schedules, and Cost | Topic E

Tools & Techniques	Description
Project management software	Provides ways of tracking planned dates vs. actual dates, and to forecast effects of changes to the project schedule.
Resource optimization techniques	Assists in making scheduling decisions when there are resource management concerns and enables optimum distribution of work among the available resources.
Modeling techniques	Analysis that involves the review of multiple scenarios and then calculating various possibilities of project durations, activity sequences, and resource loading to bring schedule in alignment with the plan.
Leads and lags	Brings the project activities, which are behind or ahead of schedule, in alignment with the plan. Working out possibilities of accelerating (adding leads to) or decelerating (adding lags to) the schedule to meet the demands of the plan.
Schedule compression	Shortens the schedule so as to align the project activities to the project plan without affecting the project scope.
Scheduling tool	Uses updated schedule data and the scheduling tool with the project management software or other methods to perform schedule network analysis and generate an updated project schedule.

A Guide to the Project Management Body of Knowledge (PMBOK® Guide) – Fifth Edition, Project Management Institute, Inc., 2013, pg. 188-190

Performance Reviews

There are four types of performance reviews that can be held to analyze schedule performance.

- Trend analysis shows the project schedule performance over time to see if there is a trend of the project slowing down or moving ahead of schedule. Adjustments can be made based on the trend being observed.
- Critical path method, showing the minimum project duration, should be reviewed to see if there is any deviation. This is the most important path to the end of the project, so the impact of a delay could be significant to the project ending on time.
- Critical chain method reviews the buffer built into the schedule to ensure that there is still enough buffer to protect the project delivery date.
- Earned Value Management (EVM) reviews schedule performance measurements such as Schedule Variance (SV) and Schedule Performance Index (SPI) to uncover variance against the schedule baseline. Significant variance needs to be addressed with schedule updates.

A Guide to the Project Management Body of Knowledge (PMBOK® Guide) – Fifth Edition, Project Management Institute, Inc., 2013, pg. 188-189

Control Schedule Outputs

There are six outputs from the Control Schedule process.

Output	Description
Work performance information	SV and SPI values calculated for WBS components are documented and communicated to the respective stakeholders.
Schedule forecasts	Schedule forecasts are adjusted based on the work performance information gathered as the project is executed.

A Guide to the Project Management Body of Knowledge (PMBOK® Guide) – Fifth Edition, Project Management Institute (PMI)®, Project Management Professional (PMP)®, and Certified Associate in Project Management (CAPM)® are registered trademarks of Project Management Institute, Inc. - Version 2.1 Published September 30, 2014

Lesson 10: Managing Project Work, Scope, Schedules, and Cost | Topic E

Output	Description
Change requests	Any changes requested to the project schedule baseline can originate from schedule variance analysis, review of progress reports, results of performance measures, and modifications to the project schedule.
Project management plan updates	Contains updated components such as the schedule baseline, schedule management plan, and cost baseline to reflect changes caused by the schedule adjustments.
Project documents updates	Contains updated project documents such as schedule data and project schedule.
Organizational process assets updates	Items documented in the organizational process assets include lessons learned about the causes of variance, the reasons why corrective actions are chosen, as well as other types of lessons learned from schedule control.

A Guide to the Project Management Body of Knowledge (PMBOK® Guide) – Fifth Edition, Project Management Institute, Inc., 2013, pg. 190-192

EVM

EVM is a method of measuring project progress by comparing actual schedule and cost performance against planned performance as laid out in the schedule and cost baselines. Assessing the value of work requires first determining what work has actually been performed and therefore what value it has contributed to the project.

Cost variances occur when the actual cost of the project (AC) and its flexible budget differ. The benefit of using EVM as opposed to just a flexible budget is the time dimension associated with earned value.

During planning, project work is broken down into work packages and activities. Each work package is assigned a budget and a schedule. Because each increment of work is time-phased, an SV results when work is not completed when it was scheduled to be completed. It is valuable to understand the monetary value of work contribution.

A Guide to the Project Management Body of Knowledge (PMBOK® Guide) – Fifth Edition, Project Management Institute, Inc., 2013, pg. 149, 189, 217-219, 538

Cost and Schedule Performance

The EVM approach to monitoring cost and schedule performance provides metrics that show variances from the baselines. Armed with this information, the project manager can identify appropriate corrective actions. When cost and schedule variance analysis is conducted at the appropriate time intervals and levels, it can be effective in controlling against further cost and schedule problems.

A Guide to the Project Management Body of Knowledge (PMBOK® Guide) – Fifth Edition, Project Management Institute, Inc., 2013, pg. 189, 199, 217-219

EVM Variables

EVM involves determining three independent variables to assess and monitor project cost and schedule performance progress. The variables include:

- Planned Value (PV)
- Earned Value (EV)
- Actual Cost (AC)

A Guide to the Project Management Body of Knowledge (PMBOK® Guide) – Fifth Edition, Project Management Institute (PMI)®, Project Management Professional (PMP)®, and Certified Associate in Project Management (CAPM)® are registered trademarks of Project Management Institute, Inc. - Version 2.1 Published September 30, 2014

Lesson 10: Managing Project Work, Scope, Schedules, and Cost | Topic E

These three variables are used to provide measures of whether or not work is being accomplished as planned and to forecast project cost at completion.

A Guide to the Project Management Body of Knowledge (PMBOK® Guide) – Fifth Edition, Project Management Institute, Inc., 2013, pg. 149, 189, 217-219, 224

PV

PV is the budgeted portion of the approved cost estimate to be spent during a particular time period to complete the scheduled project work. This amount is specified in the project's cost baseline. In simpler terms, PV indicates the value of work to be done during a particular time period.

A Guide to the Project Management Body of Knowledge (PMBOK® Guide) – Fifth Edition, Project Management Institute, Inc., 2013, pg. 189, 218, 224, 550

EV

EV is a composite measurement of both cost and time performance in relation to scheduled or planned cost and time performance. EV is calculated by multiplying the percentage of work completed by the budgeted cost for the activity as laid out in the cost baseline.

In order to determine the EV of the project work to date, you will have to look back at the cost baseline to determine how costs were assigned originally. If the PV was determined by the percentage completed to date method, you would apply the same method of assessing the EV. In other words, EV indicates the value of work actually performed during a particular time period.

A Guide to the Project Management Body of Knowledge (PMBOK® Guide) – Fifth Edition, Project Management Institute, Inc., 2013, pg. 189, 218, 224, 538

Evaluating an EV Example

The manager of a shed building project receives a project report at the end of day six, which says that the flooring task ($200) is 100 percent complete and the drywalling task ($800) is 75 percent complete. To calculate the earned value for the completed work:

EV = (100% × Flooring budget) + (75% × Drywalling budget)

EV = (100% × 200) + (75% × 800)

EV = 200 + 600

EV = $800

Therefore, the calculated EV for the project at the end of day six is $800.

A Guide to the Project Management Body of Knowledge (PMBOK® Guide) – Fifth Edition, Project Management Institute, Inc., 2013, pg. 224

AC

AC refers to the total amount of costs incurred while accomplishing work performed, either during completion of a schedule activity or during the completion of a work breakdown structure component. Actual cost is calculated and documented once the work is complete. In other words, AC indicates the actual money that has been spent for work that has been completed.

A Guide to the Project Management Body of Knowledge (PMBOK® Guide) – Fifth Edition, Project Management Institute, Inc., 2013, pg. 189, 218, 224, 527

Evaluating an AC Example

The shed building project report also states that the actual money spent on flooring is $180 and on drywalling is $700. So, the actual cost for the project as of day six is $880.

A Guide to the Project Management Body of Knowledge (PMBOK® Guide) – Fifth Edition, Project Management Institute, Inc., 2013, p. 224

EVM Measures

The most commonly used EVM measures are:

- Schedule Variance ($SV = EV - PV$).
- Schedule Performance Index ($SPI = EV / PV$).
- Cost Variance ($CV = EV - AC$).
- Cost Performance Index ($CPI = EV / AC$).

 Note: For detailed information on Cost Variance (CV) and Cost Performance Index (CPI), refer to the "Control Project Costs" topic.

A Guide to the Project Management Body of Knowledge (PMBOK® Guide) – Fifth Edition, Project Management Institute, Inc., 2013, pg. 189, 217-224

Schedule Performance Measurement

Schedule performance measurement is any technique used to determine how the project is performing in terms of time as compared to its planned performance. Schedule performance measurement tells the project manager how much variance exists between the actual work completed and the work scheduled.

Performance measurement techniques such as SV, SPI, trend analysis, and variance analysis are used to help determine if the schedule variance is potentially detrimental to the project and if corrective actions are needed to ensure on-time deliverables. By using the approved schedule baseline as the standard for measuring progress, the project manager collects reporting information for each activity and uses a bar chart to summarize the data.

A Guide to the Project Management Body of Knowledge (PMBOK® Guide) – Fifth Edition, Project Management Institute, Inc., 2013, pg. 89, 149, 182-184, 189, 218-219, 224

Conducting Schedule Performance Measurement

Consider an example of a software development project. The estimated duration of the entire project is four months. Dan, the project manager, decides early in the project life cycle that there will be eight reporting periods and that work package owners will supply schedule performance reports every two weeks.

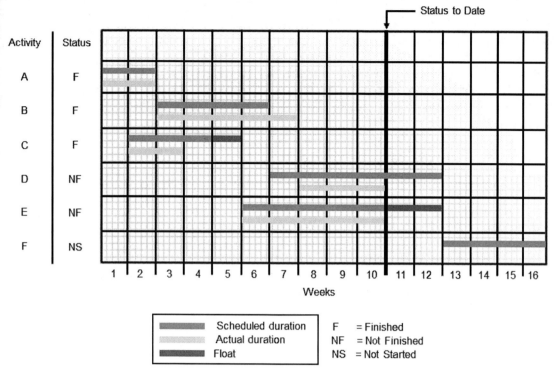

A Gantt chart of a software development project

Figure 10–11: A sample Gantt chart.

On the fifth reporting period, Dan receives the schedule reports and plots the results on a Gantt chart, shown in the software development bar chart. The bar chart shows that:

- Activities A, B, and C are finished.
- Activity B finished behind schedule.
- Activity C finished early.
- Activity D started a week late.
- Activity E is behind schedule.
- Activity F has not started yet.

The bar chart is an effective tool for providing up-to-date summary information and can be extremely helpful for analyzing the project's overall time performance. The bar chart also shows when milestones are scheduled and if those critical dates are still on track.

A Guide to the Project Management Body of Knowledge (PMBOK® Guide) – Fifth Edition, Project Management Institute, Inc., 2013, pg. 182, 542

Determining Schedule Performance Efficiency

The following table provides calculations to determine schedule performance efficiency.

Technique	Calculation
Earned Value (EV)	EV = % complete x total budget of work
Schedule Variance (SV)	SV = EV - PV
Schedule Performance Index (SPI)	SPI = EV / PV

A Guide to the Project Management Body of Knowledge (PMBOK® Guide) – Fifth Edition, Project Management Institute, Inc., 2013, pg. 149, 182-184, 189, 218-219, 224

SV

Schedule Variance (SV) is the measured difference between the actual completion of the activities in the reporting time period and the planned or scheduled completion of the activities. To calculate the SV, subtract the planned value from the earned value. A negative SV indicates that the project is behind schedule. A positive SV indicates that the project is ahead of schedule. When the SV is zero, it indicates that a project is on schedule. The formula for schedule variance is (SV = EV - PV).

A Guide to the Project Management Body of Knowledge (PMBOK® Guide) – Fifth Edition, Project Management Institute, Inc., 2013, pg. 89, 149, 189, 218, 222, 224, 561

Calculating Schedule Variance Example

A project manager for a construction project plans to calculate the schedule variance at the end of every month to measure schedule performance. The project is scheduled to last eight months and has a budget of $800,000. According to the cost baseline, by the fourth reporting period, he planned to spend $500,000 accomplishing project work. This is the PV through this reporting period. By collecting reporting data through the fourth period, he determines that only $425,000 worth of the work has actually been accomplished. This is the EV through the fourth reporting period. He subtracts $500,000 (PV) from $425,000 (EV) to determine that the project currently has an SV of -$75,000, which indicates that the project is behind schedule.

A Guide to the Project Management Body of Knowledge (PMBOK® Guide) – Fifth Edition, Project Management Institute, Inc., 2013, p. 222, 224

SPI

Another measurement of schedule performance efficiency is the *SPI*. The SPI is the ratio of work performed to work scheduled. To calculate the SPI, divide the EV by the PV. An SPI of 1.0 or 100 percent means the project is right on schedule. If the SPI is greater than 1.0 or 100 percent, the project is ahead of schedule. If the SPI is less than 1.0 or 100 percent, the project is behind schedule. The formula for schedule performance index is (SPI = EV / PV).

A Guide to the Project Management Body of Knowledge (PMBOK® Guide) – Fifth Edition, Project Management Institute, Inc., 2013, pg. 89, 149, 189, 219, 224, 561

Guidelines to Control Schedule

Continually monitoring schedule performance and controlling changes to the approved project schedule enables you to maintain the schedule baseline. To control the project schedule, follow these guidelines:

- Develop and implement a schedule change control system. Make sure your system:
  - Is integrated with the project's integrated change control system.
  - Includes the paperwork, tracking systems, and approval levels necessary for authorizing schedule changes.
  - Complies with any relevant contractual provisions when the project is done under contract.
  - Complies with the guidelines specified in the schedule management plan.
- Evaluate change requests by asking these questions:
  - What is the magnitude of the change when compared to the schedule baseline?
  - What is the impact of the change on project cost and quality objectives?
  - What are the potential risks and benefits of the change?
- Use performance measurement techniques to compare actual schedule performance to planned performance.
  - Use schedule reports to monitor schedule performance.
  - Calculate SV and SPI to determine whether the project is ahead of or behind schedule.

A Guide to the Project Management Body of Knowledge (PMBOK® Guide) – Fifth Edition, Project Management Institute (PMI)®, Project Management Professional (PMP)®, and Certified Associate in Project Management (CAPM)® are registered trademarks of Project Management Institute, Inc. - Version 2.1 Published September 30, 2014

Lesson 10: Managing Project Work, Scope, Schedules, and Cost | Topic E

- Analyze the results of your performance measurements by asking these questions:
  - What is the cause of the variance?
  - What is the magnitude of the variance? Is the activity that is causing the variance on the schedule's critical path? If so, this will indicate that your project finish date will be pushed out.
  - Is it likely that the variance can be made up in the near future without corrective action or is corrective action necessary to bring the schedule performance back in line with the baseline?
- Identify and document corrective action to take to bring expected future project performance in line with planned performance.
- Depending upon the nature of the change, you may need to revise the cost, schedule, or quality performance baselines to reflect the changes and to form a new baseline against which to measure future performance. Notify project stakeholders of any changes made to project baselines.
- Use performance measurement techniques, including trend analysis, to monitor the changes.
- Document lessons learned during schedule control for use on future projects.

A Guide to the Project Management Body of Knowledge (PMBOK® Guide) – Fifth Edition, Project Management Institute, Inc., 2013, pg. 185-192, 224

A Guide to the Project Management Body of Knowledge (PMBOK® Guide) – Fifth Edition, Project Management Institute (PMI)®, Project Management Professional (PMP)®, and Certified Associate in Project Management (CAPM)® are registered trademarks of Project Management Institute, Inc. - Version 2.1 Published September 30, 2014

Lesson 10: Managing Project Work, Scope, Schedules, and Cost | Topic E

ACTIVITY 10-5
Controlling the Project Schedule

Scenario

The Building with Heart main office is undergoing minor renovations. You have been assigned to manage the project. It is eight weeks into the project and your manager asks you whether or not the project is on schedule. The entire project is scheduled to take 16 weeks at a total cost of $25,000.

1. What calculation is used to determine schedule variance?
   - ○ EV / PV
   - ○ EV - PV
   - ○ EV - AC
   - ○ EV / AC

2. What calculation is used to determine schedule performance index?
   - ○ EV / PV
   - ○ EV - PV
   - ○ EV - AC
   - ○ EV / AC

3. According to your cost baseline for the project, you planned to spend $15,000 by the end of the eighth week. You collect reporting data for the eighth week and determine that $12,000 worth of work has actually been completed. What actions should you take with this information?
   - ☐ Bring it to the attention of the CCB with some possible solutions.
   - ☑ Use it to identify corrective action to take.
   - ☑ Use it to compare actual schedule performance to planned performance.
   - ☐ Bring it to the attention of project stakeholders.

4. The SV for the eighth week of your project is –$3,000. The SPI for this reporting period is 0.80. What is your analysis of this data and the project's schedule performance to date?

5. Using performance measurement techniques, you have determined that the project is behind schedule. What should you do with this information?

TOPIC F

Control Project Costs

You established a cost baseline for your project. Now that work results are being produced, you need to monitor project costs as your project progresses. In this topic, you will focus on the Control Costs process and use the cost baseline to control project costs.

A Guide to the Project Management Body of Knowledge (PMBOK® Guide) – Fifth Edition, Project Management Institute, Inc., 2013, pg. 215-216

The following data flow diagram illustrates how the Control Costs process relates to the other knowledge areas within the Planning Process Group.

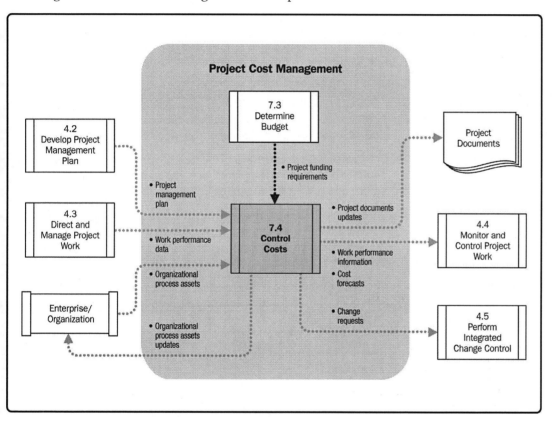

Figure 10–12: Control Costs data flow diagram.

A Guide to the Project Management Body of Knowledge (PMBOK® Guide) – Fifth Edition, Project Management Institute, Inc., 2013, p. 215

The Control Costs Process

Control costs is the process of monitoring cost performance and controlling changes to the cost baseline, while influencing the causes of changes. During this process, the project manager (along with a CCB) monitors, coordinates, and implements changes to the project's cost baseline and evaluates the impact of those changes on other performance baselines and the original scope definition. Effective cost control is to analyze the relationship between the utilization of project funds to the actual expenditures made to the work that has been completed.

A Guide to the Project Management Body of Knowledge (PMBOK® Guide) – Fifth Edition, Project Management Institute, Inc., 2013, pg. 215-216

Inputs	Tools & Techniques	Outputs
.1 Project management plan .2 Project funding requirements .3 Work performance data .4 Organizational process assets	.1 Earned value management .2 Forecasting .3 To-complete performance index (TCPI) .4 Performance reviews .5 Project management software .6 Reserve analysis	.1 Work performance information .2 Cost forecasts .3 Change requests .4 Project management plan updates .5 Project documents updates .6 Organizational process assets updates

Figure 10-13: The Control Costs process.

A Guide to the Project Management Body of Knowledge (PMBOK® Guide) – Fifth Edition, Project Management Institute, Inc., 2013, p. 215

Control Costs Inputs

Various components provide input to the Control Costs process.

Input	Description
Project management plan	Contains project documents such as the cost performance baseline and cost management plan, which provide cost control information.
Project funding requirements	All funding requirements are obtained from the cost baseline. Any funding occurs in increments. The total amount of funds includes the cost baseline plus the management contingency reserve.
Work performance data	Information collected dealing with the status and cost of project activities being performed. This information includes deliverables completed and not completed, authorized and incurred costs, and approximate estimates to complete project work.
Organizational process assets	Include cost control related policies, procedures, and guidelines, cost control tools, and monitoring and reporting methods that are to be followed.

A Guide to the Project Management Body of Knowledge (PMBOK® Guide) – Fifth Edition, Project Management Institute, Inc., 2013, pg. 216-217

Control Costs Tools and Techniques

There are numerous tools and techniques used in the Control Costs process.

Tools & Techniques	Description
Earned value management	A technique that integrates scope, cost, and schedule to measure performance of the project and its progress. The three parameters that EVM considers for monitoring are Planned Value (PV), Earned Value (EV), and Actual Cost (AC). Variances such as schedule and cost variance, and indices such as the schedule performance index and cost performance index from the approved baseline, will also be monitored.

A Guide to the Project Management Body of Knowledge (PMBOK® Guide) – Fifth Edition, Project Management Institute (PMI)®, Project Management Professional (PMP)®, and Certified Associate in Project Management (CAPM)® are registered trademarks of Project Management Institute, Inc. - Version 2.1 Published September 30, 2014

Lesson 10: Managing Project Work, Scope, Schedules, and Cost | Topic F

Tools & Techniques	Description
Forecasting	An estimate or prediction of the project's future, based on past and present knowledge. As the project progresses, forecasts get generated, updated, and reissued based on work performance. Work performance information is based on past performance and anything that could affect the project's future.
To-Complete Performance Index (TCPI)	Calculates the efficiency of cost performance on the project to achieve the Budget at Completion (BAC) or the Estimate at Completion (EAC). If it is not possible to complete the project within the BAC, then an EAC (forecast of the total cost required) is determined by the project manager.
Performance reviews	A comparison of cost performance over time, schedule activities or work packages exceeding or going under budget, and the estimated project funds required to complete work in progress.
Project management software	Determines the cause and degree of variance comparative to the cost baseline and decides on the corrective action that is required. Variance decreases as project work nears completion.
Reserve analysis	Used to examine the three parameters of EVM: Planned Value (PV), Earned Value (EV), and Actual Cost (AC). Also used to demonstrate graphical trends and forecast possible project results.

A Guide to the Project Management Body of Knowledge (PMBOK® Guide) – Fifth Edition, Project Management Institute, Inc., 2013, pg. 217-225

CV

Cost Variance (CV) is any difference between the earned value and the actual cost incurred to complete that work. To calculate the CV, subtract the Actual Cost (AC) from the EV. Actual costs are the costs incurred to accomplish the work to date. A negative CV indicates that the project is performing over budget. A positive CV indicates that the project is performing below budget. When the CV is zero, it indicates that the project is running as per the budget.

A Guide to the Project Management Body of Knowledge (PMBOK® Guide) – Fifth Edition, Project Management Institute, Inc., 2013, pg. 89, 218-219, 222, 224, 535

CPI

Cost Performance Index (CPI) is a measurement of cost performance used to determine whether the project is over or under budget. To calculate CPI, divide the Earned Value (EV) by the Actual Cost (AC); the formula is ($CPI = EV / AC$). A CPI of 1.0 means the project is right on budget. If the CPI is greater than 1.0, the project is performing under budget. If the CPI is less than 1.0, the project is over budget.

A Guide to the Project Management Body of Knowledge (PMBOK® Guide) – Fifth Edition, Project Management Institute, Inc., 2013, pg. 89, 219-220, 224, 535

Performance Measurement Analysis Techniques

The cause of variance, magnitude of variance, and corrective action for a variance are all important factors in cost control. Cost baseline, used in EVM, reviews the progress of a project and impact of variations.

Several standard values for schedule activity, work package, and control account are involved in the earned value technique, including:

- Planned Value (PV)
- Earned Value (EV)
- Actual Cost (AC)
- Estimate to Complete (ETC) and Estimate at Completion (EAC)
- Cost Variance (CV)
- Cost Performance Index (CPI)
- Budget at Completion (BAC)

A Guide to the Project Management Body of Knowledge (PMBOK® Guide) – Fifth Edition, Project Management Institute, Inc., 2013, pg. 218-221, 224

BAC Calculations

The *BAC* is the total budgeted cost of the project at completion. Projects seldom run as per the plan and they are continuously updated. It is necessary to forecast the expected cost at completion. BAC is used as a base value factored with CPI to calculate Estimate to Complete (ETC) and Estimate at Completion (EAC). The formula is: BAC = Total PV at completion.

A Guide to the Project Management Body of Knowledge (PMBOK® Guide) – Fifth Edition, Project Management Institute, Inc., 2013, pg. 89, 218-221, 224, 530

ETC Calculations

The *ETC* forecasting technique, based on an updated, mid-project estimate that is more accurate and comprehensive, is independent for all outstanding work. It also takes into consideration the performance and production of current resources.

According to the *PMBOK® Guide Fifth Edition*, you can calculate ETC for cost by using earned value by one of two methods.

- If work is proceeding on plan, the cost of completing the remaining authorized work can be calculated using the formula ETC = (EAC - AC)
- Reestimate the remaining work from the bottom up.

One downfall for using ETC and EAC is that they are not accurate in determining the remainder of work to be done in a project. The accuracy depends on accuracy of data of work completed.

A Guide to the Project Management Body of Knowledge (PMBOK® Guide) – Fifth Edition, Project Management Institute, Inc., 2013, pg. 89, 219-221, 224, 539

Forecasting

Forecasting is used to estimate the cost at completion or *EAC*. If it becomes apparent that the BAC is no longer accurate, an EAC should be determined based on the project's work performance data. This is calculated by taking the actual cost at a point in time, plus the ETC for the remaining work (EAC = AC + Bottom-up ETC). There are three common methods to do this.

EAC Method	Description
EAC = AC + ETC	EAC using a new estimate. This method requires making a new ETC for all remaining project work and adding that estimate to the ACs incurred to date. Should be used when original estimating assumptions are flawed and conditions have changed.
EAC = AC + (BAC - EV)	EAC using remaining budget. This method uses the sum of the ACs and the BAC minus the EV. Should be used when current cost variances are atypical of future variances.

A Guide to the Project Management Body of Knowledge (PMBOK® Guide) – Fifth Edition, Project Management Institute (PMI)®, Project Management Professional (PMP)®, and Certified Associate in Project Management (CAPM)® are registered trademarks of Project Management Institute, Inc. - Version 2.1 Published September 30, 2014

Lesson 10: Managing Project Work, Scope, Schedules, and Cost | Topic F

EAC Method	Description
EAC = AC + [(BAC - EV) / CPI * SPI]	EAC using CPI and SPI. This method involves adding the AC to the difference of the BAC and the EV divided by the influencing CPI and SPI multiplied. Should be used when current variances are typical of future variances.

A Guide to the Project Management Body of Knowledge (PMBOK® Guide) – Fifth Edition, Project Management Institute, Inc., 2013, pg. 220-221, 224

TCPI

The TCPI is an indicator of the usage of resources for the remainder of the project. The TCPI value can be derived by dividing the budgeted cost of remaining work by the remaining project budget to achieve either the BAC or the EAC. If management decides that the BAC is not achievable, a new EAC is created by the project manager.

TCPI based on BAC can be calculated by using the equation: (BAC - EV) / (BAC - AC). The TCPI based on EAC can be calculated by using the equation: (BAC - EV) / (EAC - AC).

The TCPI value can be either greater or less than 1 when it is compared with the CPI. If the TCPI value is greater than 1, then the project team should be utilized carefully for the remainder of the project. But if the TCPI value is less than 1, then the project team can be utilized more freely.

A Guide to the Project Management Body of Knowledge (PMBOK® Guide) – Fifth Edition, Project Management Institute, Inc., 2013, pg. 221-222, 224, 565

TSPI

The To-Schedule Performance Index (TSPI) is an indicator of efficiency at which the remaining time that is allocated for the project should be utilized by the project team. The equation to evaluate TSPI is: (BAC - EV) / (BAC - PV).

The TSPI value can either be greater or less than 1. If the value is less than 1, then it indicates the required efficiency is less than 100 percent and therefore the project team can work at a measured pace in utilizing the remaining project time. But if the TSPI value happens to be greater than 1, then it indicates the required efficiency is more than 100 percent and therefore the project team should be careful in utilizing the remaining project time and will have to work more efficiently.

Control Costs Outputs

There are various outputs from the Control Costs process.

Output	Description
Work performance information	The calculated CV, SV, CPI, and SPI values for certain WBS components, including work packages and control accounts, are documented and communicated.
Cost forecasts	A calculated or organization-reported EAC value or a bottom-up EAC value is documented and communicated to stakeholders.
Change requests	Requested changes can occur from an analysis of project performance. Any changes identified may result in an increase or decrease to the budget.
Project management plan updates	Elements of the project management plan that provide updates on cost performance baseline and cost management plan.
Project documents updates	Includes updated project documents such as the cost estimates and basis of estimates.

A Guide to the Project Management Body of Knowledge (PMBOK® Guide) – Fifth Edition, Project Management Institute (PMI)®, Project Management Professional (PMP)®, and Certified Associate in Project Management (CAPM)® are registered trademarks of Project Management Institute, Inc. - Version 2.1 Published September 30, 2014

Lesson 10: Managing Project Work, Scope, Schedules, and Cost | Topic F

Output	Description
Organizational process assets updates	Items that may need to be updated include causes of variances, reasons as to why certain corrective actions are chosen, as well as lessons learned from cost control.

A Guide to the Project Management Body of Knowledge (PMBOK® Guide) – Fifth Edition, Project Management Institute, Inc., 2013, pg. 225-226

Guidelines to Control Project Cost

Continually monitoring cost performance and controlling changes to the project's budget enables you to maintain the cost baseline. Controlling project costs also helps to avoid budget problems that may jeopardize the successful completion of a project. To control cost performance, follow these guidelines:

- Develop and implement a cost change control system. Make sure your system:
  - Is integrated with the project's integrated change control system.
  - Includes the paperwork, tracking systems, and approval levels necessary for authorizing changes to the cost baseline.
  - Complies with any relevant contractual provisions when the project is done under contract.
  - Complies with the guidelines specified in the cost management plan.
- Evaluate change requests by asking these questions:
  - What is the magnitude of the change when compared to the cost baseline?
  - What is the impact of the change on project schedule and quality objectives?
  - What are the potential risks and benefits of the change?
- Use performance measurement techniques to compare actual cost performance to planned performance.
  - Use performance reports to monitor cost performance.
  - Calculate CV and CPI to determine whether the project is performing over or under budget.
  - Use earned value analysis and management to continually measure cost and schedule performance and to assess the value of work performed to date.
- Analyze the results of your performance measurements by asking these questions:
  - What is the cause of the variance?
  - What is the magnitude of the variance? Is the activity causing the variance on the critical path?
  - Is it likely that the variance can be made up in the near future without corrective action, or is corrective action necessary to bring the cost performance back in line with the baseline?
- Identify and document corrective action to take to bring expected future cost performance in line with planned performance. Depending on the priorities of your project, consider one or more of the following alternatives:
  - Re-check cost estimates to determine whether they are still valid. Avoid the temptation to reduce estimates simply to make the cost performance look better.
  - Identify alternate, cheaper sources for materials. For example, consider using a lower-grade building material to keep the project costs on target.
  - Brainstorm ways to improve productivity. Consider using an efficiency expert to identify areas where productivity could be bolstered with training or guidance.
  - Change the schedule baseline. When a schedule change is contemplated, make sure it is done in communication with customers and other key stakeholders to determine the schedule flexibility. If finishing on time is not as important as finishing on budget, cost overruns can be corrected through schedule changes.
  - Reduce project scope. One way to reduce scope is to prioritize the remaining work and eliminate work with the lowest priority. Another option is to plan for a Phase 2 project to

A Guide to the Project Management Body of Knowledge (PMBOK® Guide) – Fifth Edition, Project Management Institute (PMI)®, Project Management Professional (PMP)®, and Certified Associate in Project Management (CAPM)® are registered trademarks of Project Management Institute, Inc. - Version 2.1 Published September 30, 2014

Lesson 10: Managing Project Work, Scope, Schedules, and Cost | Topic F cover unfinished scope items. Reducing the project scope must be done according to the integrated change control system and with approval of the customer and the sponsoring organization.

- Depending upon the nature of the change, you may need to revise the cost, schedule, or quality performance baselines to reflect the changes and to form a new baseline against which to measure future performance.

  - Review the cost management plan as you begin to monitor cost performance. Follow the systematic procedures outlined in the cost management plan as you identify the need for corrective action and baseline adjustments.
  - Notify project stakeholders of any changes made to project baselines.

- Use performance measurement techniques, including trend analysis and EAC, to monitor the changes.

  - Are the changes being properly implemented?
  - Do the changes bring about the desired results?
  - Are new risks being introduced as a result of implementing the changes?

- Document lessons learned during cost control for use on future projects. The documentation should include:

  - Causes of variances
  - Performance baselines affected by the changes
  - Rationale behind the recommended corrective action
  - Any other lessons learned during cost control

A Guide to the Project Management Body of Knowledge (PMBOK® Guide) – Fifth Edition, Project Management Institute, Inc., 2013, pg. 215-226

A Guide to the Project Management Body of Knowledge (PMBOK® Guide) – Fifth Edition, Project Management Institute (PMI)®, Project Management Professional (PMP)®, and Certified Associate in Project Management (CAPM)® are registered trademarks of Project Management Institute, Inc. - Version 2.1 Published September 30, 2014

Lesson 10: Managing Project Work, Scope, Schedules, and Cost | Topic F

ACTIVITY 10-6
Controlling Project Costs

Scenario

The BAC for the new build project is $50,000. At this point in the project, the earned value (EV) is $25,000, the actual cost (AC) is $28,000, and the planned value (PV) is $30,000. The Building with Heart CFO would like the financial status for the new build project. You need to calculate the cost and schedule variances and the cost and schedule performance indexes. Use the following formulas to help conduct the required calculations:

$$CV = EV - AC$$
$$CPI = EV / AC$$
$$SV = EV - PV$$
$$SPI = EV / PV$$
$$EAC = BAC / CPI$$
$$ETC = EAC - AC$$
$$VAC = BAC - EAC$$

(handwritten:)
EV = 25000
AC = 28000
PV = 30000
BAC = 50,000

---

1. Calculate the cost variance for the project.

   CV -3000

2. Calculate the CPI for the project.

   CPI 0.89

3. Calculate the schedule variance for the project.

   SV -5000

4. Calculate the schedule performance index for the project.

   SPI 0.83

5. With this project showing a variance, you now need to calculate the estimate at completion.

   EAC 50000/0.89 = 56179.77

6. Next, calculate the estimate to complete the project.

   ETC ~~56179.70~~ ~~28,000~~ 28,179.77

7. Finally, calculate the variance at project completion.

   VAC -6179.77

A Guide to the Project Management Body of Knowledge (PMBOK® Guide) – Fifth Edition, Project Management Institute (PMI)®, Project Management Professional (PMP)®, and Certified Associate in Project Management (CAPM)® are registered trademarks of Project Management Institute, Inc. - Version 2.1 Published September 30, 2014

Lesson 10: Managing Project Work, Scope, Schedules, and Cost | Topic F

Summary

In this lesson, you monitored and controlled project work, schedule, and cost. Monitoring and controlling the project is the only way that you can ensure that your project will meet stakeholders' expectations for time, cost, and quality performance. Without controlling schedule and costs, your project may exceed its promised deadline and go over budget. Monitoring and controlling project schedules and costs helps your organization maintain its competitive advantage in the marketplace.

When preparing for a scope verification inspection, what do you think are the steps required to make your project successful?

How could using Earned Value Management help you to control project costs on future projects?

 Note: Check your LogicalCHOICE Course screen for opportunities to interact with your classmates, peers, and the larger LogicalCHOICE online community about the topics covered in this course or other topics you are interested in. From the Course screen you can also access available resources for a more continuous learning experience.

A Guide to the Project Management Body of Knowledge (PMBOK® Guide) – Fifth Edition, Project Management Institute (PMI)®, Project Management Professional (PMP)®, and Certified Associate in Project Management (CAPM)® are registered trademarks of Project Management Institute, Inc. - Version 2.1 Published September 30, 2014

Lesson 10: Managing Project Work, Scope, Schedules, and Cost |

11 | Controlling the Project

Lesson Time: 3 hours, 30 minutes

Lesson Objectives

In this lesson, you will:

- Control project quality.

- Control project communications.

- Control project risks.

- Control project procurements.

- Control project stakeholder engagement.

Lesson Introduction

As your project work continues, you've monitored the schedule and budget baselines. Other important aspects of projects that need to be tracked and controlled are project performance, quality, communications, risks, procurements, and stakeholders. In this lesson, you'll continue tracking project performance and control project quality. You will also continue to monitor and control the project, focusing on project risk, procurements, and stakeholders.

The following diagram highlights the next process group and knowledge areas covered in this lesson.

		Project Management Process Groups			
Knowledge Areas	Initiating Process Group	Planning Process Group	Executing Process Group	Monitoring and Controlling Process Group	Closing Process Group
4. Project Integration Management	4.1 Develop Project Charter	4.2 Develop Project Management Plan	4.3 Direct and Manage Project Work	4.4 Monitor and Control Project Work 4.5 Perform Integrated Change Control	4.6 Close Project or Phase
5. Project Scope Management		5.1 Plan Scope Management 5.2 Collect Requirements 5.3 Define Scope 5.4 Create WBS		5.5 Validate Scope 5.6 Control Scope	
6. Project Time Management		6.1 Plan Schedule Management 6.2 Define Activities 6.3 Sequence Activites 6.4 Estimate Activity Resources 6.5 Estimate Activity Durations 6.6 Develop Schedule		6.7 Control Schedule	
7. Project Cost Management		7.1 Plan Cost Management 7.2 Estimate Cost 7.3 Determine Budget		7.4 Control Costs	
8. Project Quality Management		8.1 Plan Quality Management	8.2 Perform Quality Assurance	8.3 Control Quality	
9. Project Human Resource Management		9.1 Plan Human Resource Management	9.2 Acquire Project Team 9.3 Develop Project Team 9.4 Manage Project Team		
10. Project Communication Management		10.1 Plan Communications Management	10.2 Manage Communications	10.3 Control Communications	
11. Project Risk Management		11.1 Plan Risk Management 11.2 Identify Risks 11.3 Perform Qualitative Risk Analysis 11.4 Perform Quantitative Risk Analysis 11.5 Plan Risk Responses		11.6 Control Risks	
12. Project Procurement Management		12.1 Plan Procurement Management	12.2 Conduct Procurements	12.3 Control Procurements	12.4 Close Procurements
13. Project Stakeholder Management	13.1 Identify Stakeholders	13.2 Plan Stakeholder Management	13.3 Manage Stakeholder Engagement	13.4 Control Stakeholder Engagement	

TOPIC A

Control Project Quality

Your quality management plan describes how your project team will move forward. Now that your project is well under way, you need to monitor the work results to ensure that they meet the quality standards you defined in your quality management plan. In this topic, you will focus on the Control Quality process.

A Guide to the Project Management Body of Knowledge (PMBOK® Guide) – Fifth Edition, Project Management Institute, Inc., 2013, pg. 248-250

The following data flow diagram illustrates how the Control Quality process relates to the other knowledge areas within the Monitoring and Controlling Process Group.

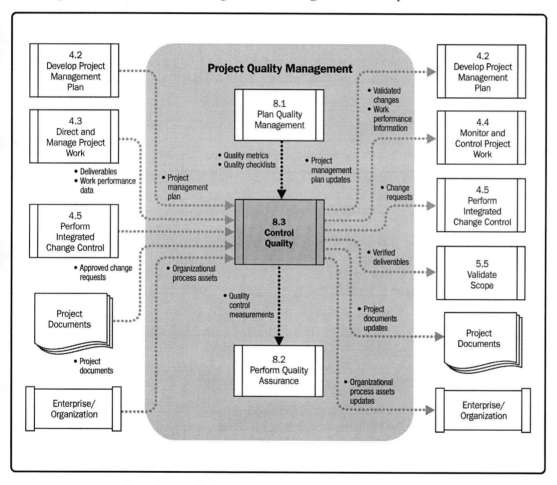

Figure 11-1: Control Quality work data flow diagram.

A Guide to the Project Management Body of Knowledge (PMBOK® Guide) – Fifth Edition, Project Management Institute, Inc., 2013, p. 249

The Control Quality Process

The *Control Quality process* involves monitoring project performance to determine if it complies with relevant quality standards and identifying ways to eliminate causes of unacceptable performance. Quality control involves continually measuring, adjusting, and monitoring. Its goal is to improve the work process and produce results that meet customer and stakeholder specifications and expectations. Quality control is normally performed by the quality control department or a similar unit.

A Guide to the Project Management Body of Knowledge (PMBOK® Guide) – Fifth Edition, Project Management Institute, Inc., 2013, pg. 248-250

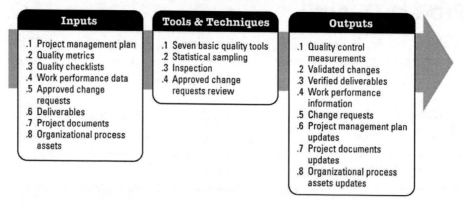

Figure 11-2: The Control Quality process.

A Guide to the Project Management Body of Knowledge (PMBOK® Guide) – Fifth Edition, Project Management Institute, Inc., 2013, p. 249

Control Quality Inputs

Various components provide input to the Control Quality process.

Input	Description
Project management plan	Contains the quality management plan, which describes the project management team's approach to implementing its quality policy. The quality management plan must include Quality Control (QC), Quality Assurance (QA), and documentation process improvements.
Quality metrics	An actual value that, for each deliverable, describes the measurements for the quality control process. Examples of quality metrics include defect density, reliability, rate of failure, and test coverage.
Quality checklists	Job aids that prompt employees to perform activities according to a consistent standard.
Work performance data	Measurements used to create the project activity metrics, which maintain actual progress vs. planned progress. Some of the metrics used are: • Planned vs. actual technical performance • Defects found and defects originated • Deliverables in progress and those completed • Planned vs. actual schedule performance • Planned vs. actual cost performance
Approved change requests	In quality control, approved change requests can include modifications to work methods and the schedule. All approved changes need to be verified.
Deliverables	A distinctive product, result, or capability used to perform a service that must be produced to complete a project, phase, or process.

A Guide to the Project Management Body of Knowledge (PMBOK® Guide) – Fifth Edition, Project Management Institute (PMI)®, Project Management Professional (PMP)®, and Certified Associate in Project Management (CAPM)® are registered trademarks of Project Management Institute, Inc. - Version 2.1 Published September 30, 2014

Lesson 11: Controlling the Project | Topic A

Input	Description
Project documents	May include agreements, quality audit reports, change logs, training plans and process documentation.
Organizational process assets	Represent formal and informal policies, procedures, plans, guidelines, and knowledge from previous projects that can influence the perform quality control process.

A Guide to the Project Management Body of Knowledge (PMBOK® Guide) – Fifth Edition, Project Management Institute, Inc., 2013, pg. 250-251

Control Quality Tools and Techniques

There are four tools and techniques used in the Control Quality process.

Tools & Techniques	Description
Seven basic quality tools	Tools used include: • Cause-and-effect diagrams • Flowcharts • Checksheets • Pareto diagrams • Histograms • Control charts • Scatter diagrams
Statistical sampling	Measures an entire population based on actual measurement of a representative sample of that population.
Inspection	An official examination of work results to verify that they meet requirements. The inspection may be conducted by an internal or external inspection team.
Approved change requests review	Ensures that all change requests are reviewed and implemented as approved during the perform integrated change control process.

A Guide to the Project Management Body of Knowledge (PMBOK® Guide) – Fifth Edition, Project Management Institute, Inc., 2013, p. 252

Control Quality Outputs

There are eight outputs from the Control Quality process.

Output	Description
Quality control measurements	The results of quality control activities that are documented in the format determined when planning for project quality. The results are fed back to the QA process for use in re-evaluating and analyzing quality standards and processes.
Validated changes	Reinspected, repaired items to be formally accepted or rejected.
Verified deliverables	QC needs to verify the accuracy of deliverables through quality control processes.

A Guide to the Project Management Body of Knowledge (PMBOK® Guide) – Fifth Edition, Project Management Institute (PMI)®, Project Management Professional (PMP)®, and Certified Associate in Project Management (CAPM)® are registered trademarks of Project Management Institute, Inc. - Version 2.1 Published September 30, 2014

Lesson 11: Controlling the Project | Topic A

Output	Description
Work performance information	Performance data collected during the quality control process such as number of requirements fulfilled, number of items rejected, number of items reworked.
Change requests	If there are any changes needed to the output of the work package, a change request should be submitted in compliance with the perform integrated change control process.
Project management plan updates	Any changes in the quality management plan through QC processes are documented in the project management plan. Any requested changes to the project management plan and its subplans are reviewed through the integrated change control process. Plans that may be subject to changes in this process include the quality management plan and process improvement plan.
Project documents updates	Documents that may need to be updated include the quality standards, quality management plan, quality baseline, and quality metrics.
Organizational process assets updates	These include completed checklists and lessons learned documentation. If checklists are used, they become part of the project's records, and any lessons learned from QC should be documented and put in a database for the current project and for the entire organization to refer to.

A Guide to the Project Management Body of Knowledge (PMBOK® Guide) – Fifth Edition, Project Management Institute, Inc., 2013, pg. 252-254

Variance

Variance is the quantifiable deviance, or amount of departure, from the expected results for any component of product and service being developed, including quality, as well as schedule and cost. Variance can be extreme or almost undetectable; it may result from many causes, such as problems with resource availability or from the skills of personnel assigned to the project. Variance may be obvious the moment a product is produced or may become obvious over time through use and exposure to environmental conditions. To control quality, you must recognize the difference between quality variance within a normal range and variance that indicates a quality error.

A Guide to the Project Management Body of Knowledge (PMBOK® Guide) – Fifth Edition, Project Management Institute, Inc., 2013, pg. 250, 566

Causes of Variance

Causes of variance in a process or item are the sources or reasons for deviations from the expected standard. There are two main types: random causes and special causes. Random or common causes are those everyday occurrences that are always present in project work; as such, they may be unavoidable. They may be either insignificant and have little impact on the overall quality performance, or they may have a dramatic effect on quality. The corrective actions taken in response to random causes of variance are typically long-term and generally involve overall changes to the process.

Special, or assignable, causes are unusual, sporadic occurrences; they are the result of some unexpected circumstance and are typically not caused by a flaw in the overall production process. Like random causes, special causes of variance can also have a dramatic effect on performance.

By analyzing instances of the occurrences of special variances, you may be able to isolate the cause and take corrective action to avoid the negative effects on quality performance. The corrective actions taken in response to special causes of variance are typically short-term and do not involve

A Guide to the Project Management Body of Knowledge (PMBOK® Guide) – Fifth Edition, Project Management Institute (PMI)®, Project Management Professional (PMP)®, and Certified Associate in Project Management (CAPM)® are registered trademarks of Project Management Institute, Inc. - Version 2.1 Published September 30, 2014

Lesson 11: Controlling the Project | Topic A

overall changes to the process. Special causes do not occur frequently but it can sometimes be decided not to act upon them, as the cost of action may be much more than the benefit.

The Analyzing Variances Task

The analyzing variances task involves taking data concerning work results and measuring that data against the specifications and operational definitions included in the project plan. Any variances must be analyzed to determine whether they are acceptable or if they merit corrective action to keep the performance within specifications.

A Guide to the Project Management Body of Knowledge (PMBOK® Guide) – Fifth Edition, Project Management Institute, Inc., 2013, pg. 139, 222, 352, 566

Tolerances

Tolerances are the measurement values that determine if a product or service is acceptable or unacceptable. They are the standards against which data collected will be analyzed. Tolerances are typically expressed in ranges. If the result of the test falls within the range specified by the tolerance, it is acceptable. If not, it is considered unacceptable. Tolerances are specified in the quality management plan.

For example, the tolerance for a product's weight may be 5.8 grams ± 0.2 grams. If a product weighs more than 6.0 grams, or less than 5.6 grams, it is considered unacceptable because it exceeds the tolerance and does not meet specification.

A Guide to the Project Management Body of Knowledge (PMBOK® Guide) – Fifth Edition, Project Management Institute, Inc., 2013, pg. 250, 565

The 6-Sigma Limit

All processes include some variability. Project managers use control charts to determine when a process is experiencing normal variation (it is "in control") and when it is experiencing abnormal variation (it is "out of control"). If a process is out of control, the project management needs to take action to bring the process back in control.

In a typical control chart, the upper control limit (UCL) is set to three standard deviations (3 sigmas) about the mean and the lower control limit (LCL) is set to three standard deviations below the mean. Warning limits are set to two standard deviations (2 sigmas) above and below the mean. Normal variation is set to one standard deviation (1 sigma) above and below the mean.

However, control charts can be set with much higher tolerances, such as plus or minus 6 sigmas. This is termed as the *6-Sigma limit.* In terms of controlling processes, the 6-Sigma limit is significant because it provides a generally accepted guideline for monitoring quality and improving it.

The 6-Sigma Process

6-Sigma has also evolved into a business management strategy that seeks to improve the quality of process outputs by identifying and removing the causes of defects and variability in processes. To achieve 6-Sigma, a process must not produce more than 3.4 defects per million opportunities.

The 3-Sigma Rule

The 3-Sigma rule, an empirical rule, states that for normal distribution almost all values lie within three standard deviations of mean. The values in the normal distribution will exhibit deviation as follows:

- About 68 percent of the values lie within one standard deviation of the mean.
- About 95 percent of the values lie within two standard deviations of the mean.
- About 99.7 percent of the values lie within three standard deviations of the mean.

A Guide to the Project Management Body of Knowledge (PMBOK® Guide) – Fifth Edition, Project Management Institute (PMI)®, Project Management Professional (PMP)®, and Certified Associate in Project Management (CAPM)® are registered trademarks of Project Management Institute, Inc. - Version 2.1 Published September 30, 2014

Lesson 11: Controlling the Project | *Topic A*

Variability Indications

Measurements that exceed the range between the upper and lower control limits are considered to be an indication of instability. The variability expressed is atypical for the process and may be an indication of a special source of variance. It is important to remember that, while control charts can effectively show variability, they cannot indicate the source of the variability or show performance in relation to an expected performance. The control chart shows only the capability of the process to produce similar products. It does not show the conformity of that process to a customer's specifications.

A Guide to the Project Management Body of Knowledge (PMBOK® Guide) – Fifth Edition, Project Management Institute, Inc., 2013, p. 238, 250, 566

Pareto Diagrams

A *Pareto diagram* is a histogram that is used to rank causes of problems in a hierarchical format. The goal is to narrow down the primary causes of variance on a project, and focus the energy and efforts into tackling the most significant sources of variance. The variables in the diagram are ordered by frequency of occurrence.

A Guide to the Project Management Body of Knowledge (PMBOK® Guide) – Fifth Edition, Project Management Institute, Inc., 2013, pg. 237, 548

Pareto Analysis

The analysis used to develop Pareto diagrams is referred to as a Pareto analysis, after Vilfredo Pareto, an Italian economist of the late 19th and early 20th century. In his analysis, Vilfredo Pareto found that 80 percent of the country's wealth was concentrated in the hands of 20 percent of the population.

During a Pareto analysis, data is collected in various forms, such as reports, inspections, and surveys. This data is then analyzed to isolate the major causes of project variance and is assigned a frequency or percentage value. The resulting diagram is a histogram that identifies specific sources of variance and ranks them according to their effect on the quality performance. Pareto diagrams can be very useful tools throughout the entire project for prioritizing and focusing corrective actions. Comparative analysis of Pareto diagrams at different points in the project can be an effective tool for determining and communicating the effect corrective actions have had on curtailing or eliminating variability.

The 80/20 Rule

Pareto diagrams are based on Pareto's law, also known as the 80/20 rule. The 80/20 rule is a general guideline with many applications; in terms of controlling processes, it contends that a relatively large number of problems or defects, typically 80 percent, are commonly due to a relatively small number of causes, typically 20 percent.

Statistical Sampling

Statistical sampling is a technique used to determine characteristics of an entire population based on actual measurement of a representative sample of that population. Sampling is a way to determine if large batches of a product should be accepted or rejected without having to test every single item produced. Its goal is to produce a process that does not require inspection of every item. The size of samples and the frequency and cost of sampling must be determined when planning for project quality.

A Guide to the Project Management Body of Knowledge (PMBOK® Guide) – Fifth Edition, Project Management Institute, Inc., 2013, pg. 240, 252, 564

80% problem are due to 20% causes

Determining Sample Size

Sample size can affect the accuracy of results. Generally speaking, the larger the sample size, the higher the likelihood the sample will truly represent the variability of the population. In quality terms, the larger the sample size, the more confidence you can have that your measurements reflect the quality level of the entire product population.

The Statistical Sampling Process

The *statistical sampling process* involves dividing sampling data into two categories—attribute and variable—each of which is gathered according to sampling plans. As corrective actions are taken in response to analysis of statistical sampling and other quality control activities, and as trend analysis is performed, defects and process variability should be reduced. The use of statistical sampling during quality control can reduce overall quality cost by helping to forecast and prevent errors before they occur.

Attribute Sampling Data

Attribute sampling data is data from the sample that is counted, such as the:

* Number of employees participating in profit sharing
* Number of customer complaint calls
* Number of returned items

Attribute sampling uses no scale. It simply tells you whether or not a standard has been met. Implementing an attribute sampling plan is fairly simple. Team members may be required to count the number of items that do not conform to a quality specification or that show evidence of a quality defect. If the number exceeds a certain limit, the sample fails to meet quality specifications.

A Guide to the Project Management Body of Knowledge (PMBOK® Guide) – Fifth Edition, Project Management Institute, Inc., 2013, pg. 250, 529

Variable Sampling Data

Variable sampling data is data from the sample that is measured on a continuous scale, such as:

* Time
* Temperature
* Weight

For variable data, the compliance to specifications is rated on a continuous scale. Measurements can fall between an upper and lower range. To implement a variable sampling plan, you would collect a sample of product and take some specific measurement to determine if the sample meets quality specifications. Variable samples typically provide the same level of accuracy as attribute samples with much smaller sample sizes.

A Guide to the Project Management Body of Knowledge (PMBOK® Guide) – Fifth Edition, Project Management Institute, Inc., 2013, p. 250

Guidelines to Control Project Quality

Monitoring and controlling project quality ensures that the quality complies with relevant quality standards. Meeting quality standards enhances the team's ability to deliver an overall project performance that meets the project objectives. To effectively control project quality, follow these guidelines:

* Conduct inspections to detect quality errors as project work is ongoing.

    * Consult the quality management plan for the procedures and guidelines to use during quality control.

A Guide to the Project Management Body of Knowledge (PMBOK® Guide) – Fifth Edition, Project Management Institute (PMI)®, Project Management Professional (PMP)®, and Certified Associate in Project Management (CAPM)® are registered trademarks of Project Management Institute, Inc. - Version 2.1 Published September 30, 2014

Lesson 11: Controlling the Project | *Topic A*

- Check work results against relevant operational definitions and checklists. Document the results.
- Use statistical sampling to determine whether large batches of a product should be accepted or rejected based on the quality of the sample(s). Ensure that samples are chosen randomly and that the sample size is large enough to demonstrate the variability of the entire group.
- Use Pareto diagrams to focus corrective actions on the problems having the greatest effect on overall quality performance and to measure and monitor the effect of corrective actions over time.
- Use control charts to analyze and communicate the variability of a process or project activity over time. As you analyze performance with control charts, you must not only look for variability outside the control limits, but you should also analyze patterns of data within control limits.
- Identify ways to eliminate causes of unsatisfactory results in order to minimize rework and bring nonconforming items into compliance.
- Use flowcharts to identify redundancies, missed steps, or the source of quality performance problems.
- Initiate process adjustments by implementing corrective or preventive actions necessary to bring the quality of work results to an acceptable level. Major adjustments must be made according to the project's change control system.
- Continue to monitor, measure, and adjust quality throughout the project life cycle.

A Guide to the Project Management Body of Knowledge (PMBOK® Guide) – Fifth Edition, Project Management Institute, Inc., 2013, pg. 248-254

A Guide to the Project Management Body of Knowledge (PMBOK® Guide) – Fifth Edition, Project Management Institute (PMI)®, Project Management Professional (PMP)®, and Certified Associate in Project Management (CAPM)® are registered trademarks of Project Management Institute, Inc. - Version 2.1 Published September 30, 2014

Lesson 11: Controlling the Project | Topic A

ACTIVITY 11-1
Controlling Project Quality

Scenario

The HVAC contractors are completing the work for the installation of the heating and cooling system. Your team had developed operational definitions and checklists for this work, and you have provided these to the lead quality control engineer. Historically, on similar projects, there has been no more than an average variance of one degree between floors. The quality inspections reveal that the second floor is three degrees cooler than the first floor.

---

1. Given that there is a significant variation in temperature between the first and second floor, what should be done?

   ○ Report this information to the appropriate people, according to the project's change control system.

   ⊘ Because of the potentially high re-work cost, finding a solution should be a top priority.

   ○ Initiate process adjustments.

   ○ Continue to monitor quality as the HVAC installation continues.

2. The quality management plan documented acceptability of the installation with a tolerance of a one degree variance between floors. What would you do to determine the reasons for the variance in quality tests?

3. After researching the cause of the variance, you discover that the testing was done by one quality control engineer. You then meet with the contract supervisor to investigate the process. You discover that the duct work on the second floor was installed over a weekend by a different, less experienced crew. What should your next step be?

A Guide to the Project Management Body of Knowledge (PMBOK® Guide) – Fifth Edition, Project Management Institute (PMI)®, Project Management Professional (PMP)®, and Certified Associate in Project Management (CAPM)® are registered trademarks of Project Management Institute, Inc. - Version 2.1 Published September 30, 2014

Lesson 11: Controlling the Project | Topic A

TOPIC B

Control Communications

Communication is key in the success of a project. All aspects of a project depend on good effective communication among team members. Now that your project is in full swing, it's important to control all communications on a regular basis. In this topic, you will control project communications.

A Guide to the Project Management Body of Knowledge (PMBOK® Guide) – Fifth Edition, Project Management Institute, Inc., 2013, pg. 303-304

The following data flow diagram illustrates how the Control Communications process relates to the other knowledge areas within the Monitoring and Controlling Process Group.

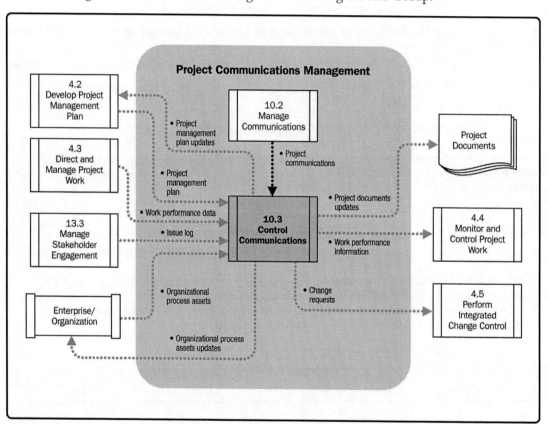

Figure 11-3: Control Communications work data flow diagram.

A Guide to the Project Management Body of Knowledge (PMBOK® Guide) – Fifth Edition, Project Management Institute, Inc., 2013, p. 304

The Control Communications Process

The *Control Communications process* monitors and controls communications to ensure that the information needs of the stakeholders are met throughout the life cycle of the project. It provides optimal information flow at any point in time to all communication participants. Project communications should be managed so that the right message is delivered to the right people at the right time.

A Guide to the Project Management Body of Knowledge (PMBOK® Guide) – Fifth Edition, Project Management Institute, Inc., 2013, pg. 303-304

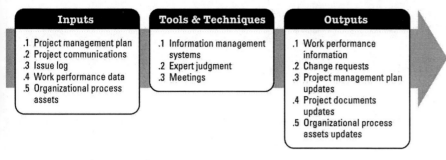

Figure 11-4: The Control Communications process.

A Guide to the Project Management Body of Knowledge (PMBOK® Guide) – Fifth Edition, Project
Management Institute, Inc., 2013, p. 303

Control Communications Inputs

Various components provide input to the Control Communications process.

Input	Description
Project management plan	Provides information such as stakeholder communications requirements, reason for distribution of information, time frame and frequency of information distribution, who is responsible for communicating information and who receives information.
Project communications	Includes the activities for information and communications to be monitored, acted upon, and released to stakeholders.
Issue log	Used to document issues and the resolution of those issues.
Work performance data	Contains organized and summarized information and presents the results of comparative analysis to the performance measurement baseline.
Organizational process assets	Organizational process assets that can influence this process include report templates, communications policies, standards and procedures, communications technologies, allowed communications media, record retention policies, and security requirements.

A Guide to the Project Management Body of Knowledge (PMBOK® Guide) – Fifth Edition, Project
Management Institute, Inc., 2013, pg. 304-306

Control Communications Tools and Techniques

There are three tools and techniques used in the Control Communications process.

Tools & Techniques	Description
Information management systems	Provide a set of standard tools to capture, store, and distribute project information to stakeholders, including costs, schedule, and performance.
Expert judgment	Used to assess the impact of project communications, need for action, and what, who, and when action should be taken.
Meetings	Used to discuss the most appropriate way to update and communicate project performance and respond to stakeholder requests for this information.

A Guide to the Project Management Body of Knowledge (PMBOK® Guide) – Fifth Edition, Project Management Institute, Inc., 2013, pg. 306-307

Control Communications Outputs

There are five outputs from the Control Communications process.

Output	Description
Work performance information	Organizes and summarizes the project performance data.
Change requests	May be generated for communications requirements adjustment, action, or intervention.
Project management plan updates	Documents that may need updating include the communications, human resource, and stakeholder management plans.
Project documents updates	Documents that may need updating include forecasts, performance reports, and the issue log.
Organizational process assets updates	Documents that may need updating include report formats and lessons learned documentation.

A Guide to the Project Management Body of Knowledge (PMBOK® Guide) – Fifth Edition, Project Management Institute, Inc., 2013, pg. 307-308

Guidelines to Control Communications

Guidelines to controlling communications are as follows:

- Review the project management plan for information such as stakeholder communications requirements, reason for distribution of information, time frame and frequency of information distribution, who is responsible for communicating information and who receives information.
- Review the project communications for the activities for information and communications to be monitored, acted upon, and released to stakeholders.
- Review the issue log for issues and the resolution of those issues.
- Review the work performance data that contains organized and summarized information and presents the results of comparative analysis to the performance measurement baseline.
- Review the organizational process assets such as report templates, communications policies, standards and procedures, communications technologies, allowed communications media, record retention policies, and security requirements.
- Use tools and techniques such as information management systems, expert judgment, and meetings to control the project communications.
- Communicate the work performance information and change requests to the project team and update project documents.
- Ask the stakeholders if the communication that was planned for the project is working for them.

A Guide to the Project Management Body of Knowledge (PMBOK® Guide) – Fifth Edition, Project Management Institute, Inc., 2013, pg. 303-308

ACTIVITY 11-2
Discussing Controlling Project Communications

Scenario

In this activity, you will discuss project communications.

---

1. How could you control communications during the home build project?

2. What could happen if this process is completed throughout the course of a project?

3. You have received approval for the adjustment to the railings of the new house build. After checking the project schedule, you realize that the railing installation work was to be completed today. How would you communicate this change to the team?

TOPIC C

Control Project Risks

In prior process groups, you developed a risk management plan and a risk response plan to control project risks. During project execution, you will need to implement those plans. In this topic, you will monitor and control project risks.

A Guide to the Project Management Body of Knowledge (PMBOK® Guide) – Fifth Edition, Project Management Institute, Inc., 2013, pg. 349-350

The following data flow diagram illustrates how the Control Risks process relates to the other knowledge areas within the Monitoring and Controlling Process Group.

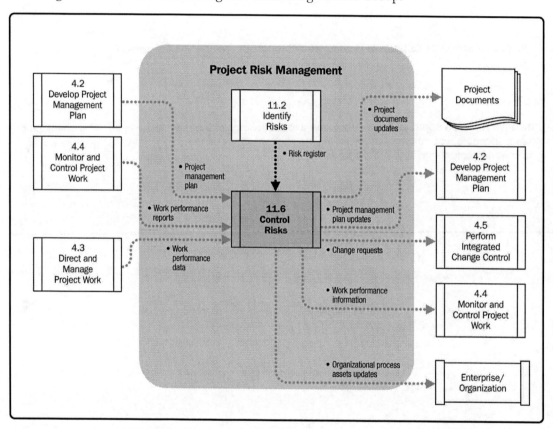

Figure 11–5: Control risk work data flow diagram.

A Guide to the Project Management Body of Knowledge (PMBOK® Guide) – Fifth Edition, Project Management Institute, Inc., 2013, p. 349

The Control Risks Process

The *Control Risks process* is the process of responding to identified and unforeseen risks. It involves tracking identified risks, identifying new risks, implementing risk response plans, and monitoring their effectiveness. During the monitor and control risks process, you will constantly monitor your project for the introduction of new risks in addition to monitoring triggers for the risks already identified. When new risks surface, they must be documented and analyzed, and a response plan must be selected using the risk analysis and response planning processes. As the project progresses, risks change. Constant monitoring is essential. Risk monitoring and control is iterative and ongoing, and takes place throughout the project life cycle.

A Guide to the Project Management Body of Knowledge (PMBOK® Guide) – Fifth Edition, Project Management Institute (PMI)®, Project Management Professional (PMP)®, and Certified Associate in Project Management (CAPM)® are registered trademarks of Project Management Institute, Inc. - Version 2.1 Published September 30, 2014

Lesson 11: Controlling the Project | Topic C

A Guide to the Project Management Body of Knowledge (PMBOK® Guide) – Fifth Edition, Project
Management Institute, Inc., 2013, pg. 349-350

Figure 11-6: The Control Risks process.

A Guide to the Project Management Body of Knowledge (PMBOK® Guide) – Fifth Edition, Project
Management Institute, Inc., 2013, p. 349

Control Risks Inputs

Various components provide input to the Control Risks process.

Input	Description
Project management plan	Contains the risk management plan, which includes risk tolerances, risk owners, protocols, human resources, time, and other resources allocated for project risk management.
Risk register	Identifies risks, risk owners, actions to respond to risks, characteristics of risks, and a watch list of risks of low priority.
Work performance data	Items relating to risk monitoring and control such as deliverable status, corrective action, and performance reports.
Work performance reports	Information on project work performance that may affect the processes of risk management or the actual occurrence of risk.

A Guide to the Project Management Body of Knowledge (PMBOK® Guide) – Fifth Edition, Project
Management Institute, Inc., 2013, pg. 350-351

Control Risks Tools and Techniques

There are various tools and techniques used in the Control Risks process.

Tools & Techniques	Description
Risk reassessment	The risk register should be reassessed at project team status meetings. This will be done by the risk management team, if there is one for the project. Tasks in risk assessment require the identification of new risks, reassessment of current risks for their probability and impact, and the closure of outdated risks. The extent of risk assessment at the status meetings depends on how the project is flowing compared to its objectives. For example, if an unanticipated risk develops, it may be necessary to have additional response planning.

A Guide to the Project Management Body of Knowledge (PMBOK® Guide) – Fifth Edition, Project Management Institute (PMI)®, Project Management Professional
(PMP)®, and Certified Associate in Project Management (CAPM)® are registered trademarks of Project Management Institute, Inc. - Version 2.1 Published September 30, 2014

Lesson 11: Controlling the Project | *Topic C*

Tools & Techniques	Description
Risk audits	Examines effectiveness of the team's risk response efforts. Risk audits are performed as per the risk management plan schedules and are conducted during project review meetings or in separate risk audit meetings.
Variance and trend analysis	Project trends should be reviewed by using data collected on performance. Results from trend analysis may forecast a difference of cost and schedule from their initial targets. Any variation from the plan may result in threats or lost opportunities on the project.
Technical performance measurement	A comparison of the project's technical accomplishments to the planned accomplishments as outlined in the project plan. Any differences can help predict if the project scope will be achieved.
Reserve analysis	Makes a comparison of the amount of contingency reserves to the remaining amount of risk to decide if the reserve is sufficient.
Meetings	Project risk management should be on the to-do list at project status meetings and at meetings with the risk management team. The time it takes to address the issue depends on what risks have been identified, their priority, and complexity of response.

A Guide to the Project Management Body of Knowledge (PMBOK® Guide) – Fifth Edition, Project Management Institute, Inc., 2013, pg. 351-352

Project Risk Audits

A *project risk audit* is the process of examining the project team or risk management team's ability to identify risks, the effectiveness of risk response plans, and of the performance of risk owners. The audit may be conducted by a third party, by the project's risk officer, or by other qualified personnel.

The auditor reviews the risk response plan and data concerning project work results to determine whether the planned responses to identified risks are producing the desired results in terms of avoiding, transferring, or mitigating risk. In addition, the auditor evaluates the performance of the risk owner in implementing the response plan. The auditor documents the results of the audit and makes recommendations for improvement in the project's risk management efforts.

A Guide to the Project Management Body of Knowledge (PMBOK® Guide) – Fifth Edition, Project Management Institute, Inc., 2013, p. 351, 354, 559

Control Risks Outputs

There are five outputs from the Control Risks process.

Output	Description
Work performance information	Includes results from risk assessments, risk audits, and periodic risk reviews that may include updates to probability, impact, priority, response plans, ownership, and risks that are no longer active; also includes results of project risks that can help in future risk planning. This will complete the records of risk management, and is part of the close project or phase process and project closure documents.

A Guide to the Project Management Body of Knowledge (PMBOK® Guide) – Fifth Edition, Project Management Institute (PMI)®, Project Management Professional (PMP)®, and Certified Associate in Project Management (CAPM)® are registered trademarks of Project Management Institute, Inc. - Version 2.1 Published September 30, 2014

Lesson 11: Controlling the Project | Topic C

Output	Description
Change requests	Anything that deviates from the project baseline results in changes to the project management plan. These changes are submitted through the perform integrated change control process as an output of the monitor and control risks process. Approved changes become inputs to the direct and manage project execution process and monitor and control risks process. Change requests can include recommended corrective actions, namely contingency plans and workaround plans. Change requests can also include recommended preventive actions that are used to make sure the project is following the guidelines of the project management plan.
Project management plan updates	The project management plan needs to be revised and reissued if any approved changes have an effect on risk management processes.
Project documents updates	Various project documents that require updates include the assumptions log, technical documentation, contract terms, and the schedule and cost baselines.
Organizational process assets updates	Project risk management processes should be documented in the organizational process assets to be referenced in future projects. The probability and impact matrix, risk register, and risk breakdown structure can be updated at project close-out, or at the closing of each phase or milestone for longer projects. Lessons learned from project risk management activities can be added to the lessons learned database. Cost and project activity length can be added to the organization's database.

A Guide to the Project Management Body of Knowledge (PMBOK® Guide) – Fifth Edition, Project Management Institute, Inc., 2013, pg. 353-354

Guidelines to Control Project Risk

Controlling project risks ensures that appropriate responses to risk events are implemented. To effectively control project risks, follow these guidelines:

- When an event affects the project objectives, consult the risk response plan to execute actions as mentioned in the risk response plan.
- Monitor the environment for any new risks that may arise due to:
  - Changes in the project objectives. Any change to the overall cost, schedule, or quality/performance level of your project will change your overall risk picture.
  - Changes to scope. Whether the scope of the project increases or decreases, the risk picture changes. For example, increasing the scope of the project without assessing the impact on time or cost can spell disaster. Changes in scope require iterating the risk management process.
  - Changes within the organization, such as restructuring within functional departments. Such a change could mean some of the resources you were counting on will no longer be available for assignment to the project.
  - Changes outside of the organization, such as technological changes, changes in industry standards, economic or market changes, or legal/regulatory changes.
- Monitor the effectiveness of the risk response plan, as well as the contingency and fallback plans laid out in the risk response plan. Make sure your monitoring is done in accordance with the policies and procedures defined in the risk management plan.
  - Conduct project risk response audits to examine and document the effectiveness of the risk response plan and the performance of the risk owner.

A Guide to the Project Management Body of Knowledge (PMBOK® Guide) – Fifth Edition, Project Management Institute (PMI)®, Project Management Professional (PMP)®, and Certified Associate in Project Management (CAPM)® are registered trademarks of Project Management Institute, Inc. - Version 2.1 Published September 30, 2014

Lesson 11: Controlling the Project | *Topic C*

- Perform earned value analysis to monitor overall project performance against the baselines. If the project is deviating significantly from the baseline, reiterate the risk identification and analysis processes.
- Conduct periodic project risk reviews that are part of the project schedule to communicate risk response effectiveness and to identify new risks or triggers that may require additional response planning.
- Measure technical performance to determine whether variances are significant enough to warrant additional risk response planning.
- If the response plans are not effective in reducing or eliminating risk, consider implementing the fallback plan.
- Deal with unforeseen risks by systematically planning a reasoned response.
  - Develop workarounds for risks with low impact.
  - Perform additional response planning for risks with significant impact on project objectives.
- Update project documentation as changes are indicated.
  - Keep the risk response plan up-to-date as risks occur and response plans are changed or added.
  - Issue change requests in accordance with the integrated change control system.
  - Update performance baselines if the changes are significant.
  - Update risk identification checklists to help manage risk in future projects.
- Manage the contingency reserve so that the additional time, money, and resources are utilized as planned.

A Guide to the Project Management Body of Knowledge (PMBOK® Guide) – Fifth Edition, Project Management Institute, Inc., 2013, pg. 349-354

ACTIVITY 11-3
Controlling Project Risks

Scenario

During the course of the 122 East Main build, you receive an email from the electrical contractor outlining a three-week delay in the Install and Terminate Electrical Devices activity, due to defective materials. The electrical contractor's SOW states that if there is a potential delay, all subcontractors must inform you in writing within 48 hours of the onset of the delay, and the email meets this requirement. The project has already been significantly delayed due to severe weather conditions. Although your risk analysis included a schedule contingency for weather conditions and the receipt of defective materials, this is a serious problem that threatens to further delay the project.

---

1. What action should you take in regard to the material delay?

    ○ Monitor the environment for new risks.

    ○ Conduct a project risk response audit.

    ○ Update performance baselines.

    ○ Consult the risk response plan.

2. You have developed a very robust risk response plan in the risk register. Based on the vendor performance report, you notice that chances of delay have now become very high (from an earlier rating of high). You now need to decide what would be your next step.

    ○ Consult the risk response plan.

    ○ Follow the risk management process.

    ○ Implement the fallback plan.

    ○ Develop a workaround.

3. The contractor suggests that it might ultimately be more cost-effective to buy materials from another contractor, although the initial cost of materials will be higher. Do you think this is an effective solution?

A Guide to the Project Management Body of Knowledge (PMBOK® Guide) – Fifth Edition, Project Management Institute (PMI)®, Project Management Professional (PMP)®, and Certified Associate in Project Management (CAPM)® are registered trademarks of Project Management Institute, Inc. - Version 2.1 Published September 30, 2014

TOPIC D

Control Project Procurements

You selected a vendor to fulfill your project's procurement requirements. Now you need to ensure that the vendor's performance meets the contract requirements. In this topic, you will control project procurements.

A Guide to the Project Management Body of Knowledge (PMBOK® Guide) – Fifth Edition, Project Management Institute, Inc., 2013, pg. 379-381

The following data flow diagram illustrates how the Control Procurements process relates to the other knowledge areas within the Monitoring and Controlling Process Group.

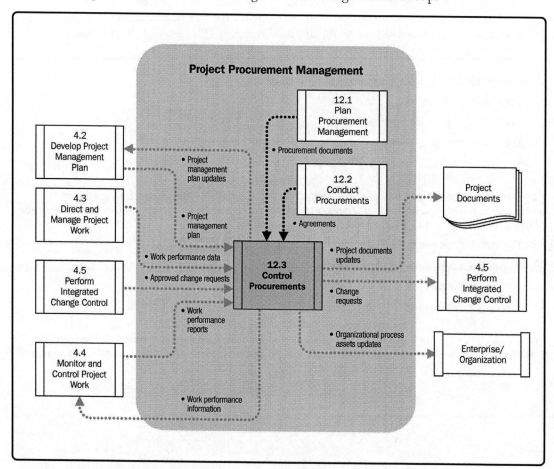

Figure 11–7: Control procurements work data flow diagram.

A Guide to the Project Management Body of Knowledge (PMBOK® Guide) – Fifth Edition, Project Management Institute, Inc., 2013, p. 380

The Control Procurements Process

The *Control Procurements process* is the process of managing the relationship with the seller. During control procurements, the project manager applies other project management processes to the contractual relationship and integrates the coordination of the outputs from these processes into the overall management of the project. The other project management processes include:

- Project plan execution to formally sanction the seller's work to begin at the appropriate time.

A Guide to the Project Management Body of Knowledge (PMBOK® Guide) – Fifth Edition, Project Management Institute (PMI)®, Project Management Professional (PMP)®, and Certified Associate in Project Management (CAPM)® are registered trademarks of Project Management Institute, Inc. - Version 2.1 Published September 30, 2014

Lesson 11: Controlling the Project | Topic D

- Performance reporting to monitor seller cost, schedule, and technical performance.
- Quality control to ensure that the quality of the seller's service or product meets contract objectives.
- Change control to ensure that changes to the contract are carefully managed and properly approved.
- Monitor and control the project risks to ensure that the risks are properly managed.

A Guide to the Project Management Body of Knowledge (PMBOK® Guide) – Fifth Edition, Project Management Institute, Inc., 2013, pg. 379-381

Figure 11–8: The Control Procurements process.

A Guide to the Project Management Body of Knowledge (PMBOK® Guide) – Fifth Edition, Project Management Institute, Inc., 2013, p. 379

Control Procurements Inputs

Various components provide input to the Control Procurements process.

Input	Description
Project management plan	Describes every management step of the procurement process starting with development and ending with closing the contract.
Procurement documents	The instructions that you provide to prospective sellers so that they can completely and accurately respond to your request. These include the procurement SOW with description of the goods or services to be purchased.
Agreements	A mutually binding agreement that details the obligations of the buyer and seller. One is given to each selected seller.
Approved change requests	Any changes to the current contract may include the procurement statement of work, price, and the description of products, services, or results. All changes need to be in writing and approved before implementation. Any verbal, undocumented changes are not required to be processed or implemented.
Work performance reports	Performance evaluation documentation for providers includes technical documentation and other deliverables that are provided and meet the needs of the contract. Past performance records when dealing with a vendor figure heavily in the decision making for current and future vendor solicitation.
Work performance data	Includes amount of costs incurred, how quality standards are being met and followed, and invoices. Performance reports show what deliverables have been completed and which still need to be accomplished. Invoices must be submitted to request payment. All documentation on invoices are established within the contract.

A Guide to the Project Management Body of Knowledge (PMBOK® Guide) – Fifth Edition, Project Management Institute, Inc., 2013, pg. 381-382

Control Procurements Tools and Techniques

There are various tools and techniques used in the Control Procurements process.

Tools & Techniques	Description
Contract change control system	A contract change control system is an offshoot of the overall change control system, but dedicated specifically to controlling contract changes.
Procurements performance reviews	A review of the seller's performance on project scope, quality, and the project's associated schedule and costs as compared to the contract. It can include a review of documentation submitted by the seller, inspections, or quality audits. The purpose of this review is to identify strengths and weaknesses with project performance, and to monitor the progress of schedules and tasks.
Inspections and audits	Can be conducted during the project to identify weaknesses in how the seller conducts work. This is outlined in the contract. Some contracts allow buyer procurement personnel as part of their inspection and audit teams.
Performance reporting	Performance reporting for administer procurements provides the project management team with information about how the seller is doing in regard to meeting the contractual obligations. The contract performance reporting system is an offshoot of the overall project performance reporting system, but dedicated specifically to reporting contract performance.
Payment systems	Payments to the seller are made contingent on the acceptance of the delivered goods or services, and on the receipt of a valid invoice for the goods or services. Typically, invoices are sent to the organization's accounts payable department. They, in turn, check with the project organization to verify that goods or services were delivered and accepted, and then authorize payment.
Claims administration	When buyers and sellers cannot agree on changes, these disputes are referred to as claims or appeals. Claims are handled in accordance with contract terms, and are managed throughout the term of the contract. If the buyer and seller do not resolve the claim, it will be handled according to the dispute resolution procedures in the contract. Contract clauses may include arbitration or litigation and may be brought up after contract closure.
Records management system	Contains processes and controls functions and automation tools. It is used by the project manager to control procurement and contract documentation and records. This system is used to keep track of and retrieve documents and correspondence.

A Guide to the Project Management Body of Knowledge (PMBOK® Guide) – Fifth Edition, Project Management Institute, Inc., 2013, pg. 383-384

Contract Change Control System

Either party can propose contract change requests for any of the contract terms, including scope, cost, delivery date, or quality of goods or services.

Contract Change	Description
Administrative changes	These are non-substantive changes to the way the contract is administered. This is the most common type of contract change. Administrative changes should be documented and written notification sent to the seller with a clear expectation that the seller will approve and return the change document. Administrative changes require no adjustment in payment.
Contract modification	This is a substantive change to the contract requirements, such as a new deadline or a change to the product requirements. Contract modifications should be documented and a formal change order should be sent to the seller. Contract modifications may result in claims for payment adjustment.
Supplemental agreement	This is an additional agreement related to the contract but negotiated separately. A supplemental agreement requires the signatures of both buyer and seller. A separate payment schedule is attached for the work in a supplemental agreement.
Constructive changes	These are changes that the seller may have caused through action or inaction. As a result of constructive changes, a seller is required to change the way the contract is fulfilled. The seller may claim a payment adjustment as a result of constructive changes.
Termination of contract	A contract may be terminated due to seller default or for customer convenience. Defaults are typically due to non-performance such as late deliveries, poor quality, or non-performance of some or all project requirements. Termination due to customer convenience may result due to major changes in the contract plans, through no fault of the seller.

A Guide to the Project Management Body of Knowledge (PMBOK® Guide) – Fifth Edition, Project Management Institute, Inc., 2013, p. 384, 533

Control Procurements Outputs

There are five outputs from the Control Procurements process.

Output	Description
Work performance information	Includes identification of current or potential issues to support later claims or new procurement, vendor performance, and compliance of contracts.
Change requests	Can include changes in project direction by the buyer or through a change in seller actions. These changes can affect the project management plan and subsidiary plans, the project schedule, and the procurement management plan. Any changes need to be identified and documented in project correspondence.

A Guide to the Project Management Body of Knowledge (PMBOK® Guide) – Fifth Edition, Project Management Institute (PMI)®, Project Management Professional (PMP)®, and Certified Associate in Project Management (CAPM)® are registered trademarks of Project Management Institute, Inc. - Version 2.1 Published September 30, 2014

Lesson 11: Controlling the Project | *Topic D*

Output	Description
Project management plan updates	The procurement management plan is modified to include approved change requests affecting procurement management. Each contract management plan is modified to include approved change requests affecting contract administration. The baseline schedule is modified to reflect slippages that affect the overall project performance and also the current expectations. Further, updates to the project management plan include any changes to the contracts, human resource requirements, and the project scope or cost baselines.
Project documents updates	Includes the contract, schedules, and approved and unapproved change requests. It can also include technical documentation, deliverables, seller performance reports, warranties, financial documents, and results of contract inspections.
Organizational process assets updates	There are several assets to update: • Correspondence: Contract terms and conditions often need documentation of communications between the buyer and seller. Some documentation may include warnings of bad performance and contract change requests or verifications. A complete written record of all communication between the buyer and seller is given to both parties. • Payment schedules and requests: This is required if the project has an external payment system. If an internal system is used, the output would just be payments. • Seller performance evaluation documentation: Prepared by the buyer to document the seller's ability to comply with the contract, to indicate if the seller will be hired for future projects, or to rate the quality of the seller's work on the project. These documents can indicate early contract termination, or determine how contract penalties, fees, or incentives are administered. Any results can be used in the qualified sellers list.

A Guide to the Project Management Body of Knowledge (PMBOK® Guide) – Fifth Edition, Project Management Institute, Inc., 2013, pg. 384-386

Legal Issues

Project managers should be familiar with some of the common legal issues related to procurement administration.

• Warranty: A promise, explicit or implied, that goods or services will meet a predetermined standard. The standard may cover features such as reliability, fitness for use, and safety.
• Waiver: The giving up of a contract right, even inadvertently.
• Breach of contract: Failure to meet some or all of the obligations of a contract. It may result in damages paid to the injured party, litigation, or other ramifications.

A Guide to the Project Management Body of Knowledge (PMBOK® Guide) – Fifth Edition, Project Management Institute, Inc., 2013, pg. 380-381

Types of Warranties

As a project manager, you may encounter several types of warranties.

A Guide to the Project Management Body of Knowledge (PMBOK® Guide) – Fifth Edition, Project Management Institute (PMI)®, Project Management Professional (PMP)®, and Certified Associate in Project Management (CAPM)® are registered trademarks of Project Management Institute, Inc. - Version 2.1 Published September 30, 2014

Lesson 11: Controlling the Project | Topic D

Type	Description
Express warranty	If the pre-determined standard for quality or performance is specified, either in a formal warranty or in the manufacturer's description of the product, it is considered an express warranty.
Implied warranty	If the pre-determined standard for quality or performance exists but is not specified, it is considered an implied warranty. This type of warranty takes effect if the buyer depends on the seller's expertise when making a purchasing decision. If you purchase items that are widely available on the market, it is assumed that you are relying on the seller's expertise in determining that the goods are merchantable and fit for a particular purpose.
	On the other hand, if you are a technical expert, and you require an unusual modification to the product or you intend to use the standard product in an unusual way, you won't be able to claim implied warranties.
	Similarly, if you provide detailed product specifications and the seller meets them, you won't be able to claim that the seller breached an express warranty if the goods do not meet your needs.
Warranties of merchantability	Implied warranties that require goods to be fit for ordinary usage. Any sale of an item is subject to warranties of merchantability. The sale of an item for use in a particular project would mean that the item was also subject to warranty of fitness if it can be proven that the seller knew how it would be used.
Warranties of fitness for purpose	Implied warranties that require goods to be fit for the usage that was intended by the buyer.

Types of Waivers

It is possible for a party to a contract to explicitly waive a contract right. However, project managers should be particularly aware of the ways in which they can inadvertently waive their contract rights. These include:

* Accepting a product that fails to meet standards for quality or performance.
* Accepting late deliveries.
* Overlooking some other aspect of non-conformance to contractual obligations.

To protect against losses incurred by an inadvertent waiver of contract rights, some contracts are written to specifically exclude the possibility of waiving a specified right.

Breaches of Contract

Project managers may encounter different types of breaches of contracts.

* Anticipatory breach: An unavoidable indication that the other party will not be able to produce the performance necessary to fulfill the contract.
* Fundamental breach: A breach so serious that it negates the very foundation of the contract.
* Material breach: A serious breach that prevents the injured party from benefiting from the contract. In a material breach, the injured party can claim damages, but is no longer obligated to fulfill any contract commitments.
* Immaterial breach: The contract has been breached in such a way that there is no resulting damage to the injured party; because there are no damages, the injured party is not entitled to receive compensation. This is also called a minor breach.

A Guide to the Project Management Body of Knowledge (PMBOK® Guide) – Fifth Edition, Project Management Institute (PMI)®, Project Management Professional (PMP)®, and Certified Associate in Project Management (CAPM)® are registered trademarks of Project Management Institute, Inc. - Version 2.1 Published September 30, 2014

Lesson 11: Controlling the Project | Topic D

Legal Expertise

Project managers should have a general understanding of contracts and breaches of contracts, but they are not expected to be legal experts. The best way to protect yourself, your project, and your organization is to make sure that your legal department has reviewed and approved any contracts before you sign them. As a general guideline, you should never sign a contract unless you are sure that you understand all of its terms.

The Force Majeure Clause

Force majeure, or superior force, is a common clause added to contracts that addresses the actions from both the parties when an extraordinary circumstance beyond the control of either party occurs. The extraordinary circumstances include war, strike, riot, crime, or a natural disaster (a so-called "Act of God" that includes floods, earthquakes, and storms) that prevent one or both parties from fulfilling their obligations under the contract. However, the force majeure clause is not intended to excuse negligence or other misconduct by the parties and the nonperformance is caused by the usual and natural consequences.

Guidelines to Control Project Procurements

Regardless of project size, the project manager is responsible for administering procurements for the project. Experienced project managers always rely heavily on the contract administration expertise of their organizations' procurement, purchasing, and legal departments. Effective procurement control ensures that the seller's performance meets contractual requirements and objectives. To control procurements, follow these guidelines:

- Index and store all contract correspondence for ease of retrieval.
- Develop and implement an effective contract change control system. The system should be integrated with the project's overall change control system and should include these elements:
  - Forms and paperwork required to request a contract change.
  - Contract performance-tracking mechanisms.
  - Procedures for submitting and approving change requests, including approval levels based on cost or impact of change.
  - Procedures for reviewing and resolving contract disputes.
- Evaluate the risk of each contract change request.
- Document all contract changes and incorporate any effects of the changes into the project plan.
- Develop and implement an effective performance reporting system for the seller. The performance reporting system should include these elements:
  - Baseline time, cost, and quality specifications.
  - Actual time, cost, and quality specifications.
  - Procedures for determining contract performance, including status reporting, on-site visits, and product inspection.
  - Procedures for determining acceptance or non-acceptance of delivered goods or services. These might include the options to accept the entire delivery, reject the entire delivery, or accept part of a delivery.
- Spell out in the contract any performance reporting specifications to be imposed on the seller.
- Set performance milestones to monitor project progress.
  - Depending on your project, you might use partial deliveries, completion of selected portions of the product, or preliminary versions of the finished product as milestones.
  - Make sure the milestones are arranged and agreed upon with the seller ahead of time.
  - Negotiate a deadline for each milestone, as well as quality and completeness specifications for the milestone.
  - If work is performed at another site, conduct site visits to determine how the seller's work is progressing.

A Guide to the Project Management Body of Knowledge (PMBOK® Guide) – Fifth Edition, Project Management Institute (PMI)®, Project Management Professional (PMP)®, and Certified Associate in Project Management (CAPM)® are registered trademarks of Project Management Institute, Inc. - Version 2.1 Published September 30, 2014

Lesson 11: Controlling the Project | Topic D

- Be sensitive to the cost of site visits in terms of time and impact on vendor relationships.
- Schedule the visits up-front, set an agenda for each visit, and use only the time required.
- Submit approved invoices for payment in accordance with the contract and the project's payment system.

A Guide to the Project Management Body of Knowledge (PMBOK® Guide) – Fifth Edition, Project Management Institute, Inc., 2013, pg. 379-386

ACTIVITY 11–4
Controlling Project Procurements

Scenario

The 122 East Main project is continuing through the execution processes. You have selected a landscaper to supply and install the from lawn and shrubs. You have been asked to administer the contract. The supplier has worked with Building with Heart in the past with good results. However, because the driveway and sidewalk installation depends on the landscaping being completed on time, you want to carefully monitor the work to stay ahead of problems and take actions early to mitigate the risk of delays.

---

1. The work done by the landscaper is scheduled to be completed in three phases. What action can you take to ensure that these deadlines are met?
   - ○ Set performance milestones
   - ○ Document contract changes
   - ○ Implement a contract change control system
   - ○ Index all contract correspondence

2. Your landscaping contact informs you that their primary on-site coordinator has resigned. They have asked to push the lawn installation date out a week to get another coordinator up to speed. What action should you take?
   - ○ Document contract changes
   - ○ Conduct an on-site visit
   - ○ Consult the contract change control system
   - ○ Negotiate a milestone deadline

3. The landscaper has informed you that they have completed the site prep phase as specified in the contract. It is your responsibility as project manager to verify that all work was completed to spec. Upon your review, you notice that some of the property was not prepped. What action should you take?

TOPIC E

Control Stakeholder Engagement

With your project progressing through the monitoring and controlling phases, you must make sure to properly control the project stakeholder engagement. The next process will take you through the process to keep stakeholders involved in the project. In this topic, you will control stakeholder engagement.

A Guide to the Project Management Body of Knowledge (PMBOK® Guide) – Fifth Edition, Project Management Institute, Inc., 2013, pg. 409-410

The following data flow diagram illustrates how the Control Stakeholder Engagement process relates to the other knowledge areas within the Monitoring and Controlling Process Group.

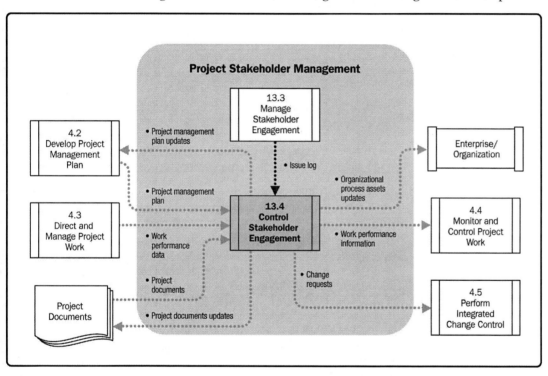

Figure 11–9: The Control Stakeholder Engagement work data flow diagram.

A Guide to the Project Management Body of Knowledge (PMBOK® Guide) – Fifth Edition, Project Management Institute, Inc., 2013, p. 410

The Control Stakeholder Engagement Process

The *Control Stakeholder Engagement process* monitors and controls the project stakeholder relationships during the course of a project. You want to use engagement strategies and plans for keeping stakeholders engaged from the start of the project until the close of the project. This process should be continuous throughout the life of the project.

A Guide to the Project Management Body of Knowledge (PMBOK® Guide) – Fifth Edition, Project Management Institute, Inc., 2013, pg. 409-410

A Guide to the Project Management Body of Knowledge (PMBOK® Guide) – Fifth Edition, Project Management Institute (PMI)®, Project Management Professional (PMP)®, and Certified Associate in Project Management (CAPM)® are registered trademarks of Project Management Institute, Inc. - Version 2.1 Published September 30, 2014

Lesson 11: Controlling the Project | Topic E

Inputs	Tools & Techniques	Outputs
.1 Project management plan .2 Issue log .3 Work performance data .4 Project documents	.1 Information management systems .2 Expert judgment .3 Meetings	.1 Work performance information .2 Change requests .3 Project management plan updates .4 Project documents updates .5 Organizational process assets updates

Figure 11-10: The Control Stakeholder Engagement process.

A Guide to the Project Management Body of Knowledge (PMBOK® Guide) – Fifth Edition, Project Management Institute, Inc., 2013, p. 410

Control Stakeholder Engagement Inputs

Various components provide input to the Control Stakeholder Engagement process.

Input	Description
Project management plan	Provides details outlined in the stakeholder management plan.
Issues log	Provides list of new issues and resolved issues that could involve project stakeholders.
Work performance data	Provides measurements on project activities and deliverables that can be useful when managing stakeholders.
Project documents	Documents include project schedule, stakeholder register, issues log, change log, and project communications

A Guide to the Project Management Body of Knowledge (PMBOK® Guide) – Fifth Edition, Project Management Institute, Inc., 2013, pg. 411-412

Control Stakeholder Engagement Tools and Techniques

There are various tools and techniques used in the Control Stakeholder Engagement process.

Tools & Techniques	Description
Information management systems	A tool to capture, store, and distribute project information to stakeholders.
Expert judgment	Used to identify new and reassess current stakeholders.
Meetings	Used to exchange and analyze information about stakeholder engagement.

A Guide to the Project Management Body of Knowledge (PMBOK® Guide) – Fifth Edition, Project Management Institute, Inc., 2013, pg. 412- 413

Control Stakeholder Engagement Outputs

There are five outputs from the Control Stakeholder Engagement process.

A Guide to the Project Management Body of Knowledge (PMBOK® Guide) – Fifth Edition, Project Management Institute (PMI)®, Project Management Professional (PMP)®, and Certified Associate in Project Management (CAPM)® are registered trademarks of Project Management Institute, Inc. - Version 2.1 Published September 30, 2014

Lesson 11: Controlling the Project | Topic E

Output	Description
Work performance information	Includes performance data from various controlling processes that is communicated to stakeholders.
Change requests	Changes generated by stakeholders for preventive and corrective actions.
Project management plan updates	Documents that may need updating include the change management, communications, cost, human resource, procurement, quality, requirements, risk, schedule, scope, and stakeholder management plans.
Project documents updates	Documents that may need updating include the stakeholder register and issue log.
Organizational process assets updates	Documents that may need updating include stakeholder notifications, project reports, project presentations, project records, feedback from stakeholders, and lessons learned documentation.

A Guide to the Project Management Body of Knowledge (PMBOK® Guide) – Fifth Edition, Project Management Institute, Inc., 2013, pg. 413- 415

Guidelines to Control Stakeholder Engagement

Keeping the stakeholders engaged throughout the project is key in a successful project. To do this, follow these guidelines:

- Review the project management plan for information in the stakeholder management plan.
- Review the issue log for a list of issues including new issues and resolved issues.
- Review the work performance data for the measurements on project activities and deliverables.
- Review the project documents such as the project schedule, stakeholder register, issues log, change log, and project communications.
- Use tools and techniques such as information management systems, expert judgment, and meetings to control the stakeholder engagement.
- Communicate the work performance information and change requests to the project team and stakeholders, and update project documents.

A Guide to the Project Management Body of Knowledge (PMBOK® Guide) – Fifth Edition, Project Management Institute, Inc., 2013, pg. 409- 415

ACTIVITY 11–5
Discussing Project Stakeholder Engagement

Scenario

In this activity, you will discuss project stakeholder engagement.

1. Why is it important to the project to control stakeholder engagement?

2. What things could you be communicating to the project stakeholders to keep them engaged in the house build project?

3. What could happen if you do not control stakeholder engagement?

A Guide to the Project Management Body of Knowledge (PMBOK® Guide) – Fifth Edition, Project Management Institute (PMI)®, Project Management Professional (PMP)®, and Certified Associate in Project Management (CAPM)® are registered trademarks of Project Management Institute, Inc. - Version 2.1 Published September 30, 2014

Summary

In this lesson, you controlled various aspects of the project including quality, communications, risks, procurements, and stakeholder engagement. As the project manager, you are responsible for monitoring many areas of your project, controlling them appropriately, and executing the project contracts effectively so that you can successfully bring your project to its conclusion.

Why is it important to monitor and control each of the processes covered in this lesson?

What quality control methods have you used in the past? Were they effective? Why or why not?

Note: Check your LogicalCHOICE Course screen for opportunities to interact with your classmates, peers, and the larger LogicalCHOICE online community about the topics covered in this course or other topics you are interested in. From the Course screen you can also access available resources for a more continuous learning experience.

A Guide to the Project Management Body of Knowledge (PMBOK® Guide) – Fifth Edition, Project Management Institute (PMI)®, Project Management Professional (PMP)®, and Certified Associate in Project Management (CAPM)® are registered trademarks of Project Management Institute, Inc. - Version 2.1 Published September 30, 2014

Lesson 11: Controlling the Project |

12 | Closing a Project

Lesson Time: 2 hours

Lesson Objectives

In this lesson, you will:

- Close a project or phase.

- Close procurements.

Lesson Introduction

In this course, you have been through a number of different project management processes and experienced the impact each process has on a project. With all that in mind, you are ready to officially close a project. Closing a project out is as important as initiating a project. The lessons learned during the course of a project are analyzed and addressed in the close-out phase so that the same mistakes or known issues will not occur again. In this lesson, you will close a project.

The following diagram highlights the next process group and knowledge areas covered in this lesson.

	Project Management Process Groups				
Knowledge Areas	**Initiating Process Group**	**Planning Process Group**	**Executing Process Group**	**Monitoring and Controlling Process Group**	**Closing Process Group**
4. Project Integration Management	4.1 Develop Project Charter	4.2 Develop Project Management Plan	4.3 Direct and Manage Project Work	4.4 Monitor and Control Project Work 4.5 Perform Integrated Change Control	4.6 Close Project or Phase
5. Project Scope Management		5.1 Plan Scope Management 5.2 Collect Requirements 5.3 Define Scope 5.4 Create WBS		5.5 Validate Scope 5.6 Control Scope	
6. Project Time Management		6.1 Plan Schedule Management 6.2 Define Activities 6.3 Sequence Activites 6.4 Estimate Activity Resources 6.5 Estimate Activity Durations 6.6 Develop Schedule		6.7 Control Schedule	
7. Project Cost Management		7.1 Plan Cost Management 7.2 Estimate Cost 7.3 Determine Budget		7.4 Control Costs	
8. Project Quality Management		8.1 Plan Quality Management	8.2 Perform Quality Assurance	8.3 Control Quality	
9. Project Human Resource Management		9.1 Plan Human Resource Management	9.2 Acquire Project Team 9.3 Develop Project Team 9.4 Manage Project Team		
10. Project Communication Management		10.1 Plan Communications Management	10.2 Manage Communications	10.3 Control Communications	
11. Project Risk Management		11.1 Plan Risk Management 11.2 Identify Risks 11.3 Perform Qualitative Risk Analysis 11.4 Perform Quantitative Risk Analysis 11.5 Plan Risk Responses		11.6 Control Risks	
12. Project Procurement Management		12.1 Plan Procurement Management	12.2 Conduct Procurements	12.3 Control Procurements	12.4 Close Procurements
13. Project Stakeholder Management	13.1 Identify Stakeholders	13.2 Plan Stakeholder Management	13.3 Manage Stakeholder Engagement	13.4 Control Stakeholder Engagement	

TOPIC A

Close Project or Phase

Closing a project or project phase is one of the last steps in completing a project or phase. Because a project is a unique, one-time activity, the formal closing out of the project is essential. In some cases, without an official close-out of a project or phase, the next related activity, phase, or project will not get started. This happens often when there are multiple projects managed within a program.

A Guide to the Project Management Body of Knowledge (PMBOK® Guide) – Fifth Edition, Project Management Institute, Inc., 2013, pg. 100-101

The following data flow diagram illustrates how the Close a Project or Phase process relates to the other project management processes.

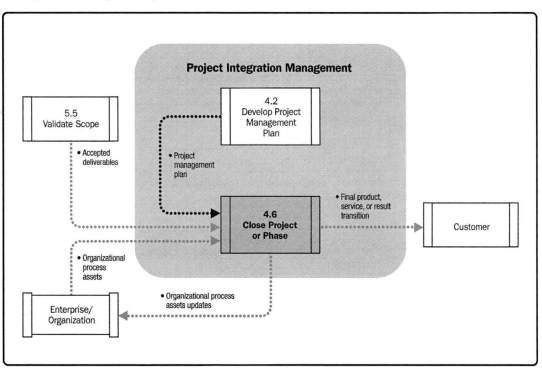

Figure 12–1: The Close a Project or Phase data flow diagram.

A Guide to the Project Management Body of Knowledge (PMBOK® Guide) – Fifth Edition, Project Management Institute, Inc., 2013, p. 101

The Close a Project or Phase Process

The *close a project or phase process* finalizes any project documentation, makes sure all invoices are paid, contracts are closed out, project lessons learned are discussed and documented, and any other loose ends are wrapped up so that the project is complete and resources (people, equipment, facilities, and money) can be released to work on new projects or project phases. This process ensures that the activities across all of the project management process groups are finalized to signify the formal ending of the project work and the project or phase. The project manager reviews all project information to verify that all project work is complete and the project has delivered its objectives. The scope baseline is also reviewed to confirm completion. If a project is terminated before completion, this process analyzes and documents the reasons for the early ending.

A Guide to the Project Management Body of Knowledge (PMBOK® Guide) – Fifth Edition, Project Management Institute (PMI)®, Project Management Professional (PMP)®, and Certified Associate in Project Management (CAPM)® are registered trademarks of Project Management Institute, Inc. - Version 2.1 Published September 30, 2014

Lesson 12: Closing a Project | Topic A

A Guide to the Project Management Body of Knowledge (PMBOK® Guide) – Fifth Edition, Project Management Institute, Inc., 2013, pg. 100-101

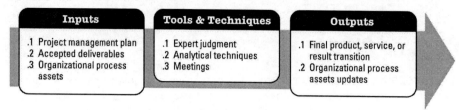

Figure 12-2: The close a project or phase process.

A Guide to the Project Management Body of Knowledge (PMBOK® Guide) – Fifth Edition, Project Management Institute, Inc., 2013, p. 100

Close a Project or Phase Inputs

Various components provide input to the Close a Project or Phase process.

Input	Description
Project management plan	The project management plan is the agreement between the project manager and the project sponsor, defining what determines project completion.
Accepted deliverables	Examples include approved product specifications, paid invoices, and work performance documents.
Organizational process assets	Organizational process assets that can influence this process include project or phase closure guidelines or requirements, historical information, and lessons learned.

A Guide to the Project Management Body of Knowledge (PMBOK® Guide) – Fifth Edition, Project Management Institute, Inc., 2013, p. 102

Close a Project or Phase Tools and Techniques

There are three tools and techniques used in the Close a Project or Phase process.

Tools & Techniques	Description
Expert judgment	Expert judgment is used to ensure the project or phase closure is performed to the expected standards. Experts include other project managers within the organization, the PMO, and professional and technical associations.
Analytical techniques	Analytical techniques that can be used in project close-out include regression analysis and trend analysis.
Meetings	Lessons learned, close-out, user group, and review meetings are held by project team members and stakeholders.

A Guide to the Project Management Body of Knowledge (PMBOK® Guide) – Fifth Edition, Project Management Institute, Inc., 2013, pg. 102-103

Close a Project or Phase Outputs

There are two outputs from the Close a Project or Phase process.

Output	Description
Final product, service, or result transition	The official delivery and acceptance by the customer or sponsor. Ideally, this acceptance is documented in writing for storage in the project archives.
Organizational process assets updates	Organizational process assets that are updated now can include project files, project or phase closure documents, and historical information.

A Guide to the Project Management Body of Knowledge (PMBOK® Guide) – Fifth Edition, Project Management Institute, Inc., 2013, p. 103

Affected Organizational Assets

During the Close a Project or Phase process, there are a number of assets that may need to be updated as a result of the process. These can include:

- Project files including documentation from the project's activities, the scope, cost, schedule, and project calendars in the project management plan, risk registers and change management documentation, actual risk response actions and impact.
- Project or phase closure documents are formal documents that demonstrate the completion of the project or phase, and confirm the transfer of the completed project deliverables to others who will use those deliverables. The project manager reviews the customer acceptance documentation from the validate scope process to confirm deliverable acceptance and also confirms that the project requirements in the contract are complete. If the project was terminated early, the reasons why and the how to transfer the finished and unfinished deliverables to others needs to be documented.
- Historical information and lessons learned are documented for use by future projects or phases.

A Guide to the Project Management Body of Knowledge (PMBOK® Guide) – Fifth Edition, Project Management Institute, Inc., 2013, p. 104

Administrative Closure

Administrative closure involves verifying and documenting project results to formalize project or phase completion. During the administrative closure process, the project team gathers and updates project documentation and relevant records and reports. Project results are compared against customer and stakeholder expectations and requirements. A properly completed administrative closure process ensures that the project or phase requirements were met and formal acceptance was granted.

A Guide to the Project Management Body of Knowledge (PMBOK® Guide) – Fifth Edition, Project Management Institute, Inc., 2013, pg. 57-58, 103-104

Archiving

During administrative closure, it may be beneficial to archive selected project records such as:

- The project management plan with its subsidiary plans and supporting detail
- Project performance records, audit reports, and financial records
- Contract documentation
- Copies of all communications, status reports, meeting minutes, and change requests
- Relevant project databases
- Staff evaluations
- Lessons learned reports and the final project report
- Formal acceptance documentation

A Guide to the Project Management Body of Knowledge (PMBOK® Guide) – Fifth Edition, Project Management Institute (PMI)®, Project Management Professional (PMP)®, and Certified Associate in Project Management (CAPM)® are registered trademarks of Project Management Institute, Inc. - Version 2.1 Published September 30, 2014

Lesson 12: Closing a Project | *Topic A*

Outstanding Items

It may be helpful to construct a checklist of outstanding items that must be resolved, addressed, or completed before the customer will accept the final work results. Make sure to include the actions taken to resolve any outstanding issues and any time frames associated with completion.

Lessons Learned Reports

Lessons learned reports are documents that capture salient and helpful information about the work done in a project or a project phase; they identify both the project team's strengths and areas for improvement. They can be formal or informal, depending on the organizational norms or requirements. They are compiled for the benefit of future project teams, so that people can capitalize on the organization's knowledge base about work that has already been done and avoid repeating mistakes, and also benefit from ongoing organizational learning.

A Guide to the Project Management Body of Knowledge (PMBOK® Guide) – Fifth Edition, Project Management Institute, Inc., 2013, p. 544

Considerations of Lessons Learned

During administrative closure, project managers should take into account some of the following considerations of lessons learned:

- Scheduling lessons learned include any relevant scheduling problems or issues. They also document the management strategies that were implemented to deal with schedule or resource constraints.

- Conflict management lessons learned include any issues that arose within the team or between the team and customers. They include documentation of the nature and source of the conflict, as well as the impact that the conflict had on the project. The documentation should also specify how management intervened in response to the conflict.

- Sellers lessons learned include seller experience and performance documented and provided to the procurement department.

- Customer lessons learned can include useful information such as customers that are excessively litigious or unreasonable to work with. This information should be conveyed to the sales and legal departments, as well as documented in the lessons learned repository.

- Strategic lessons learned are those that typically impact some aspect of the organization's project management methodology or significantly improve a template, form, or process. These address the questions: Can we reuse this project's artifact to get more done with the same resources and/or deliver work sooner?

- Tactical lessons learned answer the question: If we were to do this type of project again, what should we stop, start, and continue so that we can execute flawlessly? They focus on developing recommendations, reviewing recommendations with other managers in other departments, developing implementation plans, and implementing those plans.

- Other aspects of lessons learned include scope, schedule, cost, quality, and customer satisfaction, as well as any corrective action taken in response to issues.

A Guide to the Project Management Body of Knowledge (PMBOK® Guide) – Fifth Edition, Project Management Institute, Inc., 2013, pg. 254, 303, 389, 409, 415

Close-Out Meetings

Close-out meetings are sessions held at the end of a project or phase; they involve discussing the work and capturing lessons learned. Close-out meetings may include stakeholders, team members, project resources, and customers. They typically follow a formal agenda and may require official minutes to be recorded. Not all organizations or projects require close-out meetings. Some organizations require the minutes from close-out meetings to be completed in full, approved by management, and preserved in a specific manner.

A Guide to the Project Management Body of Knowledge (PMBOK® Guide) – Fifth Edition, Project Management Institute (PMI)®, Project Management Professional (PMP)®, and Certified Associate in Project Management (CAPM)® are registered trademarks of Project Management Institute, Inc. - Version 2.1 Published September 30, 2014

Lesson 12: Closing a Project | Topic A

Note: To explore how to give an effective briefing, you can access the LearnTO **Give a Briefing** presentation from the **LearnTO** tile on the LogicalCHOICE Course screen.

A Guide to the Project Management Body of Knowledge (PMBOK® Guide) – Fifth Edition, Project Management Institute, Inc., 2013, p. 103

Varieties of Close–Out Meetings

Some organizations require official close-out meetings so that they can obtain the customers' formal project acceptance, while others use them as an opportunity to discuss the project with the customers as a prelude to soliciting additional business. Other organizations use close-out meetings for internal purposes, for the edification of the staff and improvement of internal processes. From an organizational standpoint, good endings lead to good beginnings on subsequent projects.

Guidelines to Close Out a Project or Project Phase

Each phase of the project must be properly closed to ensure that valuable information is safeguarded for future projects. To properly close a phase or project, do the following:

- Review the project management plan, accepted deliverables, and organizational process assets to confirm that the activities for the project are complete.
- Some organizations and application areas have a project termination checklist that may be useful when closing out a project or phase. You may find it useful to prepare one if there is not one available. This helps to ensure that you are thorough in your administrative close-out.
- Gather and organize performance measurement documentation, product documentation, and other relevant project records for ease of review by stakeholders.
- Release project resources.
- Update records to ensure that they reflect final specifications.
- Be sure to update the resource pool database to reflect new skills and increased levels of proficiency.
- Analyze project success and effectiveness and document lessons learned.
- Prepare lessons learned reports and a final project report.
- Obtain project approval and formal project acceptance. Demonstrate to the customer or sponsor that the deliverables meet the defined acceptance criteria to obtain formal acceptance of the phase or project. This may involve preparing an end-of-project report or giving a presentation.
- Archive a complete set of indexed project records.
- Celebrate the success of the project with the team and other stakeholders.

A Guide to the Project Management Body of Knowledge (PMBOK® Guide) – Fifth Edition, Project Management Institute, Inc., 2013, p. 100-104

A Guide to the Project Management Body of Knowledge (PMBOK® Guide) – Fifth Edition, Project Management Institute (PMI)®, Project Management Professional (PMP)®, and Certified Associate in Project Management (CAPM)® are registered trademarks of Project Management Institute, Inc. - Version 2.1 Published September 30, 2014

Lesson 12: Closing a Project | *Topic A*

ACTIVITY 12–1
Closing a Project or Phase

Scenario

Your good project planning and control has resulted in the 122 East Main project coming to a successful close. The final project deliverable is complete. You have collected the performance measurement reports and updated product documents and other relevant project records for archiving. Before you can close your project, you need to obtain formal project approval from the project sponsor. You have scheduled a meeting for the following afternoon.

1. Are your project records ready for review by the project sponsor? Why or why not?

2. What document will you prepare before obtaining formal acceptance from your project sponsor to officially complete the project?

3. In this case, what might constitute formal acceptance?

4. What types of documentation or computer files should you store in the project archives?

A Guide to the Project Management Body of Knowledge (PMBOK® Guide) – Fifth Edition, Project Management Institute (PMI)®, Project Management Professional (PMP)®, and Certified Associate in Project Management (CAPM)® are registered trademarks of Project Management Institute, Inc. - Version 2.1 Published September 30, 2014

Lesson 12: Closing a Project | Topic A

TOPIC B

Close Procurements

You and your project team have successfully carried out your project plan, produced work results, and controlled the project's performance baselines. You also need to close any contracts with service providers and sellers who contracted for part of the project. In this topic, you'll examine the Close Procurements process and close the necessary contracts.

A Guide to the Project Management Body of Knowledge (PMBOK® Guide) – Fifth Edition, Project Management Institute, Inc., 2013, pg. 386-387

The following data flow diagram illustrates how the Close Procurements process relates to the other project management processes.

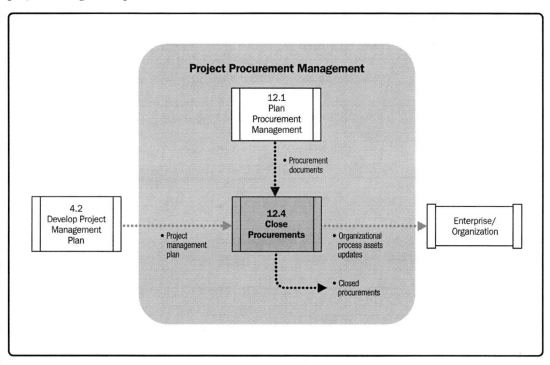

Figure 12-3: The Close Procurements process data flow diagram.

A Guide to the Project Management Body of Knowledge (PMBOK® Guide) – Fifth Edition, Project Management Institute, Inc., 2013, p. 387

The Close Procurements Process

The *close procurements process* ensures that each procurement is complete and documents project agreements and related documentation for future reference on new projects. It also involves administrative activities such as finalizing open claims, updating records to reflect final results, and archiving this information for future use. Each contract needs to be reviewed to ensure compliance to contract terms. Early termination of a contract needs to be evaluated and agreed upon.

A Guide to the Project Management Body of Knowledge (PMBOK® Guide) – Fifth Edition, Project Management Institute, Inc., 2013, pg. 386-387

A Guide to the Project Management Body of Knowledge (PMBOK® Guide) – Fifth Edition, Project Management Institute (PMI)®, Project Management Professional (PMP)®, and Certified Associate in Project Management (CAPM)® are registered trademarks of Project Management Institute, Inc. - Version 2.1 Published September 30, 2014

Lesson 12: Closing a Project | *Topic B*

Figure 12-4: The Close Procurements process.

A Guide to the Project Management Body of Knowledge (PMBOK® Guide) – Fifth Edition, Project
Management Institute, Inc., 2013, p. 386

Close Procurements Inputs

Various components provide input to the Close Procurements process.

Input	Description
Project management plan	Includes criteria for fulfillment of procurement contracts (such as outsourcing or equipment rental), and documentation as to whether these contracts have been satisfied.
Procurement documents	Contains information about vendor performances on cost, scope, quality, contract change notes, approved and rejected changes, payment notifications, and claims. These indexed documents are acknowledged and validated for contract closure. The documentation is created when administering project procurements.

A Guide to the Project Management Body of Knowledge (PMBOK® Guide) – Fifth Edition, Project
Management Institute, Inc., 2013, p. 388

Close Procurements Tools and Techniques

There are three tools and techniques used in the Close Procurements process.

Tools & Techniques	Description
Procurement audits	Evaluations of the effectiveness of the seller, as well as the procurement process itself.
Procurement negotiations	The primary goal is the final equitable settlement on all outstanding issues, claims, and disputes by negotiation. If a settlement cannot be agreed to, some form of alternative dispute resolution (ADR), such as mediation or arbitration, may be necessary to resolve the issue. The least desired option is litigation in court.
Records management system	The project manager uses a records management system to manage contract and procurement documentation and records, and archive the project's contract documents.

A Guide to the Project Management Body of Knowledge (PMBOK® Guide) – Fifth Edition, Project
Management Institute, Inc., 2013, pg. 388-389

Procurement Audits

A *procurement audit* is a formal evaluation of both the seller's performance of the contract, and the
effectiveness of the procurement process itself. The goal of the audit is to establish a record that
may be used to shape procurement practices in other contracts for this project, or for other projects.

A Guide to the Project Management Body of Knowledge (PMBOK® Guide) – Fifth Edition, Project Management Institute (PMI)®, Project Management Professional
(PMP)®, and Certified Associate in Project Management (CAPM)® are registered trademarks of Project Management Institute, Inc. - Version 2.1 Published September 30, 2014

Lesson 12: Closing a Project | Topic B

A Guide to the Project Management Body of Knowledge (PMBOK® Guide) – Fifth Edition, Project Management Institute, Inc., 2013, p. 388, 552

Elements of Procurement Audits

Procurement audits seek to answer several questions about the procurement process:

- Were the seller's responses in bids or proposals useful in conducting pre-contract assessments for consistency and compliance with rules and standards?
- Were the contract specifications completed as specified, and were all terms and conditions met?
- Was the quality, timeliness, and cost acceptable?
- Were the seller's project management, contract management, financial management, and communications management practices acceptable?
- Was the seller able to accommodate requested changes?
- Was the seller ensuring conformance during process audits?
- Were the members of the seller's staff acceptable? Did any individuals merit special recognition?
- Was there anyone you would not recommend for future assignments?
- Were there areas for improvements?
- What were the lessons learned from this contract?

Procurement Audit Lessons Learned

The lessons learned from a procurement audit can be invaluable information for future contracts. For example, the contract structure or payment terms that seemed appropriate at the start of the contract may have acted as disincentives to performance during the contract itself. By including as much anecdotal detail in the lessons learned as possible, you help others in the organization apply the learning to their situations.

Close Procurements Outputs

There are two outputs from the Close Procurements process.

Output	Description
Closed procurements	Usually, the contract spells out the terms for contract acceptance and closure. At minimum, the seller should receive a written notice of contract completion.
Organizational process assets updates	Organizational process assets that could be updated now include project files, project or phase closure documents, and historical information.

A Guide to the Project Management Body of Knowledge (PMBOK® Guide) – Fifth Edition, Project Management Institute, Inc., 2013, pg. 388-389

Organizational Process Assets for Procurement Closure

During the Close Procurements process, there may be some updates to organizational processes. These can include any of the following documents:

- Procurement files are a complete set of indexed contract documentation, including the closed contract, which are archived with the final project files.
- Deliverables acceptance is documentation of formal acceptance of the seller-provided deliverables. This agreement contains requirements for the acceptance criteria for the deliverables and how any nonconforming deliverables will be addressed.
- Lessons learned documentation contains what has been experienced on the project, and any process improvement recommendations to improve future procurements.

A Guide to the Project Management Body of Knowledge (PMBOK® Guide) – Fifth Edition, Project Management Institute (PMI)®, Project Management Professional (PMP)®, and Certified Associate in Project Management (CAPM)® are registered trademarks of Project Management Institute, Inc. - Version 2.1 Published September 30, 2014

Lesson 12: Closing a Project | *Topic B*

A Guide to the Project Management Body of Knowledge (PMBOK® Guide) – Fifth Edition, Project Management Institute, Inc., 2013, p. 389

Closed Procurements

A *closed procurement* is a written notice that is provided from the buyer to the seller once a contract is complete. This is usually documented in the terms and conditions that were specified in the contract and the procurement management plan.

A Guide to the Project Management Body of Knowledge (PMBOK® Guide) – Fifth Edition, Project Management Institute, Inc., 2013, p. 389

Guidelines to Close Procurements

Guidelines to closing procurements are as follows:

*   Ensure that all required products or services were provided by the seller.
*   Make sure that any buyer-furnished property or information was returned to the buyer.
*   Settle any outstanding contracting issues. Are there any claims or investigations pending on this contract?
*   Conduct a procurement audit to identify successes and failures of the procurement process and to evaluate the performance of the seller.
*   Address any outstanding invoices and payments.
*   Archive the complete contract file with the project archives.
*   Provide the seller with formal written notice that the contract has been completed.
*   Communicate that all procurements are closed and update organizational process asset documents as needed.

A Guide to the Project Management Body of Knowledge (PMBOK® Guide) – Fifth Edition, Project Management Institute, Inc., 2013, pg. 386-389

A Guide to the Project Management Body of Knowledge (PMBOK® Guide) – Fifth Edition, Project Management Institute (PMI)®, Project Management Professional (PMP)®, and Certified Associate in Project Management (CAPM)® are registered trademarks of Project Management Institute, Inc. - Version 2.1 Published September 30, 2014

Lesson 12: Closing a Project | Topic B

ACTIVITY 12-2
Closing Procurements

Data Files

C:\095001Data\Closing a Project\Cement_Quote.doc

Scenario

The landscape work package for the 122 East Main project is wrapping up. According to the landscape SOW document, the sidewalk is complete and the landscape architect's plans have been returned. You receive a final invoice from the subcontractor for the concrete work based on their quote for the job (as detailed in the Cement Quote document). You also receive a telephone call from the site manager, who tells you there is excess concrete and other debris left in the driveway and a small crack in the new sidewalk.

---

1. Based on the information you have, can you close out the contract with the subcontractor?

   ○ Yes, the contract has been fulfilled.

   ○ No, the contract has not been fulfilled.

   ○ You cannot determine this until a procurement audit has been completed.

   ○ You cannot determine this until the seller completes a staff evaluation.

2. What would you do to resolve incorrect or unsatisfactory contract work in the situation described in the scenario?

3. The cement contractor returned to the work site and resolved the outstanding contract issues and completed the cement work correctly and satisfactorily. Can you close out the contract? Why or why not?

4. Would you include a seller evaluation in your procurement audit? Why or why not?

A Guide to the Project Management Body of Knowledge (PMBOK® Guide) – Fifth Edition, Project Management Institute (PMI)®, Project Management Professional (PMP)®, and Certified Associate in Project Management (CAPM)® are registered trademarks of Project Management Institute, Inc. - Version 2.1 Published September 30, 2014

Lesson 12: Closing a Project | Topic B

Summary

Closing a project or project phase is the last step in completing a project or phase. Because a project is a unique, one-time activity, the formal closing out of the project is essential. In some cases, without an official close-out of a project or phase, the next related activity, phase, or project will not get started. This happens often when there are multiple projects managed within a program.

What steps do you plan to take to improve the project closure process in the future?

Why is collecting and documenting lessons learned an important activity?

Note: Check your LogicalCHOICE Course screen for opportunities to interact with your classmates, peers, and the larger LogicalCHOICE online community about the topics covered in this course or other topics you are interested in. From the Course screen you can also access available resources for a more continuous learning experience.

A Guide to the Project Management Body of Knowledge (PMBOK® Guide) – Fifth Edition, Project Management Institute (PMI)®, Project Management Professional (PMP)®, and Certified Associate in Project Management (CAPM)® are registered trademarks of Project Management Institute, Inc. - Version 2.1 Published September 30, 2014

Lesson 12: Closing a Project |

Course Follow-Up

Congratulations! You have completed the *Project Management Professional (PMP)® Training: Aligned with PMBOK® Guide Fifth Edition* course!

In this course, you discovered how to manage projects by applying the generally recognized project management knowledge and processes acknowledged by the PMI. You now have the skills and knowledge you need to successfully manage projects in your organization by applying a standards-based approach to most projects, most of the time, across industry groups. You can use these widely recognized tools and techniques on the job to effectively initiate, plan, execute, control and monitor, and close projects across application areas and industries.

 Note: To further explore SkyDrive, you can access the LearnTO **Prepare for the PMP Exam** presentation from the **LearnTO** tile on the LogicalCHOICE Course screen

What's Next?

This course provided you with a solid foundation in the generally recognized good practices on most projects, most of the time, across industries including Construction, Manufacturing, Education, Government, Engineering, Health Services, Consulting, and Information Technology. To expand your breadth of knowledge, consider taking the *Project+* course, which delves into the unique challenges of managing IT projects and may help you to prepare for professional certification in CompTIA Project+. Also consider taking both *Microsoft® Project 2013: Part 1* and *Microsoft® Project 2013: Part 2* to expand on your experience using project management tools.

You can also consider taking the following Logical Operations courses to better equip yourself with conducting business in today's world of technology:

- *iPad® for Business Use*
- *Microsoft® Windows® 8 Tablet for Business Use*

PMP® Certification Mapping

Project Management Professional (PMP)® Certification: PMBOK® Guide Fifth Edition maps directly to the objectives of the PMP® Certification Exam and aligns to the Knowledge Areas and Project Management Process Groups outlines in the *PMBOK® Guide Fifth Edition.* The following table lists the project management tasks that will be assessed on the PMP Certification Exam and where they are covered in this course.

PMP® Certification Objective	Covered In
1 INTRODUCTION	
1.1 Purpose of the PMBOK® Guide	Topic 1-A
1.2 What is a Project?	Topic 1-A
1.3 What is Project Management?	Topic 1-A
1.4 Relationships Among Portfolio Management, Program Management, Project Management, and Organizational Project Management	Topic 1-A
1.5 Relationship Between Project Management, Operations Management, and Organizational Strategy	Topic 1-B
1.6 Business Value	Topic 1-B
1.7 Role of the Project Manager	Topic 1-A
1.8 Project Manager Body of Knowledge	Topic 1-A
2 ORGANIZATIONAL INFLUENCES AND PROJECT LIFE CYCLE	
2.1 Organizational Influences on Project Management	Topic 2-A
2.2 Project Stakeholders and Governance	Topic 2-B
2.3 Project Team	Topic 2-C
2.4 Project Life Cycle	Topic 2-D
3 PROJECT MANAGEMENT PROCESSES	
3.1 Common Project Management Process Interactions	Topic 3-A
3.2 Project Management Process Groups	Topic 3-A
3.3 Initiating Process Group	Topic 3-A
3.4 Planning Process Group	Topic 3-A
3.5 Executing Process Group	Topic 3-A

PMP® Certification Objective	Covered In
3.6 Monitoring and Controlling Process Group	Topic 3-A
3.7 Closing Process Group	Topic 3-A
3.8 Project Information	Topic 3-B
3.9 Role of the Knowledge Areas	Topic 3-A
4 PROJECT INTEGRATION MANAGEMENT	
4.1 Develop Project Charter	Topic 4-A
4.2 Develop Project Management Plan	Topic 5-A
4.3 Direct and Manage Project Work	Topic 9-A
4.4 Monitor and Control Project Work	Topic 10-A
4.5 Perform Integrated Change Control	Topic 10-B
4.6 Close Project or Phase	Topic 12-A
5 PROJECT SCOPE MANAGEMENT	
5.1 Plan Scope Management	Topic 5-B
5.2 Collect Requirements	Topic 5-C
5.3 Define Scope	Topic 5-D
5.4 Create WBS	Topic 5-E
5.5 Validate Scope	Topic 10-C
5.6 Control Scope	Topic 10-D
6 PROJECT TIME MANAGEMENT	
6.1 Plan Schedule Management	Topic 6-A
6.2 Define Activities	Topic 6-B
6.3 Sequence Activities	Topic 6-C
6.4 Estimate Activity Resources	Topic 6-D
6.5 Estimate Activity Durations	Topic 6-E
6.6 Develop Schedule	Topic 6-F
6.7 Control Schedule	Topic 10-E
7 PROJECT COST MANAGEMENT	
7.1 Plan Cost Management	Topic 7-A
7.2 Estimate Costs	Topic 7-B
7.3 Determine Budget	Topic 7-C
7.4 Control Costs	Topic 10-F
8 PROJECT QUALITY MANAGEMENT	
8.1 Plan Quality Management	Topic 7-D
8.2 Perform Quality Assurance	Topic 9-B
8.3 Control Quality	Topic 11-A
9 PROJECT HUMAN RESOURCE MANAGEMENT	

A Guide to the Project Management Body of Knowledge (PMBOK® Guide) – Fifth Edition, Project Management Institute (PMI)®, Project Management Professional (PMP)®, and Certified Associate in Project Management (CAPM)® are registered trademarks of Project Management Institute, Inc. - Version 2.1 Published September 30, 2014

Appendix A : PMP® Certification Mapping |

PMP® Certification Objective	Covered In
9.1 Plan Human Resource Management	Topic 7-E
9.2 Acquire Project Team	Topic 9-C
9.3 Develop Project Team	Topic 9-D
9.4 Manage Project Team	Topic 9-E
10 PROJECT COMMUNICATIONS MANAGEMENT	
10.1 Plan Communications Management	Topic 7-F
10.2 Manage Communications	Topic 9-F
10.3 Control Communications	Topic 11-B
11 PROJECT RISK MANAGEMENT	
11.1 Plan Risk Management	Topic 8-A
11.2 Identify Risks	Topic 8-B
11.3 Perform Qualitative Risk Analysis	Topic 8-C
11.4 Perform Quantitative Risk Analysis	Topic 8-D
11.5 Plan Risk Responses	Topic 8-E
11.6 Control Risks	Topic 11-C
12 PROJECT PROCUREMENT MANAGEMENT	
12.1 Plan Procurement Management	Topic 8-F
12.2 Conduct Procurements	Topic 9-G
12.3 Control Procurements	Topic 11-D
12.4 Close Procurements	Topic 12-B
13 PROJECT STAKEHOLDER MANAGEMENT	
13.1 Identify Stakeholders	Topic 4-B
13.2 Plan Stakeholder Management	Topic 8-G
13.3 Manage Stakeholder Engagement	Topic 9-H
13.4 Control Stakeholder Engagement	Topic 11-E

A Guide to the Project Management Body of Knowledge (PMBOK® Guide) – Fifth Edition, Project Management Institute (PMI)®, Project Management Professional (PMP)®, and Certified Associate in Project Management (CAPM)® are registered trademarks of Project Management Institute, Inc. - Version 2.1 Published September 30, 2014

Appendix A : PMP® Certification Mapping |

Lesson Labs

Lesson labs are provided for certain lessons as additional learning resources for this course. Lesson labs are developed for selected lessons within a course in cases when they seem most instructionally useful as well as technically feasible. In general, labs are supplemental, optional unguided practice and may or may not be performed as part of the classroom activities. Your instructor will consider setup requirements, classroom timing, and instructional needs to determine which labs are appropriate for you to perform, and at what point during the class. If you do not perform the labs in class, your instructor can tell you if you can perform them independently as self-study, and if there are any special setup requirements.

Lesson Lab 1–1
Testing Your Knowledge of Project Management Fundamentals

Scenario

The following questions are meant to test your knowledge of the content from this lesson.

1. The ABC Engineering firm has decided to have a group of subject matter experts gather to plan and execute work to replace their CRM system. It has been decided that the one they have been using does not provide all the information different managers need and there have been many complaints by the users that it is hard to manipulate the information. The data is not stored in such a way to be able to retrieve reports with the information they need, and there are many pieces of information they would like to capture that are missing. The work to replace the old system will require input from many different people throughout the organization. It is expected to take about two years to complete the work, and roll out a new system for use. What is this group of people working on?

   ○ Process

   ○ Database development

   ✓ Project

   ○ Production system

2. Which of the following correctly describes the project management process?

   ○ A linear approach.

   ✓ An iterative, cyclical process that involves back and forth progression through many of the processes and phases.

   ✓ A model which contains the data, activity dependencies and durations, and calculations to determine the project timeline.

   ○ A continuing area including the activities and processes needed to identify, define, combine, unify, and coordinate all of the various processes and project management activities.

A Guide to the Project Management Body of Knowledge (PMBOK® Guide) – Fifth Edition, Project Management Institute (PMI)®, Project Management Professional (PMP)®, and Certified Associate in Project Management (CAPM)® are registered trademarks of Project Management Institute, Inc. - Version 2.1 Published September 30, 2014

Lesson Labs

3. The executive committee was interested in knowing more about the structure of project management as it applied to the organization's strategic objectives and how the projects all fit together. The project manager was asked to make a presentation for the executive committee to explain this. Which of the following would be the correct way that the project manager would go about explaining this structure during the presentation?

○ The relationship of portfolios, programs, and project is such that a portfolio is a collection of projects, programs, sub-portfolios, and operations managed as a group to achieve strategic business results. Programs are grouped in a portfolio and are made up of subprograms, projects, or other work that supports that portfolio. Individual projects that are either within or outside of a program are still considered part of a portfolio.

○ The relationship of portfolios, programs, and project is such that a program is a collection of projects, portfolios, sub-portfolios, and operations managed as a group to achieve strategic business results. Portfolios are grouped in a program and are made up of subprograms, projects, or other work that supports that program. Individual projects that are either within or outside of a program are still considered part of a program.

○ The relationship of portfolios, programs, and project is such that a project is a collection of activities, programs, sub-portfolios, and operations managed as a group to achieve strategic business results. Programs are grouped in a portfolio and are made up of subprograms, projects, or other work that supports that portfolio. Individual programs that are either within or outside of a portfolio are still considered part of a project.

○ The relationship of portfolios, programs, and project is such that a sub-portfolio is a collection of projects, programs, portfolios, and operations managed as a group to achieve strategic business results. Programs are grouped in a portfolio and are made up of subprograms, projects, or other work that supports that portfolio. Individual projects that are either within or outside of a program are still considered part of a portfolio.

4. When viewing the work going on within the company, it was discovered that there were multiple projects being run individually, as well as several that were being managed in a coordinated way along with some other work. It was determined that this should be considered a program. What is a program?

○ A group of programs, projects, and other work such as production, coordinated in such a way to achieve company success.

○ A group of processes needed to produce the products that the company sells in order to achieve the corporate strategic objectives.

○ A group of related portfolios, projects, and other work managed distinctly independently in order to gain the most benefit which would support the corporate strategic objectives.

○ A group of related projects, subprograms, and program activities managed in a coordinated way to achieve benefits not available from managing them individually.

5. The company has many departments including HR, Finance, Legal, Engineering, and also a department that requires project managers to use specific templates, forms, and tools, and conform to governance. What type of department is that?

○ Controlling PMO

○ Directive PMO

○ Supportive PMO

○ Department of Project Management

6. A company was hiring for certain positions. For one position, they were asking for people with skills such as leadership, team building, motivation, conflict management, influencing, negotiating, and several others. This position would require the individual to lead efforts to satisfy specific objectives and complete them in a timely manner within budget constraints. What job position were they trying to fill and what is a description of the skills they were looking for?

○ Head of the PMO and communication skills

○ Project manager and management skills

○ Project manager and interpersonal skills

○ Program manager and business skills

A Guide to the Project Management Body of Knowledge (PMBOK® Guide) – Fifth Edition, Project Management Institute (PMI)®, Project Management Professional (PMP)®, and Certified Associate in Project Management (CAPM)® are registered trademarks of Project Management Institute, Inc. - Version 2.1 Published September 30, 2014

Lesson Labs

7. The Project Management Institute *Code of Ethics and Professional Conduct* describes the ethical and professional behavior expectations of any individual working as a project management professional. What are the values as defined in the *Code of Ethics and Professional Conduct?*

   ○ Being responsible, being respectful, being fair, and being honest

   ○ Being reasonable, being respectful, being fair, and being honest

   ○ Being responsible, being respectful, being fair, and being trustworthy

   ○ Being responsible, being reasonable, being trustworthy, and being honest

8. What is *A Guide to the Project Management Body of Knowledge (PMBOK® Guide) - Fifth Edition*, and what does it provide?

   ○ It is a nationally recognized standard that describes the established norms, methods, processes, and practices that provide a base of best practices for the program management profession. It provides guidelines for managing projects and programs and defines project management concepts. It describes the project management life cycle and its processes, and the project life cycle.

   ○ It is a nationally recognized standard that describes the established norms, methods, processes, and practices that provide a base of best practices for the project management profession. It provides guidelines for managing individual projects and defines project management concepts. It describes the project management life cycle and its processes, and the project life cycle.

   ○ It is a globally recognized standard that describes the established norms, methods, processes, and practices that provide a base of best practices for the program management profession. It provides guidelines for managing projects and programs and defines project management concepts. It describes the project management life cycle and its processes, and the project life cycle.

   ○ It is a globally recognized standard that describes the established norms, methods, processes, and practices that provide a base of best practices for the project management profession. It provides guidelines for managing individual projects and defines project management concepts. It describes the project management life cycle and its processes, and the project life cycle.

9. What is the difference between the PMP certification exam and the CAPM certification exam?

   ○ Passing the CAPM demonstrates that you have the experience, education, and competency to lead and direct projects. The PMP is an entry-level certification for project practitioners with little or no project experience, that demonstrates understanding of the fundamental knowledge, terminology, and processes of effective project management.

   ○ Passing the PMP demonstrates that you have the experience, education, and competency to lead and direct projects. The CAPM is an entry-level certification for project practitioners with little or no project experience, that demonstrates understanding of the fundamental knowledge, terminology, and processes of effective project management.

   ○ Passing the PMP demonstrates that you have the experience, education, and competency to lead and direct programs. The CAPM is an entry-level certification for project practitioners with little or no project experience, that demonstrates understanding of the fundamental knowledge, terminology, and processes of effective project management.

   ○ Passing the PMP demonstrates that you have the experience, education, and competency to lead and direct projects. The CAPM is an entry-level certification for project practitioners with project experience, that demonstrates understanding of the different types of project management theories.

A Guide to the Project Management Body of Knowledge (PMBOK® Guide) – Fifth Edition, Project Management Institute (PMI)®, Project Management Professional (PMP)®, and Certified Associate in Project Management (CAPM)® are registered trademarks of Project Management Institute, Inc. - Version 2.1 Published September 30, 2014

10. A project manager engages with many different people who are interested in the project and has many conversations to find out what is important to these people about the project. By gathering all that information he/she is able to confer with subject matter experts and people who will perform the work to satisfy the project and explain what the desired outcome of the project should be. By performing this work, what role is the project manager playing within the organization?

○ The project manager is the link between what the business must have and the project team that will produce deliverables to meet the project objectives.

○ The project manager is working as a business analyst to develop a detailed list of requirements and a list of activities the team members will perform.

○ The project manager is acting as a leader making decisions about which requirements should be included in the work the team members will perform.

○ The project manager is influencing what the people are asking for from the project and what strategic objectives they want satisfied, so that the work the team members will perform is acceptable to them. Therefore, increasing their skills and knowledge as a result of the project.

A Guide to the Project Management Body of Knowledge (PMBOK® Guide) – Fifth Edition, Project Management Institute (PMI)®, Project Management Professional (PMP)®, and Certified Associate in Project Management (CAPM)® are registered trademarks of Project Management Institute, Inc. - Version 2.1 Published September 30, 2014

Lesson Lab 2-1
Testing Your Knowledge of Project Management and the Organization

Scenario

The following questions are meant to test your knowledge of the content from this lesson.

---

1. The project manager is busy looking for the appropriate people to add to the staff for the new project. There are several types of work skills that will be needed for the project and he wants to be sure that the best people with each skill will be assigned to the project. To do this, he is meeting with several department heads to discuss the timing of the project and the possible availability and assignment of certain individuals to the project. He is using his influencing interpersonal skills to convince these department heads to assign the best person that they supervise to the project. What organizational structure is the project manager working within?

   - ☑ Functional
   - ○ Strong matrix
   - ○ Projectized
   - ○ Hybrid

2. The project manager is working for a company where there are many project managers and they all share the resources between projects as needed, and there are no distinct departments in which people work. The people will complete their work on one project and then be assigned to another project, and possibly a different project manager to whom they report. What organizational structure does this represent?

   - ○ Functional
   - ☒ Weak matrix
   - ☑ Projectized
   - ○ Hybrid

3. A team member is trying to balance their workload and is not sure of the priorities of her assignments. In order to determine what work needs to be completed first, she schedules a meeting with both her functional manager and the project manager to discuss the matter and get help in determining this. What organizational structure does this represent?

   - ○ Functional
   - ☑ Balanced matrix
   - ○ Projectized
   - ○ Hybrid

4. **For this project, the team may develop its own set of operating procedures, and operate outside the standard formalized reporting structure during the project. What organizational structure does this represent?**

    ○ Functional

    ○ Composite

    ○ Projectized

    ○ Matrix

5. **Early in the establishment of the project, the project manager spends some time looking for historical data that might be helpful in planning the new project. She is looking for examples of project documents in similar projects that have been completed, that she might be able to use as templates for the new project. She is also looking for information about established processes and procedures that will help the project run more smoothly. What is the term used to define these?**

    ○ Organizational process assets

    ○ Enterprise environmental factors

    ○ Progressive elaboration

    ○ Organizational project management

6. **Which of the following would not be a list of project stakeholders?**

    ○ Sponsor, project manager, team members, people who have an interest in the deliverable

    ○ Customers, business partners, sellers

    ○ People who will benefit from a successful outcome of the project, functional managers, other departments who are impacted by the project

    ○ Individuals who are not assigned to the project as team members, end users of other products, sellers who were not selected

7. **What provides the structure, processes, decision-making models, and tools for the project manager and team to manage the project?**

    ○ Project governance

    ○ Project overhead

    ○ Senior management

    ○ Enterprise environmental factors

8. **The project manager is trying to determine who to include, how long people will be involved, if anyone will be part-time or full-time, who has knowledge of specific subjects, and who has unique skills that the project will need. What is the project manager working on?**

    ○ Project team composition

    ○ Project team development

    ○ Project team building

    ○ Project stakeholders

9. **A project is being planned, and by looking at the type of work being done, the planning team can see that there are distinct stages of work that must be defined and moved through in a sequential manner. They intend to begin with a feasibility phase, followed by a design phase, and then build and test. By determining all of this, what is being determined?**

    ○ Project life cycle

    ○ Project performance criteria

    ○ Project schedule

    ○ Project management plan

A Guide to the Project Management Body of Knowledge (PMBOK® Guide) – Fifth Edition, Project Management Institute (PMI)®, Project Management Professional (PMP)®, and Certified Associate in Project Management (CAPM)® are registered trademarks of Project Management Institute, Inc. - Version 2.1 Published September 30, 2014

10. Which of the following is true regarding project risk and the cost of changes?
    - ○ At the end, risk is high and the cost of changes is high.
    - ○ At the beginning, risk is low and the cost of changes is high.
    - ○ At the beginning, risk is high and the cost of changes is low.
    - ○ At the beginning risk is well-defined, and at the end the cost of changes is undetermined.

11. A project manager is working on the project plan with the planning team of subject matter experts. While reviewing how the work will be laid out, they discover that the project contains phases that start prior to the previous phase ending. What does this mean?
    - ○ The phase to phase relationship in this case is overlapping.
    - ○ There will be a need to have more resources available than originally planned.
    - ○ There is potentially less risk and less rework involved.
    - ○ This phase to phase relationship reduces the level of uncertainty.

12. As the project moves along in time, there are many instances where successive layers of detail are added to the plans as the project progresses. That is because you learn more about the project the further you get in to it. What is the term that define this process?
    - ○ Precedence relationship
    - ○ Hammock activities
    - ○ Start to finish relationships
    - ○ Progressive elaboration

13. Which of the following is the preferred cycle when the project outcomes are well understood and known?
    - ○ Iterative
    - ○ Rolling wave
    - ○ Predictive
    - ○ Adaptive

14. A project manager and his planning team are trying to determine the type of cycle for the new project. They know that there will be rapid, high levels of change and ongoing stakeholder involvement in the project. Which type of cycle should they consider establishing to have the most control of this particular project?
    - ○ Predictive
    - ○ Iterative
    - ○ Rolling wave
    - ○ Adaptive

15. Which of the following cycles is best when there is a highly flexible, interactive, adaptive organization where project outcomes are realized while the project work is being completed, not at the beginning of the project?
    - ○ Predictive
    - ○ Iterative
    - ○ Rolling wave
    - ○ Agile

A Guide to the Project Management Body of Knowledge (PMBOK® Guide) – Fifth Edition, Project Management Institute (PMI)®, Project Management Professional (PMP)®, and Certified Associate in Project Management (CAPM)® are registered trademarks of Project Management Institute, Inc. - Version 2.1 Published September 30, 2014

Lesson Lab 3–1

Testing Your Knowledge of Working with Project Management Processes

Scenario

The following questions are meant to test your knowledge of the content from this lesson.

---

1. The project has been going along fairly smoothly as the team is performing the project work, but something in quality control indicates that a change needs to be made. Once the change is approved, the project plan has to be updated to reflect that change, and then the team will continue to execute work based on the new plan. What does this scenario describe?

   - ○ Project management process group interactions
   - ○ A poorly planned project because changes should not be needed once it is in execution
   - ○ The end of a phase and the beginning of the next phase
   - ○ The change control process

2. The initial scope of a new project or phase is defined and financial resources are committed. Internal and external stakeholders are identified and the project manager is selected. What project management phase does this represent?

   - ○ Planning and organizational process assets
   - ○ Initiation and enterprise environmental factors
   - ○ Initiation and charter
   - ○ Feasibility and scope statement

3. Currently, the total scope of the project is established, the objectives are defined and refined, and a course of action to obtain the project objectives is being developed. What project management process group does this represent and what is one of the major outputs?

   - ○ Planning and the project management plan
   - ○ Planning and the charter
   - ○ Initiating and the budget
   - ○ Designing and the project schedule

4. The project manager is involved in coordinating people and resources, and managing stakeholder expectations; and the team is performing the activities of the project based on the project management plan. What project management process group does this represent and what is one of the major outputs?

   - ○ Planning and change requests
   - ○ Execution and deliverables
   - ○ Execution and communication problems
   - ○ Monitoring and controlling, and change requests

A Guide to the Project Management Body of Knowledge (PMBOK® Guide) – Fifth Edition, Project Management Institute (PMI)®, Project Management Professional (PMP)®, and Certified Associate in Project Management (CAPM)® are registered trademarks of Project Management Institute, Inc. - Version 2.1 Published September 30, 2014

Lesson Labs

5. At this time, project performance is measured, tracked, reviewed, and the project manager is orchestrating the progress and performance of the project, identifying areas in which changes to the plan are needed, and initiating those changes. What project management process group does this represent and what is one of the major outputs?

   ○ Executing and deliverables

   ○ Monitor and controlling, and deliverables

   ⊙ Monitor and controlling, and change requests

   ○ Implementation and change requests

6. The project work is complete and before the resources are released, the project manager asks them to collect and document lessons learned; and then they have a party to celebrate their success. What project management process group does this represent and what is not one of the major outputs?

   ⊗ Closing and final product

   ○ Closing and phase completion

   ○ Closing and completed contracts

   ⊙ Closing and change requests

7. Which knowledge area is concerned with developing a project plan as a result of a project charter, and controlling the work being done while executing that work, making sure changes consider all constraints and that everything is finalized in closing?

   ⊙ Integration

   ○ Scope

   ○ Implementation

   ⊗ Change control

8. The project team is busy performing the work of the project. The project manager is given a report indicating the work is satisfactory and the quality being obtained meets the requirements of the original scope statement. What process group is this?

   ⊙ Monitor and control

   ○ Execution

   ○ Closing

   ○ Testing

9. The quality report indicates that the original standards that were chosen to build the project were not appropriate and the project manager needs to determine different standards. What process group does this indicate the project manager will be engaged in?

   ○ Execution

   ⊙ Planning

   ○ Monitor and Control

   ⊗ Closing

A Guide to the Project Management Body of Knowledge (PMBOK® Guide) – Fifth Edition, Project Management Institute (PMI)®, Project Management Professional (PMP)®, and Certified Associate in Project Management (CAPM)® are registered trademarks of Project Management Institute, Inc. - Version 2.1 Published September 30, 2014

10. The project team is using the project plan and the resulting schedule to work on project activities. Their work is being measured to ensure it meets requirements. Some aspects of the original plan need to be adjusted, which results in a new and updated project management plan. The team then continues to work, but now they do so according to the updated plan. What does this situation represent?

- ○ A failure to plan correctly in the first place.
- ○ The team members are underperforming.
- ○ The futility of wasting time planning.
- ○ The iterative relationship between planning, executing, and monitor and control.

11. During what process group does the schedule and budget get created and what are the outputs as a result of doing this work?

- ○ Initiating and a charter
- ○ Planning and change requests
- ○ Planning and a schedule and budget
- ○ Initiating and an authorized project

12. The project manager and team are working with activities, their durations, and dependencies. Which knowledge area is being addressed?

- ○ Time
- ○ Scope
- ○ Execution
- ○ Quality

13. When the project manager is discussing what will be included in the project with the project planning team, she includes aspects of project management, as well as the product of the project. What knowledge area is being addressed?

- ○ Monitor and Control
- ○ Execution
- ○ Quality
- ○ Scope

14. The project team is discussing several things they are worried about that could impact the success of the project. They are trying to come up with ideas as to how to minimize those potential problems. What knowledge area is being addressed?

- ○ Risk
- ○ Schedule
- ○ Monitor and Control
- ○ Initiation

15. The project manager is meeting with members of the executive committee to gain their insights as to some of the people who are interested in the project. He wants to know what they think is the best way to manage those people and who of them are the most influential. What knowledge area is being addressed?

- ○ Risk management
- ○ Stakeholder engagement
- ○ Communication
- ○ Initiation

A Guide to the Project Management Body of Knowledge (PMBOK® Guide) – Fifth Edition, Project Management Institute (PMI)®, Project Management Professional (PMP)®, and Certified Associate in Project Management (CAPM)® are registered trademarks of Project Management Institute, Inc. - Version 2.1 Published September 30, 2014

Lesson Labs

Lesson Lab 4–1
Testing Your Knowledge of Initiating a Project

Scenario

The following questions are meant to test your knowledge of the content from this lesson.

---

1. The project manager has been meeting with the project sponsor to discuss various aspects of the project. As a result, the project manager has created a document and the sponsor has signed it. This document states the high-level requirements, summary budget, and cost. What is this document and what are some of its inputs?

   - ○ Charter, enterprise environmental factors, organizational process assets, business case, project SOW

   - ○ Scope statement, enterprise environmental factors, organizational process assets, business case, project SOW

   - ○ Business case, enterprise environmental factors, organizational process assets, risk register

   - ○ Project SOW, enterprise environmental factors, organizational process assets, business case, charter

2. The project manager and the sponsor need to create the project charter. The project manager wants to be sure they are stating the objectives of the project correctly, so that the charter is effective in pointing the project in the right direction. She suggests that they review the feasibility study that was prepared in order to validate the benefits of the project. What is the project manager referring to?

   - ○ The project scope statement

   - ○ The project SOWs

   - ○ The business case

   - ○ The summary project milestone schedule

3. At a very early stage in the project, the project manager is reviewing the document that is based on business needs, product, or service requirements for a particular project. He is using this information to clarify what needs to be stated on the project charter. Which document is being reviewed?

   - ○ The project scope statement

   - ○ The project SOWs

   - ○ The business case

   - ○ The summary project milestone schedule

A Guide to the Project Management Body of Knowledge (PMBOK® Guide) – Fifth Edition, Project Management Institute (PMI)®, Project Management Professional (PMP)®, and Certified Associate in Project Management (CAPM)® are registered trademarks of Project Management Institute, Inc. - Version 2.1 Published September 30, 2014

Lesson Labs

4. A financial review of a marketing plan for a new product indicates that an investment of $750,000 in development could result in potential profits of $2,000,000+ if the estimated demand of 100,000 units of the product is sold over the potential life span of the product in the near future. This kind of information might be used as a basis to determine if a new project should be initiated to develop a prototype, and then move into a new product development project. Where would this information most likely be found by a project manager and a sponsor who are trying to determine which projects are the most viable for the organization to initiate?

- ○ The business case
- ○ The project scope statement
- ○ The project SOWs
- ○ The summary projects budget

5. When a project is initiated with external customers or parties, a formal contract agreement is needed so both parties are on the same page about project information. Under what category are letters of intent considered?

- ○ Contracts
- ○ Project SOW
- ○ Business case
- ○ Agreements

6. The project manager has established several meetings with individuals who have specific knowledge about certain aspects of a potential project while working on establishing the project charter. Some of them are consultants, others are subject matter experts, and others are part of the organization's PMO. The sponsor is unclear as to why the project manager is so busy engaging in all these meetings. Why is the project manager scheduling all these meetings? Who are the people with whom he is scheduling the meetings? What is the project manager using by doing this?

- ○ The project manager wants to talk with these people to gain their buy-in and support for the project. These people are stakeholders, and the project manager is using stakeholder analysis as a technique to engage stakeholders.
- ○ The project manager wants to talk with these people to understand why they are requesting the project. These people are the business units who want the project, and the project manager is using facilitation techniques.
- ○ The project manager wants to talk with these people to help evaluate the inputs to the project charter. These people are experts, and the project manager is using expert judgment as a technique to develop the project charter.
- ○ The project manager wants to talk with these people to be sure the project maps to one of the organization's strategic goals. These people are members of the PMO and the executive committee, and the project manager is using communication skills.

7. In order to clearly understand what the project should accomplish, the project manager asked the sponsor who the project stakeholders are while developing the project charter. Which stakeholders will the sponsor relate to the project manager during this time frame, and what other times during the project will the project manager try to figure out who the stakeholders might be?

- ○ The sponsor will relate the initial high-level stakeholders that are known at this time to the project manager, and the project manager will try to find more stakeholders all throughout the project life cycle.
- ○ The sponsor will relate the initial high-level stakeholders that are known at this time to the project manager, and the project manager will try to find more stakeholders during the planning phase.
- ○ The sponsor will relate all stakeholders that are going to be affected by the project to the project manager, and the project manager will try to find more stakeholders all throughout the project life cycle.
- ○ The sponsor will relate all stakeholders that are going to affect the project to the project manager, and the project manager will try to find more stakeholders as changes in the project occur.

A Guide to the Project Management Body of Knowledge (PMBOK® Guide) – Fifth Edition, Project Management Institute (PMI)®, Project Management Professional (PMP)®, and Certified Associate in Project Management (CAPM)® are registered trademarks of Project Management Institute, Inc. - Version 2.1 Published September 30, 2014

Lesson Labs

8. **What is one of the most important reasons for issuing a project charter for every project that is undertaken within an organization?**

    ○ To assign the project manager

    ○ To state the high-level stakeholders and risks

    ○ To make the project official

    ○ To be sure the project aligns with the goals of the organization

9. **Which of the following choices best defines and provides examples of stakeholders?**

    ○ Stakeholders are people who may affect or be affected by the objectives of a project. Examples are the customer, the functional managers, the team members, and the general public.

    ○ Stakeholders are people who have submitted requirements for the project. Examples are the sponsor, the customer, and the project manager.

    ○ Stakeholders are people who may affect the objectives of a project. Examples are the customer, the functional managers, and the general public.

    ○ Stakeholders are people who may be affected by the objectives of a project. Examples are the customer, the team members, and the sponsor.

10. **The project manager is asking for expert judgment input, and is involved in several meetings as part of the process of gathering and analyzing data about people whose interests should be considered and taken into account during the life cycle of the project. What is the project manager using?**

    ○ Stakeholder assessment

    ○ Tools and techniques to identify stakeholders

    ○ Develop project charter

    ○ A review of the organizational process assets

11. **The project manager has gathered information regarding the identification, assessment, and classification of people who are interested in the project, have business expectations for the project, and can also influence the progress of the project. How should all of this information be stored?**

    ○ In a secure location with limited access

    ○ This information needs to be documented in the project charter or SOW

    ○ In a stakeholder register

    ○ This is part of the business case, documenting who wants the project

12. **There are classification models used to document stakeholder analysis results. Which of the following is one type of classification model that might be used for project management stakeholder analysis?**

    ○ Decision trees

    ○ RACI chart

    ○ Power and interest grid

    ○ Stakeholder register

13. Why would the fact that there is a procurement involved in the project to purchase goods or services from external suppliers or vendors impact information included in the Stakeholder Register?

   ○ The people involved in that contract are stakeholders because they can be affected by or can affect the project.

   ○ The fact that there is a procurement would not impact the information in the Stakeholder Register.

   ○ RFPs, IFBs, and RFQs are project documents that should be included in the register.

   ○ Because these are inputs to Stakeholder Analysis, which is an output of Identify Stakeholders.

14. The sponsor is getting annoyed with the project manager during the initiation phase of the project because the project manager is spending a great deal of time in meetings and talking with experts, and researching lessons learned and stakeholder registers from previous projects. The sponsor thinks this is a waste of time and wants to get the project work started as quickly as possible. Why is the project manager claiming that it is important to identify as many stakeholders as possible, as early as possible, and what aspects of the stakeholders is he claiming should be understood and documented?

   ○ The project manager wants to identify stakeholders early so they can't claim no one asked their opinion later on, and he wants to understand and document their interest and influence on the project.

   ○ The project manager wants to identify stakeholders early so their needs and expectations can be met, and he wants to understand and document their interest and influence on the project.

   ○ The project manager wants to identify stakeholders early so their needs and expectations can be met, and he wants to understand and document their position within the organization and how best to communicate with them.

   ○ The project manager wants to identify stakeholders early so they have no excuse as to why they did not submit their requirements, and he wants to understand and document their expectations and roles on the project.

15. The project manager wants to include the following in the project: brainstorming, conflict resolution, problem solving, and meeting management. These are all examples of what?

   ○ Facilitation techniques

   ○ Good project management

   ○ Communication methods

   ○ Ways of getting the stakeholders involved in the project

A Guide to the Project Management Body of Knowledge (PMBOK® Guide) – Fifth Edition, Project Management Institute (PMI)®, Project Management Professional (PMP)®, and Certified Associate in Project Management (CAPM)® are registered trademarks of Project Management Institute, Inc. - Version 2.1 Published September 30, 2014

Lesson Lab 5–1
Testing Your Knowledge of Planning a Project

Scenario

The following questions are meant to test your knowledge of the content from this lesson.

---

1. The project manager is working with people to help pull together all the information that will be needed to manage and control the project. This includes the subsidiary plans including baselines, the life cycle and processes, as well as a change management plan. What are these and what do they comprise?

   - ○ They are the components of the overall project management plan.
   - ○ They are inputs to the project charter.
   - ○ They are inputs to the project schedule plan.
   - ○ They are the output of develop project management plan.

2. What are subsidiary plans for the project management plan?

   - ○ Schedule, cost, and quality plans that will become the project management plan
   - ○ Individual knowledge area plans that are the output of the project management plan
   - ○ Individual knowledge area plans that will be integrated to become the project management plan
   - ○ The objectives of each knowledge area that must be met in order for the project to be declared successful

3. Once all the project plans were completed and the work began, the project manager realized that some of the decisions made during the resource planning were not correct and he will need to reassess and adjust the resources being used on the project. This will result in changes to the HR management plan. When that happens, what else will also occur?

   - ○ The cost will go up.
   - ○ The schedule will be lengthened.
   - ○ The sponsor will need to be involved in order to approve the change in resources.
   - ○ The overall project management plan will change.

A Guide to the Project Management Body of Knowledge (PMBOK® Guide) – Fifth Edition, Project Management Institute (PMI)®, Project Management Professional (PMP)®, and Certified Associate in Project Management (CAPM)® are registered trademarks of Project Management Institute, Inc. - Version 2.1 Published September 30, 2014

Lesson Labs

4. Through the life of the project, while the team members were doing the work, the customer made several requests of the team members who were working closely with them to ensure the requirements were satisfied to their specifications, as stated in the project charter and scope statement. Occasionally, the customer asked the team members to make some "minor adjustments." The team members, concerned with the success of the project, were willing to oblige the customer and performed the extra work necessary for these adjustments in an effort to keep the customer happy. What is this called and what are the potential outcomes?

   ○ Scope enhancement, which can result in decreased cost and schedule.

   ○ Scope creep, which can result in cost and schedule overruns.

   ○ Delighting the customer, which can result in performance awards.

   ○ Progressive elaboration, which can result in more information as the project develops.

5. What does configuration management address?

   ○ Activities such as keeping track of all the changes the customer makes to the product plans.

   ○ The way in which the product is configured for use to satisfy the end users and how that develops as it is being built.

   ○ Documentation of the management of configuring the product for use and how changes to the product will be incorporated into the overall project plan.

   ○ Activities such as how version control of project documents and changes to the product will be initiated, analyzed, and traced.

6. A team member who is new to the organization and working on projects has several questions and asks the project manager to meet with him to discuss these items so he is sure he understands what is going on during the planning process of the project. The project manager is delighted that this new team member is taking so much interest. The first question the team member has is: "What is the basic difference between the project requirements and the project scope?" What would the project manager's response be?

   ○ The requirements are like a wish list of everything the stakeholders would like to get from the project, and the scope is a subset of those requirements, prioritized and assessed for value to the project.

   ○ There is no real difference because what the stakeholders require to be included in the project, is what becomes the scope statement, simply re-arranged into the format of the WBS.

   ○ The scope is like a wish list of everything the stakeholders would like to get from the project and the requirements are a subset of the scope, prioritized and assessed for value to the project.

   ○ The requirements are what is stated on the project charter and is the list that is used to format the scope and build the WBS.

7. While going through all the project requirements, the planning team tries to plot them on a matrix in order to link them to the business and project objectives and to justify each. What is this matrix referred to and what purpose would it serve during the rest of the project?

   ○ This is a requirements classification table to help organize and divide the requirements which can then later be used to determine which should be included in the scope.

   ○ This is a requirements traceability matrix which can be used to verify that the output of each work package meets the quality metric as stated on the project scope statement.

   ○ This is a requirements traceability matrix which can be used to track requirements' progress through the life cycle and confirm that they have been met at project closure.

   ○ This is a requirements management plan which can be used to determine the cost and schedule of the project.

A Guide to the Project Management Body of Knowledge (PMBOK® Guide) – Fifth Edition, Project Management Institute (PMI)®, Project Management Professional (PMP)®, and Certified Associate in Project Management (CAPM)® are registered trademarks of Project Management Institute, Inc. - Version 2.1 Published September 30, 2014

Lesson Labs

8. The project manager and sponsor are actively engaged with stakeholders to determine their needs for the project. What is this process referred to as and why is it important?

    ○ This is called collect requirements. It is important as it is the foundation of all the rest of the plans. If this is not done well, all the rest of the plans will be incorrect.

    ○ This is called requirements classification. It is important as the classifications determine how the rest of the project will be assessed.

    ○ This is called stakeholder analysis. It is important to know who the stakeholders are as they are the recipients of the project output.

    ○ This is called requirements communication plan. It is important for all the stakeholders to have good communication with the project manager, so that he will know who to contact regarding changes to the scope.

9. What is the name of organized working sessions held by project managers to determine what a project's requirements are and to get all stakeholders together to agree on the project's outcomes? What are some examples?

    ○ Focus groups: JAD, VOC, QDF

    ○ Facilitated workshops: JAD, VOC, QFD

    ○ Group creativity techniques: JID, DFQ, VOC

    ○ Decision-making techniques: JAD, VOC, QFD

10. In order to make sure that best practices have been planned into the project and to generate ideas for improvement, the project manager is engaged in comparing processes and operations to those of other comparable projects of similar corporations. What is the project manager engaged in?

    ○ Observations

    ○ Benchmarking

    ○ Mind mapping

    ○ Plurality decision making technique

11. Group decision-making is a method used by a group to come to a decision. Which method is defined when everyone in the group agrees on the course of action to take?

    ○ Unanimity

    ○ Majority

    ○ Plurality

    ○ Dictatorship

12. Group decision-making is a method used by a group to come to a decision. Which method is defined when the largest batch of individuals within a group agrees on a decision?

    ○ Unanimity

    ○ Majority (more than half)

    ○ Plurality

    ○ Dictatorship

13. The project manager needs a structure to work within when determining a project's work that includes project scope, quality requirements, project deliverables, constraints, and assumptions of the project work. What part of the project plan is this?

    ○ The project charter

    ○ The project WBS

    ○ The project requirements matrix

    ○ The project scope statement

A Guide to the Project Management Body of Knowledge (PMBOK® Guide) – Fifth Edition, Project Management Institute (PMI)®, Project Management Professional (PMP)®, and Certified Associate in Project Management (CAPM)® are registered trademarks of Project Management Institute, Inc. - Version 2.1 Published September 30, 2014

Lesson Labs

14. A team member who is new to the organization and working on projects has several questions and asks the project manager to meet with him to discuss these items so he is sure he understands what is going on during the planning process of the project. The project manager is delighted that this new team member is taking so much interest. The second question the team member has is: "What is the difference between the project charter and the project scope statement?" What would the project manager's response be?

- ○ The project charter includes more high-level course objectives and goals, whereas the project scope statement focuses on the actual outcomes of the project.
- ○ The project scope statement includes more high-level course objectives and goals, whereas the project charter focuses on the actual outcomes of the project.
- ○ The project charter includes more detailed-level course objectives and goals, whereas the project scope statement focuses on the cost, quality, and schedule.
- ○ The project charter includes the stakeholder requirements, whereas the project scope statement focuses on the objectives of the project.

15. Product analysis is part of which process?
- ○ Define Scope Inputs
- ○ Define Scope Tools and Techniques
- ○ Alternatives Generation
- ○ Define Scope Outputs

16. Lateral thinking, brainstorming, and the Delphi technique are all types of what kind of method?
- ○ Nominal Group Techniques
- ○ Product Analysis
- ○ Alternatives Generation
- ○ Group Creativity Techniques

17. What is the purpose of decomposing the project work into a hierarchical WBS structure?
- ○ To create smaller more manageable chunks which can be better estimated for cost, time, and resources, and help control the project
- ○ To create a sequence of work that can be used to track progress through the life of the project, ensuring the project deadline can be met
- ○ To select the requirements that will be included in the project to the satisfaction of the stakeholders and the project sponsor
- ○ To draw out potential options to complete the work so the stakeholders and the team members agree on the methods used

18. The project manager and the team would like a way to easily track individual WBS components, which they agree would be especially helpful in the areas of performance, reporting, and cost. In order to accomplish this, what will they implement?
- ○ WBS dictionary
- ○ Code of accounts
- ○ Requirements matrix
- ○ Contingency reserve

A Guide to the Project Management Body of Knowledge (PMBOK® Guide) – Fifth Edition, Project Management Institute (PMI)®, Project Management Professional (PMP)®, and Certified Associate in Project Management (CAPM)® are registered trademarks of Project Management Institute, Inc. - Version 2.1 Published September 30, 2014

Lesson Labs

19. The project manager is leading a series of meetings with subject matter experts and the planning team in order to divide and subdivide the project scope into smaller more manageable pieces. What process are they involved in?

   ○ Product analysis

   ○ Mind mapping

   ○ Assemblage

   ○ Decomposition

20. A team member who is new to the organization and working on projects has several questions and asks the project manager to meet with him to discuss these items so he is sure he understands what is going on during the planning process of the project. The project manager is delighted that this new team member is taking so much interest. The third question the team member has is: "What is a work breakdown structure and what is the level I need to be most concerned with?" What would the project manager's response be?

   ○ A WBS defines the total scope of work required to complete the project. The individual components are at the lowest level of the hierarchy and are referred to as work packages.

   ○ A WBS defines the requirements requested for the project. The individual components are at the highest level of the hierarchy and are referred to as work packages.

   ○ A WBS defines the total scope of work required to complete the project. None of the components of the hierarchy concern individual team members.

   ○ A WBS is a way to confirm that the scope of work will satisfy the requirements of the stakeholders. You need to be concerned with the top level, which is where the work to be done is defined in work packages.

A Guide to the Project Management Body of Knowledge (PMBOK® Guide) – Fifth Edition, Project Management Institute (PMI)®, Project Management Professional (PMP)®, and Certified Associate in Project Management (CAPM)® are registered trademarks of Project Management Institute, Inc. - Version 2.1 Published September 30, 2014

Lesson Labs

Lesson Lab 6-1
Testing Your Knowledge of Planning for Project Time Management

Scenario

The following questions are meant to test your knowledge of the content from this lesson.

1. What is an element of project work that requires action to produce a deliverable?
   - ○ Work package
   - ○ Requirement
   - ⦿ Activity
   - ○ Milestone

2. Which of the following defines characteristics of activities?
   - ⦿ It has an expected duration, it consumes budget and/or human resources, and it is named in verb-noun format.
   - ○ It organizes the work to be done by control account, and provides the basis for estimating cost.
   - ○ It is the lowest level of the WBS, and it consumes budget and/or human resources.
   - ○ It has an expected duration, it is the lowest level of the WBS, and it is named in noun-verb format.

3. What lays the foundation for estimating, scheduling, executing, and monitoring and controlling the project work?
   - ○ Tasks
   - ○ Work packages
   - ○ Requirements
   - ⦿ Activities

4. What is a form of progressive elaboration where near-term work is defined at a detailed level, and future work is left at a higher level?
   - ○ Decomposition
   - ○ Task elaboration
   - ⦿ Rolling Wave Planning
   - ○ Rotation Planning

5. What is the 8/80 rule?
   - ⦿ A work package should include at least 8 but not more than 80 hours effort to complete.
   - ○ A work package should include effort that is under 8 and more than 80 hours to complete.
   - ○ That 8% of the people cause 80% of the problems.
   - ○ A guideline for planning work packages that is very useful in large projects.

A Guide to the Project Management Body of Knowledge (PMBOK® Guide) – Fifth Edition, Project Management Institute (PMI)®, Project Management Professional (PMP)®, and Certified Associate in Project Management (CAPM)® are registered trademarks of Project Management Institute, Inc. - Version 2.1 Published September 30, 2014

Lesson Labs

6. A team member who is new to the organization and working on projects has several questions and asks the project manager to meet with him to discuss these items so he is sure he understands what is going on during the planning process of the project. The project manager is delighted that this new team member is taking so much interest. One of the questions the team member has is: "What is the project schedule network diagram?" What would the project manager's response be?

   ○ A hierarchical breakdown of the work required to satisfy the requirements.

   ○ A graphical representation of the sequence of project activities and the dependencies among them.

   ○ It is the lowest level of the WBS, and it consumes budget and/or human resources.

   ○ A visual depiction of the product scope, showing a business system and how people will interact with it.

7. Which of the following correctly defines the Precedence Diagramming method?

   ○ Activities are represented as nodes and are graphically linked together by their relationships

   ○ Activities are represented as arrows and are graphically linked together by their relationships

   ○ Activities are represented as circles and are graphically linked together by their relationships

   ○ Activities are represented as icons and are graphically linked together by their hierarchical relationship from the WBS

8. There are four types of logical relationships used in the Precedence Diagramming method. What are they?

   ○ Finish to Finish, Start to Start, Top to Bottom, End to End

   ○ Finish to Start, Start to Finish, Finish to Finish, Start to Start

   ○ End to End, Front to Back, Top to Bottom, Finish to Start

   ○ Start to Finish, Finish to Finish, Bottom to Top, End to End

9. What are the four types of dependencies in a network diagram?

   ○ Incendiary, Mandatory, Required, External

   ○ Required, Discretionary, Variable, Internal

   ○ External, Internal, Written, Unspoken

   ○ Mandatory, External, Internal, Discretionary

10. Which type of dependency is usually determined by the nature of the work, or it may be due to a legal or contract requirement?

    ○ External

    ○ Discretionary

    ○ Mandatory

    ○ Internal

11. Which of the following is the name for the amount of time that needs to pass before the successor activity can begin?

    ○ Lag

    ○ Lead

    ○ Start

    ○ Float

A Guide to the Project Management Body of Knowledge (PMBOK® Guide) – Fifth Edition, Project Management Institute (PMI)®, Project Management Professional (PMP)®, and Certified Associate in Project Management (CAPM)® are registered trademarks of Project Management Institute, Inc. - Version 2.1 Published September 30, 2014

Lesson Labs

12. Which of the following is the correct definition of the critical path?
- ○ The critical path is the fastest path through the network diagram which represents the longest time in which the project can be completed.
- ○ The critical path is the shortest path through the network diagram which represents the longest time in which the project can be completed.
- ○ The critical path is the earliest path through the network diagram which represents the latest time in which the project can be completed.
- ○ The critical path is the longest path through the network diagram which represents the shortest time in which the project can be completed. ✓

13. A team member who is new to the organization and working on projects has several questions and asks the project manager to meet with him to discuss these items so he is sure he understands what is going on during the planning process of the project. The project manager is delighted that this new team member is taking so much interest. One of the questions the team member has is: "If we must complete the software code before we can create the user manual, what type of dependency exists between these two work packages?" What would the project manager's response be?
- ○ Finish to Finish
- ○ Finish to Start ✓
- ○ Start to Finish
- ○ Start to Start

14. Which of the following is the correct PERT formula to estimate duration?
- ○ Duration = (O + (4 x ML) + P) / 6 ✓
- ○ Duration = (O + ML x 4 + P) / 3
- ○ Duration = ML / 6 + (O - P)
- ○ Duration = (O x 4 + ML x 3) + P

15. The project manager and the planning team is developing the project schedule and will use the PERT method to determine project duration. The estimates include the following: Most likely is 180 hours, optimistic is 100 hours, and pessimistic is 200 hours. Which of the following is the correct PERT estimate?
- ○ 160
- ○ 80
- ○ 170 ✓
- ○ 345

$100 + (180 \times 5) + 200$

16. What method allows you to add buffers to accommodate uncertainty and limited resources?
- ○ Critical path
- ○ Resource optimization
- ○ Critical buffering
- ○ Critical chain ✓

17. Which is the correct definition of Fast Tracking?
- ○ Moving critical path activities that you had originally planned to do sequentially, and making them concurrent.
- ○ Shortening the schedule by adding resources or in some other way expediting critical path activities.
- ○ Keeping resource usages at a constant level and avoiding over-allocation.
- ○ Updating non-critical path activities that you had originally planned to do sequentially, and making them concurrent. ✓

A Guide to the Project Management Body of Knowledge (PMBOK® Guide) – Fifth Edition, Project Management Institute (PMI)®, Project Management Professional (PMP)®, and Certified Associate in Project Management (CAPM)® are registered trademarks of Project Management Institute, Inc. - Version 2.1 Published September 30, 2014

Lesson Labs

18. A process that involves expediting critical path activities by spending money is called what?
    - ○ Balancing
    - ○ Maneuvering
    - ○ Crashing
    - ○ Fast Tracking

19. The dependencies and durations for all the project activities are shown in the following table. What is the critical path duration?
    - ○ 15
    - ⊘ 19
    - ○ 21
    - ○ 16

Activity	Predecessor	Duration
X	Start	3
Y	Start	5
Z	Y	2
O	X, Z	6
T	Z, O	1
F	T	3
H	T, O	5
End	H, F	0

20. Based on the following table, how much float is there on activity F?
    - ⊘ 2
    - ○ 11
    - ○ 3
    - ○ 4

Activity	Predecessor	Duration
X	Start	3
Y	Start	5
Z	Y	2
O	X, Z	6
T	Z, O	1
F	T	3
H	T, O	5
End	H, F	0

A Guide to the Project Management Body of Knowledge (PMBOK® Guide) – Fifth Edition, Project Management Institute (PMI)®, Project Management Professional (PMP)®, and Certified Associate in Project Management (CAPM)® are registered trademarks of Project Management Institute, Inc. - Version 2.1 Published September 30, 2014

Lesson Labs

Lesson Lab 7–1

Testing Your Knowledge of Planning Project Budget, Quality, and Communications

Scenario

The following questions are meant to test your knowledge of the content from this lesson.

---

1. A team member who is new to the organization and working on projects has several questions and asks the project manager to meet with him to discuss these items so he is sure he understands what is going on during the planning process of the project. The project manager is delighted that this new team member is taking so much interest. One of the questions the team member has is: "In the projects I worked on at my old company, when we were estimating the costs, we always used the costs of a previous project with similar scope or activities to predict the cost of future activities. You don't seem to be doing that here. What method are we using for cost estimating in this company?" The project manager explained that he is using Parametric Estimating. Which of the following is the method used at the team member's former company, and what is the correct explanation of Parametric?

   ○ Expert Judgment, and a method that focuses on the cost of ensured quality.

   ○ Group Decision Making Techniques, and a method that relies on the statistical relationship that exists between historical information and variables, so as to arrive at an estimate for parameters such as duration and cost.

   ○ Analogous, and a method to use Delphi, brainstorming, and nominal group techniques.

   ○̌ Analogous, and a method that relies on the statistical relationship that exists between historical information and variables, so as to arrive at an estimate for parameters such as duration and cost.

2. What are the three aspects that Earned Value Management considers?

   ○̌ Planned Value, Earned Value, Actual Cost

   ○ Planned Cost, Earned Value, Actual Value

   ○ Value Earned, Planned Cost, Actual Plan

   ○ Planned Value, Earned Cost, Actual Amount

3. What are the three values used in Three-Point Estimate?

   ○ Optimistic, worst-case scenario, a false expectation

   ○ Best-case scenario, worst-case scenario, pre-planned scenario

   ○̌ Most likely, optimistic, pessimistic

   ○ A realistic expectation, a false expectation, an estimate of expectation

A Guide to the Project Management Body of Knowledge (PMBOK® Guide) – Fifth Edition, Project Management Institute (PMI)®, Project Management Professional (PMP)®, and Certified Associate in Project Management (CAPM)® are registered trademarks of Project Management Institute, Inc. - Version 2.1 Published September 30, 2014

Lesson Labs

4. A team member who is new to the organization and working on projects has several questions and asks the project manager to meet with him to discuss these items so he is sure he understands what is going on during the planning process of the project. The project manager is delighted that this new team member is taking so much interest. One of the questions the team member has is: "In projects at my former company, we used the cost as stated on the charter to be our cost estimate for the project. Here you are not doing that. It almost seems like you are disregarding that figure until the planning is done and then you reconcile your figures with the sponsor's on the charter. Why is that?" What would the project manager's response be?

   ○ The rough order of magnitude stated on a charter is usually developed without a basis of detailed data and is often based on very high-level historical data, expert judgment, or a costing model.

   ○ The sponsors have no idea what things cost and they just come up with a number to put something on the charter. They depend on us to come up with the correct budget figures.

   ○ The Rough Order of Magnitude is often used for appropriation purposes and has accuracy of -10% to +25%.

   ○ While the ROM has an accuracy of +/- 35 %, it is used for work that is further in the future.

5. The sponsor provides many pieces of information to the project manager to state on the project charter. One of them is the summary cost estimate. At the time the charter is being developed, what is generally the level of accuracy of the ROM as stated in the charter?

   ○ +/-35%

   ○ -50% to +100%

   ○ -5% to +10%

   ○ +/-15%

6. What are activity cost estimates made up of?

   ○ Supporting data or additional information needed to justify the cost estimates.

   ○ Estimates on probable costs necessary to finish project work including direct costs, labor, materials, equipment, facilities, services, information technology, and contingency reserves.

   ○ Estimates on probable costs necessary to finish project work based on the responsive bids obtained from vendors.

   ○ Estimates on probable costs necessary to finish project work including direct labor, materials, equipment, facilities, services, information technology, contingency reserves, or indirect costs.

7. What is the process to create a project budget?

   ○ Take the ROM and decompose it into the cost of work packages.

   ○ Combine all individual activity cost estimates and aggregate them for the entire project to produce a baseline.

   ○ Estimate costs necessary to finish project work including direct costs, labor, materials, equipment, facilities, services, information technology, and contingency reserves.

   ○ Create an S-curve with cost on the Y axis and time on the X axis.

A Guide to the Project Management Body of Knowledge (PMBOK® Guide) – Fifth Edition, Project Management Institute (PMI)®, Project Management Professional (PMP)®, and Certified Associate in Project Management (CAPM)® are registered trademarks of Project Management Institute, Inc. - Version 2.1 Published September 30, 2014

Lesson Labs

8. The project manager is using the time-phased budget to measure the cost performance. What is that budget called?

    ○ Cost baseline

    ○ Cost estimate

    ○ Rough order of magnitude

    ○ Cost consolidation

9. The project manager has a new team member who seems eager to understand the processes used at this company, since the company he came from used different processes and terminology. The project manager tells the team member to help him with the process of combining activity costs into work package costs and continue to add up through the WBS to achieve a single project cost. What tool or technique are they engaged in?

    ○ Funding limit reconciliation

    ○ Reserve analysis

    ○ Cost aggregation

    ○ Bottom down estimating

10. What is it called when funding limits are in place as a method of adjusting, spending, scheduling, and resource allocation, to regulate the outgoing capital flow and to protect against over-spending?

    ○ Budget control

    ○ Cost aggregation

    ○ Funding limit reconciliation

    ○ Reserve analysis

11. What is a quality system standard that is applicable to any product, service, or process in the world?

    ○ A quality management plan

    ○ Design of experiments

    ○ CMMI

    ○ ISO 9000 series

12. When discussing the quality of the project with a new team member, the project manager wants to be sure that the new team member is using the correct terminology that is used in this organization because it has become apparent that the team member comes from an organization where many things and terms were used differently on their projects. He asks the team member to define prevention costs. What should the team member's response be?

    ○ Upfront costs of programs or processes needed to meet customer requirements, or to design in quality.

    ○ The costs associated with evaluating whether the program or processes meet requirements.

    ○ The costs associated with making the product or service acceptable to the customer after it fails internal testing and before it's delivered to the customer.

    ○ The costs resulting from rejection of the product or service by the customer.

A Guide to the Project Management Body of Knowledge (PMBOK® Guide) – Fifth Edition, Project Management Institute (PMI)®, Project Management Professional (PMP)®, and Certified Associate in Project Management (CAPM)® are registered trademarks of Project Management Institute, Inc. - Version 2.1 Published September 30, 2014

Lesson Labs

13. When discussing the quality of the project with a new team member, the project manager wants to be sure that the new team member is using the correct terminology that is used in this organization because it has become apparent that the team member comes from an organization where many things and terms were used differently on their projects. He asks the team member to define external failure costs. What should the team member's response be?

○ Upfront costs of programs or processes needed to meet customer requirements, or to design in quality.

○ The costs resulting from rejection of the product or service by the customer.

○ The costs associated with evaluating whether the program or processes meet requirements.

○ The costs associated with making the product or service acceptable to the customer after it fails internal testing and before it's delivered to the customer.

14. What is another name for an Ishikawa diagram and what is it used for?

○ Kawasaki, used for cause and effect diagramming to find the source of problems

○ Scatter diagram, used to plot pairs to evaluate the correlation

○ Pareto, used to display the frequency of observations

○ Fishbone, used for cause and effect diagramming to find the source of problems

15. In order to test to see if the game the team is delivering is easy enough for the children of the intended age group, the team creates a prototype and then establishes their test criteria. Then the team establishes test groups of 100 boys and 100 girls, all between the ages of 3 and 5, at 50 different elementary schools across 30 states. What are they engaged in?

○ Benchmarking

○ Design of Experiments

○ Statistical sampling

○ Force field analysis

16. Training needs, rewards and recognition, compliance, and safety are all aspects of what project management plan?

○ Human resources management plan

○ Staffing management plan

○ Motivation and safety management plan

○ Process improvement plan

17. The project manager is explaining the reasons for the need to create a staffing release plan to the sponsor who is annoyed with all the plans the project manager is spending time on creating. What is the project manager's justification for doing this?

○ This will help control project costs and allows for a smooth transition to other projects.

○ This will help control the project schedule and allows for fewer individuals to be involved in the closing phase.

○ This will help let all the functional managers know how their staff will be treated while working on the project.

○ This will help the project manager remove team members who are not working up to the level of quality required to meet the project objectives.

A Guide to the Project Management Body of Knowledge (PMBOK® Guide) – Fifth Edition, Project Management Institute (PMI)®, Project Management Professional (PMP)®, and Certified Associate in Project Management (CAPM)® are registered trademarks of Project Management Institute, Inc. - Version 2.1 Published September 30, 2014

18. A team member who is new to the organization and working on projects has several questions and asks the project manager to meet with him to discuss these items so he is sure he understands what is going on during the planning process of the project. The project manager is delighted that this new team member is taking so much interest. One of the questions the team member has is: "What is involved in planning for the safety of the project staff?" He had never seen this addressed in the projects he had worked on in his previous organization. What is the correct response that the project manager should provide?

○ The project manager has had experience with team members being injured while working on the project and this has caused a worker's compensation problem.

○ Every project requires safety precautions depending on the risks of the project.

○ Some projects require safety precautions such as those being performed in non-class A office towers, those with stairs, and those that may experience winter weather conditions.

○ Some projects require safety precautions such as those being performed in nuclear power plants, construction hard hat zones, and war zones.

19. While looking at a matrix grid, the team member can understand the connection between the work package and the team members for all the work that is to be performed in the project. What type of a chart is the team member viewing?

○ Hierarchical organizational breakdown structure

○ Organizational theory chart

○ Responsibility assignment matrix (RAM)

○ Histogram

20. When planning for communication in a project, which of the following is the correct list of tools and techniques that are used?

○ Technology, methods, models

○ Requirements analysis, technology, types

○ Technology, push/pull, models

○ Requirements analysis, interactive, models

A Guide to the Project Management Body of Knowledge (PMBOK® Guide) – Fifth Edition, Project Management Institute (PMI)®, Project Management Professional (PMP)®, and Certified Associate in Project Management (CAPM)® are registered trademarks of Project Management Institute, Inc. - Version 2.1 Published September 30, 2014

Lesson Labs

Lesson Lab 8-1
Testing Your Knowledge of Planning for Risk, Procurements, and Stakeholders

Scenario

The following questions are meant to test your knowledge of the content from this lesson.

1. Which one of these is a risk?
   - ○ We have determined that our schedule is not going to meet the required deadline.
   - ○ We think it is possible there will be a sale on parts and we could spend less money than we originally thought.
   - ○ There are not enough resources to complete the work on time.
   - ○ The change in the prime rate has caused our funding source to be unable to provide the money we need in the upcoming project phase.

2. While discussing risks with the team members, one of them refers to a risk as an unknown unknown and suggests that it be referred to the management of the company. Is this correct or not, and why?
   - ○ Yes this is correct because it is up to the management of the company to help the project be successful by handing all the potential problems that could occur.
   - ○ No this is not correct because risks that are to be handled by the management are mitigated by workarounds.
   - ○ No this is not correct because all risks are known unknowns until they occur.
   - ○ Yes this is correct because large risks that cannot be handled within the project should be referred to management and are referred to as unknown unknowns.

3. What happens to the risks that are below the risk threshold level for the project? What is the risk threshold level?
   - ○ They are accepted. Risk threshold is the level of uncertainty that can be accepted.
   - ○ They are mitigated. Risk threshold is the level of uncertainty that can be accepted.
   - ○ They are accepted. Risk threshold is the degree of uncertainty that can be taken on in anticipation of a benefit.
   - ○ They are accepted. Risk threshold is the amount of risk the organization can endure.

4. During a planning meeting, the project manager displays a graph that maps the probability of occurrence and the impact of each risk so the risk management team can get an overview of how risky the project is. What is this graph called?
   - ○ Probability and impact matrix
   - ○ Probability and likeliness chart
   - ○ Impact and effect map
   - ○ RAM matrix

A Guide to the Project Management Body of Knowledge (PMBOK® Guide) – Fifth Edition, Project Management Institute (PMI)®, Project Management Professional (PMP)®, and Certified Associate in Project Management (CAPM)® are registered trademarks of Project Management Institute, Inc. - Version 2.1 Published September 30, 2014

Lesson Labs

5. A team member who is new to the organization wants to help with the risk planning. He was heavily involved in this at his old company and thinks some of their tools, which the new company does not use, were very useful. He suggests that the risk management team develop a document that is a hierarchical layout of the risks by category. What document is he referring to?

   ○ RAM

   ○ OBS

   ⊘ RBS

   ○ RACI

6. What is a risk team?

   ○ A group of stakeholders who have identified the most risks in a project.

   ○ A subset of the project team who will be the risk owners for the project.

   ○ A collection of risk responses used in previous projects that will be chosen from for the risk response plans in the current project.

   ⊘ A group of people dedicated to identify, manage, and monitor the risks in a project.

7. Early warning signs that a risk event is about to occur are stored with the risk as additional information in the risk register. What are they called and who should be aware of them?

   ⊘ Triggers, stakeholder risk owner

   ○ Warnings, the project sponsor

   ⊘ Signals, stakeholder risk owner

   ○ Triggers, the project sponsor

8. While spending time preparing for risk identification meetings, the project manager searches through the old project archives and puts together a risk checklist. There are advantages and disadvantages of this. What are they?

   ○ It creates a random way to identify risks by not using categories, but there may be other risks that do.

   ⊘ It creates a standardized way to identify risks in specific categories, but there may be additional risks that do not fall into categories on the check list.

   ○ It is a fool proof way to be sure you have covered all aspects of potential risk in the project, but it takes a long time to create.

   ○ It does not take much time or research to create, but it can only be used by the project manager.

9. When using interviewing methods to gather risk probability, what is the range of values that may be used?

   ○ 1 to 10

   ○ 10 to -1

   ○ Any range that the team wants to use, so it is not consistent across other projects

   ⊘ Lowest, most likely, highest

10. SWOT is a method used to uncover internally generated risks. What does this acronym stand for?

   ○ Strength warning original threat

   ○ Strong weak old timely

   ⊘ Strength weakness opportunity threat

   ○ Specific weakness opportunity timely

A Guide to the Project Management Body of Knowledge (PMBOK® Guide) – Fifth Edition, Project Management Institute (PMI)®, Project Management Professional (PMP)®, and Certified Associate in Project Management (CAPM)® are registered trademarks of Project Management Institute, Inc. - Version 2.1 Published September 30, 2014

Lesson Labs

11. **Which of the following is a good example of mitigating the probability of a threat risk on a project?**

    ○ Install smoke detectors

    ○ Install fire-proof components

    ○ Hire another company to do the part of the work that could result in a fire

    ○ Keep the phone number of the fire department handy

12. **The project manager has built a large table that stores a lot of information about the project risks. The team members have never seen one of these before and ask him to explain what it is and why it is important. What would be the project manager's response?**

    ○ Risk breakdown structure, to document the categories of risk in the project which helps find courses and trends and to use as lessons learned.

    ○ Risk register, to document identified risks and all attributes, as well as document the outcome of the risk management processes and share as lessons learned.

    ○ Risk register, to document all the threats to the project and the outcome of the risk management processes and share as lessons learned.

    ○ Risk register, to document the unidentified risks and their impact to the project and the outcome of the risk management processes and share as lessons learned.

13. **The members of the risk management team would like the project manager to give them a good explanation of the difference between qualitative risk analysis and quantitative risk analysis. What would be the project manager's response?**

    ○ Qualitative analysis allows us to identify time and cost contingencies, where quantitative provides a prioritization of the risks.

    ○ Qualitative analysis allows us to get the longest list of risks possible, where quantitative provides a prioritization of the risks.

    ○ Qualitative analysis provides a prioritization of the risks, where quantitative allows us to identify time and cost contingencies.

    ○ Qualitative is objective and quantitative is subjective.

14. **What is the project risk ranking used for?**

    ○ To prioritize risks within the project

    ○ To determine the level of each risk within the project

    ○ It is part of the closing process, to be sure all risks have been addressed

    ○ Comparison among other projects

15. **There is a 30% chance that there will be a sale on products and the project could save as much as $25,000. There is a 10% chance that the supplier will be late delivering, which could cost the project $85,000. There is a 25% possibility that if new equipment is bought for $3,000, the company could save $10,000. There is also a 50% likelihood that the bad weather will delay the project, which could end up costing the company $250,000. What is the total EMV?**

    ○ $125,500

    ○ $124,250

    ○ $141,500

    ○ $125,750

A Guide to the Project Management Body of Knowledge (PMBOK® Guide) – Fifth Edition, Project Management Institute (PMI)®, Project Management Professional (PMP)®, and Certified Associate in Project Management (CAPM)® are registered trademarks of Project Management Institute, Inc. - Version 2.1 Published September 30, 2014

Lesson Labs

16. The project planning team is trying to perform what–if scenarios to determine the potential outcomes for the project schedule. A team member mentions a simulation software that he has used in another company and suggests it would help. This software is used to make predictions about the optimistic, most likely, and pessimistic estimates for variables in the model and simulates various outcomes of the project schedule to provide a statistical distribution of the calculated results. What is an example of this?

   ○ Monte Carlo
   ○ Monaco Modeling
   ○ LVOS (Las Vegas Odds Simulation)
   ○ Pareto Diagramming

17. What is the difference between avoiding a threat and mitigating it?

   ○ Avoid means to reduce the impact or probability, and mitigate means to change the management plan to remove the risk.
   ○ Avoid means to outsource the work to remove the risk, and mitigate means to reduce the impact or probability.
   ○ Avoid means to change the management plan to remove the risk, and mitigate means to reduce the impact or probability.
   ○ Avoid means to change the management plan to remove the risk, and mitigate means to accept the impact or probability.

18. The project manager and his risk management team are involved in risk identification and response planning. Each time they come up with a response plan, someone points out that the contingency plan could be the cause of yet another risk. What type of risk would that be?

   ○ Subsidiary
   ○ Secondary
   ○ Unlikely
   ○ Residual

19. An architectural firm has spent a great deal of time and effort creating the design and blueprints for the building. They had to purchase materials and hire consultants and have been working on this project for six months. They have submitted all the invoices for the money they have spent on the work, as well as an invoice for the fee of $5,000. What type of contract was this?

   ○ Time and materials
   ○ CPIF
   ○ FPEPA
   ○ Cost reimbursable

20. There is a great deal of effort with regard to the stakeholders during the project planning. The sponsor would like to know what all the fuss is about and get an explanation from the project manager about what is taking so long. The project manager explains the need for a stakeholder management plan with which of the following statements?

   ○ To effectively engage stakeholders in project decisions and execution based on the analysis of their needs, interests, and potential impact
   ○ To ensure the stakeholders are receiving the reports in the format they would like
   ○ To effectively place the right people in the correct role to support achieving the project objectives on time and within budget
   ○ To be able to document which stakeholder is unaware, neutral, leading, or supportive

A Guide to the Project Management Body of Knowledge (PMBOK® Guide) – Fifth Edition, Project Management Institute (PMI)®, Project Management Professional (PMP)®, and Certified Associate in Project Management (CAPM)® are registered trademarks of Project Management Institute, Inc. - Version 2.1 Published September 30, 2014

Lesson Labs

Lesson Lab 9–1
Testing Your Knowledge of Executing a Project

Scenario

The following questions are meant to test your knowledge of the content from this lesson.

1. The project manager is working with the team as they perform the work to create the project deliverables. Some adjustments need to be made to the project plan and the baselines. What would be needed in order for the project manager to allow such changes?

    ○ Change requests

    ○ Input from stakeholders that their needs have adjusted from what was originally planned

    ○ Approved change requests

    ○ The sponsor decides on a different way to accomplish the work

2. A team member is discussing the project work with the project manager who keeps using a couple of terms that the team member is not clear on. She asks him to explain his use of the terms corrective action and preventive action. What should the project manager say in response?

    ○ Preventive action is to identify the problem ahead of time and put plans in place to prevent it from occurring, and corrective action is to have to do something over to make it right.

    ○ Preventive action is to have to do something over to make it right, and corrective action is to identify the problem ahead of time and put plans in place to prevent it from occurring.

    ○ Corrective action requires an approved change request and preventive action does not.

    ○ Preventive action requires an approved change request and corrective action does not.

3. During the execution phase of the project, the project manager meets with the team to discuss the status of work packages. As the result of one of these meetings, the project manager then calls a team member who is located in a different country to advise that team member that he can begin work on the work package he is assigned to. What is the project manager using?

    ○ Good communication skills

    ○ Work authorization system

    ○ Project Management Information System (PMIS)

    ○ Human resources management plan

A Guide to the Project Management Body of Knowledge (PMBOK® Guide) – Fifth Edition, Project Management Institute (PMI)®, Project Management Professional (PMP)®, and Certified Associate in Project Management (CAPM)® are registered trademarks of Project Management Institute, Inc. - Version 2.1 Published September 30, 2014

Lesson Labs

4. **The team member who is new to this organization continues to get confused when other team members converse and discuss deliverables. It is apparent to him that the use of this word was different in his previous job. How would you define the correct use of the term "deliverables" to this team member?**
   - ○ The final product of the project.
   - ○ The list obtained from the stakeholders at the beginning of planning stating what they want from the project.
   - ○ This is the same as the objectives, as defined in the charter.
   - ○ A product or capability produced as a result of a completed work package.

5. **Who can request changes?**
   - ○ Team members and project managers
   - ○ Sponsor
   - ○ Stakeholders
   - ○ Customer

   [handwritten: Team Member / pm, sponsor, customer all are part of stakeholders.]

6. **What is the main focus of quality assurance and what does it result in?**
   - ○ Quality assurance is focused on process and procedures used, and it results in improved quality.
   - ○ Quality assurance is focused on measuring the output of the work package, and it results in improved quality.
   - ○ Quality assurance is focused on measuring the output of the work package, and it results in better metrics.
   - ○ Quality assurance is focused on process and procedures used, and it results in a shorter schedule.

7. **The project manager is working with some specialists who can provide an unbiased perspective in an attempt to identify needed improvements to the processes used in the project. Who is the group and what are they engaged in?**
   - ○ The group is the Quality Control Department and they are engaged in process analysis.
   - ○ The group is the Quality Assurance Department and they are engaged in measuring the output of the work packages to the stated requirement metrics.
   - ○ The group is the Quality Control Department and they are engaged in a quality audit.
   - ○ The group is the Quality Assurance Department and they are engaged in process analysis.

8. **The team will be made up of several individuals who are not located at the company with the rest of the team members. What type of team does this result in and what is one of the problems associated with it?**
   - ○ This is a simulated team, and communication is more clear because they will rely on technology rather than face-to-face communication.
   - ○ This is a virtual team, and communication is more difficult and must rely on technology, as there will be few opportunities for face-to-face communication.
   - ○ This is a virtual team, and communication is more clear because they will rely on technology rather than face-to-face communication.
   - ○ This is a performing team, since there are specialists working remotely, there will be power plays due to egos.

A Guide to the Project Management Body of Knowledge (PMBOK® Guide) – Fifth Edition, Project Management Institute (PMI)®, Project Management Professional (PMP)®, and Certified Associate in Project Management (CAPM)® are registered trademarks of Project Management Institute, Inc. - Version 2.1 Published September 30, 2014

Lesson Labs

9. In reviewing the upcoming schedule of work, a team member notices that his work package is planned to be worked on when he is out of the country making a presentation at an industry conference. He is concerned about this conflict and does not understand how the project manager could have done this. What should the project manager have consulted before scheduling the work package?

○ The company calendar

○ The staffing management plan

○ The resource calendars

○ The develop project team process

10. Based on the following description of how things are going, what is the stage of development of this team? The team begins to work productively, without worrying about personal acceptance or control issues. There are still conflicts; however, they tend to be focused on process issues, rather than personality differences.

○ Forming

○ Norming

○ Adjourning

○ Performing

11. At the end of every month, the team members and the project manager would get together for a catered lunch and a two hour break from work. During that time, there were some games set up for people to play and thank-you awards announced for the team members who went above and beyond the call of duty that month. Everyone enjoyed these events and offered more ideas for new games to be played. What was the team engaged in?

○ Team building

○ Rewards and recognition

○ Frivolous waste of time

○ Co-location

12. In the conduct procurements process, project managers will obtain seller responses, select a seller, and award contracts to the identified seller for the procurement. During what stage of the project does this occur?

○ Planning

○ Monitor and Control

○ Initiation

○ Execution

13. The project manager is going to hold a bidders conference for the services they need to outsource for the project. What is the main thing that the project manager would like to ensure happens at the bidder conference?

○ That all bidders meet each other

○ That some of the bidders ask their most complex questions

○ That all the bidders ask all their questions

○ That there is enough space for all the bidders to have seats

A Guide to the Project Management Body of Knowledge (PMBOK® Guide) – Fifth Edition, Project Management Institute (PMI)®, Project Management Professional (PMP)®, and Certified Associate in Project Management (CAPM)® are registered trademarks of Project Management Institute, Inc. - Version 2.1 Published September 30, 2014

Lesson Labs

14. When problems occur in a project, they should be assigned to a team member to resolve, and the stakeholder who is concerned should be informed of the status and when the issue is resolved. What tool should be used to document all this?

- ○ Issue log
- ○ Issue register
- ○ Communication plan
- ○ Complaint department

15. The project is well underway when the project manager needs to communicate with many stakeholders regarding the status of the project. He refers to the project management plan to see what was determined to be the best method for this type of conversation. What was the choice and why is it the best?

- ○ Telecommunication is best because some people do not like to take the time to meet in person.
- ○ Face-to-face is the best and most effective method to communicate with stakeholders because the body language and other non-verbal clues can indicate more information about their level of satisfaction with the project progress.
- ○ Written formal is the best method for this type of communication so the stakeholders cannot claim that you did not keep them informed.
- ○ Phone calls and conference calls are the best method so they can talk about the project and express any concerns freely.

A Guide to the Project Management Body of Knowledge (PMBOK® Guide) – Fifth Edition, Project Management Institute (PMI)®, Project Management Professional (PMP)®, and Certified Associate in Project Management (CAPM)® are registered trademarks of Project Management Institute, Inc. - Version 2.1 Published September 30, 2014

Lesson Labs

Lesson Lab 10–1
Testing Your Knowledge of Managing Project Work, Scope, Schedules, and Cost

Scenario

The following questions are meant to test your knowledge of the content from this lesson.

1. The project manager is involved in many activities from a project management point of view. They include collecting, measuring, and distributing performance information, as well as reviewing trends. During what part of the project management life cycle would the project manager be engaged in these activities?

   ○ Execution

   ⦾ Monitor and Control

   ○ Manage and Measure

   ○ Closing

2. During the Monitor and Control process, which of the following describes the most important reason the project manager would use the project baselines created during the planning process?

   ⦾ To let the stakeholders know the status of the project

   ○ To reward the team for their efforts

   ○ To confirm that the plans were made correctly

   ⦾ To compare the actuals against

3. During the Monitor and Control process, the project manager is doing analysis and determines that one of the decisions made during the planning process was not the best. He reviews this information with some experts and team members, all of whom confirm that the decision was not right. As a result of this, what will be the output?

   ⦾ A change request.

   ○ An adjustment to the decision.

   ○ The project manager will be reprimanded by the sponsor.

   ○ The people involved in the original decision will be removed from the project.

4. There is a group of people who meet on a regular basis. When they meet, they review the input gathered for their meeting, which includes corrective and preventive action. Their job is to assess the information and make decisions about each item based on how it would impact the project constraints and if the item is beneficial to the project. The result will be communicated to appropriate stakeholders, recorded in a log, and results in updates to project documents. What is this group called?

   ○ Project team

   ⦾ Change control board

   ○ Executive committee

   ○ Stakeholders

A Guide to the Project Management Body of Knowledge (PMBOK® Guide) – Fifth Edition, Project Management Institute (PMI)®, Project Management Professional (PMP)®, and Certified Associate in Project Management (CAPM)® are registered trademarks of Project Management Institute, Inc. - Version 2.1 Published September 30, 2014

Lesson Labs

5. In the first situation, a customer forgot to mention a requirement during the planning process. Well into execution, the customer requested that the item be added to the project scope. The request was submitted to the change control board, and it was approved. In the second situation, there was another customer who neglected to mention a requirement during planning. Well into execution, the customer told the project manager that the requirement needed to be added to the scope of the project. The project manager had the request written up as a change request and submitted it to the change control board. In this case, the change was denied. What would be the reason that the first change is approved and the second is not, when they both involve a request for additional scope from a customer?

   ○   The second customer was not as influential as the first, so his request was denied.

   ○   The first customer was willing to add time and money to the project baselines to cover the item, while the second was not.

   ○   The project manager should not have gotten in the middle of the request by the second customer.

   ○   The change control board can make any decision they want and do not need to justify why.

6. A change request has been established to add scope to the project. It has been determined that this will add two weeks of time to the project schedule. In a different but similar situation, a change request was submitted to increase the quality of a deliverable in the project. In this case, it was determined that this would add two weeks to the project schedule, and $2,000 to the cost baseline, but it did not actually impact the scope. It would also add a certain amount of risk based on the project team's ability to complete both quality requests, and it would result in a change of assignment for certain team members. What is the difference between the two situations?

   ○   The first change was assessed only for time, the second change was evaluated through the integrated change control process.

   ○   The first change was not important enough to fully evaluate.

   ○   The second change came from someone with more influence than the first.

   ○   The first change was requested by someone with low influence.

7. The deliverable was completed as per the instructions in the WBS dictionary and the team member feels confident in reporting his work package as complete. Quality Control performs their job and confirms that the deliverable does indeed meet the criteria as stated. What should be the next thing to happen with the deliverable?

   ○   Have the Quality Assurance department perform their inspection.

   ○   Incorporate it into the final project.

   ○   Verify the scope of the deliverable with the sponsor or customer and gain formal acceptance.

   ○   Nothing else needs to be done with it and the team member can move on to the next work package.

8. Which of the following is not an output of Validate Scope?

   ○   Work performance information

   ○   Accepted deliverable

   ○   Change requests

   ○   Inspections

A Guide to the Project Management Body of Knowledge (PMBOK® Guide) – Fifth Edition, Project Management Institute (PMI)®, Project Management Professional (PMP)®, and Certified Associate in Project Management (CAPM)® are registered trademarks of Project Management Institute, Inc. - Version 2.1 Published September 30, 2014

Lesson Labs

9. During the first six weeks of the execution phase of the project, four work packages were scheduled to be completed. WP1 was anticipated to cost $1,100, WP2 was anticipated to cost $1,000, WP3 was anticipated to cost $950, and WP4 was anticipated to cost $1,200. As it turns out, WP1 is complete, WP2 is only 50% complete, WP3 is 75% complete, and WP4 is complete. When adding all the invoices, you can see that $1,110 was spent on WP1, $600 was spent on WP2, $750 was spent on WP3, and $1,210 was spent on WP4. Using Earned Value Management (EVM), what is the cost variance and what is the schedule variance?

   ○ CV = 0.92 and SV = 0.80

   ○ CV = $367 and SV = $425

   ○ CV = -$157.50 and SV = -$ 737.50

   ○ CV = $830.50 and SV = $250.50

10. During the first six weeks of the execution phase of the project, four work packages were scheduled to be complete. WP1 was anticipated to cost $1,100, WP2 was anticipated to cost $1,000, WP3 was anticipated to cost $950, and WP4 was anticipated to cost $1,200. As it turns out, WP1 is complete, WP2 is only 50% complete, WP3 is 75% complete, and WP4 is complete. When adding all the invoices, you can see that $1,110 was spent on WP1, $600 was spent on WP2, $750 was spent on WP3, and $1,210 was spent on WP4. Using Earned Value Management (EVM), what is the CPI and SPI?

    ○ CPI = 0.96 and SPI = 0.83

    ○ CPI = -$257.50 and SPI = -$837.50

    ○ CPI = 0.80 and SPI = 0.92

    ○ CPI = $425 and SPI = $367

11. Which of the following sets of formulas correctly shows part of EVM?

    ○ EV, SPI, SV, AC

    ○ CV, SV, SPI, CPI

    ○ SPI, CPI, CV, PV

    ○ BCWP, BCWS, CV, SV

12. During project execution, it is revealed through the use of Earned Value Management (EVM) that the project is over budget. The original budget will not be realized. Which of the following is the correct choice to represent the new higher estimate that is now anticipated to be incurred when the project is completed?

    ○ EAC

    ○ ETC

    ○ Estimate for completion

    ○ BAC

13. Which of the following is the correct nomenclature to represent what you believe the total planned value will be at the completion of the project at the end of planning?

    ○ EAC

    ○ ETC

    ○ BCWP

    ○ BAC

A Guide to the Project Management Body of Knowledge (PMBOK® Guide) – Fifth Edition, Project Management Institute (PMI)®, Project Management Professional (PMP)®, and Certified Associate in Project Management (CAPM)® are registered trademarks of Project Management Institute, Inc. - Version 2.1 Published September 30, 2014

Lesson Labs

14. During the execution phase of the project, the project manager is evaluating how things are going. She uses Earned Value Management (EVM) to calculate the status of the project schedule against the plan. She discovers that the SPI is 0.95. Which of the following is correct?

   ○ The project is behind budget.

   ○ The project is going to cost 95% of what was originally planned.

   ○ The project is behind schedule.

   ○ The actual cost has impacted the schedule.

15. During the execution phase of the project, the project manager is evaluating how things are going. She uses Earned Value Management (EVM) to calculate the status of the project's budget against the plan. She discovers that the CPI is 1.01. Which of the following is correct?

   ○ The project is 0.01 over budget.

   ○ The project is under budget.

   ○ This information is not enough to determine the status of the budget.

   ○ The CV is too high.

A Guide to the Project Management Body of Knowledge (PMBOK® Guide) – Fifth Edition, Project Management Institute (PMI)®, Project Management Professional (PMP)®, and Certified Associate in Project Management (CAPM)® are registered trademarks of Project Management Institute, Inc. - Version 2.1 Published September 30, 2014

Lesson Labs

Lesson Lab 11–1
Testing Your Knowledge of Controlling the Project

Scenario
The following questions are meant to test your knowledge of the content from this lesson.

---

1. The project manager makes sure that each team member knows which work packages they are assigned to, that they have access to the WBS dictionary for each work package, and that they have checklists. What is the purpose of checklists?

    ○ They are job aids to help employees perform activities according to a consistent standard.

    ○ They are used to make sure each employee completes all of their work packages.

    ○ They are used to track which team member is working on which work package.

    ○ They are useful in assessing the stage of development of the team.

2. What tool ensures that all change requests are reviewed and implemented as approved during the Perform Integrated Change Control process?

    ○ The change control board

    ○ Perform change audit process

    ○ Inspection

    ○ Approve change request reviews

3. During monitor and control, the work is being checked to make sure that it meets the stated objectives. One of the team members is informed that there is a variance in the deliverable on her work package. She is not sure what is meant by that and asks the project manager to explain. Which of the following is an appropriate answer that the project manager could use as a response?

    ○ A variance is a quantifiable deviance, or amount of departure, from the expected result.

    ○ A variance is a subjective observation.

    ○ She has completed the work and should move on to the next work package.

    ○ The results of the work package were compared with those similar for statistical variance.

4. The work that is performed may not exactly match what was expected. Since this is a normally occurring situation, what would you call these variances and why is it acceptable?

    ○ Assignable causes are those everyday occurrences that are always present in project work.

    ○ Special causes are sporadic and unexpected, which makes them acceptable.

    ○ Random causes are those everyday occurrences that are always present in project work.

    ○ Common causes are sporadic and are always present in project work.

A Guide to the Project Management Body of Knowledge (PMBOK® Guide) – Fifth Edition, Project Management Institute (PMI)®, Project Management Professional (PMP)®, and Certified Associate in Project Management (CAPM)® are registered trademarks of Project Management Institute, Inc. - Version 2.1 Published September 30, 2014

Lesson Labs

5. Having created the work package deliverable, it is tested for speed. The requested speed was to be 250 mph +/-2.5. What measurement value is being represented here?
   - ○ Variance
   - ○ Tolerance
   - ○ Speed
   - ○ Thrust

6. During a team meeting, a few individuals are being disruptive, which is causing negative effects on the rest of the meeting attendees. At a break in the meeting, the project manager, along with a few of the other attendees, are talking about these few individuals who are negatively impacting the meeting. One person describes the situation as "one rotten apple spoils the barrel." The project manager says that a better analogy would be that "20% of the people cause 80% of the problems." What is the project manager using as the basis for this statement?
   - ○ Statistical sampling
   - ○ 6-Sigma
   - ○ Tolerances and variances
   - ○ Pareto analysis

7. Sampling data in the statistical sampling process is divided into two categories. Which of the following correctly names those two categories?
   - ○ Tolerance and variance
   - ○ Corrective and preventive
   - ○ Attribute and tolerance
   - ○ Attribute and variable

8. A problem occurs during the project execution. It is not a big problem, but it does bother some of the stakeholders. The project manager requests that it be added to the issue log. What would be the reason for this?
   - ○ The issue log serves as a place to document problems that occur and to track their resolution.
   - ○ The issue log will be reviewed by the risk team at their next meeting to develop a contingency plan.
   - ○ The issue log will be submitted to the change control board for a change approval.
   - ○ The issue log serves as a place to document the unidentified risks.

9. A new team member has recently joined the organization. His experience on projects at his previous employer does not match up with what he sees happening at this company. He has several questions for the project manager. Today, the project manager mentioned something called a risk reassessment. The team member has never heard that term before and asks the project manager to explain. Which of the following would be the best explanation the project manager can give the team member?
   - ○ Risk reassessment needs to be done throughout the life of the project, as time changes everything and new risks will be identified, old ones will drop off, and we may need to change our response plans.
   - ○ Risk reassessment needs to be done at the beginning of the planning phase, as well as at the beginning of execution, which is the time we have just reached.
   - ○ Risk reassessment means to review all the information we have gathered in the initiation phase and use it in the risk planning step during the planning phase.
   - ○ Risk reassessment is done to compare the amount of contingency reserve we have to the amount of remaining risk.

A Guide to the Project Management Body of Knowledge (PMBOK® Guide) – Fifth Edition, Project Management Institute (PMI)®, Project Management Professional (PMP)®, and Certified Associate in Project Management (CAPM)® are registered trademarks of Project Management Institute, Inc. - Version 2.1 Published September 30, 2014

Lesson Labs

10. During the project execution phase, the team and project manager discover that one of the sellers is unable or unwilling to produce the product for which they have entered into a contractual agreement. The project manager states that this is a material breach, but one of the team members who is new to the organization has had a lot of experience with procurement at his former employer. He states that this is actually an anticipatory breach. Which of the following correctly describes the difference between the two?

○ A material breach is an unavoidable indication that the other party will not be able to produce the performance necessary to fulfill the contract. An anticipatory breach is a serious breach that prevents the injured party from benefiting from the contract.

○ An anticipatory breach is an unavoidable indication that the other party will not be able to produce the performance necessary to fulfill the contract. A material breach is a serious breach that prevents the injured party from benefiting from the contract.

○ In an anticipatory breach, the contract has been breached in such a way that there is no resulting damage to the injured. A material breach is a serious breach that prevents the injured party from benefiting from the contract.

○ An anticipatory breach is an unavoidable indication that the other party will not be able to produce the performance necessary to fulfill the contract. A material breach is a breach so serious that it negates the very foundation of the contract.

Lesson Lab 12–1
Testing Your Knowledge of Closing a Project

Scenario

The following questions are meant to test your knowledge of the content from this lesson.

---

1. In what situation would you not perform the Close Project phase?
   - ○ When a project is terminated
   - ○ When a project phase is complete
   - ○ When the customer verifies the deliverables
   - ○ When a project is complete

2. If the project was terminated early, why would the project manager insist that the team perform the close projects process?
   - ○ To document the reasons why the project was terminated early, and how to transfer the finished and unfinished deliverables to others.
   - ○ The project manager should insist this is a waste of the team members' time since no one wants the project or its output any longer.
   - ○ To make sure everyone knows that the reason for project termination was his fault or the fault of the team.
   - ○ To document lessons learned so mistakes can be repeated in future projects.

3. A team member, who was new to the company when the project started, is disappointed that the project has been terminated. She is excited to get to work on the next project assignment, when the project manager informs her that she cannot do this until the current, but terminated, project has been administratively closed. She does not have prior experience with this and asks the project manager to explain why it is necessary. What is the explanation the project manager will give to describe the value of administrative closure when the project has been terminated?
   - ○ It ensures that each procurement is complete and documents project agreements and related documentation for future reference on new projects.
   - ○ It ensures that the project or project phase requirements were met and formal acceptance was granted.
   - ○ It allows the project manager to capture salient information for the benefit of future projects.
   - ○ It is to make a checklist of all outstanding items.

4. What is involved in administrative closure?
   - ○ It involves finishing all of the work packages.
   - ○ It involves meeting with all the stakeholders to ensure all their requirements were met.
   - ○ It involves verifying and documenting project results to formalize project or phase completion.
   - ○ It involves wrapping up all of the work procured from sellers and making final payments on their invoices.

5. A team member, who was new to the company when the project started, is excited that the project has completed. She is excited to get to work on the next project assignment, but the project manager informs her that she cannot yet do this. The current project has not been completely closed, as there were many sellers involved. She does not have prior experience with this and asks the project manager to explain what needs to be done. Which of the following is the correct description of procurement closure?

   ○ It involves certifying that actual procurement costs did not exceed planned procurement costs.

   ○ It involves verifying and documenting project results to formalize project or phase completion.

   ○ It ensures that the project or project phase requirements were met and formal acceptance was granted.

   ⟲ It ensures that each procurement is complete, and documents project agreements and related documentation for future reference on new projects.

6. Part of the work that needs to be done at the end of the project is to evaluate the effectiveness of the seller, as well as the procurement process itself. What is this technique called?

   ○ Contract review

   ⟲ Procurement closure

   ○ Administrative closure

   ○ Procurement audit

7. There are several team members who have never worked on a project that had any sellers involved, so they are not familiar with the whole vendor relationship situation. During project closing, the project manager advises the team that there will be procurement audits. How would the project manager explain to the team the purpose of these procurement audits?

   ○ The goal of the audit is to provide documentation that the team was not responsible for the deliverables provided by the sellers.

   ○ The goal of the audit is to ensure the phase or project requirements were met.

   ⟲ The goal of the audit is to establish a record that may be used to shape procurement practices in other contracts.

   ○ The goal of the audit is to document why the project was terminated early.

8. The project manager wants to make sure all team members understand the importance of the whole closing process and asks if there are any more questions. One team member asks, "What would happen if this process was not done?" How should the project manager answer that question?

   ○ The customer would not be obliged to pay for the project.

   ⟲ The next related activity, phase, or project might not get started.

   ○ The stakeholders would not have any faith in the project team for future projects.

   ○ The team members would not be allowed to be assigned to future projects.

9. During the closing phase, the project manager has requested yet another document for the project. He refers to it as the "Closed Procurement." What is this?

   ⟲ It is a written notice that is usually provided by the buyer to the seller once a contract is complete.

   ○ It is a verbal notice provided by the seller to the buyer once a contract is complete.

   ○ It is a written notice provided by the seller to the sponsor once a complete contract has been agreed to.

   ○ It is a notice that is posted in the project war room indicating the terms of the contract.

A Guide to the Project Management Body of Knowledge (PMBOK® Guide) – Fifth Edition, Project Management Institute (PMI)®, Project Management Professional (PMP)®, and Certified Associate in Project Management (CAPM)® are registered trademarks of Project Management Institute, Inc. - Version 2.1 Published September 30, 2014

10. During the closing phase, the project manager has requested yet another document for the project. He refers to it as the "Closed Procurement" which is a written notice once a contract is complete. Where is the most likely place that the specifics of when and how this is done would be stated?

○ In the quality management plan, as specified by the metrics in the contract

○ In the project management plan, as specified in the contract process plan

○ In the terms and conditions set forth in the team member work authorization agreement

○ In the terms and conditions that were specified in the contract and the procurement management plan

A Guide to the Project Management Body of Knowledge (PMBOK® Guide) – Fifth Edition, Project Management Institute (PMI)®, Project Management Professional (PMP)®, and Certified Associate in Project Management (CAPM)® are registered trademarks of Project Management Institute, Inc. - Version 2.1 Published September 30, 2014

Lesson Labs

Solutions

ACTIVITY 1-1: Discussing Components of Project Management

---

1. What projects have you worked on and what was your role in those projects? Were you ever a project manager of a project?

   A: Answers will vary, but could include anything from professional projects (construction, software development and installation, clinical trials, finance, etc.) within an organization, to personal projects (home improvement, planning a wedding or party, building a house, etc.).

2. What interpersonal skills do you think are most important for a project manager to use within a project team?

   A: Answers will vary, but should include communication and negotiation with other team members and project stakeholders. Communication is 90% of a project manager's job. Being able to negotiate will ensure that you can resolve issues quickly and efficiently.

3. A large organization's PMO provides templates and other tools for the project managers to use on various projects. They also provide support to the project management team and require compliance with PMI methodologies from each project manager with respect to the project work. What type of PMO is used by this organization?

   A: Answer should be that this represents a controlling PMO. In this instance, the PMO is responsible for compliance and distributing templates and tools to the project managers throughout the company.

ACTIVITY 1-2: Discussing the Relationship Between Projects and the Business

---

1. What are operational areas?

   A: Answers will vary, but could include anything from manufacturing and engineering to different business office areas, such as accounting and human resources.

2. Describe how a past project supported or changed your organization's operational area.

   A: Answers will vary, but could include any project that improved the business and how the business was directly impacted by the completion of the project or the project outcome.

3. **Describe how a past project contributed to the business and why.**

   A: Answers will vary, but could include any project that had a positive impact and improved the business. This could be something small, such as an improved method to track employee vacation time, or a large project outcome that changes the way an organization will conduct business going forward.

LAB 1–1: Testing Your Knowledge of Project Management Fundamentals

1. The ABC Engineering firm has decided to have a group of subject matter experts gather to plan and execute work to replace their CRM system. It has been decided that the one they have been using does not provide all the information different managers need and there have been many complaints by the users that it is hard to manipulate the information. The data is not stored in such a way to be able to retrieve reports with the information they need, and there are many pieces of information they would like to capture that are missing. The work to replace the old system will require input from many different people throughout the organization. It is expected to take about two years to complete the work, and roll out a new system for use. What is this group of people working on?

   ○ Process

   ○ Database development

   ⦿ Project

   ○ Production system

2. Which of the following correctly describes the project management process?

   ○ A linear approach.

   ⦿ An iterative, cyclical process that involves back and forth progression through many of the processes and phases.

   ○ A model which contains the data, activity dependencies and durations, and calculations to determine the project timeline.

   ○ A continuing area including the activities and processes needed to identify, define, combine, unify, and coordinate all of the various processes and project management activities.

A Guide to the Project Management Body of Knowledge (PMBOK® Guide) – Fifth Edition, Project Management Institute (PMI)®, Project Management Professional (PMP)®, and Certified Associate in Project Management (CAPM)® are registered trademarks of Project Management Institute, Inc. - Version 2.1 Published September 30, 2014

Solutions

3. The executive committee was interested in knowing more about the structure of project management as it applied to the organization's strategic objectives and how the projects all fit together. The project manager was asked to make a presentation for the executive committee to explain this. Which of the following would be the correct way that the project manager would go about explaining this structure during the presentation?

⦿ The relationship of portfolios, programs, and project is such that a portfolio is a collection of projects, programs, sub-portfolios, and operations managed as a group to achieve strategic business results. Programs are grouped in a portfolio and are made up of subprograms, projects, or other work that supports that portfolio. Individual projects that are either within or outside of a program are still considered part of a portfolio.

○ The relationship of portfolios, programs, and project is such that a program is a collection of projects, portfolios, sub-portfolios, and operations managed as a group to achieve strategic business results. Portfolios are grouped in a program and are made up of subprograms, projects, or other work that supports that program. Individual projects that are either within or outside of a program are still considered part of a program.

○ The relationship of portfolios, programs, and project is such that a project is a collection of activities, programs, sub-portfolios, and operations managed as a group to achieve strategic business results. Programs are grouped in a portfolio and are made up of subprograms, projects, or other work that supports that portfolio. Individual programs that are either within or outside of a portfolio are still considered part of a project.

○ The relationship of portfolios, programs, and project is such that a sub-portfolio is a collection of projects, programs, portfolios, and operations managed as a group to achieve strategic business results. Programs are grouped in a portfolio and are made up of subprograms, projects, or other work that supports that portfolio. Individual projects that are either within or outside of a program are still considered part of a portfolio.

4. When viewing the work going on within the company, it was discovered that there were multiple projects being run individually, as well as several that were being managed in a coordinated way along with some other work. It was determined that this should be considered a program. What is a program?

○ A group of programs, projects, and other work such as production, coordinated in such a way to achieve company success.

○ A group of processes needed to produce the products that the company sells in order to achieve the corporate strategic objectives.

○ A group of related portfolios, projects, and other work managed distinctly independently in order to gain the most benefit which would support the corporate strategic objectives.

⦿ A group of related projects, subprograms, and program activities managed in a coordinated way to achieve benefits not available from managing them individually.

5. The company has many departments including HR, Finance, Legal, Engineering, and also a department that requires project managers to use specific templates, forms, and tools, and conform to governance. What type of department is that?

⦿ Controlling PMO

○ Directive PMO

○ Supportive PMO

○ Department of Project Management

6. A company was hiring for certain positions. For one position, they were asking for people with skills such as leadership, team building, motivation, conflict management, influencing, negotiating, and several others. This position would require the individual to lead efforts to satisfy specific objectives and complete them in a timely manner within budget constraints. What job position were they trying to fill and what is a description of the skills they were looking for?

○ Head of the PMO and communication skills

○ Project manager and management skills

⦿ Project manager and interpersonal skills

○ Program manager and business skills

7. **The Project Management Institute Code of Ethics and Professional Conduct describes the ethical and professional behavior expectations of any individual working as a project management professional. What are the values as defined in the Code of Ethics and Professional Conduct?**

   ◉ Being responsible, being respectful, being fair, and being honest

   ○ Being reasonable, being respectful, being fair, and being honest

   ○ Being responsible, being respectful, being fair, and being trustworthy

   ○ Being responsible, being reasonable, being trustworthy, and being honest

8. **What is A Guide to the Project Management Body of Knowledge (PMBOK® Guide) - Fifth Edition, and what does it provide?**

   ○ It is a nationally recognized standard that describes the established norms, methods, processes, and practices that provide a base of best practices for the program management profession. It provides guidelines for managing projects and programs and defines project management concepts. It describes the project management life cycle and its processes, and the project life cycle.

   ○ It is a nationally recognized standard that describes the established norms, methods, processes, and practices that provide a base of best practices for the project management profession. It provides guidelines for managing individual projects and defines project management concepts. It describes the project management life cycle and its processes, and the project life cycle.

   ○ It is a globally recognized standard that describes the established norms, methods, processes, and practices that provide a base of best practices for the program management profession. It provides guidelines for managing projects and programs and defines project management concepts. It describes the project management life cycle and its processes, and the project life cycle.

   ◉ It is a globally recognized standard that describes the established norms, methods, processes, and practices that provide a base of best practices for the project management profession. It provides guidelines for managing individual projects and defines project management concepts. It describes the project management life cycle and its processes, and the project life cycle.

9. **What is the difference between the PMP certification exam and the CAPM certification exam?**

   ○ Passing the CAPM demonstrates that you have the experience, education, and competency to lead and direct projects. The PMP is an entry-level certification for project practitioners with little or no project experience, that demonstrates understanding of the fundamental knowledge, terminology, and processes of effective project management.

   ◉ Passing the PMP demonstrates that you have the experience, education, and competency to lead and direct projects. The CAPM is an entry-level certification for project practitioners with little or no project experience, that demonstrates understanding of the fundamental knowledge, terminology, and processes of effective project management.

   ○ Passing the PMP demonstrates that you have the experience, education, and competency to lead and direct programs. The CAPM is an entry-level certification for project practitioners with little or no project experience, that demonstrates understanding of the fundamental knowledge, terminology, and processes of effective project management.

   ○ Passing the PMP demonstrates that you have the experience, education, and competency to lead and direct projects. The CAPM is an entry-level certification for project practitioners with project experience, that demonstrates understanding of the different types of project management theories.

A Guide to the Project Management Body of Knowledge (PMBOK® Guide) – Fifth Edition, Project Management Institute (PMI)®, Project Management Professional (PMP)®, and Certified Associate in Project Management (CAPM)® are registered trademarks of Project Management Institute, Inc. - Version 2.1 Published September 30, 2014

10. A project manager engages with many different people who are interested in the project and has many conversations to find out what is important to these people about the project. By gathering all that information he/she is able to confer with subject matter experts and people who will perform the work to satisfy the project and explain what the desired outcome of the project should be. By performing this work, what role is the project manager playing within the organization?

⦿ The project manager is the link between what the business must have and the project team that will produce deliverables to meet the project objectives.

○ The project manager is working as a business analyst to develop a detailed list of requirements and a list of activities the team members will perform.

○ The project manager is acting as a leader making decisions about which requirements should be included in the work the team members will perform.

○ The project manager is influencing what the people are asking for from the project and what strategic objectives they want satisfied, so that the work the team members will perform is acceptable to them. Therefore, increasing their skills and knowledge as a result of the project.

ACTIVITY 2-1: Discussing Organizational Influences on Projects

1. Describe the organizational culture, style, communication, and structure of one of your projects.

   A: Answers will vary, but may include motivation and rewards systems, such as project milestone celebrations, code of conduct, work ethic, and work hours. All of these contribute to the team's work environment.

2. If you were the project manager of the project described in the previous question, how would you work with those organizational cultures and styles? Describe the organizational process assets you have used on past projects.

   A: Answers will vary, but should relate to the answer from the previous question and should include direct improvements to working within a particular organizational culture, such as scheduling status meetings at appropriate times for a multi-time-zoned project.

3. Describe any enterprise environmental factors that you have experience with or factors that you can see coming across in the future as a project manager.

   A: Answers will vary, but may include the political climate (if you are working within a government organization), the existing IT infrastructure, and working within heath care regulations, such as HIPAA.

ACTIVITY 2-2: Discussing Project Stakeholders Roles

1. From your experience, give some examples of project stakeholders and what value they added to a project.

   A: Answers will vary, but could include any person who contributed to the project including neighbors for a new house build, the general public for public works projects such as a new water main installation, customers of new products, students for a new registration system, and so on.

2. What types of experiences have you had with project stakeholders? Were there any negative or positive impacts on the project?

   A: Answers will vary, but could include stakeholders who derailed the project by asking for out-of-scope requirements such as those that were too expensive to implement and extraneous to the main purpose and objective of the project as stated in the project charter.

A Guide to the Project Management Body of Knowledge (PMBOK® Guide) – Fifth Edition, Project Management Institute (PMI)®, Project Management Professional (PMP)®, and Certified Associate in Project Management (CAPM)® are registered trademarks of Project Management Institute, Inc. - Version 2.1 Published September 30, 2014

Solutions

3. **What responsibilities apply to project sponsors?**

   ◉ Signs and publishes the project charter

   ○ Keeps the sponsor and the stakeholders informed

   ○ Provides input to define needs for the project output

   ○ Supervises and coordinates the management of all projects in an organization

4. **What responsibilities apply to a PMO?**

   ○ Signs and publishes the project charter

   ○ Keeps the sponsor and the stakeholders informed

   ○ Provides input to define needs for the project output

   ◉ Supervises and coordinates the management of all projects in an organization

ACTIVITY 2-3: Discussing Project Teams

1. **What types of project teams have you worked with?**

   A: Answers will vary, but may include virtual teams, co-located teams, global teams, and more.

2. **What were some of the pros and cons of that team's composition?**

   A: Answers will vary, but pros might include that all team members were the same location and cons might include language barriers, time zone differences, and non–face-to-face communication.

ACTIVITY 2-4: Examining Project Life Cycles

1. **What project life cycles, if any, do you have experience with? What life cycles do you think are used most often?**

   A: Answers will vary, but may include predictive, iterative, or adaptive cycles. Experiences might include well-planned projects that had a definitive result and outcome.
   This is a good place for you to offer some examples of real-world application of the different life cycle types. You can also pose this question to the class as a whole and promote a discussion.

2. **Which project life cycle type is best suited for a fast-paced project that is always changing?**

   ○ Predictive

   ○ Iterative

   ◉ Adaptive

3. **Which life cycle type is best suited for a project that does not have well-defined deliverables?**

   ○ Predictive

   ◉ Iterative

   ○ Adaptive

A Guide to the Project Management Body of Knowledge (PMBOK® Guide) – Fifth Edition, Project Management Institute (PMI)®, Project Management Professional (PMP)®, and Certified Associate in Project Management (CAPM)® are registered trademarks of Project Management Institute, Inc. - Version 2.1 Published September 30, 2014

Solutions

4. Which life cycle type is best suited for a project that has a detailed and complete plan?
   - ◉ Predictive
   - ○ Iterative
   - ○ Adaptive

LAB 2-1: Testing Your Knowledge of Project Management and the Organization

---

1. The project manager is busy looking for the appropriate people to add to the staff for the new project. There are several types of work skills that will be needed for the project and he wants to be sure that the best people with each skill will be assigned to the project. To do this, he is meeting with several department heads to discuss the timing of the project and the possible availability and assignment of certain individuals to the project. He is using his influencing interpersonal skills to convince these department heads to assign the best person that they supervise to the project. What organizational structure is the project manager working within?
   - ◉ Functional
   - ○ Strong matrix
   - ○ Projectized
   - ○ Hybrid

2. The project manager is working for a company where there are many project managers and they all share the resources between projects as needed, and there are no distinct departments in which people work. The people will complete their work on one project and then be assigned to another project, and possibly a different project manager to whom they report. What organizational structure does this represent?
   - ○ Functional
   - ○ Weak matrix
   - ◉ Projectized
   - ○ Hybrid

3. A team member is trying to balance their workload and is not sure of the priorities of her assignments. In order to determine what work needs to be completed first, she schedules a meeting with both her functional manager and the project manager to discuss the matter and get help in determining this. What organizational structure does this represent?
   - ○ Functional
   - ◉ Balanced matrix
   - ○ Projectized
   - ○ Hybrid

4. For this project, the team may develop its own set of operating procedures, and operate outside the standard formalized reporting structure during the project. What organizational structure does this represent?
   - ○ Functional
   - ◉ Composite
   - ○ Projectized
   - ○ Matrix

A Guide to the Project Management Body of Knowledge (PMBOK® Guide) – Fifth Edition, Project Management Institute (PMI)®, Project Management Professional (PMP)®, and Certified Associate in Project Management (CAPM)® are registered trademarks of Project Management Institute, Inc. - Version 2.1 Published September 30, 2014

Solutions

5. Early in the establishment of the project, the project manager spends some time looking for historical data that might be helpful in planning the new project. She is looking for examples of project documents in similar projects that have been completed, that she might be able to use as templates for the new project. She is also looking for information about established processes and procedures that will help the project run more smoothly. What is the term used to define these?

   - ◉ Organizational process assets
   - ○ Enterprise environmental factors
   - ○ Progressive elaboration
   - ○ Organizational project management

6. Which of the following would not be a list of project stakeholders?

   - ○ Sponsor, project manager, team members, people who have an interest in the deliverable
   - ○ Customers, business partners, sellers
   - ○ People who will benefit from a successful outcome of the project, functional managers, other departments who are impacted by the project
   - ◉ Individuals who are not assigned to the project as team members, end users of other products, sellers who were not selected

7. What provides the structure, processes, decision-making models, and tools for the project manager and team to manage the project?

   - ◉ Project governance
   - ○ Project overhead
   - ○ Senior management
   - ○ Enterprise environmental factors

8. The project manager is trying to determine who to include, how long people will be involved, if anyone will be part-time or full-time, who has knowledge of specific subjects, and who has unique skills that the project will need. What is the project manager working on?

   - ◉ Project team composition
   - ○ Project team development
   - ○ Project team building
   - ○ Project stakeholders

9. A project is being planned, and by looking at the type of work being done, the planning team can see that there are distinct stages of work that must be defined and moved through in a sequential manner. They intend to begin with a feasibility phase, followed by a design phase, and then build and test. By determining all of this, what is being determined?

   - ◉ Project life cycle
   - ○ Project performance criteria
   - ○ Project schedule
   - ○ Project management plan

A Guide to the Project Management Body of Knowledge (PMBOK® Guide) – Fifth Edition, Project Management Institute (PMI)®, Project Management Professional (PMP)®, and Certified Associate in Project Management (CAPM)® are registered trademarks of Project Management Institute, Inc. - Version 2.1 Published September 30, 2014

10. Which of the following is true regarding project risk and the cost of changes?

   ○ At the end, risk is high and the cost of changes is high.

   ○ At the beginning, risk is low and the cost of changes is high.

   ◉ At the beginning, risk is high and the cost of changes is low.

   ○ At the beginning risk is well-defined, and at the end the cost of changes is undetermined.

11. A project manager is working on the project plan with the planning team of subject matter experts. While reviewing how the work will be laid out, they discover that the project contains phases that start prior to the previous phase ending. What does this mean?

   ◉ The phase to phase relationship in this case is overlapping.

   ○ There will be a need to have more resources available than originally planned.

   ○ There is potentially less risk and less rework involved.

   ○ This phase to phase relationship reduces the level of uncertainty.

12. As the project moves along in time, there are many instances where successive layers of detail are added to the plans as the project progresses. That is because you learn more about the project the further you get in to it. What is the term that define this process?

   ○ Precedence relationship

   ○ Hammock activities

   ○ Start to finish relationships

   ◉ Progressive elaboration

13. Which of the following is the preferred cycle when the project outcomes are well understood and known?

   ○ Iterative

   ○ Rolling wave

   ◉ Predictive

   ○ Adaptive

14. A project manager and his planning team are trying to determine the type of cycle for the new project. They know that there will be rapid, high levels of change and ongoing stakeholder involvement in the project. Which type of cycle should they consider establishing to have the most control of this particular project?

   ○ Predictive

   ○ Iterative

   ○ Rolling wave

   ◉ Adaptive

15. Which of the following cycles is best when there is a highly flexible, interactive, adaptive organization where project outcomes are realized while the project work is being completed, not at the beginning of the project?

   ○ Predictive

   ○ Iterative

   ○ Rolling wave

   ◉ Agile

A Guide to the Project Management Body of Knowledge (PMBOK® Guide) – Fifth Edition, Project Management Institute (PMI)®, Project Management Professional (PMP)®, and Certified Associate in Project Management (CAPM)® are registered trademarks of Project Management Institute, Inc. - Version 2.1 Published September 30, 2014

Solutions

ACTIVITY 3-1: Identifying Project Management Process Groups

1. Which process is performed to finalize all project work?
   - ○ Initiating
   - ○ Planning
   - ○ Executing
   - ○ Monitoring and Controlling
   - ◉ Closing

2. Which project management process group will you apply to regularly measure progress and identify variances from the project management plan?
   - ○ Initiating
   - ○ Planning
   - ○ Executing
   - ◉ Monitoring and Controlling
   - ○ Closing

3. Which process is performed to define a new project and get authorization to start the project?
   - ◉ Initiating
   - ○ Planning
   - ○ Executing
   - ○ Monitoring and Controlling
   - ○ Closing

4. What process is performed to actually do the project work to meet the project objectives?
   - ○ Initiating
   - ○ Planning
   - ◉ Executing
   - ○ Monitoring and Controlling
   - ○ Closing

5. Which project management process will you apply to refine program objectives and the courses of action the project team will take to meet program objectives?
   - ○ Initiating
   - ◉ Planning
   - ○ Executing
   - ○ Monitoring and Controlling
   - ○ Closing

A Guide to the Project Management Body of Knowledge (PMBOK® Guide) – Fifth Edition, Project Management Institute (PMI)®, Project Management Professional (PMP)®, and Certified Associate in Project Management (CAPM)® are registered trademarks of Project Management Institute, Inc. - Version 2.1 Published September 30, 2014

6. **What process is performed to track the progress of the project and manage changes to the project?**

   ○ Initiating

   ○ Planning

   ○ Executing

   ◉ Monitoring and Controlling

   ○ Closing

7. **What process is performed to determine the scope of the project and the activities to achieve the project objectives?**

   ○ Initiating

   ◉ Planning

   ○ Executing

   ○ Monitoring and Controlling

   ○ Closing

8. **As a project manager, why is it important to use the five process groups for your project?**

   A: Answers will vary, but might include that it provides a framework to manage projects, provides common language, and allows you to logically group your project management activities to support the project.

ACTIVITY 3-2: Identifying Project Data

1. **Which type of project information is a physical representation of electronic work performance information compiled in project documents, intended to generate decisions or raise issues, actions, or awareness?**

   ○ Work performance data

   ○ Work performance information

   ◉ Work performance reports

2. **Which type of project information is composed of raw observations and measurements identified during activities performed to carry out the project work?**

   ◉ Work performance data

   ○ Work performance information

   ○ Work performance reports

3. **Which type of project information consists of performance data collected from various controlling processes, analyzed in context, and integrated based on relationships across areas?**

   ○ Work performance data

   ◉ Work performance information

   ○ Work performance reports

A Guide to the Project Management Body of Knowledge (PMBOK® Guide) – Fifth Edition, Project Management Institute (PMI)®, Project Management Professional (PMP)®, and Certified Associate in Project Management (CAPM)® are registered trademarks of Project Management Institute, Inc. - Version 2.1 Published September 30, 2014

Solutions

LAB 3-1: Testing Your Knowledge of Working with Project Management Processes

1. The project has been going along fairly smoothly as the team is performing the project work, but something in quality control indicates that a change needs to be made. Once the change is approved, the project plan has to be updated to reflect that change, and then the team will continue to execute work based on the new plan. What does this scenario describe?

   ⦿ Project management process group interactions

   ○ A poorly planned project because changes should not be needed once it is in execution

   ○ The end of a phase and the beginning of the next phase

   ○ The change control process

2. The initial scope of a new project or phase is defined and financial resources are committed. Internal and external stakeholders are identified and the project manager is selected. What project management phase does this represent?

   ○ Planning and organizational process assets

   ○ Initiation and enterprise environmental factors

   ⦿ Initiation and charter

   ○ Feasibility and scope statement

3. Currently, the total scope of the project is established, the objectives are defined and refined, and a course of action to obtain the project objectives is being developed. What project management process group does this represent and what is one of the major outputs?

   ⦿ Planning and the project management plan

   ○ Planning and the charter

   ○ Initiating and the budget

   ○ Designing and the project schedule

4. The project manager is involved in coordinating people and resources, and managing stakeholder expectations; and the team is performing the activities of the project based on the project management plan. What project management process group does this represent and what is one of the major outputs?

   ○ Planning and change requests

   ⦿ Execution and deliverables

   ○ Execution and communication problems

   ○ Monitoring and controlling, and change requests

5. At this time, project performance is measured, tracked, reviewed, and the project manager is orchestrating the progress and performance of the project, identifying areas in which changes to the plan are needed, and initiating those changes. What project management process group does this represent and what is one of the major outputs?

   ○ Executing and deliverables

   ○ Monitor and controlling, and deliverables

   ⦿ Monitor and controlling, and change requests

   ○ Implementation and change requests

6. The project work is complete and before the resources are released, the project manager asks them to collect and document lessons learned; and then they have a party to celebrate their success. What project management process group does this represent and what is not one of the major outputs?

   ○ Closing and final product

   ○ Closing and phase completion

   ○ Closing and completed contracts

   ◉ Closing and change requests

7. Which knowledge area is concerned with developing a project plan as a result of a project charter, and controlling the work being done while executing that work, making sure changes consider all constraints and that everything is finalized in closing?

   ◉ Integration

   ○ Scope

   ○ Implementation

   ○ Change control

8. The project team is busy performing the work of the project. The project manager is given a report indicating the work is satisfactory and the quality being obtained meets the requirements of the original scope statement. What process group is this?

   ◉ Monitor and control

   ○ Execution

   ○ Closing

   ○ Testing

9. The quality report indicates that the original standards that were chosen to build the project were not appropriate and the project manager needs to determine different standards. What process group does this indicate the project manager will be engaged in?

   ○ Execution

   ◉ Planning

   ○ Monitor and Control

   ○ Closing

10. The project team is using the project plan and the resulting schedule to work on project activities. Their work is being measured to ensure it meets requirements. Some aspects of the original plan need to be adjusted, which results in a new and updated project management plan. The team then continues to work, but now they do so according to the updated plan. What does this situation represent?

    ○ A failure to plan correctly in the first place.

    ○ The team members are underperforming.

    ○ The futility of wasting time planning.

    ◉ The iterative relationship between planning, executing, and monitor and control.

11. During what process group does the schedule and budget get created and what are the outputs as a result of doing this work?

    ○ Initiating and a charter

    ○ Planning and change requests

    ◉ Planning and a schedule and budget

    ○ Initiating and an authorized project

A Guide to the Project Management Body of Knowledge (PMBOK® Guide) – Fifth Edition, Project Management Institute (PMI)®, Project Management Professional (PMP)®, and Certified Associate in Project Management (CAPM)® are registered trademarks of Project Management Institute, Inc. - Version 2.1 Published September 30, 2014

Solutions

12. The project manager and team are working with activities, their durations, and dependencies. Which knowledge area is being addressed?

   ◉ Time

   ○ Scope

   ○ Execution

   ○ Quality

13. When the project manager is discussing what will be included in the project with the project planning team, she includes aspects of project management, as well as the product of the project. What knowledge area is being addressed?

   ○ Monitor and Control

   ○ Execution

   ○ Quality

   ◉ Scope

14. The project team is discussing several things they are worried about that could impact the success of the project. They are trying to come up with ideas as to how to minimize those potential problems. What knowledge area is being addressed?

   ◉ Risk

   ○ Schedule

   ○ Monitor and Control

   ○ Initiation

15. The project manager is meeting with members of the executive committee to gain their insights as to some of the people who are interested in the project. He wants to know what they think is the best way to manage those people and who of them are the most influential. What knowledge area is being addressed?

   ○ Risk management

   ◉ Stakeholder engagement

   ○ Communication

   ○ Initiation

LAB 4-1: Testing Your Knowledge of Initiating a Project

1. The project manager has been meeting with the project sponsor to discuss various aspects of the project. As a result, the project manager has created a document and the sponsor has signed it. This document states the high-level requirements, summary budget, and cost. What is this document and what are some of its inputs?

   ◉ Charter, enterprise environmental factors, organizational process assets, business case, project SOW

   ○ Scope statement, enterprise environmental factors, organizational process assets, business case, project SOW

   ○ Business case, enterprise environmental factors, organizational process assets, risk register

   ○ Project SOW, enterprise environmental factors, organizational process assets, business case, charter

A Guide to the Project Management Body of Knowledge (PMBOK® Guide) – Fifth Edition, Project Management Institute (PMI)®, Project Management Professional (PMP)®, and Certified Associate in Project Management (CAPM)® are registered trademarks of Project Management Institute, Inc. - Version 2.1 Published September 30, 2014

2. The project manager and the sponsor need to create the project charter. The project manager wants to be sure they are stating the objectives of the project correctly, so that the charter is effective in pointing the project in the right direction. She suggests that they review the feasibility study that was prepared in order to validate the benefits of the project. What is the project manager referring to?

   ○ The project scope statement

   ○ The project SOWs

   ◉ The business case

   ○ The summary project milestone schedule

3. At a very early stage in the project, the project manager is reviewing the document that is based on business needs, product, or service requirements for a particular project. He is using this information to clarify what needs to be stated on the project charter. Which document is being reviewed?

   ○ The project scope statement

   ◉ The project SOWs

   ○ The business case

   ○ The summary project milestone schedule

4. A financial review of a marketing plan for a new product indicates that an investment of $750,000 in development could result in potential profits of $2,000,000+ if the estimated demand of 100,000 units of the product is sold over the potential life span of the product in the near future. This kind of information might be used as a basis to determine if a new project should be initiated to develop a prototype, and then move into a new product development project. Where would this information most likely be found by a project manager and a sponsor who are trying to determine which projects are the most viable for the organization to initiate?

   ◉ The business case

   ○ The project scope statement

   ○ The project SOWs

   ○ The summary projects budget

5. When a project is initiated with external customers or parties, a formal contract agreement is needed so both parties are on the same page about project information. Under what category are letters of intent considered?

   ○ Contracts

   ○ Project SOW

   ○ Business case

   ◉ Agreements

A Guide to the Project Management Body of Knowledge (PMBOK® Guide) – Fifth Edition, Project Management Institute (PMI)®, Project Management Professional (PMP)®, and Certified Associate in Project Management (CAPM)® are registered trademarks of Project Management Institute, Inc. - Version 2.1 Published September 30, 2014

Solutions

6. The project manager has established several meetings with individuals who have specific knowledge about certain aspects of a potential project while working on establishing the project charter. Some of them are consultants, others are subject matter experts, and others are part of the organization's PMO. The sponsor is unclear as to why the project manager is so busy engaging in all these meetings. Why is the project manager scheduling all these meetings? Who are the people with whom he is scheduling the meetings? What is the project manager using by doing this?

   ○ The project manager wants to talk with these people to gain their buy-in and support for the project. These people are stakeholders, and the project manager is using stakeholder analysis as a technique to engage stakeholders.

   ○ The project manager wants to talk with these people to understand why they are requesting the project. These people are the business units who want the project, and the project manager is using facilitation techniques.

   ◉ The project manager wants to talk with these people to help evaluate the inputs to the project charter. These people are experts, and the project manager is using expert judgment as a technique to develop the project charter.

   ○ The project manager wants to talk with these people to be sure the project maps to one of the organization's strategic goals. These people are members of the PMO and the executive committee, and the project manager is using communication skills.

7. In order to clearly understand what the project should accomplish, the project manager asked the sponsor who the project stakeholders are while developing the project charter. Which stakeholders will the sponsor relate to the project manager during this time frame, and what other times during the project will the project manager try to figure out who the stakeholders might be?

   ◉ The sponsor will relate the initial high-level stakeholders that are known at this time to the project manager, and the project manager will try to find more stakeholders all throughout the project life cycle.

   ○ The sponsor will relate the initial high-level stakeholders that are known at this time to the project manager, and the project manager will try to find more stakeholders during the planning phase.

   ○ The sponsor will relate all stakeholders that are going to be affected by the project to the project manager, and the project manager will try to find more stakeholders all throughout the project life cycle.

   ○ The sponsor will relate all stakeholders that are going to affect the project to the project manager, and the project manager will try to find more stakeholders as changes in the project occur.

8. What is one of the most important reasons for issuing a project charter for every project that is undertaken within an organization?

   ○ To assign the project manager

   ○ To state the high-level stakeholders and risks

   ○ To make the project official

   ◉ To be sure the project aligns with the goals of the organization

9. Which of the following choices best defines and provides examples of stakeholders?

   ◉ Stakeholders are people who may affect or be affected by the objectives of a project. Examples are the customer, the functional managers, the team members, and the general public.

   ○ Stakeholders are people who have submitted requirements for the project. Examples are the sponsor, the customer, and the project manager.

   ○ Stakeholders are people who may affect the objectives of a project. Examples are the customer, the functional managers, and the general public.

   ○ Stakeholders are people who may be affected by the objectives of a project. Examples are the customer, the team members, and the sponsor.

A Guide to the Project Management Body of Knowledge (PMBOK® Guide) – Fifth Edition, Project Management Institute (PMI)®, Project Management Professional (PMP)®, and Certified Associate in Project Management (CAPM)® are registered trademarks of Project Management Institute, Inc. - Version 2.1 Published September 30, 2014

Solutions

10. The project manager is asking for expert judgment input, and is involved in several meetings as part of the process of gathering and analyzing data about people whose interests should be considered and taken into account during the life cycle of the project. What is the project manager using?
   - ○ Stakeholder assessment
   - ◉ Tools and techniques to identify stakeholders
   - ○ Develop project charter
   - ○ A review of the organizational process assets

11. The project manager has gathered information regarding the identification, assessment, and classification of people who are interested in the project, have business expectations for the project, and can also influence the progress of the project. How should all of this information be stored?
   - ○ In a secure location with limited access
   - ○ This information needs to be documented in the project charter or SOW
   - ◉ In a stakeholder register
   - ○ This is part of the business case, documenting who wants the project

12. There are classification models used to document stakeholder analysis results. Which of the following is one type of classification model that might be used for project management stakeholder analysis?
   - ○ Decision trees
   - ○ RACI chart
   - ◉ Power and interest grid
   - ○ Stakeholder register

13. Why would the fact that there is a procurement involved in the project to purchase goods or services from external suppliers or vendors impact information included in the Stakeholder Register?
   - ◉ The people involved in that contract are stakeholders because they can be affected by or can affect the project.
   - ○ The fact that there is a procurement would not impact the information in the Stakeholder Register.
   - ○ RFPs, IFBs, and RFQs are project documents that should be included in the register.
   - ○ Because these are inputs to Stakeholder Analysis, which is an output of Identify Stakeholders.

14. The sponsor is getting annoyed with the project manager during the initiation phase of the project because the project manager is spending a great deal of time in meetings and talking with experts, and researching lessons learned and stakeholder registers from previous projects. The sponsor thinks this is a waste of time and wants to get the project work started as quickly as possible. Why is the project manager claiming that it is important to identify as many stakeholders as possible, as early as possible, and what aspects of the stakeholders is he claiming should be understood and documented?
   - ○ The project manager wants to identify stakeholders early so they can't claim no one asked their opinion later on, and he wants to understand and document their interest and influence on the project.
   - ◉ The project manager wants to identify stakeholders early so their needs and expectations can be met, and he wants to understand and document their interest and influence on the project.
   - ○ The project manager wants to identify stakeholders early so their needs and expectations can be met, and he wants to understand and document their position within the organization and how best to communicate with them.
   - ○ The project manager wants to identify stakeholders early so they have no excuse as to why they did not submit their requirements, and he wants to understand and document their expectations and roles on the project.

A Guide to the Project Management Body of Knowledge (PMBOK® Guide) – Fifth Edition, Project Management Institute (PMI)®, Project Management Professional (PMP)®, and Certified Associate in Project Management (CAPM)® are registered trademarks of Project Management Institute, Inc. - Version 2.1 Published September 30, 2014

Solutions

15. The project manager wants to include the following in the project: brainstorming, conflict resolution, problem solving, and meeting management. These are all examples of what?

   ◉ Facilitation techniques

   ○ Good project management

   ○ Communication methods

   ○ Ways of getting the stakeholders involved in the project

ACTIVITY 5-1: Researching Scope Management Plans

2. Why is it important to properly manage the scope of your project?

   A: Answers will vary, but should include: Because the scope determines what the project outcomes will be, you must make sure that it is constantly on track with the approved scope baseline.

3. Which of the following is not a component of the scope management plan?

   ○ A scope statement

   ◉ The project management plan

   ○ A process to manage changes

   ○ A process to create the WBS

   This question might be tricky, so you may need to help the students make the distinction between new requirements that could be added to a project but have not been approved by the Change Control Board and can lead to scope creep.

4. True or False? Scope creep includes new requirements that must be added to the project immediately.

   ☐ True

   ☑ False

ACTIVITY 5-3: Creating a Project Scope Statement

1. Which documents can you use as a basis for your scope statement?

   A: Answers will vary, but should include the requirements documentation and the project charter as a basis for your scope statement.

ACTIVITY 5-4: Creating a WBS

1. When creating the WBS for the 122 East Main project, what types of reference materials and other inputs could you use?

   A: You can reference the requirements documentation, project charter, project SOW, and the project scope statement. You should also determine if there is an existing WBS template that can be used.

A Guide to the Project Management Body of Knowledge (PMBOK® Guide) – Fifth Edition, Project Management Institute (PMI)®, Project Management Professional (PMP)®, and Certified Associate in Project Management (CAPM)® are registered trademarks of Project Management Institute, Inc. - Version 2.1 Published September 30, 2014

Solutions

3. As the project manager, you are asked to decompose the WBS deliverables. Which activity will you perform during decomposition?

   ○ Assign unique ID numbers to each requirement.

   ◉ Break the requirements down into smaller components.

   ○ Arrange the requirement into categories, based on risk.

   ○ Organize the requirements based on which project team is responsible for their completion.

LAB 5-1: Testing Your Knowledge of Planning a Project

1. The project manager is working with people to help pull together all the information that will be needed to manage and control the project. This includes the subsidiary plans including baselines, the life cycle and processes, as well as a change management plan. What are these and what do they comprise?

   ◉ They are the components of the overall project management plan.

   ○ They are inputs to the project charter.

   ○ They are inputs to the project schedule plan.

   ○ They are the output of develop project management plan.

2. What are subsidiary plans for the project management plan?

   ○ Schedule, cost, and quality plans that will become the project management plan

   ○ Individual knowledge area plans that are the output of the project management plan

   ◉ Individual knowledge area plans that will be integrated to become the project management plan

   ○ The objectives of each knowledge area that must be met in order for the project to be declared successful

3. Once all the project plans were completed and the work began, the project manager realized that some of the decisions made during the resource planning were not correct and he will need to reassess and adjust the resources being used on the project. This will result in changes to the HR management plan. When that happens, what else will also occur?

   ○ The cost will go up.

   ○ The schedule will be lengthened.

   ○ The sponsor will need to be involved in order to approve the change in resources.

   ◉ The overall project management plan will change.

4. Through the life of the project, while the team members were doing the work, the customer made several requests of the team members who were working closely with them to ensure the requirements were satisfied to their specifications, as stated in the project charter and scope statement. Occasionally, the customer asked the team members to make some "minor adjustments." The team members, concerned with the success of the project, were willing to oblige the customer and performed the extra work necessary for these adjustments in an effort to keep the customer happy. What is this called and what are the potential outcomes?

   ○ Scope enhancement, which can result in decreased cost and schedule.

   ◉ Scope creep, which can result in cost and schedule overruns.

   ○ Delighting the customer, which can result in performance awards.

   ○ Progressive elaboration, which can result in more information as the project develops.

A Guide to the Project Management Body of Knowledge (PMBOK® Guide) – Fifth Edition, Project Management Institute (PMI)®, Project Management Professional (PMP)®, and Certified Associate in Project Management (CAPM)® are registered trademarks of Project Management Institute, Inc. - Version 2.1 Published September 30, 2014

Solutions

5. **What does configuration management address?**

   ○   Activities such as keeping track of all the changes the customer makes to the product plans.

   ○   The way in which the product is configured for use to satisfy the end users and how that develops as it is being built.

   ○   Documentation of the management of configuring the product for use and how changes to the product will be incorporated into the overall project plan.

   ◉   Activities such as how version control of project documents and changes to the product will be initiated, analyzed, and traced.

6. **A team member who is new to the organization and working on projects has several questions and asks the project manager to meet with him to discuss these items so he is sure he understands what is going on during the planning process of the project. The project manager is delighted that this new team member is taking so much interest. The first question the team member has is: "What is the basic difference between the project requirements and the project scope?" What would the project manager's response be?**

   ◉   The requirements are like a wish list of everything the stakeholders would like to get from the project, and the scope is a subset of those requirements, prioritized and assessed for value to the project.

   ○   There is no real difference because what the stakeholders require to be included in the project, is what becomes the scope statement, simply re-arranged into the format of the WBS.

   ○   The scope is like a wish list of everything the stakeholders would like to get from the project and the requirements are a subset of the scope, prioritized and assessed for value to the project.

   ○   The requirements are what is stated on the project charter and is the list that is used to format the scope and build the WBS.

7. **While going through all the project requirements, the planning team tries to plot them on a matrix in order to link them to the business and project objectives and to justify each. What is this matrix referred to and what purpose would it serve during the rest of the project?**

   ○   This is a requirements classification table to help organize and divide the requirements which can then later be used to determine which should be included in the scope.

   ○   This is a requirements traceability matrix which can be used to verify that the output of each work package meets the quality metric as stated on the project scope statement.

   ◉   This is a requirements traceability matrix which can be used to track requirements' progress through the life cycle and confirm that they have been met at project closure.

   ○   This is a requirements management plan which can be used to determine the cost and schedule of the project.

8. **The project manager and sponsor are actively engaged with stakeholders to determine their needs for the project. What is this process referred to as and why is it important?**

   ◉   This is called collect requirements. It is important as it is the foundation of all the rest of the plans. If this is not done well, all the rest of the plans will be incorrect.

   ○   This is called requirements classification. It is important as the classifications determine how the rest of the project will be assessed.

   ○   This is called stakeholder analysis. It is important to know who the stakeholders are as they are the recipients of the project output.

   ○   This is called requirements communication plan. It is important for all the stakeholders to have good communication with the project manager, so that he will know who to contact regarding changes to the scope.

A Guide to the Project Management Body of Knowledge (PMBOK® Guide) – Fifth Edition, Project Management Institute (PMI)®, Project Management Professional (PMP)®, and Certified Associate in Project Management (CAPM)® are registered trademarks of Project Management Institute, Inc. - Version 2.1 Published September 30, 2014

Solutions

9. What is the name of organized working sessions held by project managers to determine what a project's requirements are and to get all stakeholders together to agree on the project's outcomes? What are some examples?

   ○ Focus groups: JAD, VOC, QDF
   ◉ Facilitated workshops: JAD, VOC, QFD
   ○ Group creativity techniques: JID, DFQ, VOC
   ○ Decision-making techniques: JAD, VOC, QFD

10. In order to make sure that best practices have been planned into the project and to generate ideas for improvement, the project manager is engaged in comparing processes and operations to those of other comparable projects of similar corporations. What is the project manager engaged in?

    ○ Observations
    ◉ Benchmarking
    ○ Mind mapping
    ○ Plurality decision making technique

11. Group decision-making is a method used by a group to come to a decision. Which method is defined when everyone in the group agrees on the course of action to take?

    ◉ Unanimity
    ○ Majority
    ○ Plurality
    ○ Dictatorship

12. Group decision-making is a method used by a group to come to a decision. Which method is defined when the largest batch of individuals within a group agrees on a decision?

    ○ Unanimity
    ○ Majority
    ◉ Plurality
    ○ Dictatorship

13. The project manager needs a structure to work within when determining a project's work that includes project scope, quality requirements, project deliverables, constraints, and assumptions of the project work. What part of the project plan is this?

    ○ The project charter
    ○ The project WBS
    ○ The project requirements matrix
    ◉ The project scope statement

A Guide to the Project Management Body of Knowledge (PMBOK® Guide) – Fifth Edition, Project Management Institute (PMI)®, Project Management Professional (PMP)®, and Certified Associate in Project Management (CAPM)® are registered trademarks of Project Management Institute, Inc. - Version 2.1 Published September 30, 2014

Solutions

14. A team member who is new to the organization and working on projects has several questions and asks the project manager to meet with him to discuss these items so he is sure he understands what is going on during the planning process of the project. The project manager is delighted that this new team member is taking so much interest. The second question the team member has is: "What is the difference between the project charter and the project scope statement?" What would the project manager's response be?

◉ The project charter includes more high-level course objectives and goals, whereas the project scope statement focuses on the actual outcomes of the project.

○ The project scope statement includes more high-level course objectives and goals, whereas the project charter focuses on the actual outcomes of the project.

○ The project charter includes more detailed-level course objectives and goals, whereas the project scope statement focuses on the cost, quality, and schedule.

○ The project charter includes the stakeholder requirements, whereas the project scope statement focuses on the objectives of the project.

15. Product analysis is part of which process?
○ Define Scope Inputs
◉ Define Scope Tools and Techniques
○ Alternatives Generation
○ Define Scope Outputs

16. Lateral thinking, brainstorming, and the Delphi technique are all types of what kind of method?
○ Nominal Group Techniques
○ Product Analysis
◉ Alternatives Generation
○ Group Creativity Techniques

17. What is the purpose of decomposing the project work into a hierarchical WBS structure?
◉ To create smaller more manageable chunks which can be better estimated for cost, time, and resources, and help control the project
○ To create a sequence of work that can be used to track progress through the life of the project, ensuring the project deadline can be met
○ To select the requirements that will be included in the project to the satisfaction of the stakeholders and the project sponsor
○ To draw out potential options to complete the work so the stakeholders and the team members agree on the methods used

18. The project manager and the team would like a way to easily track individual WBS components, which they agree would be especially helpful in the areas of performance, reporting, and cost. In order to accomplish this, what will they implement?
○ WBS dictionary
◉ Code of accounts
○ Requirements matrix
○ Contingency reserve

A Guide to the Project Management Body of Knowledge (PMBOK® Guide) – Fifth Edition, Project Management Institute (PMI)®, Project Management Professional (PMP)®, and Certified Associate in Project Management (CAPM)® are registered trademarks of Project Management Institute, Inc. - Version 2.1 Published September 30, 2014

Solutions

19. The project manager is leading a series of meetings with subject matter experts and the planning team in order to divide and subdivide the project scope into smaller more manageable pieces. What process are they involved in?

   ○ Product analysis

   ○ Mind mapping

   ○ Assemblage

   ◉ Decomposition

20. A team member who is new to the organization and working on projects has several questions and asks the project manager to meet with him to discuss these items so he is sure he understands what is going on during the planning process of the project. The project manager is delighted that this new team member is taking so much interest. The third question the team member has is: "What is a work breakdown structure and what is the level I need to be most concerned with?" What would the project manager's response be?

   ◉ A WBS defines the total scope of work required to complete the project. The individual components are at the lowest level of the hierarchy and are referred to as work packages.

   ○ A WBS defines the requirements requested for the project. The individual components are at the highest level of the hierarchy and are referred to as work packages.

   ○ A WBS defines the total scope of work required to complete the project. None of the components of the hierarchy concern individual team members.

   ○ A WBS is a way to confirm that the scope of work will satisfy the requirements of the stakeholders. You need to be concerned with the top level, which is where the work to be done is defined in work packages.

ACTIVITY 6-1: Researching Schedule Management Plans

3. Why is managing the project schedule important?

   A: Answers will vary, but might include that the schedule dictates all the project work and when tasks will be completed. Without proper management, tasks could slip and dependencies would then be misaligned, which could ultimately cause the project outcomes to be delayed.

4. Which of the following is not a component of the schedule management plan?

   ○ Rules for establishing percent complete

   ○ Schedule performance measurements

   ○ Control thresholds

   ◉ Cost estimates for each work package

ACTIVITY 6-2: Creating an Activity List and a Milestone List

1. The first step in creating an activity list is to gather your resource materials. Which items will be helpful in creating your list?

   ☑ The WBS

   ☐ Cost-benefit analysis

   ☑ The scope statement

   ☑ Activity lists from similar projects

A Guide to the Project Management Body of Knowledge (PMBOK® Guide) – Fifth Edition, Project Management Institute (PMI)®, Project Management Professional (PMP)®, and Certified Associate in Project Management (CAPM)® are registered trademarks of Project Management Institute, Inc. - Version 2.1 Published September 30, 2014

Solutions

ACTIVITY 6–3: Sequencing Activities

1. During a recent meeting with your project team, a decision was made to add five days between the installing plywood flooring and frame interior walls activities due to other projects that some members of the team have already committed to. Will this be a lag or lead relationship that you should account for? Please explain.

   A: There will be a five-day lag between installing plywood flooring and framing interior walls.

ACTIVITY 6–5: Estimating Activity Durations

2. Why do you think it is a good practice to use a three-point estimate for activities?

   A: Answers will vary, but might include that this formula gives a better estimate because the data used to create the estimate is more detailed.

ACTIVITY 6–6: Creating a Project Schedule

1. What other inputs will you need to have available before developing the project schedule?
   - ☑ Resource calendars
   - ☑ Project scope statement
   - ☑ Specific milestone dates that must be met
   - ☐ Schedule baseline

LAB 6–1: Testing Your Knowledge of Planning for Project Time Management

1. What is an element of project work that requires action to produce a deliverable?
   - ○ Work package
   - ○ Requirement
   - ◉ Activity
   - ○ Milestone

2. Which of the following defines characteristics of activities?
   - ◉ It has an expected duration, it consumes budget and/or human resources, and it is named in verb-noun format.
   - ○ It organizes the work to be done by control account, and provides the basis for estimating cost.
   - ○ It is the lowest level of the WBS, and it consumes budget and/or human resources.
   - ○ It has an expected duration, it is the lowest level of the WBS, and it is named in noun-verb format.

A Guide to the Project Management Body of Knowledge (PMBOK® Guide) – Fifth Edition, Project Management Institute (PMI)®, Project Management Professional (PMP)®, and Certified Associate in Project Management (CAPM)® are registered trademarks of Project Management Institute, Inc. - Version 2.1 Published September 30, 2014

3. **What lays the foundation for estimating, scheduling, executing, and monitoring and controlling the project work?**
   - ○ Tasks
   - ○ Work packages
   - ○ Requirements
   - ◉ Activities

4. **What is a form of progressive elaboration where near-term work is defined at a detailed level, and future work is left at a higher level?**
   - ○ Decomposition
   - ○ Task elaboration
   - ◉ Rolling Wave Planning
   - ○ Rotation Planning

5. **What is the 8/80 rule?**
   - ◉ A work package should include at least 8 but not more than 80 hours effort to complete.
   - ○ A work package should include effort that is under 8 and more than 80 hours to complete.
   - ○ That 8% of the people cause 80% of the problems.
   - ○ A guideline for planning work packages that is very useful in large projects.

6. **A team member who is new to the organization and working on projects has several questions and asks the project manager to meet with him to discuss these items so he is sure he understands what is going on during the planning process of the project. The project manager is delighted that this new team member is taking so much interest. One of the questions the team member has is: "What is the project schedule network diagram?" What would the project manager's response be?**
   - ○ A hierarchical breakdown of the work required to satisfy the requirements.
   - ◉ A graphical representation of the sequence of project activities and the dependencies among them.
   - ○ It is the lowest level of the WBS, and it consumes budget and/or human resources.
   - ○ A visual depiction of the product scope, showing a business system and how people will interact with it.

7. **Which of the following correctly defines the Precedence Diagramming method?**
   - ◉ Activities are represented as nodes and are graphically linked together by their relationships
   - ○ Activities are represented as arrows and are graphically linked together by their relationships
   - ○ Activities are represented as circles and are graphically linked together by their relationships
   - ○ Activities are represented as icons and are graphically linked together by their hierarchical relationship from the WBS

8. **There are four types of logical relationships used in the Precedence Diagramming method. What are they?**
   - ○ Finish to Finish, Start to Start, Top to Bottom, End to End
   - ◉ Finish to Start, Start to Finish, Finish to Finish, Start to Start
   - ○ End to End, Front to Back, Top to Bottom, Finish to Start
   - ○ Start to Finish, Finish to Finish, Bottom to Top, End to End

A Guide to the Project Management Body of Knowledge (PMBOK® Guide) – Fifth Edition, Project Management Institute (PMI)®, Project Management Professional (PMP)®, and Certified Associate in Project Management (CAPM)® are registered trademarks of Project Management Institute, Inc. - Version 2.1 Published September 30, 2014

Solutions

9. What are the four types of dependencies in a network diagram?
   - ○ Incendiary, Mandatory, Required, External
   - ○ Required, Discretionary, Variable, Internal
   - ○ External, Internal, Written, Unspoken
   - ◉ Mandatory, External, Internal, Discretionary

10. Which type of dependency is usually determined by the nature of the work, or it may be due to a legal or contract requirement?
    - ○ External
    - ○ Discretionary
    - ◉ Mandatory
    - ○ Internal

11. Which of the following is the name for the amount of time that needs to pass before the successor activity can begin?
    - ◉ Lag
    - ○ Lead
    - ○ Start
    - ○ Float

12. Which of the following is the correct definition of the critical path?
    - ○ The critical path is the fastest path through the network diagram which represents the longest time in which the project can be completed.
    - ○ The critical path is the shortest path through the network diagram which represents the longest time in which the project can be completed.
    - ○ The critical path is the earliest path through the network diagram which represents the latest time in which the project can be completed.
    - ◉ The critical path is the longest path through the network diagram which represents the shortest time in which the project can be completed.

13. A team member who is new to the organization and working on projects has several questions and asks the project manager to meet with him to discuss these items so he is sure he understands what is going on during the planning process of the project. The project manager is delighted that this new team member is taking so much interest. One of the questions the team member has is: "If we must complete the software code before we can create the user manual, what type of dependency exists between these two work packages?" What would the project manager's response be?
    - ○ Finish to Finish
    - ◉ Finish to Start
    - ○ Start to Finish
    - ○ Start to Start

14. Which of the following is the correct PERT formula to estimate duration?
    - ◉ Duration = (O + (4 x ML) + P) / 6
    - ○ Duration = (O + ML x 4 + P) / 3
    - ○ Duration = ML / 6 + (O - P)
    - ○ Duration = (O x 4 + ML x 3) + P

A Guide to the Project Management Body of Knowledge (PMBOK® Guide) – Fifth Edition, Project Management Institute (PMI)®, Project Management Professional (PMP)®, and Certified Associate in Project Management (CAPM)® are registered trademarks of Project Management Institute, Inc. - Version 2.1 Published September 30, 2014

Solutions

15. The project manager and the planning team is developing the project schedule and will use the PERT method to determine project duration. The estimates include the following: Most likely is 180 hours, optimistic is 100 hours, and pessimistic is 200 hours. Which of the following is the correct PERT estimate?
- ○ 160
- ○ 80
- ◉ 170
- ○ 345

16. What method allows you to add buffers to accommodate uncertainty and limited resources?
- ○ Critical path
- ○ Resource optimization
- ○ Critical buffering
- ◉ Critical chain

17. Which is the correct definition of Fast Tracking?
- ◉ Moving critical path activities that you had originally planned to do sequentially, and making them concurrent.
- ○ Shortening the schedule by adding resources or in some other way expediting critical path activities.
- ○ Keeping resource usages at a constant level and avoiding over-allocation.
- ○ Updating non-critical path activities that you had originally planned to do sequentially, and making them concurrent.

18. A process that involves expediting critical path activities by spending money is called what?
- ○ Balancing
- ○ Maneuvering
- ◉ Crashing
- ○ Fast Tracking

19. The dependencies and durations for all the project activities are shown in the following table. What is the critical path duration?
- ○ 15
- ◉ 19
- ○ 21
- ○ 16

Activity Predecessor Duration X Start 3 Y Start 5 Z Y 2 O X, Z 6 T Z, O 1 F T 3 H T, O 5 End H, F 0

20. Based on the following table, how much float is there on activity F?
- ◉ 2
- ○ 11
- ○ 3
- ○ 4

Activity Predecessor Duration X Start 3 Y Start 5 Z Y 2 O X, Z 6 T Z, O 1 F T 3 H T, O 5 End H, F 0

A Guide to the Project Management Body of Knowledge (PMBOK® Guide) – Fifth Edition, Project Management Institute (PMI)®, Project Management Professional (PMP)®, and Certified Associate in Project Management (CAPM)® are registered trademarks of Project Management Institute, Inc. - Version 2.1 Published September 30, 2014

Solutions

ACTIVITY 7-1: Estimating Project Costs

1. Use analogous estimating to calculate the cost of the doors for this house.

   A: Two external doors are donated, and on previous projects, internal doors cost $100, so 100 * 8 = $800.

2. What basis of estimate documentation would you provide to show how you obtained your cost estimate for all the doors?

   A: Answers will vary, but could include the donation letter for the external doors from the last project and the invoice for the internal doors from the last project to show what you based your estimates on.

3. How does the project WBS help you when estimating costs for your project?

   A: Answers will vary, but should include that the WBS provides the lowest level breakdown of the work packages and allows the project manager to estimate costs at the very lowest level.

4. What are the benefits of the parametric modeling technique?

   A: The parametric model is reliable and can provide a high level of accuracy. However, the information that forms the parameters must be accurate, quantifiable, and scalable.

ACTIVITY 7-2: Creating a Partial Budget

Use information provided for the framing work package to determine the actual costs of the materials and the supervisor resource.

A: The answer is as follows: **Supervisor**: 10 days * 8 hours * $20.00 = $1,600.00; **Plywood**: 66 sheets at $15.00 per sheet = $990.00; **2x4s**: 150 at $6.50 per board = $975.00; **30 pounds of nails** at $5.00 per pound = $150.00, which brings the total budget for the framing work package to **$3,715.00**.

ACTIVITY 7-3: Examining Quality Management

1. What are some of the costs of quality?

   A: Answers will vary, but might include paying for the inspectors, building permits, cost of certificates, and in some cases, the cost of any rework.

2. How can you prevent some of these costs to avoid exceeding your budget?

   A: Answers will vary, but could include completing a pre-inspection, scheduling all inspections together so the inspector has to make only one trip. You could also conduct volunteer training to increase skills for improved quality of work completed.

3. Which of the following seven basic quality tools should you use to identify a root cause of a quality issue?
   - ◉ Fishbone diagram
   - ○ Checksheet
   - ○ Histogram
   - ○ Pareto diagram

A Guide to the Project Management Body of Knowledge (PMBOK® Guide) – Fifth Edition, Project Management Institute (PMI)®, Project Management Professional (PMP)®, and Certified Associate in Project Management (CAPM)® are registered trademarks of Project Management Institute, Inc. - Version 2.1 Published September 30, 2014

Solutions

4. Which two of the following are costs of conformance to ensure quality?

   - ☑ Prevention costs
   - ☑ Appraisal costs
   - ☐ Failure costs
   - ☐ Warranties

ACTIVITY 7-4: Examining Human Resource Management

1. Determine what skills are needed for each work package.

   A: Answers are as follows: volunteers, site supervisor, landscapers, masons, inspectors, electricians, plumbers, framers, and window and door installers.

2. What method could you use to attain volunteers for the build project?

   A: Answers will vary, but could include the use of networking and meetings with local organizations.

3. You have reviewed the staffing management plan, and to your surprise, it appears that there are now staffing gaps due to resource reassignments. What could you do to address this problem?

   A: Answers will vary, but may include to develop some rough choices for the project sponsor in terms of acquiring new resources and lead times to fill these staffing gaps. Typically, this is where the budget and schedule get their first updates.

ACTIVITY 7-5: Discussing Communications Management

1. What communication skills can be used when working with the various people and volunteers on the build project?

   A: Answers will vary, but could include listening, coaching, resolving conflict, and educating.

2. Which item should you use to determine the communications needs of your project stakeholders?

   - ◉ Stakeholder analysis data
   - ○ Research material
   - ○ Project report deadlines
   - ○ Executive board schedule

3. Given the scenario, what would be a good technology for enhancing team member interactions and building relationships throughout the life of the project?

   - ○ Team building event at project kick-off
   - ○ Project team threaded discussion board
   - ○ Use email and databases to collect and store information
   - ◉ High-quality virtual teleconferencing on a semi-weekly or weekly basis

4. After integrating the communications management plan into the overall project plan, what would be the next logical step?

   - ○ Determining whether there will be changes to the proposed technology before the project is over
   - ○ Creating a schedule for the production of each type of communication
   - ○ Creating a description of stakeholder communication requirements
   - ◉ Distributing the plan to all the stakeholders

5. Today, at the new build site, there are 10 volunteers working, and you as the site coordinator need to communicate with all these volunteers a number of times throughout the day. How many communication paths exist today? Use the communications requirements analysis [n (n – 1) / 2] to determine the number of communication paths.

A: Answer should be 11 (11 – 1) / 2 = 55 total communication paths.
You may need to remind students that the project manager is included in the communication path calculation.

LAB 7–1: Testing Your Knowledge of Planning Project Budget, Quality, and Communications

---

1. A team member who is new to the organization and working on projects has several questions and asks the project manager to meet with him to discuss these items so he is sure he understands what is going on during the planning process of the project. The project manager is delighted that this new team member is taking so much interest. One of the questions the team member has is: "In the projects I worked on at my old company, when we were estimating the costs, we always used the costs of a previous project with similar scope or activities to predict the cost of future activities. You don't seem to be doing that here. What method are we using for cost estimating in this company?" The project manager explained that he is using Parametric Estimating. Which of the following is the method used at the team member's former company, and what is the correct explanation of Parametric?

   ○ Expert Judgment, and a method that focuses on the cost of ensured quality.

   ○ Group Decision Making Techniques, and a method that relies on the statistical relationship that exists between historical information and variables, so as to arrive at an estimate for parameters such as duration and cost.

   ○ Analogous, and a method to use Delphi, brainstorming, and nominal group techniques.

   ◉ Analogous, and a method that relies on the statistical relationship that exists between historical information and variables, so as to arrive at an estimate for parameters such as duration and cost.

2. What are the three aspects that Earned Value Management considers?

   ◉ Planned Value, Earned Value, Actual Cost

   ○ Planned Cost, Earned Value, Actual Value

   ○ Value Earned, Planned Cost, Actual Plan

   ○ Planned Value, Earned Cost, Actual Amount

3. What are the three values used in Three-Point Estimate?

   ○ Optimistic, worst-case scenario, a false expectation

   ○ Best-case scenario, worst-case scenario, pre-planned scenario

   ◉ Most likely, optimistic, pessimistic

   ○ A realistic expectation, a false expectation, an estimate of expectation

A Guide to the Project Management Body of Knowledge (PMBOK® Guide) – Fifth Edition, Project Management Institute (PMI)®, Project Management Professional (PMP)®, and Certified Associate in Project Management (CAPM)® are registered trademarks of Project Management Institute, Inc. - Version 2.1 Published September 30, 2014

Solutions

4. A team member who is new to the organization and working on projects has several questions and asks the project manager to meet with him to discuss these items so he is sure he understands what is going on during the planning process of the project. The project manager is delighted that this new team member is taking so much interest. One of the questions the team member has is: "In projects at my former company, we used the cost as stated on the charter to be our cost estimate for the project. Here you are not doing that. It almost seems like you are disregarding that figure until the planning is done and then you reconcile your figures with the sponsor's on the charter. Why is that?" What would the project manager's response be?

⦿ The rough order of magnitude stated on a charter is usually developed without a basis of detailed data and is often based on very high-level historical data, expert judgment, or a costing model.

○ The sponsors have no idea what things cost and they just come up with a number to put something on the charter. They depend on us to come up with the correct budget figures.

○ The Rough Order of Magnitude is often used for appropriation purposes and has accuracy of -10% to +25%.

○ While the ROM has an accuracy of +/- 35 %, it is used for work that is further in the future.

5. The sponsor provides many pieces of information to the project manager to state on the project charter. One of them is the summary cost estimate. At the time the charter is being developed, what is generally the level of accuracy of the ROM as stated in the charter?

○ +/-35%

⦿ -50% to +100%

○ -5% to +10%

○ +/-15%

6. What are activity cost estimates made up of?

○ Supporting data or additional information needed to justify the cost estimates.

○ Estimates on probable costs necessary to finish project work including direct costs, labor, materials, equipment, facilities, services, information technology, and contingency reserves.

○ Estimates on probable costs necessary to finish project work based on the responsive bids obtained from vendors.

⦿ Estimates on probable costs necessary to finish project work including direct labor, materials, equipment, facilities, services, information technology, contingency reserves, or indirect costs.

7. What is the process to create a project budget?

○ Take the ROM and decompose it into the cost of work packages.

⦿ Combine all individual activity cost estimates and aggregate them for the entire project to produce a baseline.

○ Estimate costs necessary to finish project work including direct costs, labor, materials, equipment, facilities, services, information technology, and contingency reserves.

○ Create an S-curve with cost on the Y axis and time on the X axis.

8. The project manager is using the time-phased budget to measure the cost performance. What is that budget called?

⦿ Cost baseline

○ Cost estimate

○ Rough order of magnitude

○ Cost consolidation

A Guide to the Project Management Body of Knowledge (PMBOK® Guide) – Fifth Edition, Project Management Institute (PMI)®, Project Management Professional (PMP)®, and Certified Associate in Project Management (CAPM)® are registered trademarks of Project Management Institute, Inc. - Version 2.1 Published September 30, 2014

Solutions

9. The project manager has a new team member who seems eager to understand the processes used at this company, since the company he came from used different processes and terminology. The project manager tells the team member to help him with the process of combining activity costs into work package costs and continue to add up through the WBS to achieve a single project cost. What tool or technique are they engaged in?

   ○ Funding limit reconciliation

   ○ Reserve analysis

   ◉ Cost aggregation

   ○ Bottom down estimating

10. What is it called when funding limits are in place as a method of adjusting, spending, scheduling, and resource allocation, to regulate the outgoing capital flow and to protect against over-spending?

    ○ Budget control

    ○ Cost aggregation

    ◉ Funding limit reconciliation

    ○ Reserve analysis

11. What is a quality system standard that is applicable to any product, service, or process in the world?

    ○ A quality management plan

    ○ Design of experiments

    ○ CMMI

    ◉ ISO 9000 series

12. When discussing the quality of the project with a new team member, the project manager wants to be sure that the new team member is using the correct terminology that is used in this organization because it has become apparent that the team member comes from an organization where many things and terms were used differently on their projects. He asks the team member to define prevention costs. What should the team member's response be?

    ◉ Upfront costs of programs or processes needed to meet customer requirements, or to design in quality.

    ○ The costs associated with evaluating whether the program or processes meet requirements.

    ○ The costs associated with making the product or service acceptable to the customer after it fails internal testing and before it's delivered to the customer.

    ○ The costs resulting from rejection of the product or service by the customer.

13. When discussing the quality of the project with a new team member, the project manager wants to be sure that the new team member is using the correct terminology that is used in this organization because it has become apparent that the team member comes from an organization where many things and terms were used differently on their projects. He asks the team member to define external failure costs. What should the team member's response be?

    ○ Upfront costs of programs or processes needed to meet customer requirements, or to design in quality.

    ◉ The costs resulting from rejection of the product or service by the customer.

    ○ The costs associated with evaluating whether the program or processes meet requirements.

    ○ The costs associated with making the product or service acceptable to the customer after it fails internal testing and before it's delivered to the customer.

A Guide to the Project Management Body of Knowledge (PMBOK® Guide) – Fifth Edition, Project Management Institute (PMI)®, Project Management Professional (PMP)®, and Certified Associate in Project Management (CAPM)® are registered trademarks of Project Management Institute, Inc. - Version 2.1 Published September 30, 2014

Solutions

14. What is another name for an Ishikawa diagram and what is it used for?

- ○ Kawasaki, used for cause and effect diagramming to find the source of problems
- ○ Scatter diagram, used to plot pairs to evaluate the correlation
- ○ Pareto, used to display the frequency of observations
- ◉ Fishbone, used for cause and effect diagramming to find the source of problems

15. In order to test to see if the game the team is delivering is easy enough for the children of the intended age group, the team creates a prototype and then establishes their test criteria. Then the team establishes test groups of 100 boys and 100 girls, all between the ages of 3 and 5, at 50 different elementary schools across 30 states. What are they engaged in?

- ○ Benchmarking
- ○ Design of Experiments
- ◉ Statistical sampling
- ○ Force field analysis

16. Training needs, rewards and recognition, compliance, and safety are all aspects of what project management plan?

- ○ Human resources management plan
- ◉ Staffing management plan
- ○ Motivation and safety management plan
- ○ Process improvement plan

17. The project manager is explaining the reasons for the need to create a staffing release plan to the sponsor who is annoyed with all the plans the project manager is spending time on creating. What is the project manager's justification for doing this?

- ◉ This will help control project costs and allows for a smooth transition to other projects.
- ○ This will help control the project schedule and allows for fewer individuals to be involved in the closing phase.
- ○ This will help let all the functional managers know how their staff will be treated while working on the project.
- ○ This will help the project manager remove team members who are not working up to the level of quality required to meet the project objectives.

18. A team member who is new to the organization and working on projects has several questions and asks the project manager to meet with him to discuss these items so he is sure he understands what is going on during the planning process of the project. The project manager is delighted that this new team member is taking so much interest. One of the questions the team member has is: "What is involved in planning for the safety of the project staff?" He had never seen this addressed in the projects he had worked on in his previous organization. What is the correct response that the project manager should provide?

- ○ The project manager has had experience with team members being injured while working on the project and this has caused a worker's compensation problem.
- ○ Every project requires safety precautions depending on the risks of the project.
- ○ Some projects require safety precautions such as those being performed in non-class A office towers, those with stairs, and those that may experience winter weather conditions.
- ◉ Some projects require safety precautions such as those being performed in nuclear power plants, construction hard hat zones, and war zones.

A Guide to the Project Management Body of Knowledge (PMBOK® Guide) – Fifth Edition, Project Management Institute (PMI)®, Project Management Professional (PMP)®, and Certified Associate in Project Management (CAPM)® are registered trademarks of Project Management Institute, Inc. - Version 2.1 Published September 30, 2014

Solutions

19. While looking at a matrix grid, the team member can understand the connection between the work package and the team members for all the work that is to be performed in the project. What type of a chart is the team member viewing?

   ○ Hierarchical organizational breakdown structure

   ○ Organizational theory chart

   ◉ Responsibility assignment matrix (RAM)

   ○ Histogram

20. When planning for communication in a project, which of the following is the correct list of tools and techniques that are used?

   ◉ Technology, methods, models

   ○ Requirements analysis, technology, types

   ○ Technology, push/pull, models

   ○ Requirements analysis, interactive, models

ACTIVITY 8-1: Researching Risk Management Plans

3. After reviewing the risk management plan for a previous project, what changes, if any, would you make in your new plan?

   A: Answers will vary, but might include: Looking at previous projects allows you to use a frame of reference to plan for your project's risks. It's considered a best practice to review previous project documents to identify patterns in risk and to identify any potential risks going forward.

4. Why do you think the roles and responsibilities section is important to include in a risk management plan?

   A: Answers will vary, but might include making sure that all risk activities are accounted for, as well as project stakeholders who are involved. By setting the roles up early in the process, you can establish good communication strategies with the project stakeholders that need to be involved in the risk management process.

ACTIVITY 8-6: Planning Project Procurements

1. When planning procurement management, what should you do first?

   A: Answers may vary, but should include reviewing all inputs to this process to identify all the goods and services that need to acquired for the project work to be done.

2. What are the three contract types and when would you use each one?

   A: The three contract types are fixed, cost reimbursable, and time and materials contracts. The use of the contracts may vary, but could include using fixed price contracts when the requirements are very well known, using cost reimbursable contracts when the scope of the work cannot be precisely defined, and using time and materials contracts (T&M) when specific deliverables cannot be determined.

3. What do you need to create a procurement statement of work document?

   A: Answers may vary, but should include enough detail on the requirements for the product or service being procured. This can include specifications, quantity, quality level, performance requirements, work location, and so on, and should be concise, clear, and complete.

A Guide to the Project Management Body of Knowledge (PMBOK® Guide) – Fifth Edition, Project Management Institute (PMI)®, Project Management Professional (PMP)®, and Certified Associate in Project Management (CAPM)® are registered trademarks of Project Management Institute, Inc. - Version 2.1 Published September 30, 2014

Solutions

4. **Why can change requests be generated from procurement planning?**

   A: Answers may vary, but should include the fact that decisions to procure items for the project can create changes to the project as originally planned.

ACTIVITY 8-7: Researching Stakeholder Management Plans

2. **Why is it important to plan for stakeholder management?**

   A: Answers will vary, but should include the stakeholders having a large impact and influence on a project and what the outcomes will be. They are always emerging as a project progresses, and so having a good management plan will enable you to react and keep all stakeholders engaged. Because most of a project's requirements come from the stakeholders, keeping good track of them along with the stakeholder who is associated with the requirements is essential to good communication and project success.

3. **Bob Jones is the manager of the accounting department of a large manufacturing firm. The organization's Information Technology department has a new initiative to upgrade and improve the existing accounting system due to new tax regulations. Bob likes the older system he's been using for more than 10 years and is questioning whether the new system will produce the same results as the old one. What classification would you use for Bob's level of involvement in this project?**

   - ⦿ Resistant
   - ○ Unaware
   - ○ Leading
   - ○ Supportive
   - ○ Neutral

LAB 8-1: Testing Your Knowledge of Planning for Risk, Procurements, and Stakeholders

1. **Which one of these is a risk?**
   - ○ We have determined that our schedule is not going to meet the required deadline.
   - ⦿ We think it is possible there will be a sale on parts and we could spend less money than we originally thought.
   - ○ There are not enough resources to complete the work on time.
   - ○ The change in the prime rate has caused our funding source to be unable to provide the money we need in the upcoming project phase.

2. **While discussing risks with the team members, one of them refers to a risk as an unknown unknown and suggests that it be referred to the management of the company. Is this correct or not, and why?**
   - ○ Yes this is correct because it is up to the management of the company to help the project be successful by handing all the potential problems that could occur.
   - ○ No this is not correct because risks that are to be handled by the management are mitigated by workarounds.
   - ○ No this is not correct because all risks are known unknowns until they occur.
   - ⦿ Yes this is correct because large risks that cannot be handled within the project should be referred to management and are referred to as unknown unknowns.

A Guide to the Project Management Body of Knowledge (PMBOK® Guide) – Fifth Edition, Project Management Institute (PMI)®, Project Management Professional (PMP)®, and Certified Associate in Project Management (CAPM)® are registered trademarks of Project Management Institute, Inc. - Version 2.1 Published September 30, 2014

Solutions

3. **What happens to the risks that are below the risk threshold level for the project? What is the risk threshold level?**
   - ◉ They are accepted. Risk threshold is the level of uncertainty that can be accepted.
   - ○ They are mitigated. Risk threshold is the level of uncertainty that can be accepted.
   - ○ They are accepted. Risk threshold is the degree of uncertainty that can be taken on in anticipation of a benefit.
   - ○ They are accepted. Risk threshold is the amount of risk the organization can endure.

4. **During a planning meeting, the project manager displays a graph that maps the probability of occurrence and the impact of each risk so the risk management team can get an overview of how risky the project is. What is this graph called?**
   - ◉ Probability and impact matrix
   - ○ Probability and likeliness chart
   - ○ Impact and effect map
   - ○ RAM matrix

5. **A team member who is new to the organization wants to help with the risk planning. He was heavily involved in this at his old company and thinks some of their tools, which the new company does not use, were very useful. He suggests that the risk management team develop a document that is a hierarchical layout of the risks by category. What document is he referring to?**
   - ○ RAM
   - ○ OBS
   - ◉ RBS
   - ○ RACI

6. **What is a risk team?**
   - ○ A group of stakeholders who have identified the most risks in a project.
   - ○ A subset of the project team who will be the risk owners for the project.
   - ○ A collection of risk responses used in previous projects that will be chosen from for the risk response plans in the current project.
   - ◉ A group of people dedicated to identify, manage, and monitor the risks in a project.

7. **Early warning signs that a risk event is about to occur are stored with the risk as additional information in the risk register. What are they called and who should be aware of them?**
   - ◉ Triggers, stakeholder risk owner
   - ○ Warnings, the project sponsor
   - ○ Signals, stakeholder risk owner
   - ○ Triggers, the project sponsor

A Guide to the Project Management Body of Knowledge (PMBOK® Guide) – Fifth Edition, Project Management Institute (PMI)®, Project Management Professional (PMP)®, and Certified Associate in Project Management (CAPM)® are registered trademarks of Project Management Institute, Inc. - Version 2.1 Published September 30, 2014

Solutions

8. While spending time preparing for risk identification meetings, the project manager searches through the old project archives and puts together a risk checklist. There are advantages and disadvantages of this. What are they?

   ○ It creates a random way to identify risks by not using categories, but there may be other risks that do.

   ◉ It creates a standardized way to identify risks in specific categories, but there may be additional risks that do not fall into categories on the check list.

   ○ It is a fool proof way to be sure you have covered all aspects of potential risk in the project, but it takes a long time to create.

   ○ It does not take much time or research to create, but it can only be used by the project manager.

9. When using interviewing methods to gather risk probability, what is the range of values that may be used?

   ○ 1 to 10

   ○ 10 to -1

   ○ Any range that the team wants to use, so it is not consistent across other projects

   ◉ Lowest, most likely, highest

10. SWOT is a method used to uncover internally generated risks. What does this acronym stand for?

    ○ Strength warning original threat

    ○ Strong weak old timely

    ◉ Strength weakness opportunity threat

    ○ Specific weakness opportunity timely

11. Which of the following is a good example of mitigating the probability of a threat risk on a project?

    ◉ Install smoke detectors

    ○ Install fire-proof components

    ○ Hire another company to do the part of the work that could result in a fire

    ○ Keep the phone number of the fire department handy

12. The project manager has built a large table that stores a lot of information about the project risks. The team members have never seen one of these before and ask him to explain what it is and why it is important. What would be the project manager's response?

    ○ Risk breakdown structure, to document the categories of risk in the project which helps find courses and trends and to use as lessons learned.

    ◉ Risk register, to document identified risks and all attributes, as well as document the outcome of the risk management processes and share as lessons learned.

    ○ Risk register, to document all the threats to the project and the outcome of the risk management processes and share as lessons learned.

    ○ Risk register, to document the unidentified risks and their impact to the project and the outcome of the risk management processes and share as lessons learned.

A Guide to the Project Management Body of Knowledge (PMBOK® Guide) – Fifth Edition, Project Management Institute (PMI)®, Project Management Professional (PMP)®, and Certified Associate in Project Management (CAPM)® are registered trademarks of Project Management Institute, Inc. - Version 2.1 Published September 30, 2014

Solutions

13. The members of the risk management team would like the project manager to give them a good explanation of the difference between qualitative risk analysis and quantitative risk analysis. What would be the project manager's response?

   ○ Qualitative analysis allows us to identify time and cost contingencies, where quantitative provides a prioritization of the risks.

   ○ Qualitative analysis allows us to get the longest list of risks possible, where quantitative provides a prioritization of the risks.

   ◉ Qualitative analysis provides a prioritization of the risks, where quantitative allows us to identify time and cost contingencies.

   ○ Qualitative is objective and quantitative is subjective.

14. What is the project risk ranking used for?

   ○ To prioritize risks within the project

   ○ To determine the level of each risk within the project

   ○ It is part of the closing process, to be sure all risks have been addressed

   ◉ Comparison among other projects

15. There is a 30% chance that there will be a sale on products and the project could save as much as $25,000. There is a 10% chance that the supplier will be late delivering, which could cost the project $85,000. There is a 25% possibility that if new equipment is bought for $3,000, the company could save $10,000. There is also a 50% likelihood that the bad weather will delay the project, which could end up costing the company $250,000. What is the total EMV?

   ○ $125,500

   ◉ $124,250

   ○ $141,500

   ○ $125,750

16. The project planning team is trying to perform what–if scenarios to determine the potential outcomes for the project schedule. A team member mentions a simulation software that he has used in another company and suggests it would help. This software is used to make predictions about the optimistic, most likely, and pessimistic estimates for variables in the model and simulates various outcomes of the project schedule to provide a statistical distribution of the calculated results. What is an example of this?

   ◉ Monte Carlo

   ○ Monaco Modeling

   ○ LVOS (Las Vegas Odds Simulation)

   ○ Pareto Diagramming

17. What is the difference between avoiding a threat and mitigating it?

   ○ Avoid means to reduce the impact or probability, and mitigate means to change the management plan to remove the risk.

   ○ Avoid means to outsource the work to remove the risk, and mitigate means to reduce the impact or probability.

   ◉ Avoid means to change the management plan to remove the risk, and mitigate means to reduce the impact or probability.

   ○ Avoid means to change the management plan to remove the risk, and mitigate means to accept the impact or probability.

18. The project manager and his risk management team are involved in risk identification and response planning. Each time they come up with a response plan, someone points out that the contingency plan could be the cause of yet another risk. What type of risk would that be?

   ○ Subsidiary

   ◉ Secondary

   ○ Unlikely

   ○ Residual

19. An architectural firm has spent a great deal of time and effort creating the design and blueprints for the building. They had to purchase materials and hire consultants and have been working on this project for six months. They have submitted all the invoices for the money they have spent on the work, as well as an invoice for the fee of $5,000. What type of contract was this?

   ○ Time and materials

   ○ CPIF

   ○ FPEPA

   ◉ Cost reimbursable

20. There is a great deal of effort with regard to the stakeholders during the project planning. The sponsor would like to know what all the fuss is about and get an explanation from the project manager about what is taking so long. The project manager explains the need for a stakeholder management plan with which of the following statements?

   ◉ To effectively engage stakeholders in project decisions and execution based on the analysis of their needs, interests, and potential impact

   ○ To ensure the stakeholders are receiving the reports in the format they would like

   ○ To effectively place the right people in the correct role to support achieving the project objectives on time and within budget

   ○ To be able to document which stakeholder is unaware, neutral, leading, or supportive

ACTIVITY 9-1: Identifying Responsibilities for Project Execution

1. You need to assist the systems analyst in the creation of a PMIS that is workable for your project. In order to design an effective PMIS, what are the inputs that a systems analyst should know about the project that the PMIS will manage?

   ☑ What people will have access to the information?

   ☑ When will the information be needed?

   ☑ Who will incorporate the information into the system?

   ☐ Who is the customer?

2. As the project manager, you have made sure all organizational policies and procedures were followed, and the contract training vendor is familiar with their responsibilities. What would you do next?

   ○ Call a meeting with the project sponsor so she can commence work.

   ◉ Issue work authorization.

   ○ Work with a systems analyst to create a PMIS.

   ○ Collect work performance information.

A Guide to the Project Management Body of Knowledge (PMBOK® Guide) – Fifth Edition, Project Management Institute (PMI)®, Project Management Professional (PMP)®, and Certified Associate in Project Management (CAPM)® are registered trademarks of Project Management Institute, Inc. - Version 2.1 Published September 30, 2014

Solutions

3. **An activity did not start on its scheduled date. The responsible team, Team 1, claimed that they could not start the activity because its predecessor activity did not show a completion date in the latest status report. Team 2 claimed that they had completed the activity on time and had followed the appropriate procedure for updating its completion status. What are some things you would do to investigate why the status report was not up to date?**

   A: Review the status for the activities in the PMIS, as it is the central point of data collection for activity status. If you discover that the completion status for the activity is not reflected in the system, alert the PMIS technical experts so that the cause can be identified. Along with the current system for activity updates, you may also ask that resources communicate their activity progress weekly through a quick email or phone call until the original system is proven.

ACTIVITY 9-2: Performing Quality Assurance

1. **The manager of quality assurance has asked you about your quality management plan. Which feature might he find problematic?**

   ◉ Any corrective actions that a project manager feels will improve the effectiveness or efficiency.

   ○ Scheduled and random quality inspections will take place, which will be conducted by an internal quality assurance engineer, as well as by the city.

   ○ Operational definitions were defined for measuring the quality of the construction work.

   ○ Occurrence of scheduled and random quality inspections during the course of the project.

2. **As construction gets under way, random inspection results of completed construction elements are unexpectedly negative. What sort of quality activities should be taking place?**

   A: Perform a random or scheduled quality audit to evaluate the quality management plan, quality testing procedures, and measurement criteria for inconsistencies in the way that the quality plan and operational definitions are being carried out.

3. **The stakeholders are questioning the amount of resources dedicated to quality assurance. How can you demonstrate to them that the benefits of quality assurance outweigh the cost?**

   ○ Perform benchmarking to compare project practices to other projects to generate ideas for improvement.

   ○ Conduct an array of experiments to identify which factors may be influencing specific variables.

   ○ Use flowcharts to see how systems relate and how various factors might be linked to problems or effects.

   ◉ Document the identified corrective actions so that their effect on project quality, cost, and schedule can be monitored during quality control.

A Guide to the Project Management Body of Knowledge (PMBOK® Guide) – Fifth Edition, Project Management Institute (PMI)®, Project Management Professional (PMP)®, and Certified Associate in Project Management (CAPM)® are registered trademarks of Project Management Institute, Inc. - Version 2.1 Published September 30, 2014

Solutions

ACTIVITY 9-3: Acquiring a Project Team

1. Three members of your project team have to be allocated to you on a part-time, 50 percent basis. What would be your first step in acquiring these resources for the project team?

   A: Answers will vary, but may include forming good relationships with the functional manager in order to identify and acquire resources, resolve problems, and manage team members. You can also discuss the specific time frames that you will need for those people.

2. The functional manager of the department informs you that, based on the time frame for your project, two of the resources that are available are new volunteers who have not yet worked in a project on their own. What should you do?

   A: Answers will vary, but may include asking the functional manager if a seasoned volunteer member of his team can serve as a mentor to the new hires, at least throughout the beginning phases of the project. You can also verify that the assigned resources will be able to perform the work required. Also, discuss who will be responsible for training the new hires. Learning to negotiate effectively with functional managers is a crucial part of the team acquisition process.

3. Why is negotiation so important when acquiring your project team?

   A: Answers will vary, but could include that negotiation helps you get the right resources for your project. Learning to negotiate effectively is important to obtain the right project team.

4. During the first meeting of the new project team, some confusion arises between two team members about their roles and responsibilities. Because this conversation is not appropriate in this forum, how might you respond?

   A: Answers will vary, but may include: As the project manager, you should identify the issue, table it, and use the human resource plan, which was developed for the project and clearly documents the roles and responsibilities and organizational structure. The two resources will be informed and once again be made aware of it. This sets the expectation that "working the problem" should be the focus, not "arguing the problem."

ACTIVITY 9-4: Developing Your Project Team

1. You notice that Rachel, a team member, has consistently met her deliverable deadlines and is always on time with her status reports. She actively participates in brainstorming sessions and makes valuable contributions to the discussions. When required, she has gone beyond her responsibilities and has helped her project manager facilitate brainstorming meetings and discussion sessions. How should you respond?

   A: Answers will vary, but may include: Consider publicly recognizing her in a team meeting to reinforce the desirable behaviors. The team may congratulate her and it may give everyone motivation to go the extra mile when needed to meet aggressive deadlines. It is also advisable to provide positive input to her functional manager for her performance appraisal. This will also boost her motivation to go the extra mile, and might lead to a raise.

2. One of your junior team members, who is assigned to gather information from supervisors through an interview process, has confided in you that he is not comfortable during the interviews. He feels that the supervisors seem impatient with the questions he is asking. The other junior team members assigned to interviews have not had any problems. What are some things you would do to address this issue?

   A: Answers will vary, but may include: As a project manager, you can talk to the team member about certain aspects of his voice, such as intonation, and his communication style, such as nonverbal cues. You need to identify if the team member has a problem in any of these aspects, which might create a negative impression while interviewing the managers.

A Guide to the Project Management Body of Knowledge (PMBOK® Guide) – Fifth Edition, Project Management Institute (PMI)®, Project Management Professional (PMP)®, and Certified Associate in Project Management (CAPM)® are registered trademarks of Project Management Institute, Inc. - Version 2.1 Published September 30, 2014

3. **What specific Develop Project Team tools and techniques could you use with the Building with Heart 122 East Main Street volunteer team?**

   A: Answers may vary, but should include training before working on the house, team building activities, ground rules, and recognition for a job well done.

ACTIVITY 9–5: Managing Project Communications

1. **An automated information retrieval system will provide stakeholders with access to project information via the intranet. What, if any, concerns do you have with relying on this type of distribution of project information to stakeholders?**

   A: Answers will vary, but may include: Although this may be a good method for making information available to stakeholders in an efficient manner, the information is left up to the stakeholders to interpret. One-on-one meetings would still be necessary to provide an overview of how the information reflects the reality of the project status. Also, the information must be carefully screened for accuracy. Consider the importance of version control; stakeholders should be able to share information without losing earlier versions of the material. Consider whether only selected people should have the ability to modify the content.

2. **As people strive to meet their deadlines, reporting the status of activities can become a low priority. This is a problem when you are trying to distribute up-to-date information on the status of the project. What are some things that you could do to make sure that people report accurate and timely information to you?**

   A: Answers may vary, but may include scheduling weekly project status meetings or meeting with resource groups on an individual basis. If they are using the same document to report their status, you may consider implementing a date-and-time stamp for version control.

3. **How could poor communication between project team members affect the overall project?**

   A: Answers may vary, but could include volunteers not showing up on the expected day and time, donations decreasing, the community being upset or concerned about a new house, city approvals not getting done on time, homeowners not ready to work, and employees not being aware of or involved in the new house builds.

4. **You are asked by your manager to provide the senior executives your project's progress to-date. Which information distribution methods would be most appropriate in this situation?**

   ○ Send an email announcing that a report is posted on the intranet site.

   ○ Make a telephone call to schedule one-on-one meetings with each executive.

   ○ Send an email based on status notes that you took over the phone while communicating with team members.

   ◉ Make a presentation to the senior executives and highlight the important points in the report.

ACTIVITY 9–6: Conducting Procurements

1. **What do you think would be the most appropriate method of finding qualified trained suppliers for the 122 East Main project?**

   A: Answers will vary, but may include: Building with Heart may have a list of suppliers that the company has used in the past.

A Guide to the Project Management Body of Knowledge (PMBOK® Guide) – Fifth Edition, Project Management Institute (PMI)®, Project Management Professional (PMP)®, and Certified Associate in Project Management (CAPM)® are registered trademarks of Project Management Institute, Inc. - Version 2.1 Published September 30, 2014

Solutions

2. **There are only two local suppliers in a 20-mile radius of the build site. You decide to expand your supplier list outside of the local area. What methods would you use to do this?**

   A: Answers will vary, but may include checking the Building with Heart records to see what additional suppliers the company has used in the past.

3. **Based on the scenario, would you conduct a bidder conference? Why or why not?**

   A: Answers will vary, but may include based on the initial feedback and queries that you get from various suppliers in response to your RFP, you may decide to conduct a bidder conference to allow prospective suppliers to ask questions and to get clarification about the deliverables and the procurement requirements for preparing their responses. However, if the proposals from various suppliers indicate a proper understanding of the requirements, you would not require a bidder conference, as this incurs additional costs, time, and effort that need not be expended.

ACTIVITY 9-7: Managing Stakeholder Engagement

1. **Stakeholders are worried about the current state of the project. How should you handle their concerns?**
   - ○ Follow processes outlined in the communications plan.
   - ○ Take corrective action.
   - ◉ Conduct a face-to-face meeting with a clear agenda targeting their specific concerns.
   - ○ Document lessons learned.

2. **Two stakeholders are out of town on a business trip and are available sporadically. Another has an extremely busy schedule and can't squeeze another lengthy meeting into his day. You know it is important to have face-to-face interaction with each stakeholder. How can you accommodate their needs? (Select all that apply.)**
   - ☑ Use video conferencing
   - ☐ Send a memo via email
   - ☐ Use an instant messaging service
   - ☑ Hold a brief summarization meeting

3. **During the face-to-face meeting with project stakeholders, you offer a recap of some contractor changes that occurred. It became necessary to add another electrical contractor to the team, which resulted in changes to the project cost baseline. While you are talking about this issue, you notice that one of the project stakeholders continually looks down at the floor and rapidly taps her pen against the table. What does her behavior indicate?**

   A: Answers will vary, but may include assessing body language provides the project manager with an opportunity to determine if the stakeholder is pleased or not with the project's progress. Based on her body language, you can determine that the project stakeholder is uncomfortable with the information you are providing to the group. Draw her into a conversation to determine what aspect of the information is unsettling to her. Her answer will tell you if there are outstanding issues to address in regards to project cost baselines, or any other issue that may be of concern to her.

A Guide to the Project Management Body of Knowledge (PMBOK® Guide) – Fifth Edition, Project Management Institute (PMI)®, Project Management Professional (PMP)®, and Certified Associate in Project Management (CAPM)® are registered trademarks of Project Management Institute, Inc. - Version 2.1 Published September 30, 2014

Solutions

LAB 9-1: Testing Your Knowledge of Executing a Project

1. The project manager is working with the team as they perform the work to create the project deliverables. Some adjustments need to be made to the project plan and the baselines. What would be needed in order for the project manager to allow such changes?

   ○ Change requests

   ○ Input from stakeholders that their needs have adjusted from what was originally planned

   ◉ Approved change requests

   ○ The sponsor decides on a different way to accomplish the work

2. A team member is discussing the project work with the project manager who keeps using a couple of terms that the team member is not clear on. She asks him to explain his use of the terms corrective action and preventive action. What should the project manager say in response?

   ◉ Preventive action is to identify the problem ahead of time and put plans in place to prevent it from occurring, and corrective action is to have to do something over to make it right.

   ○ Preventive action is to have to do something over to make it right, and corrective action is to identify the problem ahead of time and put plans in place to prevent it from occurring.

   ○ Corrective action requires an approved change request and preventive action does not.

   ○ Preventive action requires an approved change request and corrective action does not.

3. During the execution phase of the project, the project manager meets with the team to discuss the status of work packages. As the result of one of these meetings, the project manager then calls a team member who is located in a different country to advise that team member that he can begin work on the work package he is assigned to. What is the project manager using?

   ○ Good communication skills

   ◉ Work authorization system

   ○ Project Management Information System (PMIS)

   ○ Human resources management plan

4. The team member who is new to this organization continues to get confused when other team members converse and discuss deliverables. It is apparent to him that the use of this word was different in his previous job. How would you define the correct use of the term "deliverables" to this team member?

   ○ The final product of the project.

   ○ The list obtained from the stakeholders at the beginning of planning stating what they want from the project.

   ○ This is the same as the objectives, as defined in the charter.

   ◉ A product or capability produced as a result of a completed work package.

A Guide to the Project Management Body of Knowledge (PMBOK® Guide) – Fifth Edition, Project Management Institute (PMI)®, Project Management Professional (PMP)®, and Certified Associate in Project Management (CAPM)® are registered trademarks of Project Management Institute, Inc. - Version 2.1 Published September 30, 2014

Solutions

5. Who can request changes?
- ○ Team members and project managers
- ○ Sponsor
- ◉ Stakeholders
- ○ Customer

6. What is the main focus of quality assurance and what does it result in?
- ◉ Quality assurance is focused on process and procedures used, and it results in improved quality.
- ○ Quality assurance is focused on measuring the output of the work package, and it results in improved quality.
- ○ Quality assurance is focused on measuring the output of the work package, and it results in better metrics.
- ○ Quality assurance is focused on process and procedures used, and it results in a shorter schedule.

7. The project manager is working with some specialists who can provide an unbiased perspective in an attempt to identify needed improvements to the processes used in the project. Who is the group and what are they engaged in?
- ○ The group is the Quality Control Department and they are engaged in process analysis.
- ○ The group is the Quality Assurance Department and they are engaged in measuring the output of the work packages to the stated requirement metrics.
- ○ The group is the Quality Control Department and they are engaged in a quality audit.
- ◉ The group is the Quality Assurance Department and they are engaged in process analysis.

8. The team will be made up of several individuals who are not located at the company with the rest of the team members. What type of team does this result in and what is one of the problems associated with it?
- ○ This is a simulated team, and communication is more clear because they will rely on technology rather than face-to-face communication.
- ◉ This is a virtual team, and communication is more difficult and must rely on technology, as there will be few opportunities for face-to-face communication.
- ○ This is a virtual team, and communication is more clear because they will rely on technology rather than face-to-face communication.
- ○ This is a performing team, since there are specialists working remotely, there will be power plays due to egos.

9. In reviewing the upcoming schedule of work, a team member notices that his work package is planned to be worked on when he is out of the country making a presentation at an industry conference. He is concerned about this conflict and does not understand how the project manager could have done this. What should the project manager have consulted before scheduling the work package?
- ○ The company calendar
- ○ The staffing management plan
- ◉ The resource calendars
- ○ The develop project team process

A Guide to the Project Management Body of Knowledge (PMBOK® Guide) – Fifth Edition, Project Management Institute (PMI)®, Project Management Professional (PMP)®, and Certified Associate in Project Management (CAPM)® are registered trademarks of Project Management Institute, Inc. - Version 2.1 Published September 30, 2014

10. Based on the following description of how things are going, what is the stage of development of this team? The team begins to work productively, without worrying about personal acceptance or control issues. There are still conflicts; however, they tend to be focused on process issues, rather than personality differences.

   ○ Forming

   ◉ Norming

   ○ Adjourning

   ○ Performing

11. At the end of every month, the team members and the project manager would get together for a catered lunch and a two hour break from work. During that time, there were some games set up for people to play and thank-you awards announced for the team members who went above and beyond the call of duty that month. Everyone enjoyed these events and offered more ideas for new games to be played. What was the team engaged in?

   ◉ Team building

   ○ Rewards and recognition

   ○ Frivolous waste of time

   ○ Co-location

12. In the conduct procurements process, project managers will obtain seller responses, select a seller, and award contracts to the identified seller for the procurement. During what stage of the project does this occur?

   ○ Planning

   ○ Monitor and Control

   ○ Initiation

   ◉ Execution

13. The project manager is going to hold a bidders conference for the services they need to outsource for the project. What is the main thing that the project manager would like to ensure happens at the bidder conference?

   ○ That all bidders meet each other

   ○ That some of the bidders ask their most complex questions

   ◉ That all the bidders ask all their questions

   ○ That there is enough space for all the bidders to have seats

14. When problems occur in a project, they should be assigned to a team member to resolve, and the stakeholder who is concerned should be informed of the status and when the issue is resolved. What tool should be used to document all this?

   ◉ Issue log

   ○ Issue register

   ○ Communication plan

   ○ Complaint department

A Guide to the Project Management Body of Knowledge (PMBOK® Guide) – Fifth Edition, Project Management Institute (PMI)®, Project Management Professional (PMP)®, and Certified Associate in Project Management (CAPM)® are registered trademarks of Project Management Institute, Inc. - Version 2.1 Published September 30, 2014

15. The project is well underway when the project manager needs to communicate with many stakeholders regarding the status of the project. He refers to the project management plan to see what was determined to be the best method for this type of conversation. What was the choice and why is it the best?

   ○ Telecommunication is best because some people do not like to take the time to meet in person.

   ◉ Face-to-face is the best and most effective method to communicate with stakeholders because the body language and other non-verbal clues can indicate more information about their level of satisfaction with the project progress.

   ○ Written formal is the best method for this type of communication so the stakeholders cannot claim that you did not keep them informed.

   ○ Phone calls and conference calls are the best method so they can talk about the project and express any concerns freely.

ACTIVITY 10-1: Monitoring and Controlling Project Work

1. What can you do, as the project manager, to mitigate the negative effects of a staffing change?

   ○ Put the project on hold until Sarah returns from sick leave.

   ○ Rebuild the schedule to include additional time for Kevin to complete his tasks.

   ◉ Closely monitor Kevin's work to assess any possible risk.

   ○ Discuss with the team the impending change and that the team can expect to go through the team development stages again.

2. Kevin missed an important deadline. What action can you take to help Kevin get back on schedule?

   A: You might recommend that another experienced site manager be brought in to assist him. Once you've determined that project performance is not meeting the project plan, it becomes necessary to recommend corrective action. A change in head count will have an impact on cost and scheduling, and will require the monitoring of changes as they occur.

3. After he has been given extra help, Kevin manages to meet his next important deadline. What should be your next action as project manager?

   ○ Keep a private log for your own reference, detailing changes that have been made to the project.

   ◉ Update recent cost and schedule changes that may have resulted from recent changes.

   ○ Ask Kevin to closely monitor changes to the project's cost and schedule.

   ○ Ask Kevin to let you know if he has any further problems as the project progresses.

ACTIVITY 10-2: Performing Integrated Change Control

1. Who will you involve in the change control process for the new build project and what is their role in the change control process?

   A: The change control process should involve the Building with Heart senior executives and strategic planning individuals who are the key stakeholders. Their role will be to identify what will be considered a significant enough change from each baseline to require management approval. You should also include the PMO if one exists.

A Guide to the Project Management Body of Knowledge (PMBOK® Guide) – Fifth Edition, Project Management Institute (PMI)®, Project Management Professional (PMP)®, and Certified Associate in Project Management (CAPM)® are registered trademarks of Project Management Institute, Inc. - Version 2.1 Published September 30, 2014

Solutions

2. **The site manager informs you that the window and door installation will have a significant delay. In the risk register, you accounted for a delay due to the weather, but this delay is much longer than originally anticipated. What action should you take first?**

   ○ Coordinate changes across knowledge areas.

   ◉ Document the change request in a change control system.

   ○ Update the project plan to reflect changes.

   ○ Bring the information to the stakeholders for evaluation and approval.

3. **The site manager contacted the window and door supplier and was able to secure half of the windows before the next shipment. Based on your change control process, what further action, if any, should you take?**

   A: You should document the results of installing half the windows now and the remaining when the shipment arrives.

ACTIVITY 10-3: Validating Project Scope

1. **Your build team has decided to use a checklist and job aid in combination for the house build completed tasks. Before beginning the actual review, what else would you consider doing?**

   A: Before you begin the review, you should first gather all relevant scope documentation, including the WBS, scope statement, and requirements documentation. You should also communicate with the team members who will participate in the test, so they can prepare for the review.

2. **The initial build components have passed the inspection. What should be included in your review report and why?**

   A: (1) The project baseline and status comparison. This part of the report compares baseline specifications, schedules, and budgets to the actual project results. (2) Overall project status. This part of the report discusses whether or not the project as a whole is on track with the project plan. (3) Change recommendations. Recommending changes would be necessary if the review indicated that the product specification, scope, schedule, or budget goals would not be met. (4) Scope and methodology of the inspection. This part of the report explains the purpose and details of the review.

3. **You receive formal approval for the initial build components. How will you inform stakeholders?**

   A: Provide written documentation to project stakeholders indicating formal acceptance in accordance with the communications management plan.

4. **What could happen if the project scope is not validated regularly for this project?**

   A: Answers will vary, but could include the house not meeting the homeowner's needs or expectations, or the house not passing city code inspections.

A Guide to the Project Management Body of Knowledge (PMBOK® Guide) – Fifth Edition, Project Management Institute (PMI)®, Project Management Professional (PMP)®, and Certified Associate in Project Management (CAPM)® are registered trademarks of Project Management Institute, Inc. - Version 2.1 Published September 30, 2014

Solutions

ACTIVITY 10-4: Controlling the Project Scope

1. A scope change request recommending additional work site documentation has been submitted to the CCB for analysis. This change might impact the project finish date. What should be done first with this request?
   - ◉ Evaluate the request
   - ○ Ensure that new specifications are detailed
   - ○ Monitor changes
   - ○ Identify corrective action to take

2. What controlling scope input provides information on elements that can be configured, those that undergo formal change control, and the process of controlling such changes?
   - ◉ Configuration management plan
   - ○ Work performance information
   - ○ Requirements documentation
   - ○ Requirements traceability matrix

3. What controlling scope input documents how each project requirement meets the overall business need of the project?
   - ○ Configuration management plan
   - ○ Work performance information
   - ◉ Requirements documentation
   - ○ Requirements traceability matrix

4. The CCB informs you that the additional costs for the work site requests will be adjusted in the project budget. However, the project finish date must remain the same. As the project manager, what could you do to ensure that the project finishes on time?

   A: Consider assigning additional resources to effort-driven activities on the critical path.

ACTIVITY 10-5: Controlling the Project Schedule

1. What calculation is used to determine schedule variance?
   - ○ EV / PV
   - ◉ EV PV
   - ○ EV - AC
   - ○ EV / AC

2. What calculation is used to determine schedule performance index?
   - ◉ EV / PV
   - ○ EV - PV
   - ○ EV - AC
   - ○ EV / AC

A Guide to the Project Management Body of Knowledge (PMBOK® Guide) – Fifth Edition, Project Management Institute (PMI)®, Project Management Professional (PMP)®, and Certified Associate in Project Management (CAPM)® are registered trademarks of Project Management Institute, Inc. - Version 2.1 Published September 30, 2014

Solutions

3. According to your cost baseline for the project, you planned to spend $15,000 by the end of the eighth week. You collect reporting data for the eighth week and determine that $12,000 worth of work has actually been completed. What actions should you take with this information?

   ☐ Bring it to the attention of the CCB with some possible solutions.

   ☑ Use it to identify corrective action to take.

   ☑ Use it to compare actual schedule performance to planned performance.

   ☐ Bring it to the attention of project stakeholders.

4. The SV for the eighth week of your project is –$3,000. The SPI for this reporting period is 0.80. What is your analysis of this data and the project's schedule performance to date?

   A: A negative SV indicates that the project is currently behind schedule. An SPI number less than 1.0 also indicates that the project is behind schedule. You need to determine the cause of the variance and whether the activity that is behind schedule is on the critical path. You may consider talking to your resources to identify the source of the problem. You may have to change the schedule dates as well.

5. Using performance measurement techniques, you have determined that the project is behind schedule. What should you do with this information?

   A: Now that you know the project is behind schedule, you need to determine what activity is causing the problem. Once the activity has been identified, you must then determine whether it is on the critical path. If it is on the critical path, you most likely will have to take corrective action, such as fast-tracking, compression, or resource leveling to meet your milestone dates and your project deliverable deadline. Remember to analyze the impact of your corrective action on project cost and quality performance baselines. You should continue to carefully monitor the schedule performance to check the effectiveness of your corrective action.

ACTIVITY 10–6: Controlling Project Costs

1. Calculate the cost variance for the project.

   A: $25,000 - $28,000 = -$3,000

2. Calculate the CPI for the project.

   A: $25,000 / $28,000 = .89 is 89 cents of work is completed for every dollar paid out, which means the project is over budget.

3. Calculate the schedule variance for the project.

   A: $25,000 - $30,000 = -$5,000

4. Calculate the schedule performance index for the project.

   A: $25,000 / $30,000 = 83% of progress has been made on the project instead of 100%

5. With this project showing a variance, you now need to calculate the estimate at completion.

   A: $50,000 / .89 = $56,180 which is showing the project $6,180 over budget.

6. Next, calculate the estimate to complete the project.

   A: $56,180 - $28,000 = $28,180

7. Finally, calculate the variance at project completion.

   A: $50,000 - $56,180 = $6,180

A Guide to the Project Management Body of Knowledge (PMBOK® Guide) – Fifth Edition, Project Management Institute (PMI)®, Project Management Professional (PMP)®, and Certified Associate in Project Management (CAPM)® are registered trademarks of Project Management Institute, Inc. - Version 2.1 Published September 30, 2014

LAB 10-1: Testing Your Knowledge of Managing Project Work, Scope, Schedules, and Cost

1. The project manager is involved in many activities from a project management point of view. They include collecting, measuring, and distributing performance information, as well as reviewing trends. During what part of the project management life cycle would the project manager be engaged in these activities?

   ○ Execution

   ◉ Monitor and Control

   ○ Manage and Measure

   ○ Closing

2. During the Monitor and Control process, which of the following describes the most important reason the project manager would use the project baselines created during the planning process?

   ○ To let the stakeholders know the status of the project

   ○ To reward the team for their efforts

   ○ To confirm that the plans were made correctly

   ◉ To compare the actuals against

3. During the Monitor and Control process, the project manager is doing analysis and determines that one of the decisions made during the planning process was not the best. He reviews this information with some experts and team members, all of whom confirm that the decision was not right. As a result of this, what will be the output?

   ◉ A change request.

   ○ An adjustment to the decision.

   ○ The project manager will be reprimanded by the sponsor.

   ○ The people involved in the original decision will be removed from the project.

4. There is a group of people who meet on a regular basis. When they meet, they review the input gathered for their meeting, which includes corrective and preventive action. Their job is to assess the information and make decisions about each item based on how it would impact the project constraints and if the item is beneficial to the project. The result will be communicated to appropriate stakeholders, recorded in a log, and results in updates to project documents. What is this group called?

   ○ Project team

   ◉ Change control board

   ○ Executive committee

   ○ Stakeholders

A Guide to the Project Management Body of Knowledge (PMBOK® Guide) – Fifth Edition, Project Management Institute (PMI)®, Project Management Professional (PMP)®, and Certified Associate in Project Management (CAPM)® are registered trademarks of Project Management Institute, Inc. - Version 2.1 Published September 30, 2014

5. In the first situation, a customer forgot to mention a requirement during the planning process. Well into execution, the customer requested that the item be added to the project scope. The request was submitted to the change control board, and it was approved. In the second situation, there was another customer who neglected to mention a requirement during planning. Well into execution, the customer told the project manager that the requirement needed to be added to the scope of the project. The project manager had the request written up as a change request and submitted it to the change control board. In this case, the change was denied. What would be the reason that the first change is approved and the second is not, when they both involve a request for additional scope from a customer?

   ○ The second customer was not as influential as the first, so his request was denied.

   ◉ The first customer was willing to add time and money to the project baselines to cover the item, while the second was not.

   ○ The project manager should not have gotten in the middle of the request by the second customer.

   ○ The change control board can make any decision they want and do not need to justify why.

6. A change request has been established to add scope to the project. It has been determined that this will add two weeks of time to the project schedule. In a different but similar situation, a change request was submitted to increase the quality of a deliverable in the project. In this case, it was determined that this would add two weeks to the project schedule, and $2,000 to the cost baseline, but it did not actually impact the scope. It would also add a certain amount of risk based on the project team's ability to complete both quality requests, and it would result in a change of assignment for certain team members. What is the difference between the two situations?

   ◉ The first change was assessed only for time, the second change was evaluated through the integrated change control process.

   ○ The first change was not important enough to fully evaluate.

   ○ The second change came from someone with more influence than the first.

   ○ The first change was requested by someone with low influence.

7. The deliverable was completed as per the instructions in the WBS dictionary and the team member feels confident in reporting his work package as complete. Quality Control performs their job and confirms that the deliverable does indeed meet the criteria as stated. What should be the next thing to happen with the deliverable?

   ○ Have the Quality Assurance department perform their inspection.

   ○ Incorporate it into the final project.

   ◉ Verify the scope of the deliverable with the sponsor or customer and gain formal acceptance.

   ○ Nothing else needs to be done with it and the team member can move on to the next work package.

8. Which of the following is not an output of Validate Scope?

   ○ Work performance information

   ○ Accepted deliverable

   ○ Change requests

   ◉ Inspections

A Guide to the Project Management Body of Knowledge (PMBOK® Guide) – Fifth Edition, Project Management Institute (PMI)®, Project Management Professional (PMP)®, and Certified Associate in Project Management (CAPM)® are registered trademarks of Project Management Institute, Inc. - Version 2.1 Published September 30, 2014

Solutions

9. During the first six weeks of the execution phase of the project, four work packages were scheduled to be completed. WP1 was anticipated to cost $1,100, WP2 was anticipated to cost $1,000, WP3 was anticipated to cost $950, and WP4 was anticipated to cost $1,200. As it turns out, WP1 is complete, WP2 is only 50% complete, WP3 is 75% complete, and WP4 is complete. When adding all the invoices, you can see that $1,110 was spent on WP1, $600 was spent on WP2, $750 was spent on WP3, and $1,210 was spent on WP4. Using Earned Value Management (EVM), what is the cost variance and what is the schedule variance?

- ○ CV = 0.92 and SV = 0.80
- ○ CV = $367 and SV = $425
- ◉ CV = -$157.50 and SV = -$ 737.50
- ○ CV = $830.50 and SV = $250.50

10. During the first six weeks of the execution phase of the project, four work packages were scheduled to be complete. WP1 was anticipated to cost $1,100, WP2 was anticipated to cost $1,000, WP3 was anticipated to cost $950, and WP4 was anticipated to cost $1,200. As it turns out, WP1 is complete, WP2 is only 50% complete, WP3 is 75% complete, and WP4 is complete. When adding all the invoices, you can see that $1,110 was spent on WP1, $600 was spent on WP2, $750 was spent on WP3, and $1,210 was spent on WP4. Using Earned Value Management (EVM), what is the CPI and SPI?

- ◉ CPI = 0.96 and SPI = 0.83
- ○ CPI = -$257.50 and SPI = -$837.50
- ○ CPI = 0.80 and SPI = 0.92
- ○ CPI = $425 and SPI = $367

11. Which of the following sets of formulas correctly shows part of EVM?

- ○ EV, SPI, SV, AC
- ◉ CV, SV, SPI, CPI
- ○ SPI, CPI, CV, PV
- ○ BCWP, BCWS, CV, SV

12. During project execution, it is revealed through the use of Earned Value Management (EVM) that the project is over budget. The original budget will not be realized. Which of the following is the correct choice to represent the new higher estimate that is now anticipated to be incurred when the project is completed?

- ◉ EAC
- ○ ETC
- ○ Estimate for completion
- ○ BAC

13. Which of the following is the correct nomenclature to represent what you believe the total planned value will be at the completion of the project at the end of planning?

- ○ EAC
- ○ ETC
- ○ BCWP
- ◉ BAC

A Guide to the Project Management Body of Knowledge (PMBOK® Guide) – Fifth Edition, Project Management Institute (PMI)®, Project Management Professional (PMP)®, and Certified Associate in Project Management (CAPM)® are registered trademarks of Project Management Institute, Inc. - Version 2.1 Published September 30, 2014

Solutions

14. During the execution phase of the project, the project manager is evaluating how things are going. She uses Earned Value Management (EVM) to calculate the status of the project schedule against the plan. She discovers that the SPI is 0.95. Which of the following is correct?

○ The project is behind budget.

○ The project is going to cost 95% of what was originally planned.

◉ The project is behind schedule.

○ The actual cost has impacted the schedule.

15. During the execution phase of the project, the project manager is evaluating how things are going. She uses Earned Value Management (EVM) to calculate the status of the project's budget against the plan. She discovers that the CPI is 1.01. Which of the following is correct?

○ The project is 0.01 over budget.

◉ The project is under budget.

○ This information is not enough to determine the status of the budget.

○ The CV is too high.

ACTIVITY 11–1: Controlling Project Quality

1. Given that there is a significant variation in temperature between the first and second floor, what should be done?

○ Report this information to the appropriate people, according to the project's change control system.

◉ Because of the potentially high re-work cost, finding a solution should be a top priority.

○ Initiate process adjustments.

○ Continue to monitor quality as the HVAC installation continues.

2. The quality management plan documented acceptability of the installation with a tolerance of a one degree variance between floors. What would you do to determine the reasons for the variance in quality tests?

A: You will need to determine the source of the variability so that appropriate corrective action can be taken. Take a closer look at how the HVAC installation is being distributed among the contractors. Also consider how the quality testing is being done. Is the same quality control engineer inspecting all of the floors?

3. After researching the cause of the variance, you discover that the testing was done by one quality control engineer. You then meet with the contract supervisor to investigate the process. You discover that the duct work on the second floor was installed over a weekend by a different, less experienced crew. What should your next step be?

A: Recommend corrective action to the supervisor to bring in the first floor crew to troubleshoot the variance between floors. It is important that you consider the impact any corrective action may have on the project budget and schedule. Major adjustments must be made according to the project's change control system.

A Guide to the Project Management Body of Knowledge (PMBOK® Guide) – Fifth Edition, Project Management Institute (PMI)®, Project Management Professional (PMP)®, and Certified Associate in Project Management (CAPM)® are registered trademarks of Project Management Institute, Inc. - Version 2.1 Published September 30, 2014

Solutions

ACTIVITY 11-2: Discussing Controlling Project Communications

1. How could you control communications during the home build project?

   A: Answers may vary, but could include monitoring the project communications to ensure that the right message is being communicated to the right people at the right time.

2. What could happen if this process is completed throughout the course of a project?

   A: Answers may vary, but could include that the project may fall behind schedule, have increased cost, be of lower quality than expected, and may not finish on time if the right communications are not happening.

3. You have received approval for the adjustment to the railings of the new house build. After checking the project schedule, you realize that the railing installation work was to be completed today. How would you communicate this change to the team?

   A: Answers may vary, but should include going to the work site to see what the status is on the railing installation and communicate in person to the people working on that task to make an adjustment in the spacing of the spindles. An email needs to go to purchasing to order more spindles, and this additional work must be put on the schedule.

ACTIVITY 11-3: Controlling Project Risks

1. What action should you take in regard to the material delay?
   - ○ Monitor the environment for new risks.
   - ○ Conduct a project risk response audit.
   - ○ Update performance baselines.
   - ◉ Consult the risk response plan.

2. You have developed a very robust risk response plan in the risk register. Based on the vendor performance report, you notice that chances of delay have now become very high (from an earlier rating of high). You now need to decide what would be your next step.
   - ◉ Consult the risk response plan.
   - ○ Follow the risk management process.
   - ○ Implement the fallback plan.
   - ○ Develop a workaround.

3. The contractor suggests that it might ultimately be more cost-effective to buy materials from another contractor, although the initial cost of materials will be higher. Do you think this is an effective solution?

   A: Answers will vary, but may include: Although the cost of materials will be higher when purchased in this manner, the cost of the schedule delay might be even more expensive. By buying materials right away, you will forestall any additional work delays.

A Guide to the Project Management Body of Knowledge (PMBOK® Guide) – Fifth Edition, Project Management Institute (PMI)®, Project Management Professional (PMP)®, and Certified Associate in Project Management (CAPM)® are registered trademarks of Project Management Institute, Inc. - Version 2.1 Published September 30, 2014

Solutions

ACTIVITY 11–4: Controlling Project Procurements

1. The work done by the landscaper is scheduled to be completed in three phases. What action can you take to ensure that these deadlines are met?

   ⦿ Set performance milestones

   ◯ Document contract changes

   ◯ Implement a contract change control system

   ◯ Index all contract correspondence

2. Your landscaping contact informs you that their primary on-site coordinator has resigned. They have asked to push the lawn installation date out a week to get another coordinator up to speed. What action should you take?

   ◯ Document contract changes

   ◯ Conduct an on-site visit

   ⦿ Consult the contract change control system

   ◯ Negotiate a milestone deadline

3. The landscaper has informed you that they have completed the site prep phase as specified in the contract. It is your responsibility as project manager to verify that all work was completed to spec. Upon your review, you notice that some of the property was not prepped. What action should you take?

   A: You might review your contract with the owner of the landscape organization for guidance on the timelines and deadlines for completing the various work phases. Consult the performance reporting system to determine how to handle this problem. The procedure for determining acceptance or nonacceptance of the assessment documents is documented in the performance reporting system.

ACTIVITY 11–5: Discussing Project Stakeholder Engagement

1. Why is it important to the project to control stakeholder engagement?

   A: Answers may vary, but should include that these are the people who have a vested interest in the project and its outcome or are affected by the project deliverables. They have provided requirements for the project deliverables, so keeping them engaged throughout the project life cycle will prevent any surprises and reduce the risk of not meeting the project objectives.

2. What things could you be communicating to the project stakeholders to keep them engaged in the house build project?

   A: Answers may vary, but could include weekly updates on the progress of the house with photos posted to the Building with Heart website.

3. What could happen if you do not control stakeholder engagement?

   A: Answers may vary, but could include a delay to your project completion from lack of interest from stakeholders. And in the bigger picture, fewer volunteers for the next project, fewer donations in the future, concerns from the neighboring community, and city officials not supporting and promoting future builds.

A Guide to the Project Management Body of Knowledge (PMBOK® Guide) – Fifth Edition, Project Management Institute (PMI)®, Project Management Professional (PMP)®, and Certified Associate in Project Management (CAPM)® are registered trademarks of Project Management Institute, Inc. - Version 2.1 Published September 30, 2014

LAB 11-1: Testing Your Knowledge of Controlling the Project

1. The project manager makes sure that each team member knows which work packages they are assigned to, that they have access to the WBS dictionary for each work package, and that they have checklists. What is the purpose of checklists?

   ◉ They are job aids to help employees perform activities according to a consistent standard.

   ○ They are used to make sure each employee completes all of their work packages.

   ○ They are used to track which team member is working on which work package.

   ○ They are useful in assessing the stage of development of the team.

2. What tool ensures that all change requests are reviewed and implemented as approved during the Perform Integrated Change Control process?

   ○ The change control board

   ○ Perform change audit process

   ○ Inspection

   ◉ Approve change request reviews

3. During monitor and control, the work is being checked to make sure that it meets the stated objectives. One of the team members is informed that there is a variance in the deliverable on her work package. She is not sure what is meant by that and asks the project manager to explain. Which of the following is an appropriate answer that the project manager could use as a response?

   ◉ A variance is a quantifiable deviance, or amount of departure, from the expected result.

   ○ A variance is a subjective observation.

   ○ She has completed the work and should move on to the next work package.

   ○ The results of the work package were compared with those similar for statistical variance.

4. The work that is performed may not exactly match what was expected. Since this is a normally occurring situation, what would you call these variances and why is it acceptable?

   ○ Assignable causes are those everyday occurrences that are always present in project work.

   ○ Special causes are sporadic and unexpected, which makes them acceptable.

   ◉ Random causes are those everyday occurrences that are always present in project work.

   ○ Common causes are sporadic and are always present in project work.

5. Having created the work package deliverable, it is tested for speed. The requested speed was to be 250 mph +/-2.5. What measurement value is being represented here?

   ○ Variance

   ◉ Tolerance

   ○ Speed

   ○ Thrust

A Guide to the Project Management Body of Knowledge (PMBOK® Guide) – Fifth Edition, Project Management Institute (PMI)®, Project Management Professional (PMP)®, and Certified Associate in Project Management (CAPM)® are registered trademarks of Project Management Institute, Inc. - Version 2.1 Published September 30, 2014

Solutions

6. During a team meeting, a few individuals are being disruptive, which is causing negative effects on the rest of the meeting attendees. At a break in the meeting, the project manager, along with a few of the other attendees, are talking about these few individuals who are negatively impacting the meeting. One person describes the situation as "one rotten apple spoils the barrel." The project manager says that a better analogy would be that "20% of the people cause 80% of the problems." What is the project manager using as the basis for this statement?

   ○ Statistical sampling

   ○ 6-Sigma

   ○ Tolerances and variances

   ◉ Pareto analysis

7. Sampling data in the statistical sampling process is divided into two categories. Which of the following correctly names those two categories?

   ○ Tolerance and variance

   ○ Corrective and preventive

   ○ Attribute and tolerance

   ◉ Attribute and variable

8. A problem occurs during the project execution. It is not a big problem, but it does bother some of the stakeholders. The project manager requests that it be added to the issue log. What would be the reason for this?

   ◉ The issue log serves as a place to document problems that occur and to track their resolution.

   ○ The issue log will be reviewed by the risk team at their next meeting to develop a contingency plan.

   ○ The issue log will be submitted to the change control board for a change approval.

   ○ The issue log serves as a place to document the unidentified risks.

9. A new team member has recently joined the organization. His experience on projects at his previous employer does not match up with what he sees happening at this company. He has several questions for the project manager. Today, the project manager mentioned something called a risk reassessment. The team member has never heard that term before and asks the project manager to explain. Which of the following would be the best explanation the project manager can give the team member?

   ◉ Risk reassessment needs to be done throughout the life of the project, as time changes everything and new risks will be identified, old ones will drop off, and we may need to change our response plans.

   ○ Risk reassessment needs to be done at the beginning of the planning phase, as well as at the beginning of execution, which is the time we have just reached.

   ○ Risk reassessment means to review all the information we have gathered in the initiation phase and use it in the risk planning step during the planning phase.

   ○ Risk reassessment is done to compare the amount of contingency reserve we have to the amount of remaining risk.

10. During the project execution phase, the team and project manager discover that one of the sellers is unable or unwilling to produce the product for which they have entered into a contractual agreement. The project manager states that this is a material breach, but one of the team members who is new to the organization has had a lot of experience with procurement at his former employer. He states that this is actually an anticipatory breach. Which of the following correctly describes the difference between the two?

   ○ A material breach is an unavoidable indication that the other party will not be able to produce the performance necessary to fulfill the contract. An anticipatory breach is a serious breach that prevents the injured party from benefiting from the contract.

   ◉ An anticipatory breach is an unavoidable indication that the other party will not be able to produce the performance necessary to fulfill the contract. A material breach is a serious breach that prevents the injured party from benefiting from the contract.

   ○ In an anticipatory breach, the contract has been breached in such a way that there is no resulting damage to the injured. A material breach is a serious breach that prevents the injured party from benefiting from the contract.

   ○ An anticipatory breach is an unavoidable indication that the other party will not be able to produce the performance necessary to fulfill the contract. A material breach is a breach so serious that it negates the very foundation of the contract.

ACTIVITY 12-1: Closing a Project or Phase

1. Are your project records ready for review by the project sponsor? Why or why not?

   A: Yes, because you have collected performance measurement and product documentation as well as other relevant project records to archive.

2. What document will you prepare before obtaining formal acceptance from your project sponsor to officially complete the project?

   A: You should prepare a final project report. You should also complete a lessons learned report.

3. In this case, what might constitute formal acceptance?

   A: Answers will vary, but may include a formal presentation to stakeholders followed by a memo from the project sponsor that the project is complete. Formal acceptance documentation should be distributed to the appropriate stakeholders and stored with the project archives. If the customer was external, you might also need to receive their formal acceptance in writing.

4. What types of documentation or computer files should you store in the project archives?

   A: Answers will vary, but may include the project plan, project performance records, contract records, names of team members, and/or financial records.

ACTIVITY 12-2: Closing Procurements

1. Based on the information you have, can you close out the contract with the subcontractor?

   ○ Yes, the contract has been fulfilled.

   ◉ No, the contract has not been fulfilled.

   ○ You cannot determine this until a procurement audit has been completed.

   ○ You cannot determine this until the seller completes a staff evaluation.

A Guide to the Project Management Body of Knowledge (PMBOK® Guide) – Fifth Edition, Project Management Institute (PMI)®, Project Management Professional (PMP)®, and Certified Associate in Project Management (CAPM)® are registered trademarks of Project Management Institute, Inc. - Version 2.1 Published September 30, 2014

Solutions

2. **What would you do to resolve incorrect or unsatisfactory contract work in the situation described in the scenario?**

   A: Answers will vary, but may include: Make arrangements to meet the subcontractor at the work site to evaluate what outstanding work is required to finish the job correctly and satisfactorily; call the subcontractor and direct him to return to the work site, clean up the debris, and repair the crack in the sidewalk; or conduct a procurement audit to ensure that the contract work was properly completed.

3. **The cement contractor returned to the work site and resolved the outstanding contract issues and completed the cement work correctly and satisfactorily. Can you close out the contract? Why or why not?**

   A: Yes. This contract can be closed out because the seller resolved the outstanding contract issues and completed the cement work correctly and satisfactorily.

4. **Would you include a seller evaluation in your procurement audit? Why or why not?**

   A: Yes, because it is important to document the seller's performance for use in future similar procurements.

LAB 12-1: Testing Your Knowledge of Closing a Project

1. **In what situation would you not perform the Close Project phase?**
   - ○ When a project is terminated
   - ○ When a project phase is complete
   - ◉ When the customer verifies the deliverables
   - ○ When a project is complete

2. **If the project was terminated early, why would the project manager insist that the team perform the close projects process?**
   - ◉ To document the reasons why the project was terminated early, and how to transfer the finished and unfinished deliverables to others.
   - ○ The project manager should insist this is a waste of the team members' time since no one wants the project or its output any longer.
   - ○ To make sure everyone knows that the reason for project termination was his fault or the fault of the team.
   - ○ To document lessons learned so mistakes can be repeated in future projects.

3. **A team member, who was new to the company when the project started, is disappointed that the project has been terminated. She is excited to get to work on the next project assignment, when the project manager informs her that she cannot do this until the current, but terminated, project has been administratively closed. She does not have prior experience with this and asks the project manager to explain why it is necessary. What is the explanation the project manager will give to describe the value of administrative closure when the project has been terminated?**
   - ○ It ensures that each procurement is complete and documents project agreements and related documentation for future reference on new projects.
   - ◉ It ensures that the project or project phase requirements were met and formal acceptance was granted.
   - ○ It allows the project manager to capture salient information for the benefit of future projects.
   - ○ It is to make a checklist of all outstanding items.

A Guide to the Project Management Body of Knowledge (PMBOK® Guide) – Fifth Edition, Project Management Institute (PMI)®, Project Management Professional (PMP)®, and Certified Associate in Project Management (CAPM)® are registered trademarks of Project Management Institute, Inc. - Version 2.1 Published September 30, 2014

Solutions

4. What is involved in administrative closure?
   - ○ It involves finishing all of the work packages.
   - ○ It involves meeting with all the stakeholders to ensure all their requirements were met.
   - ◉ It involves verifying and documenting project results to formalize project or phase completion.
   - ○ It involves wrapping up all of the work procured from sellers and making final payments on their invoices.

5. A team member, who was new to the company when the project started, is excited that the project has completed. She is excited to get to work on the next project assignment, but the project manager informs her that she cannot yet do this. The current project has not been completely closed, as there were many sellers involved. She does not have prior experience with this and asks the project manager to explain what needs to be done. Which of the following is the correct description of procurement closure?
   - ○ It involves certifying that actual procurement costs did not exceed planned procurement costs.
   - ○ It involves verifying and documenting project results to formalize project or phase completion.
   - ○ It ensures that the project or project phase requirements were met and formal acceptance was granted.
   - ◉ It ensures that each procurement is complete, and documents project agreements and related documentation for future reference on new projects.

6. Part of the work that needs to be done at the end of the project is to evaluate the effectiveness of the seller, as well as the procurement process itself. What is this technique called?
   - ○ Contract review
   - ○ Procurement closure
   - ○ Administrative closure
   - ◉ Procurement audit

7. There are several team members who have never worked on a project that had any sellers involved, so they are not familiar with the whole vendor relationship situation. During project closing, the project manager advises the team that there will be procurement audits. How would the project manager explain to the team the purpose of these procurement audits?
   - ○ The goal of the audit is to provide documentation that the team was not responsible for the deliverables provided by the sellers.
   - ○ The goal of the audit is to ensure the phase or project requirements were met.
   - ◉ The goal of the audit is to establish a record that may be used to shape procurement practices in other contracts.
   - ○ The goal of the audit is to document why the project was terminated early.

8. The project manager wants to make sure all team members understand the importance of the whole closing process and asks if there are any more questions. One team member asks, "What would happen if this process was not done?" How should the project manager answer that question?
   - ○ The customer would not be obliged to pay for the project.
   - ◉ The next related activity, phase, or project might not get started.
   - ○ The stakeholders would not have any faith in the project team for future projects.
   - ○ The team members would not be allowed to be assigned to future projects.

A Guide to the Project Management Body of Knowledge (PMBOK® Guide) – Fifth Edition, Project Management Institute (PMI)®, Project Management Professional (PMP)®, and Certified Associate in Project Management (CAPM)® are registered trademarks of Project Management Institute, Inc. - Version 2.1 Published September 30, 2014

Solutions

9. **During the closing phase, the project manager has requested yet another document for the project. He refers to it as the "Closed Procurement." What is this?**

   ◉ It is a written notice that is usually provided by the buyer to the seller once a contract is complete.

   ○ It is a verbal notice provided by the seller to the buyer once a contract is complete.

   ○ It is a written notice provided by the seller to the sponsor once a complete contract has been agreed to.

   ○ It is a notice that is posted in the project war room indicating the terms of the contract.

10. **During the closing phase, the project manager has requested yet another document for the project. He refers to it as the "Closed Procurement" which is a written notice once a contract is complete. Where is the most likely place that the specifics of when and how this is done would be stated?**

    ○ In the quality management plan, as specified by the metrics in the contract

    ○ In the project management plan, as specified in the contract process plan

    ○ In the terms and conditions set forth in the team member work authorization agreement

    ◉ In the terms and conditions that were specified in the contract and the procurement management plan

A Guide to the Project Management Body of Knowledge (PMBOK® Guide) – Fifth Edition, Project Management Institute (PMI)®, Project Management Professional (PMP)®, and Certified Associate in Project Management (CAPM)® are registered trademarks of Project Management Institute, Inc. - Version 2.1 Published September 30, 2014

Solutions

Glossary

360-degree feedback
The collection of performance data from several key sources, including peers, managers, and subordinates.

6-Sigma limit
In a control chart, setting the upper and lower control limits at six standard deviations above and below the mean. Generally accepted guideline for monitoring quality and improving it

AC
(Actual Cost) Total amount of costs incurred while accomplishing work performed, either during completion of a schedule activity or during the completion of a work breakdown structure component.

accept
Strategy for managing negative risks or opportunities that involves acknowledging a risk and not taking any action until the risk occurs.

acquire project team process
Process that involves making the identified resources available to the project.

activity
Element of project work that requires action to produce a deliverable.

activity attributes
Descriptions of every activity on the activity list.

activity dependency
A logical relationship that exists between two project activities. The relationship indicates whether the start of an activity is contingent upon an event or input from outside the activity.

activity duration estimates
The likely number of time periods that are needed to complete an activity.

activity list
Document that includes all the activities for the project.

activity resource requirements
Estimates that determine the types and quantities of the resources that are needed for each project activity.

activity resources
Any useful material object or individual needed for the project work to be completed.

administrative closure
Process that involves verifying and documenting project results to formalize project or phase completion.

agile project management
Refers to taking an iterative approach to managing a project throughout its life cycle. It allows the project manager to continually re-evaluate progress, development, and priorities and make adjustments as needed.

agreements

Statements, which are often but not always written, that are used to document the intent of a project. Examples include contracts, memorandums of understanding (MOUs), service level agreements (SLAs), letters of agreement, letters of intent, verbal agreements, email, or other written agreements.

alternative analysis

Technique used to identify different ways of accomplishing activities and the different resources required by each method.

alternatives generation

Method used to draw out potential options to complete project work.

analogous estimation

Estimate activity durations technique that uses historical data from similar projects to estimate duration for the current project activities.

AON

(Activity-On-Node) The most commonly used graphical representation of activities in project management software.

approved change requests

Change requests that have been reviewed and approved by the change control board (CCB) and are ready to be scheduled for implementation.

assumptions analysis

Process that explores the validity of the project assumptions and identifies risks from any incompleteness or inaccuracy of these project assumptions.

avoid

Strategy for managing negative risks or threats that involves changing the project management plan to remove the risk entirely by extending the schedule, changing the strategy, increasing the funding, or reducing the scope.

BAC

(Budget at Completion) Total budgeted cost of the project at completion.

bar charts

Type of project schedule that shows activities on the vertical axis and dates on the horizontal axis with durations shown as bars with start and end dates. Bar charts are also known as Gantt charts.

benchmarking

Method used to evaluate processes or practices against another organization's standard.

bottom-up estimating

Process used to decompose work in an activity to the last executable level that generates activity resource estimates by adding the resources required by each activity.

brainstorm session

A meeting where a facilitator helps the group identify project risks in a free-form session where ideas are generated, built on, and recorded.

business case

The document that captures the reasoning for initiating a project or task from a financial perspective. It documents the investment needed to make the project successful and determines whether or not the deliverables from the project are worth the investment to the overall business.

business value

The entire value of a business, the total sum of all tangible and intangible elements.

CAPM

(Certified Associate in Project Management) A valuable entry-level certification for project practitioners with little or no project experience that demonstrates your understanding of the fundamental knowledge, terminology, and processes of effective project management.

A Guide to the Project Management Body of Knowledge (PMBOK® Guide) – Fifth Edition, Project Management Institute (PMI)®, Project Management Professional (PMP)®, and Certified Associate in Project Management (CAPM)® are registered trademarks of Project Management Institute, Inc. - Version 2.1 Published September 30, 2014

Glossary

CCM

(Critical Chain Method) A schedule network analysis method that allows you to consider resource limitations and adjust the schedule as appropriate to work within those limitations.

change control system

Collection of formal, documented procedures for changing official project documents; it specifies how project deliverables will be controlled, changed, and approved.

checklist analysis

Process that involves reviewing and analyzing previous project documents and checklists.

close a project or phase process

Process that finalizes any project documentation, makes sure all invoices are paid, contracts are closed out, project lessons learned are discussed and documented, and any other loose ends are wrapped up so that the project or project phase is complete and resources (people, equipment, facilities, and money) can be released to work on new projects or project phases.

close procurements process

Process that ensures that each procurement is complete and documents project agreements and related documentation for future reference on new projects.

close-out meetings

Sessions held at the end of a project or phase; they involve discussing the work and capturing lessons learned.

closed procurements

Written notice that is provided from the buyer to the seller once a contract is complete.

Closing Process Group

The processes performed to finalize all activities across all project management process groups to formally complete the project, phase, or contractual obligations.

co-location

The practice of positioning most or all key team members in the same physical location to make communication easier and enhance team performance and team spirit.

coaching

The act of giving guidance and direction to another person so that he or she can make better decisions in the future.

code of accounts

Any system for numbering the elements in a WBS.

Code of Ethics and Professional Conduct

PMI publication that describes the ethical and professional behavior expectations of any individual working as a project management professional.

collect requirements process

The process used to gather, analyze, document, and manage all the needs of a project. The requirements are assembled directly from the project stakeholders and the outcomes for a project.

communication

The process of imparting or interchanging information, thoughts, ideas, and opinions through a variety of media, such as speech, documentation, email, and telecommunications.

communication models

Theories used to facilitate communications and information exchange.

communication requirements analysis

An investigation that leads to a clear articulation of the stakeholders' communications needs and helps the project manager make effective choices regarding the technologies to be recommended in the communications management plan.

communication technology

Tool set that includes various methods used to transfer information.

communications management plan

Component of the project management plan that documents how project communications will be planned, structured, monitored, and controlled throughout the life of the project.

communications requirements

The project stakeholders' documented communications needs.

conduct procurements process

The process through which project managers will obtain seller responses, select a seller, and award contracts to the identified seller for the procurement of the required product, service, or result from the seller.

configuration management

Tool used to manage changes to a product or service being produced as well as changes to any of the project documents, such as schedule updates.

configuration management system

Tool that contains procedures that help provide technical and administrative guidance for: identifying and recording the characteristics of a product or service; controlling changes made to the characteristics; documenting the changes and the status of implementation; and verifying the product's conformance to the requirements.

conflict management

The application of one or more strategies for dealing with disagreements that may be detrimental to team performance.

context diagram

A visual representation of a product's scope. The diagram includes the business process, equipment, or computer system and what roles interact with those systems.

contingency plan

Risk response strategy developed in advance, before risks occur; it is meant to be used if and when identified risks become reality.

contingency reserve

Predetermined amount of time in the schedule baseline that is allocated for known risks that are accepted.

contracts

Mutually binding agreements that detail the obligations of both parties; in terms of procuring work, they relate to both the buyer and the seller.

control accounts

Points within the WBS that are tracked by finance to verify that costs are within budget. These accounts are associated with different work packages within the WBS that can be tracked and verified against the earned value of a project to check performance.

control communications process

Process that monitors and controls communications to ensure that the information needs of the stakeholders are met throughout the life cycle of the project.

control procurements process

Process of managing the relationship with the seller.

control quality process

Process that involves monitoring project performance to determine if it complies with relevant quality standards and identifying ways to eliminate causes of unacceptable performance.

control risks process

Process of responding to identified and unforeseen risks. It involves tracking identified risks, identifying new risks, implementing risk response plans, and monitoring their effectiveness.

control stakeholder engagement process

Process that monitors and controls the project stakeholder relationships during the course of a project.

controlling PMO

Type of PMO that provides support and requires compliance through various means. Compliance may involve adopting project management frameworks or methodologies, using specific templates, forms, and tools, or conformance to governance.

COQ

(Cost of Quality) Refers to the total cost of effort needed to achieve an acceptable level of quality in the project's product or service.

cost aggregation

Determine a budget technique that combines activity costs into work package costs, which are then aggregated up the WBS until a single project cost is produced.

cost baseline

A time-phased budget that will be used to monitor and measure cost performance throughout the project life cycle.

cost benefit analysis

Plan quality management technique that considers the trade-offs and the benefit of meeting quality requirements of higher productivity and lower costs while increasing stakeholder satisfaction.

cost management plan

A subsidiary plan of the project management plan that defines the processes, procedures, tools, and techniques to effectively manage the cost of a project.

cost of conformance

The money spent during a project to avoid failures. This includes prevention costs that build a quality product, and appraisal costs that assess the quality.

cost of non-conformance

The money spent after a project is complete because of failures. This includes internal and external failure costs.

cost reimbursable contract

Type of contract that provides sellers a refund of the expenses incurred while providing a service, plus a fee representing seller profit.

CPAF contract

(Cost Plus Award Fee contract) Type of contract that ensures the seller is reimbursed for all legitimate costs. The majority of the fee is earned based on the satisfaction of certain broad subjective performance criteria defined and incorporated into the contract. The determination of the fee is based on the buyer's subjective determination of seller performance and is generally not subject to appeals.

CPFF contract

(Cost Plus Fixed Fee contract) Type of contract that ensures the seller is reimbursed for all allowable costs for performing the contract work. The seller receives a fixed fee payment calculated based on the initial estimated project costs. This fixed fee does not change due to seller performance.

CPI

(Cost Performance Index) Measurement of cost performance used to determine whether the project is over or under budget.

CPIF contract

(Cost Plus Incentive Fee contract) Type of contract that ensures that the seller is reimbursed for all allowable costs for performing the contract work. The seller also receives a predetermined target fee.

CPM

(Critical Path Method) A schedule network analysis method that uses a sequential finish-to-start network logic and calculates one early and late start and finish date for each activity using a single duration estimate.

crash cost plotting methods

Techniques for analyzing the crash costs through creating a graph or a visual representation that clearly illustrates those costs.

crashing

Schedule compression method that analyzes cost and schedule trade-offs to determine how to obtain the greatest schedule compression for the least incremental cost.

critical activities

The activities that are on the critical path.

critical chain

The basis of the critical chain method, which is established by analyzing the critical path alongside the resources that are actually available.

A Guide to the Project Management Body of Knowledge (PMBOK® Guide) – Fifth Edition, Project Management Institute (PMI)®, Project Management Professional (PMP)®, and Certified Associate in Project Management (CAPM)® are registered trademarks of Project Management Institute, Inc. - Version 2.1 Published September 30, 2014

Glossary

critical path

The network path that has the longest total duration.

CV

(Cost Variance) The difference between the Earned Value (EV) and the Actual Cost (AC) incurred to complete that work.

decision making

The process of selecting a course of action from among multiple options.

decomposition

The process of breaking down of project scope and requirements into smaller more manageable chunks.

define activities process

Process that determines the activities that need to take place to deliver the project objectives and outputs which need to be defined and documented.

define scope process

Process that is used to evaluate all the requirements collected during the collect requirements process, and to determine what requirements will be included within the project scope and which ones will not.

deliverable

The product, result, or capability produced as a result of completed work packages that were determined in the WBS creation process.

Delphi technique

Information gathering technique that can be used to reach consensus of a group of experts. A facilitator uses a questionnaire to anonymously solicit ideas about important project risks. The responses are summarized and recirculated for further comment.

design of experiments

A statistical method of identifying the factors that may influence certain product or process variables.

develop project team process

An ongoing effort to build a cohesive team that benefits from good communication and a foundation of trust.

develop schedule process

Process of analyzing the activity sequences, durations, resource requirements, and time constraints to develop the project schedule.

dictatorship

Group decision-making method in which a single member of the group can override a group's decision. In most cases, this person will consider the larger group's ideas and decisions, and will then make their decision based on the best decision.

direct and manage project work process

Process that involves carrying out the project management plan to produce a product or provide a service so as to meet the project objectives.

directive PMO

Type of PMO that takes control of projects by directly managing the projects.

discretionary dependencies

Type of activity dependencies that are a desired sequence of activities that make sense for the project.

document analysis

A technique used to gain project requirements from current documentation evaluation.

documentation reviews

Structured reviews of project plans and related documents used to identify previously identified risks that might apply to your existing project.

EAC

(Estimate at Completion) Expected total cost of completing all of the project work. It is expressed as the sum of the Actual Cost (AC) to date and the Estimate to Complete (ETC).

effort

The number of person-hours or person-days required for completion of an activity.

elapsed time

The actual calendar time required for an activity from start to finish.

EMV
(Expected Monetary Value) Method of calculating the average outcome when the future is uncertain.

enhance
Strategy for managing positive risks or opportunities that involves increasing the probability that the opportunity will happen or the impact it will have by identifying and maximizing enablers of these opportunities.

enterprise environmental factors
Internal or external conditions, not under the control of the project, that influence, constrain, or direct the project.

estimate activity durations process
The act of estimating the duration of work that will be needed to complete individual project activities using the available resources.

Estimate Activity Resources
Process that facilitates the estimation of the type and quantity of resources needed for each project activity. These resources can include people, materials, supplies, and equipment.

estimate costs
The process of projecting the total expenditures necessary for the completion of your project.

ETC
(Estimate to Complete) The estimated cost of finishing all the remaining project work.

EVM
(Earned Value Management) Method of measuring project progress by comparing actual schedule and cost performance against planned performance as laid out in the schedule and cost baselines.

Executing Process Group
The processes performed to complete the work defined in the project management plan to satisfy the project objectives.

expert judgment
Contributed opinion or perspective that is used to evaluate the inputs used to document the project charter. Expert judgment can be given by any group or individual that has specific knowledge about the objectives of the project.

exploit
Strategy for managing positive risks or opportunities that involves attempting to make sure that the opportunity happens.

external dependencies
Type of activity dependencies that exist between project activities and non-project activities and can be out of the project's control.

facilitated workshops
Organized working sessions held by project managers to determine what a project's requirements are and to get all stakeholders together to agree on the project's outcomes.

fast-tracking
The process of compressing total project duration by performing some activities concurrently that were originally scheduled sequentially.

FFP contract
(Firm Fixed Price contract) Type of contract that is favored by most buying organizations because the price for products or services is set at the outset and not subject to change unless the scope of work changes.

finish-to-finish (FF) relationship
Type of precedence relationship between two activities in which the successor activity cannot finish until the predecessor activity has finished.

finish-to-start (FS) relationship
Type of precedence relationship between two activities in which the successor activity cannot start until the predecessor activity has finished.

fishbone diagrams
Cause-and-effect diagrams that can help identify the causes of risks (see also: *Ishikawa diagram*).

fixed price contract
Type of contract that establishes a total price for a product or service. The seller agrees to perform the work at the negotiated contract

A Guide to the Project Management Body of Knowledge (PMBOK® Guide) – Fifth Edition, Project Management Institute (PMI)®, Project Management Professional (PMP)®, and Certified Associate in Project Management (CAPM)® are registered trademarks of Project Management Institute, Inc. - Version 2.1 Published September 30, 2014

Glossary

value. This is also known as a lump-sum contract.

float

The amount of time an activity can be delayed from its early start date without delaying the project finish date or the consecutive activities.

focus groups

Small events or discussions that are designed to be less structured and more information sharing sessions within a small group of people.

forecasting

Process used to estimate the cost at completion or Estimate at Completion (EAC).

FPEPA contract

(Fixed Price with Economic Price Adjustment contract) Type of fixed-price contract with special provisions to allow pre-defined final adjustments to the contract price due to changed conditions, such as inflation changes, or cost increases or decreases for specific commodities such as fuel, and for currency fluctuations.

FPIF contract

(Fixed Price Incentive Fee contract) Type of contract that is flexible in that it allows for deviation from performance. Financial incentives are tied to achieving metrics that are agreed to earlier.

free float

The amount of time an activity can be delayed without delaying the early start date of any activity that immediately follows it.

functional organization

A hierarchy with each employee reporting to a specific supervisor or manager. In this structure, employees are typically grouped by specialty or function, such as engineering, production, and sales.

funding limit reconciliation

Method of adjusting, spending, scheduling, and resource allocation in order to bring expenditures into alignment with budgetary constraints.

group decision–making

Method used by a group to come to a decision. This technique is an assessment process that can have multiple alternatives and can lead to many outcomes.

human resource management

The processes used to organize, manage, and lead the people on the project team.

human resource management plan

A subsidiary plan of the project management plan that defines project roles, responsibilities, required skills, reporting relationships, and a staff management plan for the project.

identify risks process

Process used to evaluate and determine what risks may affect the project so you can understand them and document their signs and attributes.

IFB

(Invitation for Bid) Type of procurement document that is most commonly used when deliverables are commodities for which there are clear specifications and when the quantities are very large. The invitation is usually advertised and any seller may submit a bid. Negotiation is typically not anticipated. These are sometimes used interchangeably with Requests for Proposals (RFPs).

incremental life cycle

Type of project life cycle in which the high-level scope is determined as early in the project as possible, but the time and cost estimates are frequently adjusted as the project moves through its various phases (see also: *iterative life cycle*).

influence diagrams

Graphical representations of decision situations that show causal influences, time ordering of events, and other relationships among variables and outcomes that support team decision analysis.

influencing

The act of presenting a good case to explain why an idea, decision, or problem should be

A Guide to the Project Management Body of Knowledge (PMBOK® Guide) – Fifth Edition, Project Management Institute (PMI)®, Project Management Professional (PMP)®, and Certified Associate in Project Management (CAPM)® are registered trademarks of Project Management Institute, Inc. - Version 2.1 Published September 30, 2014

Glossary

handled a certain way, without resistance from other individuals.

information gathering

Process of determining what areas of the project will be most susceptible for risk.

Initiating Process Group

The processes performed to define a new project or a new phase of an existing project by obtaining authorization to start the project or phase.

inputs

The information and data that project managers draw on, create, or gather to guide their work for a specific process to achieve project goals.

inspection

Official examination of work results to verify that requirements are met.

integrated change control

Process of identifying, documenting, approving or rejecting, and controlling any changes to the project baselines.

interactive communications

An exchange of information between two or more people that ensures common understanding for everyone participating in that exchange.

internal dependencies

Type of activity dependencies that exist between project activities and are usually under the project's control.

interpersonal skills

Unique abilities that an individual possesses to conduct themselves in a professional manner when interacting with others.

interview

A formal or informal meeting or discussion that can be used to gather and document needed information from stakeholders by talking with them directly and asking targeted questions to generate discussion.

interviewing

The process of querying experienced project participants, stakeholders, and subject matter experts to gather information related to the project.

Invitation for Negotiation

Type of procurement document that is commonly used to verify all interested parties are involved. This is a documented attempt to make sure that everyone who may have an interest in contracting with the offering party has a chance to do so.

Ishikawa diagrams

Cause-and-effect diagrams that can help identify the causes of risks (see also: *fishbone diagram*).

ISO 9000 Series

A quality system standard that is applicable to any product, service, or process in the world. It was developed by ISO, which is a consortium of approximately 100 of the world's industrial nations.

iterative life cycle

Type of project life cycle in which the high-level scope is determined as early in the project as possible, but the time and cost estimates are frequently adjusted as the project moves through its various phases (see also: *incremental life cycle*).

job shadowing

See *observations*.

knowledge areas

Complete sets of concepts, terms, and activities that make up the field of project management or other professional fields. There are 10 project management knowledge areas.

known risks

Risks that have been identified and analyzed so that they can have a planned risk response.

lag

The amount of time whereby a successor activity will be delayed with respect to a predecessor activity.

A Guide to the Project Management Body of Knowledge (PMBOK® Guide) – Fifth Edition, Project Management Institute (PMI)®, Project Management Professional (PMP)®, and Certified Associate in Project Management (CAPM)® are registered trademarks of Project Management Institute, Inc. - Version 2.1 Published September 30, 2014

Glossary

lead
The amount of time whereby a successor activity can be advanced with respect to predecessor activity.

leadership
The ability to step up and guide others to help you achieve results. Leadership abilities are gained through experience, building relationships, and taking on initiatives.

lessons learned reports
Documents that capture salient and helpful information about the work done in a project or a project phase; they identify both the project team's strengths and areas for improvement.

majority
Group decision-making method in which a majority of group members agree on the course of action to take.

make or buy analysis
Technique used to determine whether it would be more cost effective to produce a product or service in-house or to procure it from an outside seller.

manage communications process
Process that involves getting the right information to the right people, both internally and externally, at the right time.

manage project team process
Process used to monitor individual performance, give feedback, solve issues, and organize changes to improve project performance.

mandatory dependencies
Type of activity dependencies that are legally or contractually required, or are due to the nature of the work.

milestone charts
Type of project schedule bar chart that only includes milestone or major deliverables as a point in time.

milestone list
Document that contains the significant points or events in a project.

mitigate
Strategy for managing negative risks or threats that involves taking action to reduce the probability of occurrence or the impact of a risk.

monitor and control work process
Process that involves tracking, reviewing, and regulating the project processes to meet the project's performance objectives.

Monitoring and Controlling Process Group
The processes required to track, review, and orchestrate the progress and performance of the project, identify areas in which changes to the plan are needed, and initiate those changes.

Monte Carlo analysis
Technique used by project managers to make predictions about the optimistic, most likely, and pessimistic estimates for variables in the model and simulates various outcomes of the project schedule to provide a statistical distribution of the calculated results.

Monte Carlo simulation
A computerized, statistical probability analysis software application that allows project managers to account for risk in quantitative analysis and decision-making.

motivation
Inner drive that keeps people involved and wanting to complete work of high quality in a timely fashion.

multi–criteria decision analysis
Process that uses multiple weighted criteria to rate or score potential team members to ensure the best selection to meet the project's objectives.

negotiation
An approach used by more than one individual to come to an agreement or resolution.

networking
The interaction between people to expand their knowledge about business topics. It can take place in an organization, industry, or professional environment.

normal distribution PDF

Probability Density Function that results when there is a symmetrical range or variation in the probabilities of each outcome. Visually, the data is distributed symmetrically in the shape of a bell with a single peak, resulting in the common term "bell curve."

observations

Techniques used in order to gain knowledge of a specific job role, task, or function in order to understand and determine project requirements. This is also known as job shadowing.

operations management

A business function that is responsible for overseeing, directing, and controlling business operations.

OPM

(Organizational Project Management) A strategy execution framework that relies on project, program, and portfolio management and organizational practices to deliver a robust organizational strategy that will ultimately produce better organization-wide performance and results.

opportunities

Type of risk that can have a positive impact on the overall project.

organization charts and position descriptions

Documentation that states team members' roles and responsibilities on the project.

organizational process assets

The assets and resources that are specific to an organization, and that the organization will use throughout the life of the project.

organizational theory

The study of how people, teams, and organizations behave to look for common themes for the purpose of maximizing efficiency and productivity, problem solving, and meeting the stakeholder requirements of a project.

outputs

The end results and deliverables achieved during project management processes. Outputs can become inputs into subsequent processes.

overlapping relationships

Type of phase-to-phase relationships that contain phases that start prior to the previous phase ending.

parametric estimation

Estimate activity durations technique that uses an algorithm to calculate duration, budget, or cost based on historical data and project parameters.

Pareto diagram

Histogram that is used to rank causes of problems in a hierarchical format.

PBO

(Project Based Organization) Organizational forms that create temporary systems for carrying out their work.

PDM

(Precedence Diagramming Method) Method used to sequence activities to create a schedule model, which is the first pass at creating a schedule and may be adjusted until it fits the project as best as possible, for the project.

PDUs

(Professional Development Units) Units of time spent extending your project management knowledge of the process areas of knowledge by taking classes, researching, and providing expertise.

perform integrated change control process

Formal method of governing and organizing the manner in which changes will be requested, reviewed, approved or rejected, implemented, controlled, and coordinated.

perform qualitative risk analysis process

Process used to assess each risk for the probability of occurrence and its potential impact on the project.

A Guide to the Project Management Body of Knowledge (PMBOK® Guide) – Fifth Edition, Project Management Institute (PMI)®, Project Management Professional (PMP)®, and Certified Associate in Project Management (CAPM)® are registered trademarks of Project Management Institute, Inc. - Version 2.1 Published September 30, 2014

Glossary

perform quality assurance process

Process that ensures that the project quality standards and operational definitions are being used, by auditing the quality requirements and results from quality control measurements.

perform quantitative risk analysis process

Process used to numerically analyze the effect for each identified risk against the project objectives.

plan communications management process

Process that identifies and documents the way the project team will communicate efficiently and effectively with the stakeholders.

plan human resource management process

The process that identifies and documents the peoples' roles, responsibilities, necessary skills, and reporting relationships for the project, and that creates a staffing plan for the project.

plan procurement management process

Process that allows project managers to document project purchasing decisions, specify the approach to be followed for project procurements, and identify potential sellers to meet the purchase requirements of the project.

plan quality management process

Process that involves developing a quality management plan to identify the quality requirements for the project process and its deliverables and to plan how to achieve compliance of these requirements.

plan risk management process

Process that defines how to conduct risk management activities for a project. It makes sure that the degree, type, and visibility of the risk management is at an appropriate level for the importance of the project to the organization.

plan risk responses process

Process that determines and documents options and specific actions to take to reduce the threats and enhance the opportunities to project objectives.

plan schedule management process

Process that documents the policies, procedures, and documentation for planning, developing, managing, executing, and controlling the project schedule. It determines how the project schedule and any schedule contingencies will be managed throughout the project life cycle.

planning package

A placeholder within a control account for work that is yet to be determined by a requirement.

Planning Process Group

The processes performed to establish the total scope of the project, define and refine the objectives, and develop a course of action to obtain the project objectives.

plurality

Group decision-making method in which the largest sub-group within a group agrees on a decision. This method is useful when the number of options is more than two.

PMBOK® Guide

(A Guide to the Project Management Body of Knowledge) Publication that provides guidelines for managing individual projects and defines project management concepts. It describes the project management life cycle and its processes, and the project life cycle. It is a globally recognized standard that describes the established norms, methods, processes, and practices that provide a base of best practices for the project management profession.

PMIS

(Project Management Information System) An automated or manual system used by a project team to gather, analyze, communicate, and store project information.

PMO

(Project Management Office) A management structure that standardizes the project-related governance processes and facilitates the sharing of resources, methodologies, tools, and

A Guide to the Project Management Body of Knowledge (PMBOK® Guide) – Fifth Edition, Project Management Institute (PMI)®, Project Management Professional (PMP)®, and Certified Associate in Project Management (CAPM)® are registered trademarks of Project Management Institute, Inc. - Version 2.1 Published September 30, 2014

Glossary

techniques. PMOs are more common in larger organizations because of the amount of projects that can be in process all at the same time.

PMP

(Project Management Professional) The most important industry-recognized certification for project managers. Globally recognized and demanded, the PMP demonstrates that you have the experience, education, and competency to lead and direct projects.

portfolio

A collection of projects, programs, sub-portfolios, and operations managed as a group to achieve organizational strategic results.

portfolio management

The centralized management of one or more portfolios to achieve strategic objectives.

precedence relationship

Logical relationship between two activities that describes the sequence in which the activities should be carried out.

predictive life cycles

Type of project life cycle in which the project scope, time, and cost are determined as early in the project as possible.

probability and impact matrix

Grid used to assign a numerical value or risk score to each risk from the risk assessment.

probability distribution

The scattering of values assigned to likelihood in a sample population. It can be visually depicted in the form of a Probability Density Function (PDF).

process

A set of interrelated actions and activities performed to create a specific product, service, or result.

process improvement plan

A subsidiary plan of the project management plan. It documents the steps to take a look at the project management processes and the product development processes in order to

identify ways to enhance their value to the project and the organization.

process improvement planning

The process of analyzing and identifying areas of improvement in project processes and enumerating an action plan based on the project goals and identified issues.

procurement

The acquisition of goods and services from an external organization, vendor, or supplier to enable the deliverables of the project.

procurement audit

Formal evaluation of both the seller's performance of the contract, and the effectiveness of the procurement process itself.

procurement document

Document that is submitted to prospective sellers and service providers to solicit their proposals for the work needed.

procurement management plan

Document that outlines the specifications for procuring work from outside sources; it specifies the types of contracts that will be used, describes the process for obtaining and evaluating bids, mandates the standardized procurement documents that must be used, and describes how multiple providers will be managed.

procurement negotiation

Process of bargaining to come to a mutual agreement regarding the terms and conditions of a contract.

procurement SOW

Detailed narrative description of the resources, goods, or services that are being sought from external sources to fulfill a project's requirements.

product analysis

Analysis method used for projects that have a product as the deliverable. This method examines the product specification requirements in order to help define the scope of the project.

A Guide to the Project Management Body of Knowledge (PMBOK® Guide) – Fifth Edition, Project Management Institute (PMI)®, Project Management Professional (PMP)®, and Certified Associate in Project Management (CAPM)® are registered trademarks of Project Management Institute, Inc. - Version 2.1 Published September 30, 2014

program
A group of related projects, subprograms, and program activities managed in a coordinated way to achieve benefits not available from managing them individually. A project may or may not be part of a program, but a program will always have projects.

progressive elaboration
A method used to arrange project life cycle phases in a specific way to allow for successive layers of detail to be added to the plans as the project progresses.

project
A temporary effort to create a unique product, service, or result. It has a defined beginning and end.

project calendars
Calendars that show work days and shifts that are available for scheduling activities.

project charter
The document, developed by the project manager and approved by a project sponsor to formally authorize the existence of a project, which authorizes the project manager to apply organizational resources, such as people and dollars, to project activities.

project communications management
Project management knowledge area that includes the processes that enable project managers to effectively and efficiently manage the communications of a project.

project cost management
Project management knowledge area that includes the processes required to plan, estimate, budget, finance, fund, manage, and control the project costs.

project funding requirements
Determine a budget output that states how a project will be funded.

project governance
A comprehensive methodology that provides oversight on the project life cycle for the organization and ensures its success. It provides the structure, processes, decision-

making models, and tools for the project manager and team to manage the project.

project human resources management
Project management knowledge area that contains the processes used to organize, manage, and lead the people on the project team.

project information
The raw data that is collected and gathered at each stage of a project. This data is then turned into information on which decisions can be made and is ultimately reported to stakeholders.

project integration management
Project management knowledge area that includes the activities and processes needed to identify, define, combine, unify, and coordinate all of the various processes and project management activities in the Project Management Process Groups.

project life cycle
The entire body of project phases of a particular project.

project management
The "application of knowledge, skills, tools, and techniques to plan activities to meet the project requirements."

project management processes
All of the activities that underlie the effective practice of project management; these include all of the phases of initiating, planning, executing, monitoring and controlling, and closing a project.

project management software
Computer application that helps plan, organize, and manage project resources and develop resource estimates for activities.

project manager
The individual assigned by an organization to lead the team that is responsible for carrying out and achieving the project objectives.

A Guide to the Project Management Body of Knowledge (PMBOK® Guide) – Fifth Edition, Project Management Institute (PMI)®, Project Management Professional (PMP)®, and Certified Associate in Project Management (CAPM)® are registered trademarks of Project Management Institute, Inc. - Version 2.1 Published September 30, 2014

Glossary

project phases
Individual sections of a project that represent activities that produce one or more deliverables.

project procurement management
Project management knowledge area comprised of the process used to properly manage the purchase or acquisition of the products, services, or results needed to perform project work external to the project team.

project quality management
Project management knowledge area that includes processes that enable a project to meet expectations on the quality of its project work and deliverables.

project risk audit
Process of examining the project team or risk management team's ability to identify risks, the effectiveness of risk response plans, and of the performance of risk owners.

project risk management
Project management knowledge area that includes conducting risk management planning, identification, analysis, response planning, and controlling risk on a project.

project risk ranking
The overall risk ranking for producing the final deliverable of the product or service of the project.

project risks
Uncertain events that may or may not occur within a project.

project schedule
The visual presentation of the project team's plan for starting and finishing activities on specific dates and in a certain sequence.

project schedule network diagram
Graphical representation of the sequence of project activities and the dependencies among them.

project scope
The approved requirements that will be implemented through the project work, but not

exceeded by the project work. The scope of a project gives the project manager a structure to work within when determining a project's work.

project scope management
Project management knowledge area that includes the processes used to identify project work and make sure that project work stays within the identified boundaries of a project.

project scope statement
A document that provides a description that includes the project scope, quality requirements, project deliverables, constraints, and assumptions of the project work.

project stakeholder
An individual who, or a group or organization that has a business interest in the outcome of a project.

project stakeholder management
Project management knowledge area that includes processes used to ensure that the project stakeholders are engaged, involved, and communicated with throughout the processes.

project team composition
Refers to the flavor of the team and how the team members are brought together or combined on the team. The project team contains people from different groups who possess knowledge on specific subjects or who have unique skill sets to carry out project work.

project time management
Project management knowledge area that includes the processes used to manage the time to complete a project.

prototyping
Method used to create and distribute a mocked-up model of a potential project outcome.

pull communications
Messages that require the interested people to access the information based on their own initiative.

A Guide to the Project Management Body of Knowledge (PMBOK® Guide) – Fifth Edition, Project Management Institute (PMI)®, Project Management Professional (PMP)®, and Certified Associate in Project Management (CAPM)® are registered trademarks of Project Management Institute, Inc. - Version 2.1 Published September 30, 2014

push communications

Messages that are sent out to people who need to receive information.

PV

(Planned Value) Budgeted portion of the approved cost estimate to be spent during a particular time period to complete the scheduled project work.

qualified sellers

Sellers who are approved to deliver the products, services, or results based on the procurement requirements identified for a project.

qualitative risk analysis

Technique used to determine the probability of occurrence and the impact of identified risk.

quality

The totality of features and characteristics of a product or services that bear on its ability to satisfy stated or implied needs.

quality assurance plan

Document that specifies a project's parameters and standards for quality, identifies how testing will be carried out, and describes how, when, in what manner, and to what degree the project will be reviewed and evaluated against quality criteria.

quality audit

An independent evaluation, inspection, or review of a project's quality assurance system to improve quality performance of a project.

quality checklists

Tool used to confirm that a set of steps has been performed.

quality management plan

A subsidiary plan of the project management plan. It documents and defines how the organization's quality policies and processes will be implemented for the project, how the project's quality requirements will be met, and how the quality aspect of the project will be managed.

quality metric

Standard that describes a project attribute and how it will be measured.

quantitative analysis methods

Processes that allow project managers to consistently determine the probability and impact of each risk.

quantitative risk analysis

Technique used to assess the risk exposure events to overall project objectives and determine the confidence levels of achieving the project objectives.

questionnaires and surveys

Distributed forms that are used to get feedback and ideas quickly from a large group of people.

regulations

Compliance-mandatory characteristics for specific products, services, or processes.

requirements documentation

An output in the collect requirements process. The documentation is comprised of all the individual requirements needed in order for a project to meet the business and/or stakeholder needs for a project.

requirements management plan

A component of the project management plan that states how requirements will be analyzed, documented, and managed.

requirements traceability matrix

A grid-based representation of project requirements that were determined and mapped directly to the outcomes of a project. The purpose of the matrix is to justify each requirement determined and to link it directly to the business and project objectives.

residual risks

Risks that remain after risk responses have been taken.

resource breakdown structure

A hierarchical representation of resources by category and type.

A Guide to the Project Management Body of Knowledge (PMBOK® Guide) – Fifth Edition, Project Management Institute (PMI)®, Project Management Professional (PMP)®, and Certified Associate in Project Management (CAPM)® are registered trademarks of Project Management Institute, Inc. - Version 2.1 Published September 30, 2014

Glossary

resource leveling

One of the two resource optimization techniques. Resource leveling is used to even out the resource demand for critical or shared resources in the schedule. This technique looks at the usage of each resource and adjusts the schedule to accommodate resource modifications. This often extends the critical path.

resource optimization techniques

Set of two techniques used to analyze the schedule model. They allow you to readjust the work as appropriate, so that people are not overly allocated. They are also used to address scheduling activities when critical resources are only available at certain times.

resource smoothing

One of the two resource optimization techniques. Resource smoothing adjusts the schedule so that resources do not exceed predefined resource limits. This does not impact the critical path, as float is used to accommodate these changes.

reward and recognition system

Formal system used to reinforce performance or behavior.

RFI

(Request for Information) Type of procurement document that is commonly used to develop lists of qualified sellers and to gain more input for resource availability.

RFP

(Request for Proposal) Type of procurement document that is commonly used when deliverables are not well-defined or when other selection criteria will be used in addition to price. Sellers are often encouraged to offer suggestions and alternative approaches to meet the project goals. Negotiation is typically expected.

RFQ

(Request for Quotation) Type of procurement document that is commonly used when deliverables are commodities for which there are clear specifications, and when price will be the primary determining factor. Unlike an RFB, this solicited price quote is used for comparison purposes and is not a formal bid for work.

risk

An uncertain event that may have either a positive or negative effect on the project.

risk appetite

The degree of uncertainty a person or group is willing to take on in anticipation of a benefit.

risk attitude

The willingness of organizations and stakeholders to accept varying degrees of risk.

risk breakdown structure

A documented breakdown of identified project risks. The risks are represented in a hierarchy according to the category assigned.

risk categories

Risk classifications that divide project risks into areas reflecting common sources of the risk.

risk categorization

Process used to group and organize risks into specific categories so you can evaluate them by urgency, or other designated values.

risk data quality assessment

Technique used to examine how well each risk is understood and assesses the accuracy, quality, reliability, and integrity of the data about the risk.

risk impact

The likely effect on project objectives if a risk event occurs.

risk management plan

A component of the project management plan that describes the team's approach to identifying risks. It identifies the methodology, approaches, and tools that will be used, documents the roles and responsibilities of those involved, identifies the budgeting and the scheduling for risk management activities, and identifies risk categories.

risk probability

The likelihood that a risk event will occur or prove true during the project.

A Guide to the Project Management Body of Knowledge (PMBOK® Guide) – Fifth Edition, Project Management Institute (PMI)®, Project Management Professional (PMP)®, and Certified Associate in Project Management (CAPM)® are registered trademarks of Project Management Institute, Inc. - Version 2.1 Published September 30, 2014

Glossary

risk register

Document that identifies and categorizes risks and potential risk responses, and their triggers or warning signs.

risk threshold

The level of uncertainty or impact that a stakeholder can accept.

risk tolerance

The amount of risk an organization or individual will endure.

risk urgency assessment

Technique used to determine the urgency of project risks.

rolling wave planning

An iterative planning technique where near-term work is defined at a detailed level and future work is left at a higher level, until it becomes the near-term work. It is a form of progressive elaboration of developing the work packages into activities as more is known about those work packages.

root cause analysis

Process used to identify a problem, determine the underlying causes that led to that problem, and determine actions to prevent the risk.

schedule compression

The shortening of the project schedule without affecting the project scope.

schedule data

The information that describes and controls the schedule.

schedule management plan

A subsidiary plan of the project management plan. It identifies a scheduling method and scheduling tool that will be used for a project.

scheduling tool

Automatic scheduling program that generates the project schedule from the submitted start and finish dates.

scope baseline

The approved version of a scope statement and a work breakdown structure (WBS), and its associated WBS dictionary, that is used to monitor and measure against throughout a project.

sensitivity analysis

Method of assessing the relative impact of changing a variable in the project to gain insight into possible outcomes of one or more potential courses of action.

sequence activities process

Process that examines each activity on the activity list to determine the relationship between the activities. A logical sequence of activities is determined so that the project can be worked with the greatest efficiency, given any project constraints.

sequential relationships

Type of phase-to-phase relationships that contain consecutive phases that only start when the previous phase is complete.

share

Strategy for managing positive risks or opportunities that involves allocating some or all of the ownership of the opportunity to a third party.

simulation

Technique that uses computer models and estimates of risk to translate uncertainties at a detailed level into their potential impact on project objectives.

simulation technique

Modelling technique that enables you to calculate different schedules based on different assumptions that you are considering for the project.

source selection criteria

The standards used to rate or score proposals, quotes, or bids and form a part of the procurement solicitation documents.

SPI

(Schedule Performance Index) Ratio of work performed to work scheduled.

staff management plan

Component of the human resource management plan that forecasts what types of staff will work on the project, when they will

A Guide to the Project Management Body of Knowledge (PMBOK® Guide) – Fifth Edition, Project Management Institute (PMI)®, Project Management Professional (PMP)®, and Certified Associate in Project Management (CAPM)® are registered trademarks of Project Management Institute, Inc. - Version 2.1 Published September 30, 2014

Glossary

be needed, how they will be recruited onto the project, and when they will be released from the project.

stakeholder analysis
The process of gathering and analyzing data about people whose interests should be considered and taken into account during the life cycle of the project.

stakeholder classification
Technique used to classify project stakeholders into smaller groups that are rated based on a classification level. Stakeholder engagement and involvement will vary with every project.

stakeholder management plan
A subsidiary plan of the project management plan that defines the processes, procedures, tools, and techniques to effectively engage stakeholders in project decisions and execution based on the analysis of their needs, interests, and potential impact.

stakeholder register
Document that contains specific stakeholder information, such as name, contact information, location, job role or position, and project involvement.

stakeholders
The people who may affect or be affected by the objectives of a project.

standards
Voluntary guidelines or characteristics that have been approved by a recognized body of experts, such as the International Organization for Standardization (ISO).

start-to-finish (SF) relationship
Type of precedence relationship between two activities in which the predecessor activity cannot finish until the successor activity has started.

start-to-start (SS) relationship
Type of precedence relationship between two activities in which the successor activity cannot start until the predecessor activity has started.

statement of work
The document that describes the products, services, or results that will be delivered by the project. This document is based on business needs, product, or service requirements for a particular project.

statistical sampling
Plan quality management tool that selects a subset of a population for inspection that is representative of the whole population.

statistical sampling process
Process that involves dividing sampling data into two categories—attribute and variable—each of which is gathered according to sampling plans. As corrective actions are taken in response to analysis of statistical sampling and other quality control activities, and as trend analysis is performed, defects and process variability should be reduced.

storyboarding
Prototyping method that uses visuals or images to illustrate a process or represent a project outcome. Storyboards are useful to illustrate how a product, service, or application will function or operate when it's complete.

summary activity
A group of related activities that, for reporting purposes, is shown as a single aggregate activity in a bar chart or graph.

supportive PMO
Type of PMO that provides a consultative role to projects by supplying templates, best practices, training, access to information, and lessons learned from other projects.

SV
(Schedule Variance) Measured difference between the actual completion of the activities in the reporting time period and the planned or scheduled completion of the activities.

SWOT analysis
Technique that examines the project by its strengths, weaknesses, opportunities, and threats (SWOT) to uncover any internally generated risks.

A Guide to the Project Management Body of Knowledge (PMBOK® Guide) – Fifth Edition, Project Management Institute (PMI)®, Project Management Professional (PMP)®, and Certified Associate in Project Management (CAPM)® are registered trademarks of Project Management Institute, Inc. - Version 2.1 Published September 30, 2014

Glossary

T & M contract

(Time and Material contact) Type of contract that includes aspects of both fixed-price and cost-reimbursable contracts. The buyer pays the seller a negotiated hourly rate and full reimbursement for materials used to complete the project. This contract is used for staff augmentation, acquisition of experts, and any outside support when a precise statement of work cannot be quickly prescribed. Many organizations include not-to-exceed values and time limits in T & M contracts to prevent unlimited cost growth.

tailoring

The act of determining which processes are appropriate for a particular project or project phase.

team building

The process of continually supporting and working collaboratively with team members in order to enable a team to work together to solve problems, diffuse interpersonal issues, share information, and tackle project objectives as a unified force.

team–building activities

The specific functions or actions taken to help the team to develop into a mature, productive team. They can be formal or informal, brief or extended, and facilitated by the project manager or a group facilitator.

three–point estimating

Estimate activity durations technique that takes estimation uncertainty and risk into consideration by providing three estimates instead of a single point. This concept is from the program evaluation and review technique (PERT).

tolerances

The measurement values that determine if a product or service is acceptable or unacceptable.

tools and techniques

The methods, templates, or approaches that project managers employ within a particular process, using a combination of inputs, to achieve stated goals.

total float

A type of float where the total amount of time an activity requires can be delayed without delaying the project finish date.

training

An activity in which team members acquire new or enhanced skills, knowledge, or attitudes.

transfer

Strategy for managing negative risks or threats that involves shifting the impact and ownership of the risk to a third party and paying a risk premium to the party taking on the liability of the risk.

triangular distribution PDF

Probability Density Function that results when there is an asymmetrical distribution of probabilities. Visually, the data is skewed to one side, indicating that an activity or element presents relatively little risk to project objectives.

triggers

Early warning signs or indications that a project risk is likely to occur.

trust building

The process of developing and fostering a sense of confidence and belief among a group of individuals.

unanimity

Group decision-making method in which everyone in the group agrees on the course of action to take.

uniform distribution PDF

Probability Density Function that results when all outcomes are equally likely to occur, so the data is shown in a straight line.

unique identification code

Specific configuration of a code of accounts that assigns a particular alphanumeric sequence of characters to each element of a WBS.

unknown risks

Risks that cannot be identified and so they cannot be managed proactively and may have a management reserve.

A Guide to the Project Management Body of Knowledge (PMBOK® Guide) – Fifth Edition, Project Management Institute (PMI)®, Project Management Professional (PMP)®, and Certified Associate in Project Management (CAPM)® are registered trademarks of Project Management Institute, Inc. - Version 2.1 Published September 30, 2014

Glossary

validate scope process
Process that demonstrates to stakeholders that they have received what they have been promised in a given deliverable and formalizes their acceptance.

variance
The quantifiable deviance, or amount of departure, from the expected results for any component of product and service being developed, including quality, as well as schedule and cost.

virtual team
Team that is distributed across multiple locations.

WBS
(Work Breakdown Structure) A logical grouping of project deliverables arranged in a hierarchical structure. A WBS defines the total scope of work required to complete the project.

WBS dictionary
Document that retains all WBS component information, such as deliverables, activities, code assignments, and scheduling information.

weighting system
Method for quantifying qualitative data to minimize the influence of personal bias on source selection.

what-if scenario analysis
Modelling technique that allows you to consider different situations that might occur and influence the schedule; it assesses the feasibility of the schedule under various adverse conditions.

work authorization system
A tool used to communicate official permission to begin working on an activity or work package. It is a function, or component, of the PMIS.

work packages
A small set of "to do's" or work that needs to be done, resulting in a small deliverable that must exist to support the satisfaction of a requirement.

A Guide to the Project Management Body of Knowledge (PMBOK® Guide) – Fifth Edition, Project Management Institute (PMI)®, Project Management Professional (PMP)®, and Certified Associate in Project Management (CAPM)® are registered trademarks of Project Management Institute, Inc. - Version 2.1 Published September 30, 2014

Glossary

Index

A Guide to the Project Management Body of Knowledge (PMBOK® Guide) – Fifth Edition, Project Management Institute (PMI)®, Project Management Professional (PMP)®, and Certified Associate in Project Management (CAPM)® are registered trademarks of Project Management Institute, Inc. - Version 2.1 Published September 30, 2014

Index

A Guide to the Project Management Body of Knowledge (PMBOK® Guide) – Fifth Edition, Project Management Institute (PMI)®, Project Management Professional (PMP)®, and Certified Associate in Project Management (CAPM)® are registered trademarks of Project Management Institute, Inc. - Version 2.1 Published September 30, 2014

Index

A Guide to the Project Management Body of Knowledge (PMBOK® Guide) – Fifth Edition, Project Management Institute (PMI)®, Project Management Professional (PMP)®, and Certified Associate in Project Management (CAPM)® are registered trademarks of Project Management Institute, Inc. - Version 2.1 Published September 30, 2014

Index

A Guide to the Project Management Body of Knowledge (PMBOK® Guide) – Fifth Edition, Project Management Institute (PMI)®, Project Management Professional (PMP)®, and Certified Associate in Project Management (CAPM)® are registered trademarks of Project Management Institute, Inc. - Version 2.1 Published September 30, 2014

Index

A Guide to the Project Management Body of Knowledge (PMBOK® Guide) – Fifth Edition, Project Management Institute (PMI)®, Project Management Professional (PMP)®, and Certified Associate in Project Management (CAPM)® are registered trademarks of Project Management Institute, Inc. - Version 2.1 Published September 30, 2014

Index

095001S rev 2.1
ISBN-13 978-1-4246-2118-7
ISBN-10 1-4246-2118-6

9 781424 621187